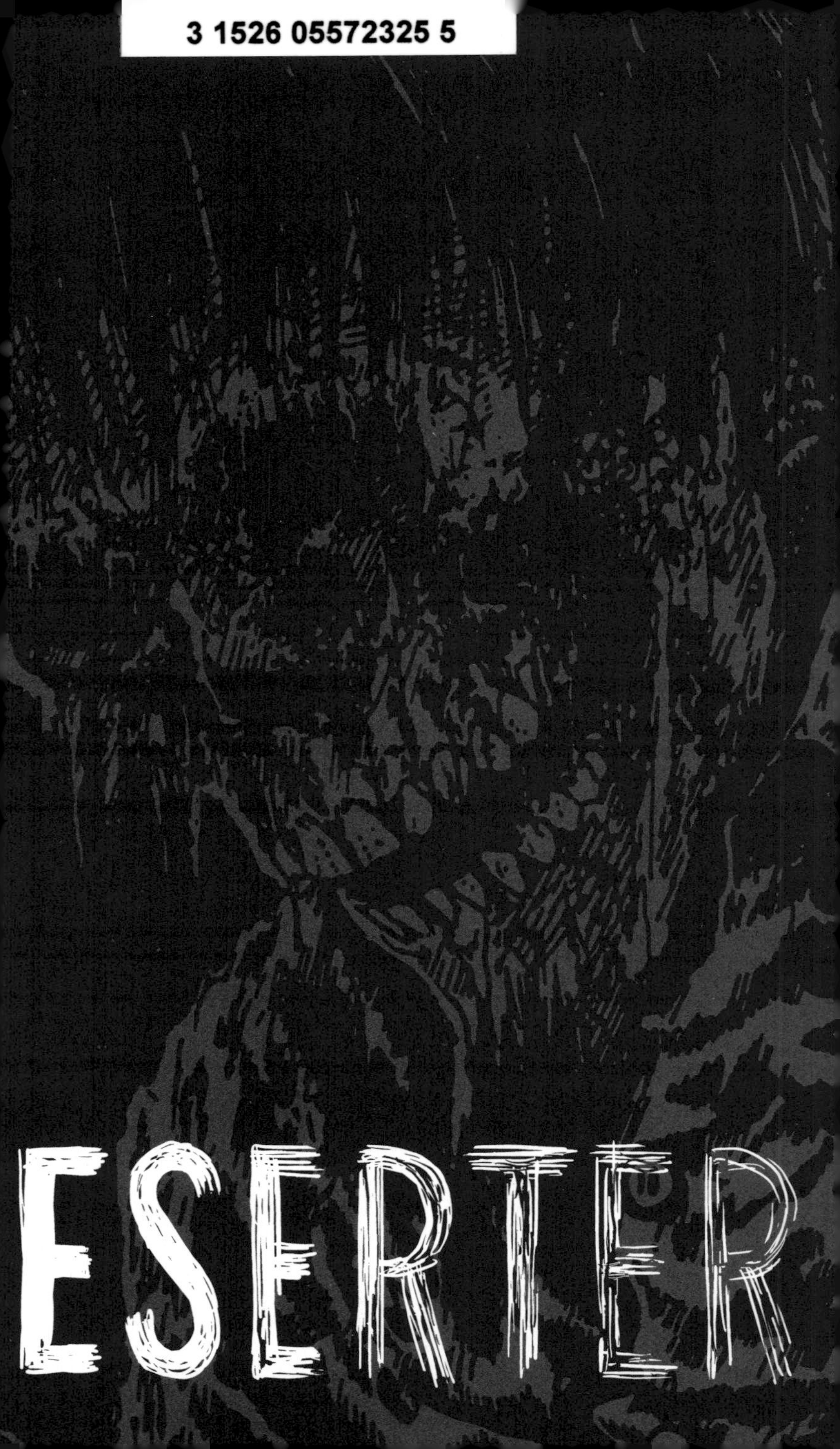
ESERTER

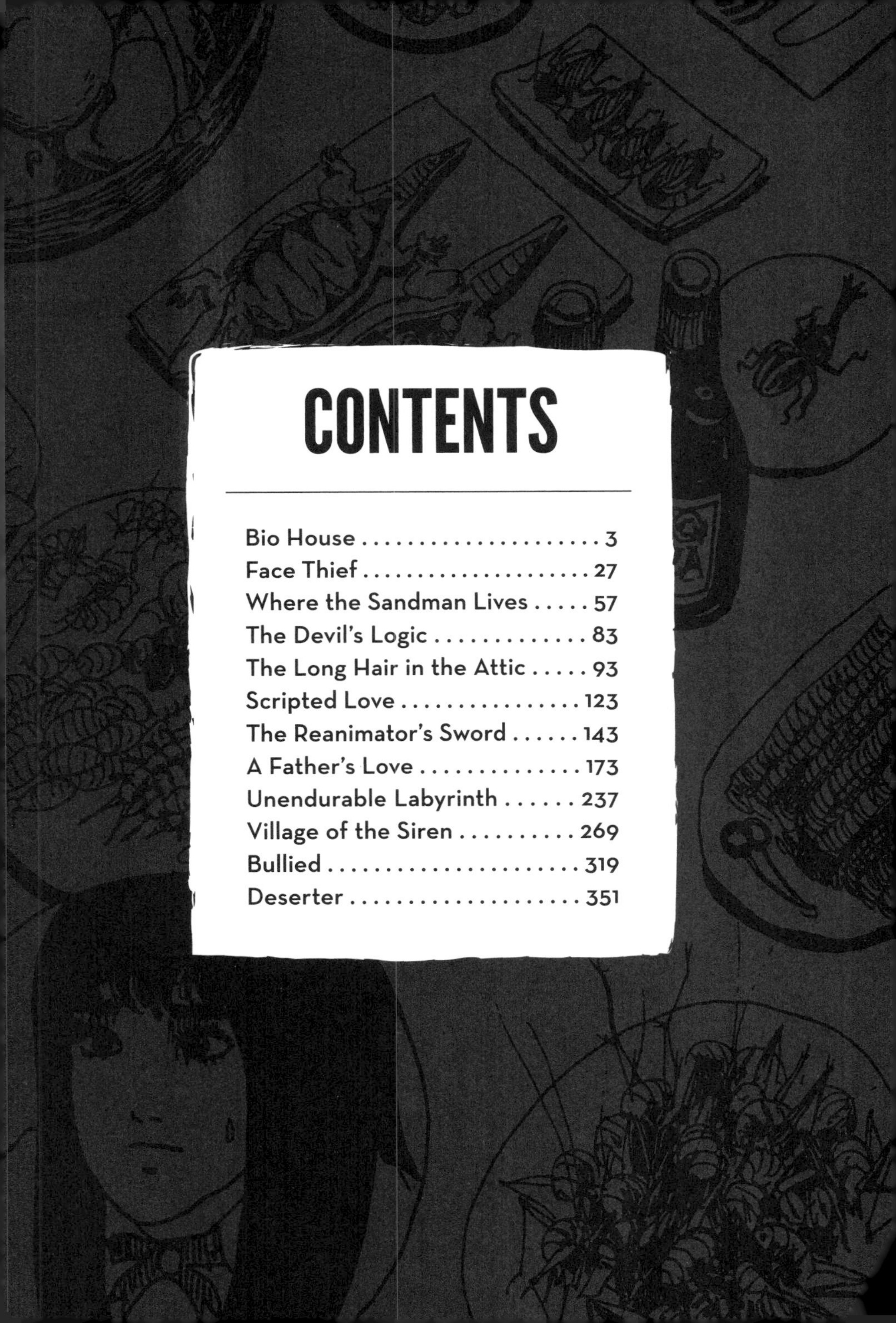

CONTENTS

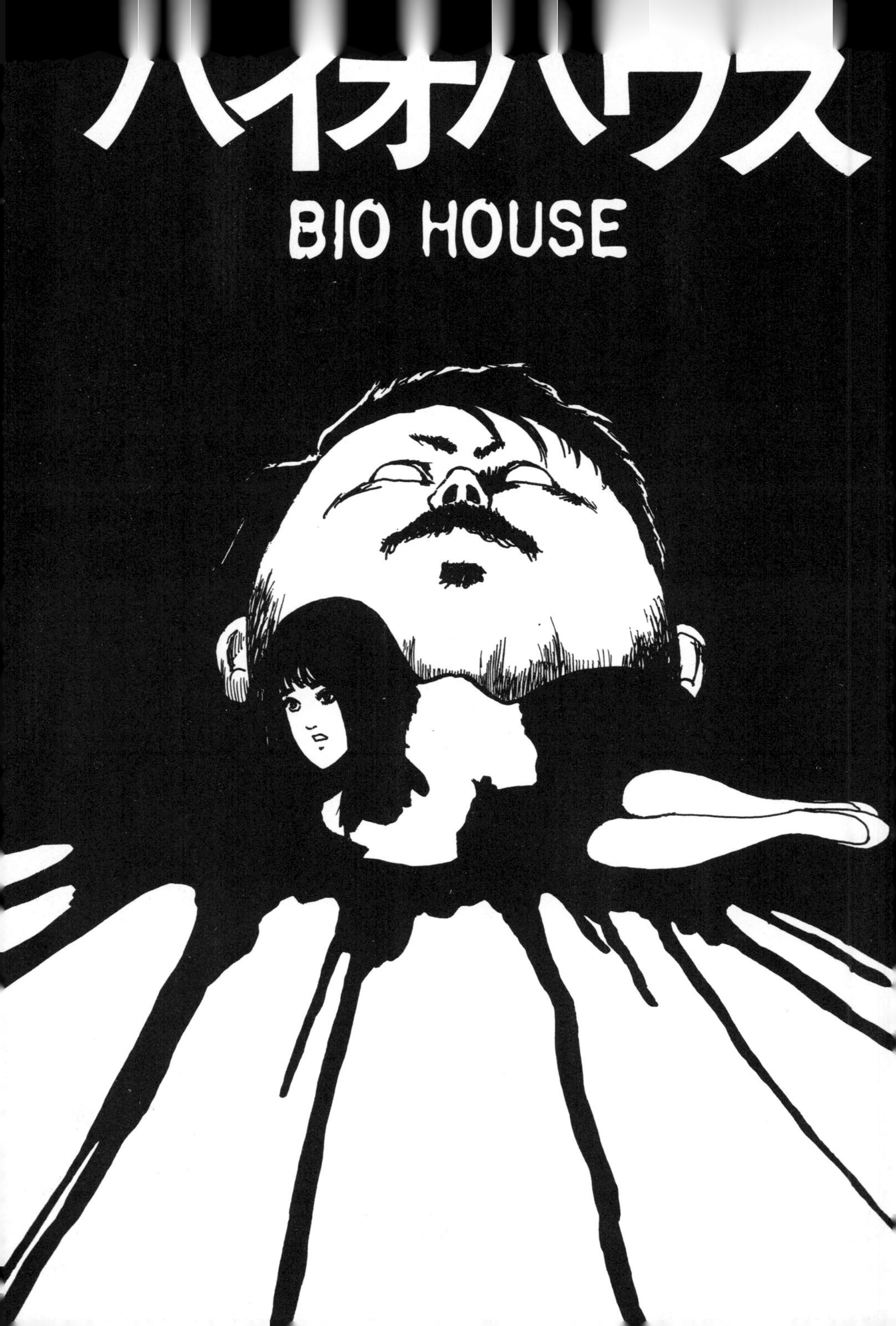
バイオハウス
BIO HOUSE

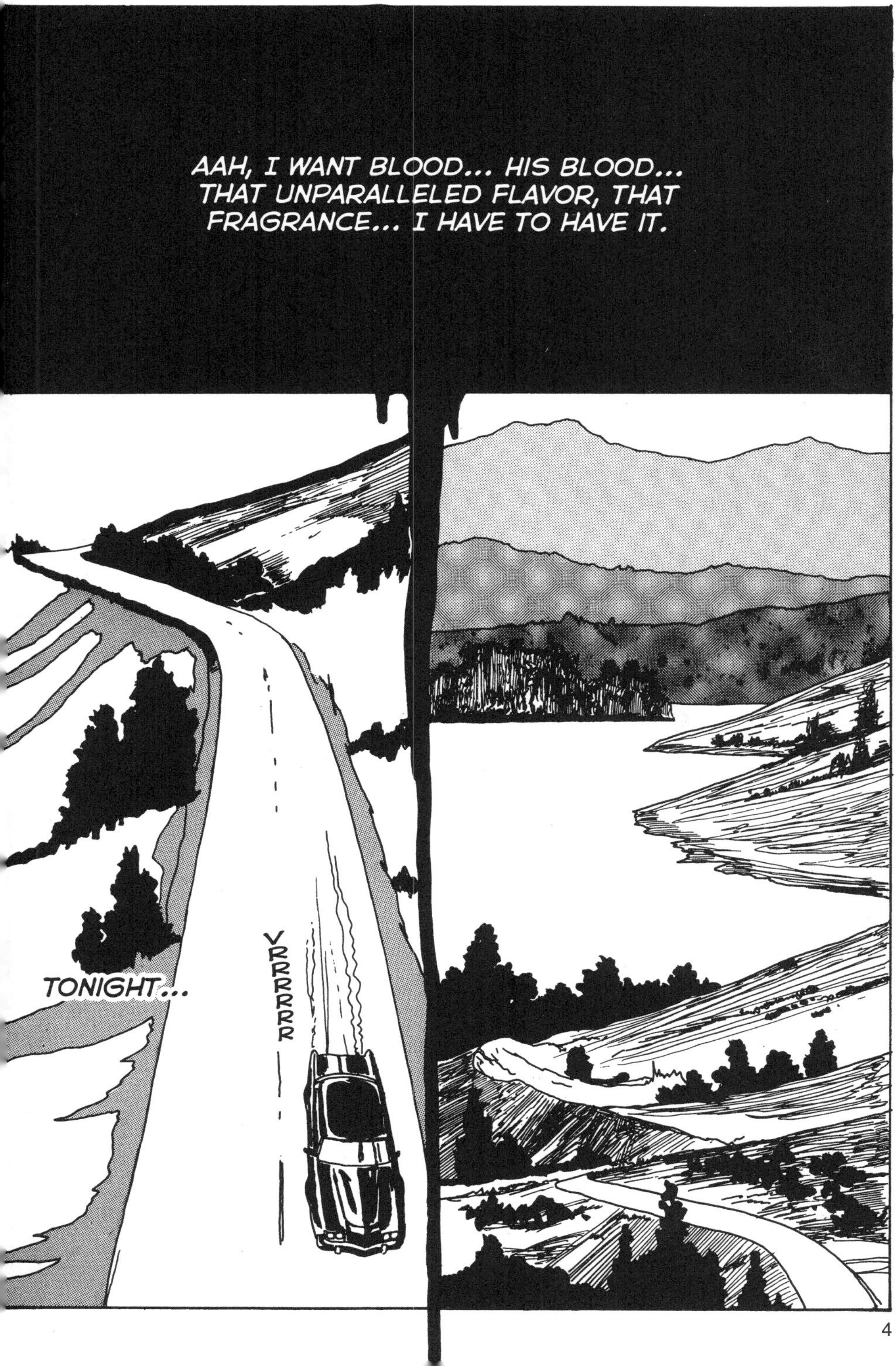
AAH, I WANT BLOOD... HIS BLOOD... THAT UNPARALLELED FLAVOR, THAT FRAGRANCE... I HAVE TO HAVE IT.
VRRRRR
TONIGHT...

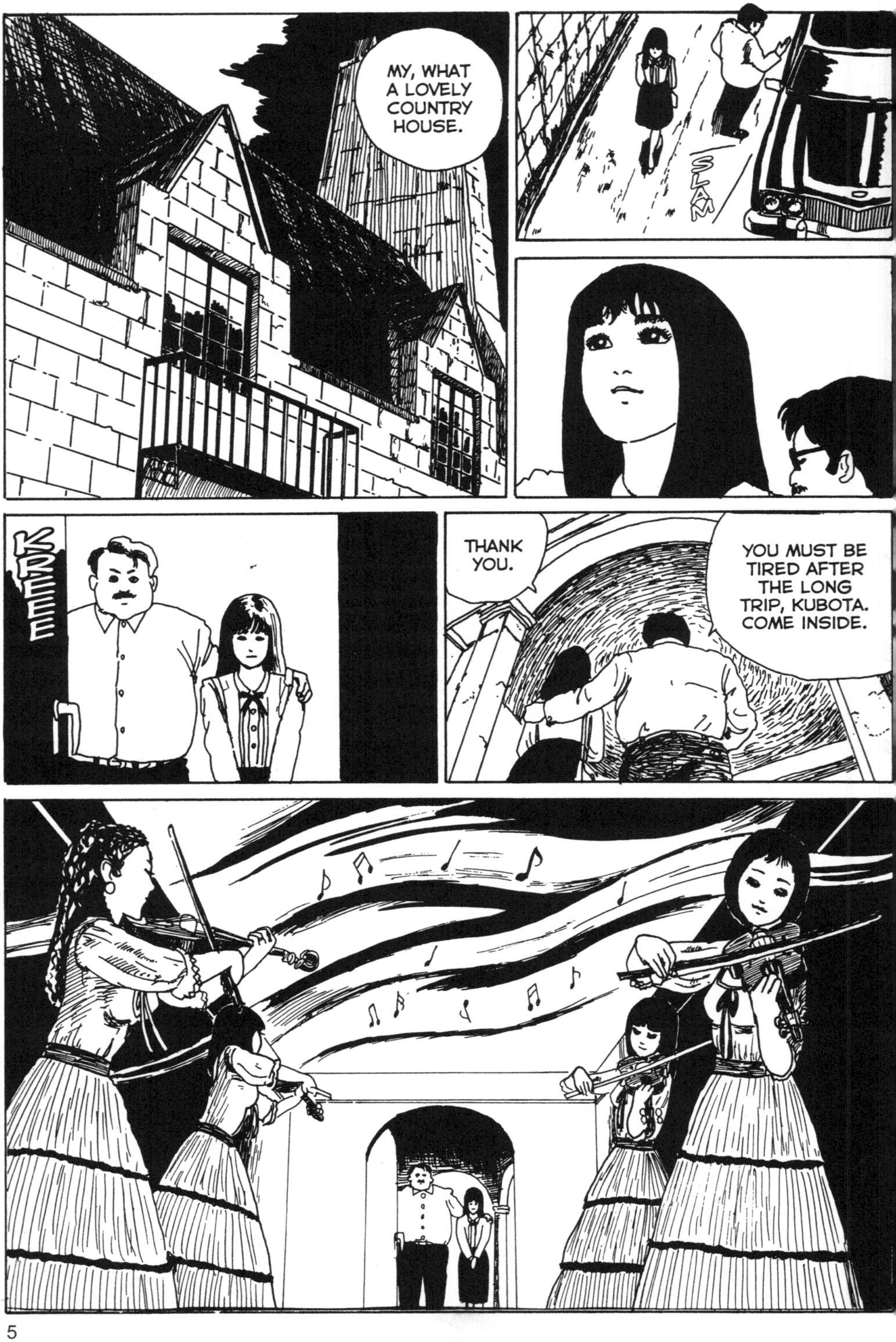
SLAM
MY, WHAT A LOVELY COUNTRY HOUSE.
YOU MUST BE TIRED AFTER THE LONG TRIP, KUBOTA. COME INSIDE.
THANK YOU.
KREEE

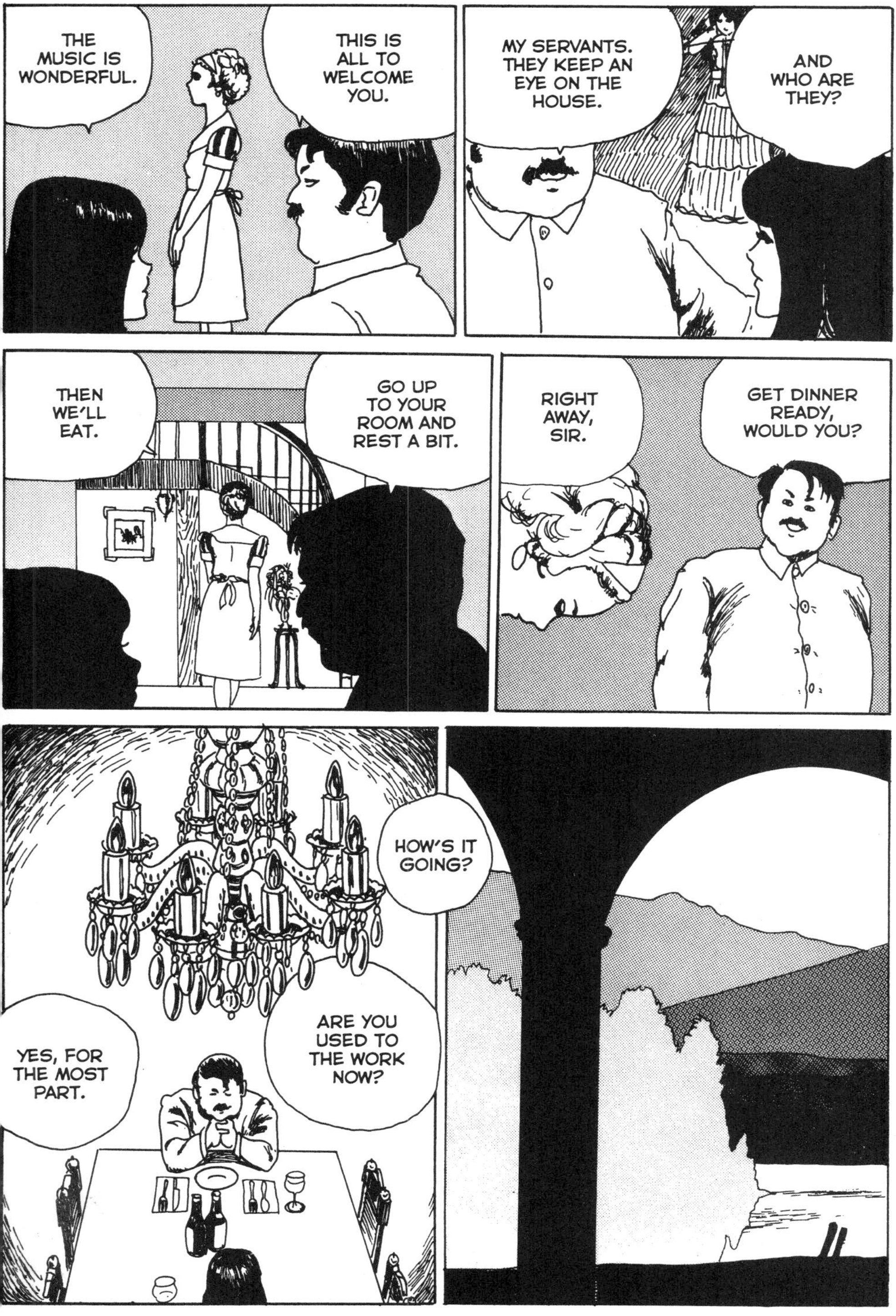
AND WHO ARE THEY?
MY SERVANTS. THEY KEEP AN EYE ON THE HOUSE.
THIS IS ALL TO WELCOME YOU.
THE MUSIC IS WONDERFUL.
GET DINNER READY, WOULD YOU?
RIGHT AWAY, SIR.
GO UP TO YOUR ROOM AND REST A BIT.
THEN WE'LL EAT.
HOW'S IT GOING?
ARE YOU USED TO THE WORK NOW?
YES, FOR THE MOST PART.

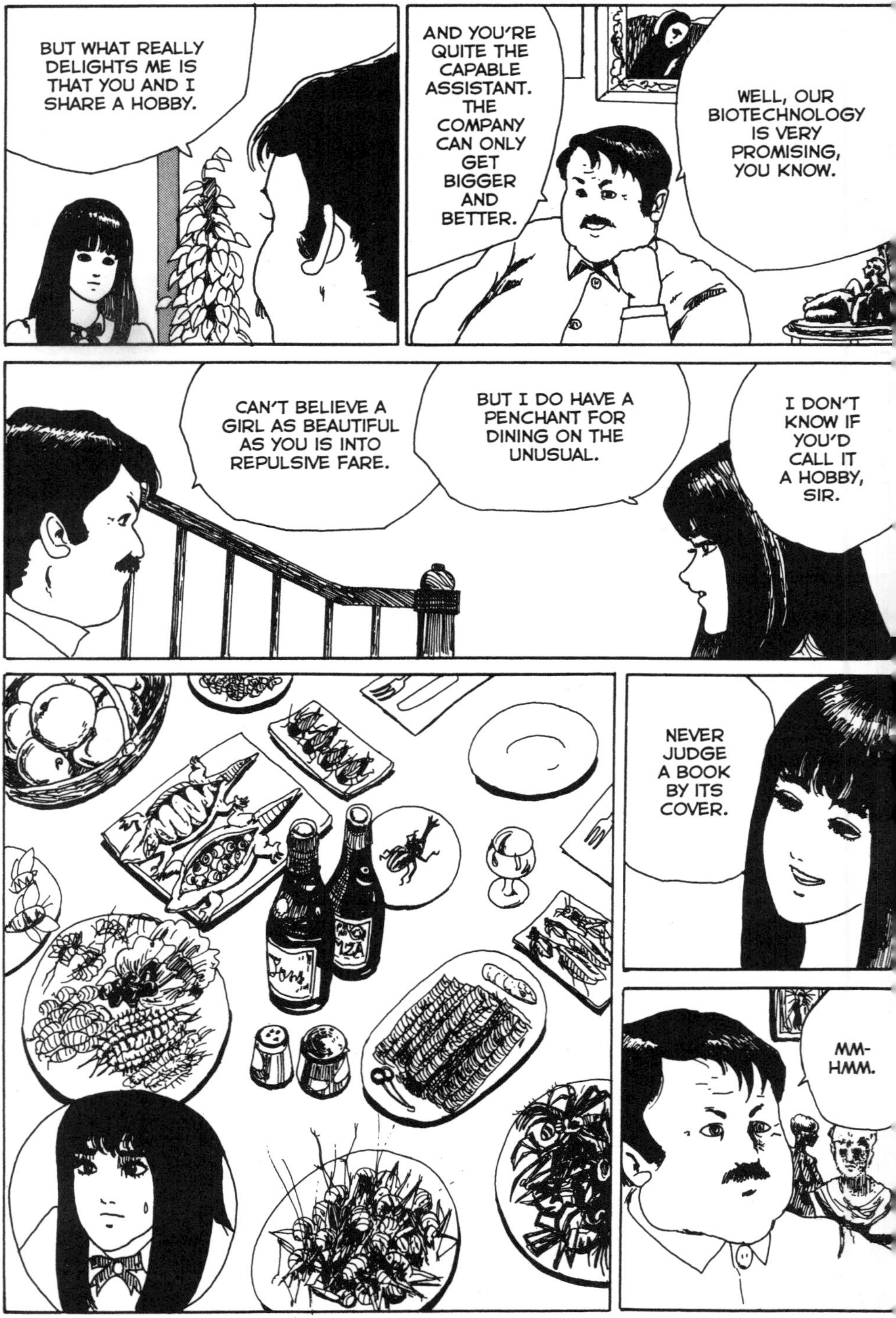
WELL, OUR BIOTECHNOLOGY IS VERY PROMISING, YOU KNOW.
AND YOU'RE QUITE THE CAPABLE ASSISTANT. THE COMPANY CAN ONLY GET BIGGER AND BETTER.
BUT WHAT REALLY DELIGHTS ME IS THAT YOU AND I SHARE A HOBBY.
I DON'T KNOW IF YOU'D CALL IT A HOBBY, SIR.
BUT I DO HAVE A PENCHANT FOR DINING ON THE UNUSUAL.
CAN'T BELIEVE A GIRL AS BEAUTIFUL AS YOU IS INTO REPULSIVE FARE.
NEVER JUDGE A BOOK BY ITS COVER.
MM-HMM.

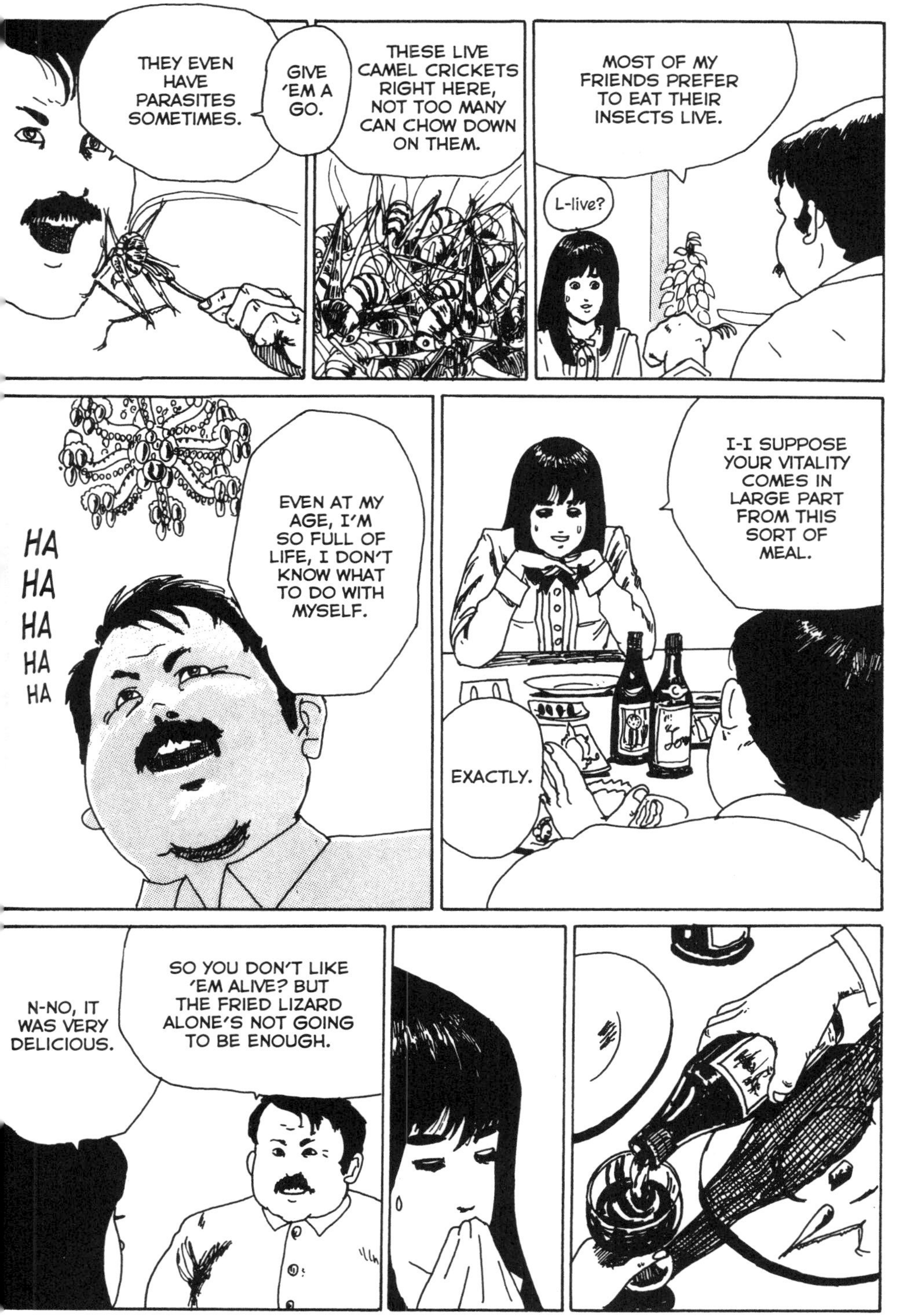
MOST OF MY FRIENDS PREFER TO EAT THEIR INSECTS LIVE.
L-live?
THESE LIVE CAMEL CRICKETS RIGHT HERE, NOT TOO MANY CAN CHOW DOWN ON THEM.
GIVE 'EM A GO.
THEY EVEN HAVE PARASITES SOMETIMES.
I-I SUPPOSE YOUR VITALITY COMES IN LARGE PART FROM THIS SORT OF MEAL.
EXACTLY.
EVEN AT MY AGE, I'M SO FULL OF LIFE, I DON'T KNOW WHAT TO DO WITH MYSELF.
HA HA HA HA HA
SO YOU DON'T LIKE 'EM ALIVE? BUT THE FRIED LIZARD ALONE'S NOT GOING TO BE ENOUGH.
N-NO, IT WAS VERY DELICIOUS.

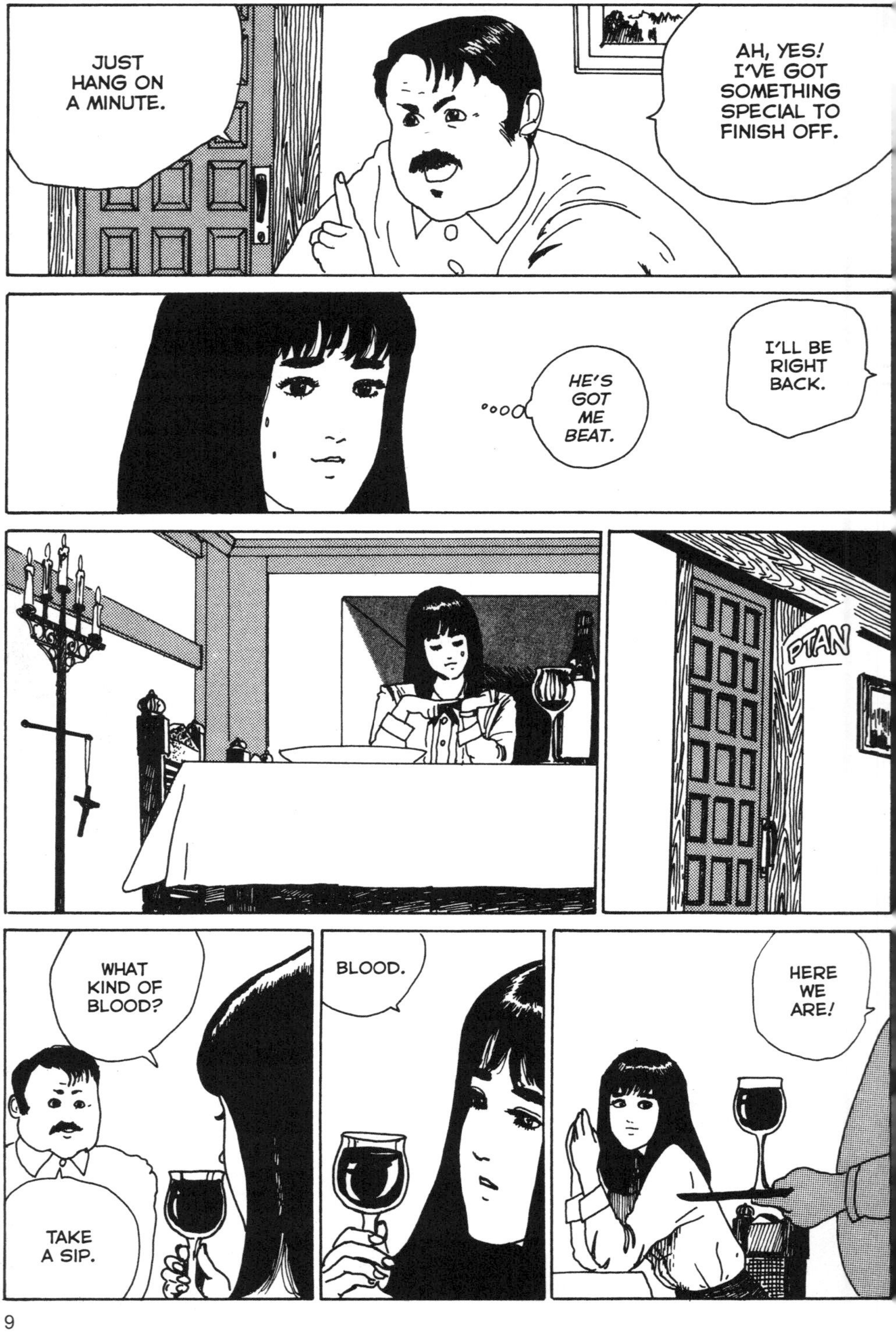
AH, YES! I'VE GOT SOMETHING SPECIAL TO FINISH OFF.
JUST HANG ON A MINUTE.
I'LL BE RIGHT BACK.
HE'S GOT ME BEAT.
PTAN
HERE WE ARE!
BLOOD.
WHAT KIND OF BLOOD?
TAKE A SIP.

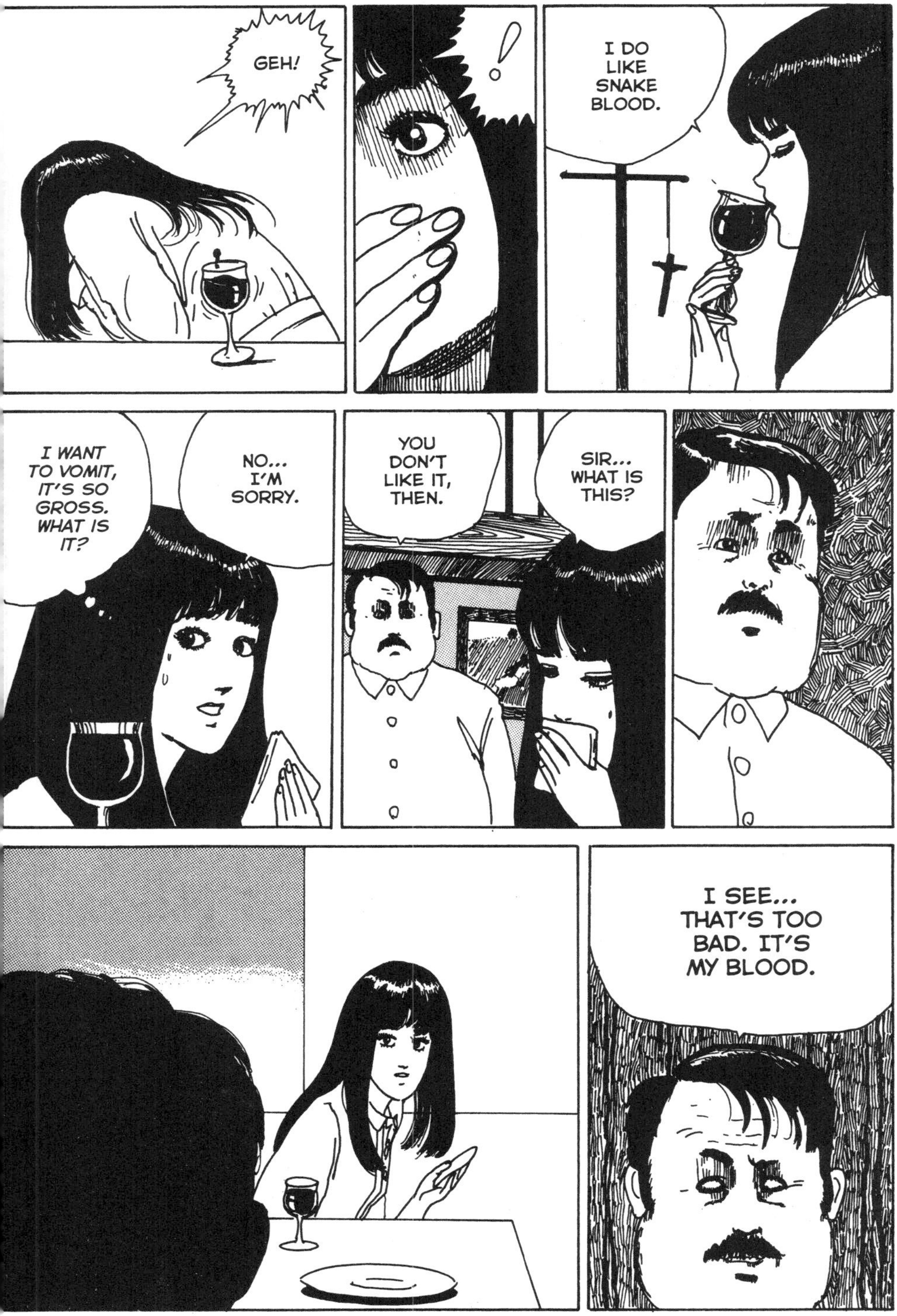
I DO LIKE SNAKE BLOOD.
!
GEH!
SIR... WHAT IS THIS?
YOU DON'T LIKE IT, THEN.
NO... I'M SORRY.
I WANT TO VOMIT, IT'S SO GROSS. WHAT IS IT?
I SEE... THAT'S TOO BAD. IT'S MY BLOOD.

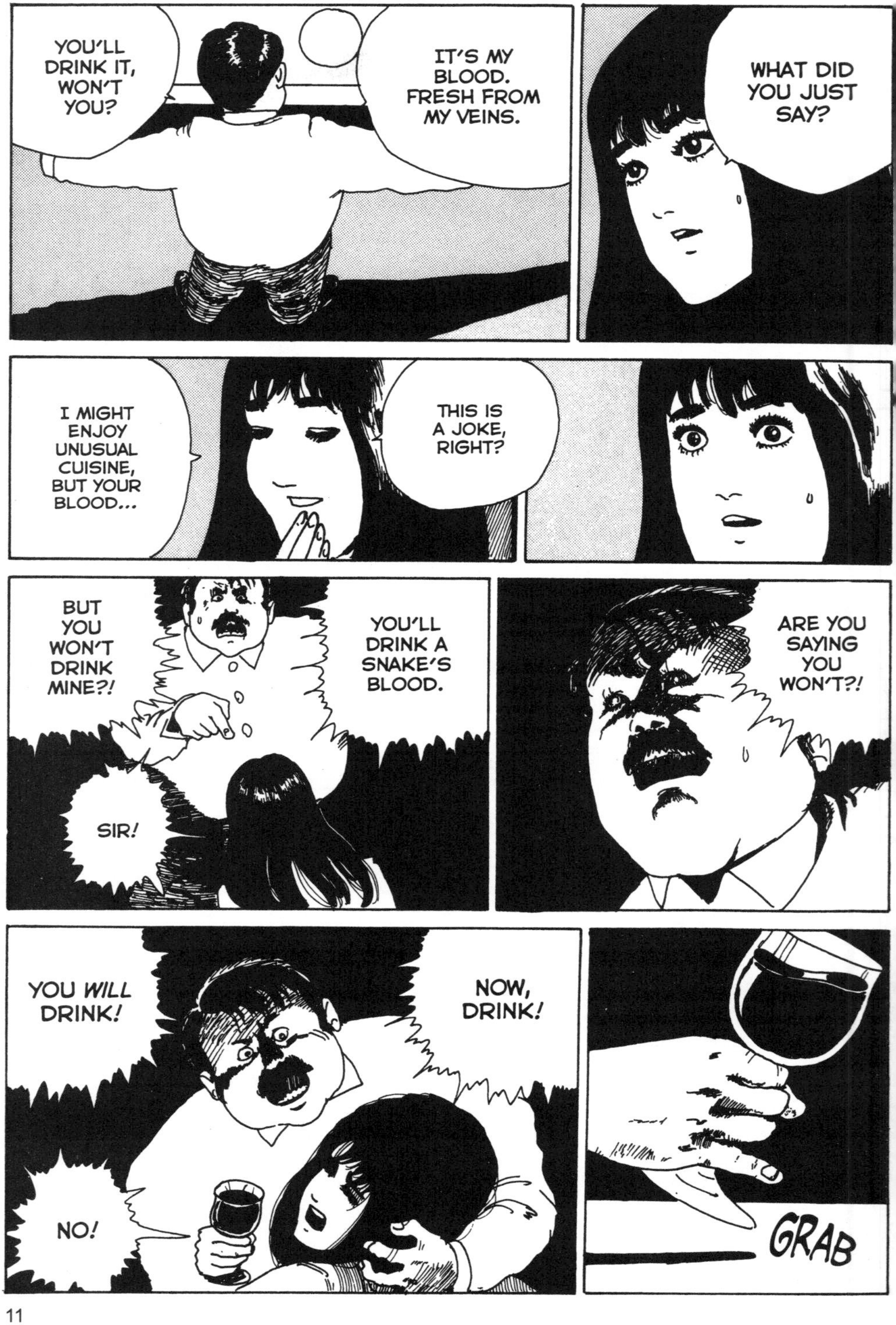
WHAT DID YOU JUST SAY?
IT'S MY BLOOD. FRESH FROM MY VEINS.
YOU'LL DRINK IT, WON'T YOU?
THIS IS A JOKE, RIGHT?
I MIGHT ENJOY UNUSUAL CUISINE, BUT YOUR BLOOD...
ARE YOU SAYING YOU WON'T?!
YOU'LL DRINK A SNAKE'S BLOOD.
BUT YOU WON'T DRINK MINE?!
SIR!
GRAB
NOW, DRINK!
YOU *WILL* DRINK!
NO!

I WON'T!

YOU DARE DEFY ME?!

Y—

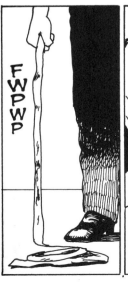

FWPWP

DO YOU KNOW WHAT HAPPENS TO PEOPLE WHO DEFY ME?!

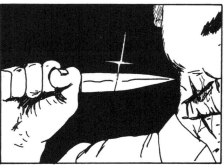
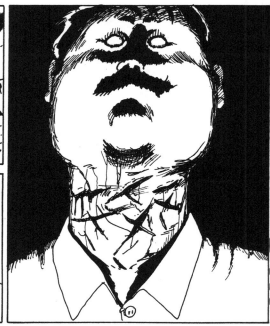

SIR
!!

SPRRRRT

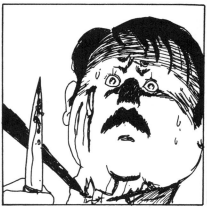

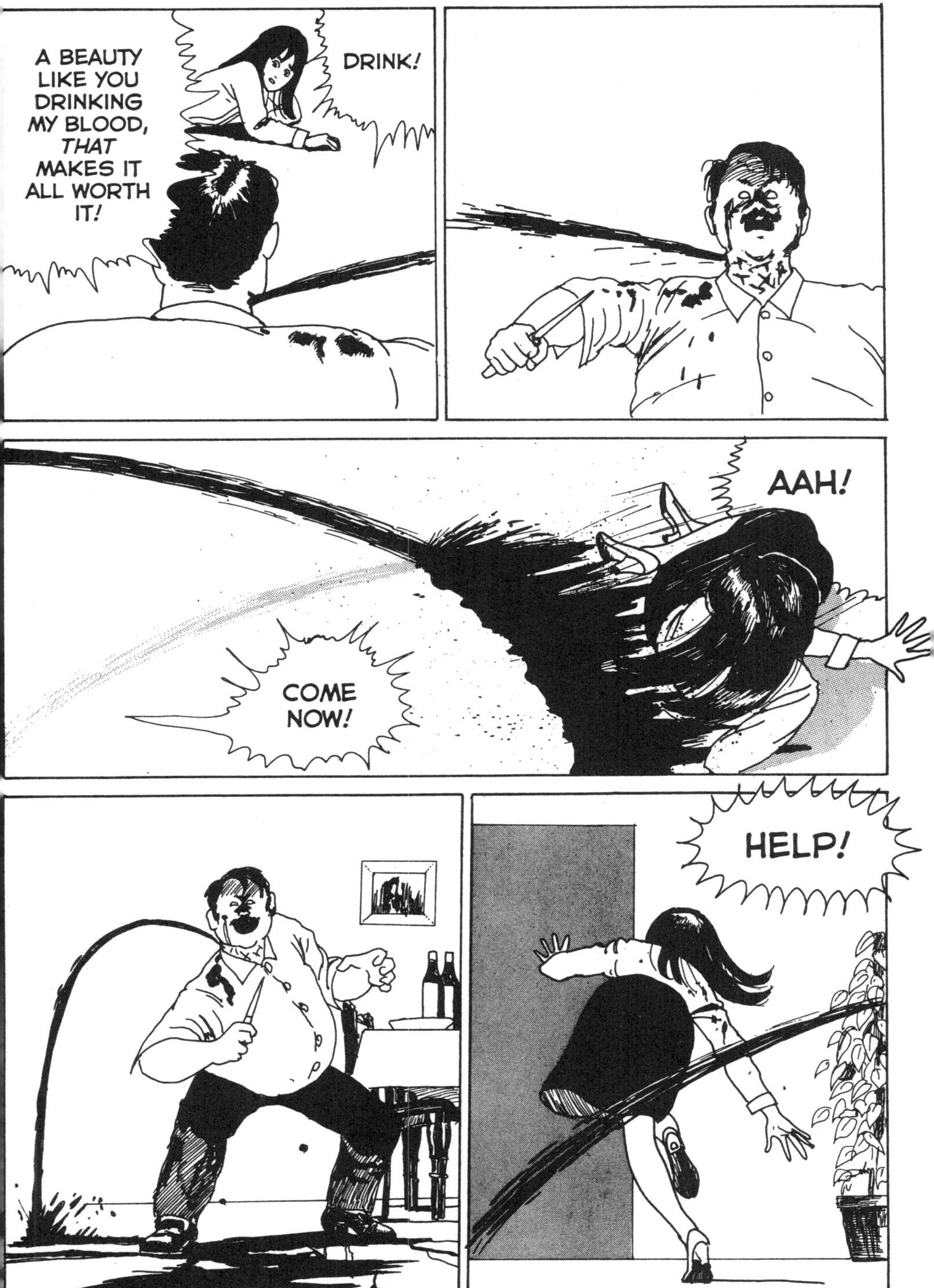
DRINK!
A BEAUTY LIKE YOU DRINKING MY BLOOD, *THAT* MAKES IT ALL WORTH IT!
AAH!
COME NOW!
HELP!

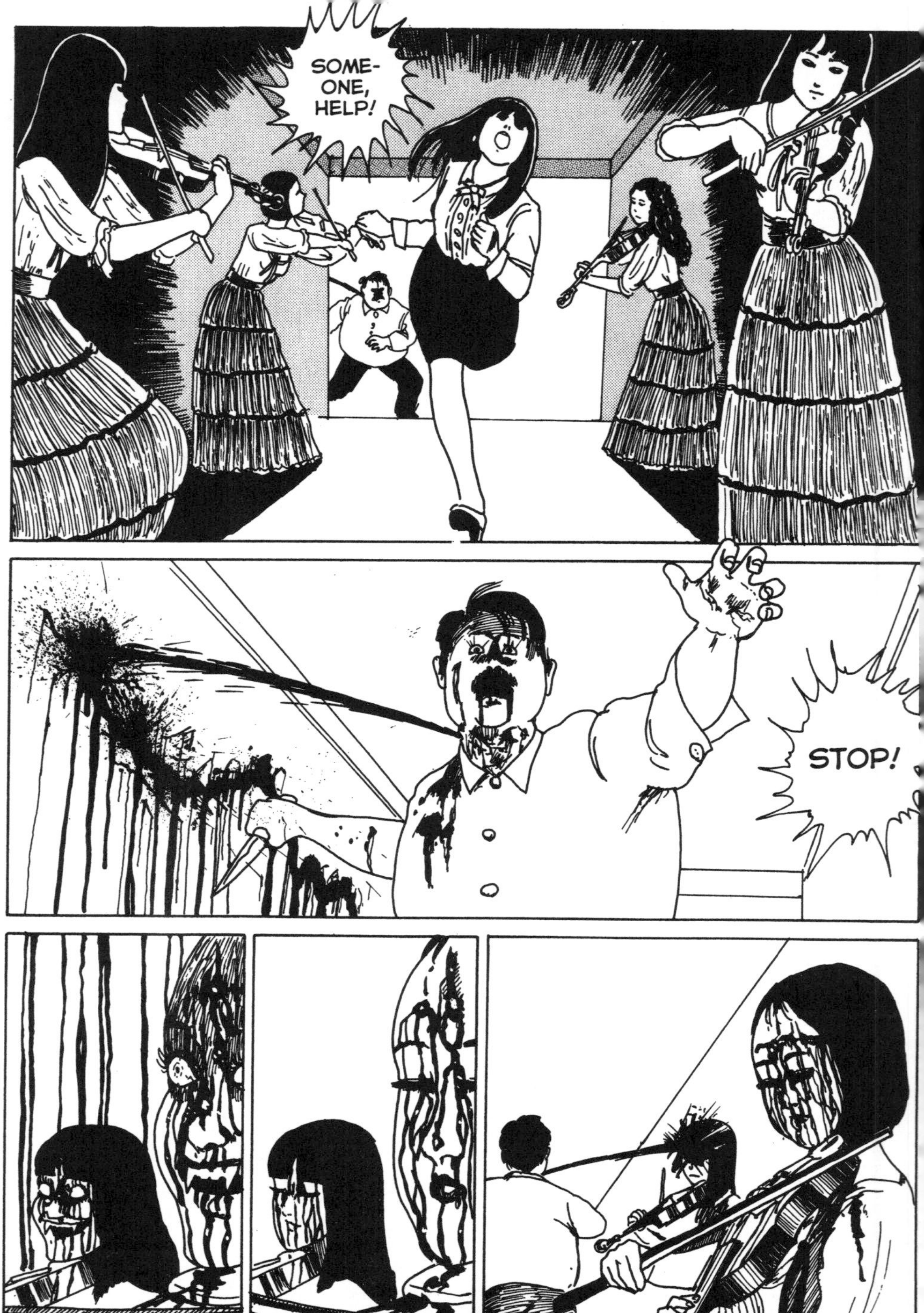
SOME-ONE, HELP!
STOP!

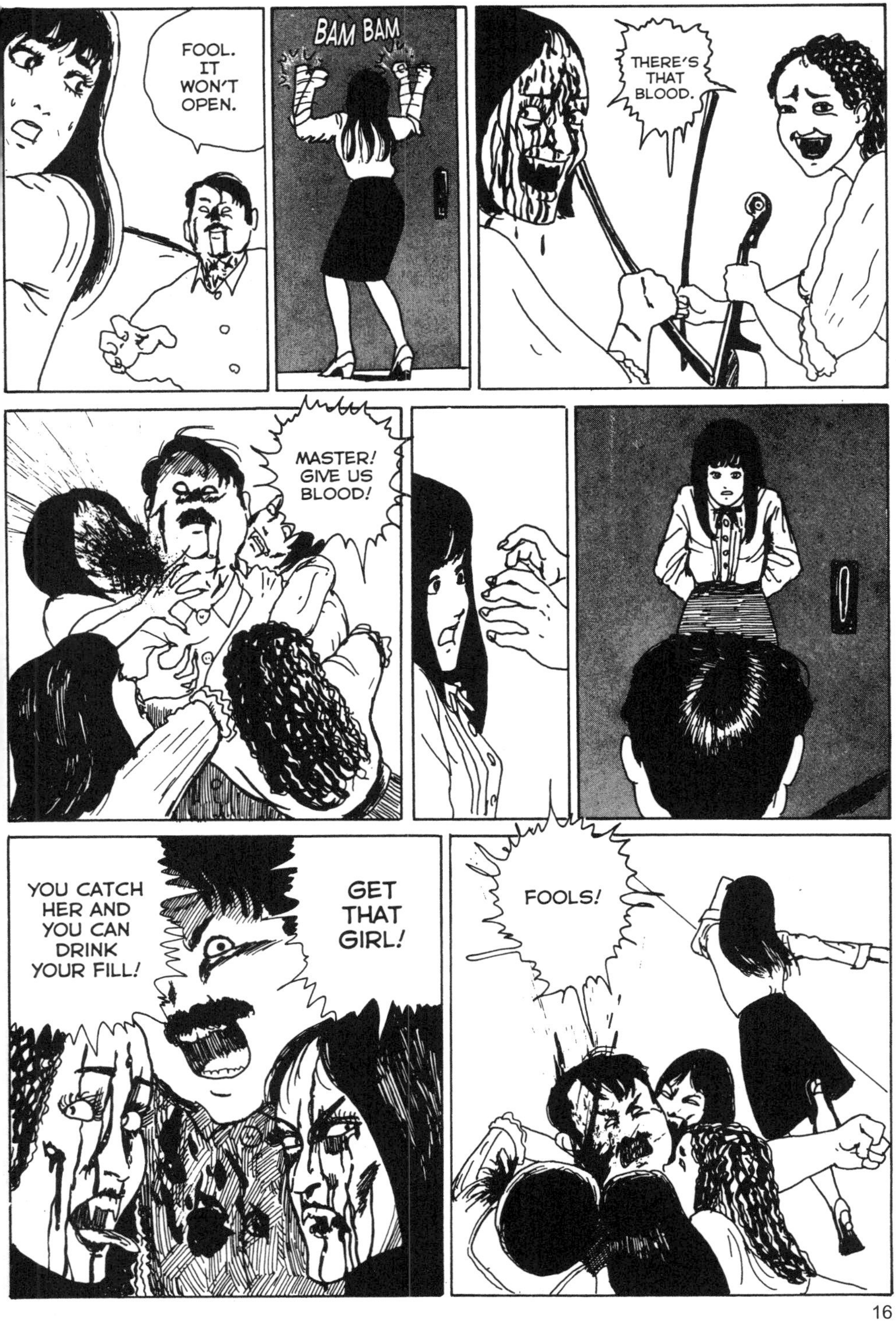
THERE'S THAT BLOOD.
BAM BAM
FOOL. IT WON'T OPEN.
MASTER! GIVE US BLOOD!
FOOLS!
GET THAT GIRL!
YOU CATCH HER AND YOU CAN DRINK YOUR FILL!

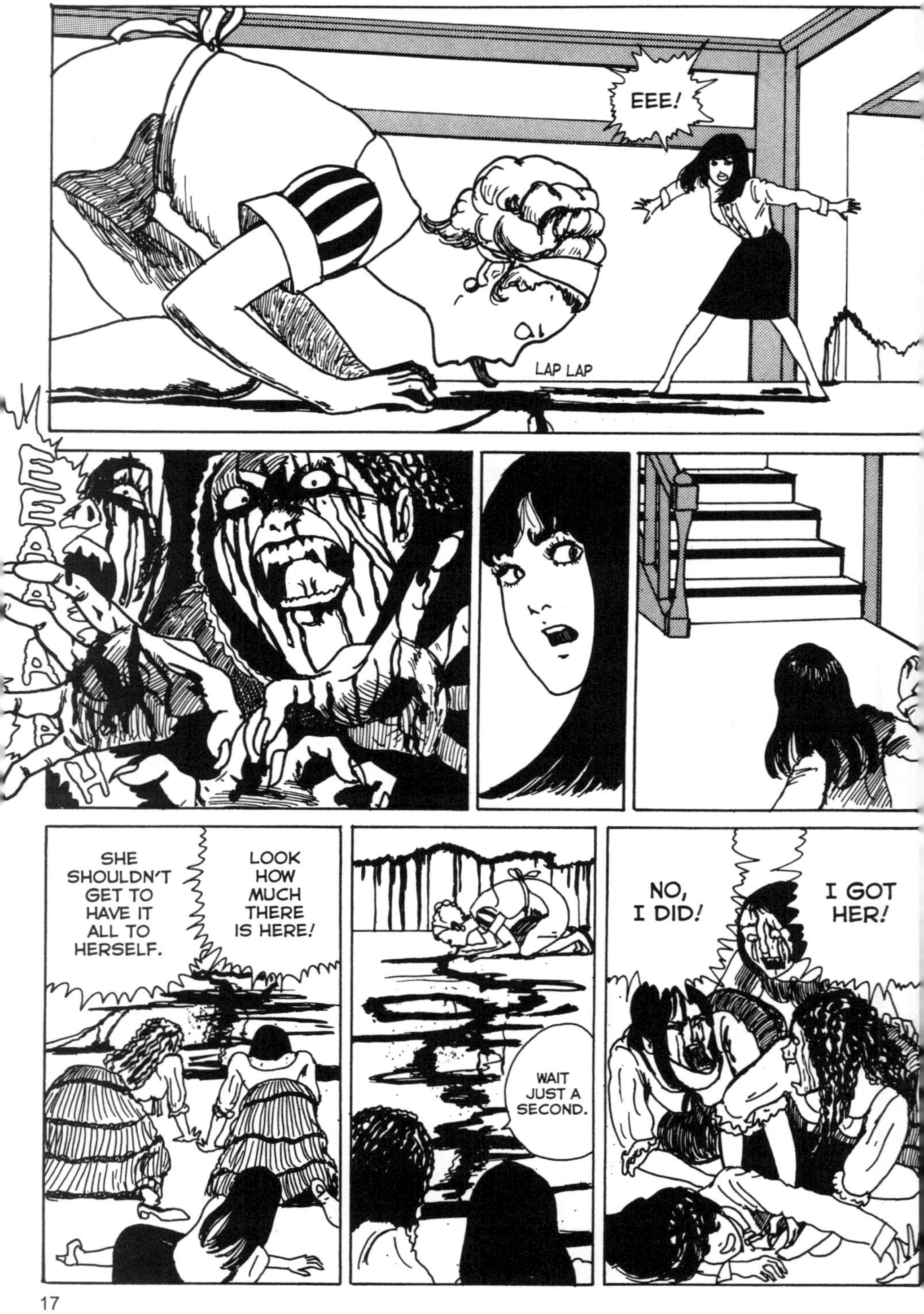
EEE!
LAP LAP
EEAAAAH
I GOT HER!
NO, I DID!
WAIT JUST A SECOND.
LOOK HOW MUCH THERE IS HERE!
SHE SHOULDN'T GET TO HAVE IT ALL TO HERSELF.

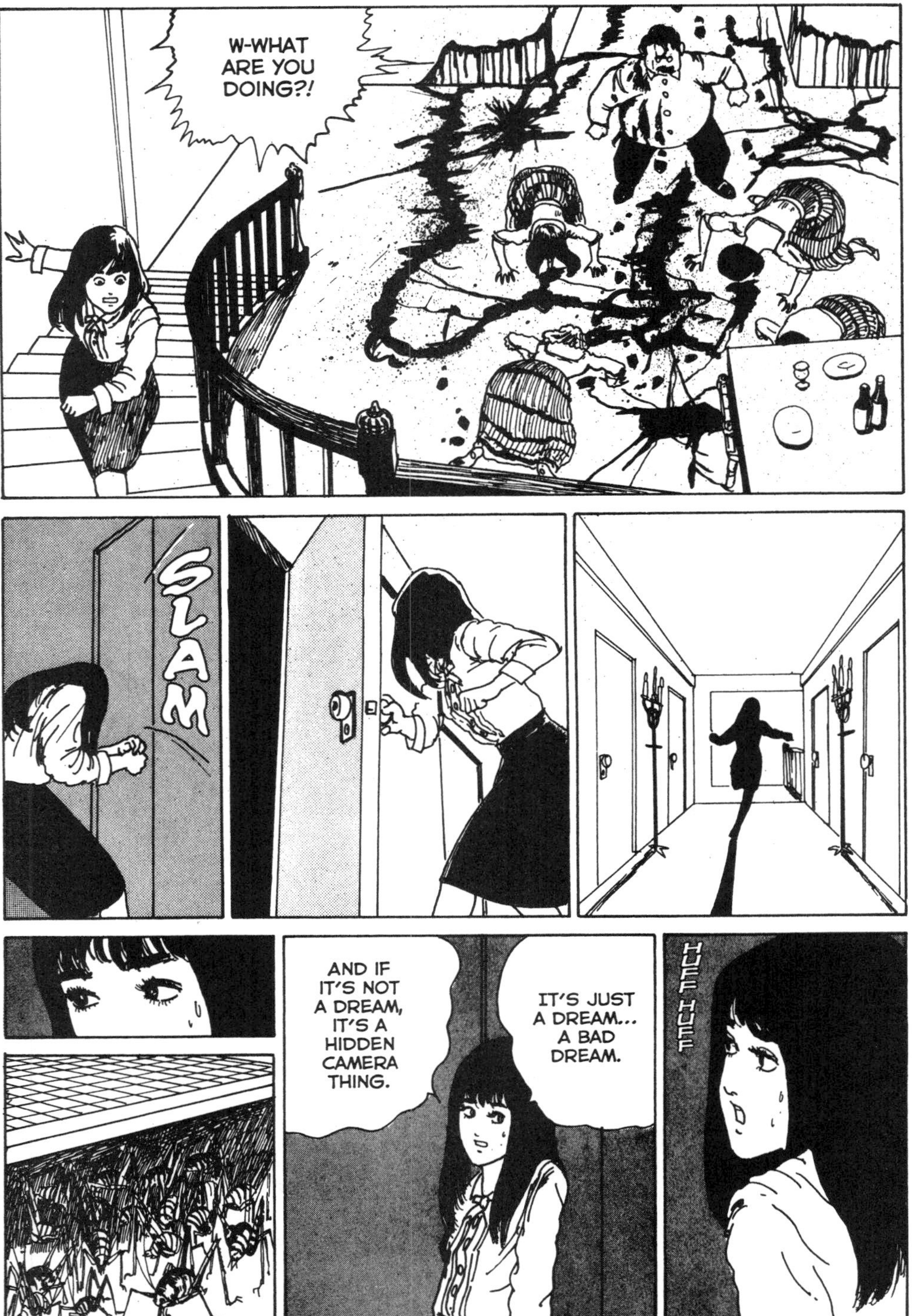
W-WHAT ARE YOU DOING?!
SLAM
HUFF HUFF
IT'S JUST A DREAM... A BAD DREAM.
AND IF IT'S NOT A DREAM, IT'S A HIDDEN CAMERA THING.

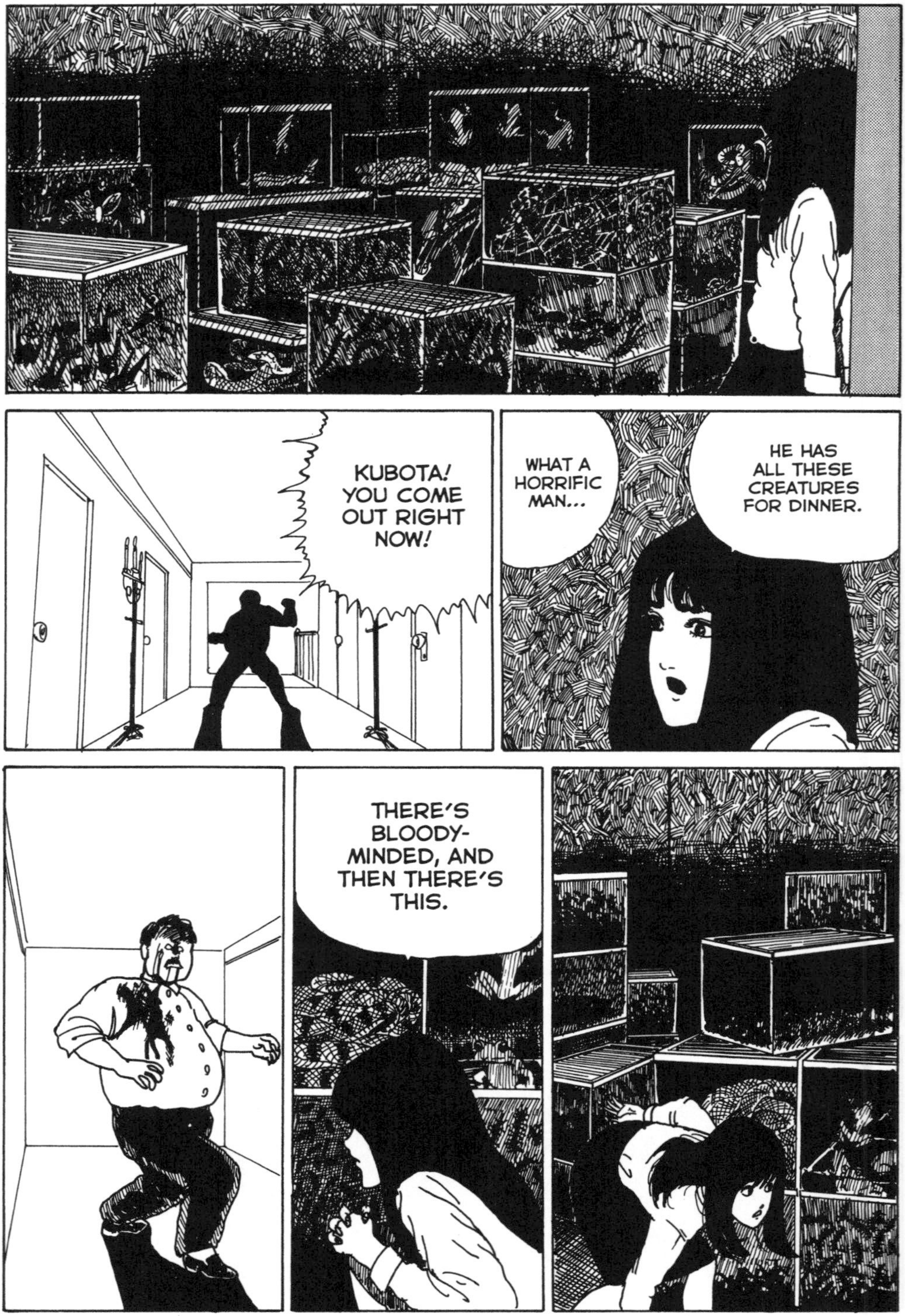
HE HAS ALL THESE CREATURES FOR DINNER.
WHAT A HORRIFIC MAN...
KUBOTA! YOU COME OUT RIGHT NOW!
THERE'S BLOODY-MINDED, AND THEN THERE'S THIS.

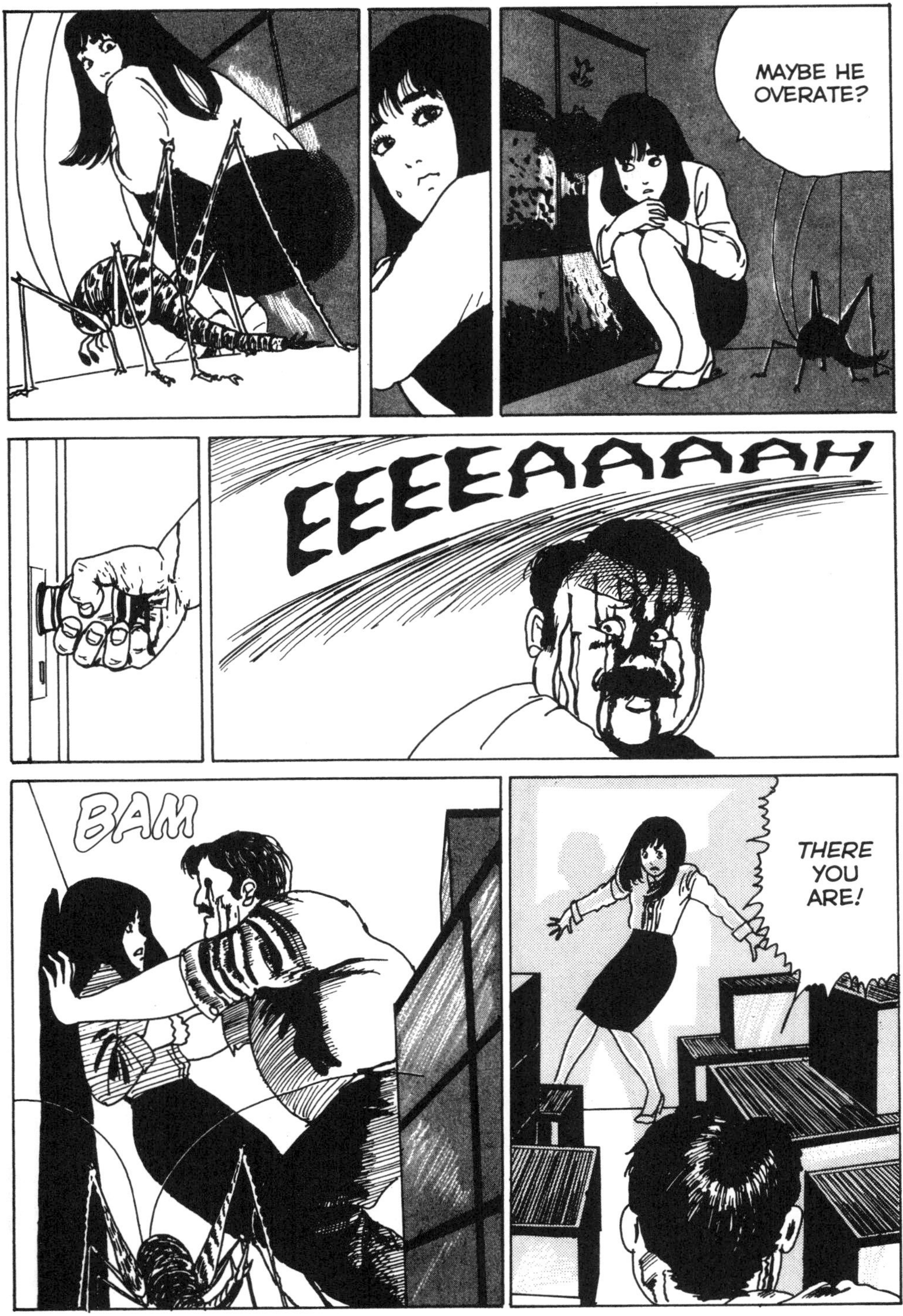
MAYBE HE OVERATE?
EEEEAAAAAH
THERE YOU ARE!
BAM

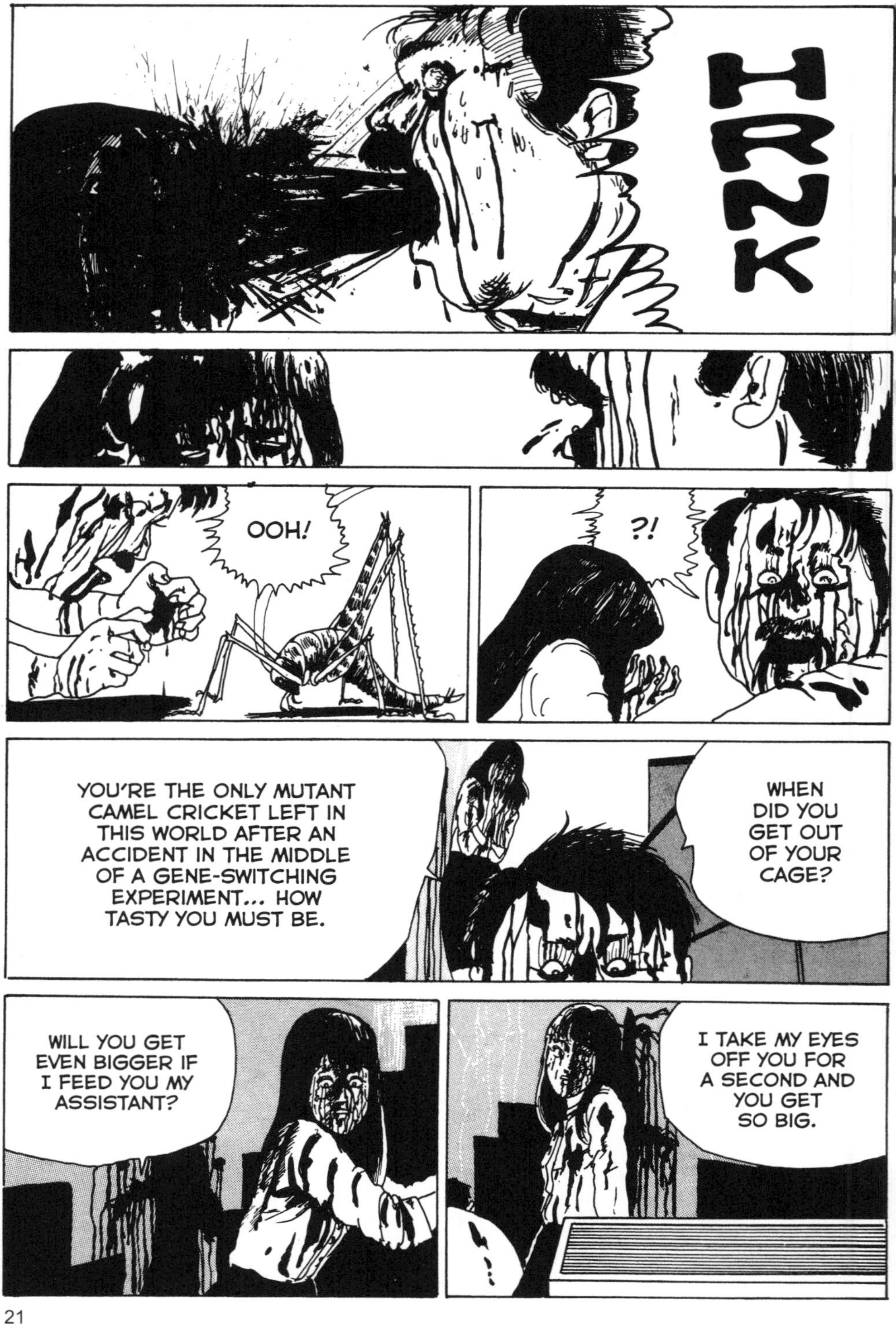
HRNK
?!
OOH!
WHEN DID YOU GET OUT OF YOUR CAGE?
YOU'RE THE ONLY MUTANT CAMEL CRICKET LEFT IN THIS WORLD AFTER AN ACCIDENT IN THE MIDDLE OF A GENE-SWITCHING EXPERIMENT... HOW TASTY YOU MUST BE.
I TAKE MY EYES OFF YOU FOR A SECOND AND YOU GET SO BIG.
WILL YOU GET EVEN BIGGER IF I FEED YOU MY ASSISTANT?

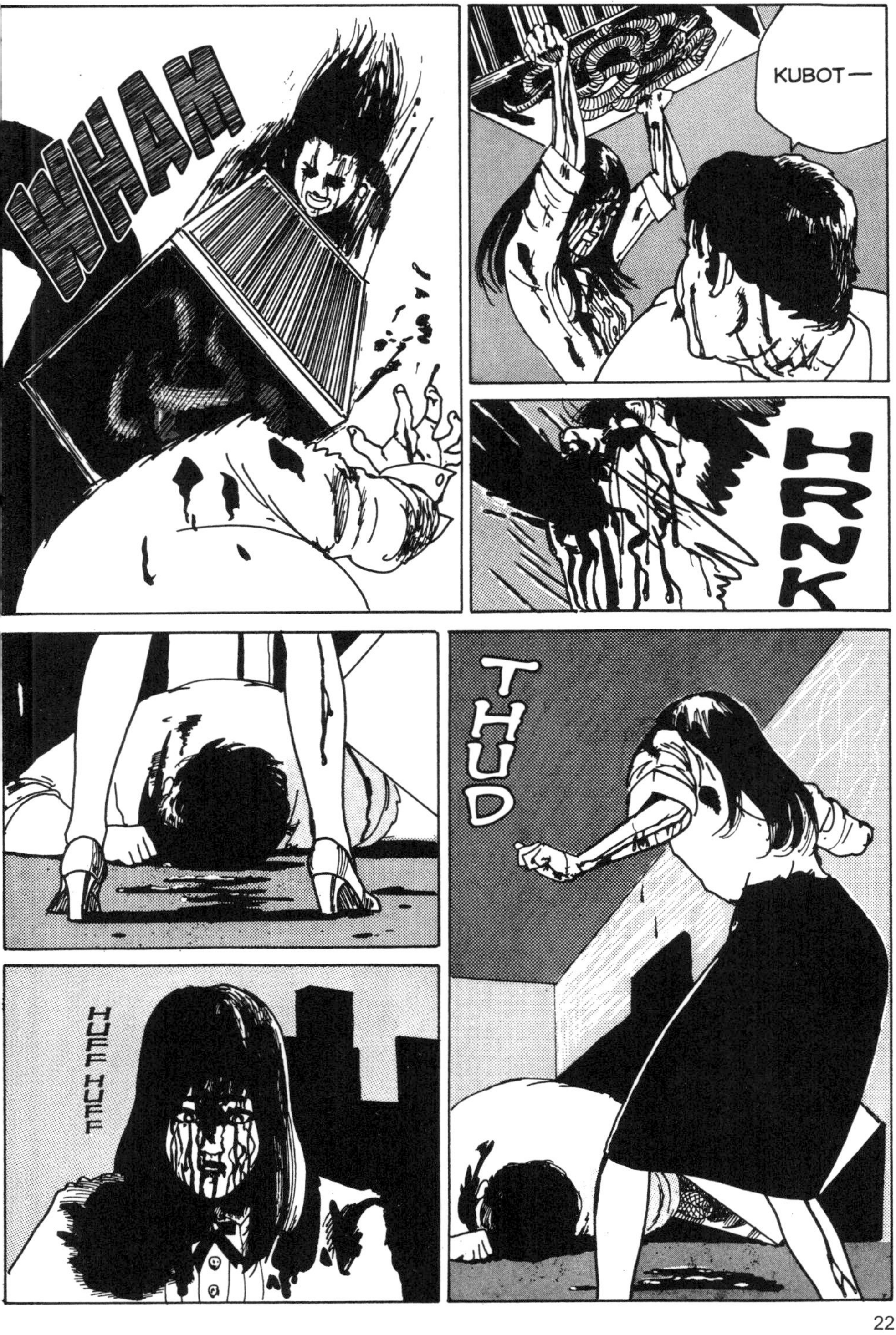
KUBOT—
HRNK
WHAM
THUD
HUFF HUFF

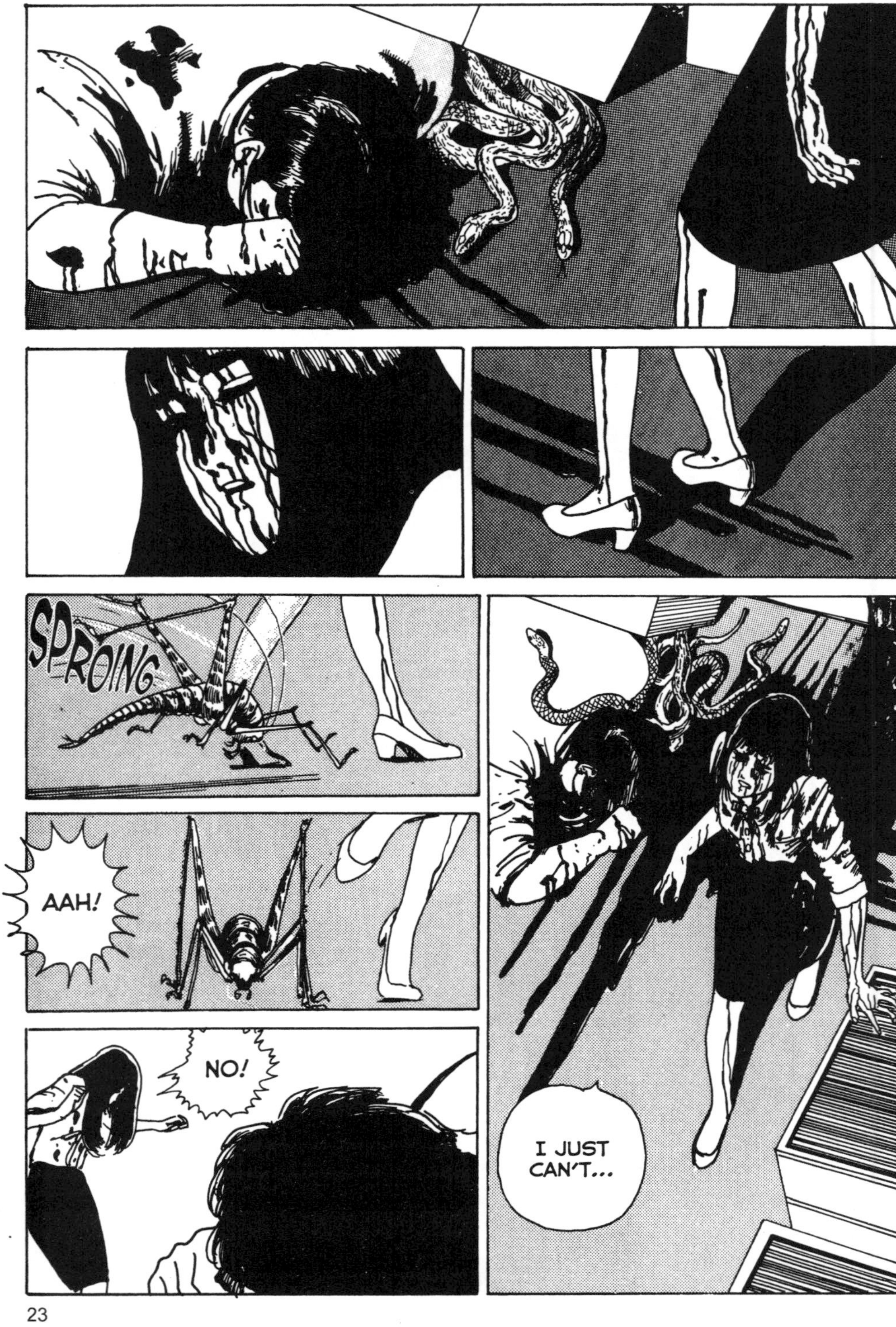
I JUST CAN'T...
SPROING
AAH!
NO!

THIS THING!
MWAH HA HA HA HA HA HA HA HA HA!
AAAAAH!
THD THD
THD

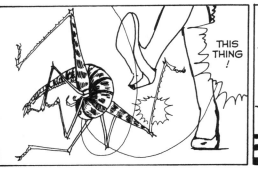

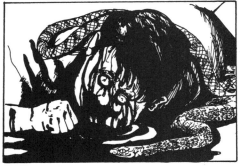

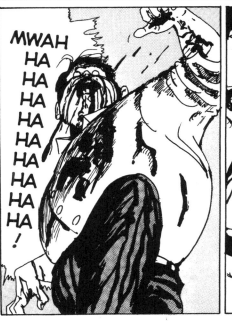

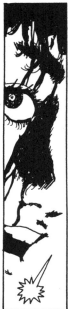

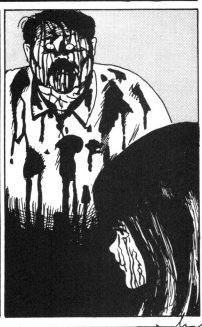

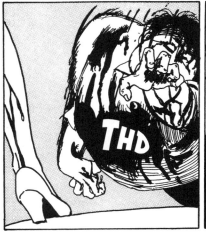

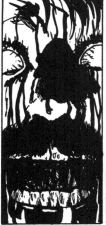

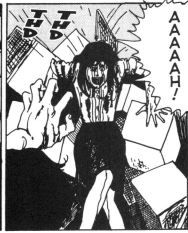

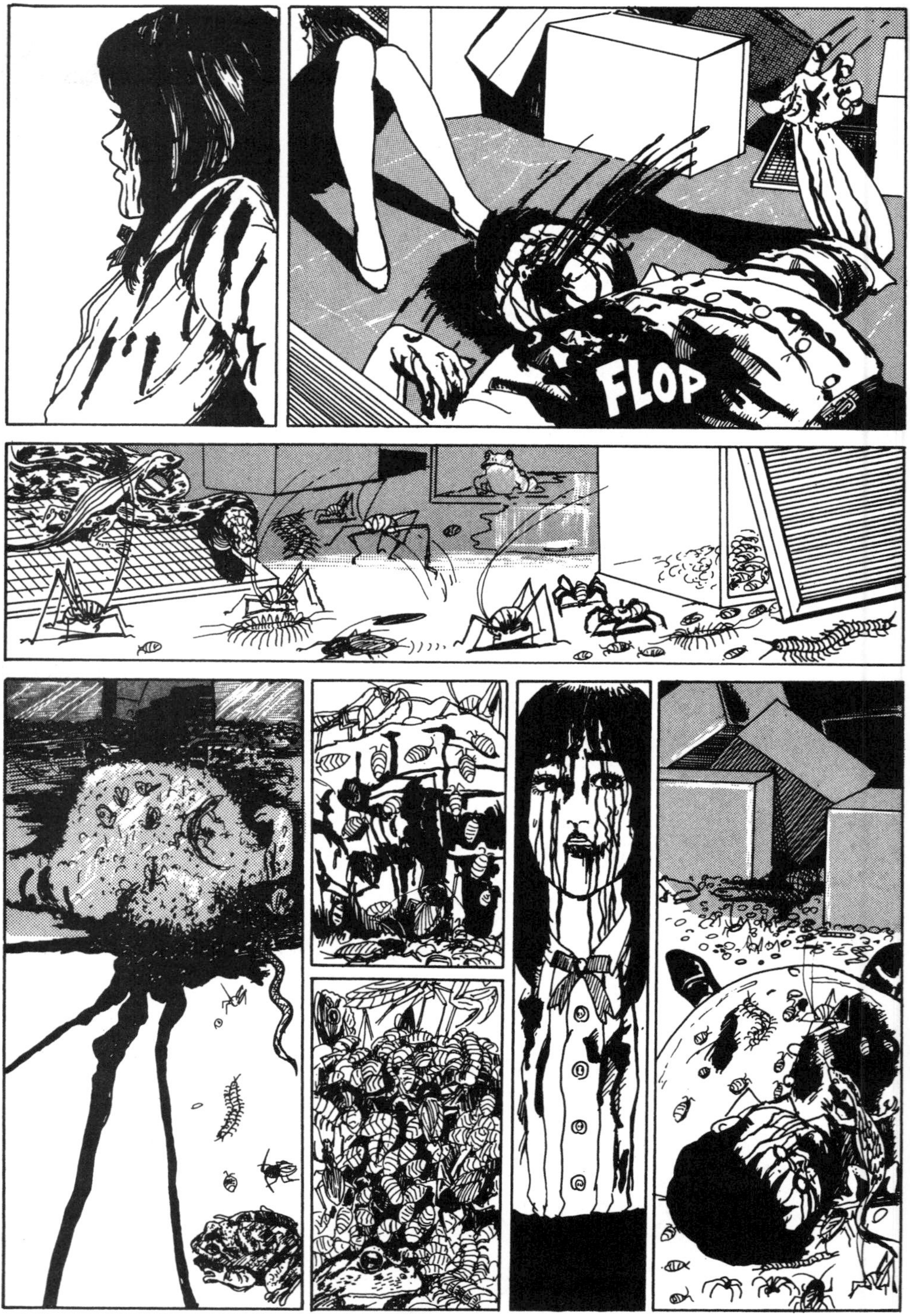
FLOP

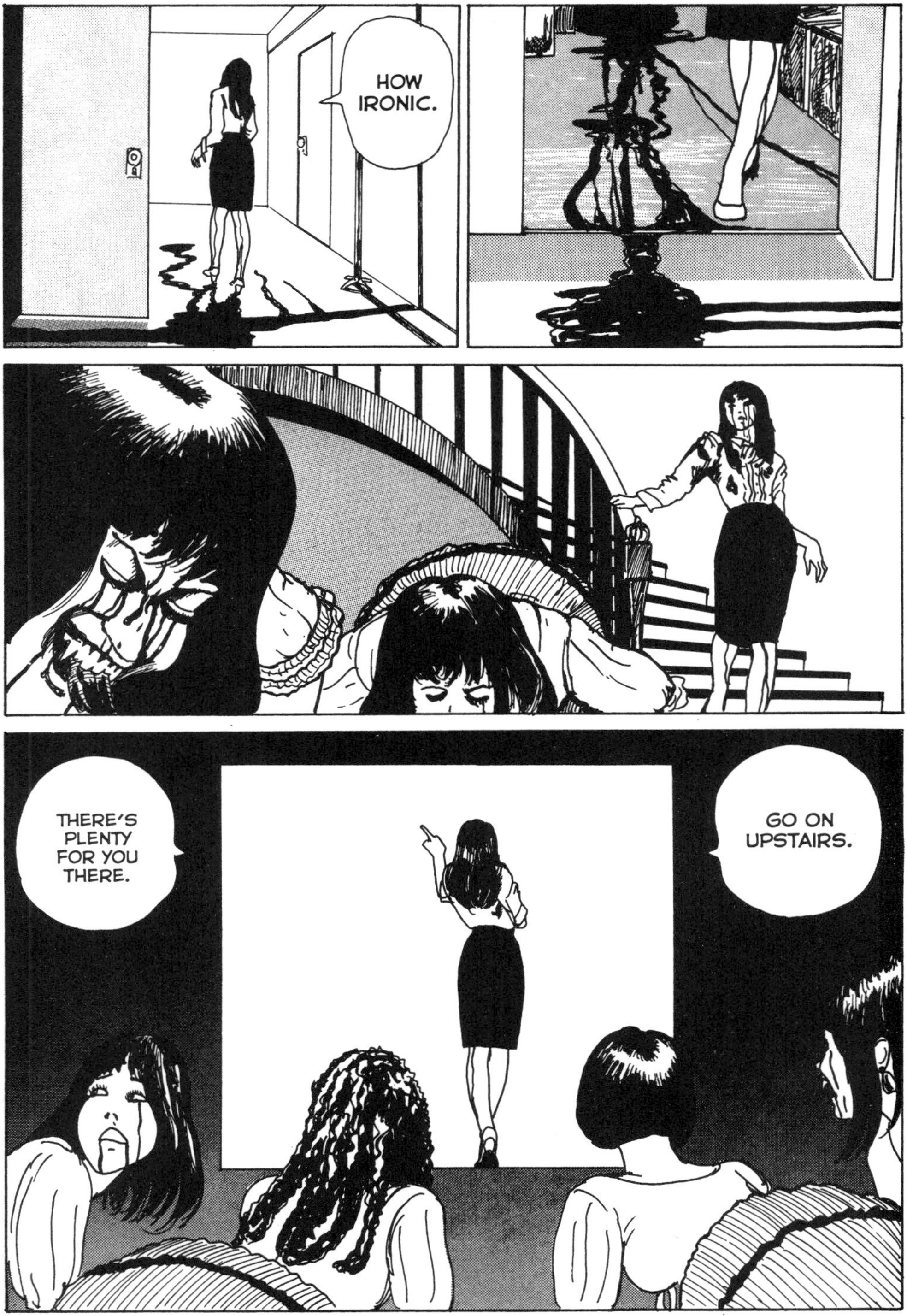
HOW IRONIC.
GO ON UPSTAIRS.
THERE'S PLENTY FOR YOU THERE.

かお　どろ　ぼう

顔泥棒

FACE THIEF

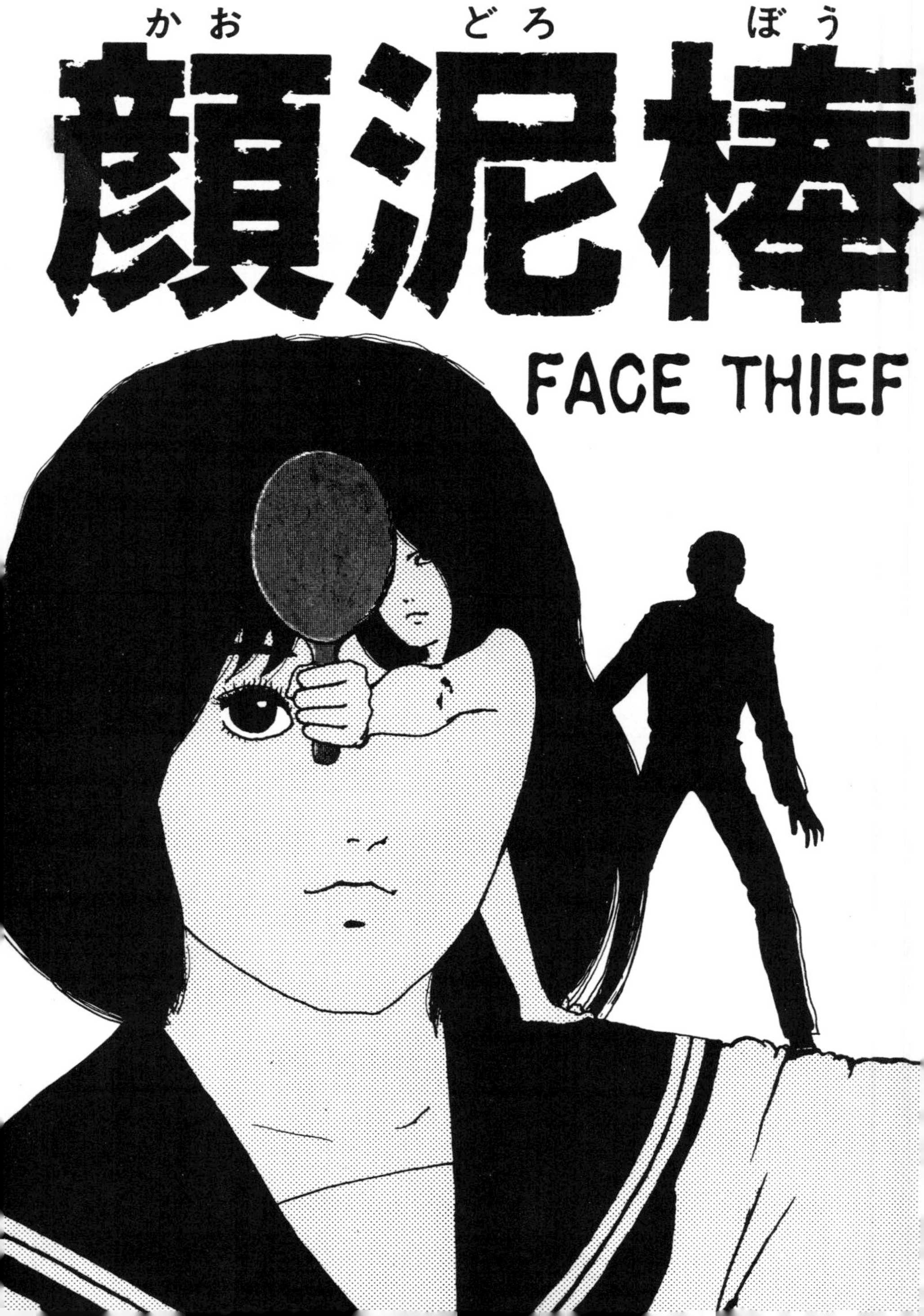

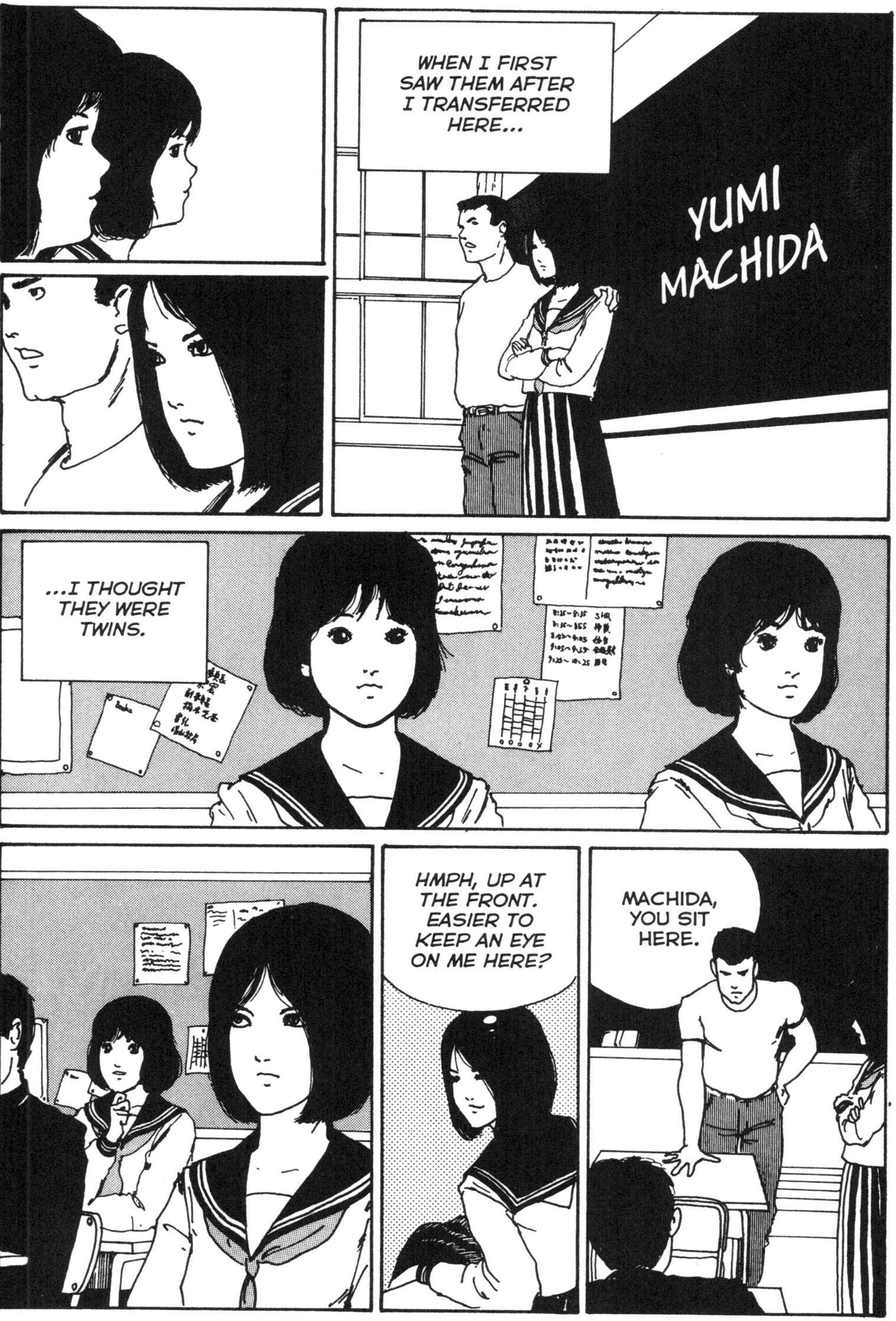

WHEN I FIRST SAW THEM AFTER I TRANSFERRED HERE...
YUMI MACHIDA
...I THOUGHT THEY WERE TWINS.
MACHIDA, YOU SIT HERE.
HMPH, UP AT THE FRONT. EASIER TO KEEP AN EYE ON ME HERE?

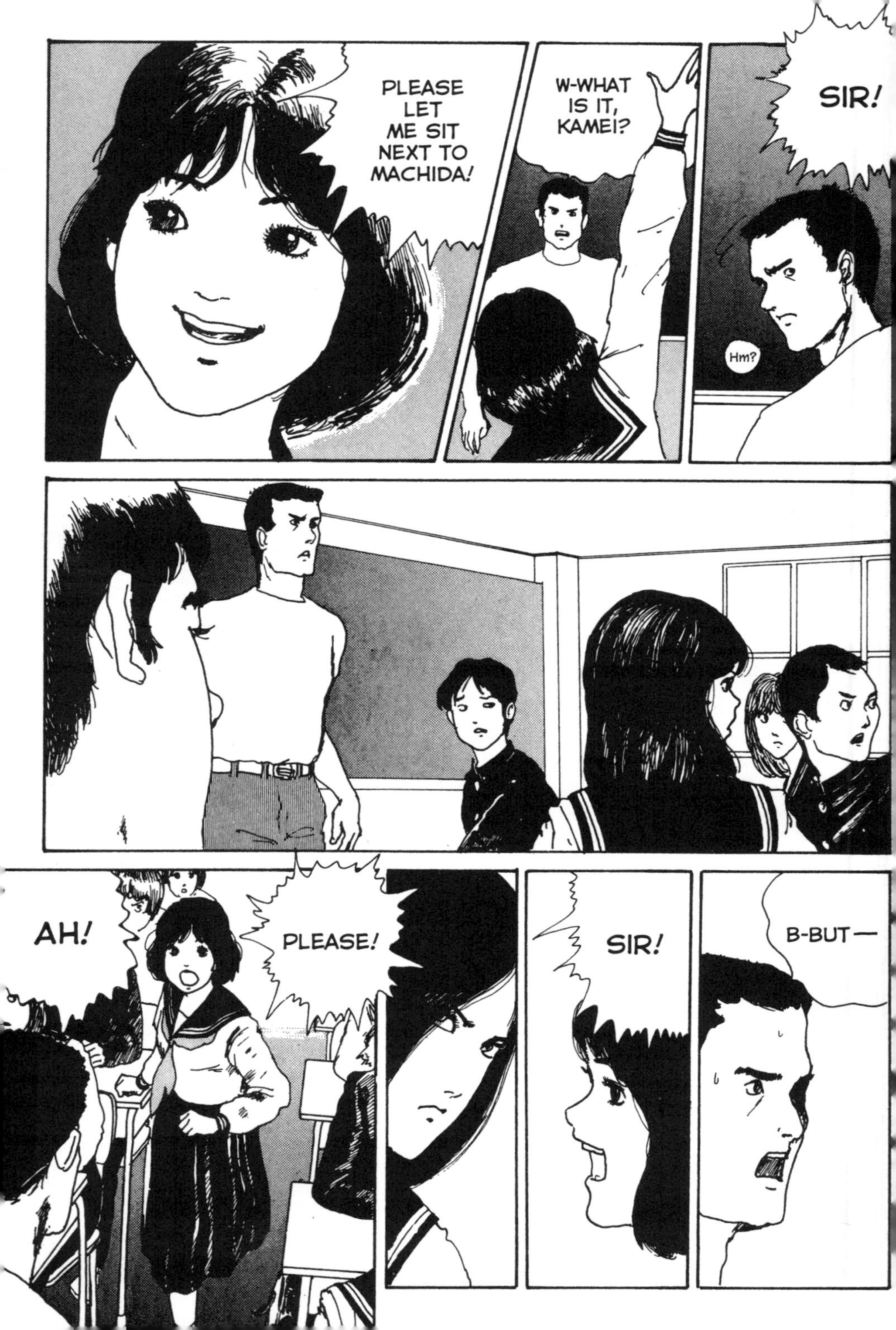
SIR!
Hm?
W-WHAT IS IT, KAMEI?
PLEASE LET ME SIT NEXT TO MACHIDA!
B-BUT—
SIR!
PLEASE!
AH!

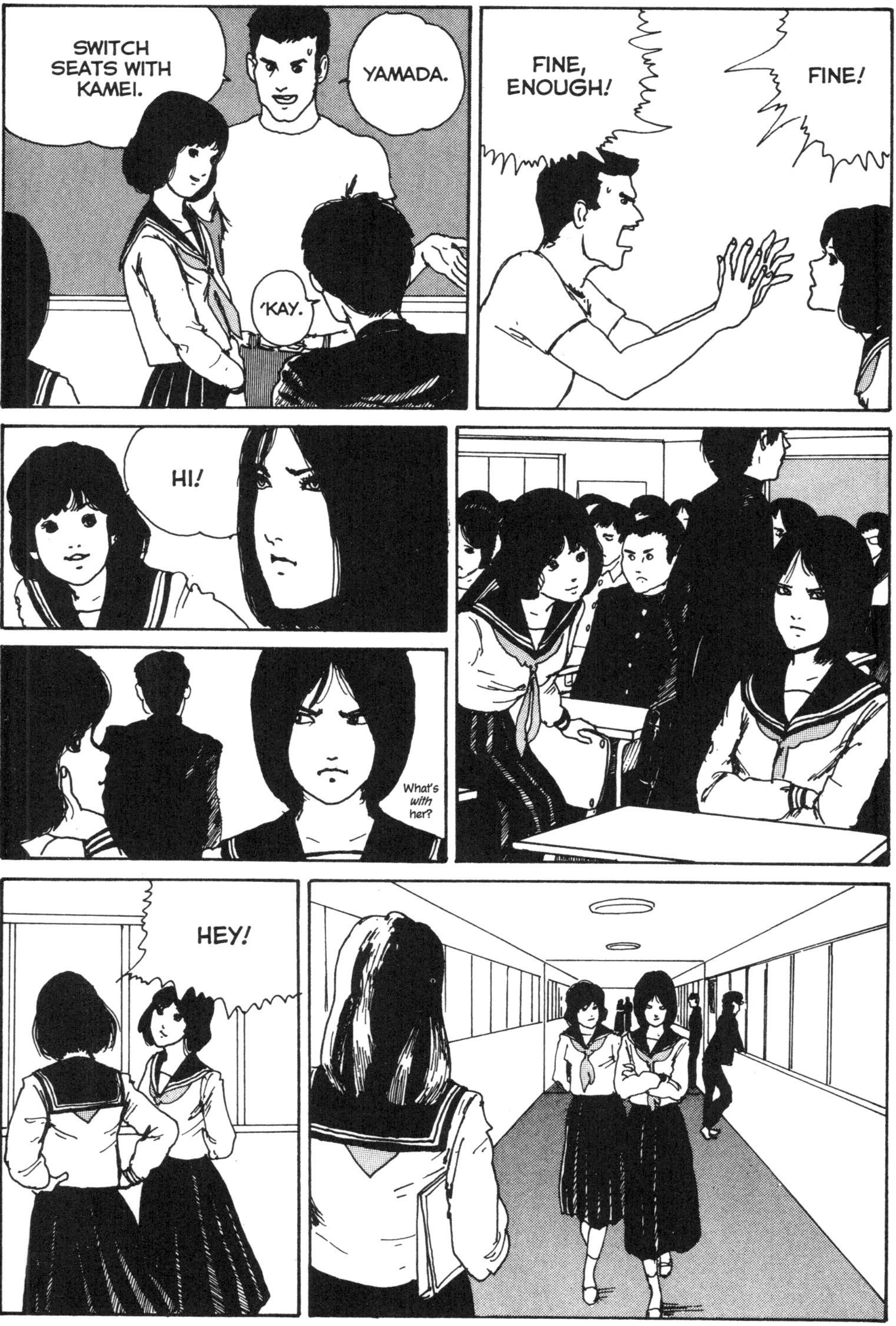
FINE!
FINE, ENOUGH!
YAMADA.
SWITCH SEATS WITH KAMEI.
'KAY.
HI!
What's with her?
HEY!

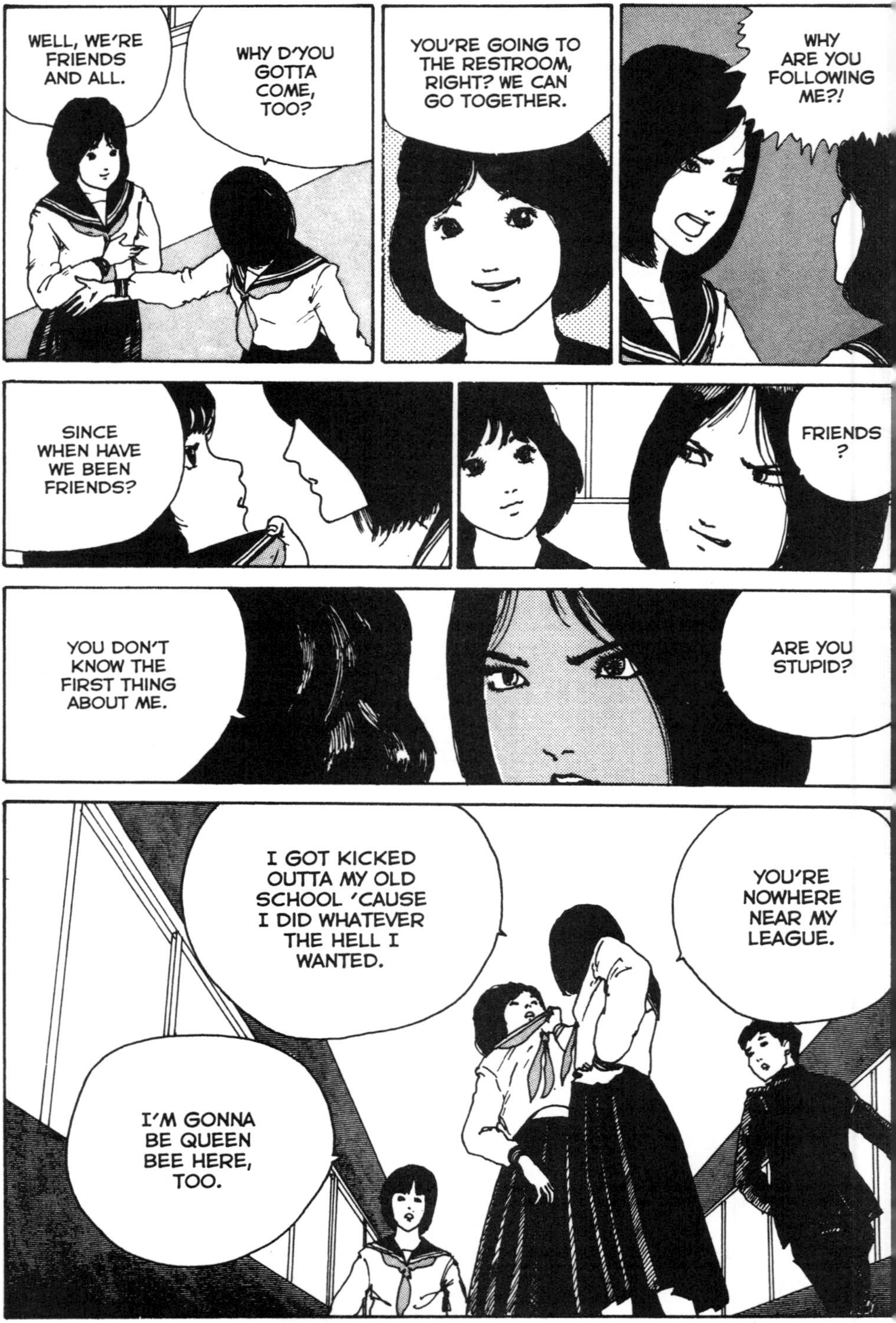
WHY ARE YOU FOLLOWING ME?!
YOU'RE GOING TO THE RESTROOM, RIGHT? WE CAN GO TOGETHER.
WHY D'YOU GOTTA COME, TOO?
WELL, WE'RE FRIENDS AND ALL.
FRIENDS?
SINCE WHEN HAVE WE BEEN FRIENDS?
ARE YOU STUPID?
YOU DON'T KNOW THE FIRST THING ABOUT ME.
YOU'RE NOWHERE NEAR MY LEAGUE.
I GOT KICKED OUTTA MY OLD SCHOOL 'CAUSE I DID WHATEVER THE HELL I WANTED.
I'M GONNA BE QUEEN BEE HERE, TOO.

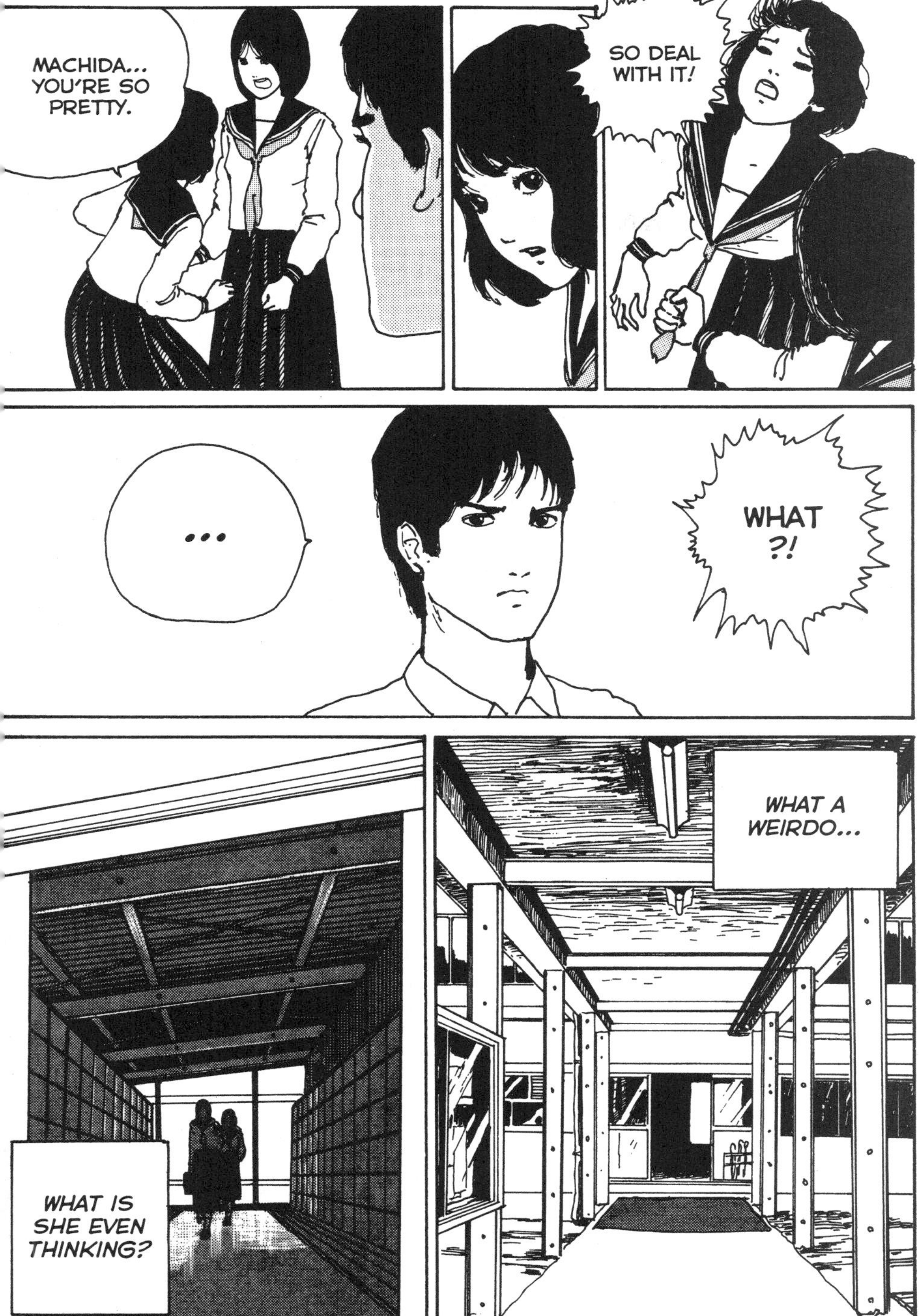
SO DEAL WITH IT!
MACHIDA... YOU'RE SO PRETTY.
WHAT ?!
...
WHAT A WEIRDO...
WHAT IS SHE EVEN THINKING?

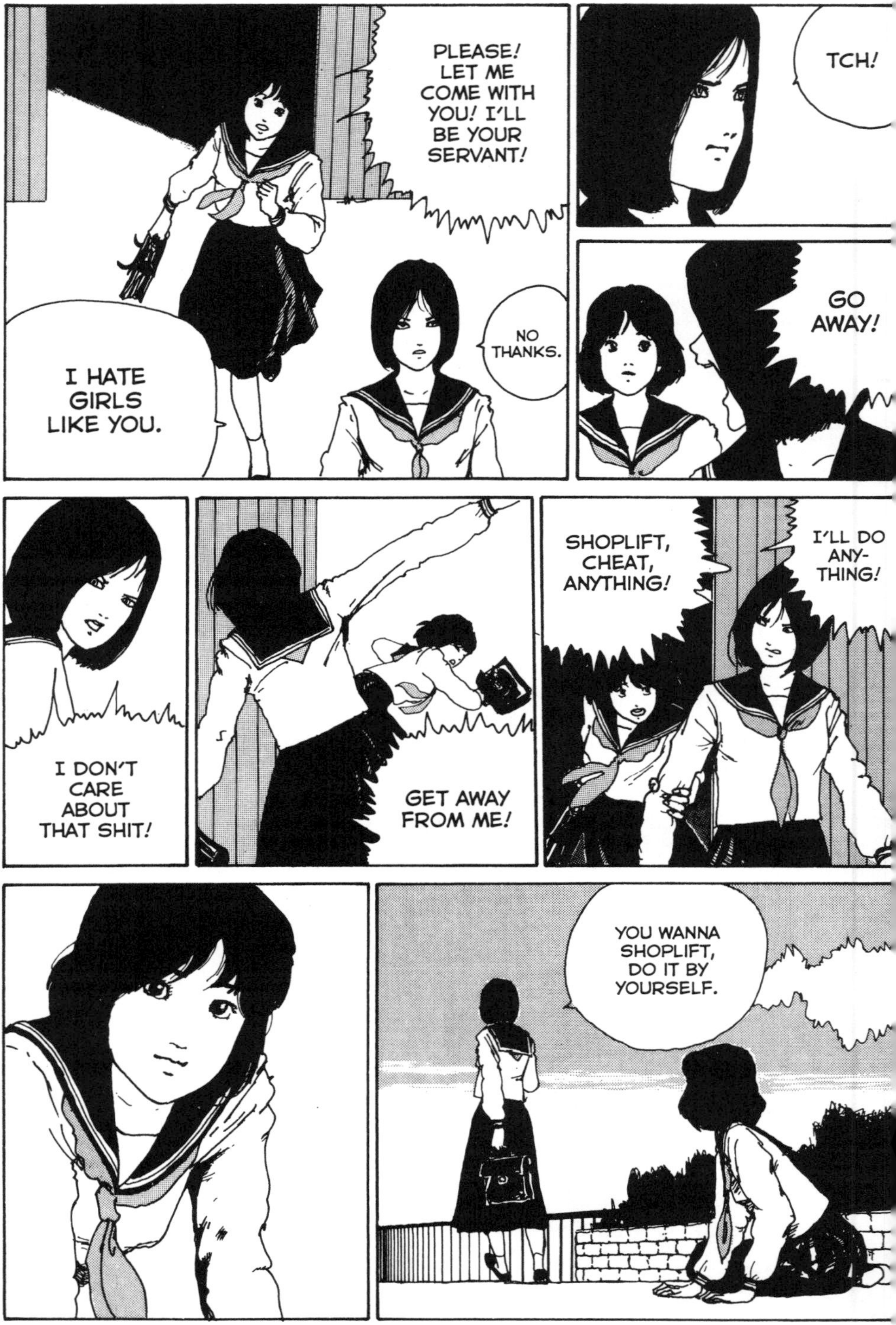
TCH!
GO AWAY!
PLEASE! LET ME COME WITH YOU! I'LL BE YOUR SERVANT!
NO THANKS.
I HATE GIRLS LIKE YOU.
I'LL DO ANY-THING!
SHOPLIFT, CHEAT, ANYTHING!
GET AWAY FROM ME!
I DON'T CARE ABOUT THAT SHIT!
YOU WANNA SHOPLIFT, DO IT BY YOURSELF.

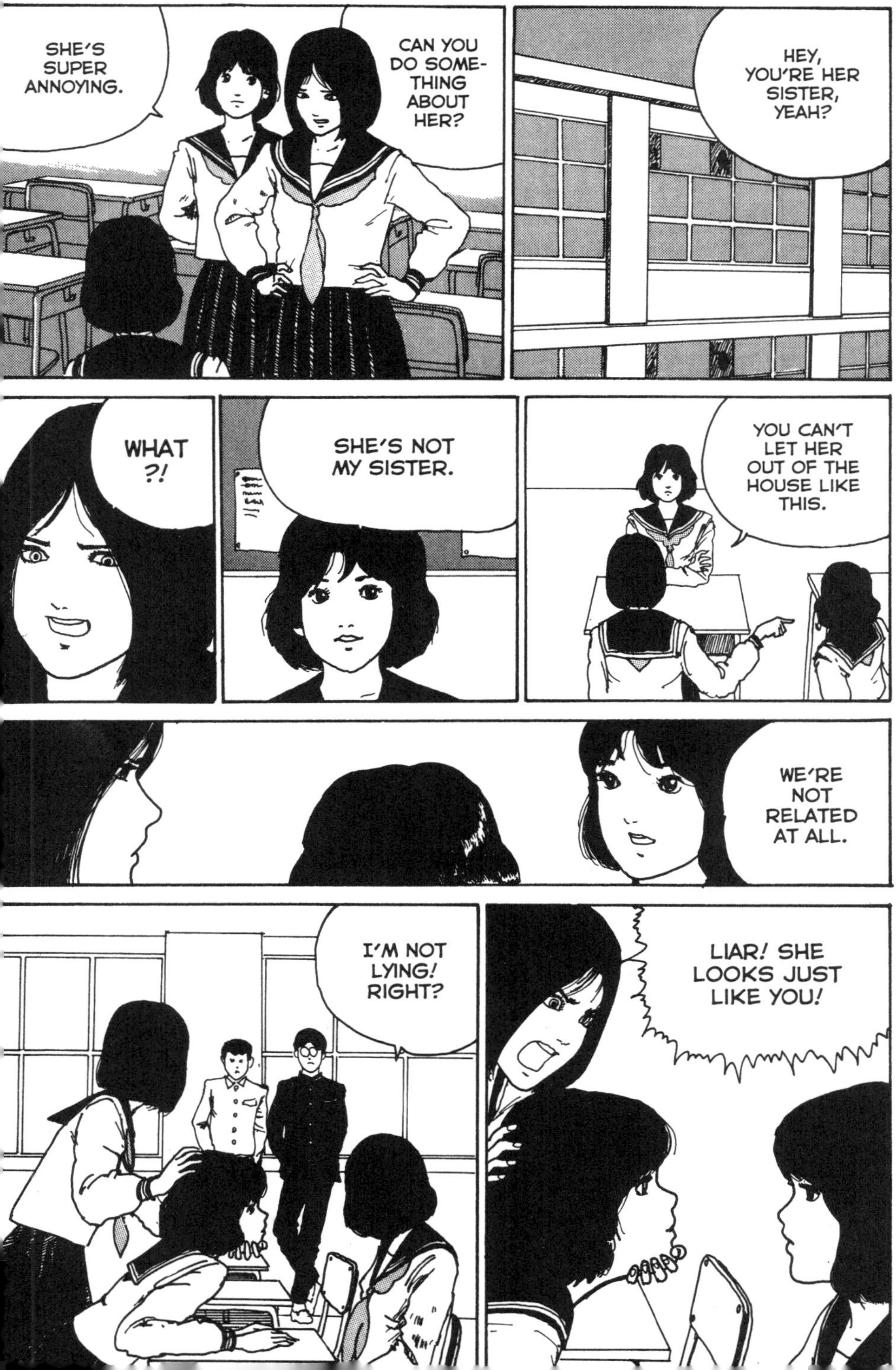
HEY, YOU'RE HER SISTER, YEAH?
CAN YOU DO SOME-THING ABOUT HER?
SHE'S SUPER ANNOYING.
YOU CAN'T LET HER OUT OF THE HOUSE LIKE THIS.
SHE'S NOT MY SISTER.
WHAT ?!
WE'RE NOT RELATED AT ALL.
LIAR! SHE LOOKS JUST LIKE YOU!
I'M NOT LYING! RIGHT?

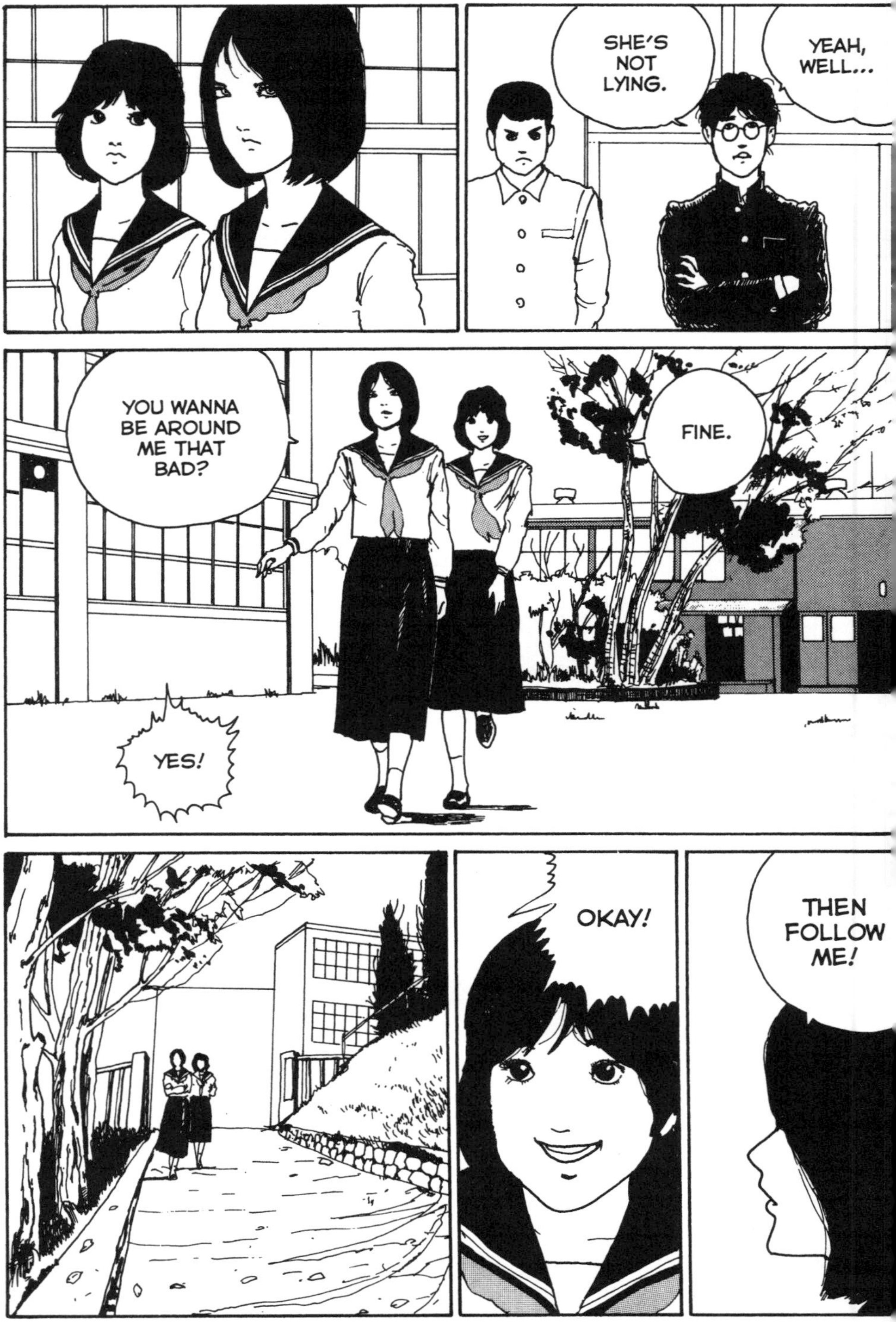
YEAH, WELL...
SHE'S NOT LYING.
FINE.
YOU WANNA BE AROUND ME THAT BAD?
YES!
THEN FOLLOW ME!
OKAY!

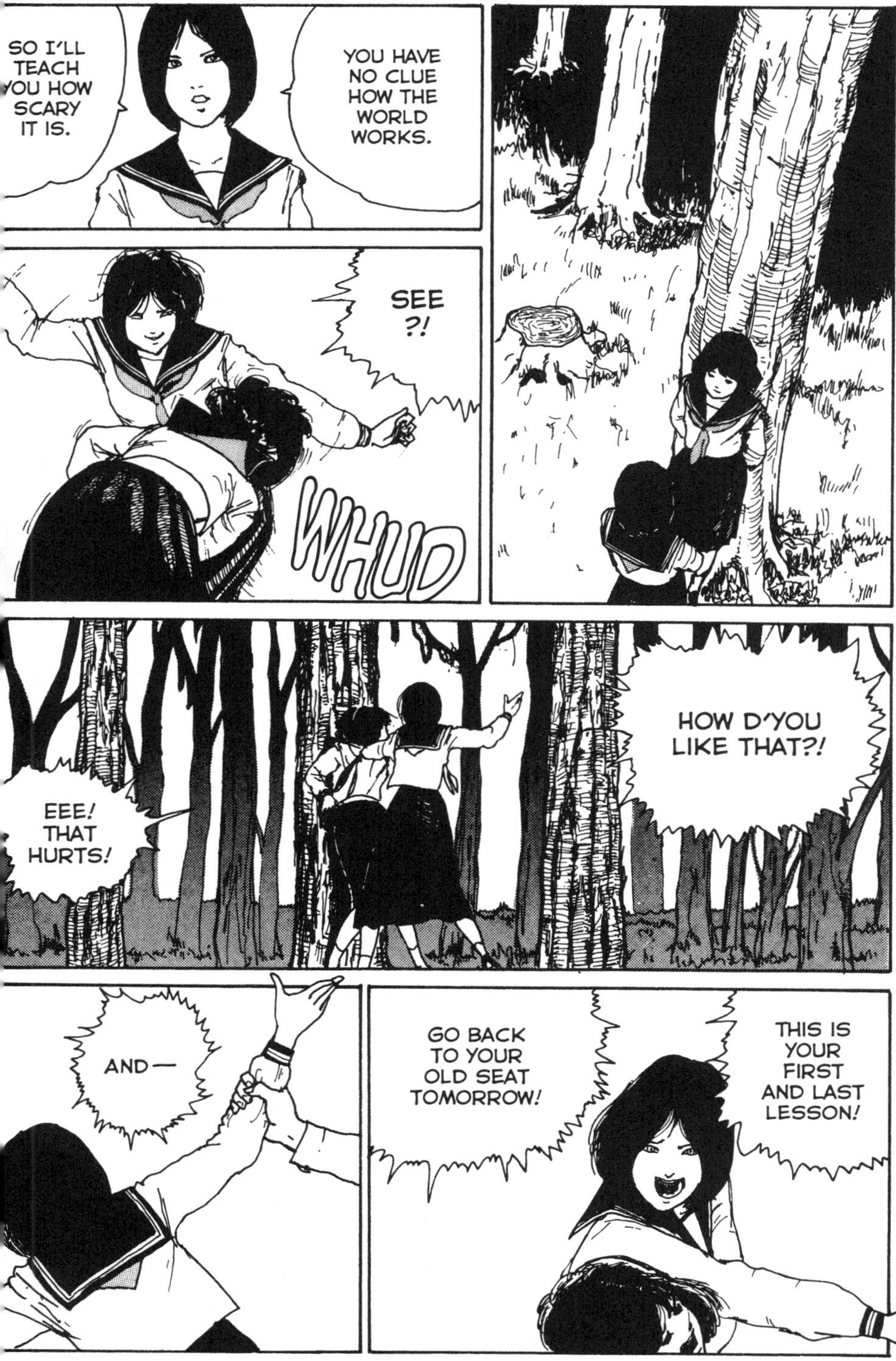
YOU HAVE NO CLUE HOW THE WORLD WORKS.
SO I'LL TEACH YOU HOW SCARY IT IS.
SEE?!
WHUD
HOW D'YOU LIKE THAT?!
EEE! THAT HURTS!
THIS IS YOUR FIRST AND LAST LESSON!
GO BACK TO YOUR OLD SEAT TOMORROW!
AND—

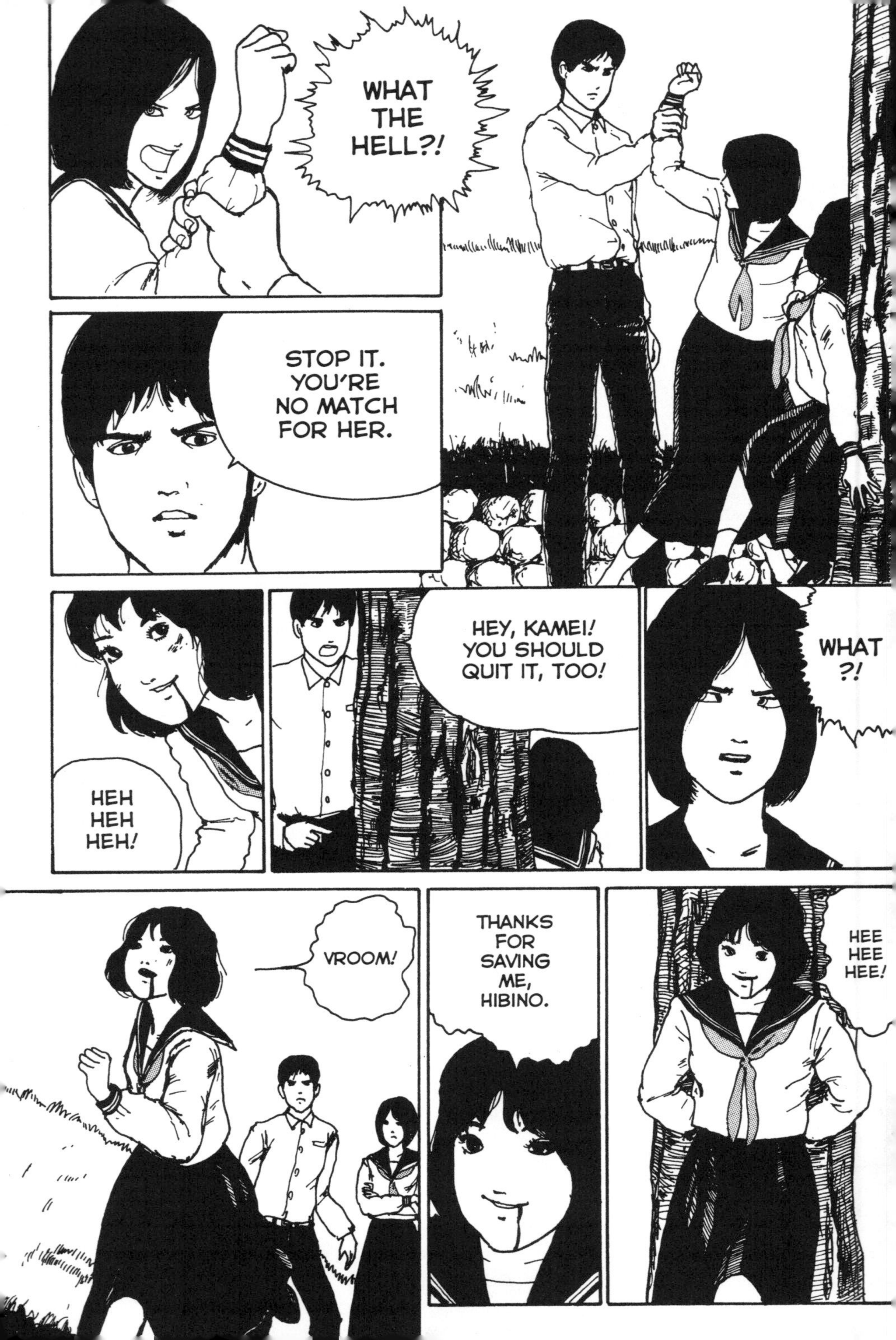
WHAT THE HELL?!
STOP IT. YOU'RE NO MATCH FOR HER.
WHAT ?!
HEY, KAMEI! YOU SHOULD QUIT IT, TOO!
HEH HEH HEH!
HEE HEE HEE!
THANKS FOR SAVING ME, HIBINO.
VROOM!

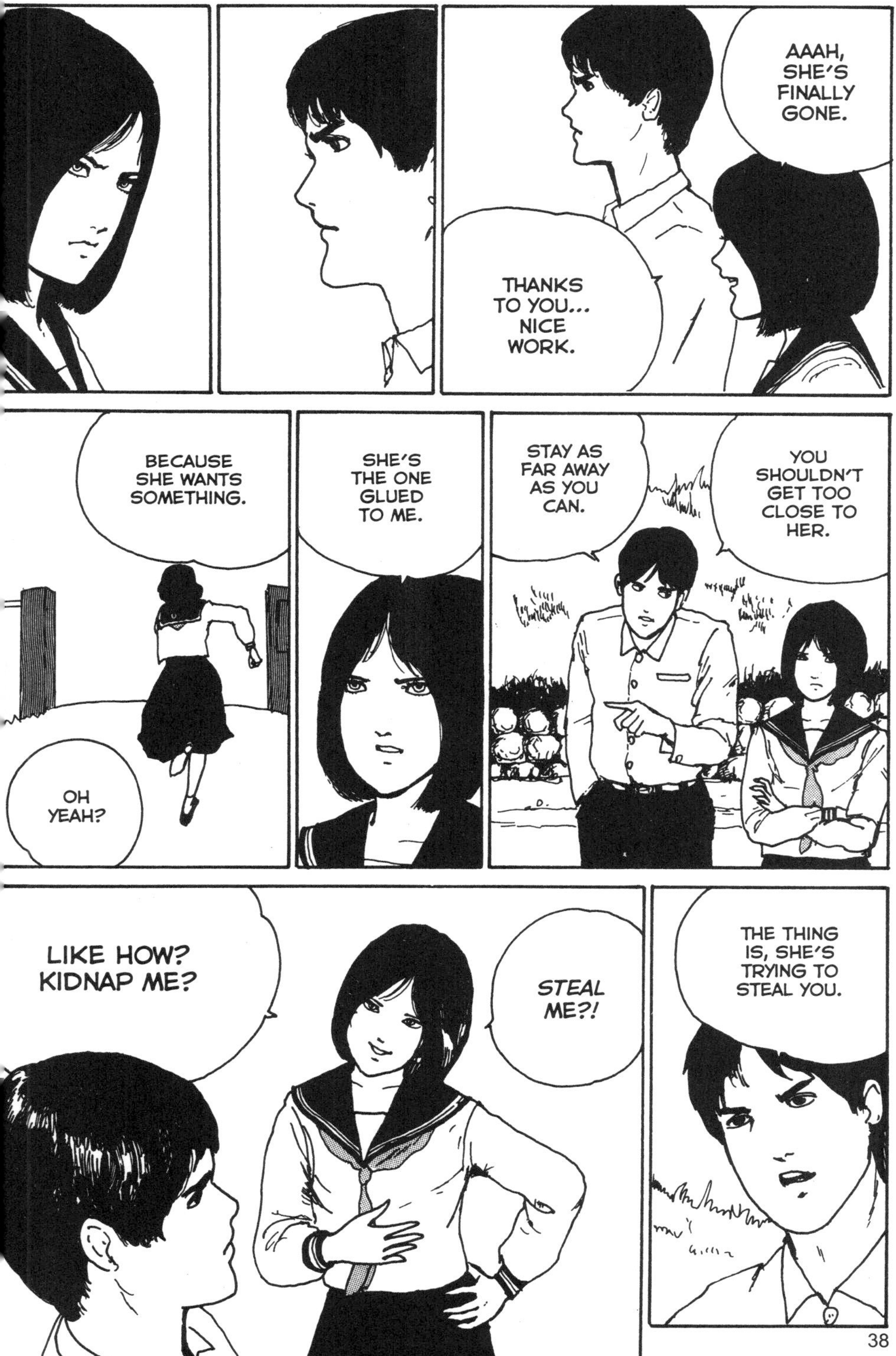
AAAH, SHE'S FINALLY GONE.
THANKS TO YOU... NICE WORK.
YOU SHOULDN'T GET TOO CLOSE TO HER.
STAY AS FAR AWAY AS YOU CAN.
SHE'S THE ONE GLUED TO ME.
BECAUSE SHE WANTS SOMETHING.
OH YEAH?
THE THING IS, SHE'S TRYING TO STEAL YOU.
STEAL ME?!
LIKE HOW? KIDNAP ME?

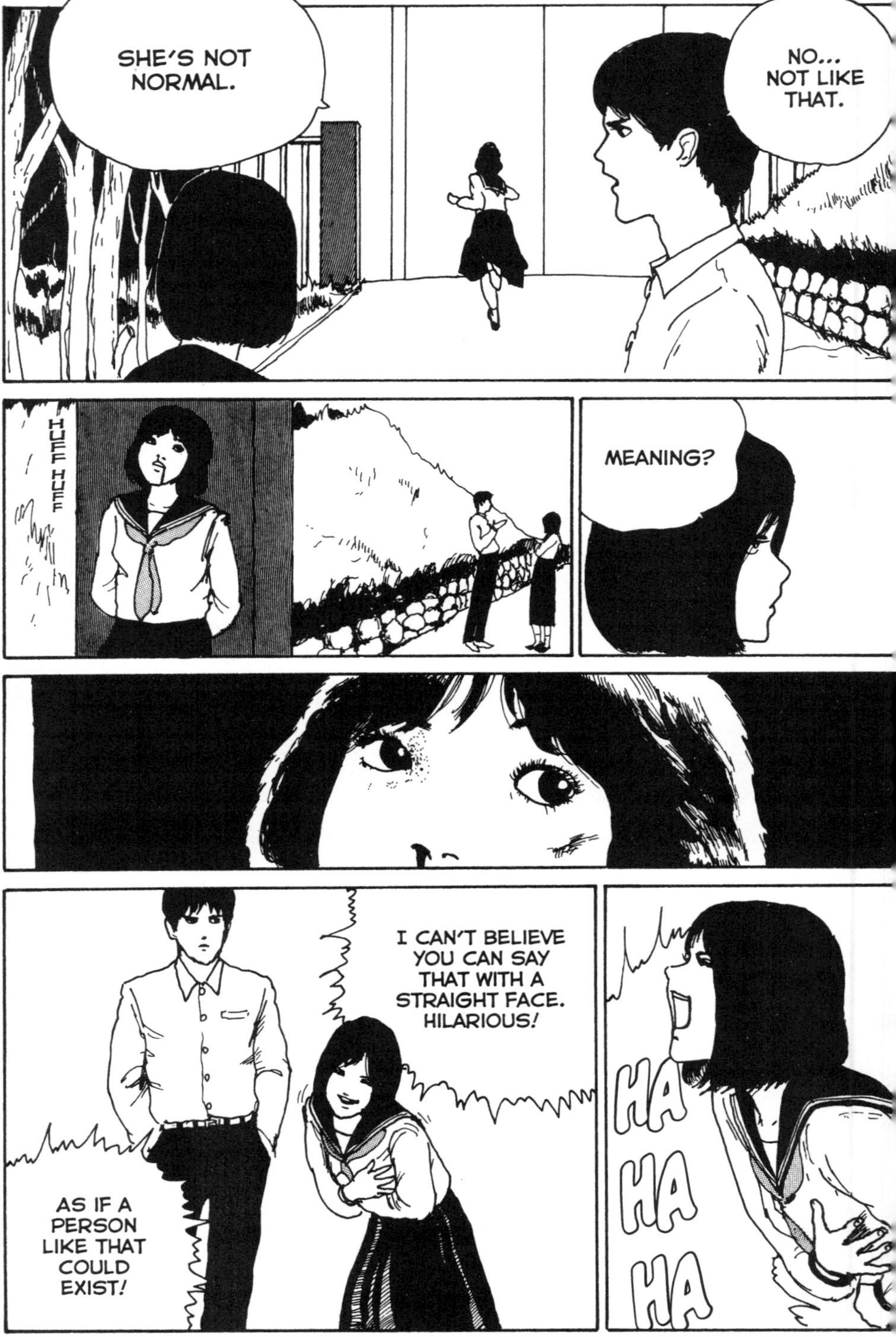
NO... NOT LIKE THAT.
SHE'S NOT NORMAL.
MEANING?
HUFF HUFF
HA HA HA
I CAN'T BELIEVE YOU CAN SAY THAT WITH A STRAIGHT FACE. HILARIOUS!
AS IF A PERSON LIKE THAT COULD EXIST!

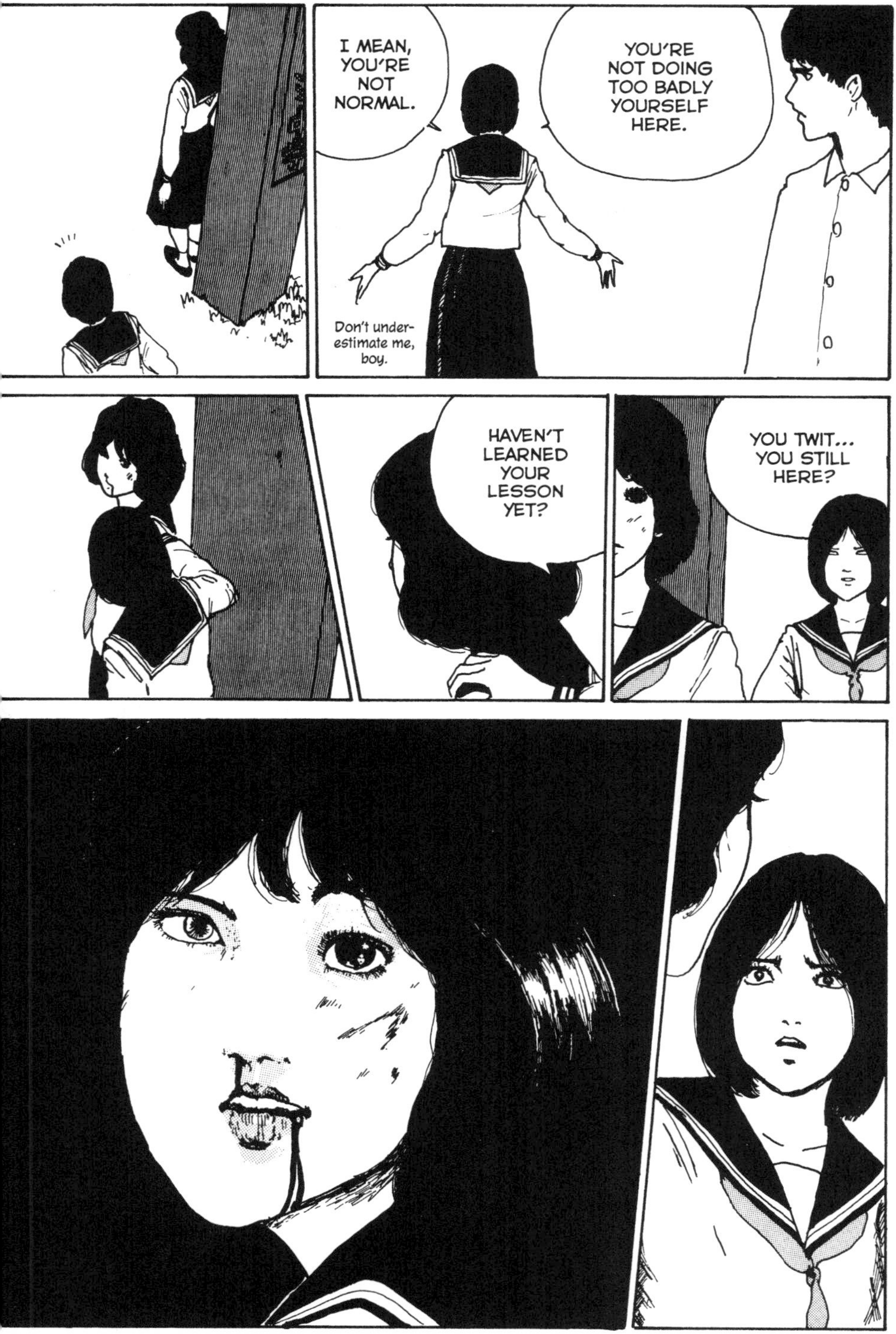
YOU'RE NOT DOING TOO BADLY YOURSELF HERE.
I MEAN, YOU'RE NOT NORMAL.
Don't under-estimate me, boy.
YOU TWIT... YOU STILL HERE?
HAVEN'T LEARNED YOUR LESSON YET?

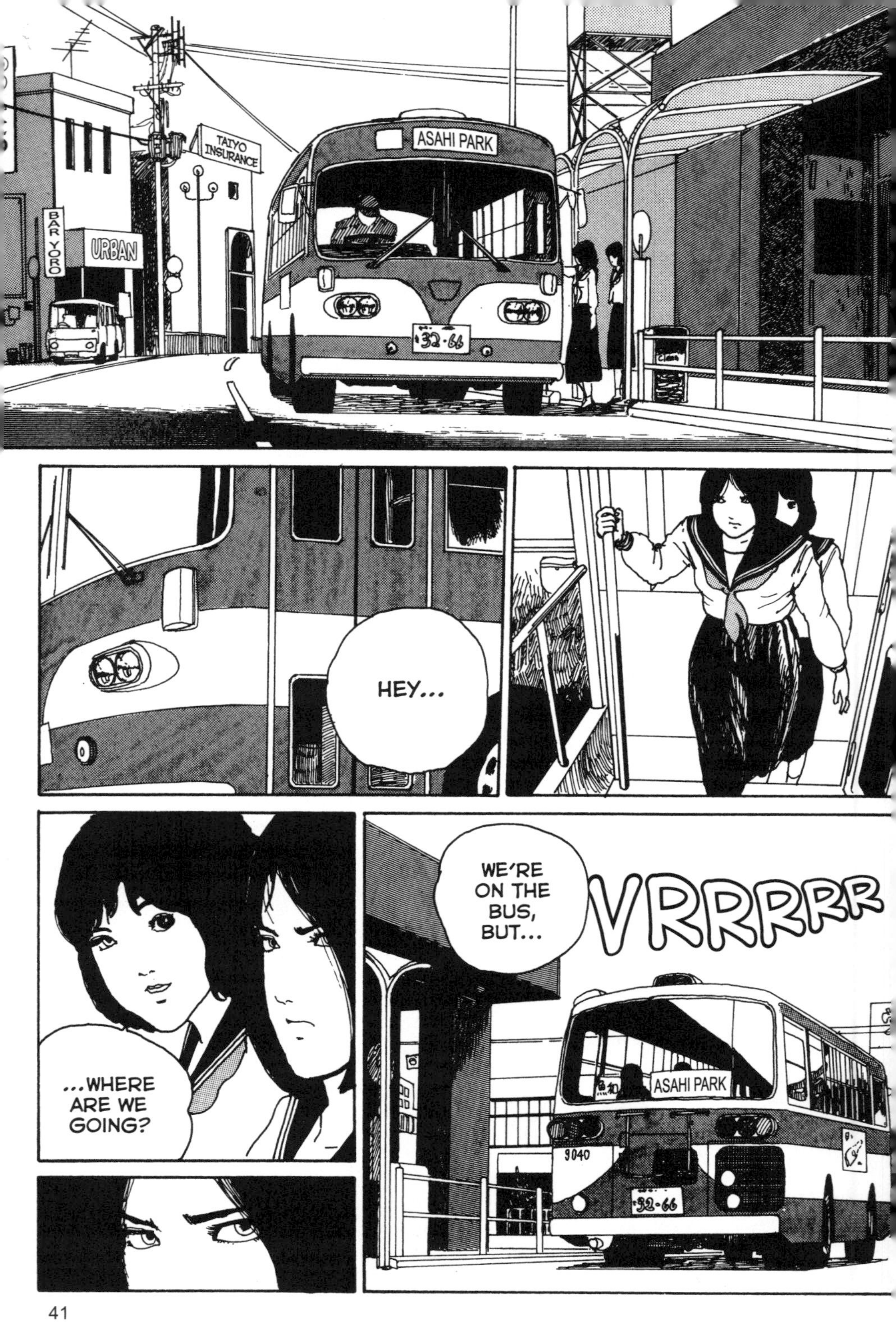
ASAHI PARK
TAIYO INSURANCE
BAR YORO
URBAN
32·66
HEY...
WE'RE ON THE BUS, BUT...
VRRRRR
ASAHI PARK
9040
32·66
...WHERE ARE WE GOING?

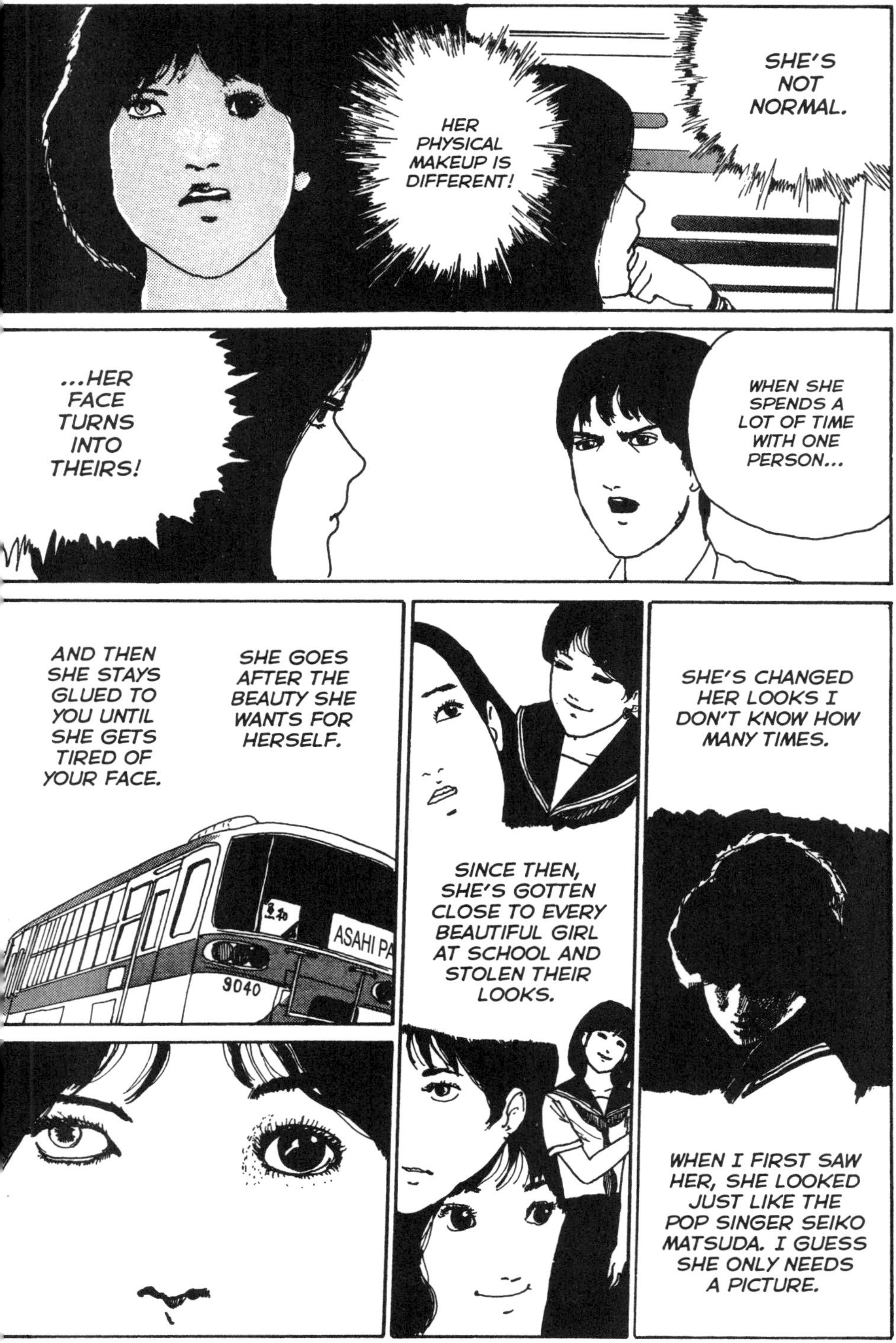
SHE'S NOT NORMAL.
HER PHYSICAL MAKEUP IS DIFFERENT!
WHEN SHE SPENDS A LOT OF TIME WITH ONE PERSON...
...HER FACE TURNS INTO THEIRS!
SHE'S CHANGED HER LOOKS I DON'T KNOW HOW MANY TIMES.
WHEN I FIRST SAW HER, SHE LOOKED JUST LIKE THE POP SINGER SEIKO MATSUDA. I GUESS SHE ONLY NEEDS A PICTURE.
SINCE THEN, SHE'S GOTTEN CLOSE TO EVERY BEAUTIFUL GIRL AT SCHOOL AND STOLEN THEIR LOOKS.
SHE GOES AFTER THE BEAUTY SHE WANTS FOR HERSELF.
AND THEN SHE STAYS GLUED TO YOU UNTIL SHE GETS TIRED OF YOUR FACE.
ASAHI PA
9040

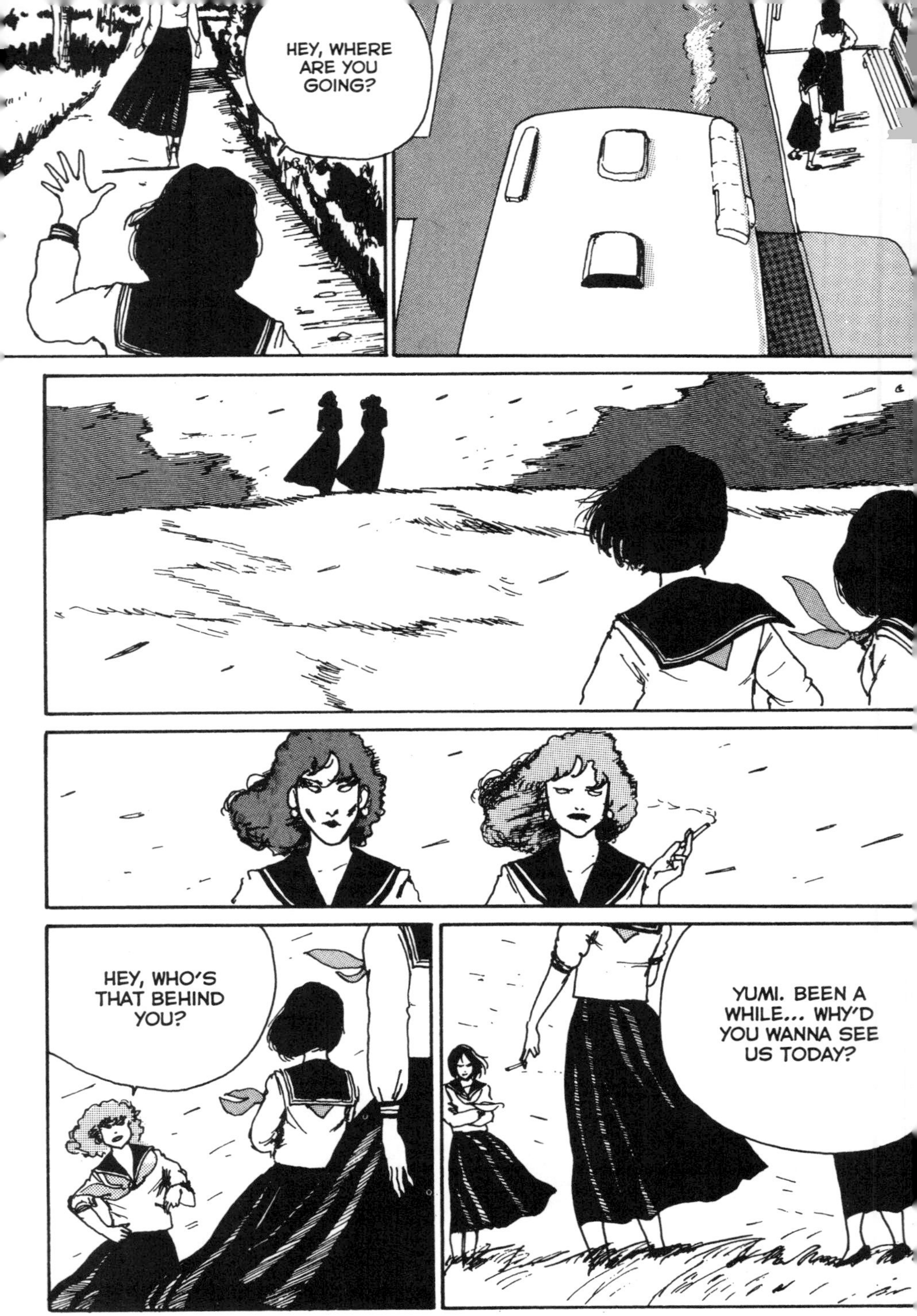
HEY, WHERE ARE YOU GOING?
YUMI. BEEN A WHILE... WHY'D YOU WANNA SEE US TODAY?
HEY, WHO'S THAT BEHIND YOU?

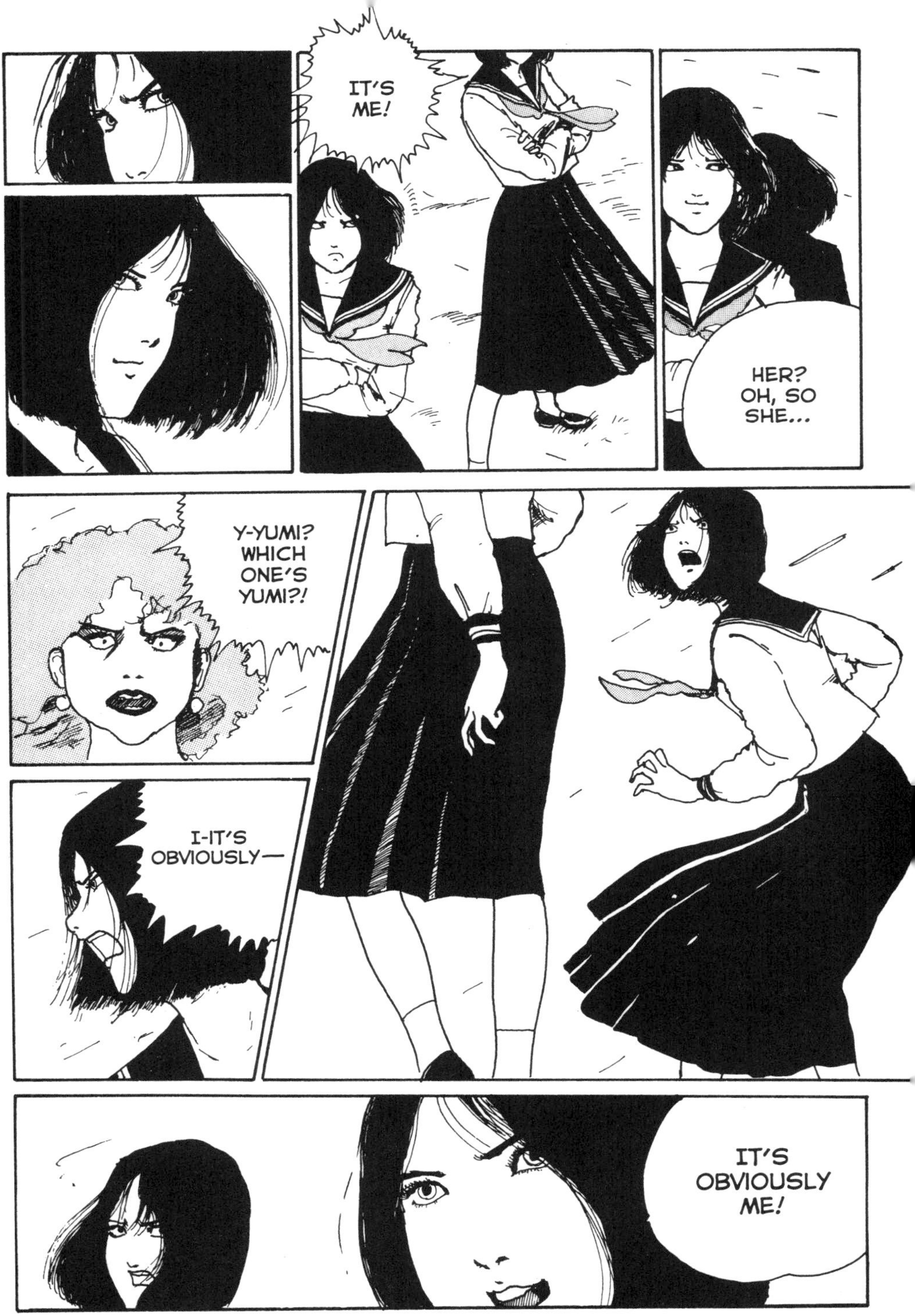
HER? OH, SO SHE...
IT'S ME!
Y-YUMI? WHICH ONE'S YUMI?!
I-IT'S OBVIOUSLY—
IT'S OBVIOUSLY ME!

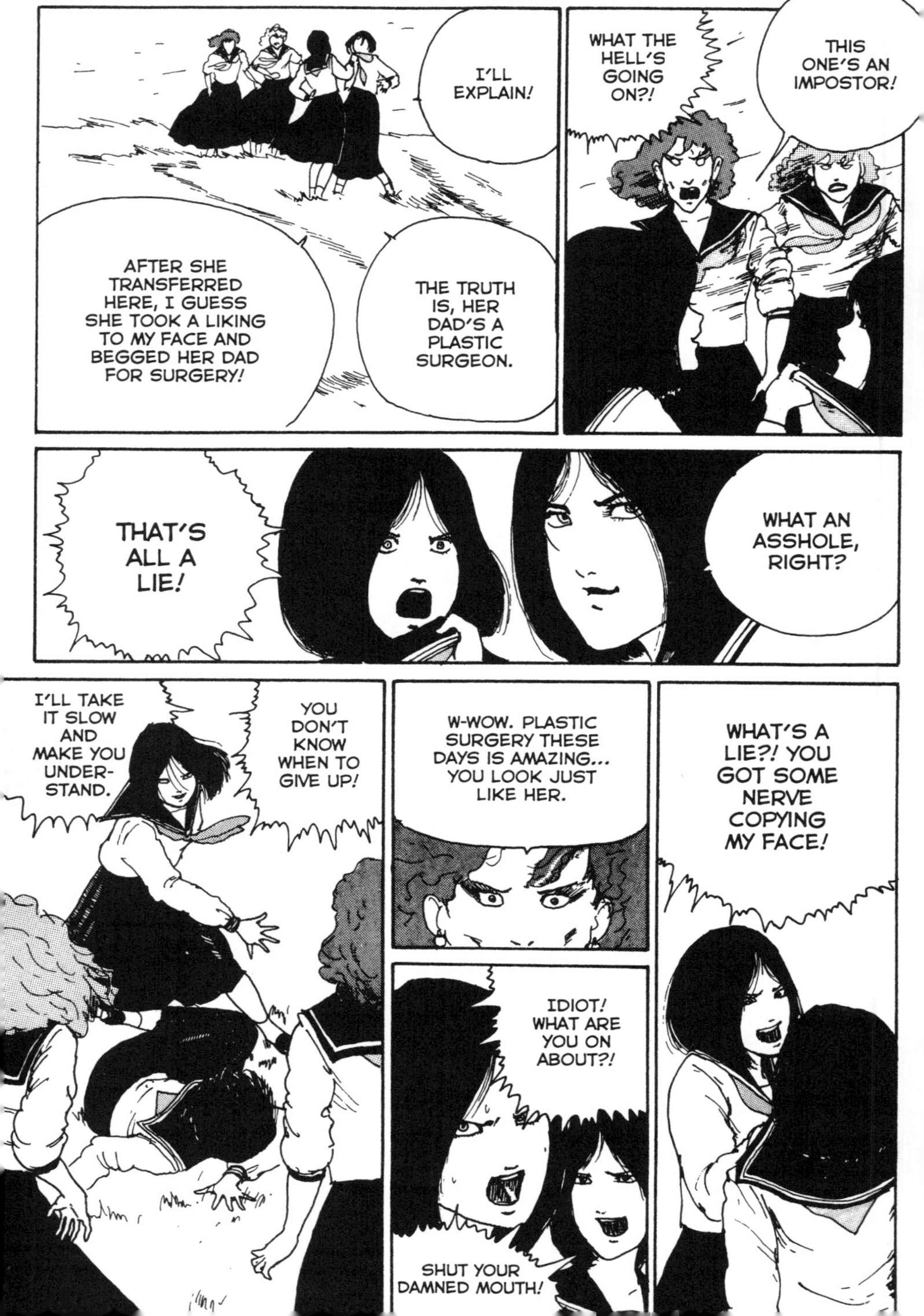
THIS ONE'S AN IMPOSTOR!
WHAT THE HELL'S GOING ON?!
I'LL EXPLAIN!
THE TRUTH IS, HER DAD'S A PLASTIC SURGEON.
AFTER SHE TRANSFERRED HERE, I GUESS SHE TOOK A LIKING TO MY FACE AND BEGGED HER DAD FOR SURGERY!
WHAT AN ASSHOLE, RIGHT?
THAT'S ALL A LIE!
WHAT'S A LIE?! YOU GOT SOME NERVE COPYING MY FACE!
W-WOW. PLASTIC SURGERY THESE DAYS IS AMAZING... YOU LOOK JUST LIKE HER.
IDIOT! WHAT ARE YOU ON ABOUT?!
SHUT YOUR DAMNED MOUTH!
YOU DON'T KNOW WHEN TO GIVE UP!
I'LL TAKE IT SLOW AND MAKE YOU UNDER-STAND.

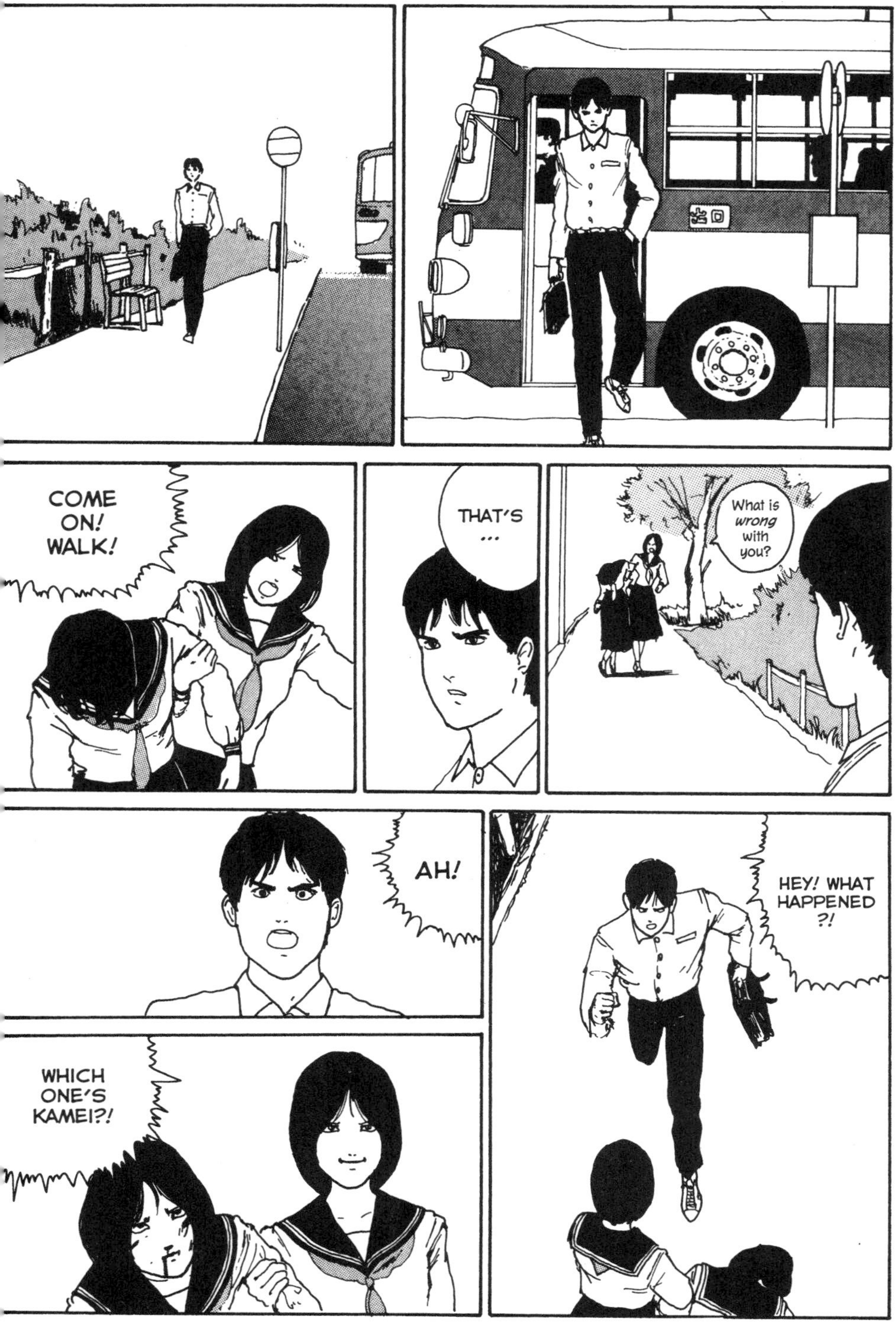
What is *wrong* with you?
THAT'S ...
COME ON! WALK!
HEY! WHAT HAPPENED ?!
AH!
WHICH ONE'S KAMEI?!

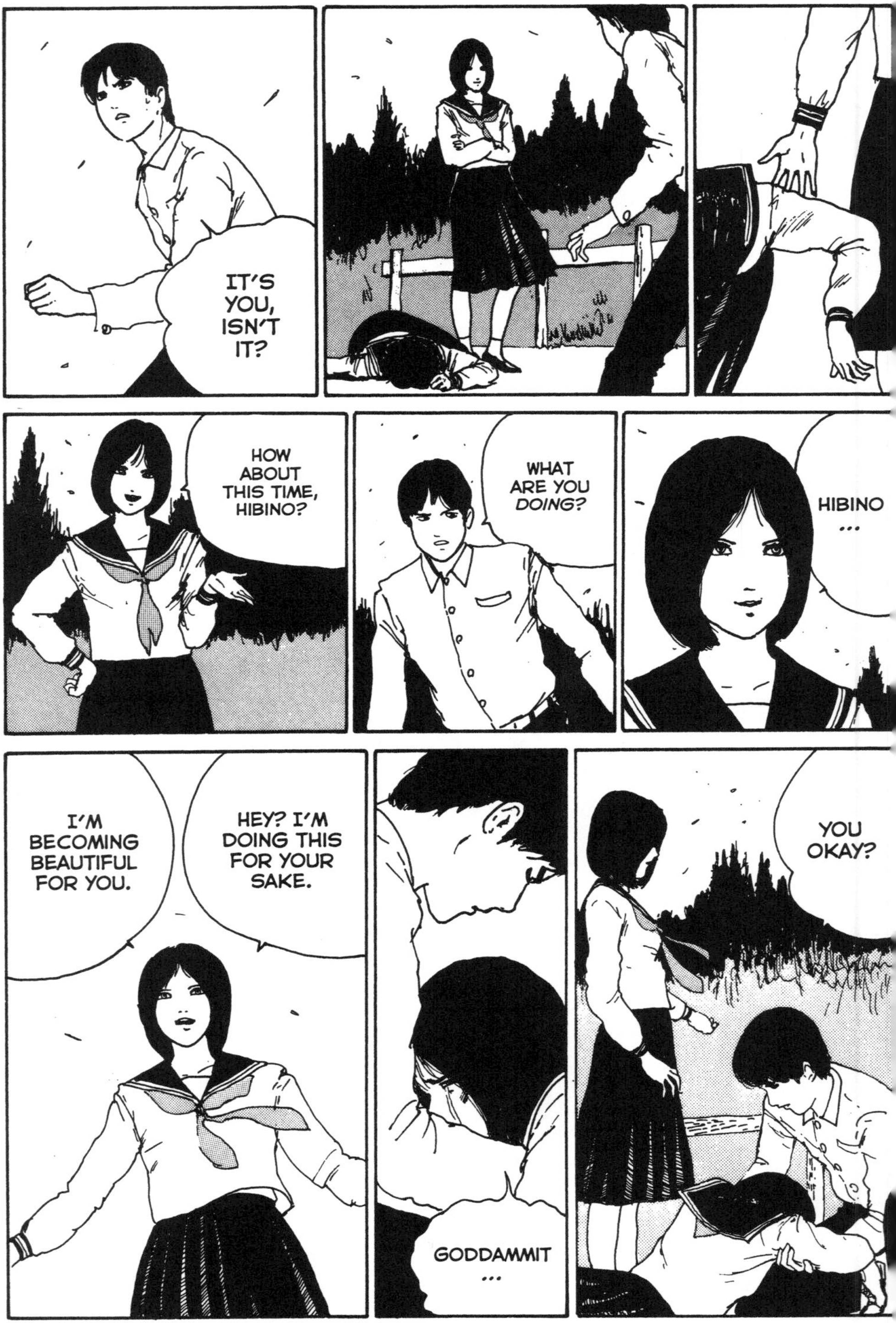
IT'S YOU, ISN'T IT?
HIBINO ...
WHAT ARE YOU *DOING*?
HOW ABOUT THIS TIME, HIBINO?
YOU OKAY?
GODDAMMIT ...
HEY? I'M DOING THIS FOR YOUR SAKE.
I'M BECOMING BEAUTIFUL FOR YOU.

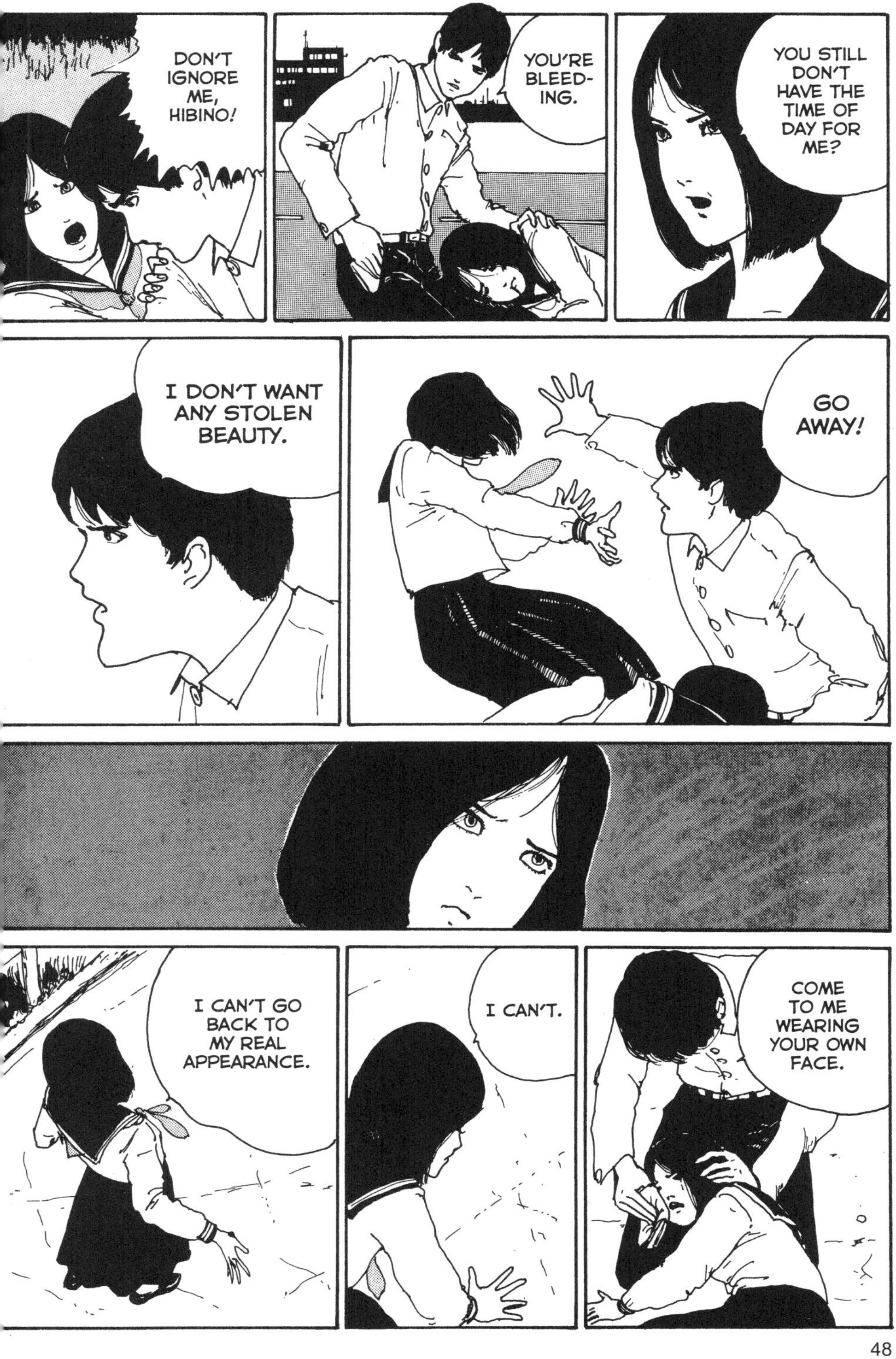
YOU STILL DON'T HAVE THE TIME OF DAY FOR ME?
YOU'RE BLEEDING.
DON'T IGNORE ME, HIBINO!
GO AWAY!
I DON'T WANT ANY STOLEN BEAUTY.
COME TO ME WEARING YOUR OWN FACE.
I CAN'T.
I CAN'T GO BACK TO MY REAL APPEARANCE.

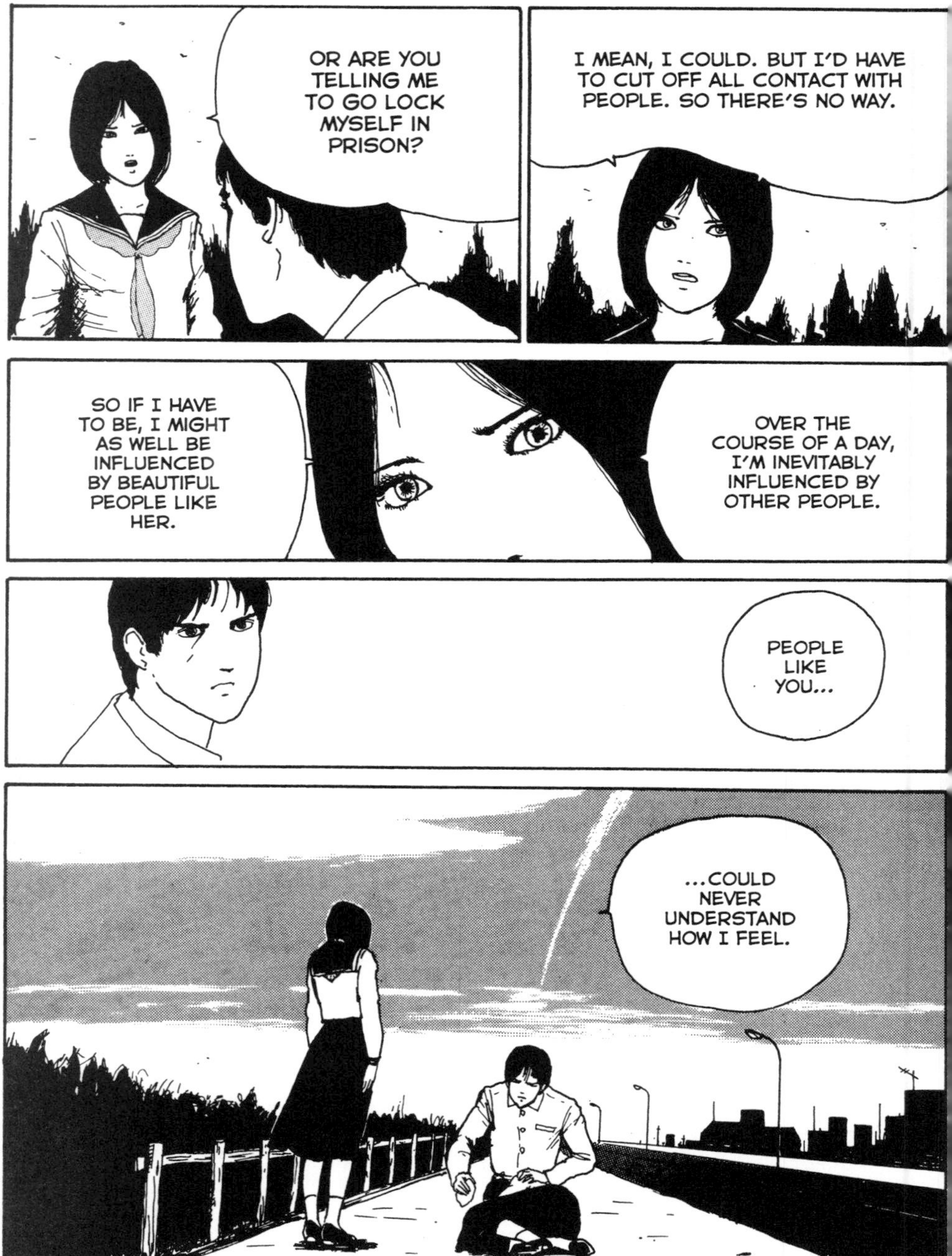
I MEAN, I COULD. BUT I'D HAVE TO CUT OFF ALL CONTACT WITH PEOPLE. SO THERE'S NO WAY.
OR ARE YOU TELLING ME TO GO LOCK MYSELF IN PRISON?
OVER THE COURSE OF A DAY, I'M INEVITABLY INFLUENCED BY OTHER PEOPLE.
SO IF I HAVE TO BE, I MIGHT AS WELL BE INFLUENCED BY BEAUTIFUL PEOPLE LIKE HER.
PEOPLE LIKE YOU...
...COULD NEVER UNDERSTAND HOW I FEEL.

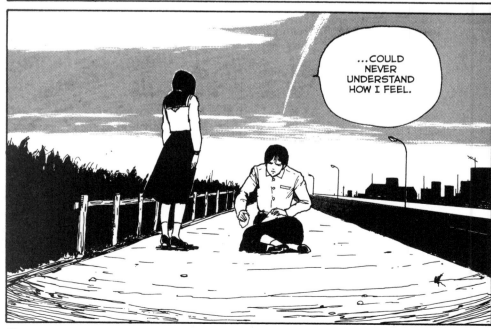

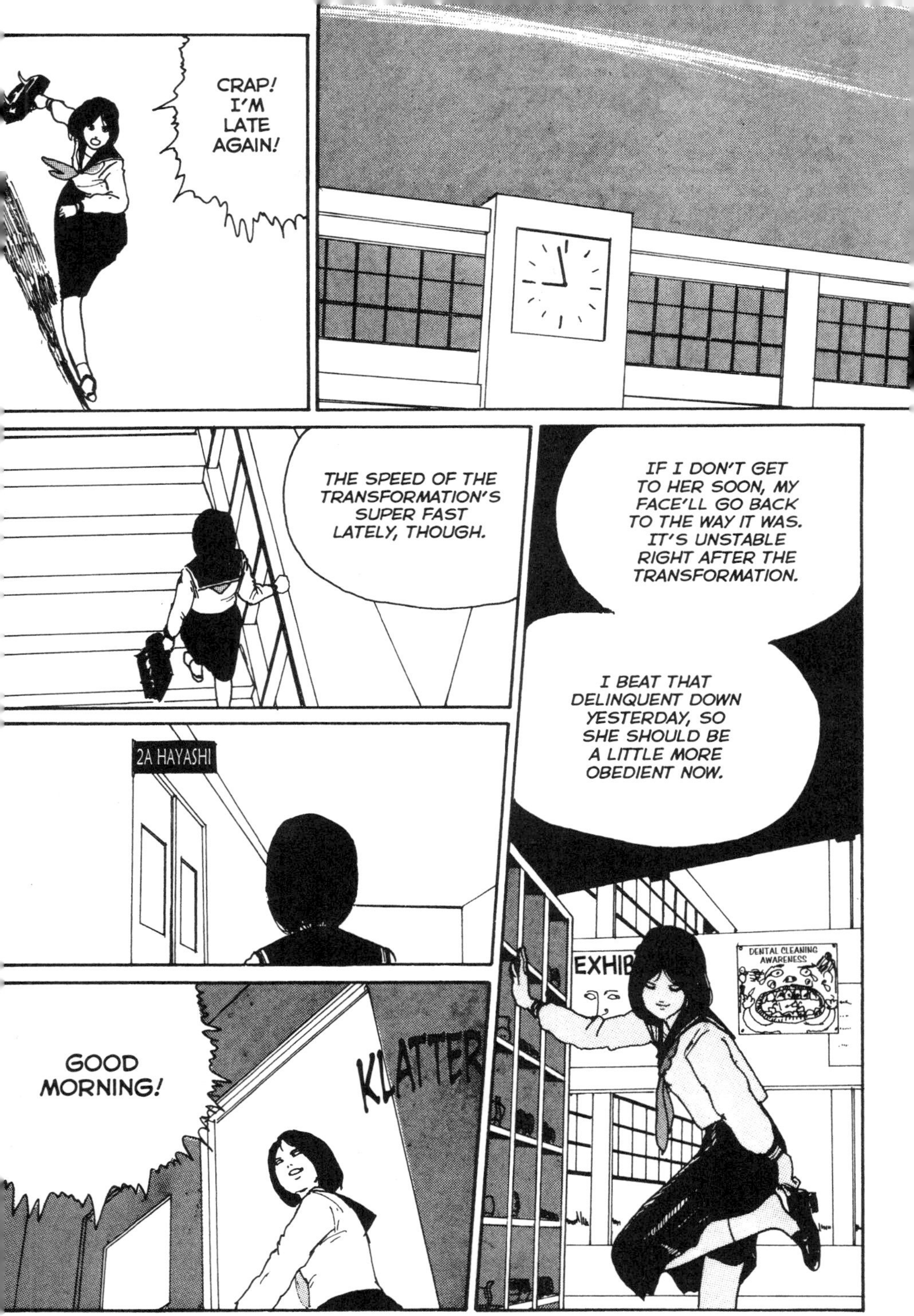
CRAP! I'M LATE AGAIN!
IF I DON'T GET TO HER SOON, MY FACE'LL GO BACK TO THE WAY IT WAS. IT'S UNSTABLE RIGHT AFTER THE TRANSFORMATION.
I BEAT THAT DELINQUENT DOWN YESTERDAY, SO SHE SHOULD BE A LITTLE MORE OBEDIENT NOW.
DENTAL CLEANING AWARENESS
EXHIB
THE SPEED OF THE TRANSFORMATION'S SUPER FAST LATELY, THOUGH.
2A HAYASHI
KLATTER
GOOD MORNING!

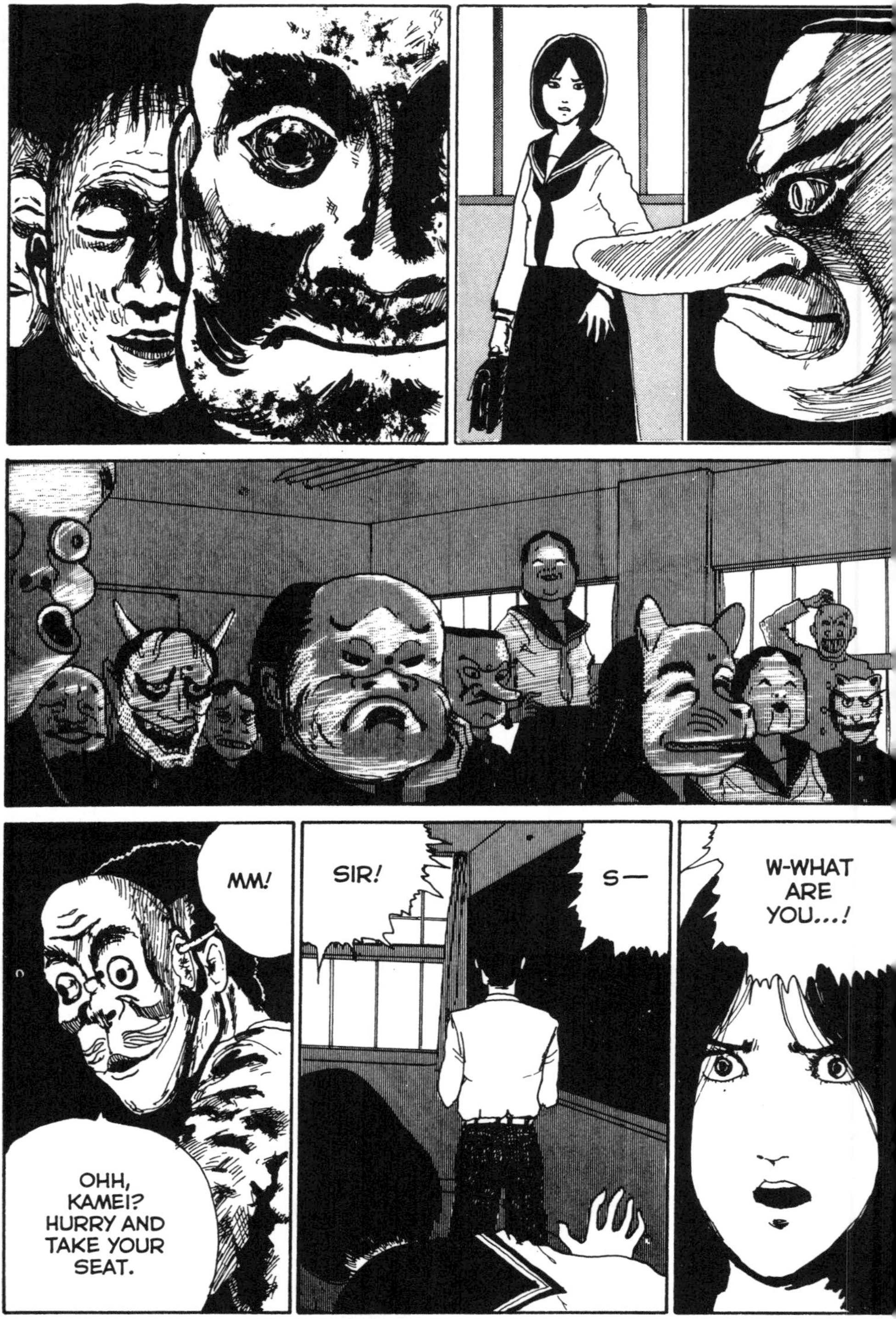
W-WHAT ARE YOU...!
S—
SIR!
MM!
OHH, KAMEI? HURRY AND TAKE YOUR SEAT.

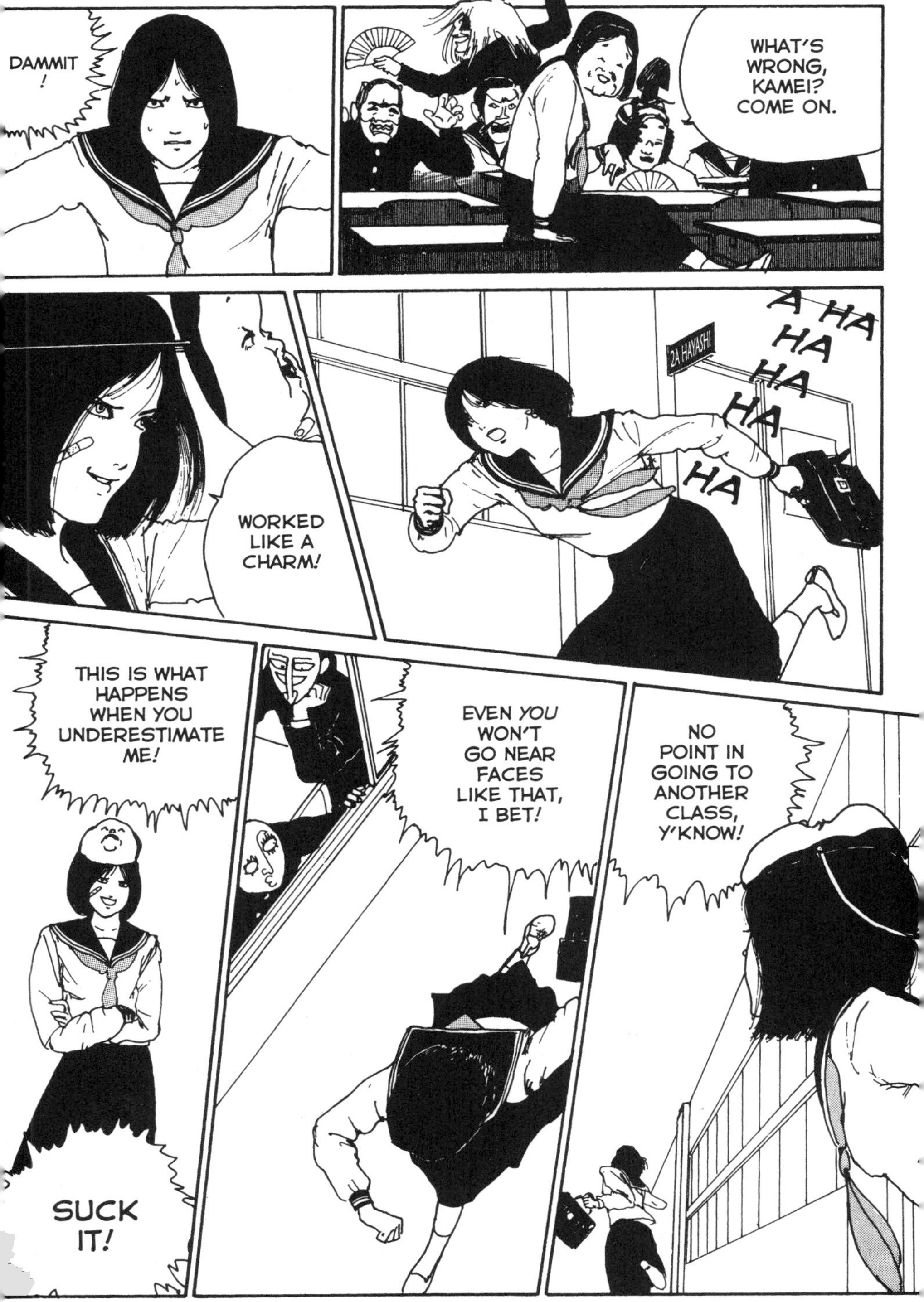
WHAT'S WRONG, KAMEI? COME ON.
DAMMIT!
2A HAYASHI
A HA HA HA HA HA
WORKED LIKE A CHARM!
NO POINT IN GOING TO ANOTHER CLASS, Y'KNOW!
EVEN *YOU* WON'T GO NEAR FACES LIKE THAT, I BET!
THIS IS WHAT HAPPENS WHEN YOU UNDERESTIMATE ME!
SUCK IT!

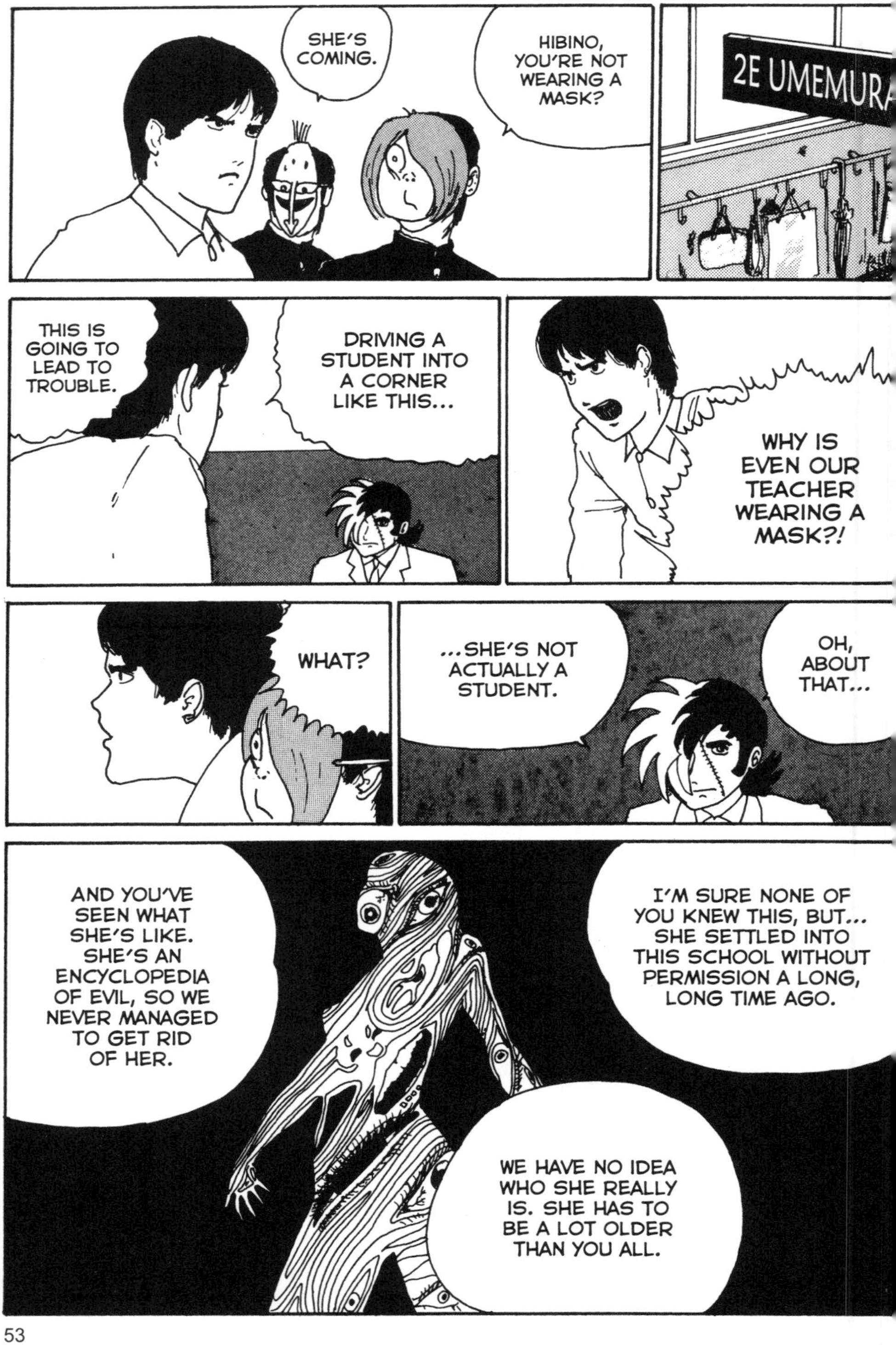
2E UMEMURA
HIBINO, YOU'RE NOT WEARING A MASK?
SHE'S COMING.
WHY IS EVEN OUR TEACHER WEARING A MASK?!
DRIVING A STUDENT INTO A CORNER LIKE THIS...
THIS IS GOING TO LEAD TO TROUBLE.
OH, ABOUT THAT...
...SHE'S NOT ACTUALLY A STUDENT.
WHAT?
I'M SURE NONE OF YOU KNEW THIS, BUT... SHE SETTLED INTO THIS SCHOOL WITHOUT PERMISSION A LONG, LONG TIME AGO.
AND YOU'VE SEEN WHAT SHE'S LIKE. SHE'S AN ENCYCLOPEDIA OF EVIL, SO WE NEVER MANAGED TO GET RID OF HER.
WE HAVE NO IDEA WHO SHE REALLY IS. SHE HAS TO BE A LOT OLDER THAN YOU ALL.

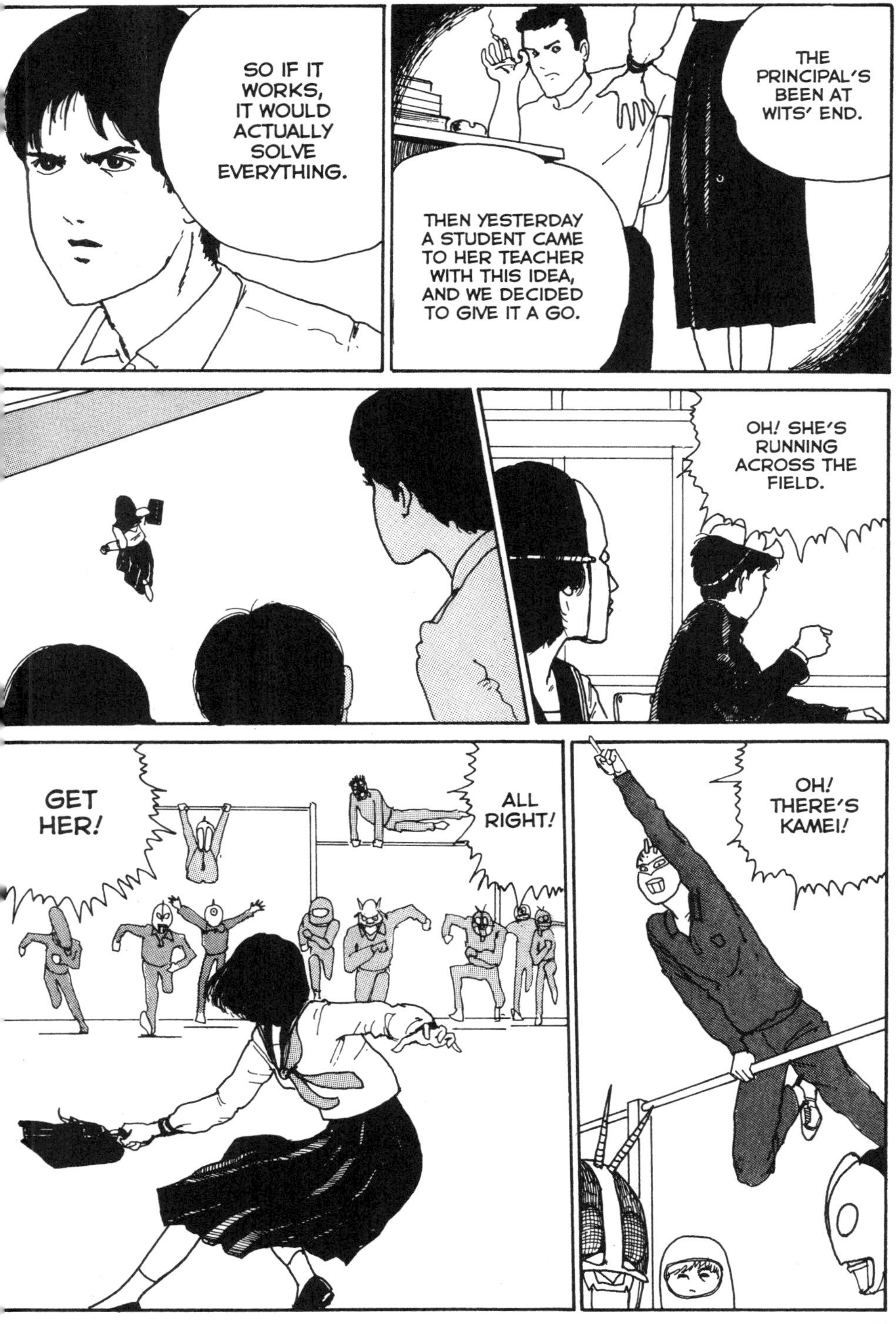
THE PRINCIPAL'S BEEN AT WITS' END.
THEN YESTERDAY A STUDENT CAME TO HER TEACHER WITH THIS IDEA, AND WE DECIDED TO GIVE IT A GO.
SO IF IT WORKS, IT WOULD ACTUALLY SOLVE EVERYTHING.
OH! SHE'S RUNNING ACROSS THE FIELD.
OH! THERE'S KAMEI!
ALL RIGHT!
GET HER!

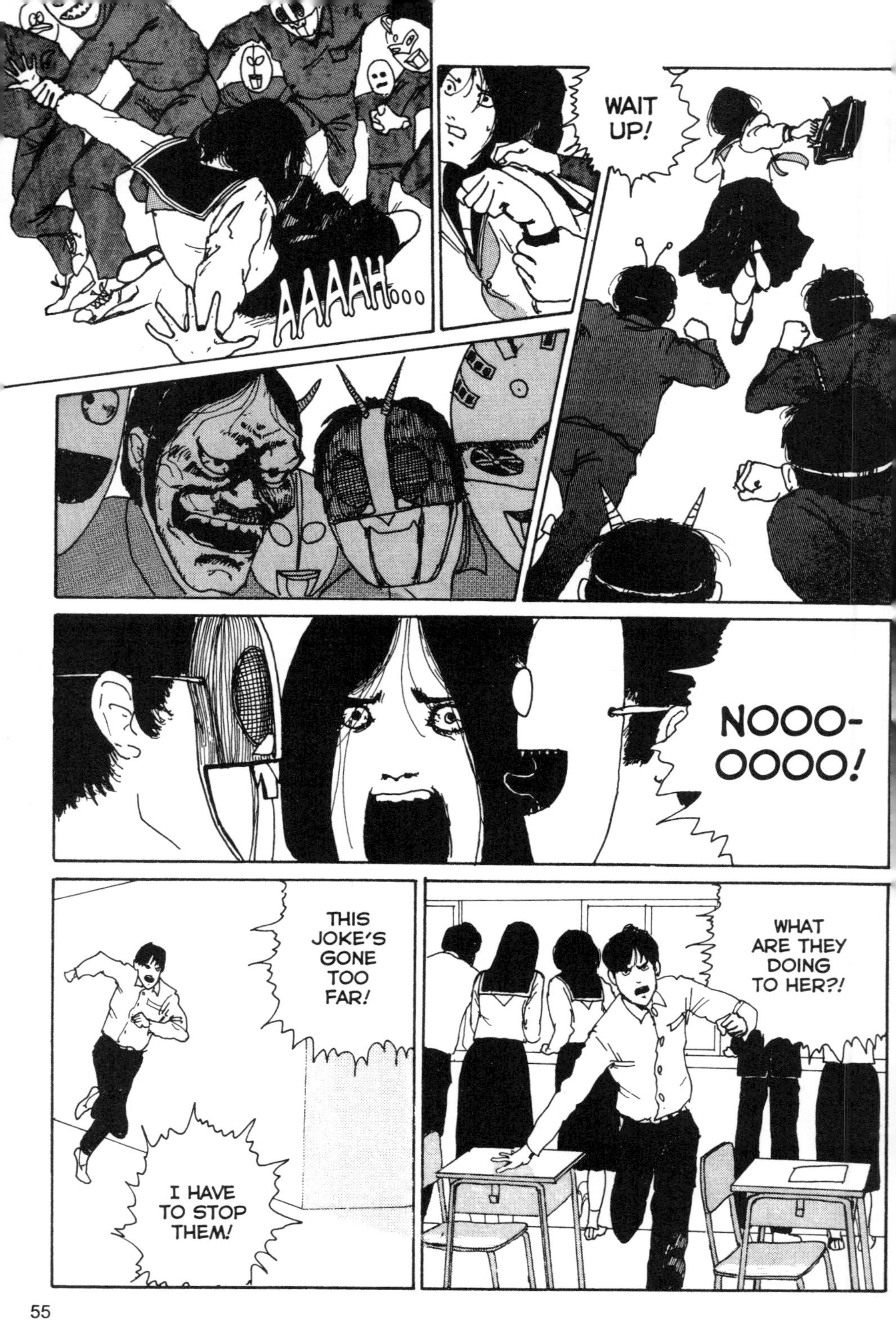
WAIT UP!
AAAAH...
NOOO-OOOO!
WHAT ARE THEY DOING TO HER?!
THIS JOKE'S GONE TOO FAR!
I HAVE TO STOP THEM!

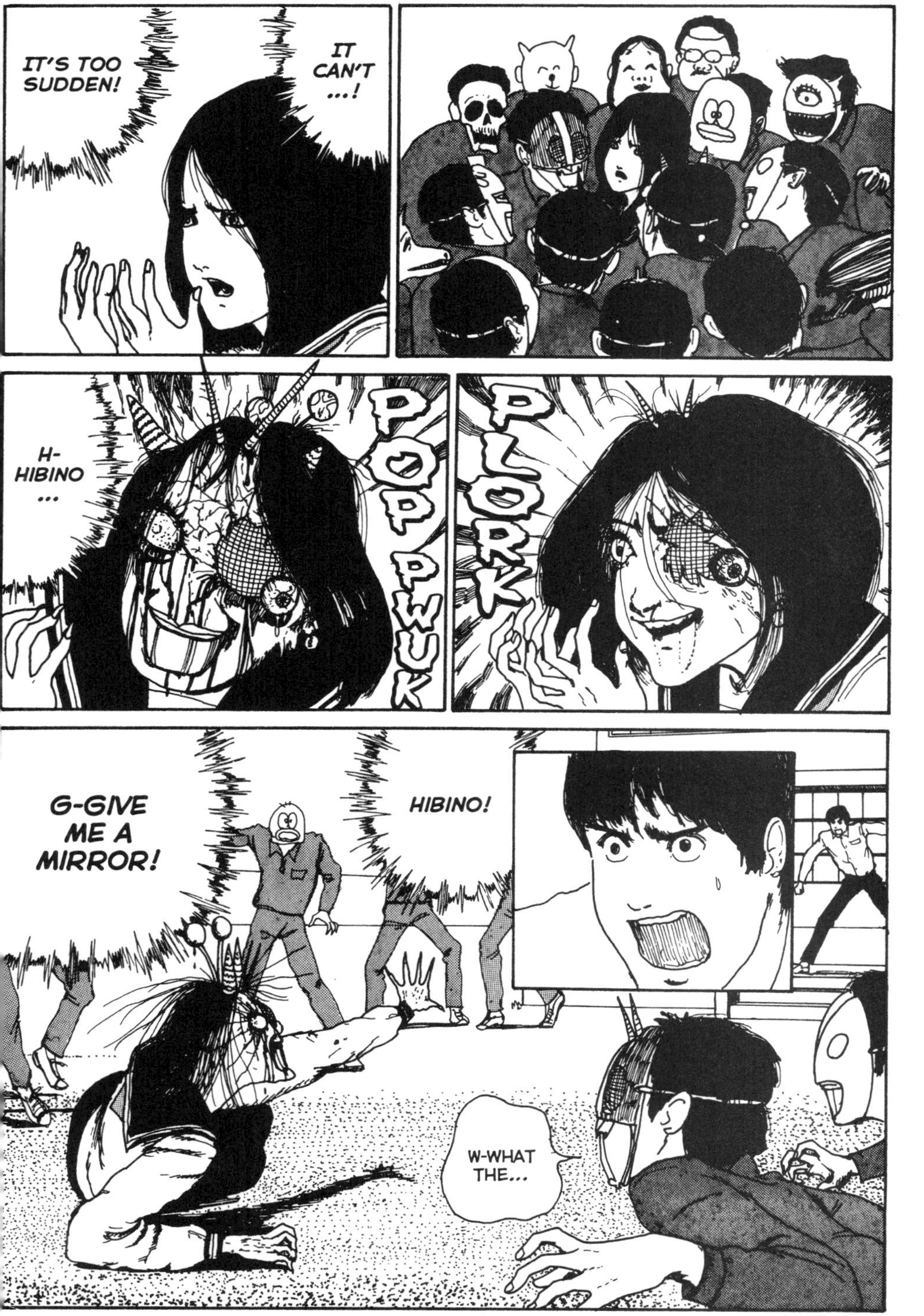
IT CAN'T ...!
IT'S TOO SUDDEN!
PLORK
POP PWUK
H-HIBINO ...
HIBINO!
G-GIVE ME A MIRROR!
W-WHAT THE...

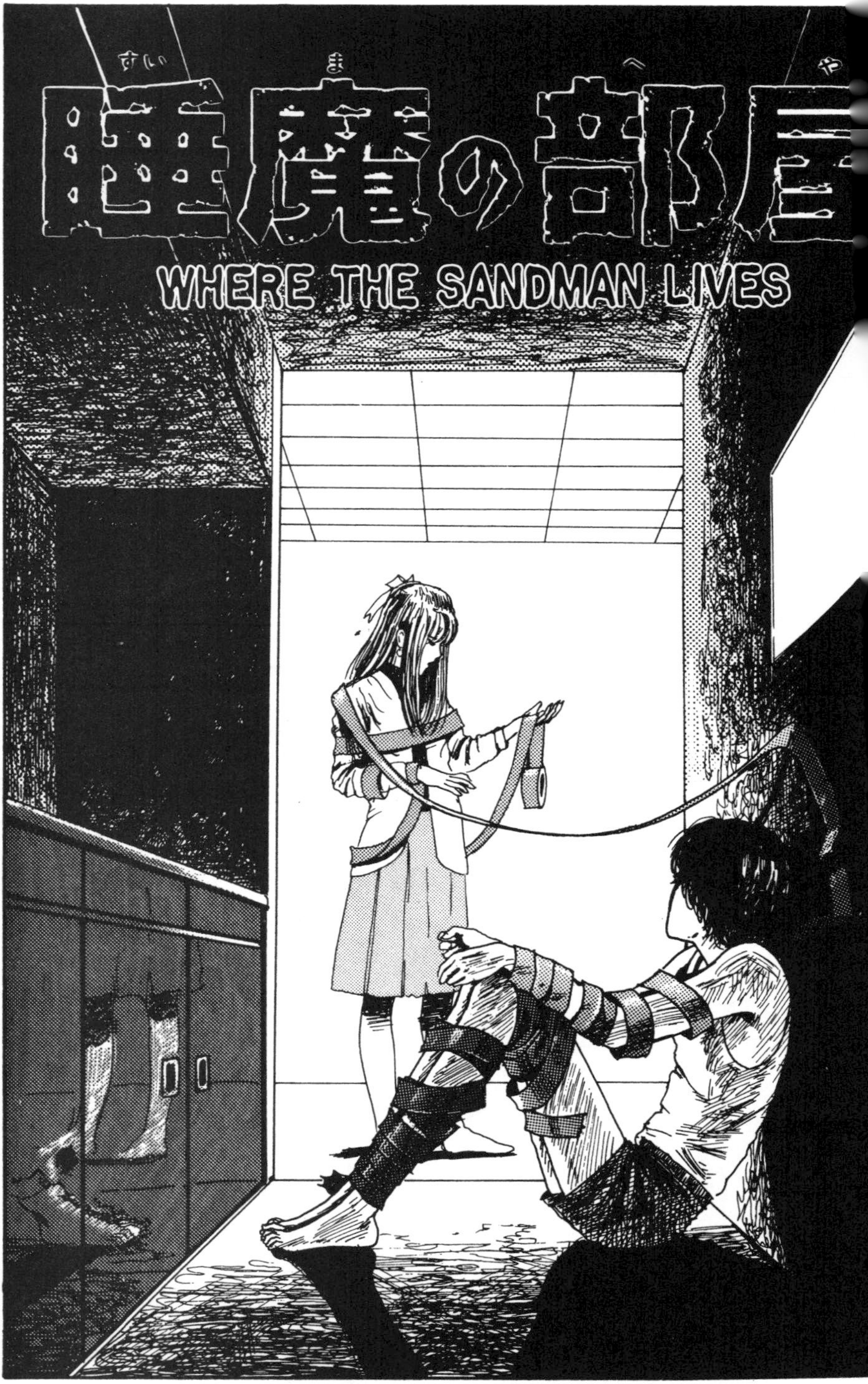
睡魔の部屋
WHERE THE SANDMAN LIVES

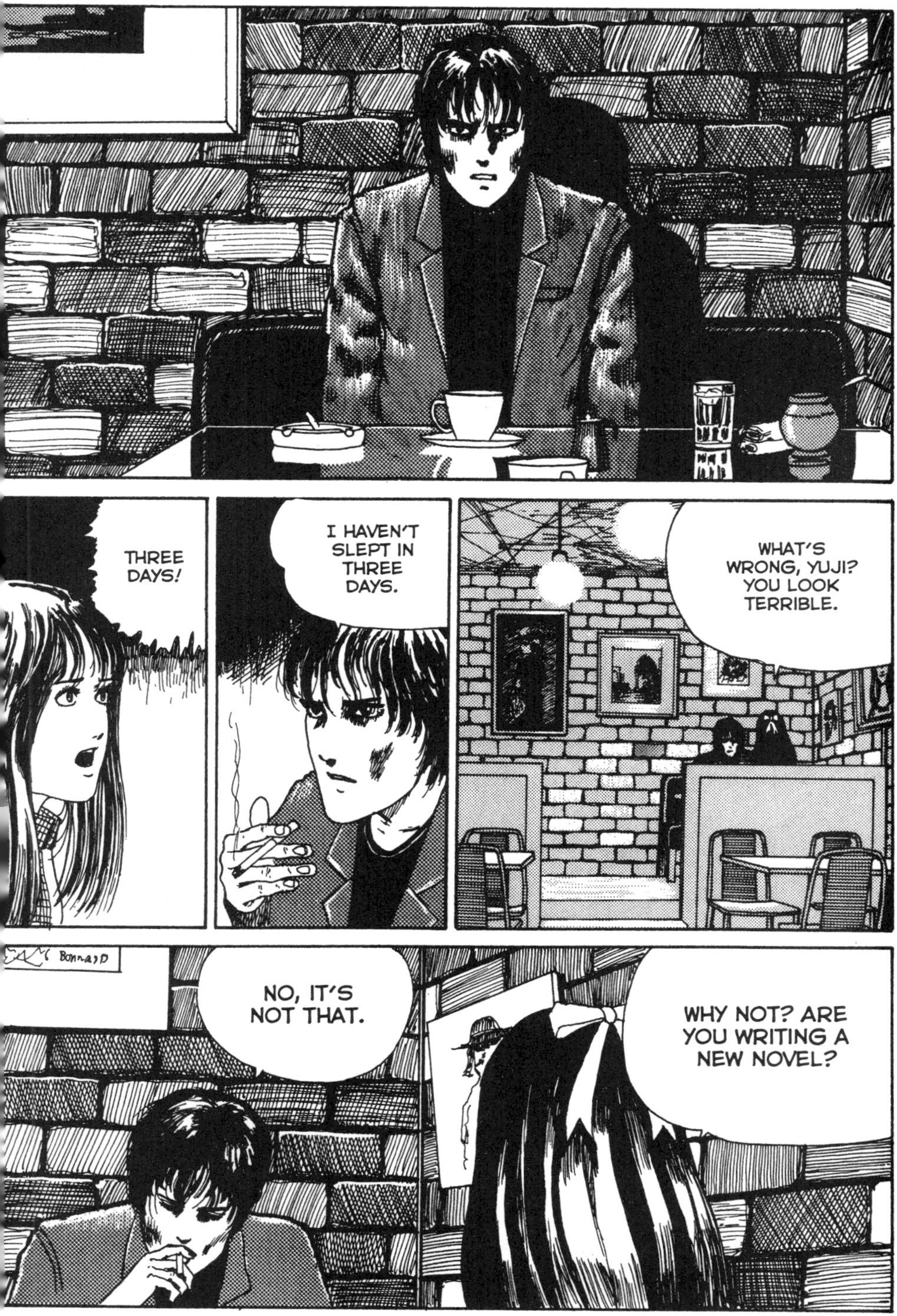
WHAT'S WRONG, YUJI? YOU LOOK TERRIBLE.
I HAVEN'T SLEPT IN THREE DAYS.
THREE DAYS!
WHY NOT? ARE YOU WRITING A NEW NOVEL?
NO, IT'S NOT THAT.

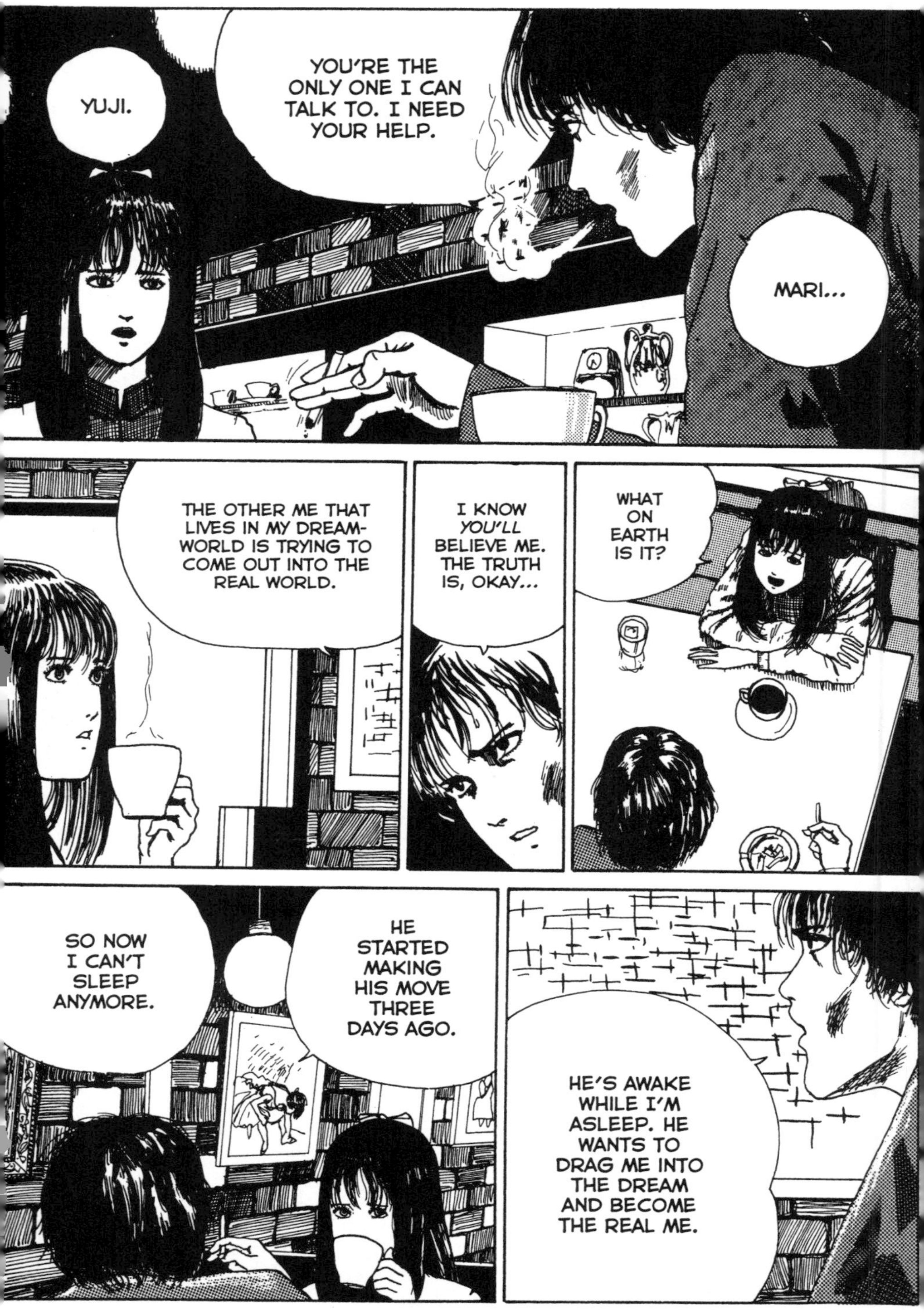
MARI...
YOU'RE THE ONLY ONE I CAN TALK TO. I NEED YOUR HELP.
YUJI.
WHAT ON EARTH IS IT?
I KNOW *YOU'LL* BELIEVE ME. THE TRUTH IS, OKAY...
THE OTHER ME THAT LIVES IN MY DREAM-WORLD IS TRYING TO COME OUT INTO THE REAL WORLD.
HE'S AWAKE WHILE I'M ASLEEP. HE WANTS TO DRAG ME INTO THE DREAM AND BECOME THE REAL ME.
HE STARTED MAKING HIS MOVE THREE DAYS AGO.
SO NOW I CAN'T SLEEP ANYMORE.

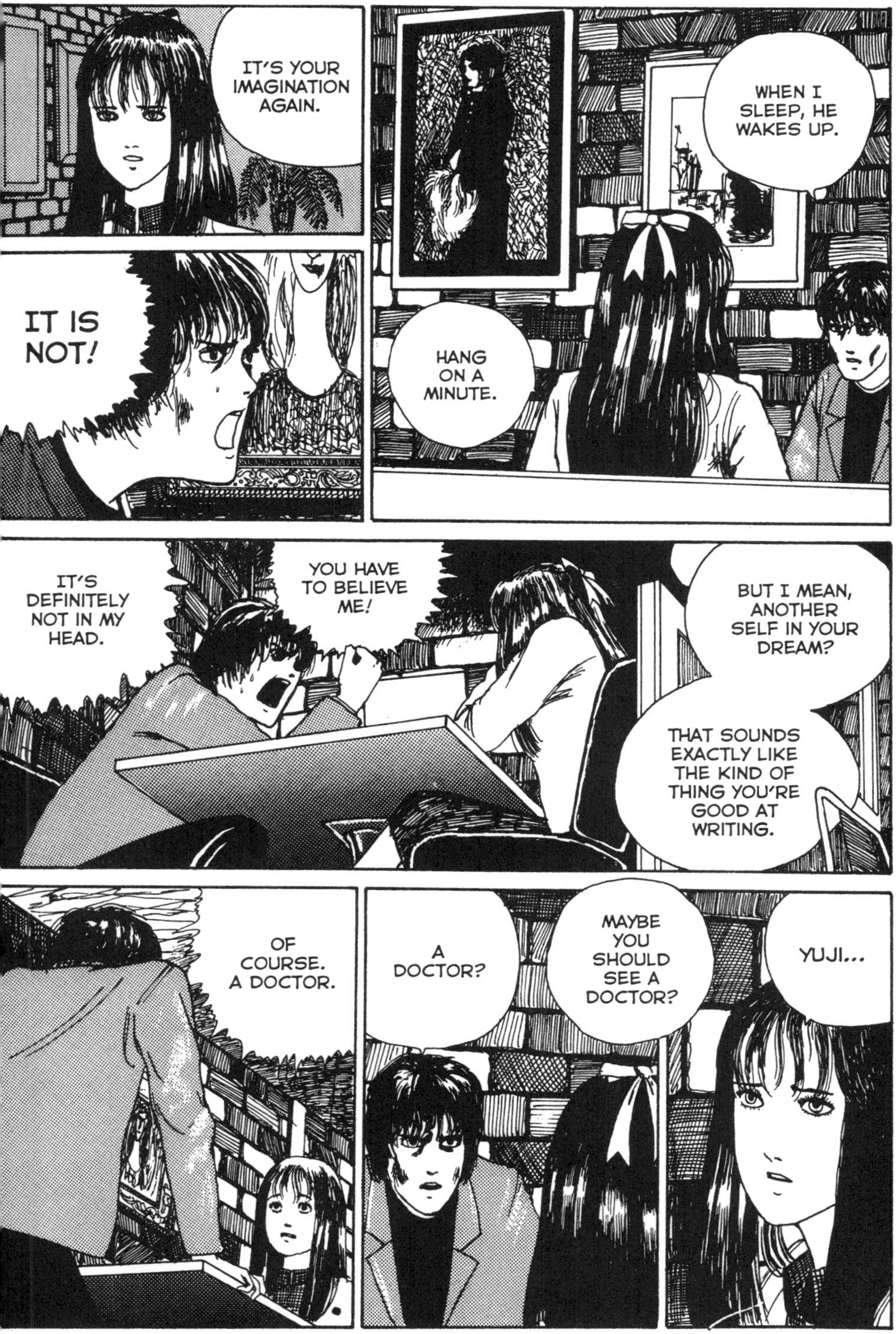
WHEN I SLEEP, HE WAKES UP.
HANG ON A MINUTE.
IT'S YOUR IMAGINATION AGAIN.
IT IS NOT!
BUT I MEAN, ANOTHER SELF IN YOUR DREAM?
THAT SOUNDS EXACTLY LIKE THE KIND OF THING YOU'RE GOOD AT WRITING.
YOU HAVE TO BELIEVE ME!
IT'S DEFINITELY NOT IN MY HEAD.
YUJI...
MAYBE YOU SHOULD SEE A DOCTOR?
A DOCTOR?
OF COURSE. A DOCTOR.

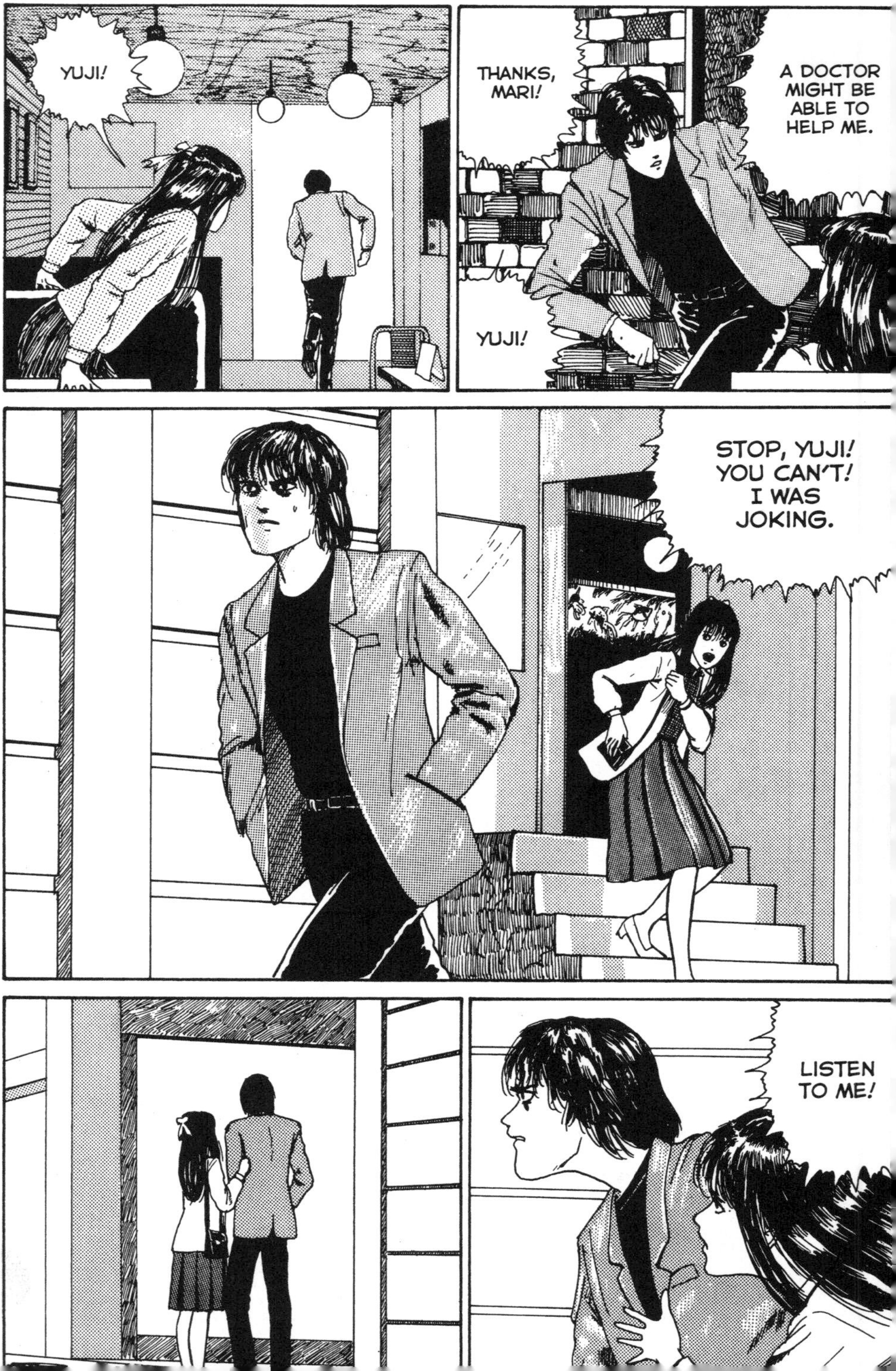
A DOCTOR MIGHT BE ABLE TO HELP ME.
THANKS, MARI!
YUJI!
YUJI!
STOP, YUJI! YOU CAN'T! I WAS JOKING.
LISTEN TO ME!

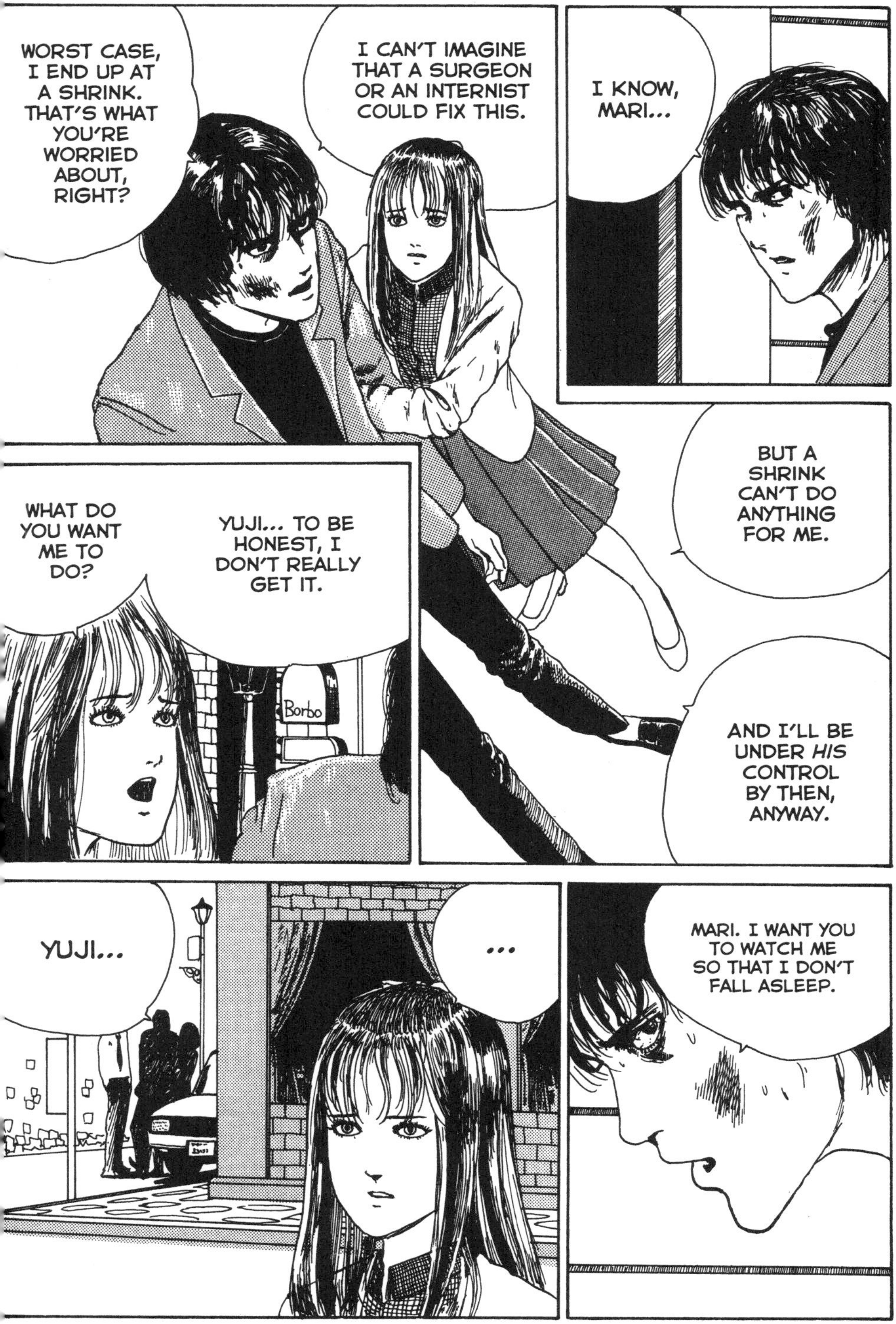
I KNOW, MARI...
I CAN'T IMAGINE THAT A SURGEON OR AN INTERNIST COULD FIX THIS.
WORST CASE, I END UP AT A SHRINK. THAT'S WHAT YOU'RE WORRIED ABOUT, RIGHT?
BUT A SHRINK CAN'T DO ANYTHING FOR ME.
AND I'LL BE UNDER *HIS* CONTROL BY THEN, ANYWAY.
YUJI... TO BE HONEST, I DON'T REALLY GET IT.
WHAT DO YOU WANT ME TO DO?
Borbo
MARI. I WANT YOU TO WATCH ME SO THAT I DON'T FALL ASLEEP.
...
YUJI...

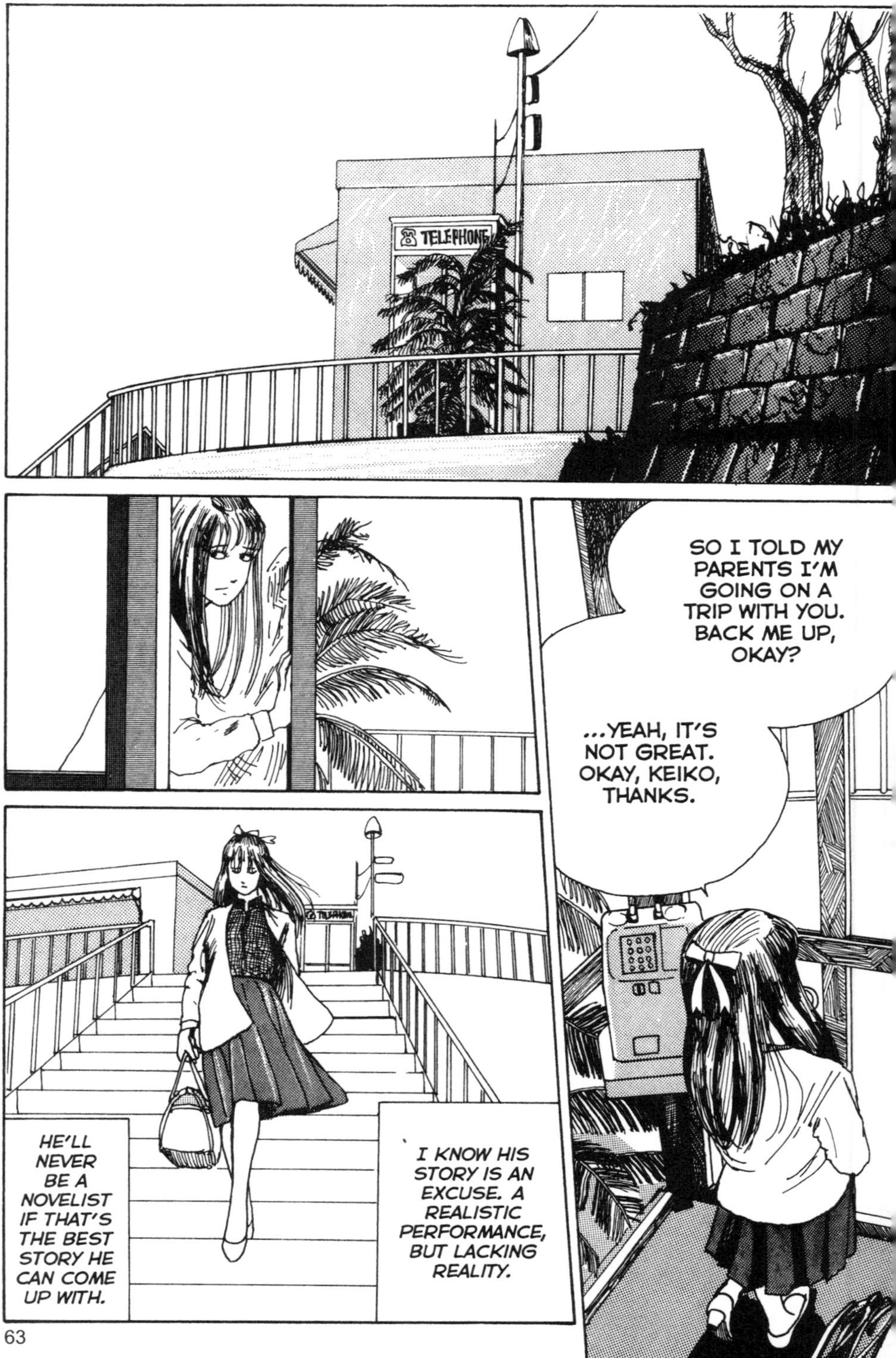
SO I TOLD MY PARENTS I'M GOING ON A TRIP WITH YOU. BACK ME UP, OKAY?
...YEAH, IT'S NOT GREAT. OKAY, KEIKO, THANKS.
I KNOW HIS STORY IS AN EXCUSE. A REALISTIC PERFORMANCE, BUT LACKING REALITY.
HE'LL NEVER BE A NOVELIST IF THAT'S THE BEST STORY HE CAN COME UP WITH.

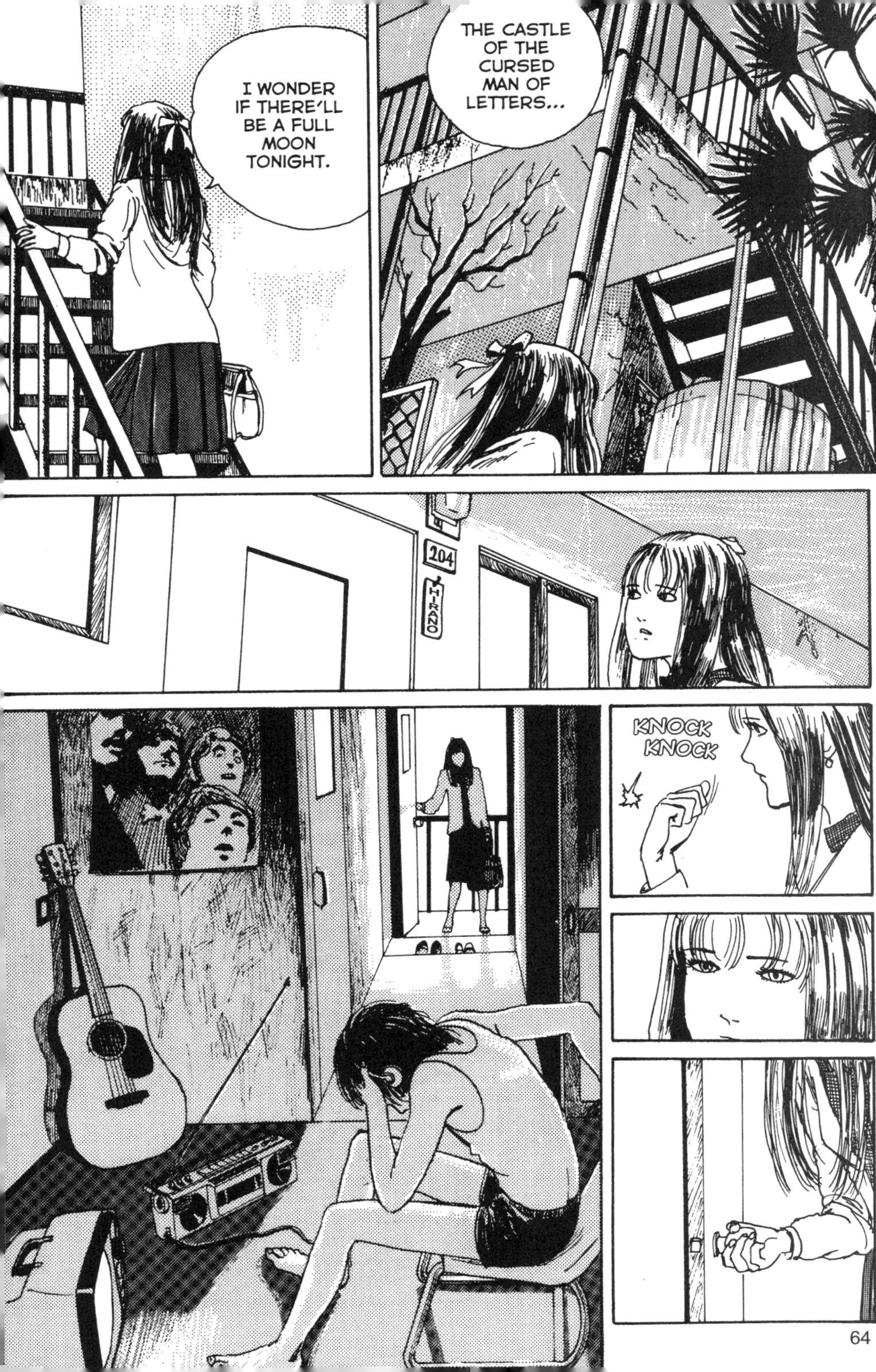
THE CASTLE OF THE CURSED MAN OF LETTERS...
I WONDER IF THERE'LL BE A FULL MOON TONIGHT.
204
HIRANO
KNOCK KNOCK

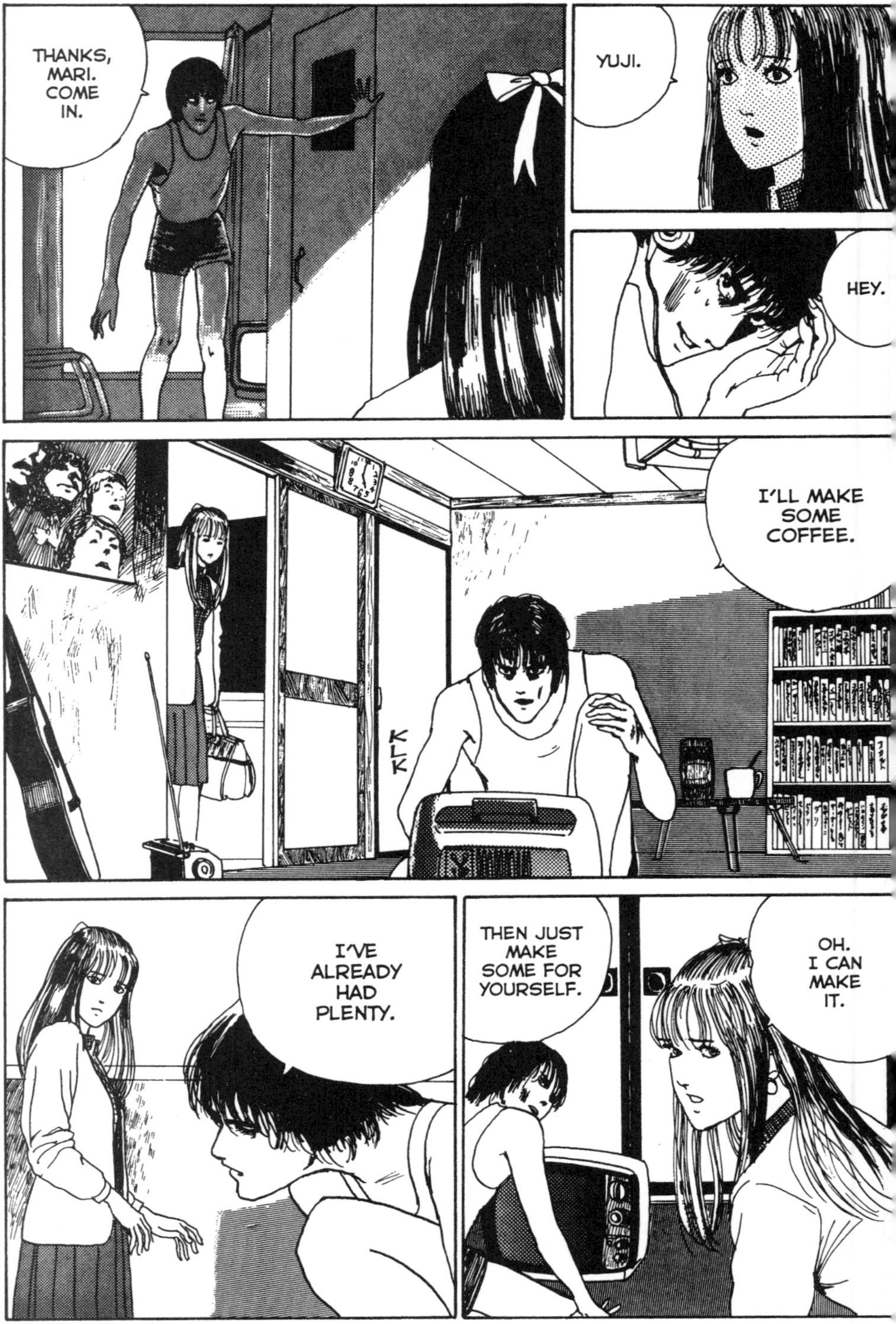
YUJI.
HEY.
THANKS, MARI. COME IN.
I'LL MAKE SOME COFFEE.
KLK KLK
OH. I CAN MAKE IT.
THEN JUST MAKE SOME FOR YOURSELF.
I'VE ALREADY HAD PLENTY.

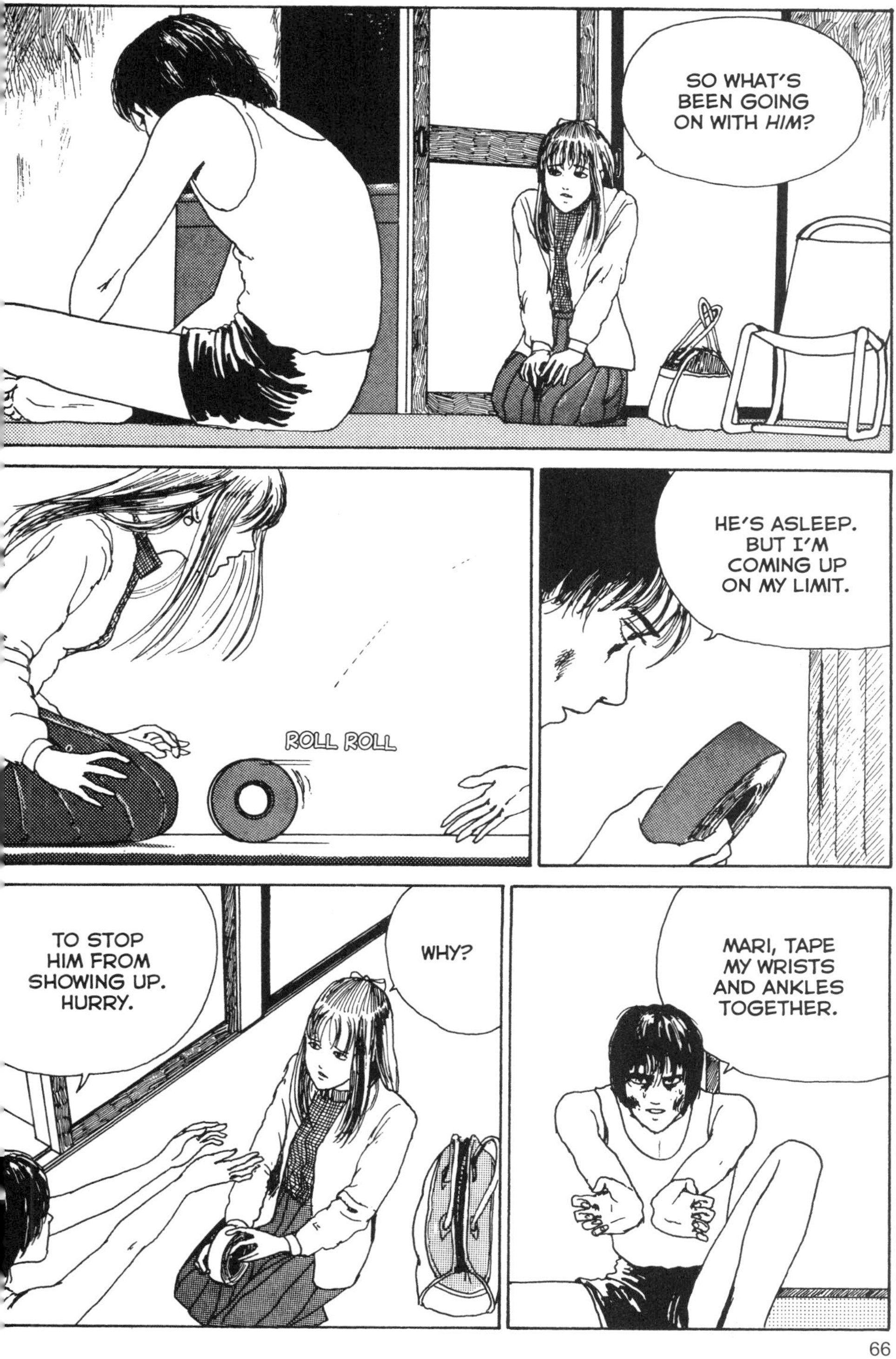
SO WHAT'S BEEN GOING ON WITH *HIM*?
HE'S ASLEEP. BUT I'M COMING UP ON MY LIMIT.
ROLL ROLL
MARI, TAPE MY WRISTS AND ANKLES TOGETHER.
WHY?
TO STOP HIM FROM SHOWING UP. HURRY.

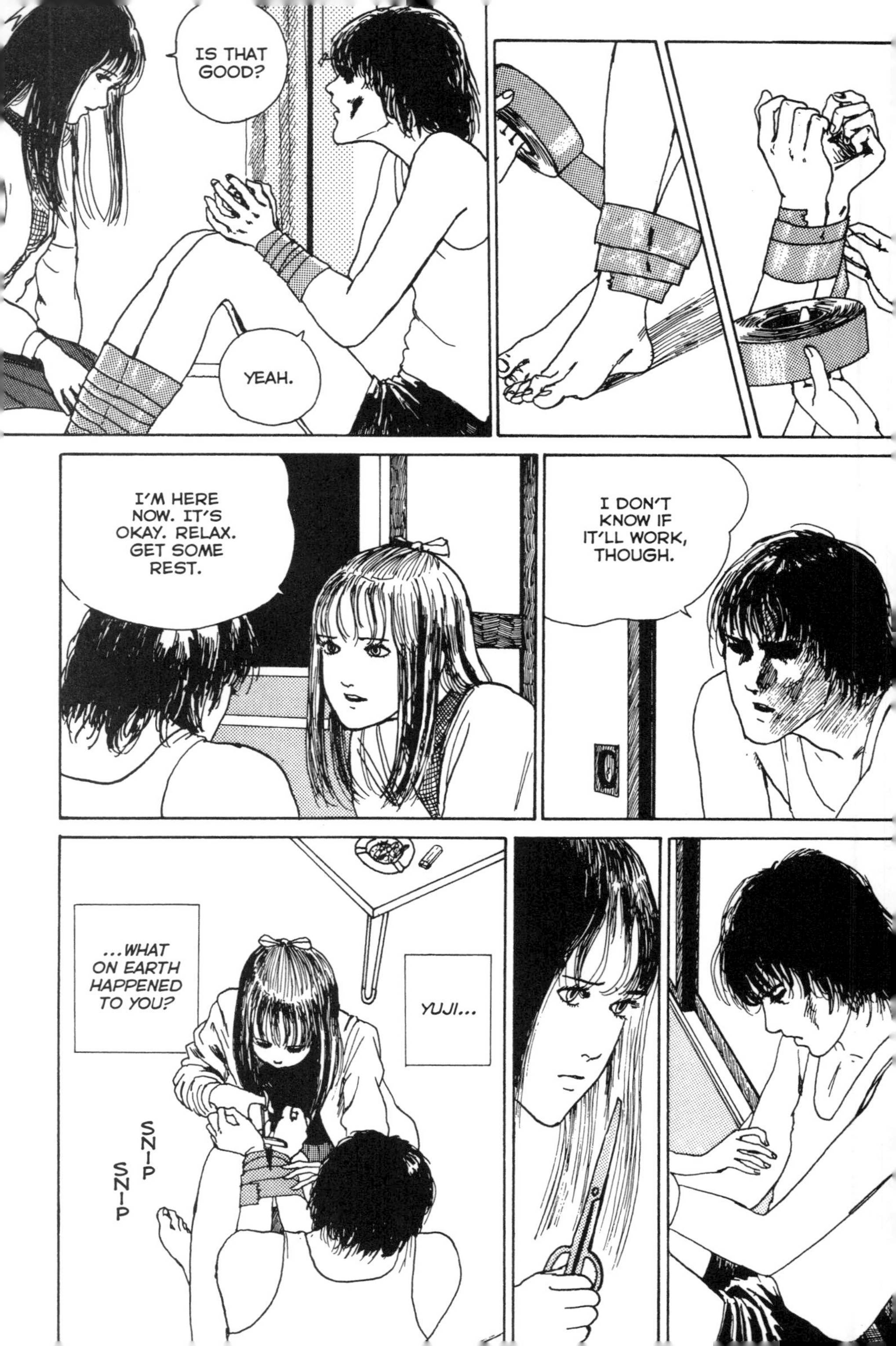
IS THAT GOOD?
YEAH.
I DON'T KNOW IF IT'LL WORK, THOUGH.
I'M HERE NOW. IT'S OKAY. RELAX. GET SOME REST.
YUJI...
...WHAT ON EARTH HAPPENED TO YOU?
SNIP
SNIP

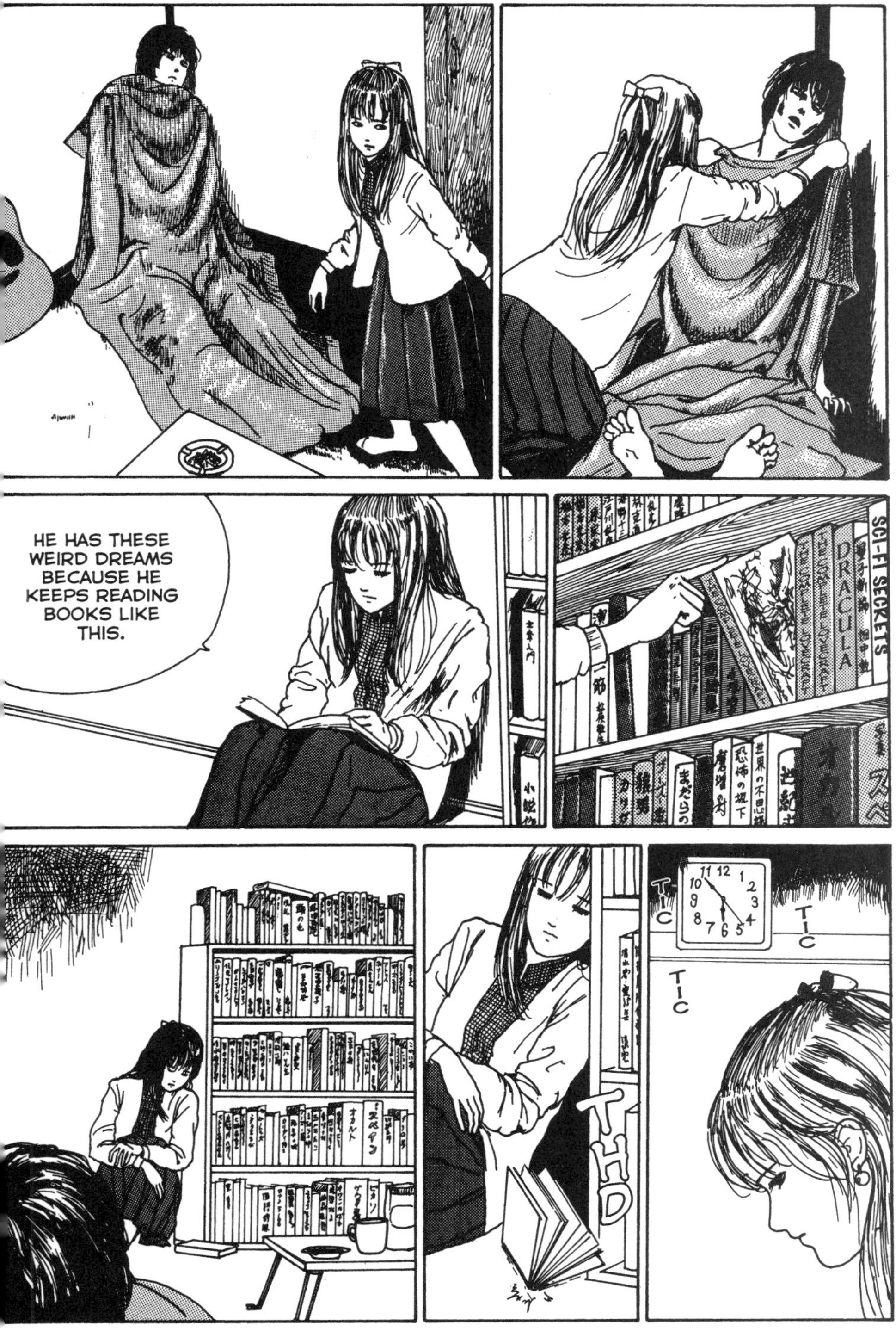
SCI-FI SECKETS
DRACULA
HE HAS THESE WEIRD DREAMS BECAUSE HE KEEPS READING BOOKS LIKE THIS.
TIC
TIC
TIC
THUD

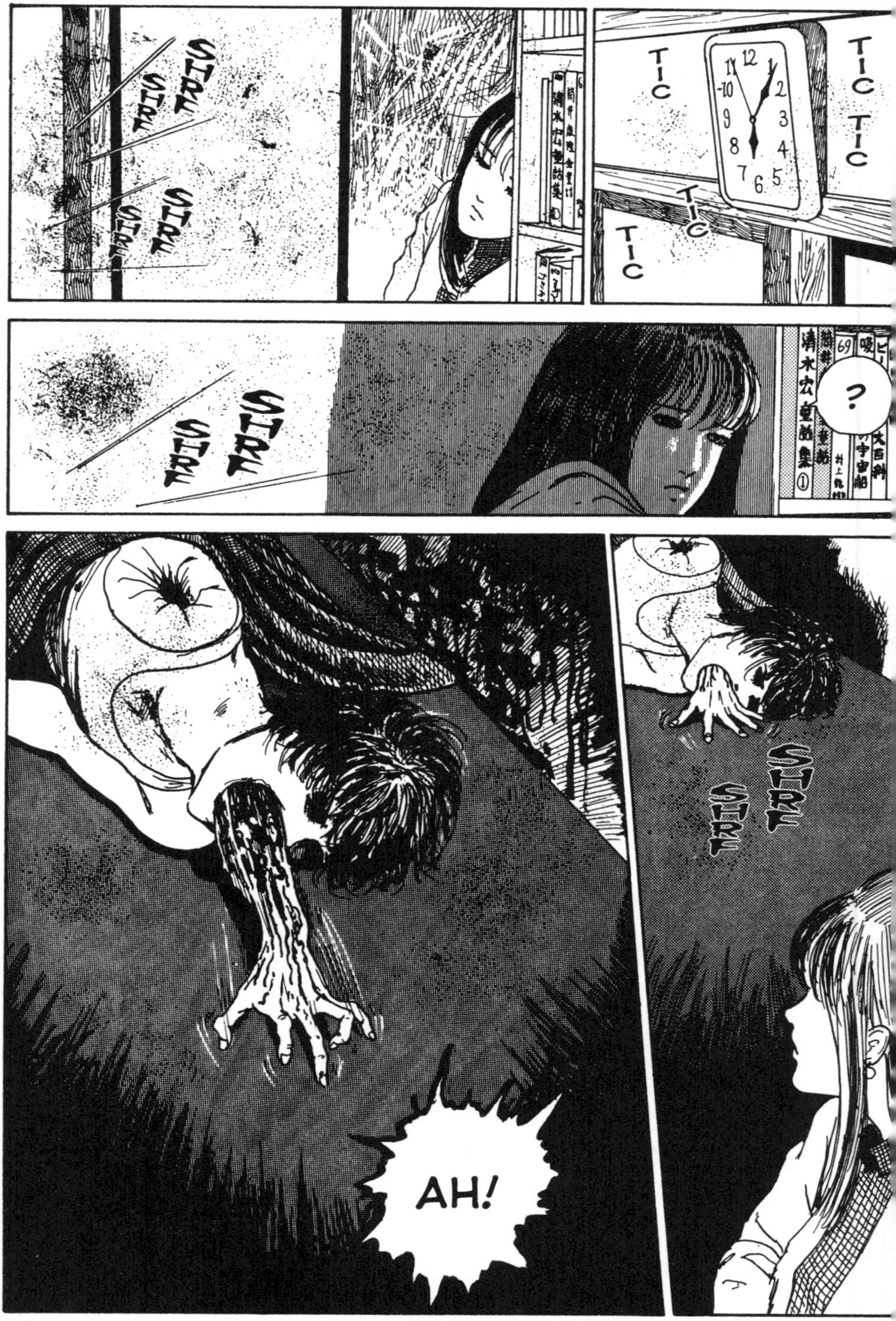
TIC
TIC
TIC
TIC
TIC
SHRF
SHRF
SHRF
SHRF
?
清水宏童話集①
SHRF
SHRF
SHRF
SHRF
AH!

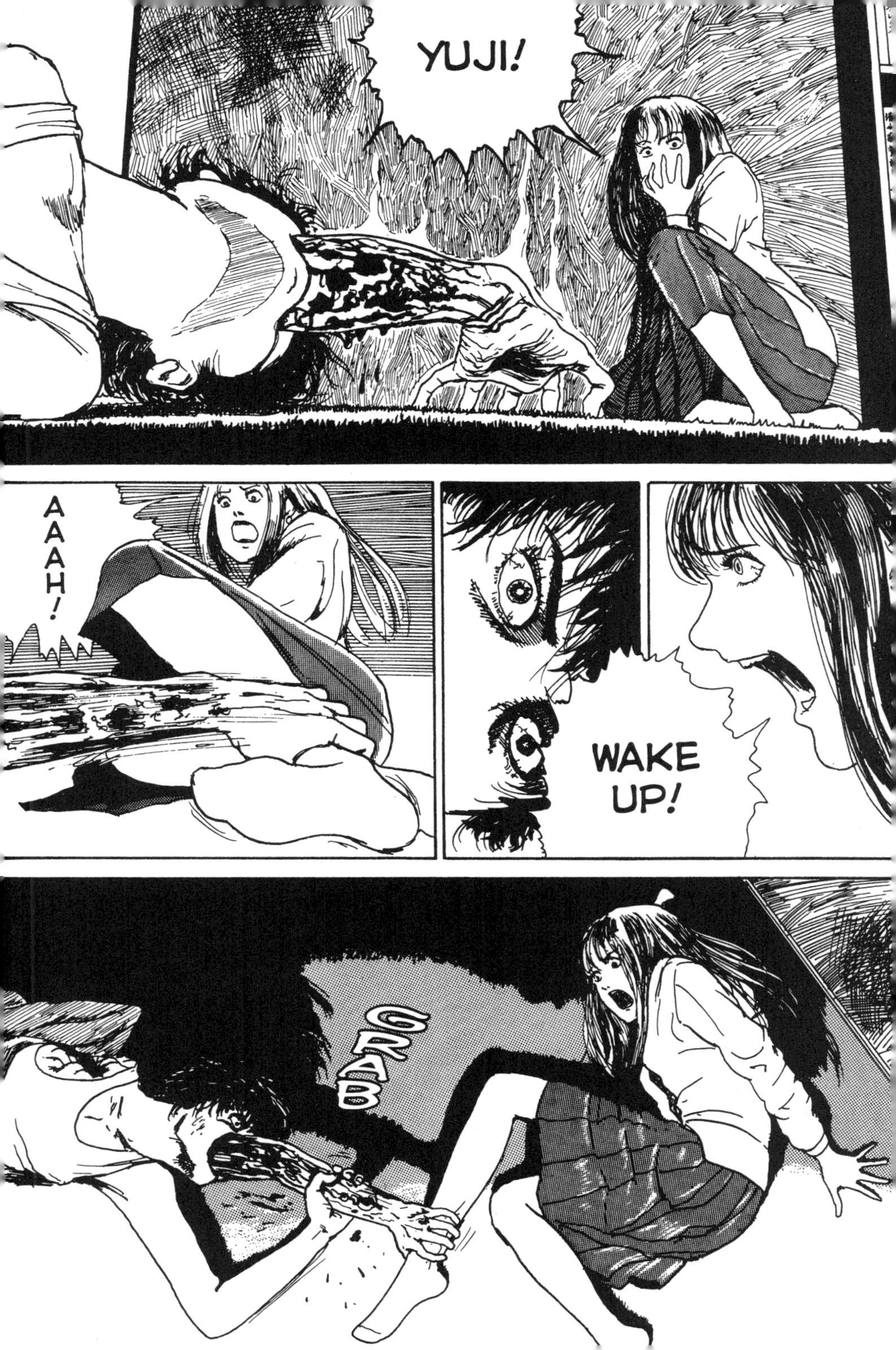
YUJI!
WAKE UP!
AAAAH!
GRAB

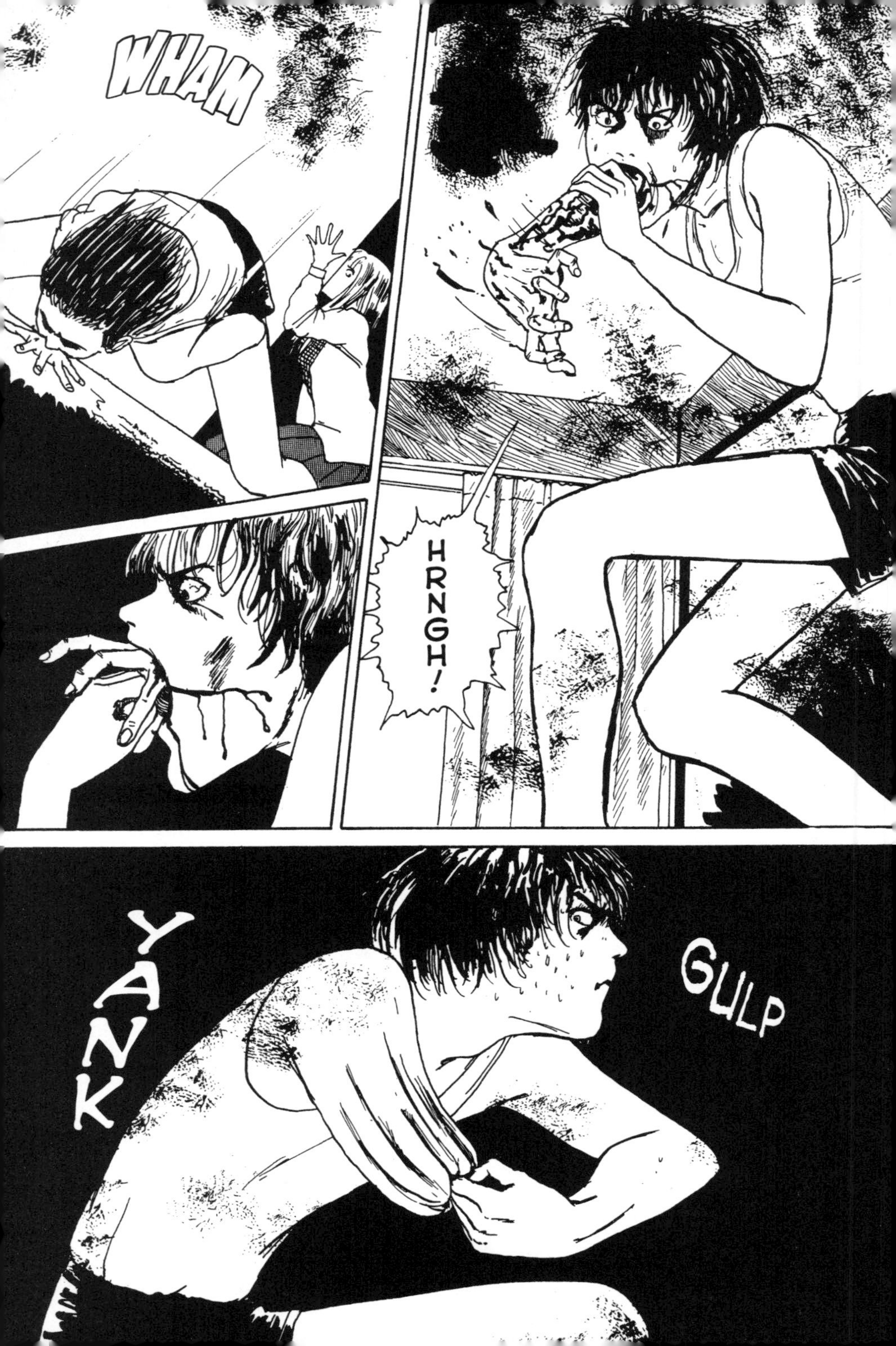
HRNGH!
WHAM
GULP
YANK

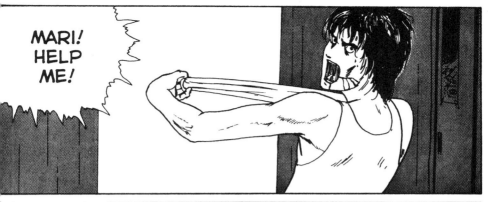

MARI!
HELP
ME!

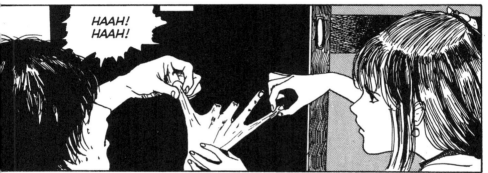

HAAH!
HAAH!

YOU
TOOK
THE TAPE
OFF?

AAAH.

YUJI...
WHAT *WAS*
THAT?

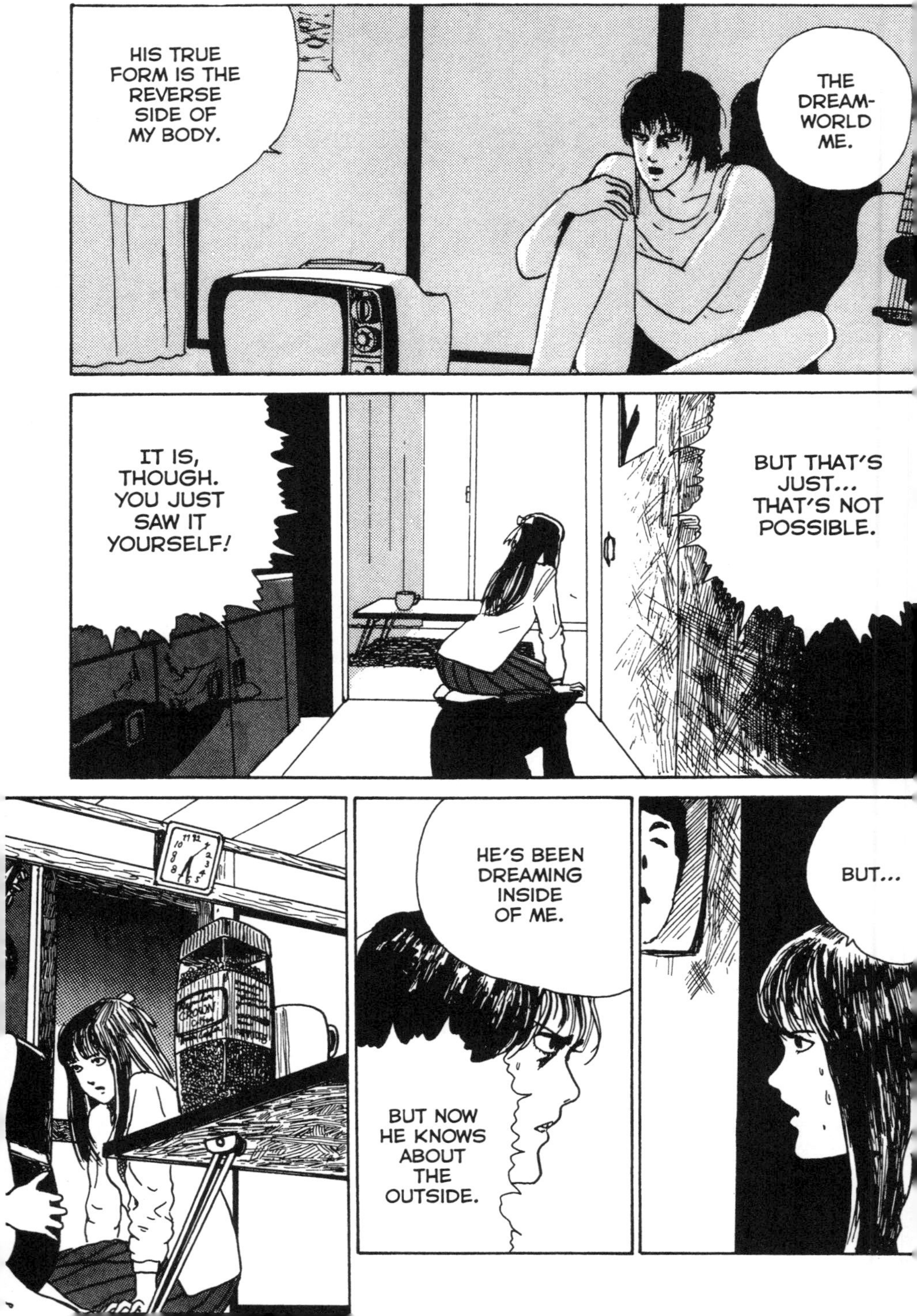
THE DREAM-WORLD ME.
HIS TRUE FORM IS THE REVERSE SIDE OF MY BODY.
BUT THAT'S JUST... THAT'S NOT POSSIBLE.
IT IS, THOUGH. YOU JUST SAW IT YOURSELF!
BUT...
HE'S BEEN DREAMING INSIDE OF ME.
BUT NOW HE KNOWS ABOUT THE OUTSIDE.

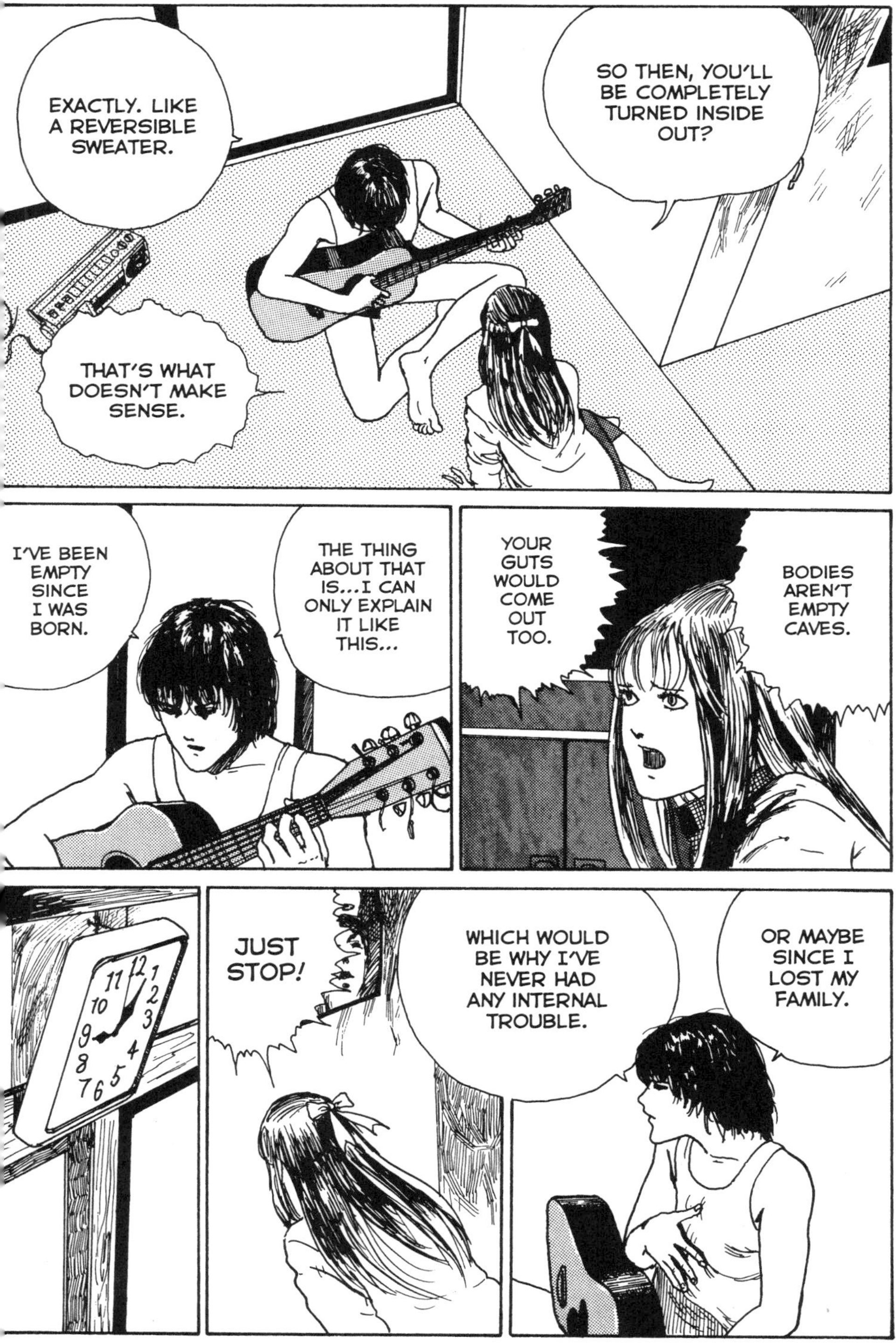
SO THEN, YOU'LL BE COMPLETELY TURNED INSIDE OUT?
EXACTLY. LIKE A REVERSIBLE SWEATER.
THAT'S WHAT DOESN'T MAKE SENSE.
BODIES AREN'T EMPTY CAVES.
YOUR GUTS WOULD COME OUT TOO.
THE THING ABOUT THAT IS...I CAN ONLY EXPLAIN IT LIKE THIS...
I'VE BEEN EMPTY SINCE I WAS BORN.
OR MAYBE SINCE I LOST MY FAMILY.
WHICH WOULD BE WHY I'VE NEVER HAD ANY INTERNAL TROUBLE.
JUST STOP!

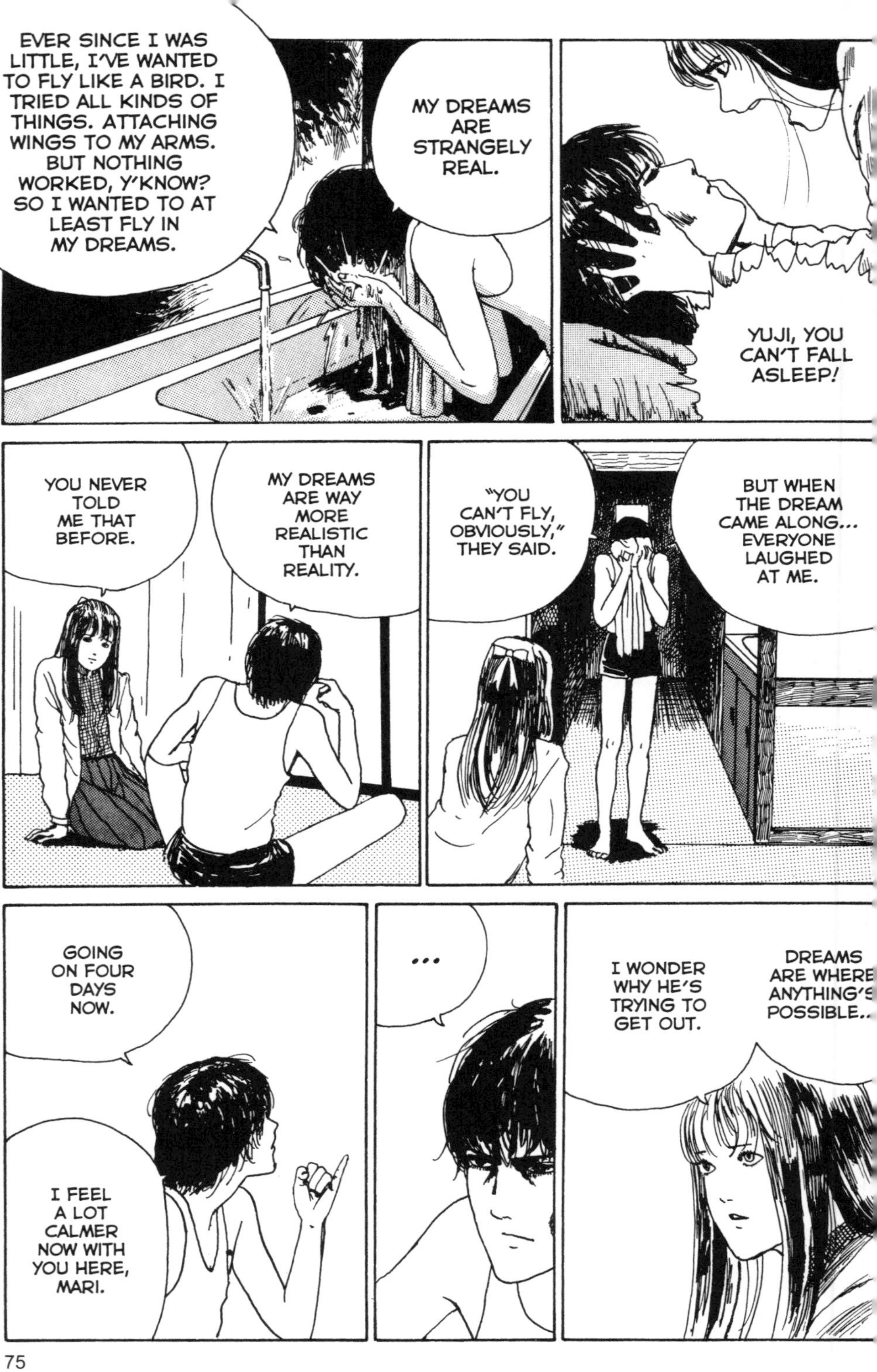
YUJI, YOU CAN'T FALL ASLEEP!
MY DREAMS ARE STRANGELY REAL.
EVER SINCE I WAS LITTLE, I'VE WANTED TO FLY LIKE A BIRD. I TRIED ALL KINDS OF THINGS. ATTACHING WINGS TO MY ARMS. BUT NOTHING WORKED, Y'KNOW? SO I WANTED TO AT LEAST FLY IN MY DREAMS.
BUT WHEN THE DREAM CAME ALONG... EVERYONE LAUGHED AT ME.
"YOU CAN'T FLY, OBVIOUSLY," THEY SAID.
MY DREAMS ARE WAY MORE REALISTIC THAN REALITY.
YOU NEVER TOLD ME THAT BEFORE.
DREAMS ARE WHERE ANYTHING'S POSSIBLE..
I WONDER WHY HE'S TRYING TO GET OUT.
...
GOING ON FOUR DAYS NOW.
I FEEL A LOT CALMER NOW WITH YOU HERE, MARI.

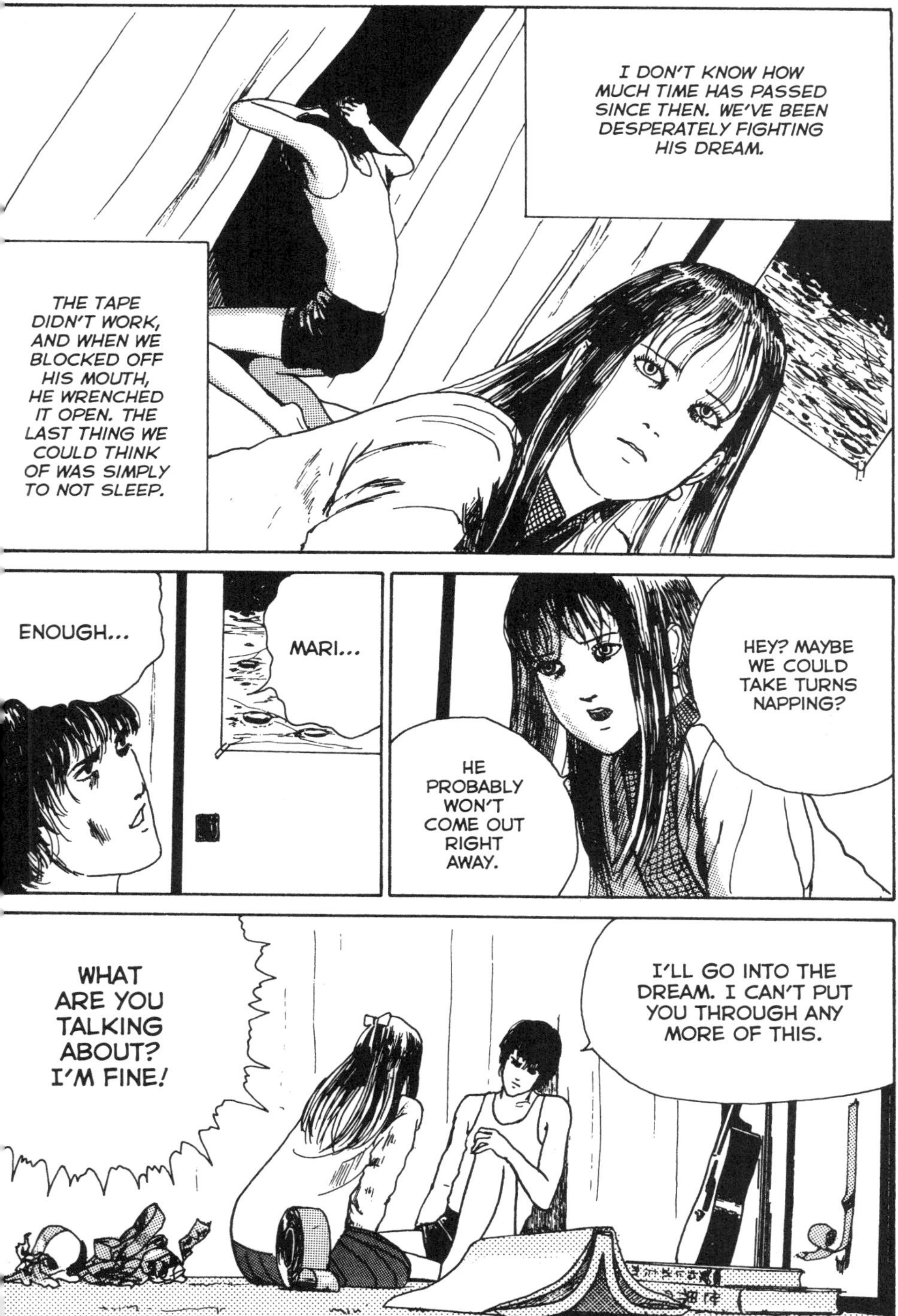
I DON'T KNOW HOW MUCH TIME HAS PASSED SINCE THEN. WE'VE BEEN DESPERATELY FIGHTING HIS DREAM.
THE TAPE DIDN'T WORK, AND WHEN WE BLOCKED OFF HIS MOUTH, HE WRENCHED IT OPEN. THE LAST THING WE COULD THINK OF WAS SIMPLY TO NOT SLEEP.
HEY? MAYBE WE COULD TAKE TURNS NAPPING?
HE PROBABLY WON'T COME OUT RIGHT AWAY.
MARI...
ENOUGH...
I'LL GO INTO THE DREAM. I CAN'T PUT YOU THROUGH ANY MORE OF THIS.
WHAT ARE YOU TALKING ABOUT? I'M FINE!

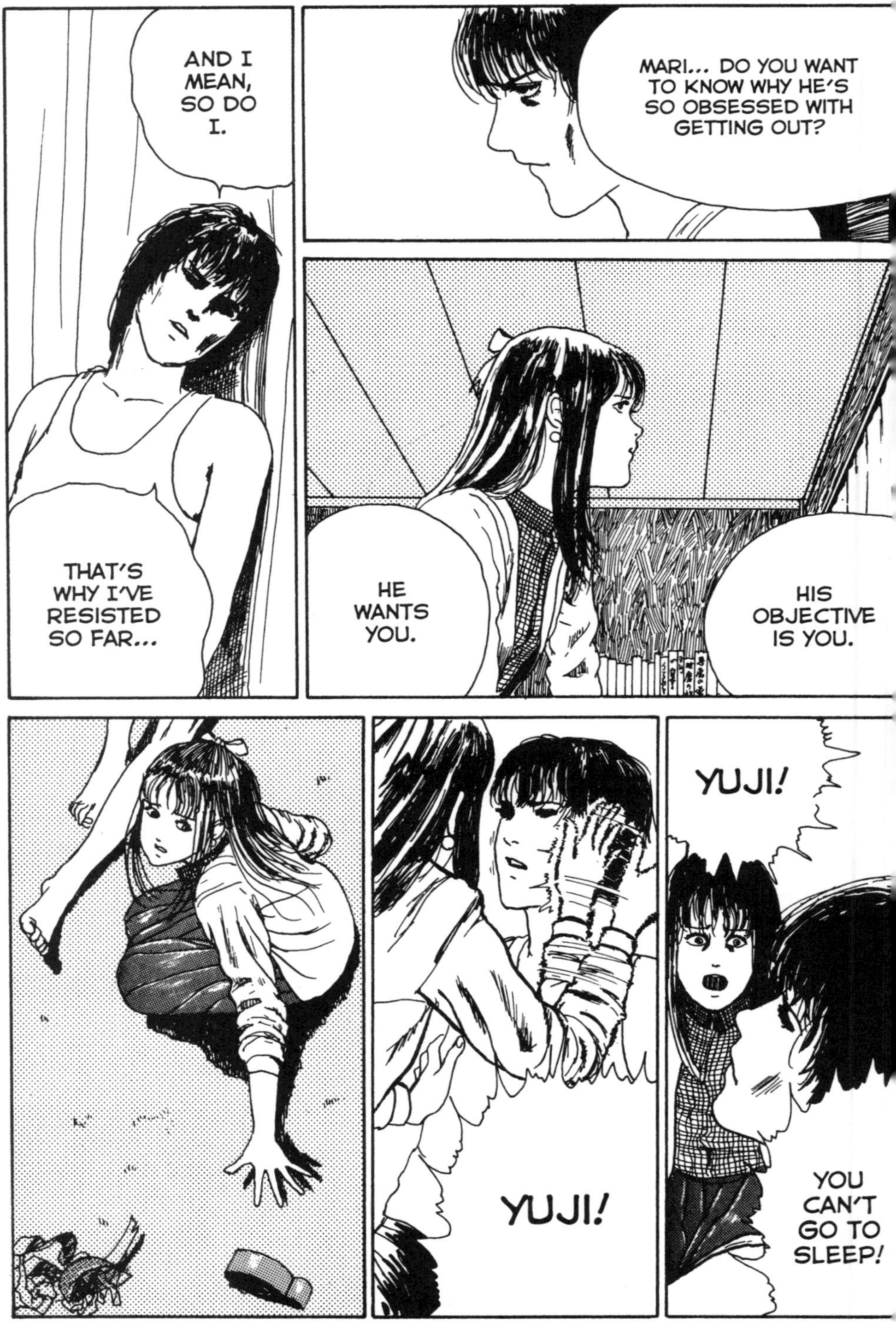
MARI... DO YOU WANT TO KNOW WHY HE'S SO OBSESSED WITH GETTING OUT?
HIS OBJECTIVE IS YOU.
HE WANTS YOU.
AND I MEAN, SO DO I.
THAT'S WHY I'VE RESISTED SO FAR...
YUJI!
YOU CAN'T GO TO SLEEP!
YUJI!

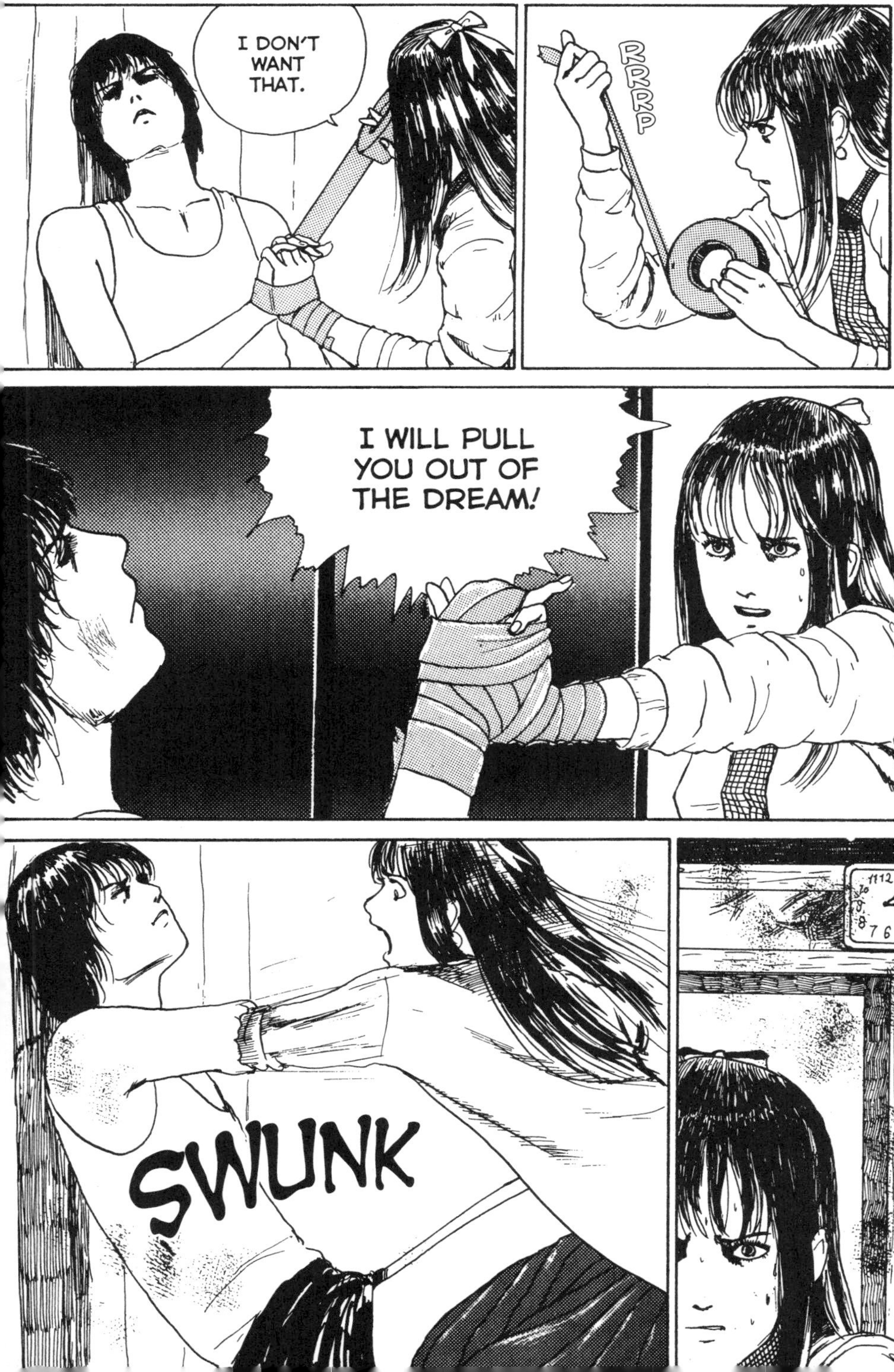
RRRP
I DON'T WANT THAT.
I WILL PULL YOU OUT OF THE DREAM!
SWUNK

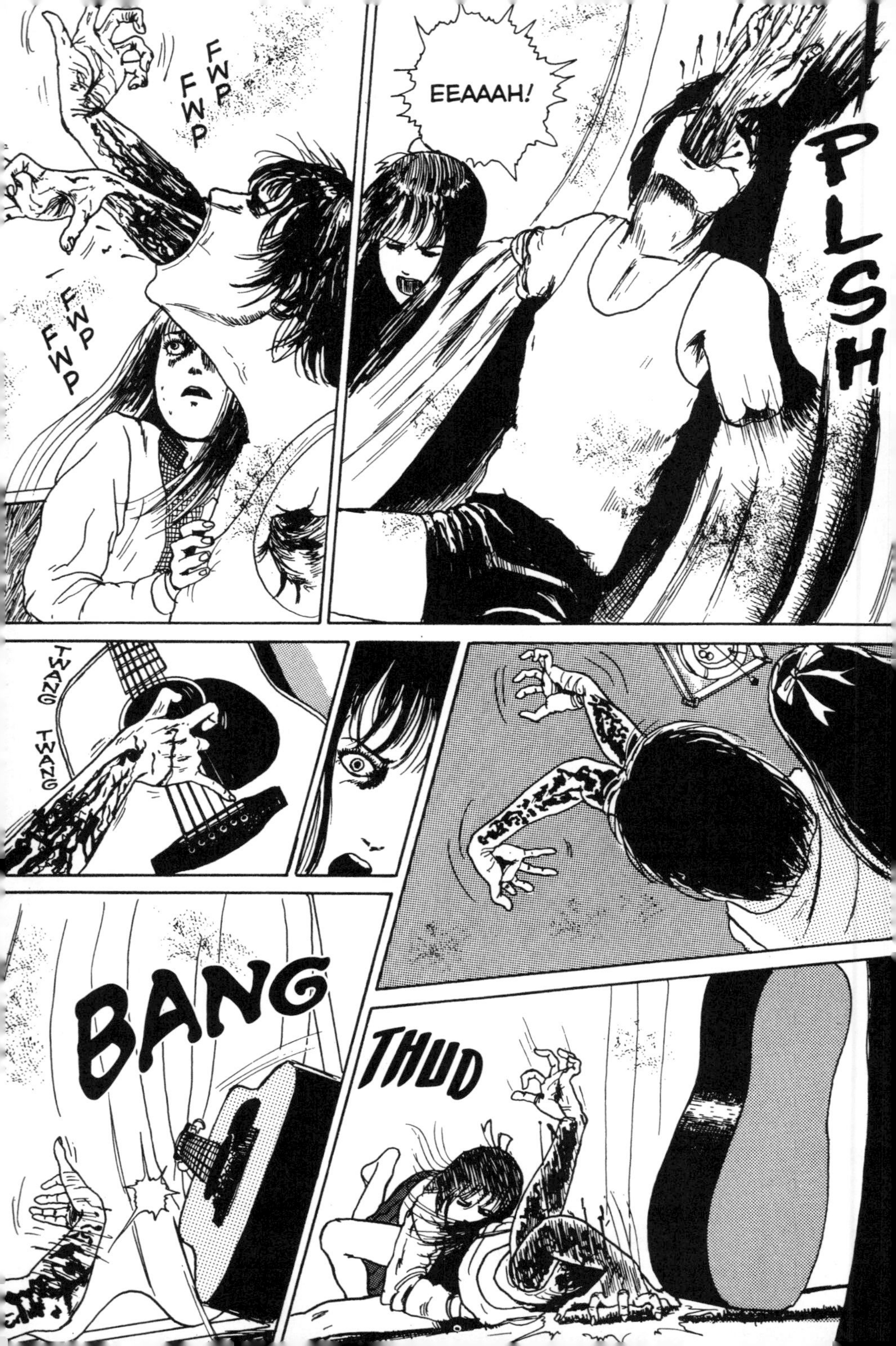
EEAAAH!
PLSH
FWP FWP
FWP FWP
TWANG TWANG
THUD
BANG

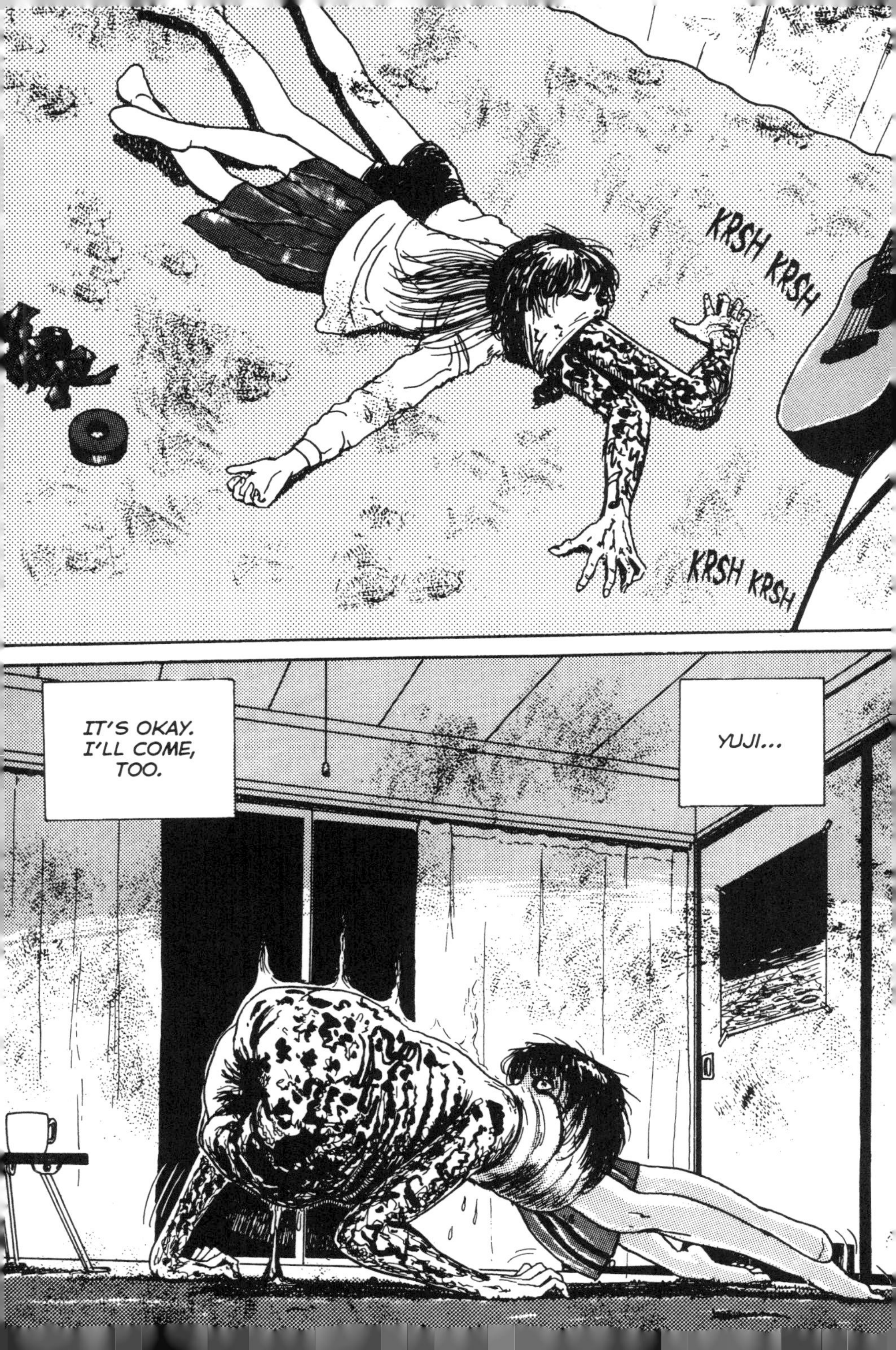
KRSH KRSH
KRSH KRSH
YUJI...
IT'S OKAY. I'LL COME, TOO.

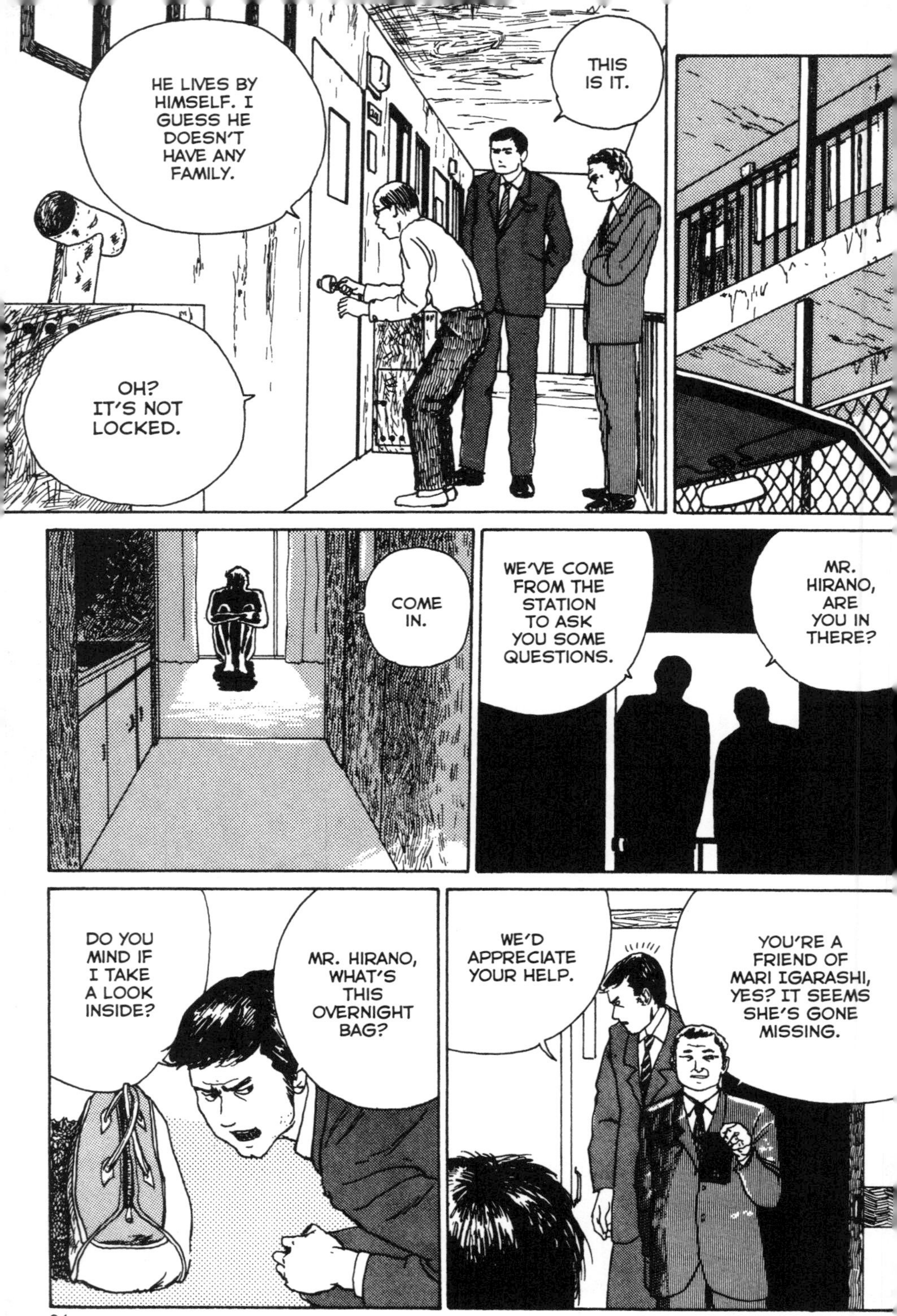
THIS IS IT.
HE LIVES BY HIMSELF. I GUESS HE DOESN'T HAVE ANY FAMILY.
OH? IT'S NOT LOCKED.
MR. HIRANO, ARE YOU IN THERE?
WE'VE COME FROM THE STATION TO ASK YOU SOME QUESTIONS.
COME IN.
YOU'RE A FRIEND OF MARI IGARASHI, YES? IT SEEMS SHE'S GONE MISSING.
WE'D APPRECIATE YOUR HELP.
MR. HIRANO, WHAT'S THIS OVERNIGHT BAG?
DO YOU MIND IF I TAKE A LOOK INSIDE?

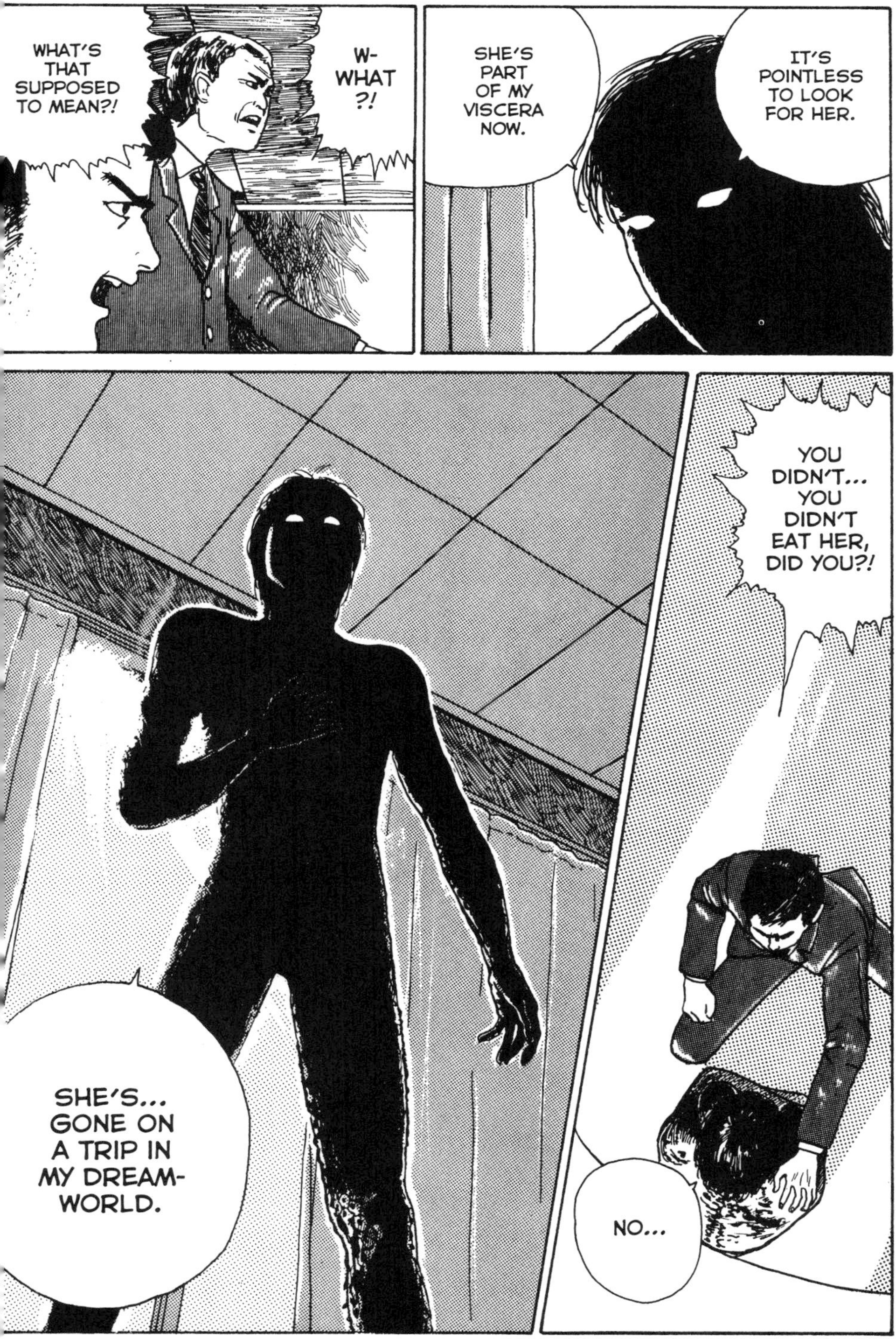
IT'S POINTLESS TO LOOK FOR HER.
SHE'S PART OF MY VISCERA NOW.
W-WHAT?!
WHAT'S THAT SUPPOSED TO MEAN?!
YOU DIDN'T... YOU DIDN'T EAT HER, DID YOU?!
NO...
SHE'S... GONE ON A TRIP IN MY DREAM-WORLD.

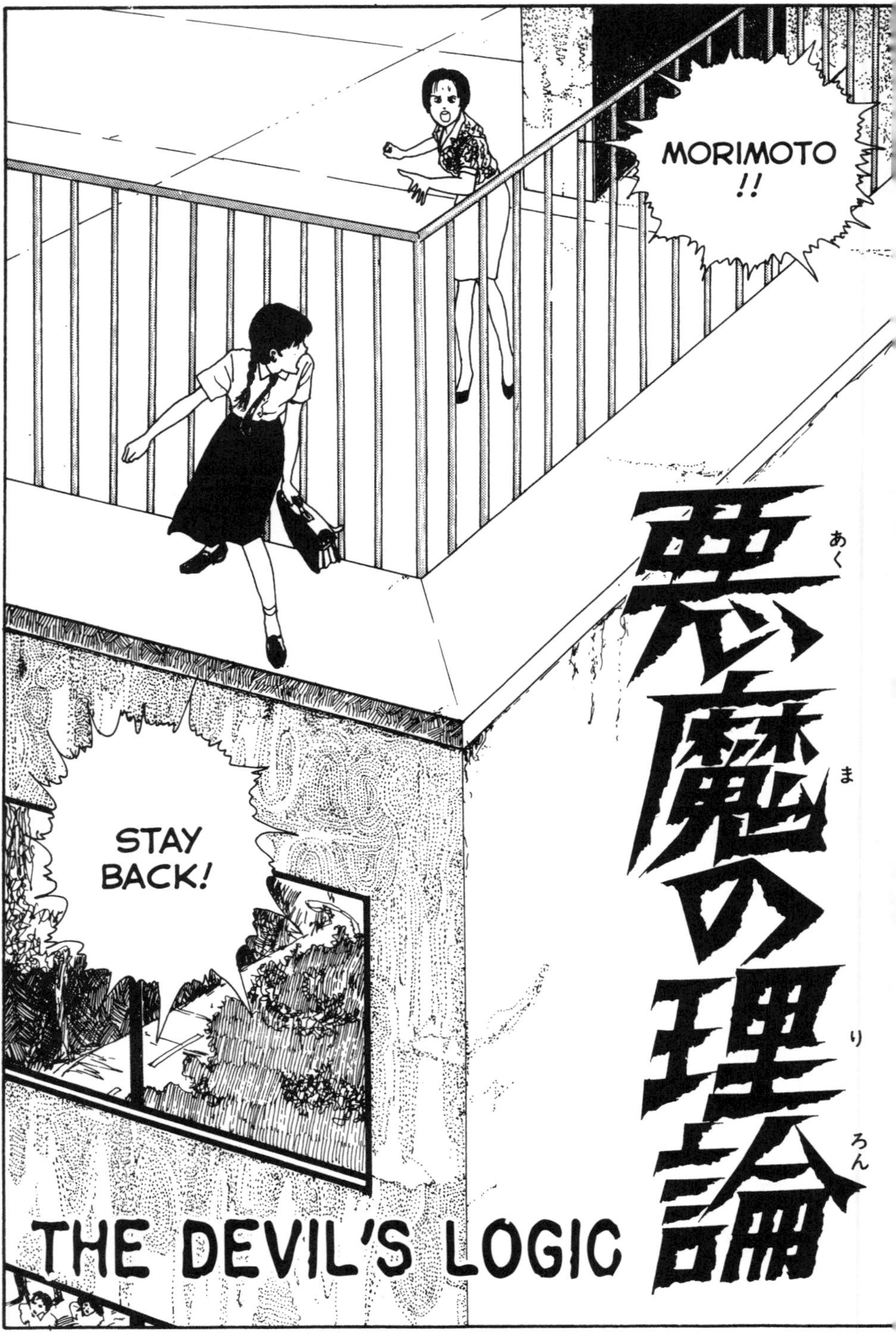
悪魔の理論
あくまのりろん
THE DEVIL'S LOGIC
MORIMOTO !!
STAY BACK!

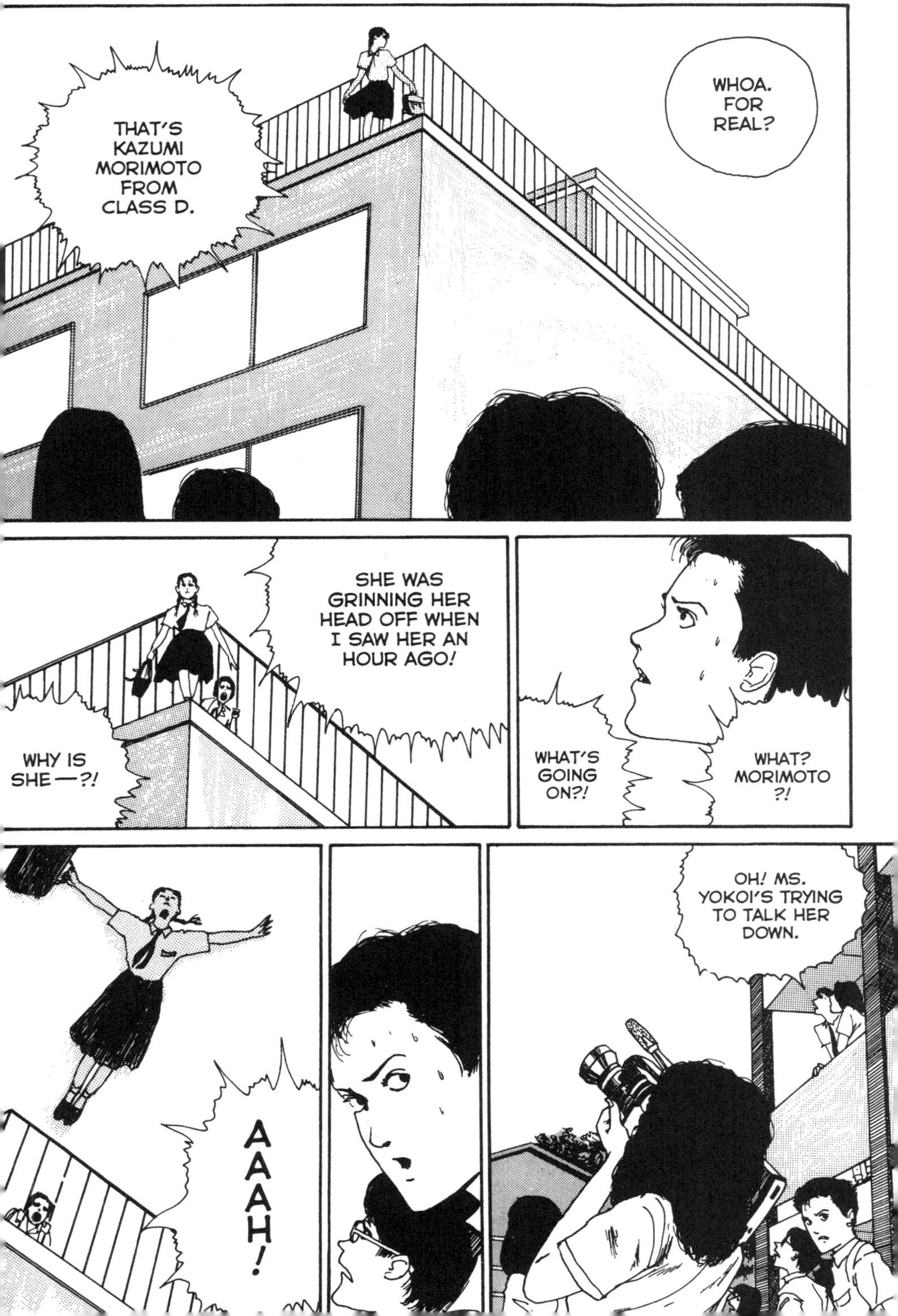

WHOA. FOR REAL?
THAT'S KAZUMI MORIMOTO FROM CLASS D.
WHAT? MORIMOTO ?!
WHAT'S GOING ON?!
SHE WAS GRINNING HER HEAD OFF WHEN I SAW HER AN HOUR AGO!
WHY IS SHE—?!
OH! MS. YOKOI'S TRYING TO TALK HER DOWN.
AAAH!

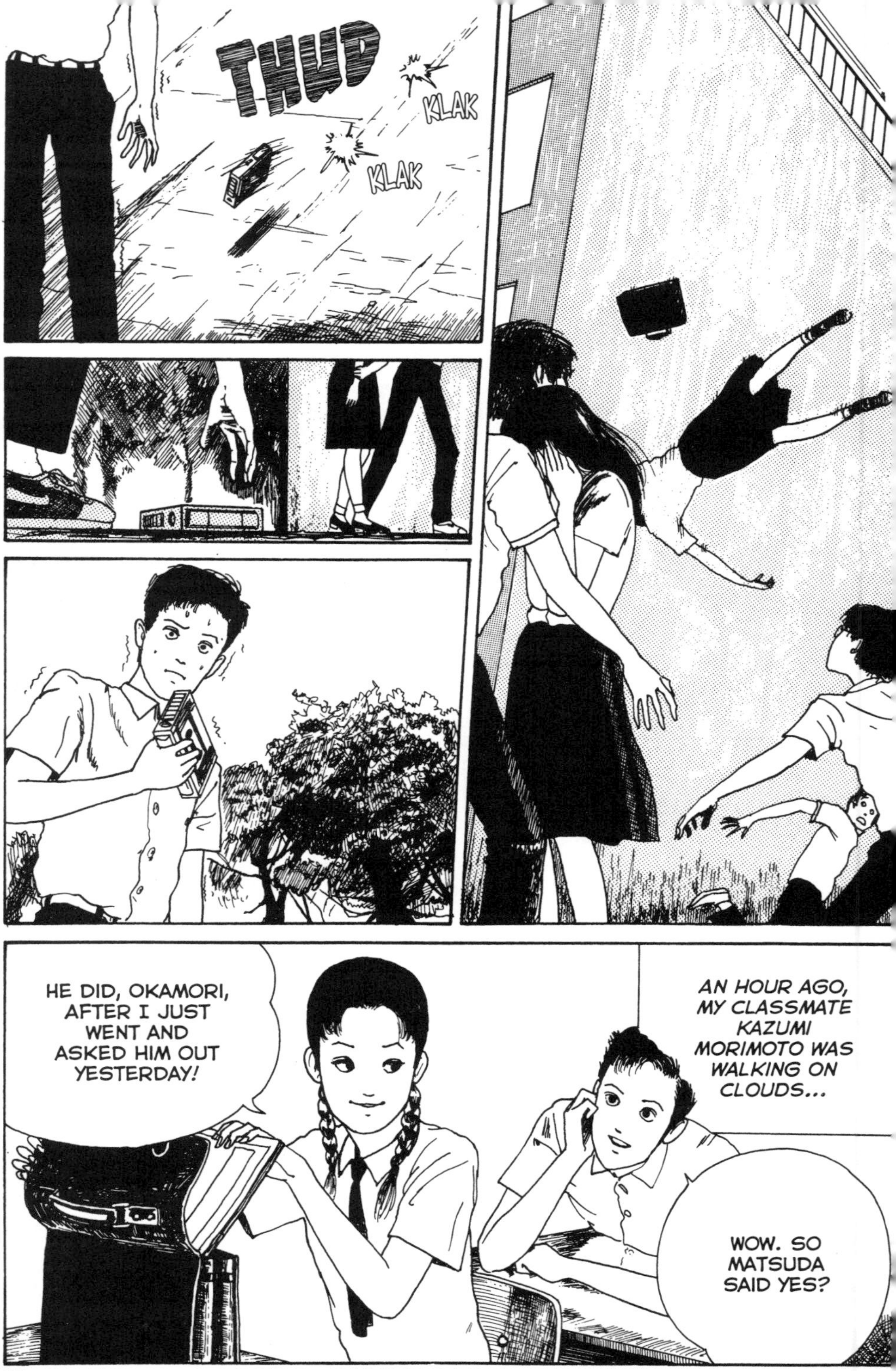
THUD
KLAK
KLAK
AN HOUR AGO, MY CLASSMATE KAZUMI MORIMOTO WAS WALKING ON CLOUDS...
WOW. SO MATSUDA SAID YES?
HE DID, OKAMORI, AFTER I JUST WENT AND ASKED HIM OUT YESTERDAY!

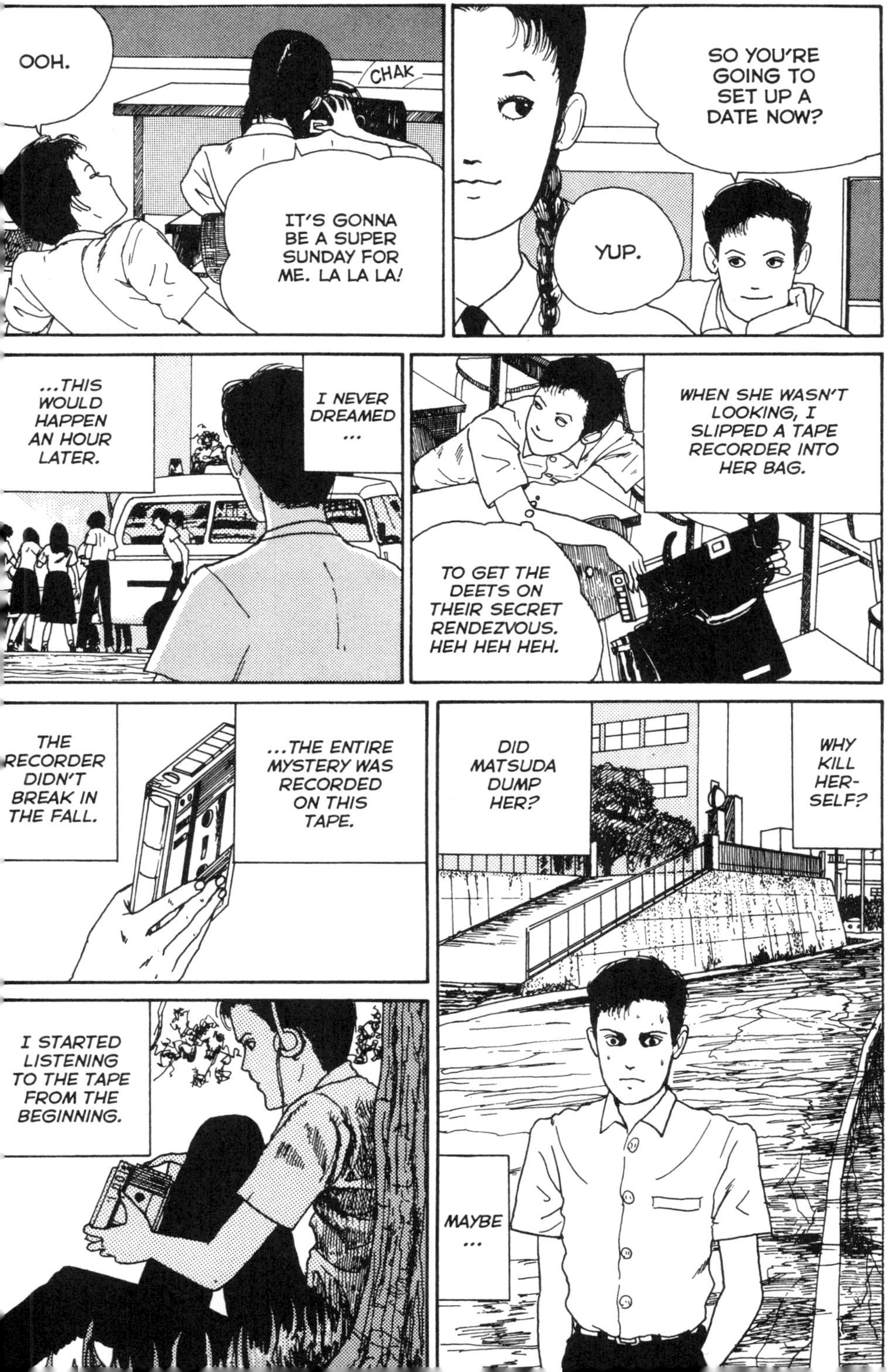
SO YOU'RE GOING TO SET UP A DATE NOW?
YUP.
CHAK
OOH.
IT'S GONNA BE A SUPER SUNDAY FOR ME. LA LA LA!
WHEN SHE WASN'T LOOKING, I SLIPPED A TAPE RECORDER INTO HER BAG.
TO GET THE DEETS ON THEIR SECRET RENDEZVOUS. HEH HEH HEH.
I NEVER DREAMED ...
...THIS WOULD HAPPEN AN HOUR LATER.
WHY KILL HER-SELF?
DID MATSUDA DUMP HER?
MAYBE ...
...THE ENTIRE MYSTERY WAS RECORDED ON THIS TAPE.
THE RECORDER DIDN'T BREAK IN THE FALL.
I STARTED LISTENING TO THE TAPE FROM THE BEGINNING.

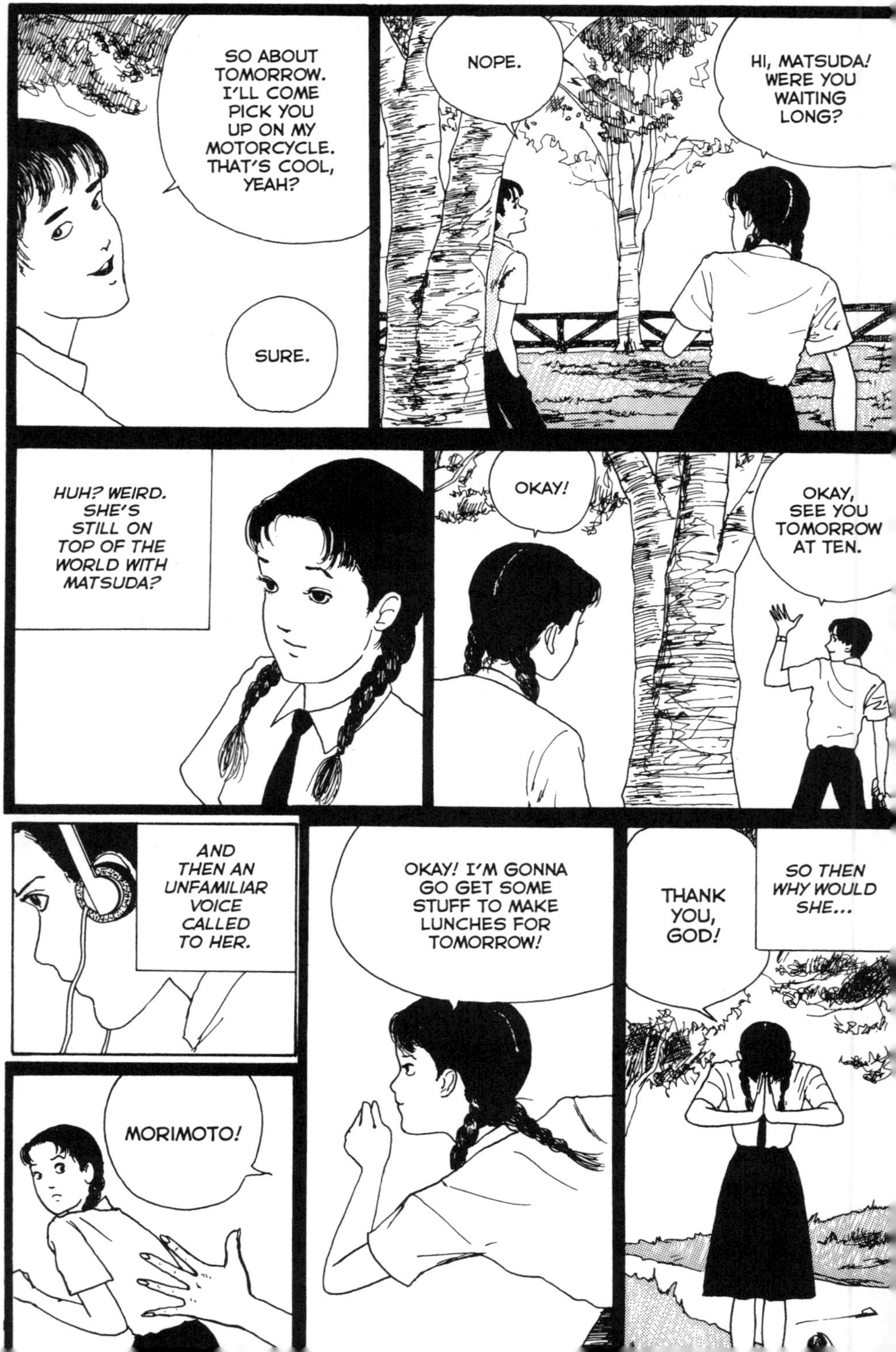
HI, MATSUDA! WERE YOU WAITING LONG?
NOPE.
SO ABOUT TOMORROW. I'LL COME PICK YOU UP ON MY MOTORCYCLE. THAT'S COOL, YEAH?
SURE.
OKAY, SEE YOU TOMORROW AT TEN.
OKAY!
HUH? WEIRD. SHE'S STILL ON TOP OF THE WORLD WITH MATSUDA?
SO THEN WHY WOULD SHE...
THANK YOU, GOD!
OKAY! I'M GONNA GO GET SOME STUFF TO MAKE LUNCHES FOR TOMORROW!
AND THEN AN UNFAMILIAR VOICE CALLED TO HER.
MORIMOTO!

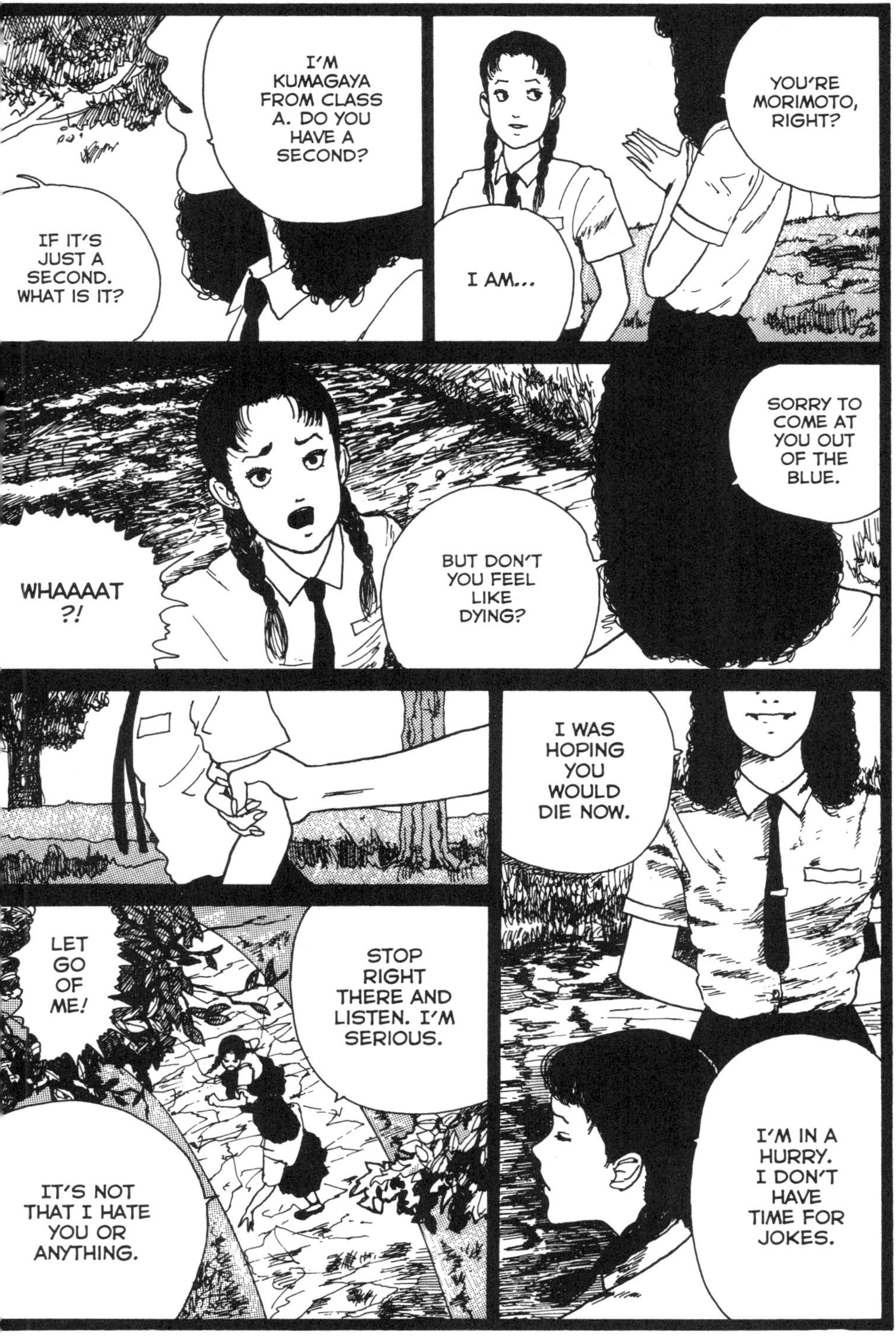
YOU'RE MORIMOTO, RIGHT?
I AM...
I'M KUMAGAYA FROM CLASS A. DO YOU HAVE A SECOND?
IF IT'S JUST A SECOND. WHAT IS IT?
SORRY TO COME AT YOU OUT OF THE BLUE.
BUT DON'T YOU FEEL LIKE DYING?
WHAAAAT?!
I WAS HOPING YOU WOULD DIE NOW.
I'M IN A HURRY. I DON'T HAVE TIME FOR JOKES.
STOP RIGHT THERE AND LISTEN. I'M SERIOUS.
LET GO OF ME!
IT'S NOT THAT I HATE YOU OR ANYTHING.

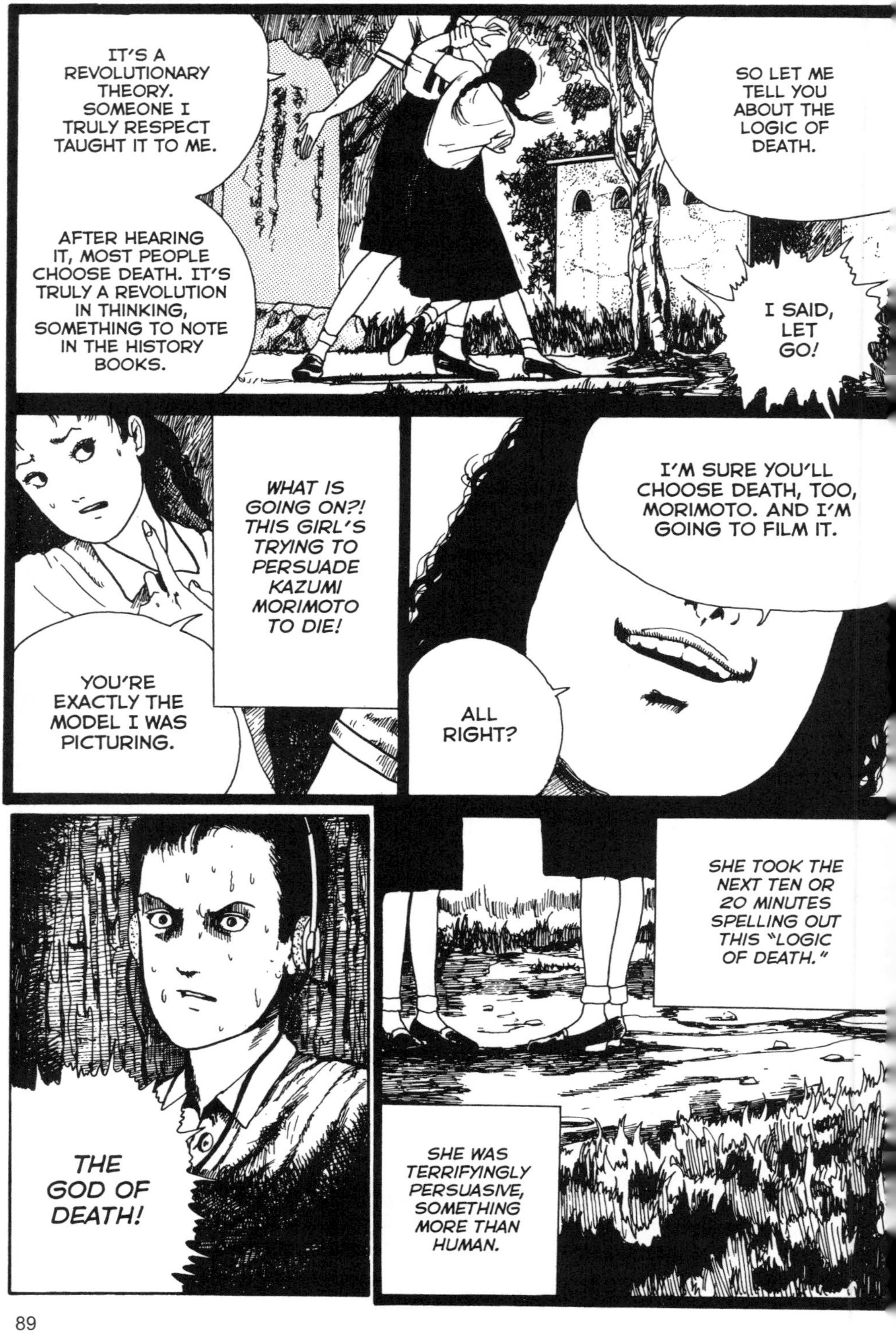
SO LET ME TELL YOU ABOUT THE LOGIC OF DEATH.
I SAID, LET GO!
IT'S A REVOLUTIONARY THEORY. SOMEONE I TRULY RESPECT TAUGHT IT TO ME.
AFTER HEARING IT, MOST PEOPLE CHOOSE DEATH. IT'S TRULY A REVOLUTION IN THINKING, SOMETHING TO NOTE IN THE HISTORY BOOKS.
I'M SURE YOU'LL CHOOSE DEATH, TOO, MORIMOTO. AND I'M GOING TO FILM IT.
ALL RIGHT?
WHAT IS GOING ON?! THIS GIRL'S TRYING TO PERSUADE KAZUMI MORIMOTO TO DIE!
YOU'RE EXACTLY THE MODEL I WAS PICTURING.
SHE TOOK THE NEXT TEN OR 20 MINUTES SPELLING OUT THIS "LOGIC OF DEATH."
SHE WAS TERRIFYINGLY PERSUASIVE, SOMETHING MORE THAN HUMAN.
THE GOD OF DEATH!

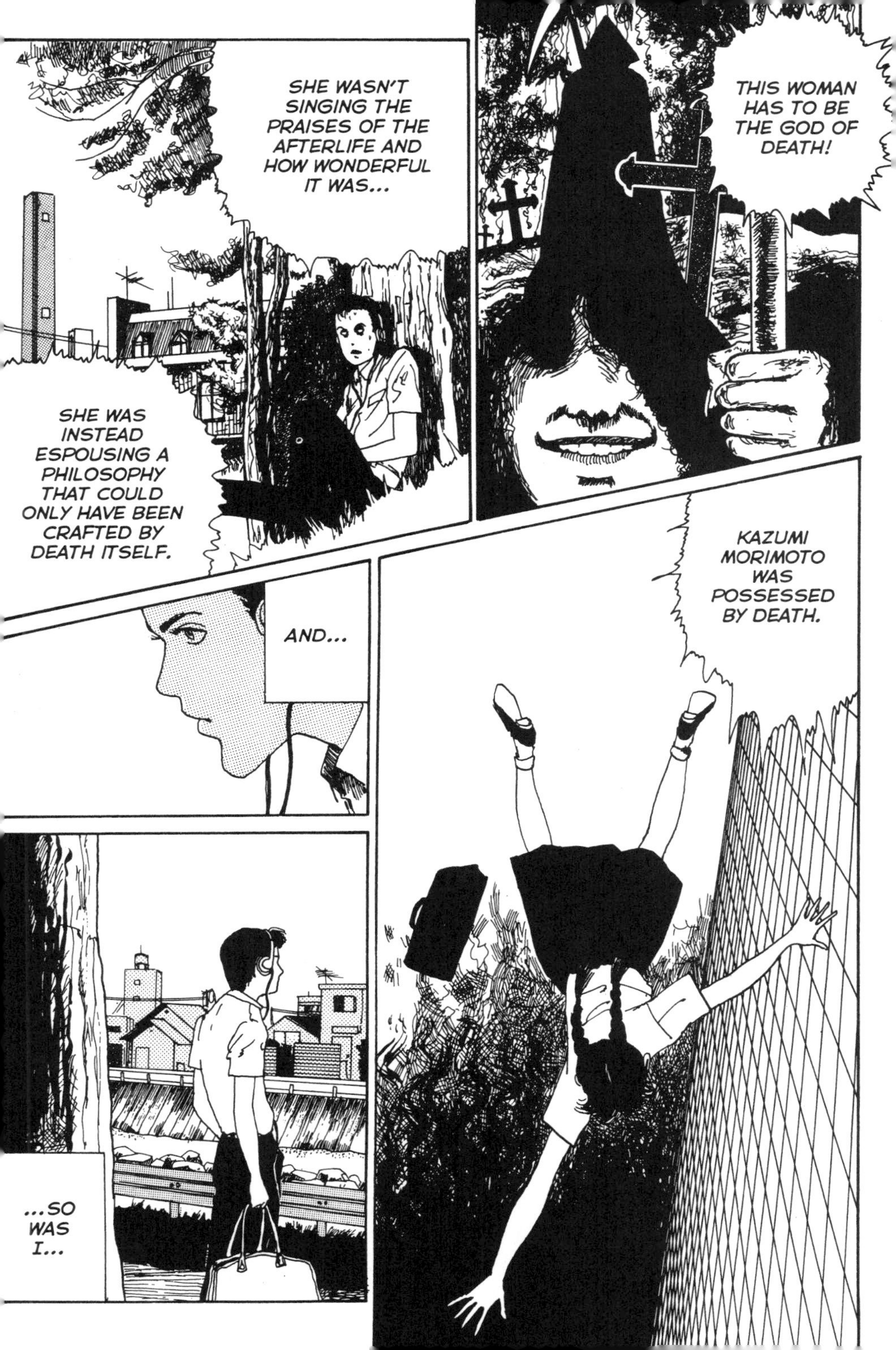
THIS WOMAN HAS TO BE THE GOD OF DEATH!
SHE WASN'T SINGING THE PRAISES OF THE AFTERLIFE AND HOW WONDERFUL IT WAS...
SHE WAS INSTEAD ESPOUSING A PHILOSOPHY THAT COULD ONLY HAVE BEEN CRAFTED BY DEATH ITSELF.
KAZUMI MORIMOTO WAS POSSESSED BY DEATH.
AND...
...SO WAS I...

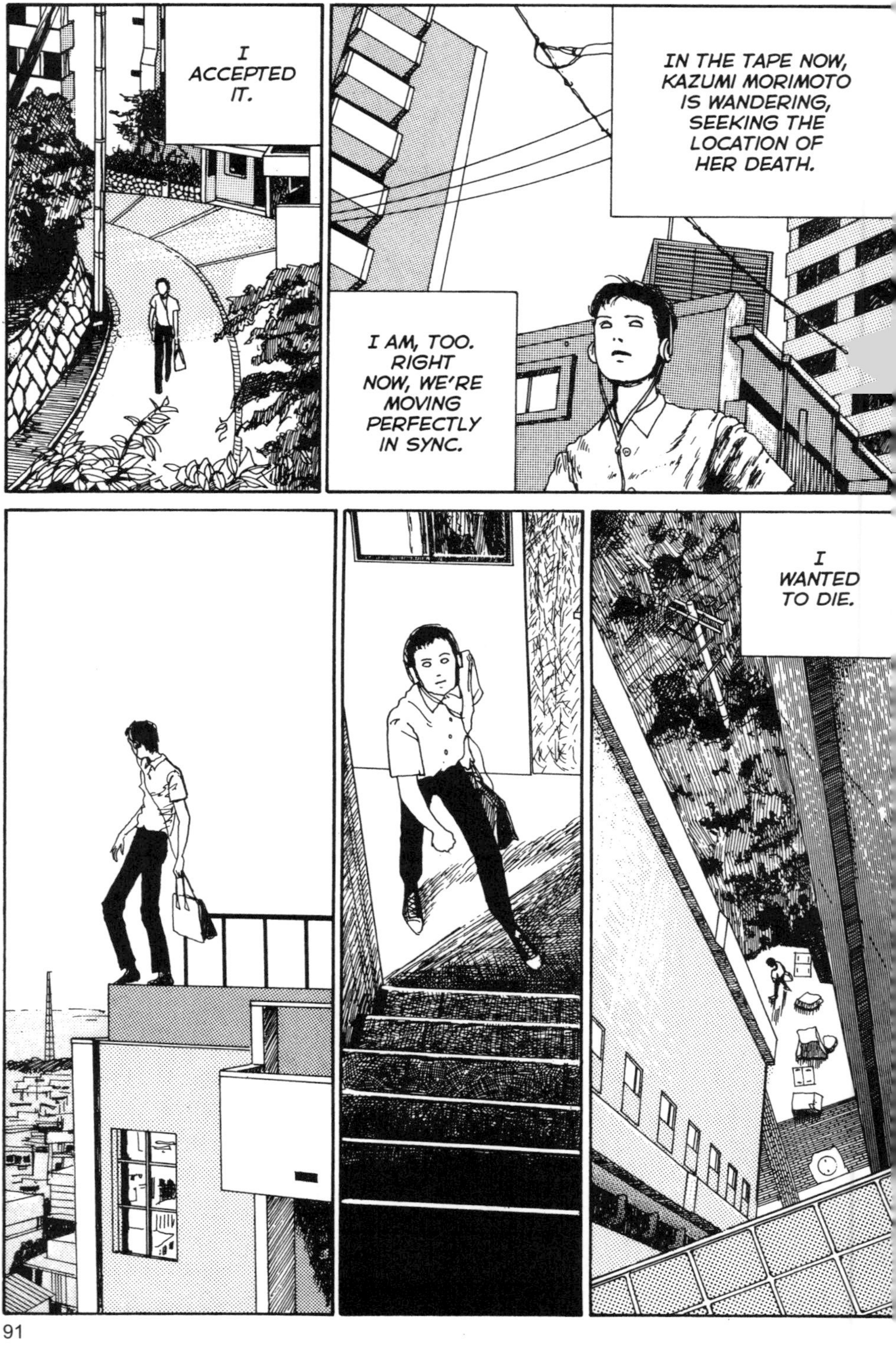
IN THE TAPE NOW, KAZUMI MORIMOTO IS WANDERING, SEEKING THE LOCATION OF HER DEATH.
I AM, TOO. RIGHT NOW, WE'RE MOVING PERFECTLY IN SYNC.
I ACCEPTED IT.
I WANTED TO DIE.

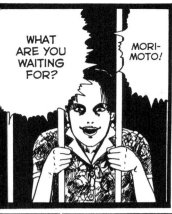

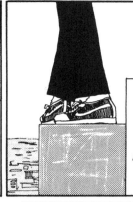

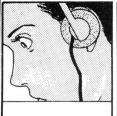

BUT ACTUALLY FACED WITH IT, I HESITATED.
AND THEN MS. YOKOI'S VOICE CAME OVER THE TAPE SUDDENLY.
MORI-MOTO!
WHAT ARE YOU WAITING FOR?
GO ON AND JUMP.
THERE'S NOTHING TO BE SCARED OF. EVERYONE IN THE WORLD WILL BE DEAD SOON.
THAT'S RIGHT... I'M DEATH'S ADVOCATE.
I'M HERE TO TELL EVERYONE IN THE WORLD WHY THEY SHOULD DIE!

THE DEVIL'S LOGIC/END

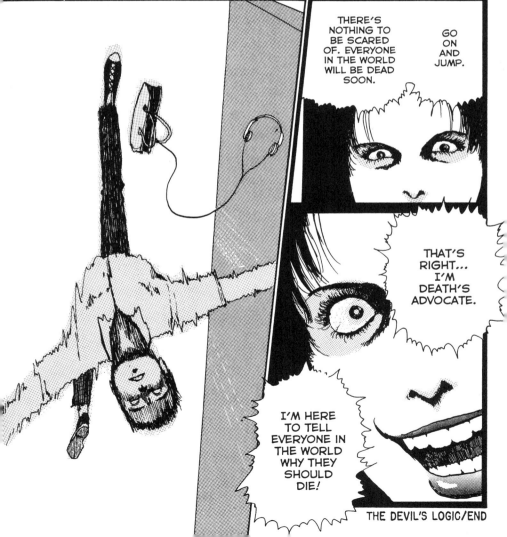

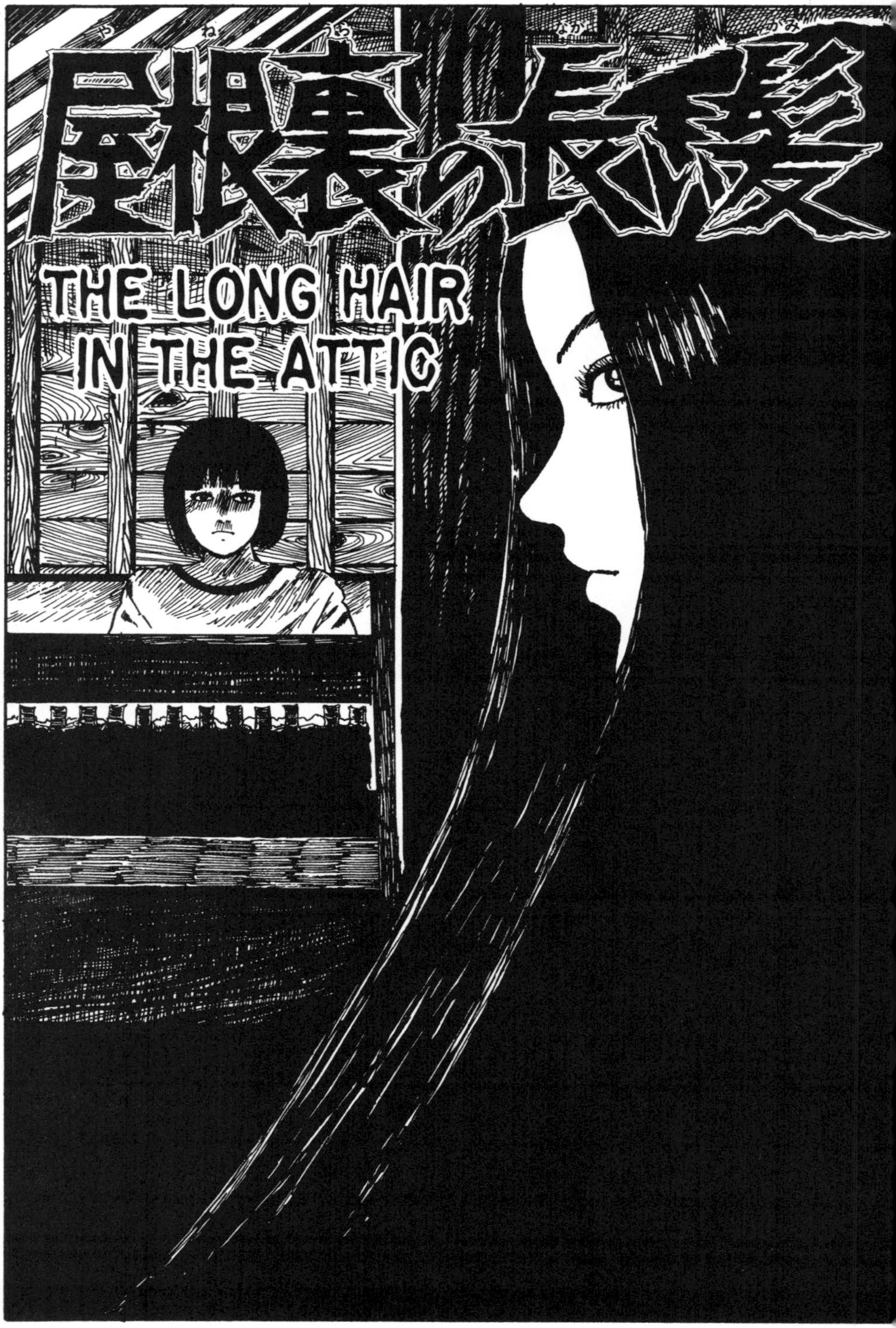
屋根裏の長髪
THE LONG HAIR IN THE ATTIC

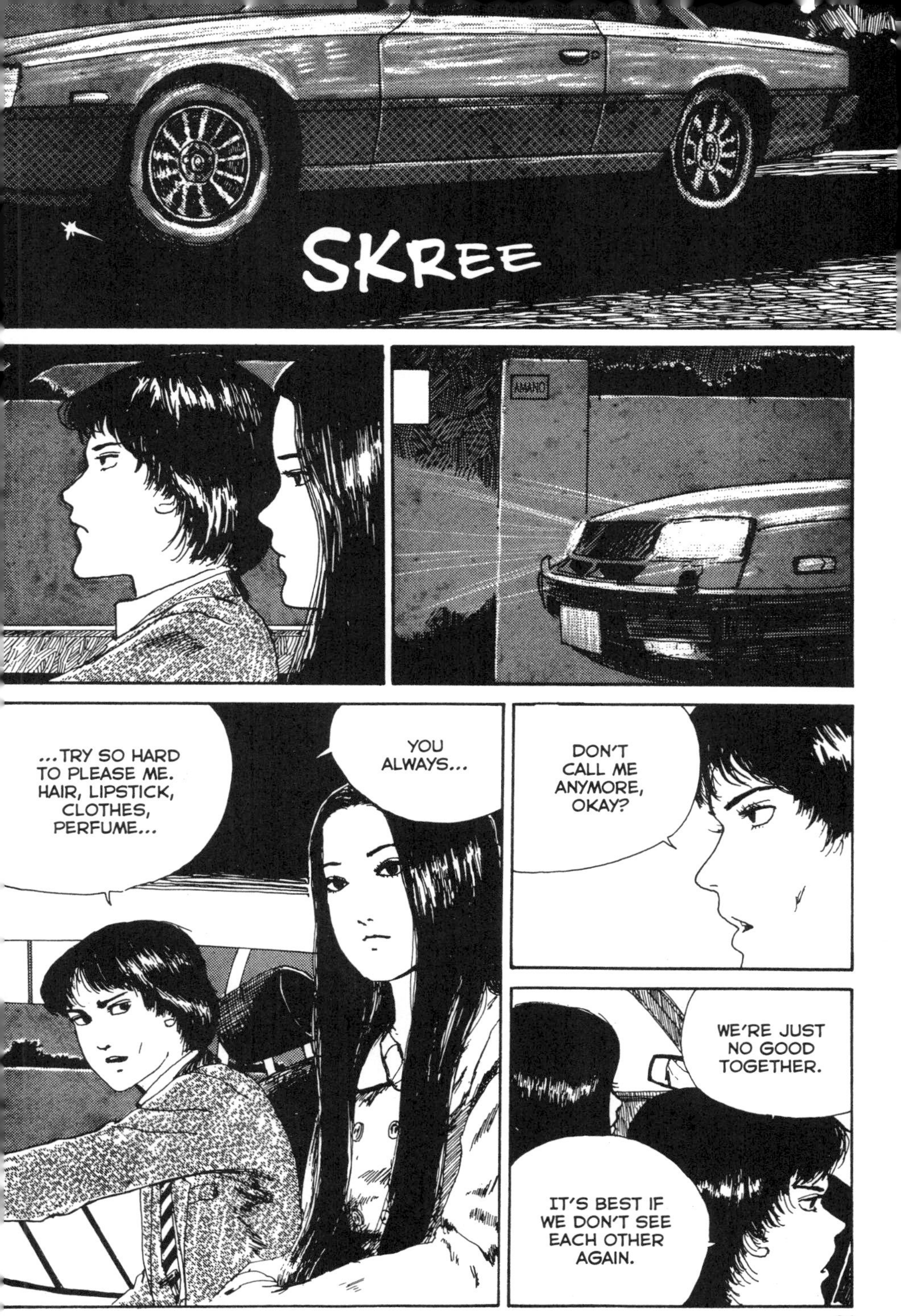
SKREE
AMANO
DON'T CALL ME ANYMORE, OKAY?
WE'RE JUST NO GOOD TOGETHER.
IT'S BEST IF WE DON'T SEE EACH OTHER AGAIN.
YOU ALWAYS...
...TRY SO HARD TO PLEASE ME. HAIR, LIPSTICK, CLOTHES, PERFUME...

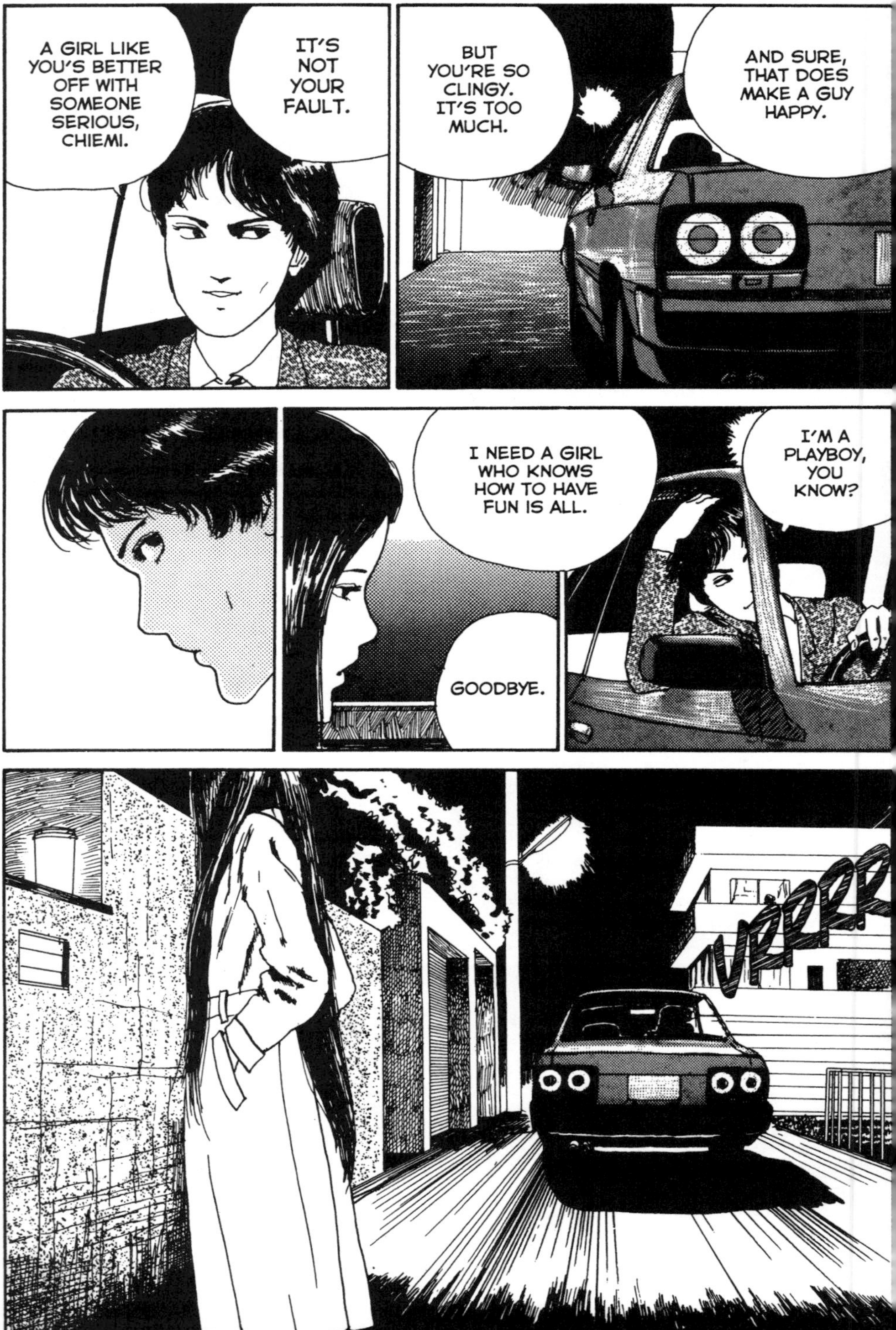
AND SURE, THAT DOES MAKE A GUY HAPPY.
BUT YOU'RE SO CLINGY. IT'S TOO MUCH.
IT'S NOT YOUR FAULT.
A GIRL LIKE YOU'S BETTER OFF WITH SOMEONE SERIOUS, CHIEMI.
I'M A PLAYBOY, YOU KNOW?
I NEED A GIRL WHO KNOWS HOW TO HAVE FUN IS ALL.
GOODBYE.
VRRRR

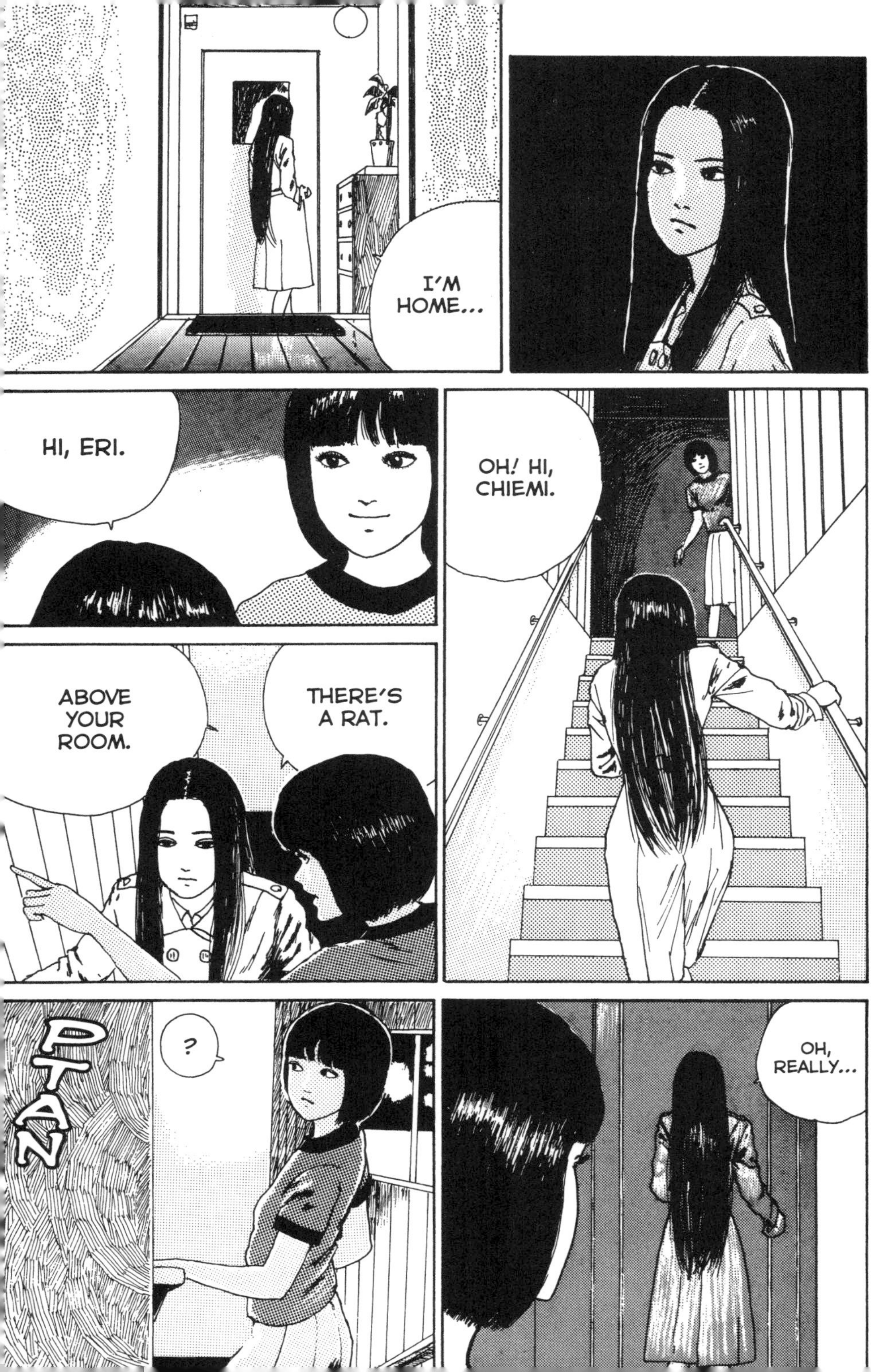
I'M HOME...
OH! HI, CHIEMI.
HI, ERI.
THERE'S A RAT.
ABOVE YOUR ROOM.
OH, REALLY...
?
PTAN

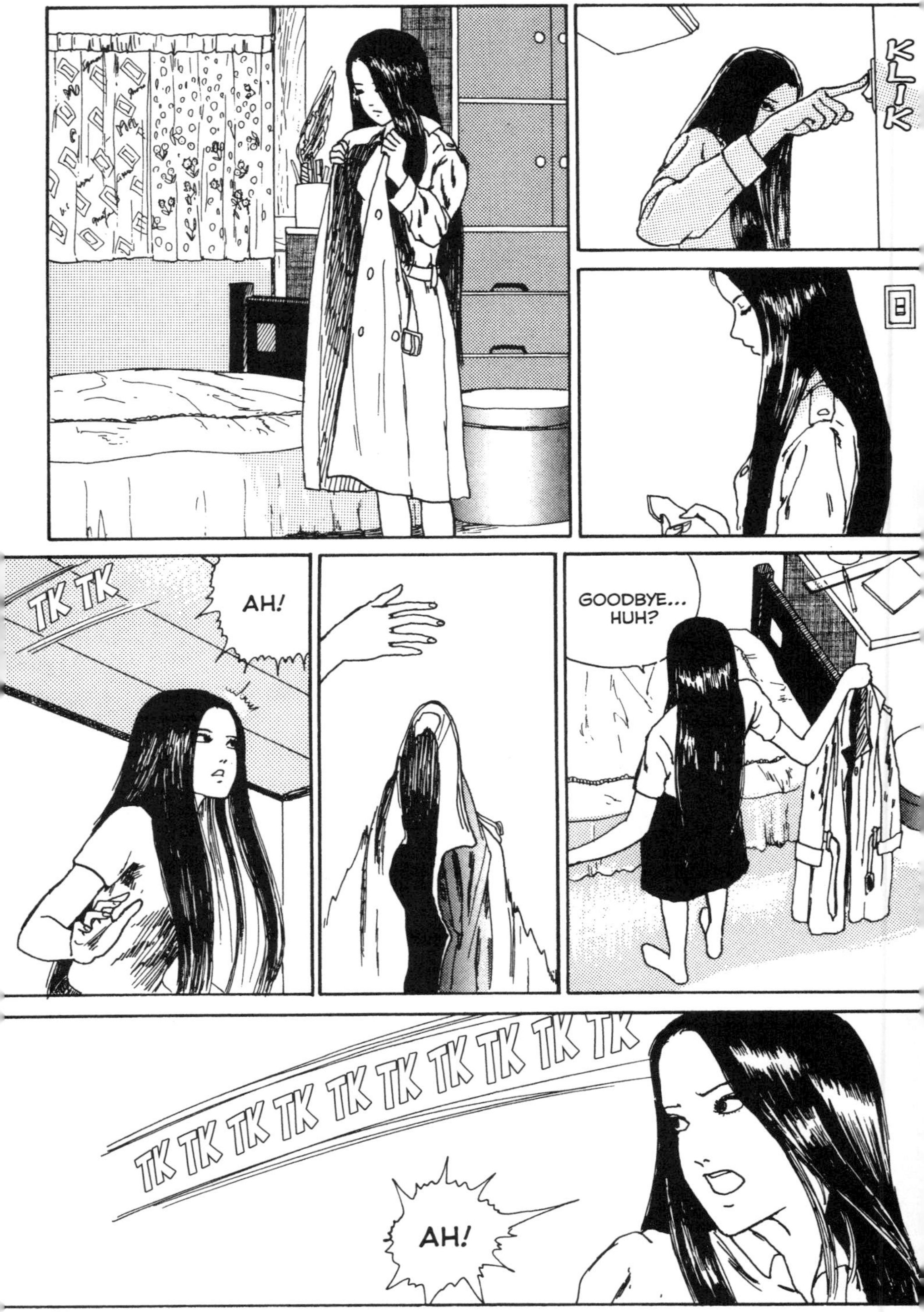
KLIK
GOODBYE... HUH?
TK TK
AH!
TK TK TK TK TK TK TK TK TK TK
AH!

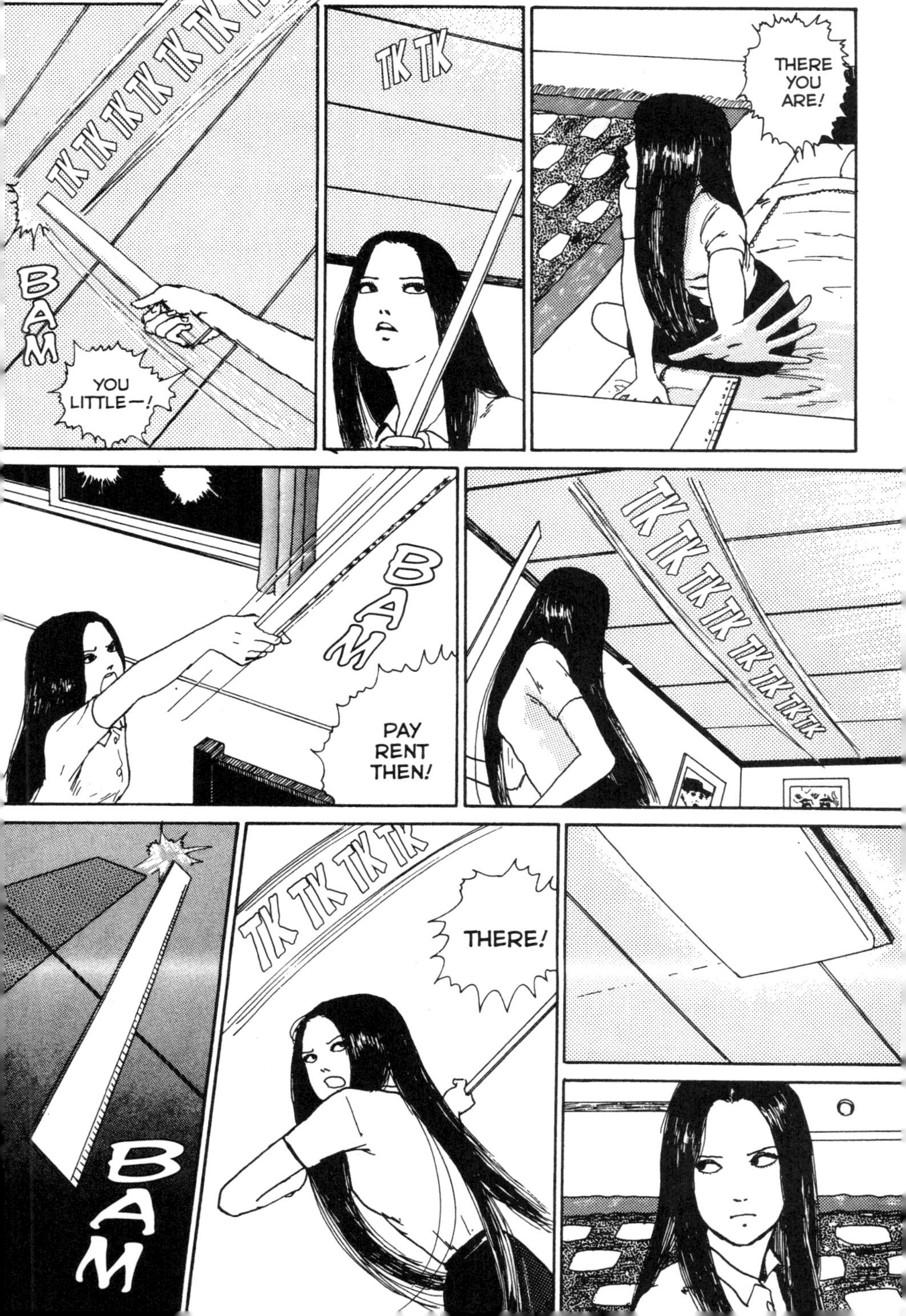
THERE YOU ARE!
TK TK
TK TK TK TK TK TK TK
BAM
YOU LITTLE—!
TK TK TK TK TK TK TK TK
BAM
PAY RENT THEN!
TK TK TK TK
THERE!
BAM

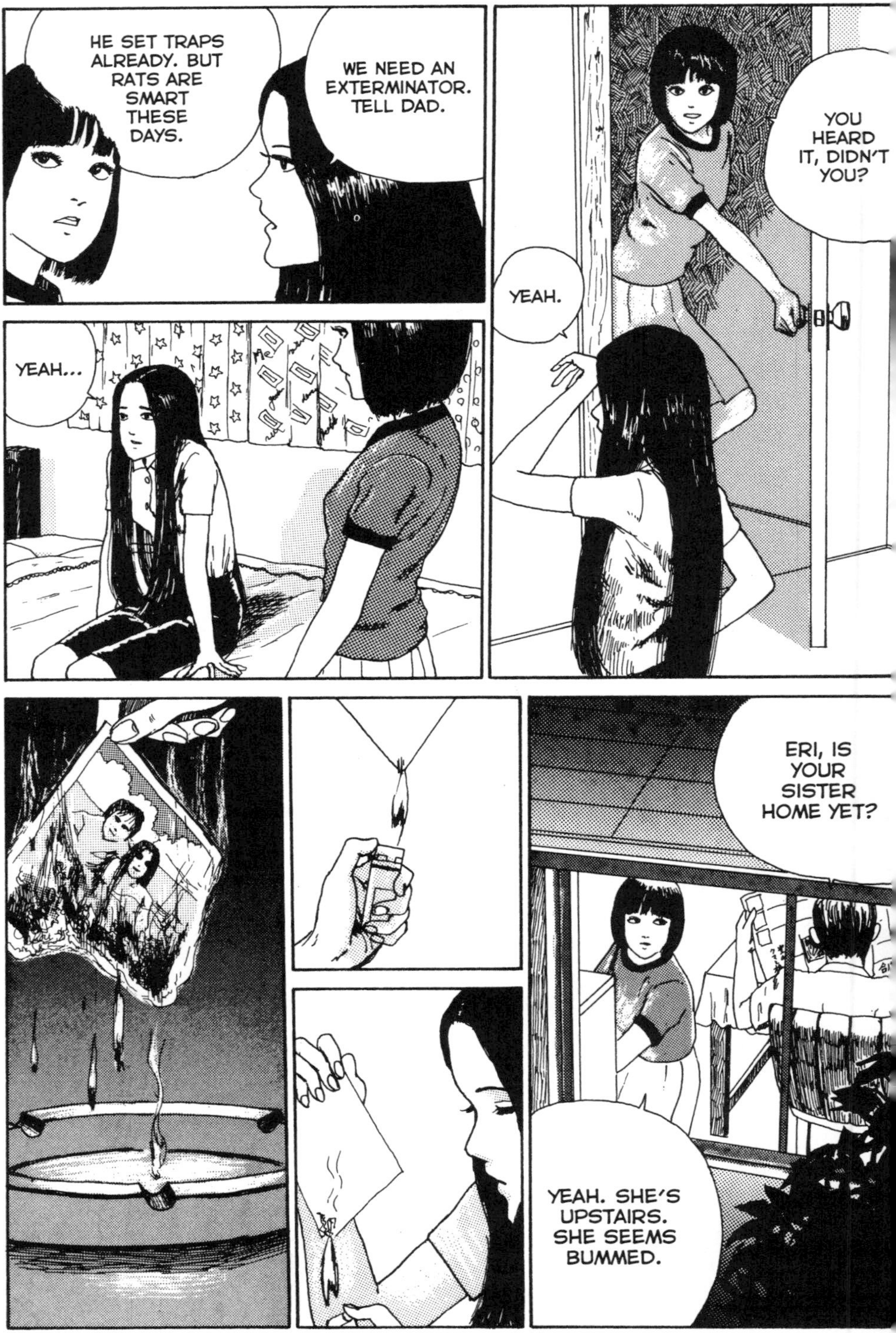

YOU HEARD IT, DIDN'T YOU?
YEAH.
WE NEED AN EXTERMINATOR. TELL DAD.
HE SET TRAPS ALREADY. BUT RATS ARE SMART THESE DAYS.
YEAH...
ERI, IS YOUR SISTER HOME YET?
YEAH. SHE'S UPSTAIRS. SHE SEEMS BUMMED.

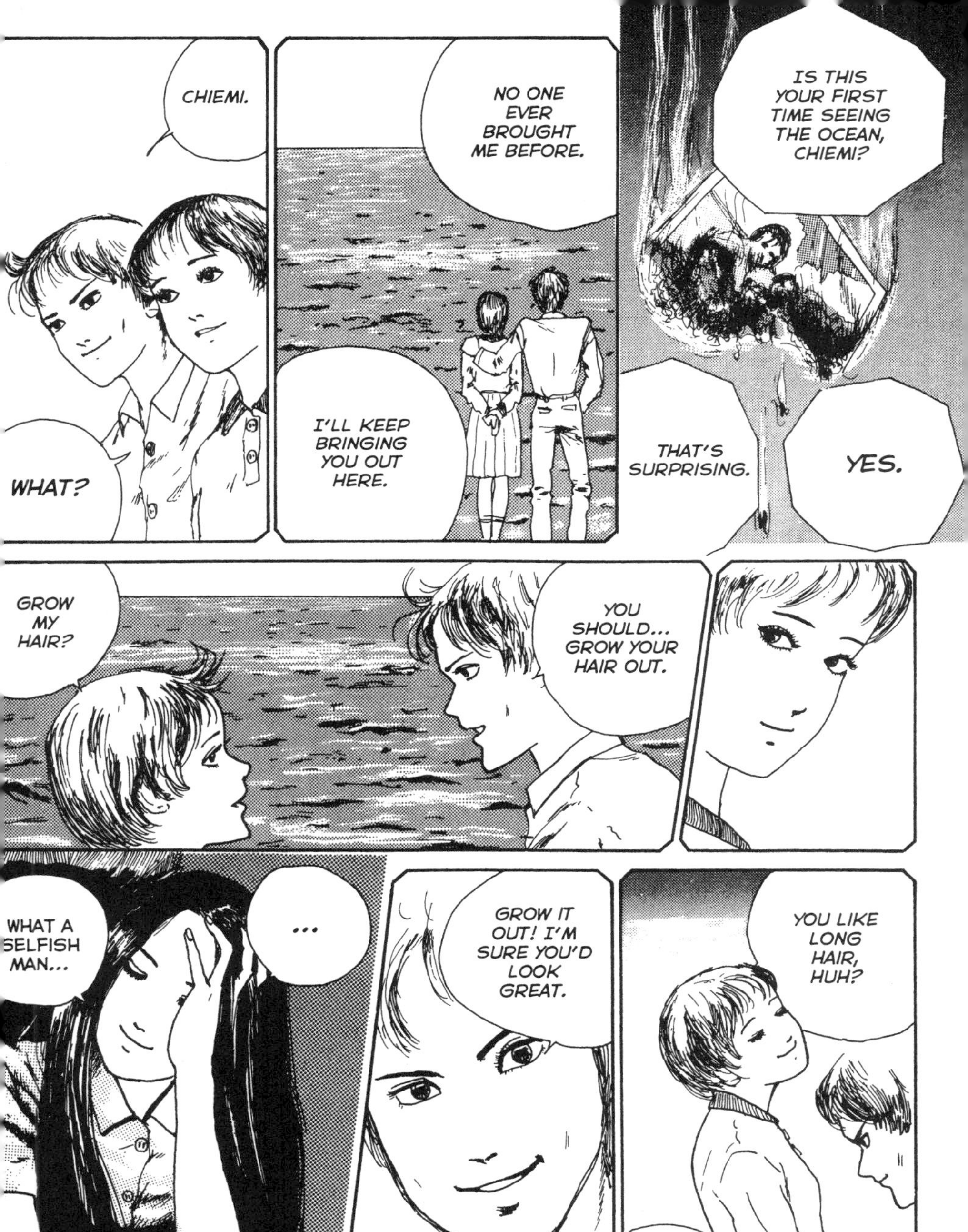
IS THIS YOUR FIRST TIME SEEING THE OCEAN, CHIEMI?
YES.
THAT'S SURPRISING.
NO ONE EVER BROUGHT ME BEFORE.
I'LL KEEP BRINGING YOU OUT HERE.
CHIEMI.
WHAT?
YOU SHOULD... GROW YOUR HAIR OUT.
GROW MY HAIR?
YOU LIKE LONG HAIR, HUH?
YEAH. DOWN TO ABOUT HERE.
GROW IT OUT! I'M SURE YOU'D LOOK GREAT.
...
WHAT A SELFISH MAN...

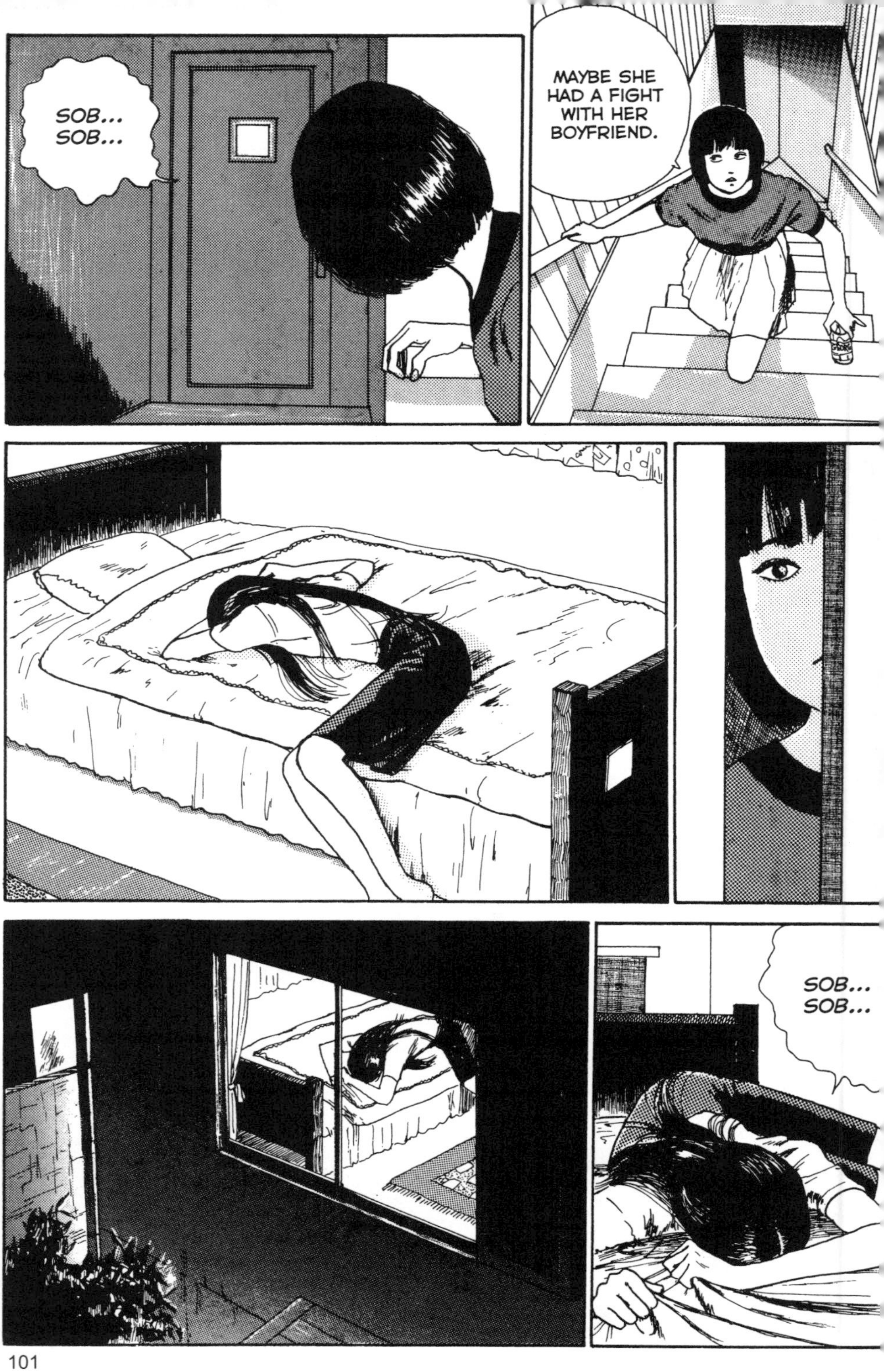
MAYBE SHE HAD A FIGHT WITH HER BOYFRIEND.
SOB... SOB...
SOB... SOB...

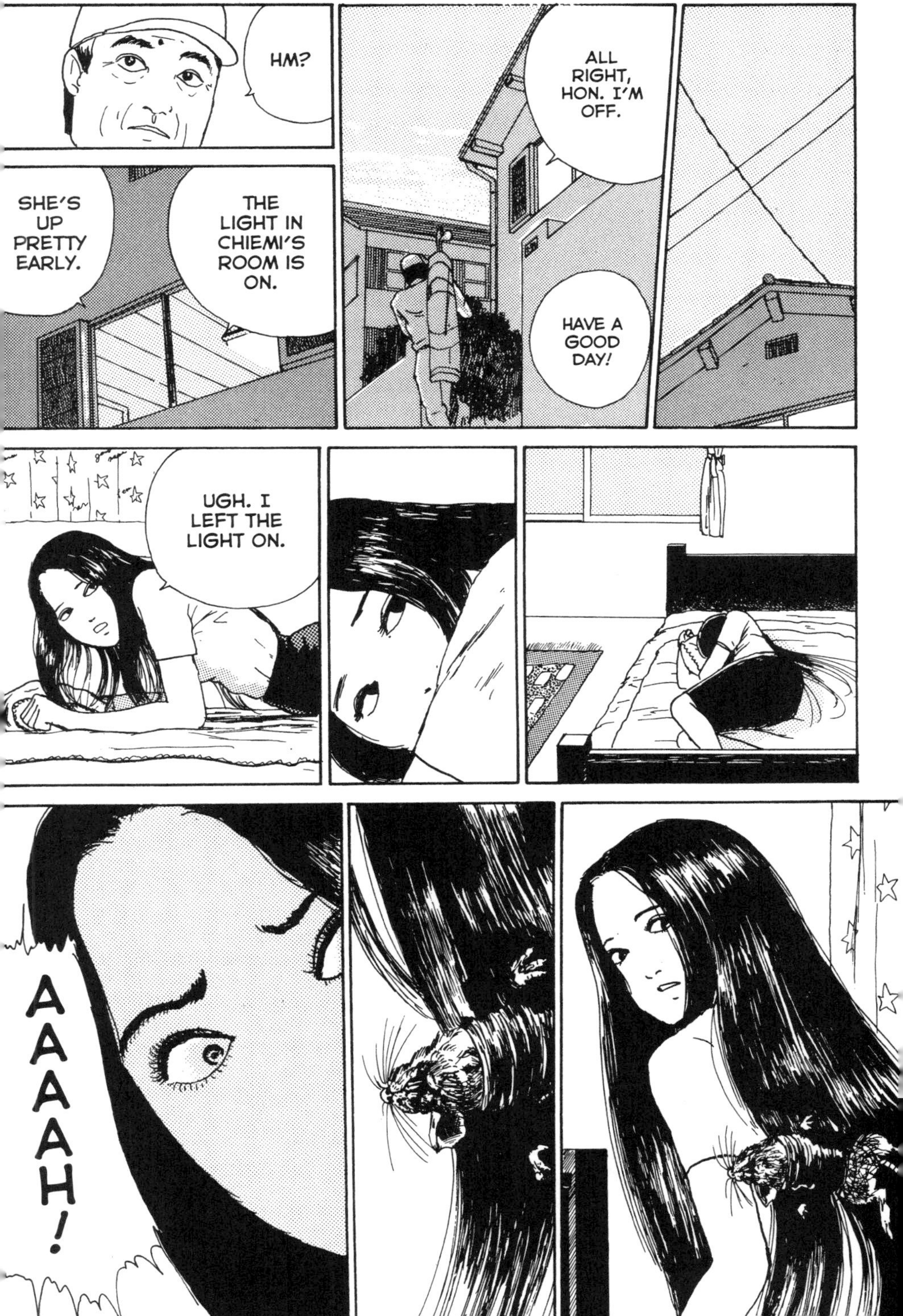
ALL RIGHT, HON. I'M OFF.
HAVE A GOOD DAY!
HM?
THE LIGHT IN CHIEMI'S ROOM IS ON.
SHE'S UP PRETTY EARLY.
UGH. I LEFT THE LIGHT ON.
AAAAH!

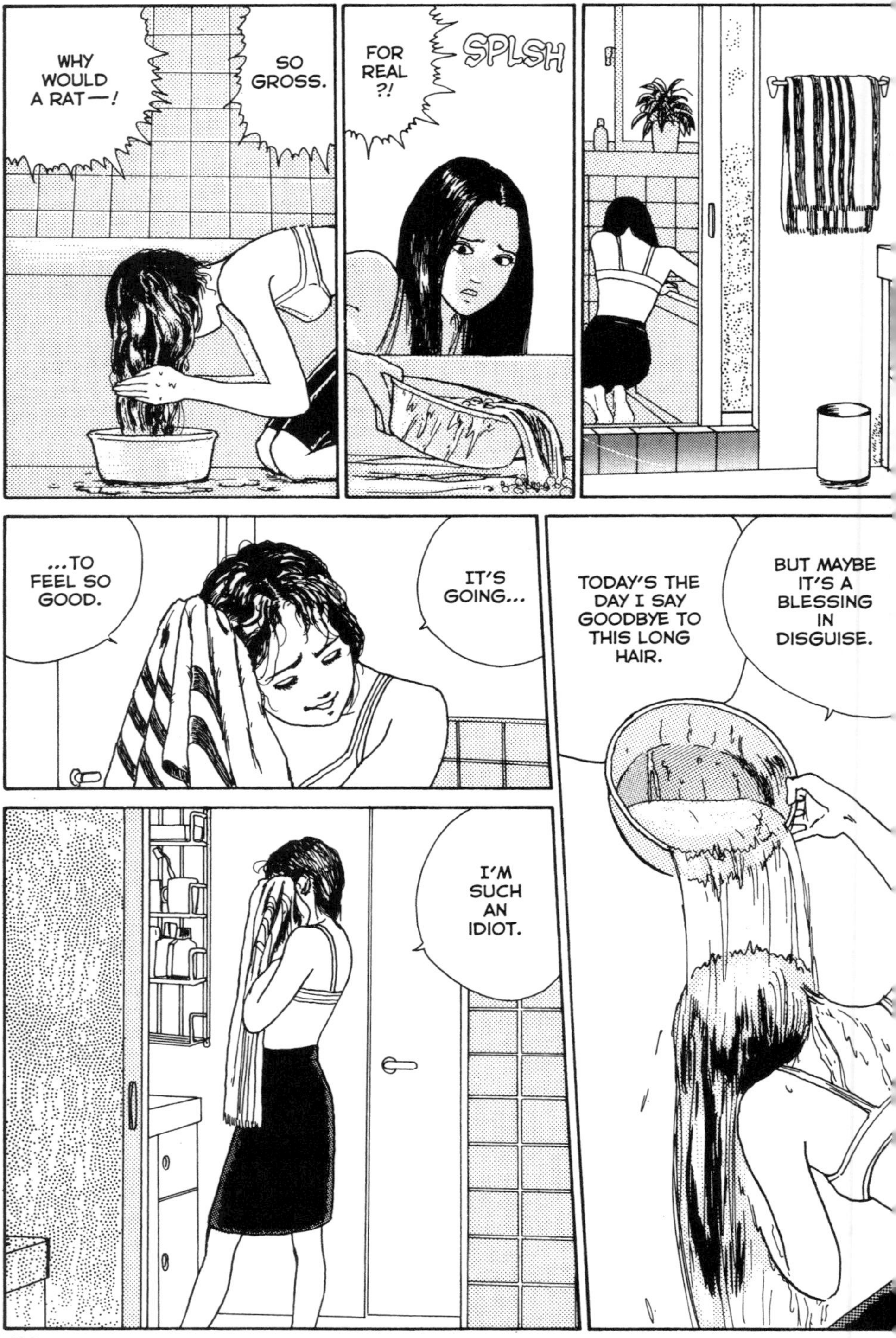
SPLSH
FOR REAL ?!
SO GROSS.
WHY WOULD A RAT—!
BUT MAYBE IT'S A BLESSING IN DISGUISE.
TODAY'S THE DAY I SAY GOODBYE TO THIS LONG HAIR.
IT'S GOING...
...TO FEEL SO GOOD.
I'M SUCH AN IDIOT.

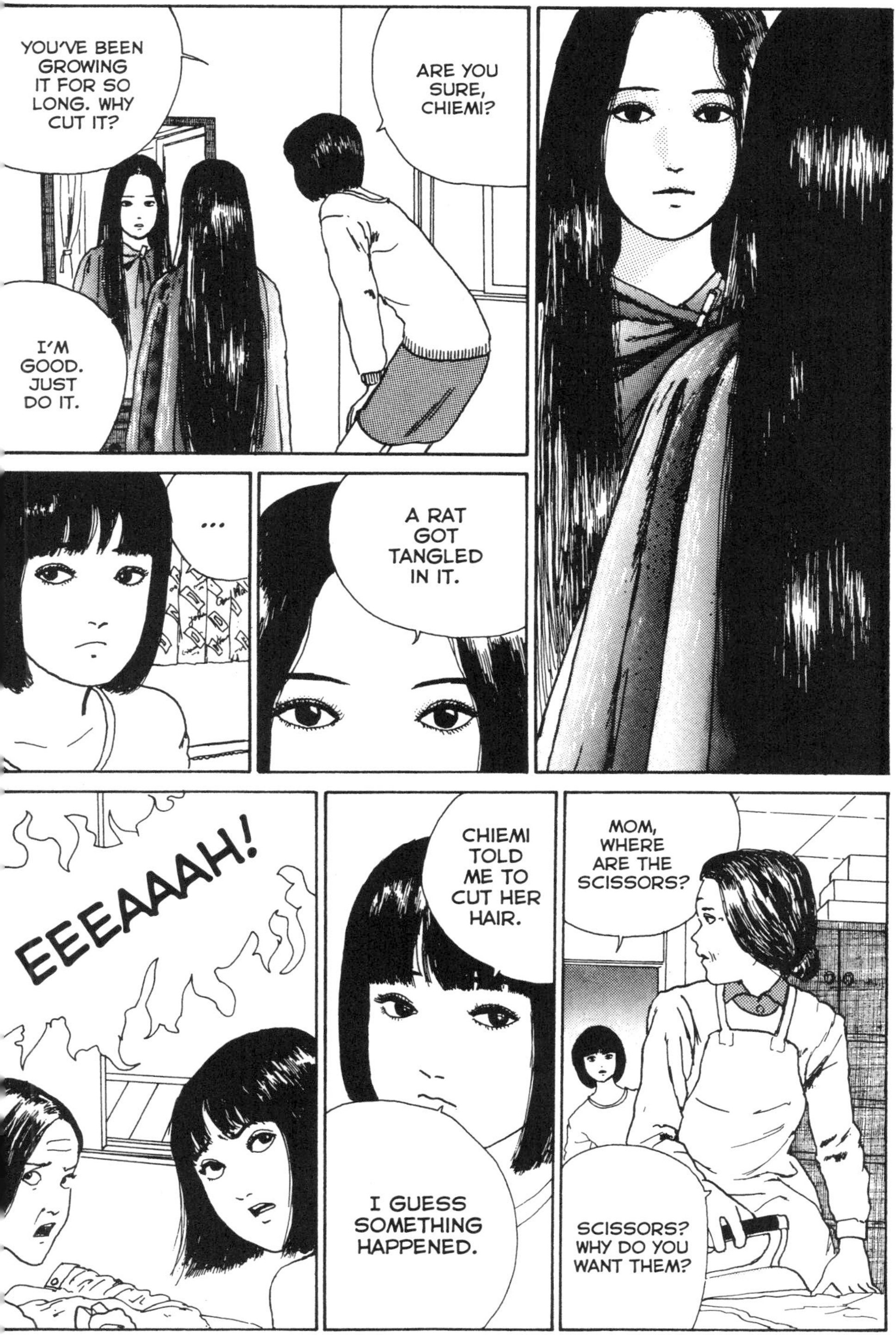
ARE YOU SURE, CHIEMI?
YOU'VE BEEN GROWING IT FOR SO LONG. WHY CUT IT?
I'M GOOD. JUST DO IT.
A RAT GOT TANGLED IN IT.
...
MOM, WHERE ARE THE SCISSORS?
SCISSORS? WHY DO YOU WANT THEM?
CHIEMI TOLD ME TO CUT HER HAIR.
I GUESS SOMETHING HAPPENED.
EEEAAAH!

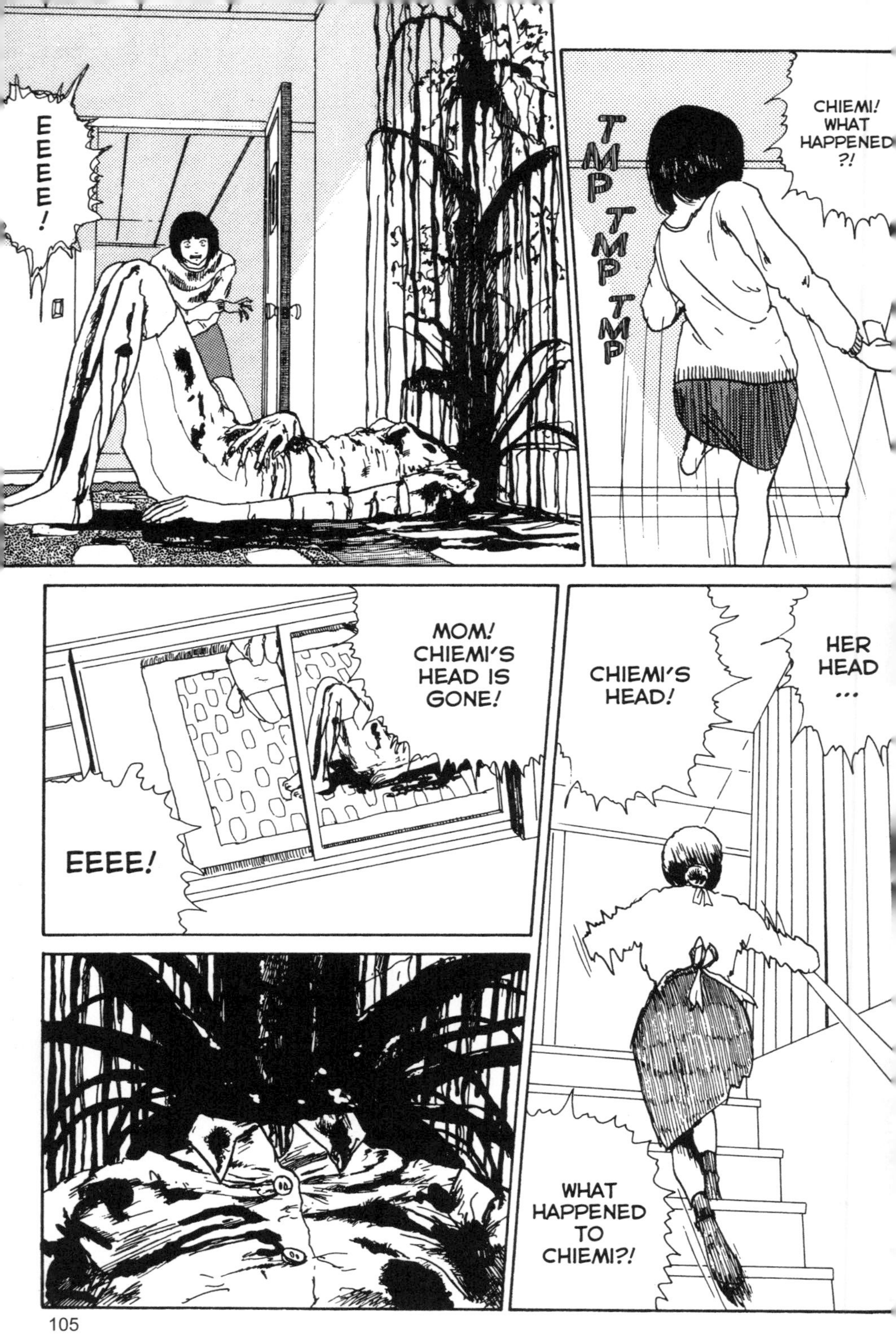
CHIEMI! WHAT HAPPENED ?!
TMP TMP TMP
EEEEE!
HER HEAD ...
CHIEMI'S HEAD!
WHAT HAPPENED TO CHIEMI?!
MOM! CHIEMI'S HEAD IS GONE!
EEEE!

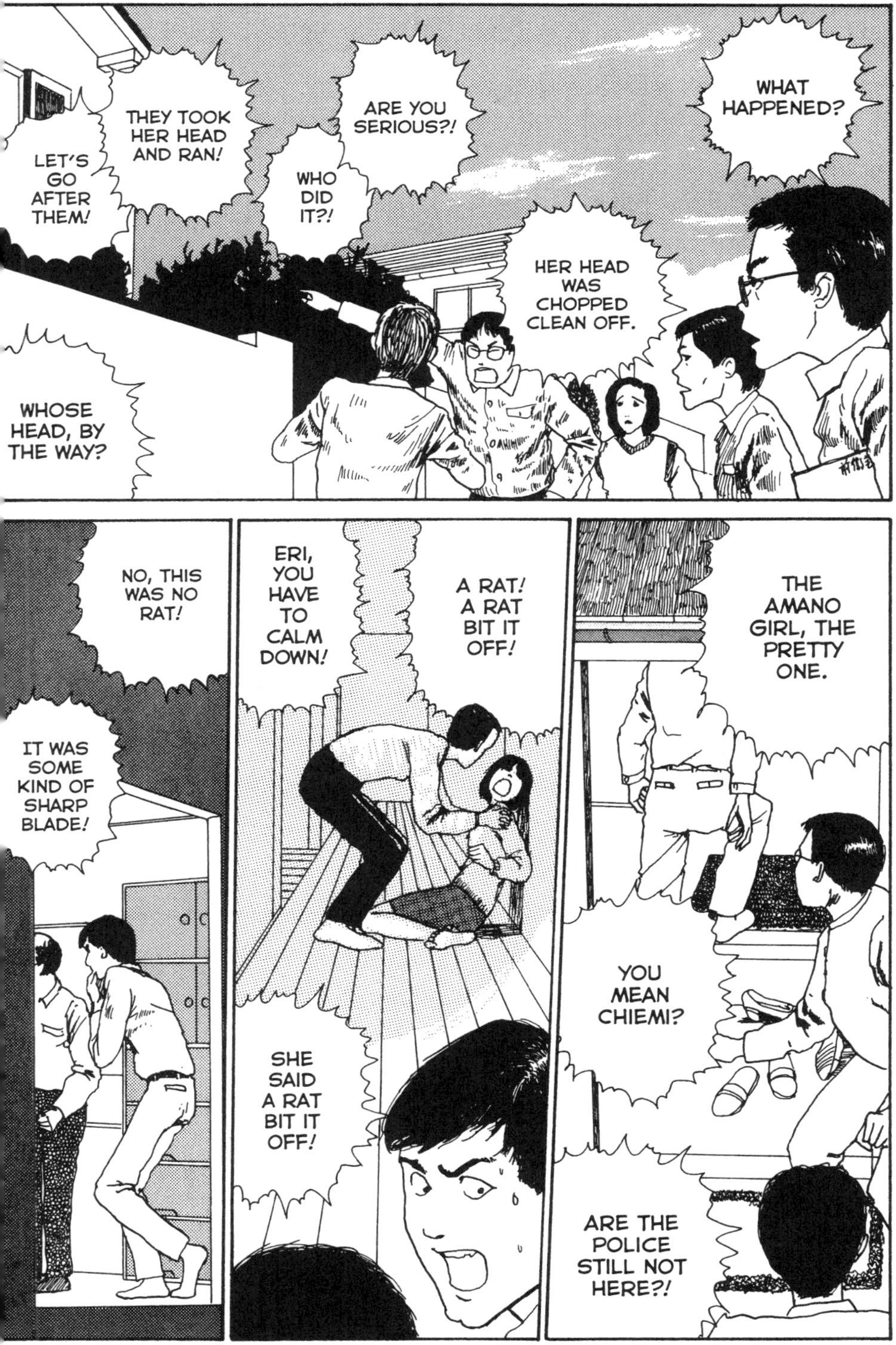
WHAT HAPPENED?
HER HEAD WAS CHOPPED CLEAN OFF.
ARE YOU SERIOUS?!
WHO DID IT?!
THEY TOOK HER HEAD AND RAN!
LET'S GO AFTER THEM!
WHOSE HEAD, BY THE WAY?
THE AMANO GIRL, THE PRETTY ONE.
YOU MEAN CHIEMI?
ARE THE POLICE STILL NOT HERE?!
A RAT! A RAT BIT IT OFF!
ERI, YOU HAVE TO CALM DOWN!
SHE SAID A RAT BIT IT OFF!
NO, THIS WAS NO RAT!
IT WAS SOME KIND OF SHARP BLADE!

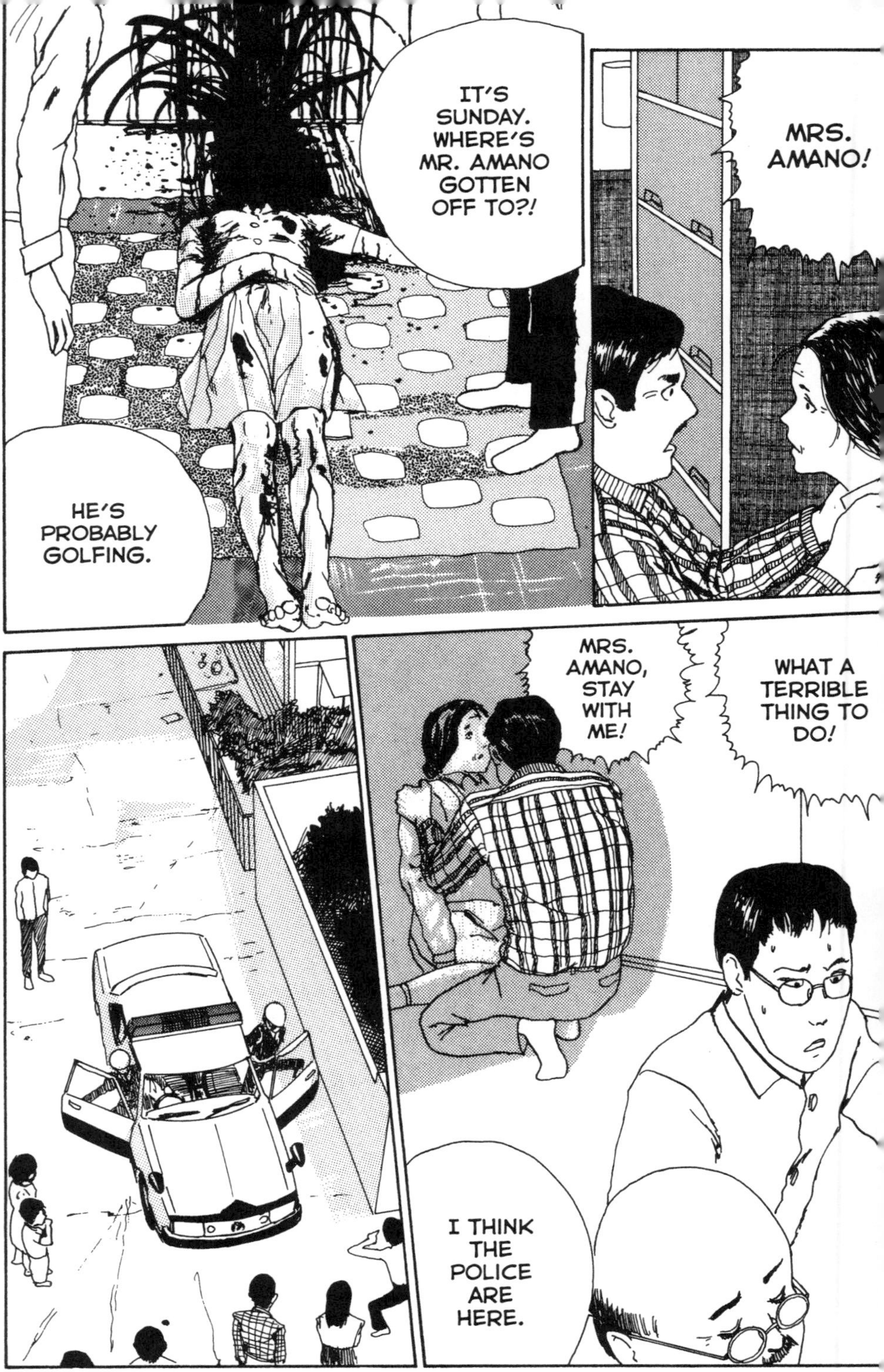
MRS. AMANO!
IT'S SUNDAY. WHERE'S MR. AMANO GOTTEN OFF TO?!
HE'S PROBABLY GOLFING.
WHAT A TERRIBLE THING TO DO!
MRS. AMANO, STAY WITH ME!
I THINK THE POLICE ARE HERE.

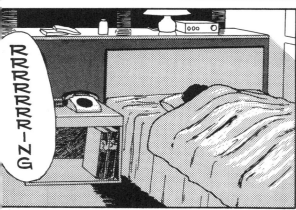

HELLO?

RRK

JESUS. DO
THEY KNOW
WHAT TIME
IT IS?

RRRRRRRING

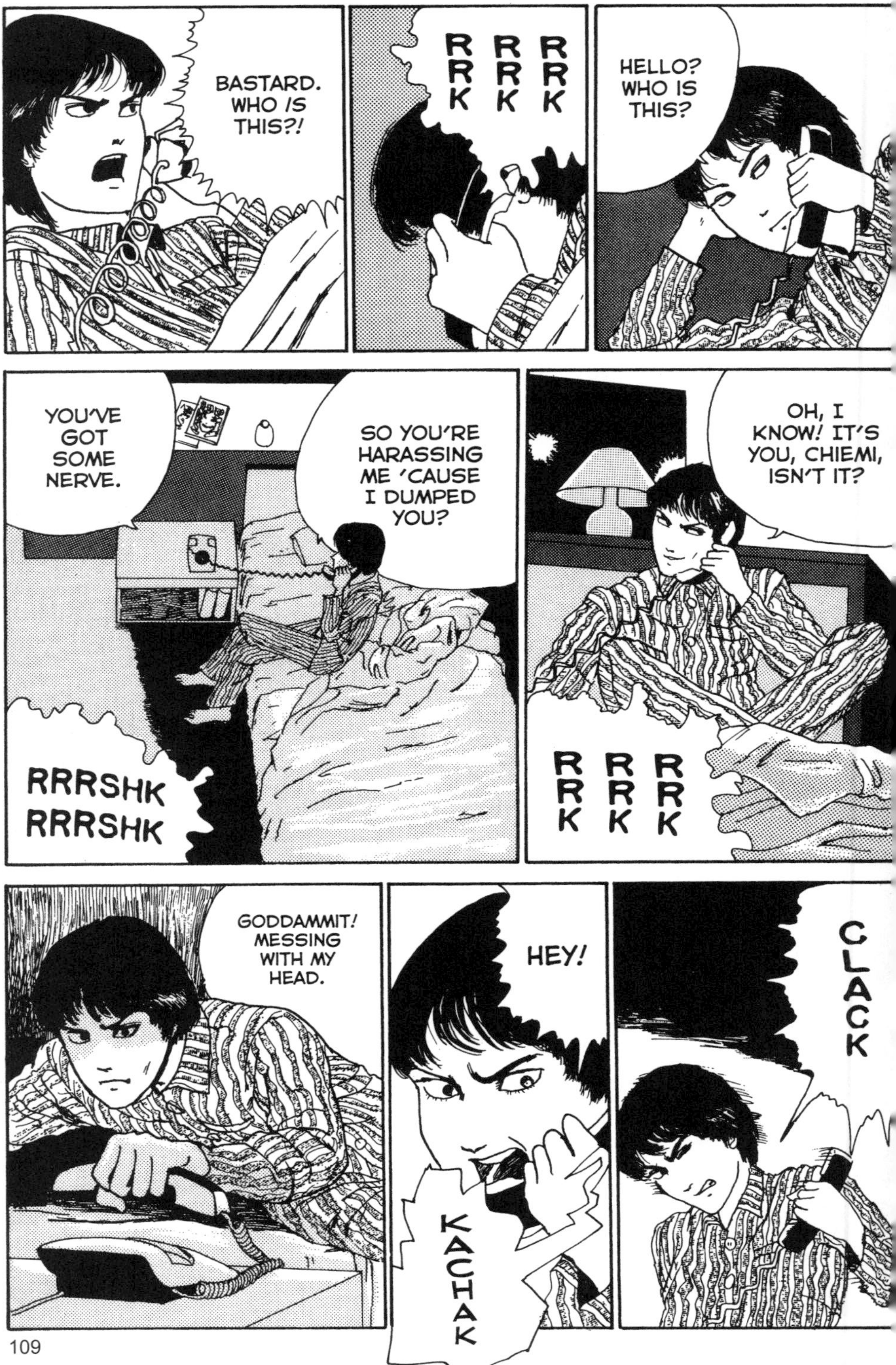
HELLO? WHO IS THIS?
RRK RRK RRK
BASTARD. WHO *IS* THIS?!
OH, I KNOW! IT'S YOU, CHIEMI, ISN'T IT?
RRK RRK RRK
SO YOU'RE HARASSING ME 'CAUSE I DUMPED YOU?
YOU'VE GOT SOME NERVE.
RRRSHK RRRSHK
CLACK
HEY!
KACHAK
GODDAMMIT! MESSING WITH MY HEAD.

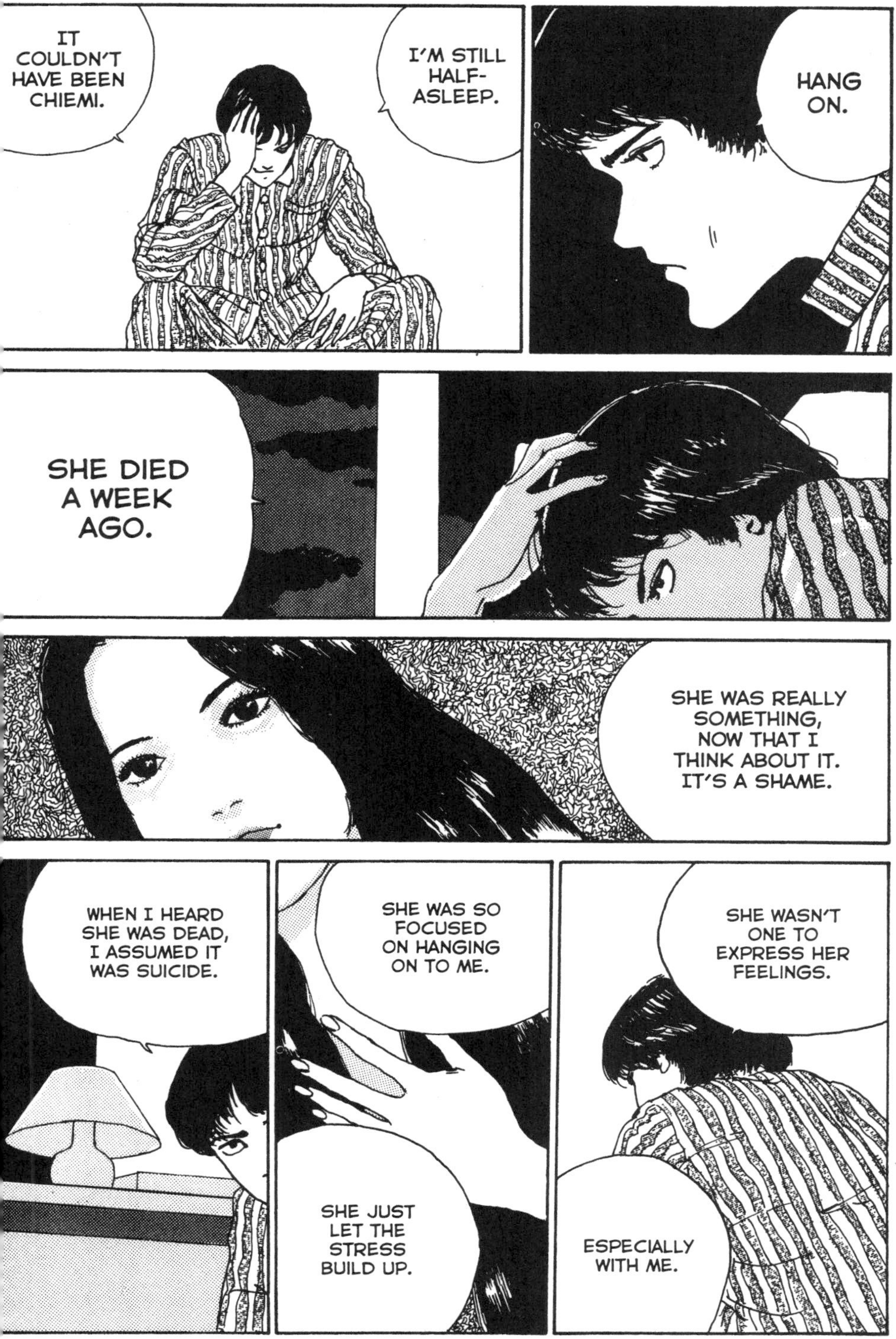
HANG ON.
I'M STILL HALF-ASLEEP.
IT COULDN'T HAVE BEEN CHIEMI.
SHE DIED A WEEK AGO.
SHE WAS REALLY SOMETHING, NOW THAT I THINK ABOUT IT. IT'S A SHAME.
SHE WASN'T ONE TO EXPRESS HER FEELINGS.
ESPECIALLY WITH ME.
SHE WAS SO FOCUSED ON HANGING ON TO ME.
SHE JUST LET THE STRESS BUILD UP.
WHEN I HEARD SHE WAS DEAD, I ASSUMED IT WAS SUICIDE.

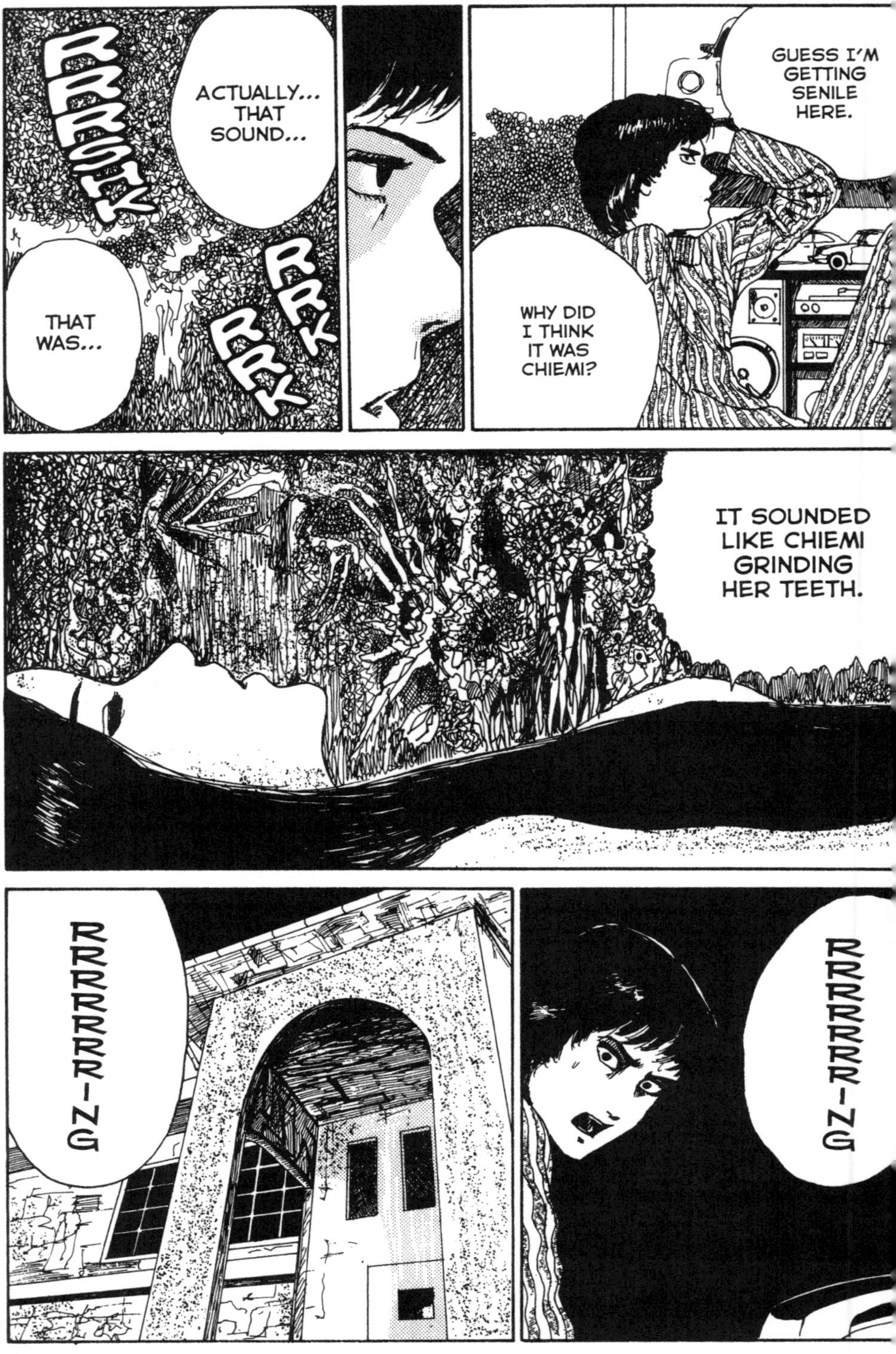
GUESS I'M GETTING SENILE HERE.
WHY DID I THINK IT WAS CHIEMI?
ACTUALLY... THAT SOUND...
RRRSTK
THAT WAS...
RRK RRK
IT SOUNDED LIKE CHIEMI GRINDING HER TEETH.
RRRRRRR-I-NG
RRRRRRR-I-NG

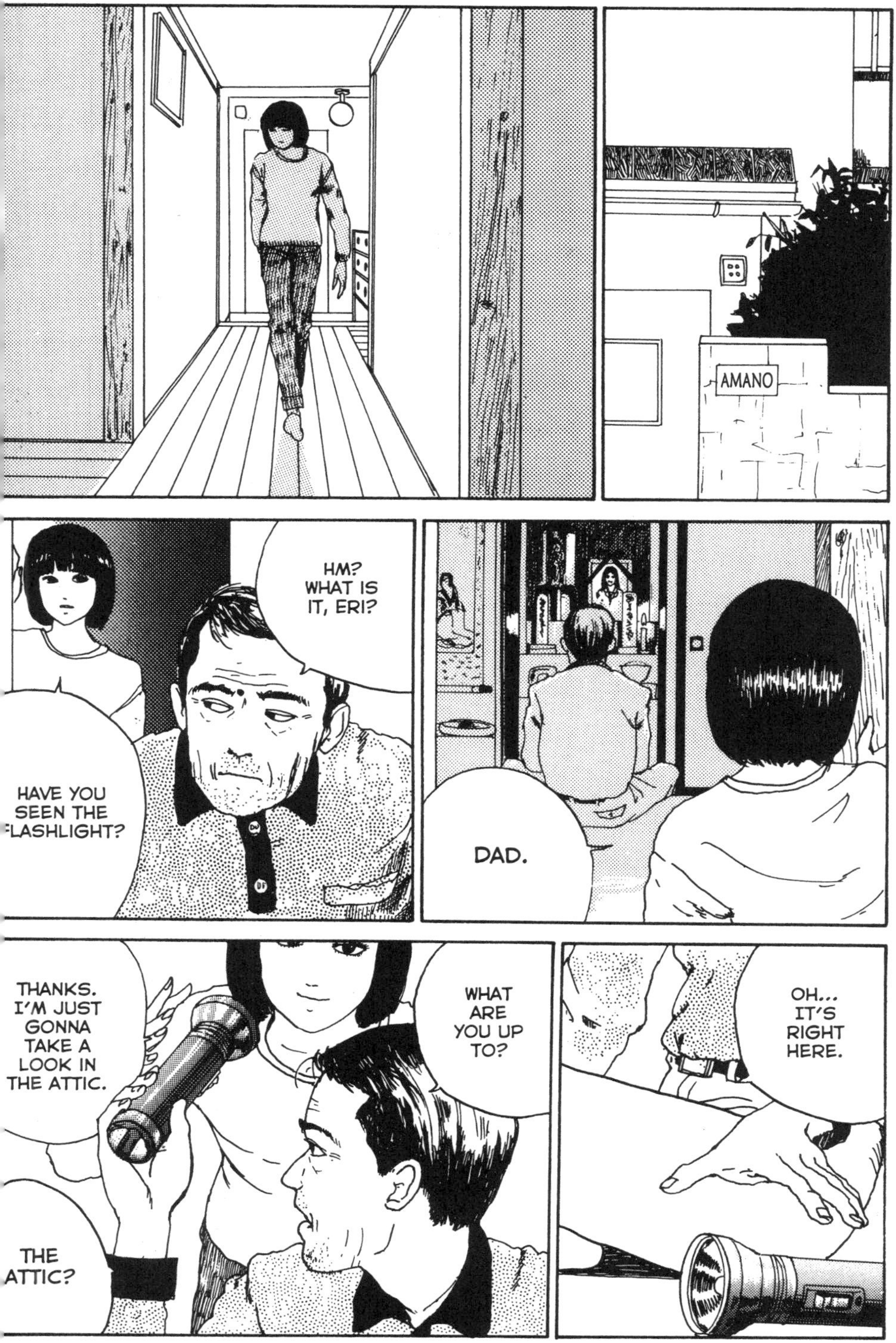
AMANO
DAD.
HM? WHAT IS IT, ERI?
HAVE YOU SEEN THE FLASHLIGHT?
OH... IT'S RIGHT HERE.
THANKS. I'M JUST GONNA TAKE A LOOK IN THE ATTIC.
THE ATTIC?
WHAT ARE YOU UP TO?

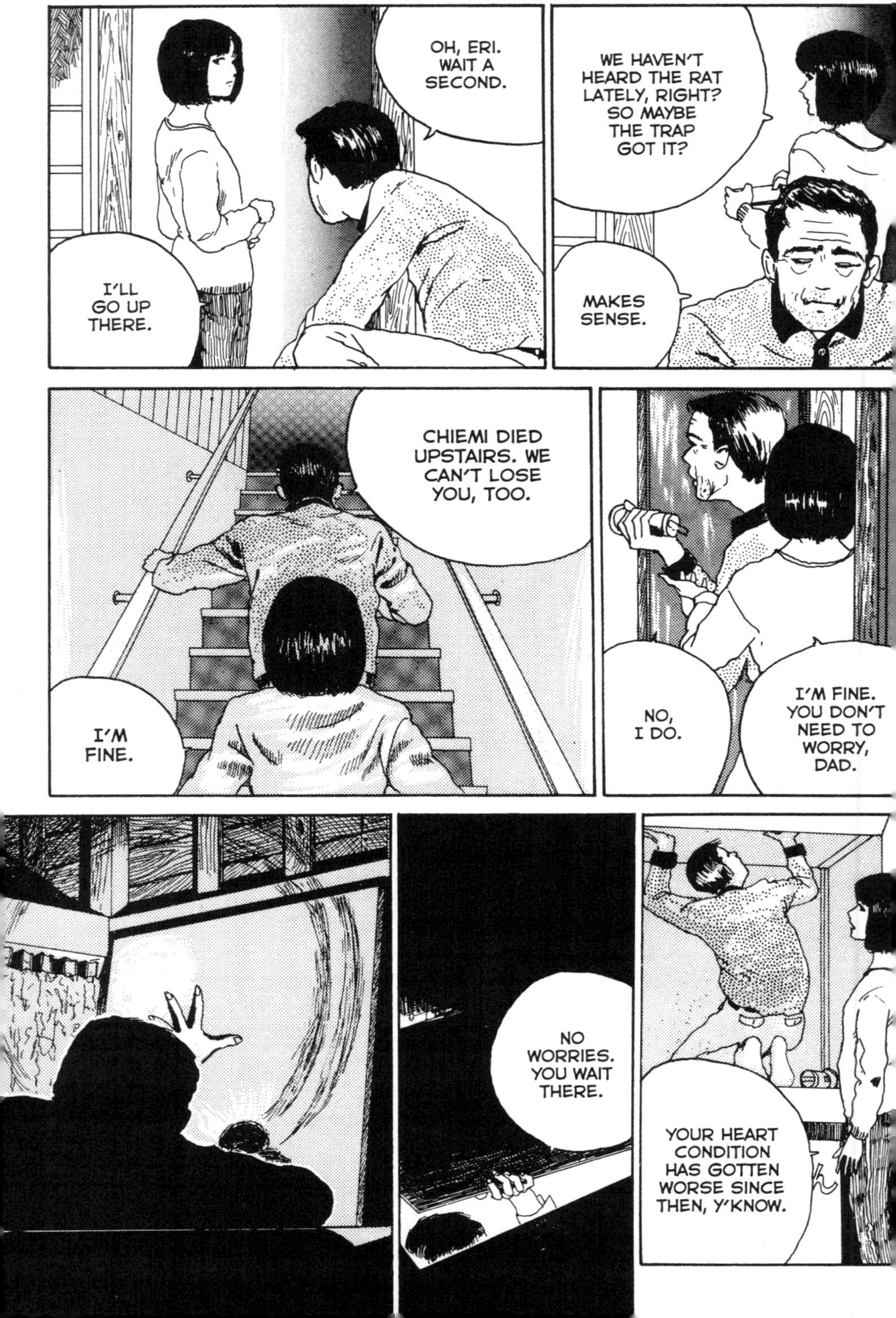
WE HAVEN'T HEARD THE RAT LATELY, RIGHT? SO MAYBE THE TRAP GOT IT?
MAKES SENSE.
OH, ERI. WAIT A SECOND.
I'LL GO UP THERE.
I'M FINE. YOU DON'T NEED TO WORRY, DAD.
NO, I DO.
CHIEMI DIED UPSTAIRS. WE CAN'T LOSE YOU, TOO.
I'M FINE.
YOUR HEART CONDITION HAS GOTTEN WORSE SINCE THEN, Y'KNOW.
NO WORRIES. YOU WAIT THERE.

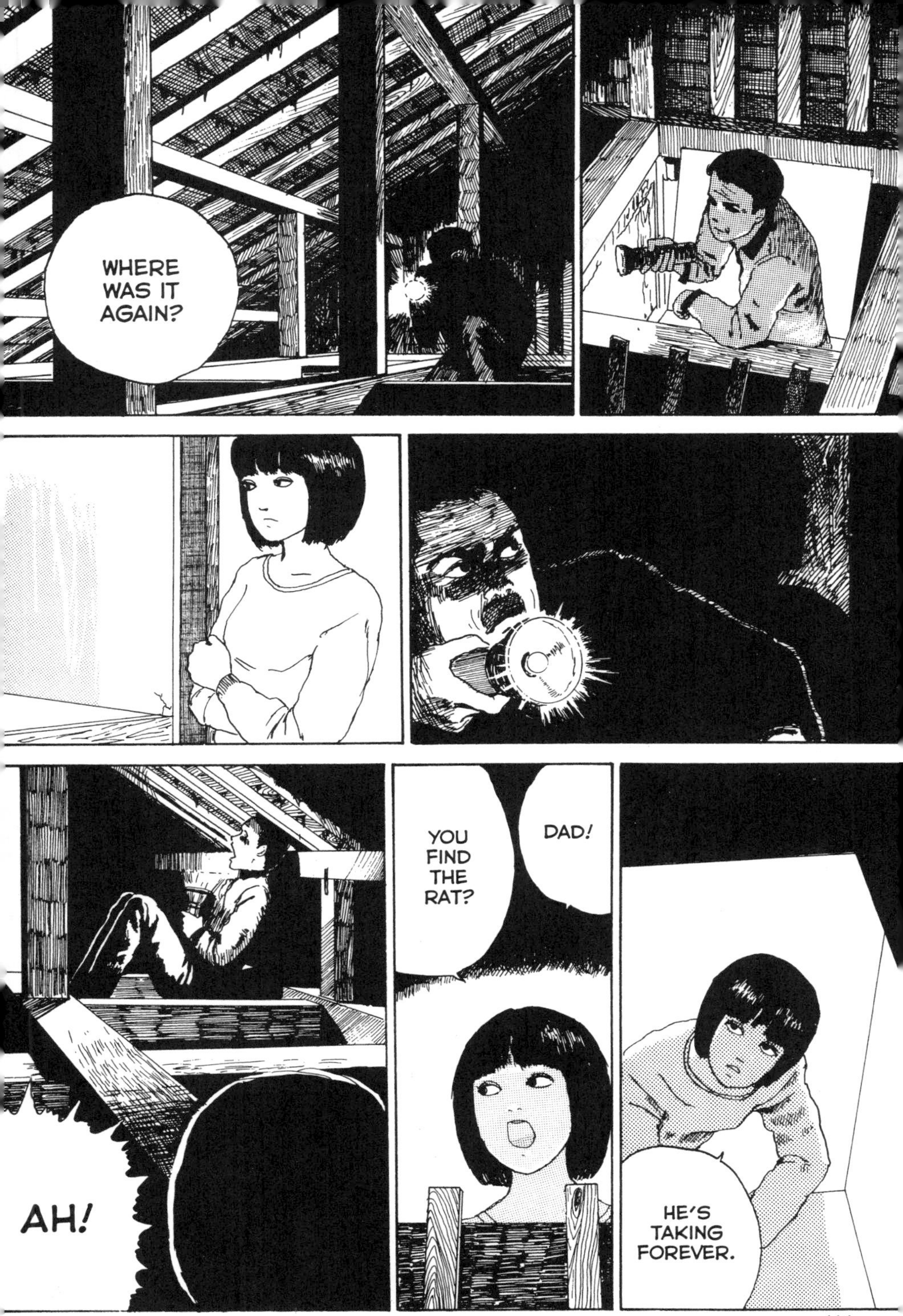
WHERE WAS IT AGAIN?
HE'S TAKING FOREVER.
DAD!
YOU FIND THE RAT?
AH!

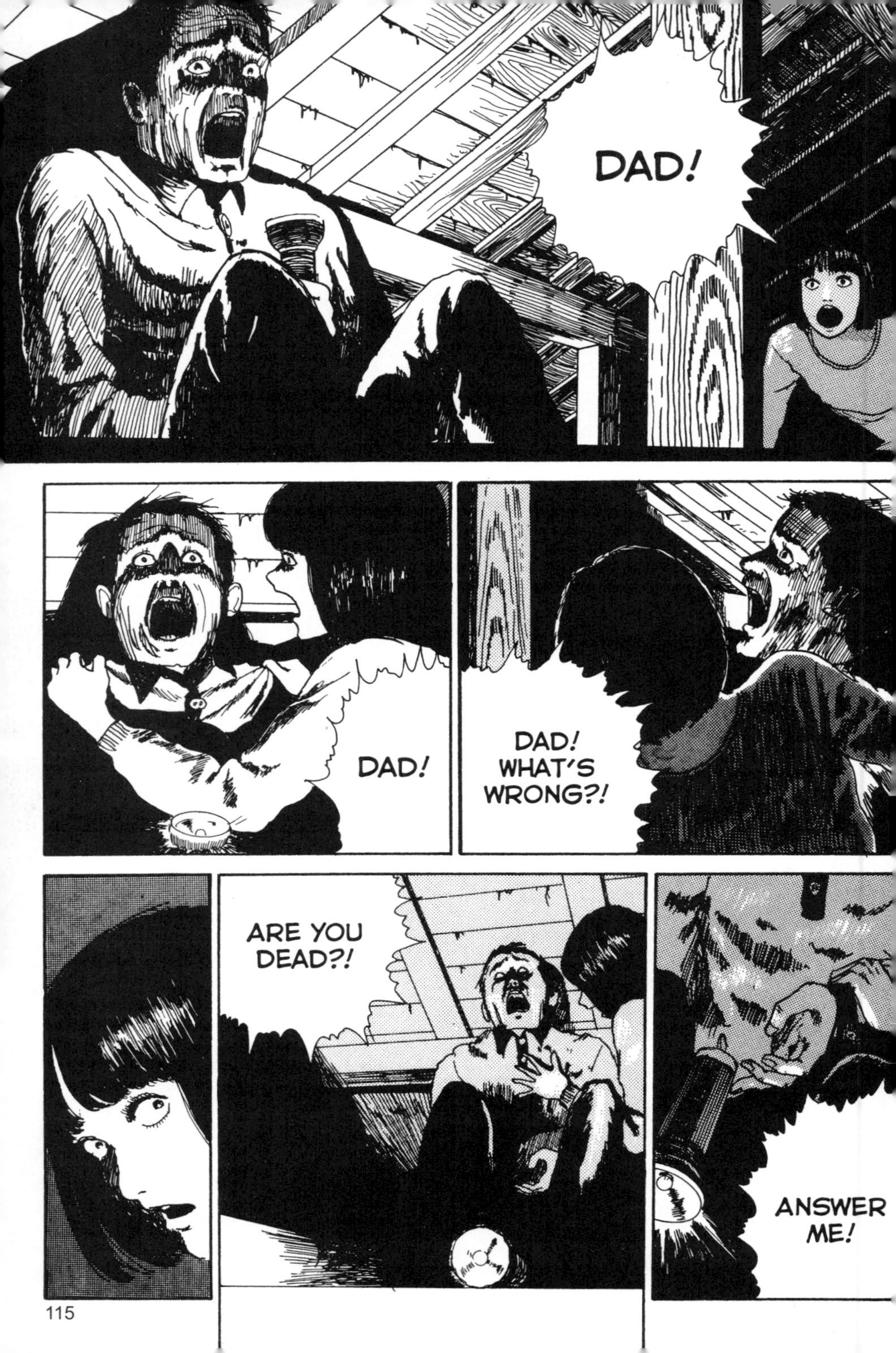
DAD!
DAD!
WHAT'S
WRONG?!
DAD!
ANSWER
ME!
ARE YOU
DEAD?!

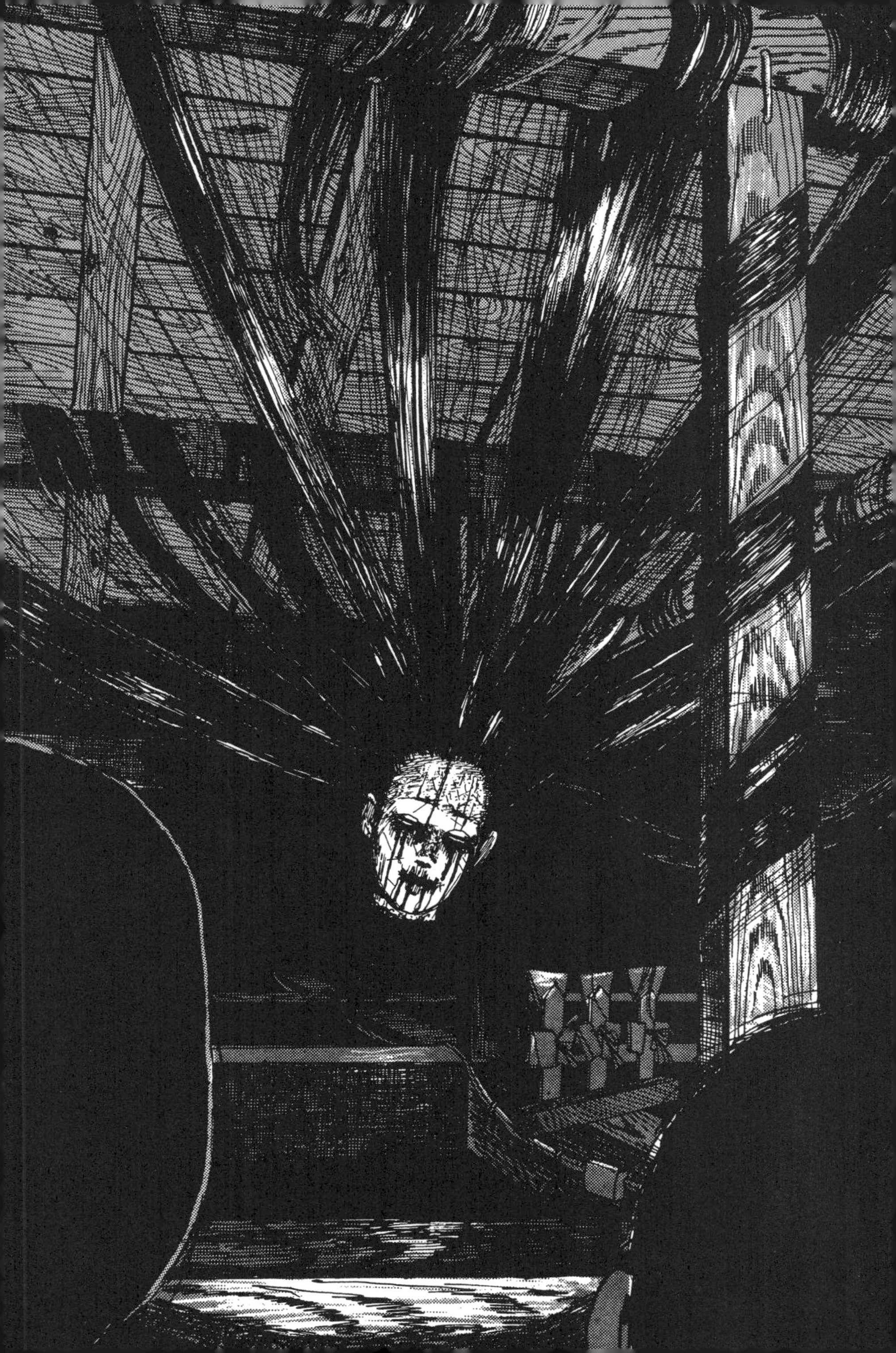

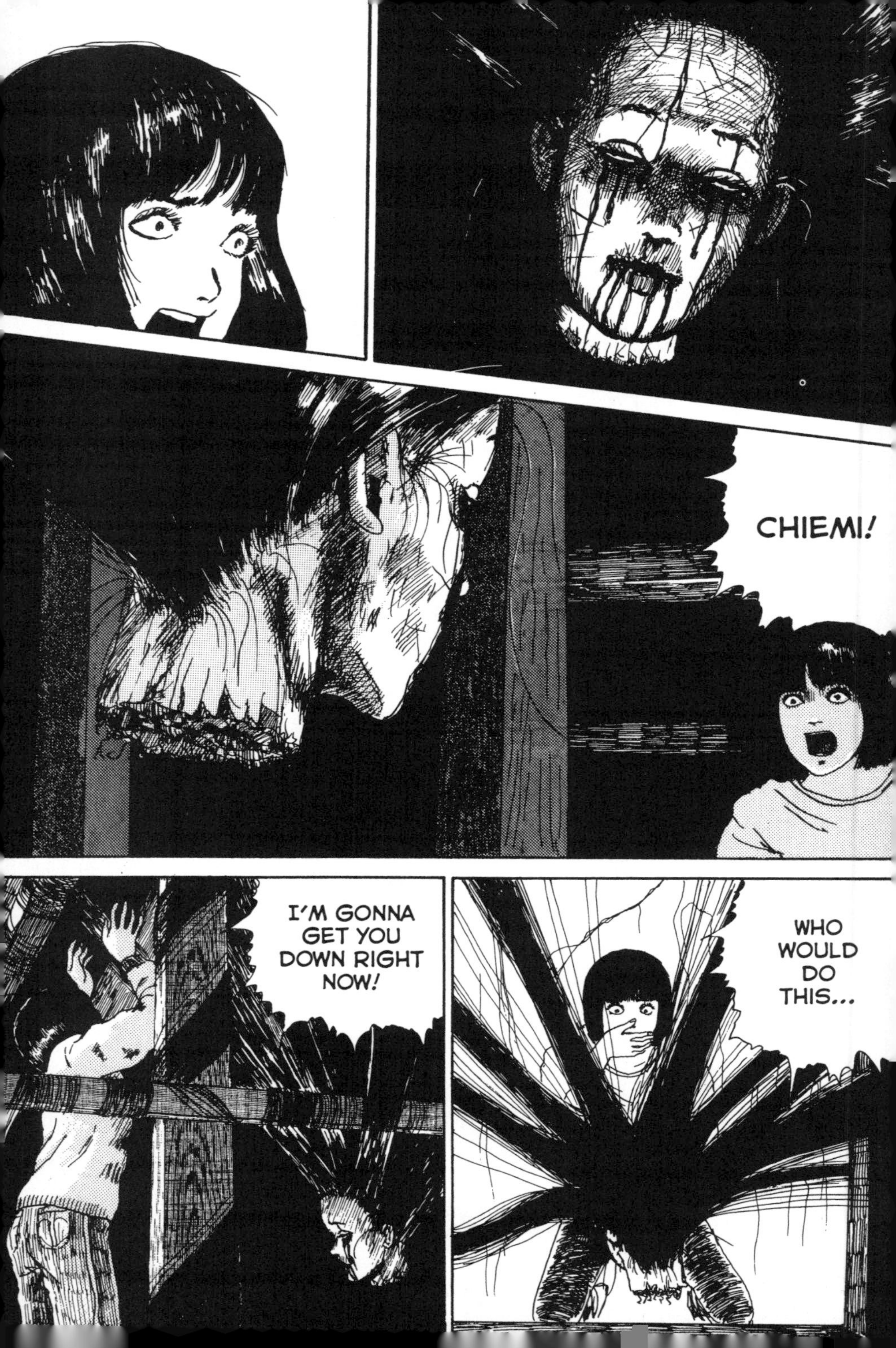
CHIEMI!
WHO WOULD DO THIS...
I'M GONNA GET YOU DOWN RIGHT NOW!

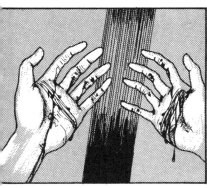

IT WON'T COME LOOSE!

S-SCISSORS. WE NEED SCISSORS.

• • •

MY HANDS • • •

RRK
RRK

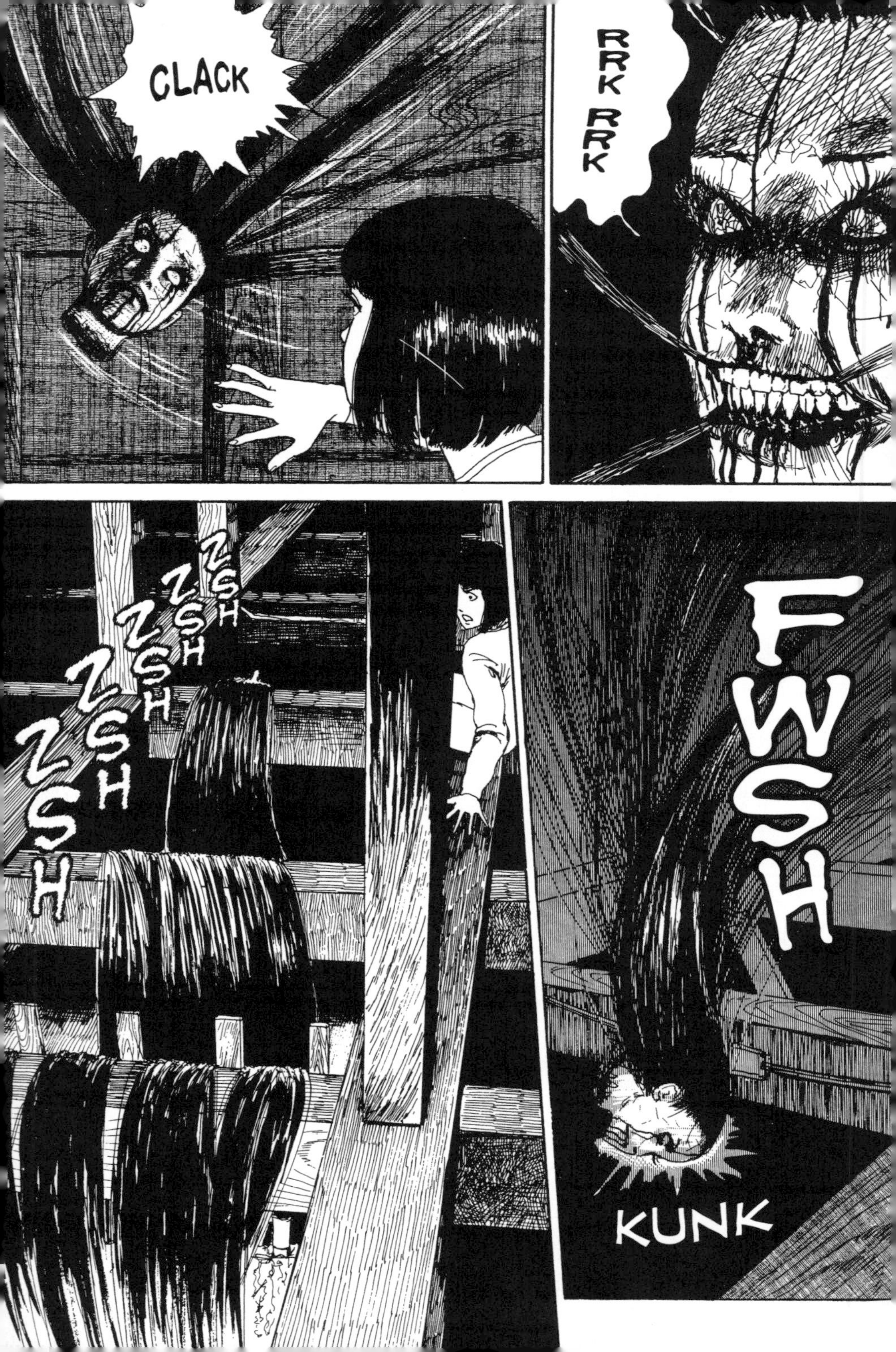
RRK RRK
CLACK
FWSH
KUNK
ZSH ZSH ZSH ZSH ZSH ZSH

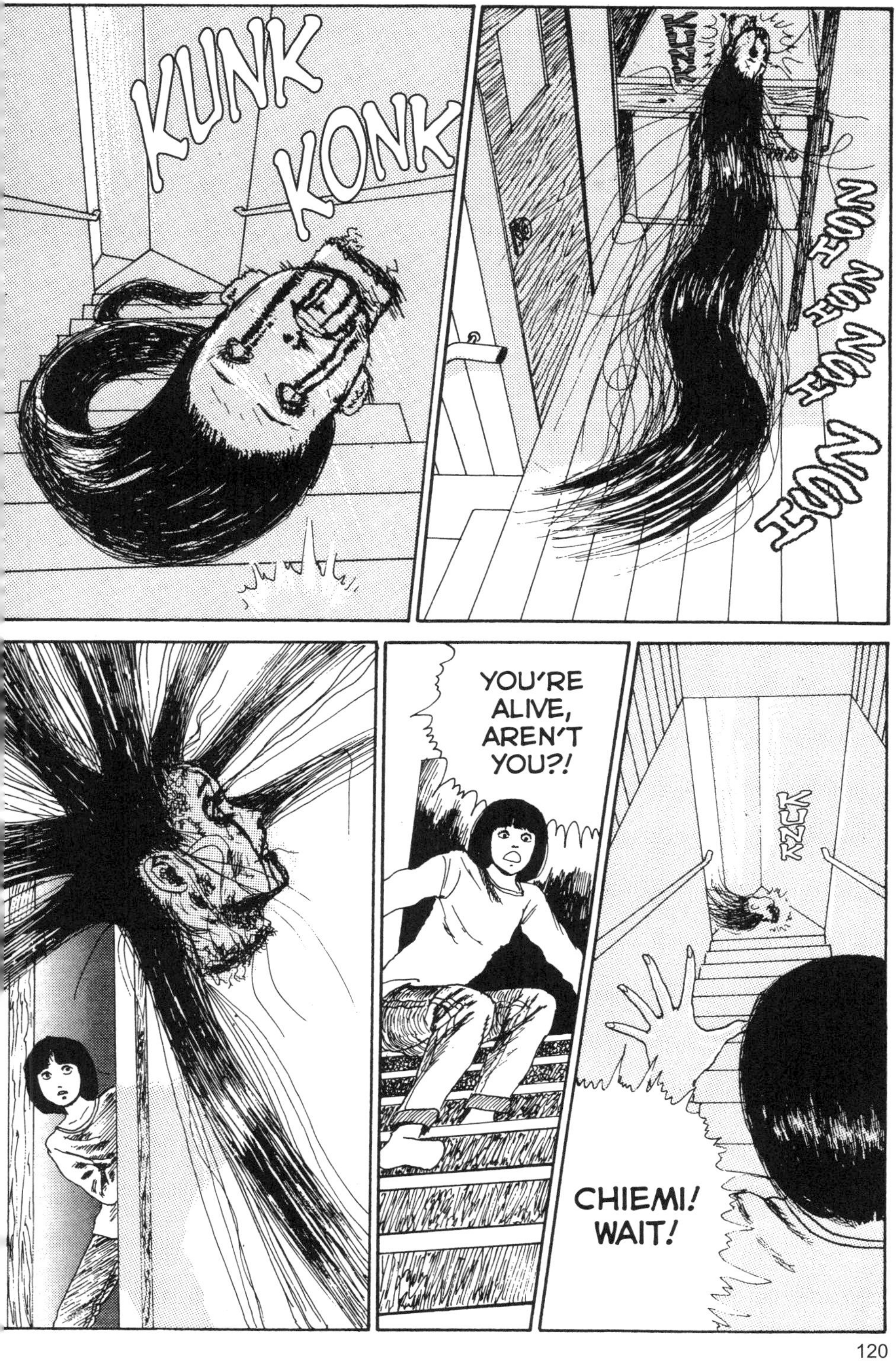
KUNK
HOON HON HON
KUNK
KONK
KUNK
CHIEMI! WAIT!
YOU'RE ALIVE, AREN'T YOU?!

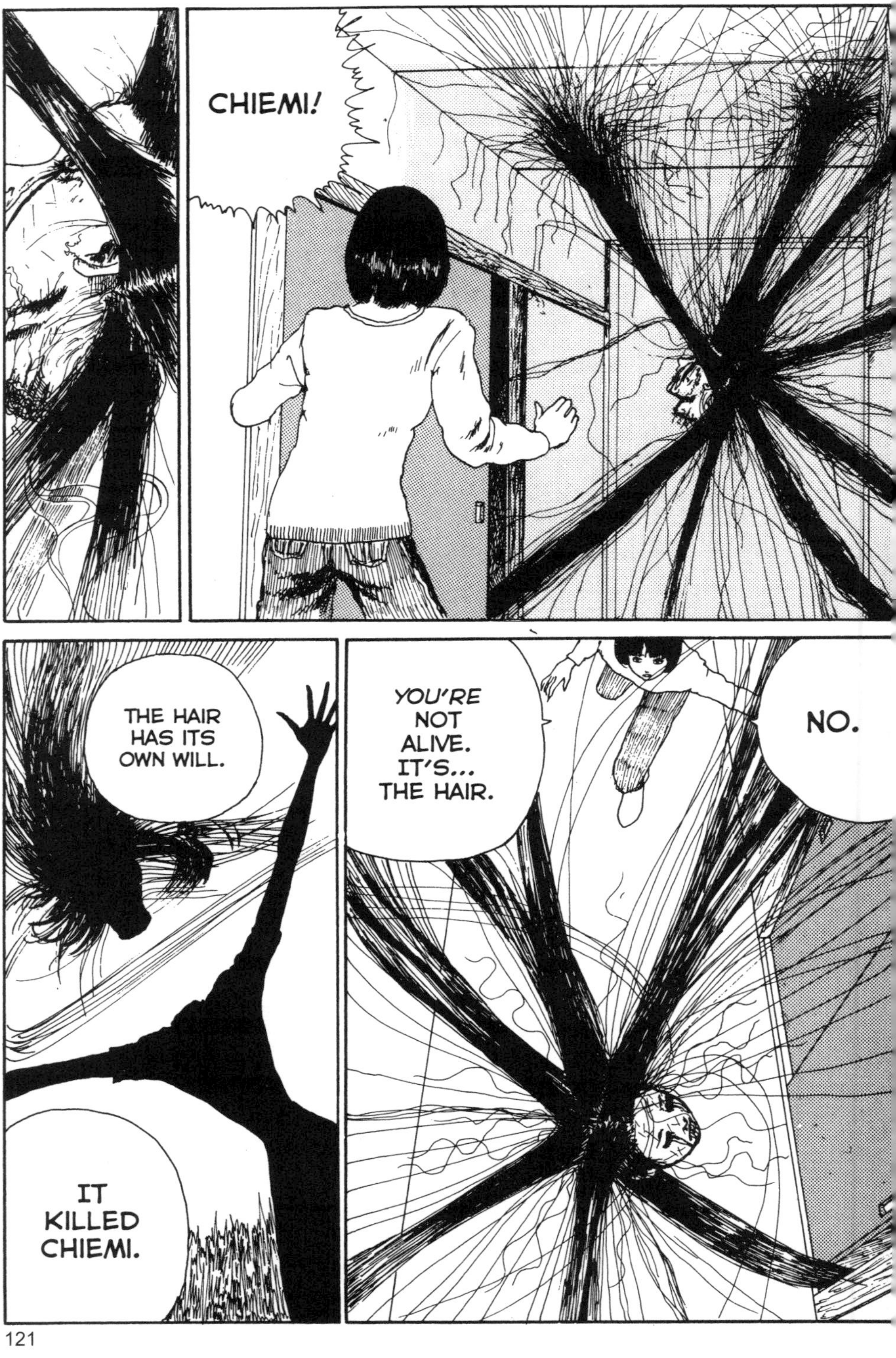
CHIEMI!
NO.
YOU'RE NOT ALIVE. IT'S... THE HAIR.
THE HAIR HAS ITS OWN WILL.
IT KILLED CHIEMI.

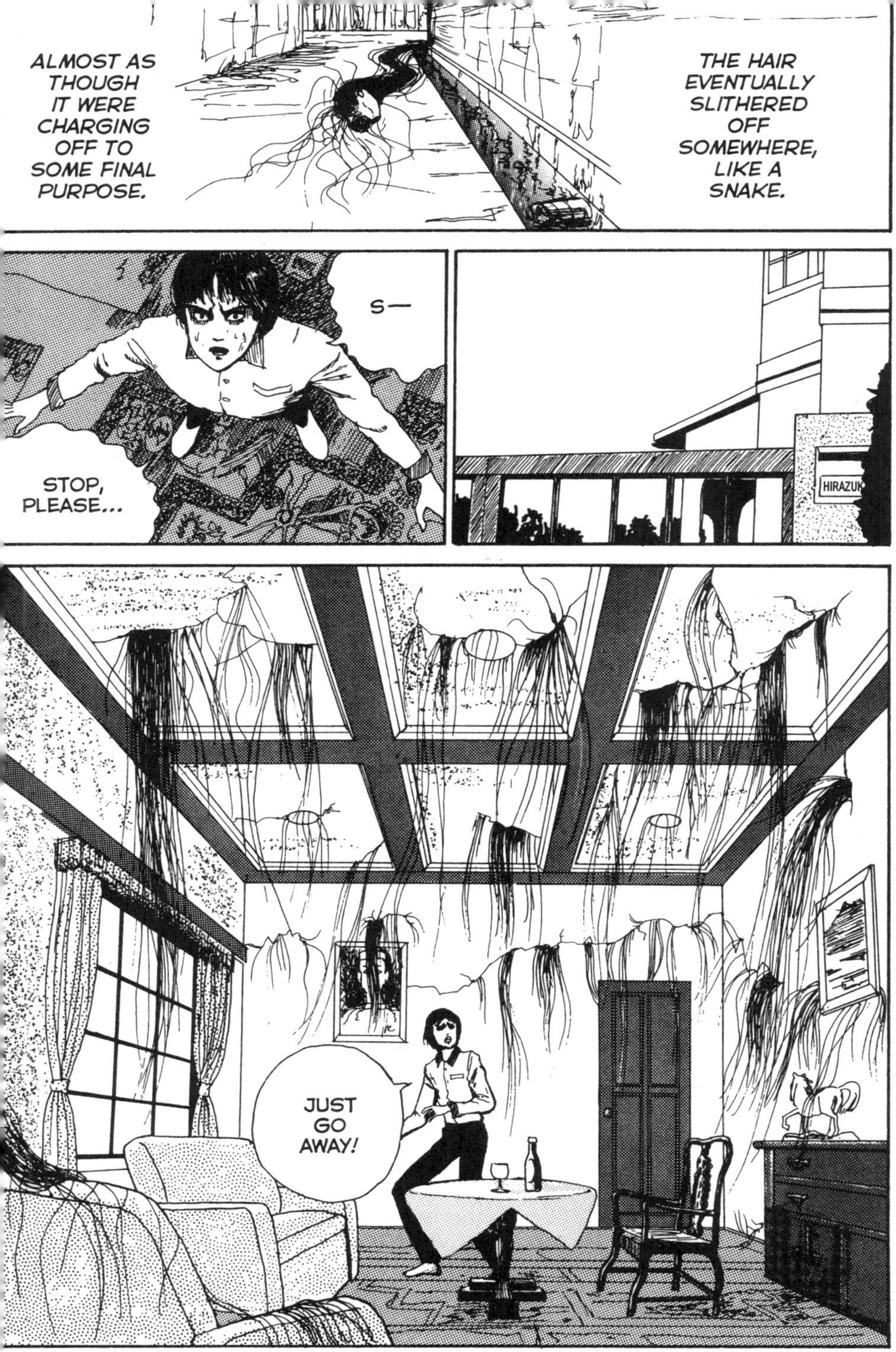
THE HAIR EVENTUALLY SLITHERED OFF SOMEWHERE, LIKE A SNAKE.
ALMOST AS THOUGH IT WERE CHARGING OFF TO SOME FINAL PURPOSE.
HIRAZUK
S—
STOP, PLEASE...
JUST GO AWAY!

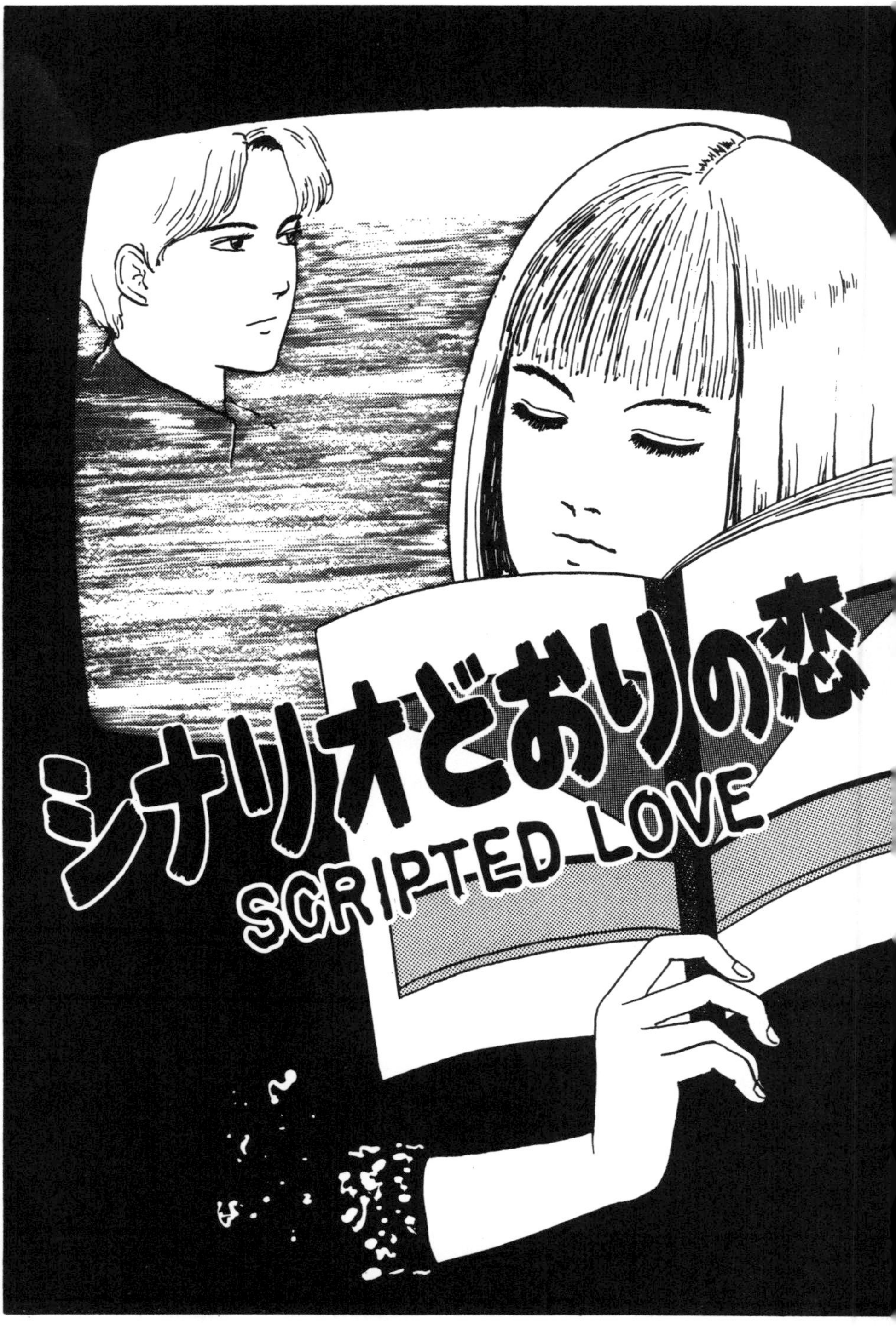
シナリオどおりの恋
SCRIPTED LOVE

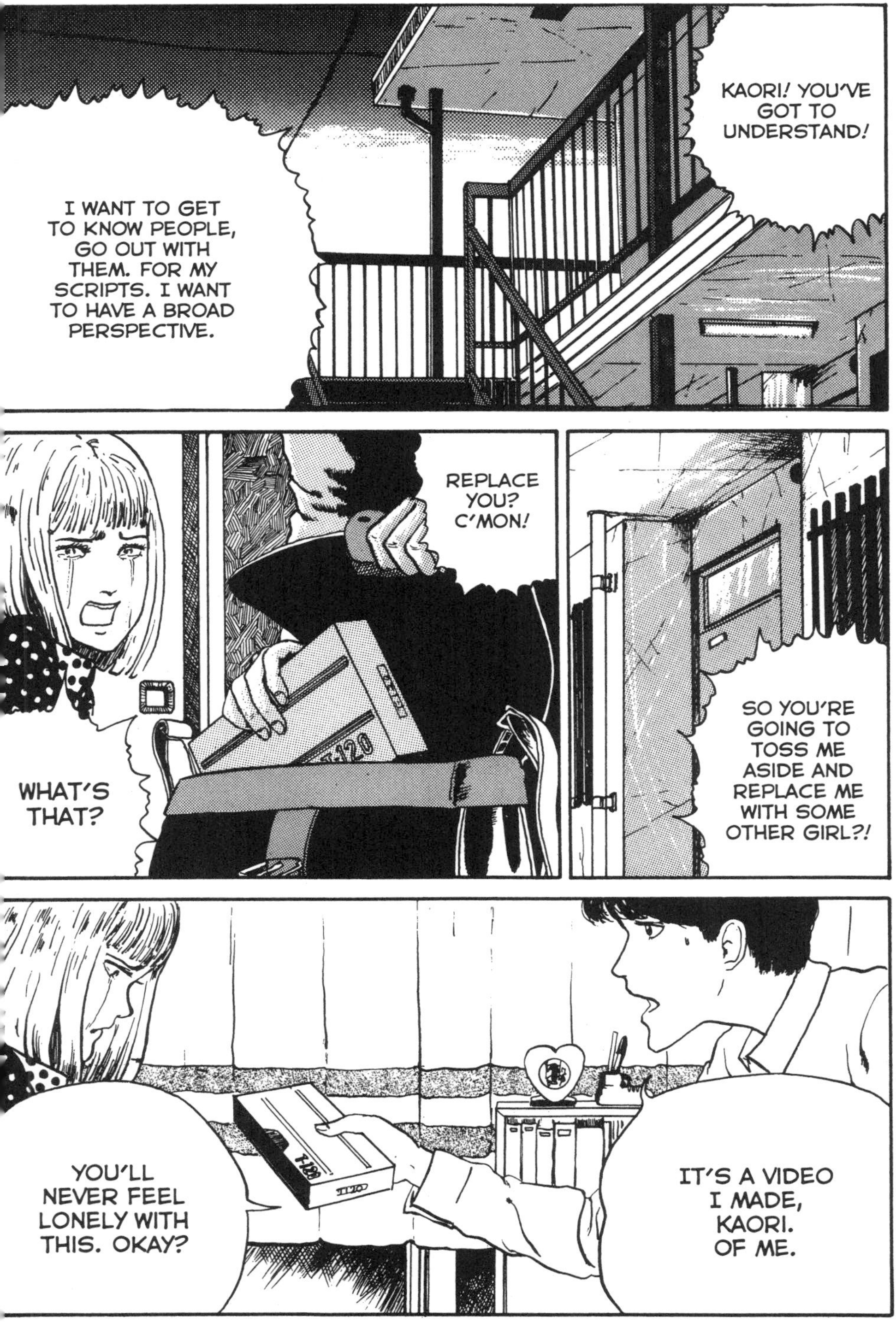
KAORI! YOU'VE GOT TO UNDERSTAND!
I WANT TO GET TO KNOW PEOPLE, GO OUT WITH THEM. FOR MY SCRIPTS. I WANT TO HAVE A BROAD PERSPECTIVE.
SO YOU'RE GOING TO TOSS ME ASIDE AND REPLACE ME WITH SOME OTHER GIRL?!
REPLACE YOU? C'MON!
WHAT'S THAT?
IT'S A VIDEO I MADE, KAORI. OF ME.
YOU'LL NEVER FEEL LONELY WITH THIS. OKAY?

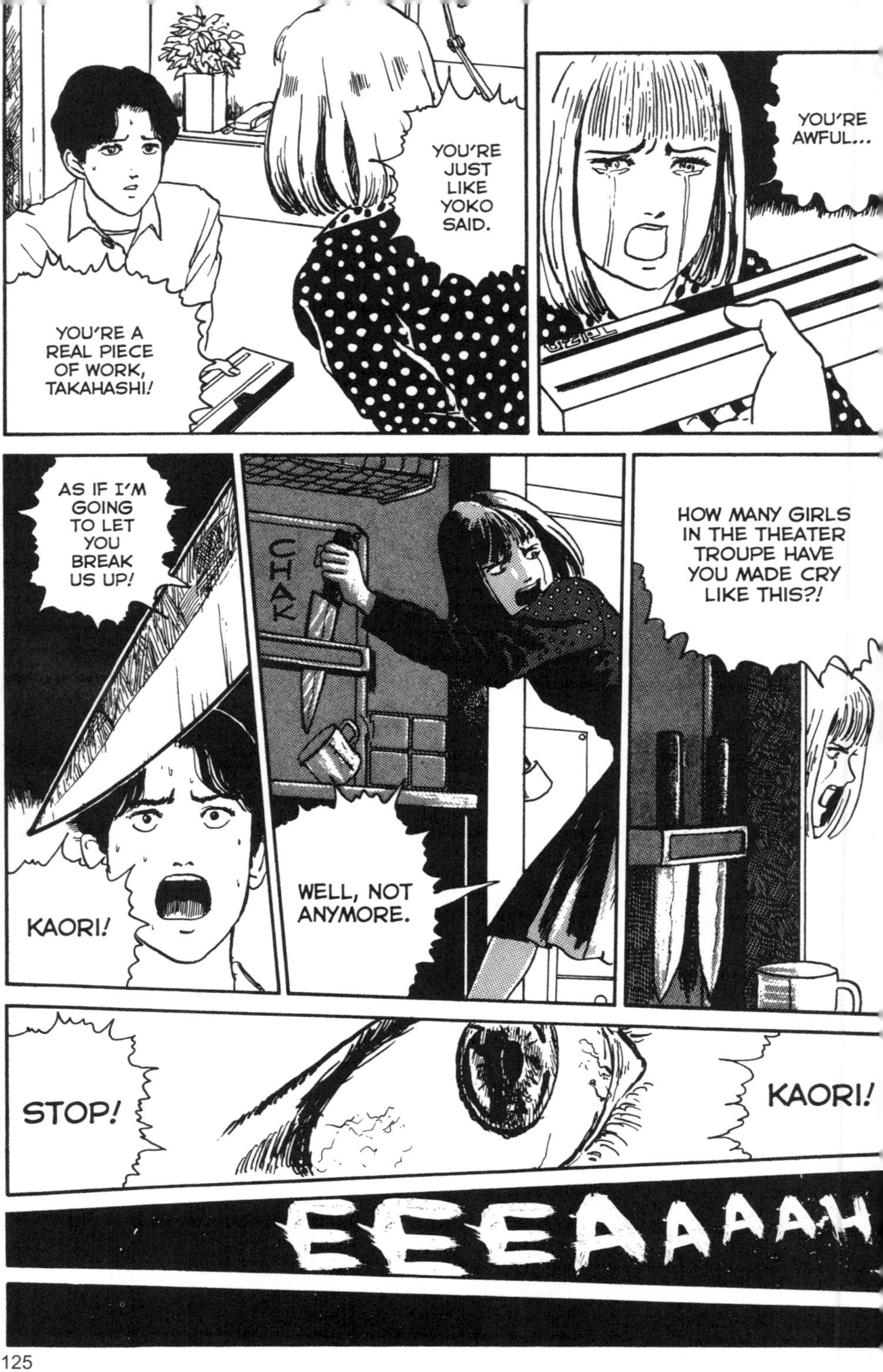
YOU'RE AWFUL...
YOU'RE JUST LIKE YOKO SAID.
YOU'RE A REAL PIECE OF WORK, TAKAHASHI!
HOW MANY GIRLS IN THE THEATER TROUPE HAVE YOU MADE CRY LIKE THIS?!
CHAK
WELL, NOT ANYMORE.
AS IF I'M GOING TO LET YOU BREAK US UP!
KAORI!
KAORI!
STOP!
EEEAAAAH

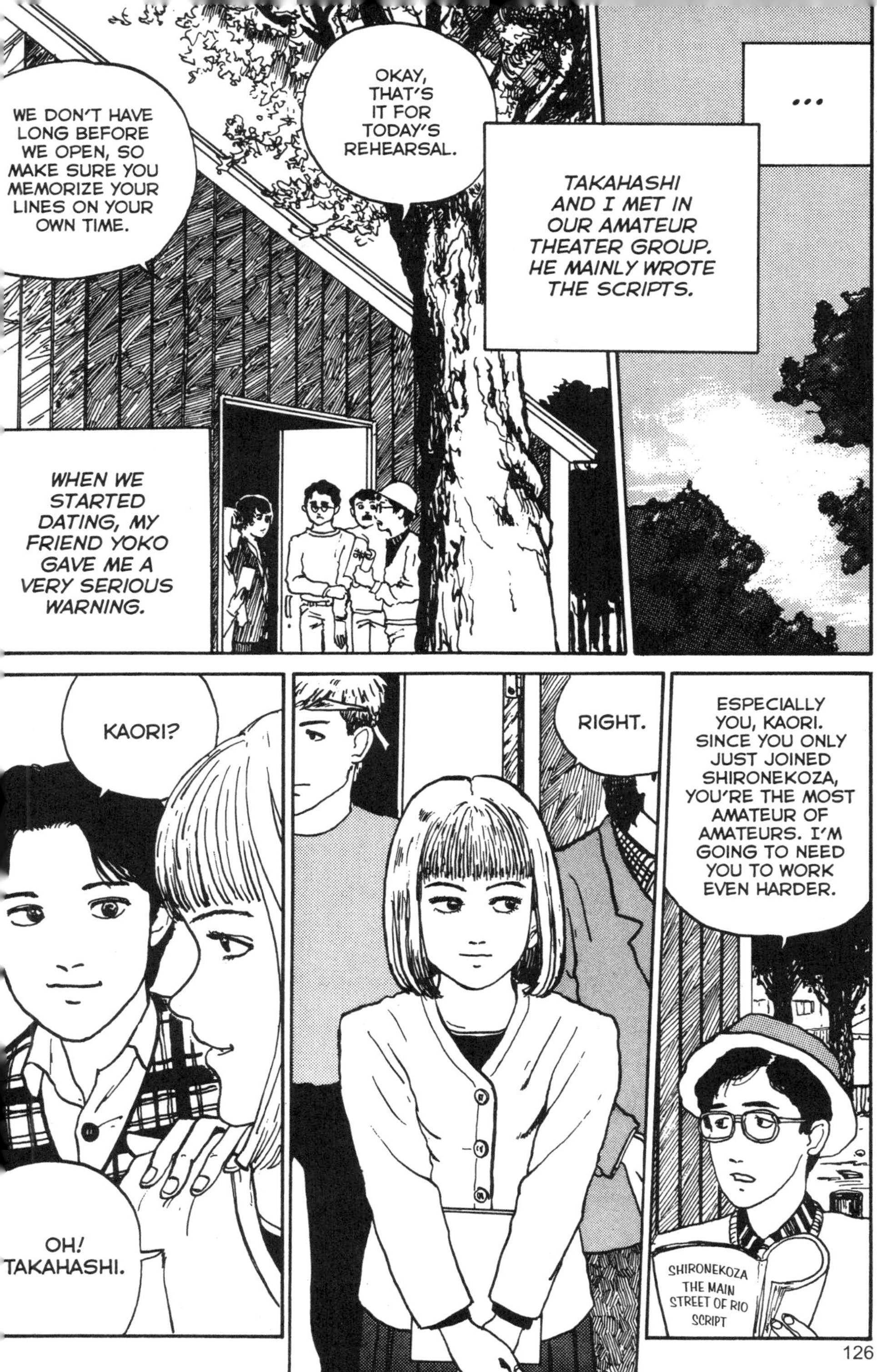
...
TAKAHASHI AND I MET IN OUR AMATEUR THEATER GROUP. HE MAINLY WROTE THE SCRIPTS.
OKAY, THAT'S IT FOR TODAY'S REHEARSAL.
WE DON'T HAVE LONG BEFORE WE OPEN, SO MAKE SURE YOU MEMORIZE YOUR LINES ON YOUR OWN TIME.
WHEN WE STARTED DATING, MY FRIEND YOKO GAVE ME A VERY SERIOUS WARNING.
ESPECIALLY YOU, KAORI. SINCE YOU ONLY JUST JOINED SHIRONEKOZA, YOU'RE THE MOST AMATEUR OF AMATEURS. I'M GOING TO NEED YOU TO WORK EVEN HARDER.
SHIRONEKOZA THE MAIN STREET OF RIO SCRIPT
RIGHT.
KAORI?
OH! TAKAHASHI.

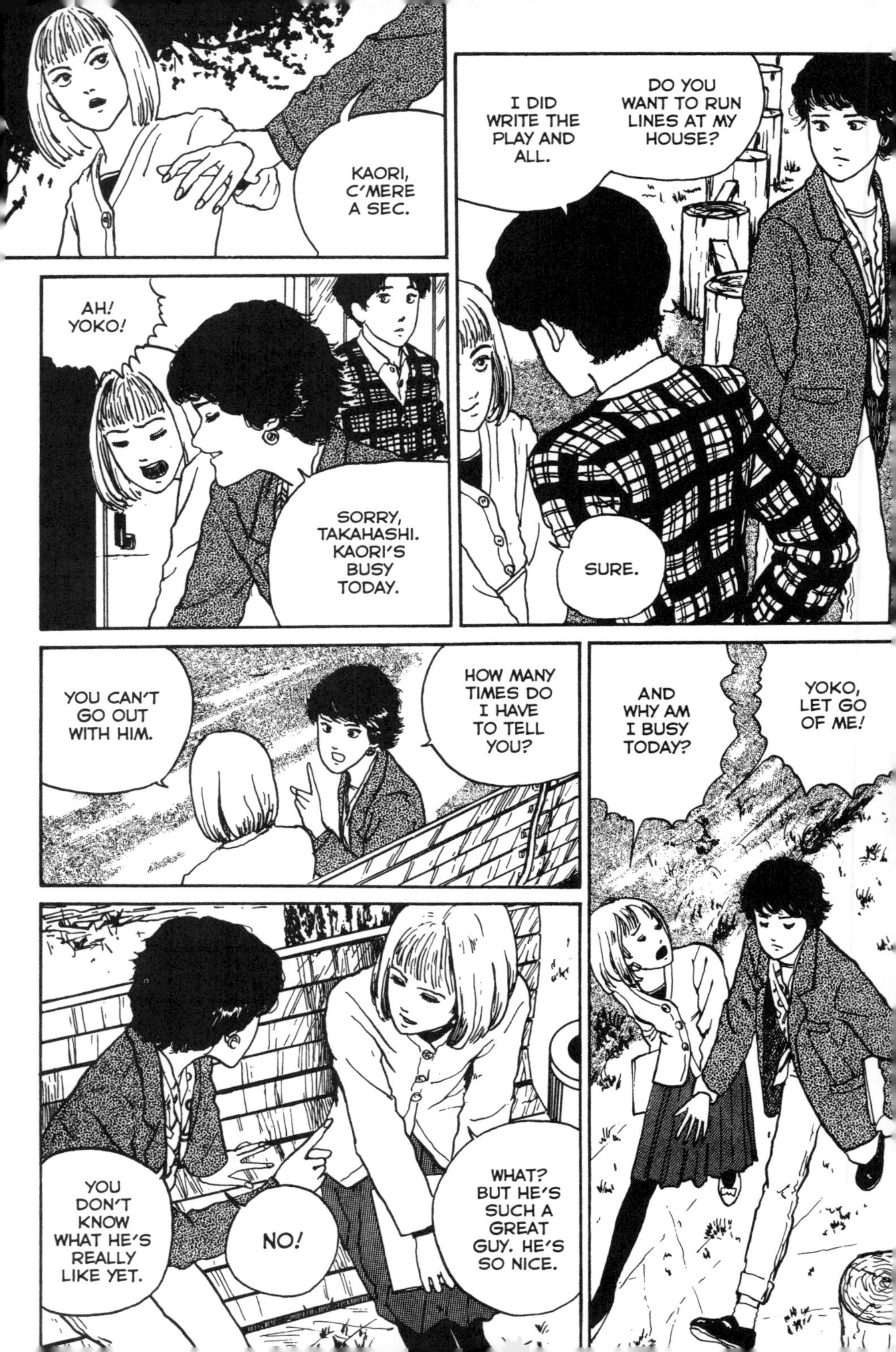
DO YOU WANT TO RUN LINES AT MY HOUSE?
I DID WRITE THE PLAY AND ALL.
SURE.
KAORI, C'MERE A SEC.
AH! YOKO!
SORRY, TAKAHASHI. KAORI'S BUSY TODAY.
YOKO, LET GO OF ME!
AND WHY AM I BUSY TODAY?
HOW MANY TIMES DO I HAVE TO TELL YOU?
YOU CAN'T GO OUT WITH HIM.
WHAT? BUT HE'S SUCH A GREAT GUY. HE'S SO NICE.
NO!
YOU DON'T KNOW WHAT HE'S REALLY LIKE YET.

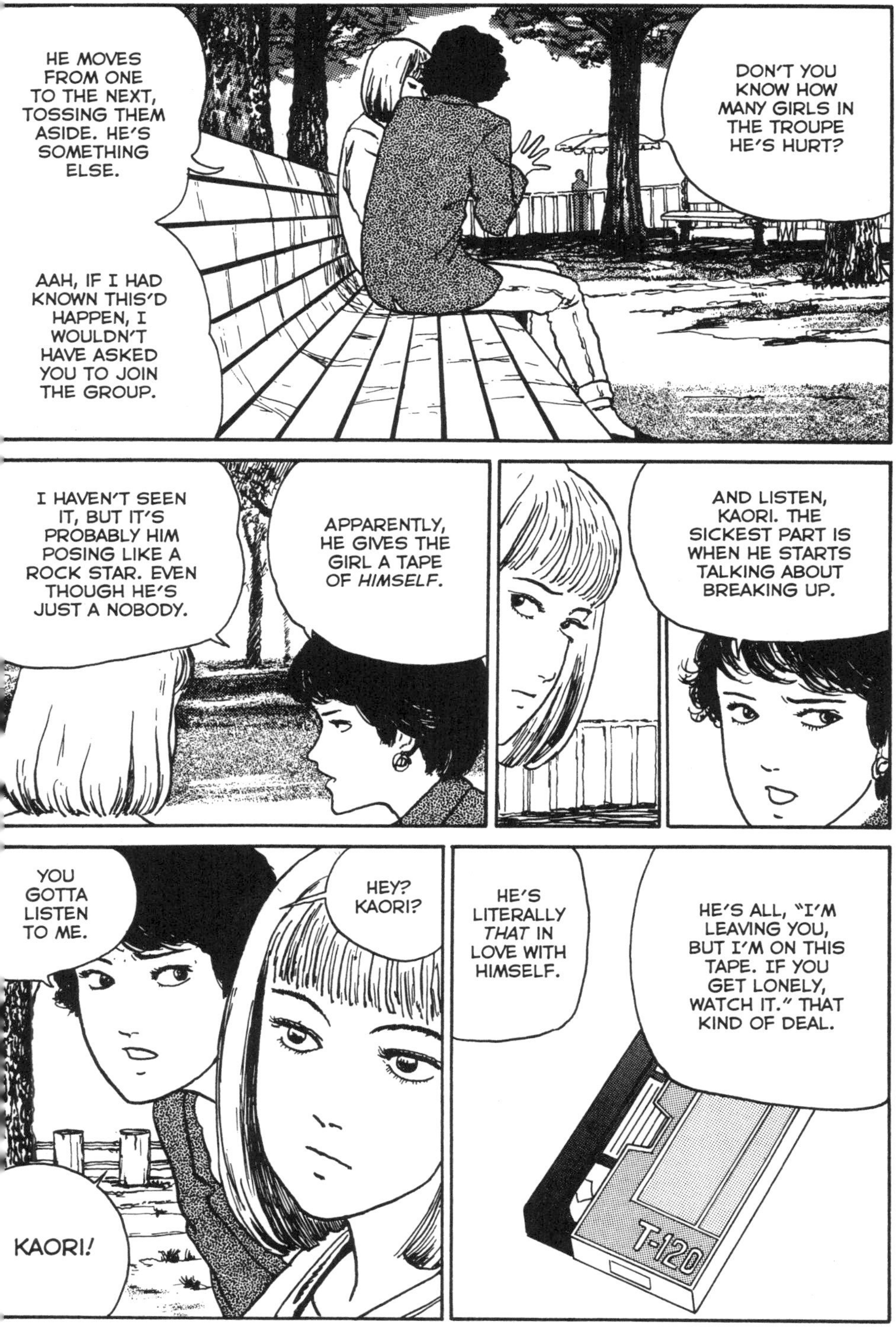
DON'T YOU KNOW HOW MANY GIRLS IN THE TROUPE HE'S HURT?
HE MOVES FROM ONE TO THE NEXT, TOSSING THEM ASIDE. HE'S SOMETHING ELSE.
AAH, IF I HAD KNOWN THIS'D HAPPEN, I WOULDN'T HAVE ASKED YOU TO JOIN THE GROUP.
AND LISTEN, KAORI. THE SICKEST PART IS WHEN HE STARTS TALKING ABOUT BREAKING UP.
APPARENTLY, HE GIVES THE GIRL A TAPE OF *HIMSELF*.
I HAVEN'T SEEN IT, BUT IT'S PROBABLY HIM POSING LIKE A ROCK STAR. EVEN THOUGH HE'S JUST A NOBODY.
HE'S ALL, "I'M LEAVING YOU, BUT I'M ON THIS TAPE. IF YOU GET LONELY, WATCH IT." THAT KIND OF DEAL.
HE'S LITERALLY *THAT* IN LOVE WITH HIMSELF.
T-120
HEY? KAORI?
YOU GOTTA LISTEN TO ME.
KAORI!

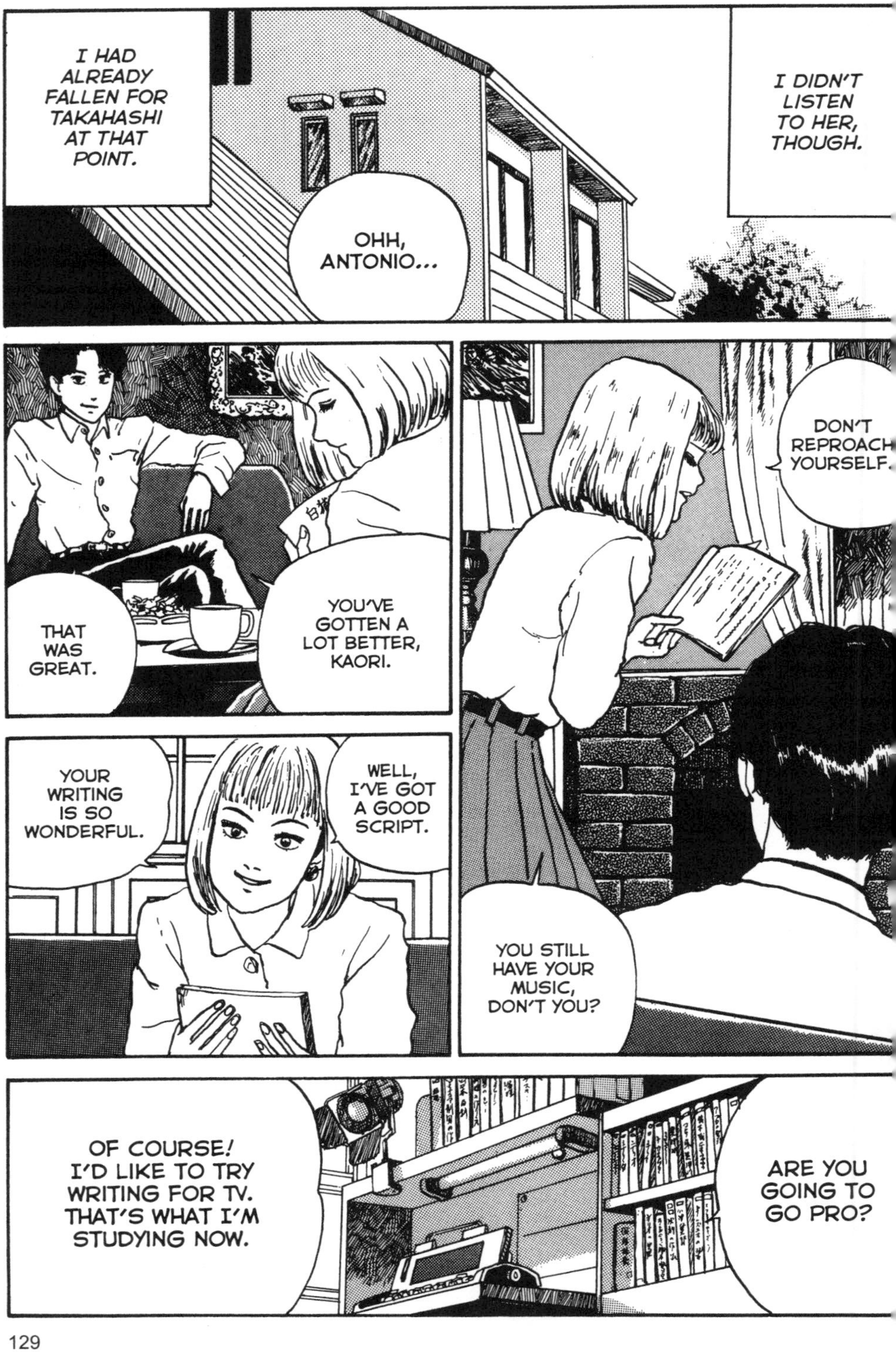
I DIDN'T LISTEN TO HER, THOUGH.
OHH, ANTONIO...
I HAD ALREADY FALLEN FOR TAKAHASHI AT THAT POINT.
DON'T REPROACH YOURSELF.
YOU STILL HAVE YOUR MUSIC, DON'T YOU?
YOU'VE GOTTEN A LOT BETTER, KAORI.
THAT WAS GREAT.
WELL, I'VE GOT A GOOD SCRIPT.
YOUR WRITING IS SO WONDERFUL.
ARE YOU GOING TO GO PRO?
OF COURSE! I'D LIKE TO TRY WRITING FOR TV. THAT'S WHAT I'M STUDYING NOW.

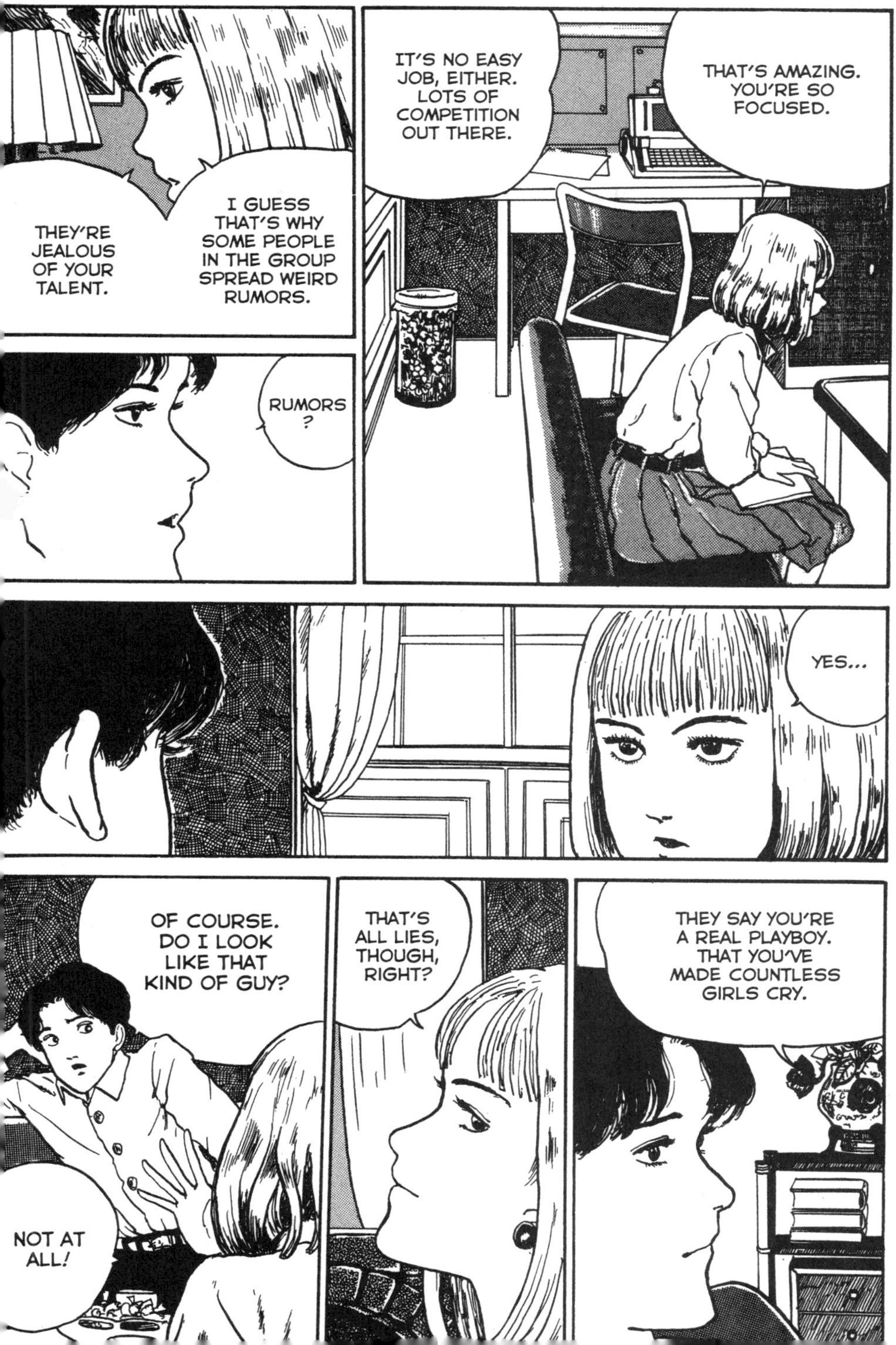
THAT'S AMAZING. YOU'RE SO FOCUSED.
IT'S NO EASY JOB, EITHER. LOTS OF COMPETITION OUT THERE.
I GUESS THAT'S WHY SOME PEOPLE IN THE GROUP SPREAD WEIRD RUMORS.
THEY'RE JEALOUS OF YOUR TALENT.
RUMORS?
YES...
THEY SAY YOU'RE A REAL PLAYBOY. THAT YOU'VE MADE COUNTLESS GIRLS CRY.
THAT'S ALL LIES, THOUGH, RIGHT?
OF COURSE. DO I LOOK LIKE THAT KIND OF GUY?
NOT AT ALL!

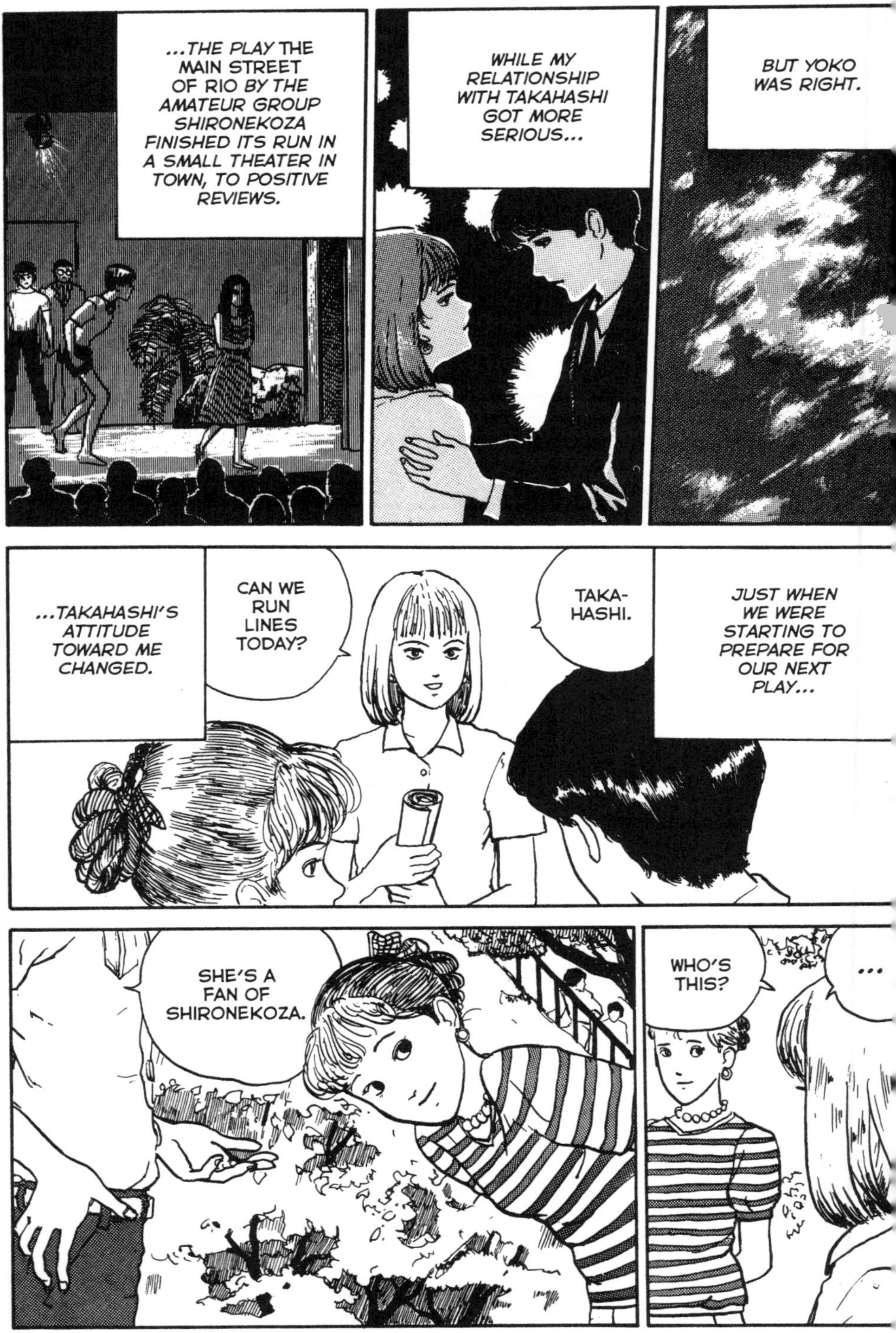
BUT YOKO WAS RIGHT.
WHILE MY RELATIONSHIP WITH TAKAHASHI GOT MORE SERIOUS...
...THE PLAY THE MAIN STREET OF RIO BY THE AMATEUR GROUP SHIRONEKOZA FINISHED ITS RUN IN A SMALL THEATER IN TOWN, TO POSITIVE REVIEWS.
JUST WHEN WE WERE STARTING TO PREPARE FOR OUR NEXT PLAY...
TAKA-HASHI.
CAN WE RUN LINES TODAY?
...TAKAHASHI'S ATTITUDE TOWARD ME CHANGED.
...
WHO'S THIS?
SHE'S A FAN OF SHIRONEKOZA.

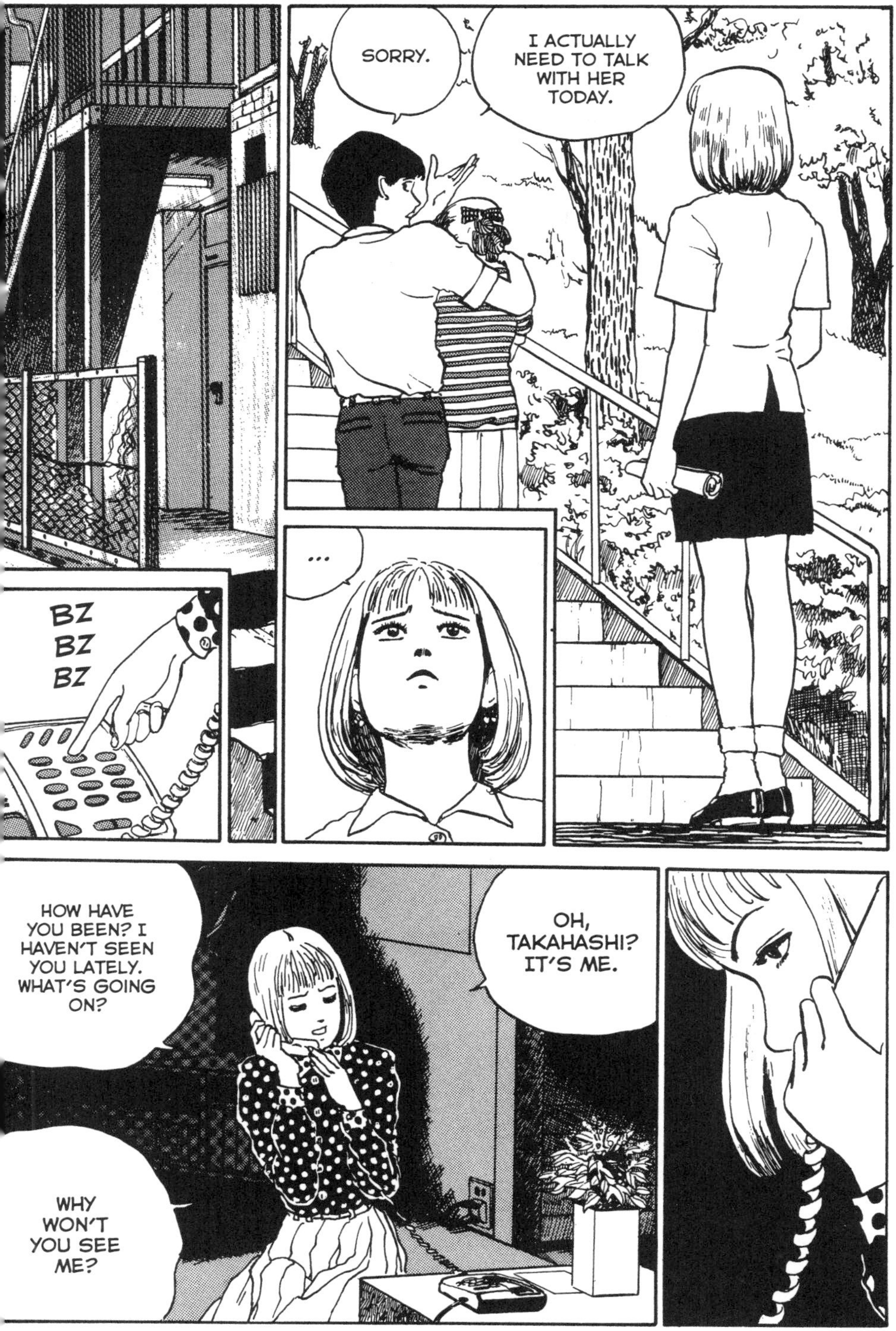
I ACTUALLY NEED TO TALK WITH HER TODAY.
SORRY.
...
BZ BZ BZ
OH, TAKAHASHI? IT'S ME.
HOW HAVE YOU BEEN? I HAVEN'T SEEN YOU LATELY. WHAT'S GOING ON?
WHY WON'T YOU SEE ME?

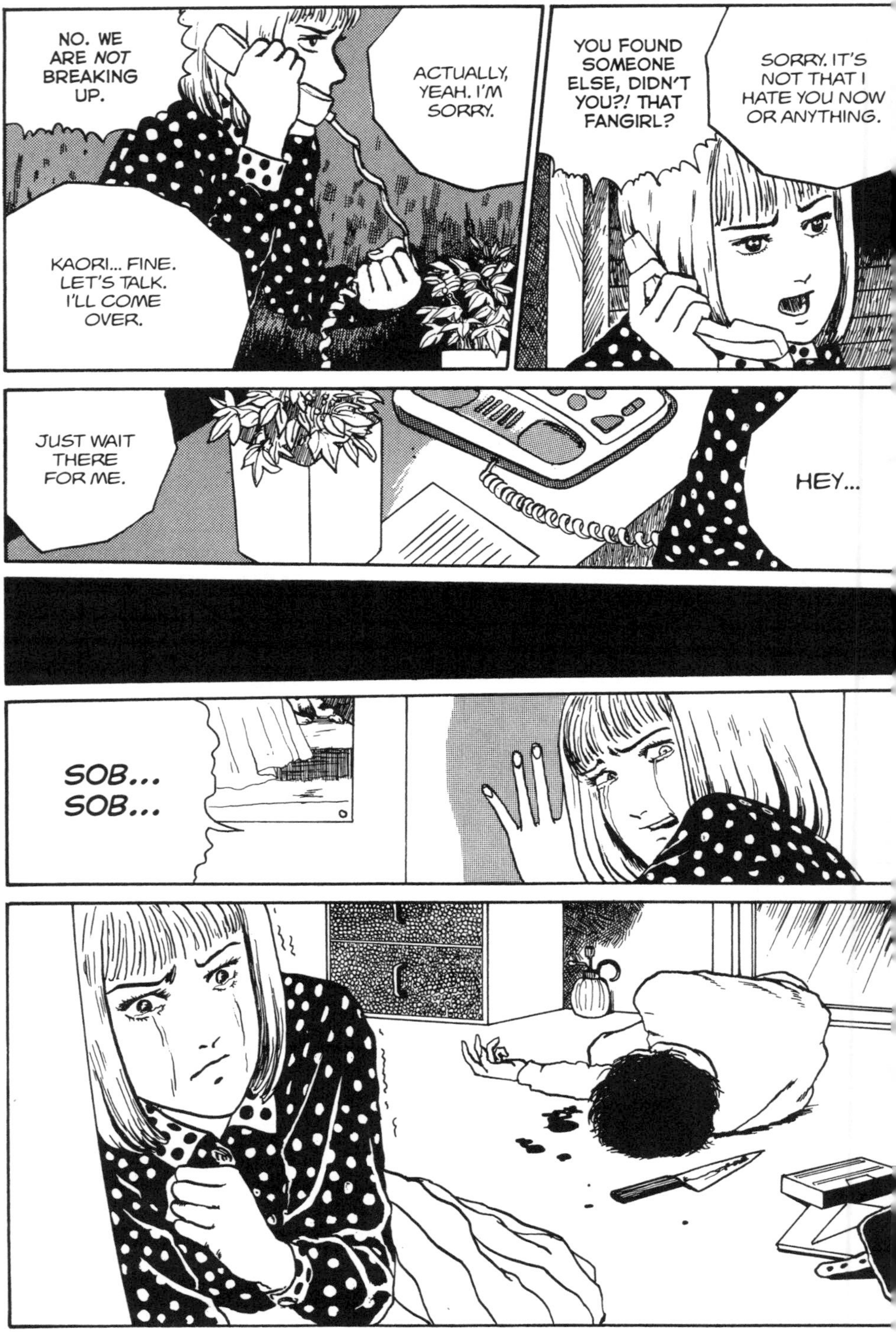
SORRY. IT'S NOT THAT I HATE YOU NOW OR ANYTHING.
YOU FOUND SOMEONE ELSE, DIDN'T YOU?! THAT FANGIRL?
ACTUALLY, YEAH. I'M SORRY.
NO. WE ARE *NOT* BREAKING UP.
KAORI... FINE. LET'S TALK. I'LL COME OVER.
HEY...
JUST WAIT THERE FOR ME.
SOB... SOB...

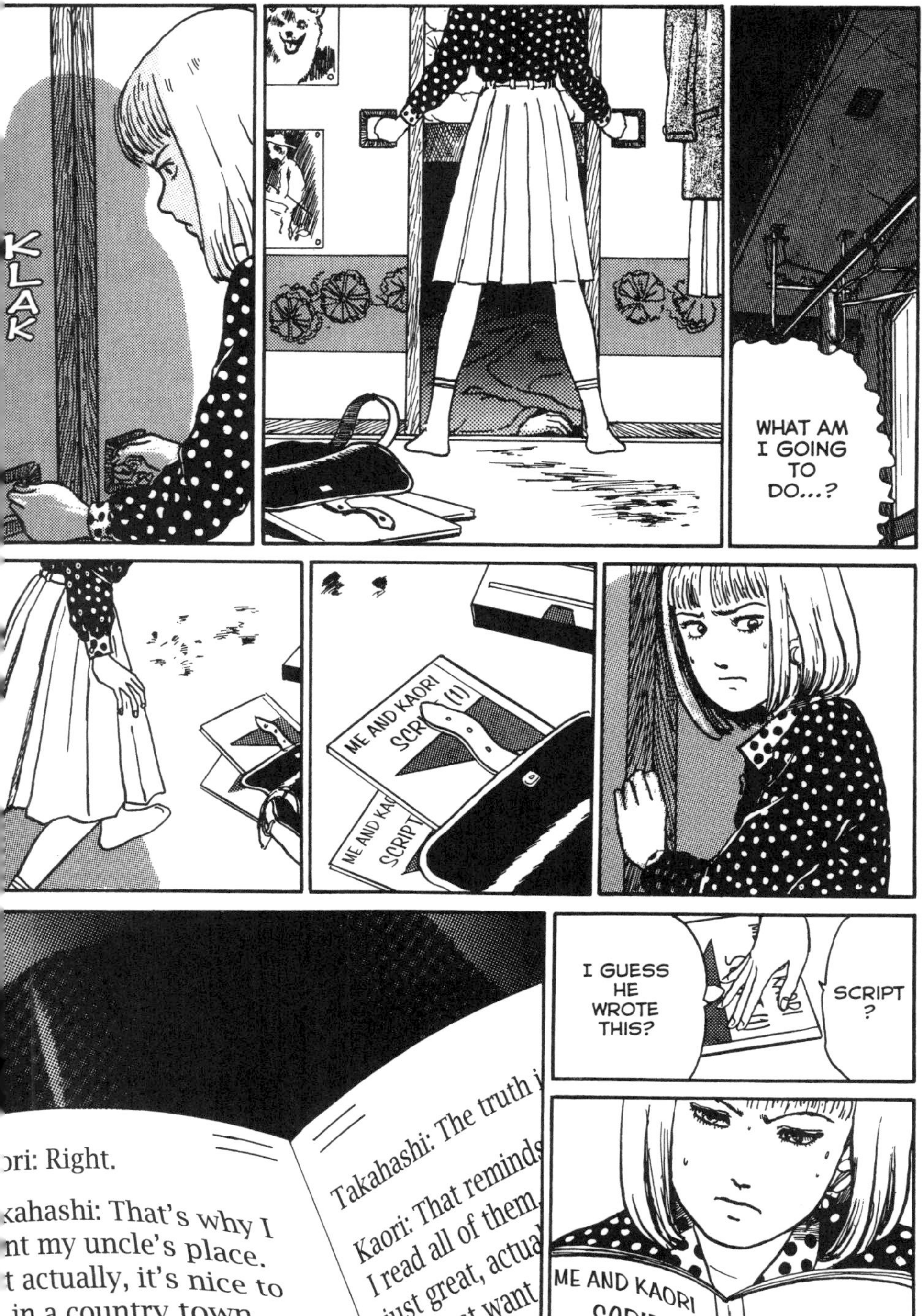

WHAT AM I GOING TO DO...?
KLAK
ME AND KAORI SCRIPT (1)
SCRIPT?
I GUESS HE WROTE THIS?
ME AND KAORI SCRIPT (1)
ori: Right.
kahashi: That's why I
nt my uncle's place.
t actually, it's nice to
in a country town
d the water's really good.
Takahashi: The truth
Kaori: That reminds
I read all of them,
just great, actua
I almost want

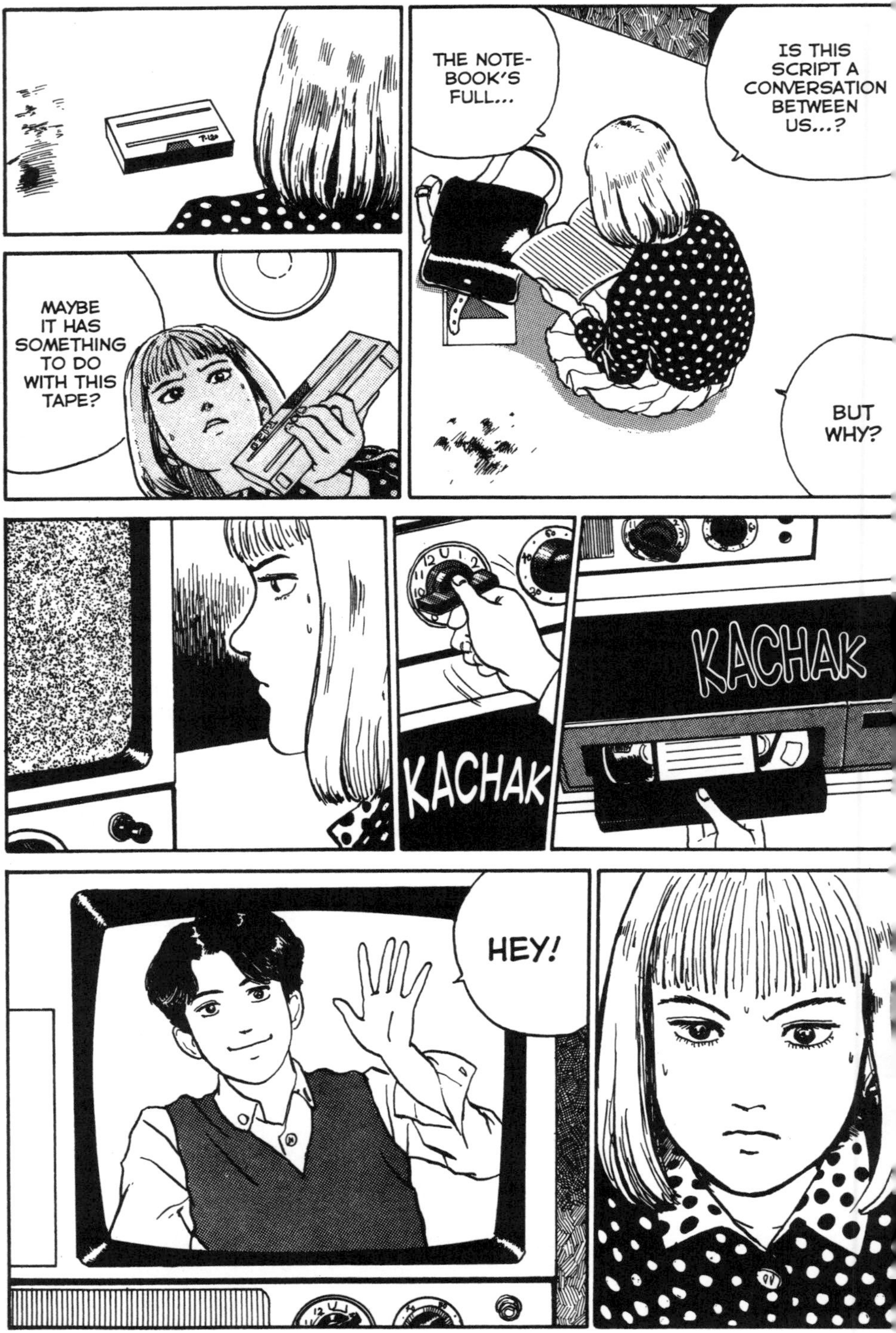
IS THIS SCRIPT A CONVERSATION BETWEEN US...?
THE NOTE-BOOK'S FULL...
BUT WHY?
MAYBE IT HAS SOMETHING TO DO WITH THIS TAPE?
KACHAK
KACHAK
HEY!

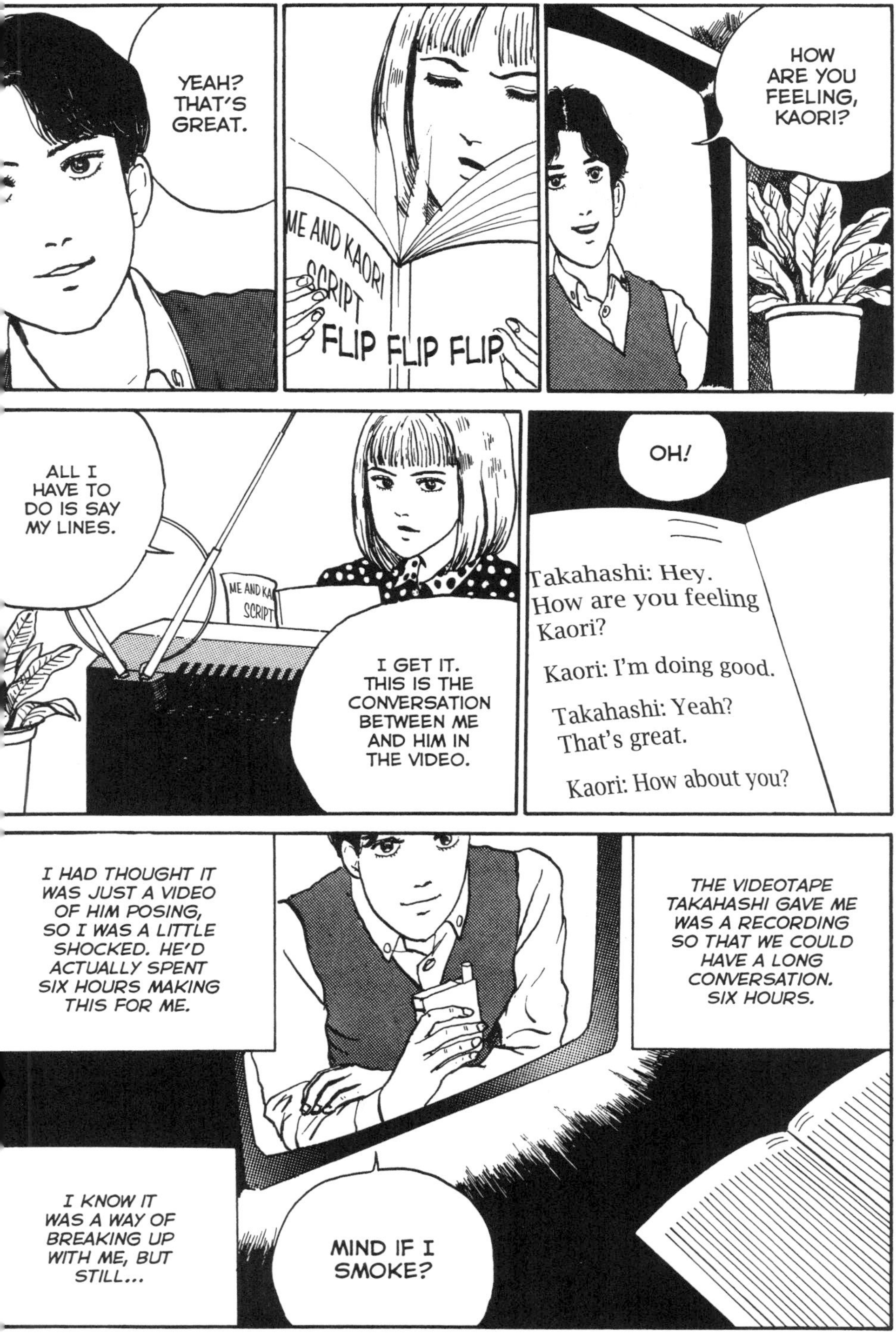
HOW ARE YOU FEELING, KAORI?
ME AND KAORI SCRIPT
FLIP FLIP FLIP
YEAH? THAT'S GREAT.
OH!
Takahashi: Hey. How are you feeling Kaori?
Kaori: I'm doing good.
Takahashi: Yeah? That's great.
Kaori: How about you?
I GET IT. THIS IS THE CONVERSATION BETWEEN ME AND HIM IN THE VIDEO.
ALL I HAVE TO DO IS SAY MY LINES.
THE VIDEOTAPE TAKAHASHI GAVE ME WAS A RECORDING SO THAT WE COULD HAVE A LONG CONVERSATION. SIX HOURS.
I HAD THOUGHT IT WAS JUST A VIDEO OF HIM POSING, SO I WAS A LITTLE SHOCKED. HE'D ACTUALLY SPENT SIX HOURS MAKING THIS FOR ME.
MIND IF I SMOKE?
I KNOW IT WAS A WAY OF BREAKING UP WITH ME, BUT STILL...

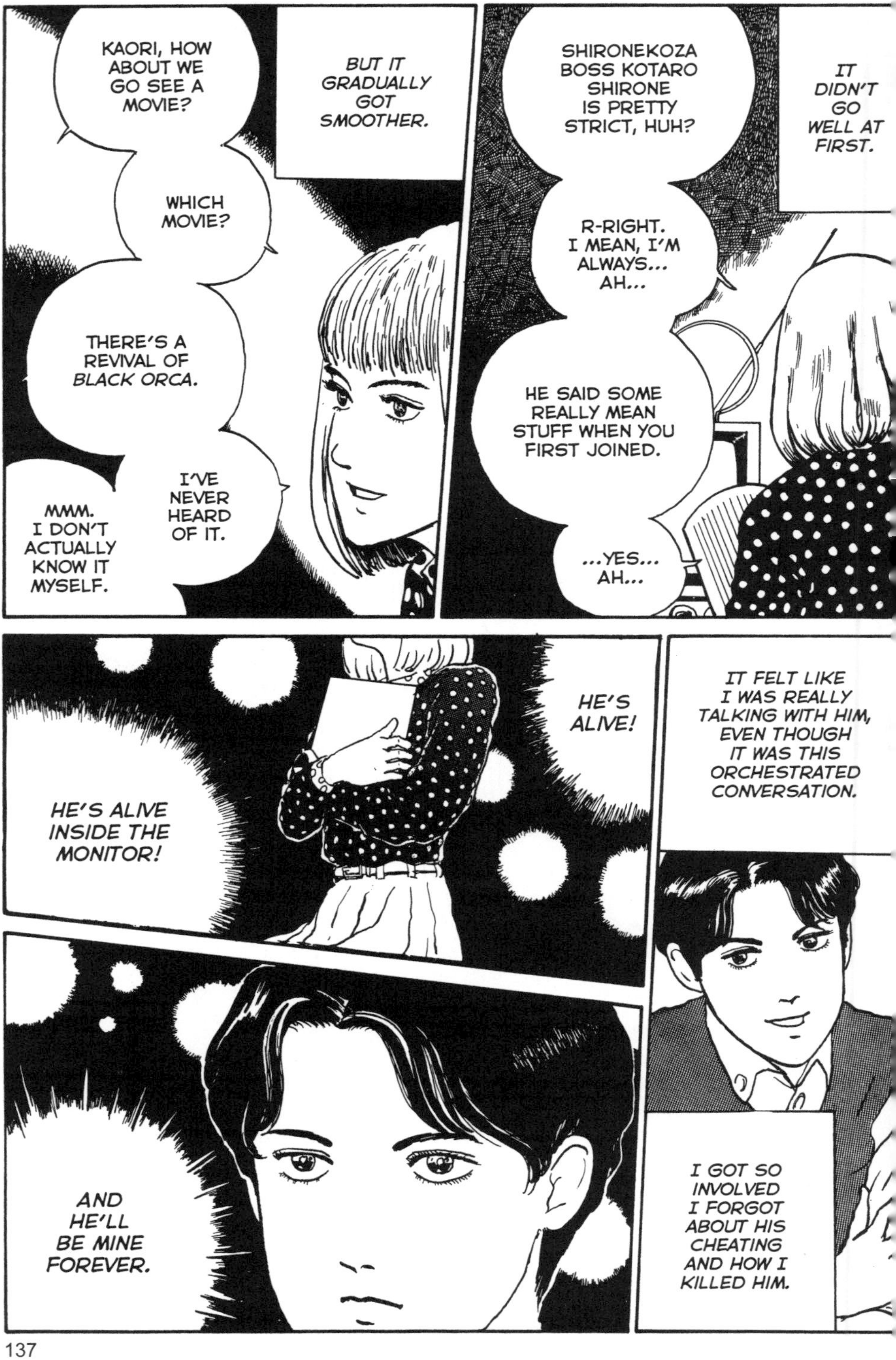
IT DIDN'T GO WELL AT FIRST.
SHIRONEKOZA BOSS KOTARO SHIRONE IS PRETTY STRICT, HUH?
R-RIGHT. I MEAN, I'M ALWAYS... AH...
HE SAID SOME REALLY MEAN STUFF WHEN YOU FIRST JOINED.
...YES... AH...
BUT IT GRADUALLY GOT SMOOTHER.
KAORI, HOW ABOUT WE GO SEE A MOVIE?
WHICH MOVIE?
THERE'S A REVIVAL OF *BLACK ORCA*.
I'VE NEVER HEARD OF IT.
MMM. I DON'T ACTUALLY KNOW IT MYSELF.
IT FELT LIKE I WAS REALLY TALKING WITH HIM, EVEN THOUGH IT WAS THIS ORCHESTRATED CONVERSATION.
I GOT SO INVOLVED I FORGOT ABOUT HIS CHEATING AND HOW I KILLED HIM.
HE'S ALIVE!
HE'S ALIVE INSIDE THE MONITOR!
AND HE'LL BE MINE FOREVER.

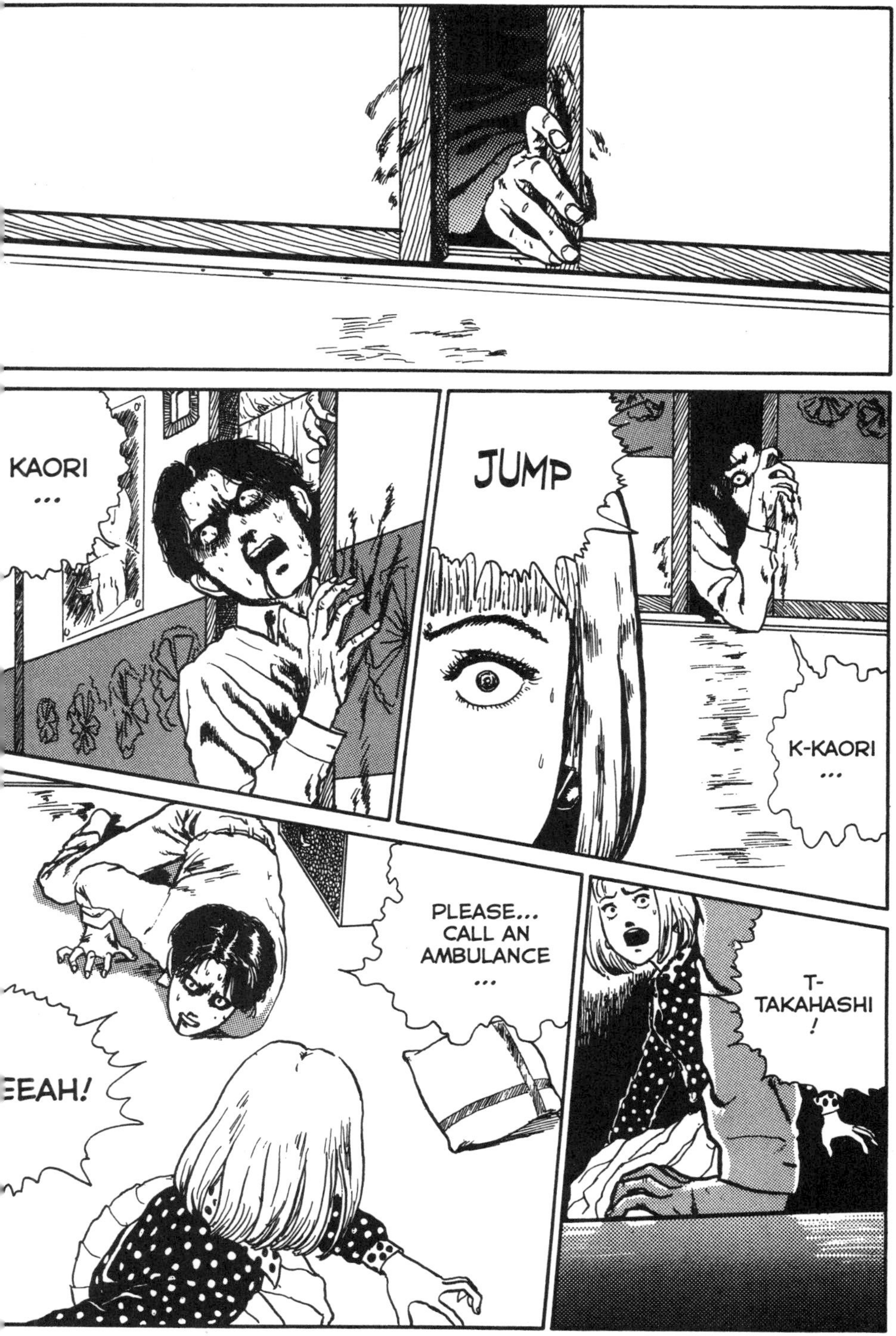
K-KAORI ...
JUMP
KAORI ...
T-TAKAHASHI!
PLEASE... CALL AN AMBULANCE ...
EEAH!

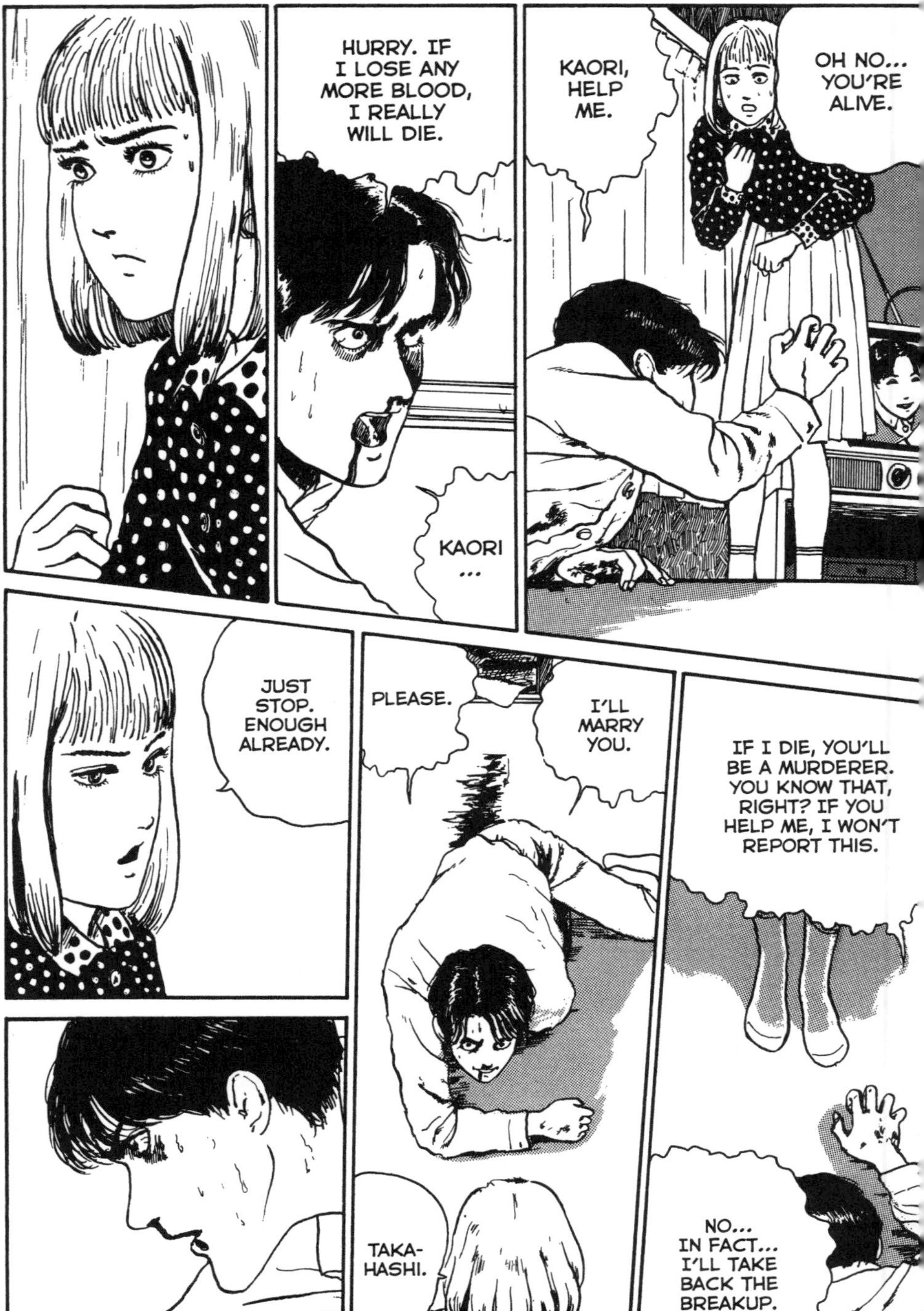

OH NO... YOU'RE ALIVE.
KAORI, HELP ME.
HURRY. IF I LOSE ANY MORE BLOOD, I REALLY WILL DIE.
KAORI ...
IF I DIE, YOU'LL BE A MURDERER. YOU KNOW THAT, RIGHT? IF YOU HELP ME, I WON'T REPORT THIS.
NO... IN FACT... I'LL TAKE BACK THE BREAKUP.
I'LL MARRY YOU.
PLEASE.
TAKA-HASHI.
JUST STOP. ENOUGH ALREADY.

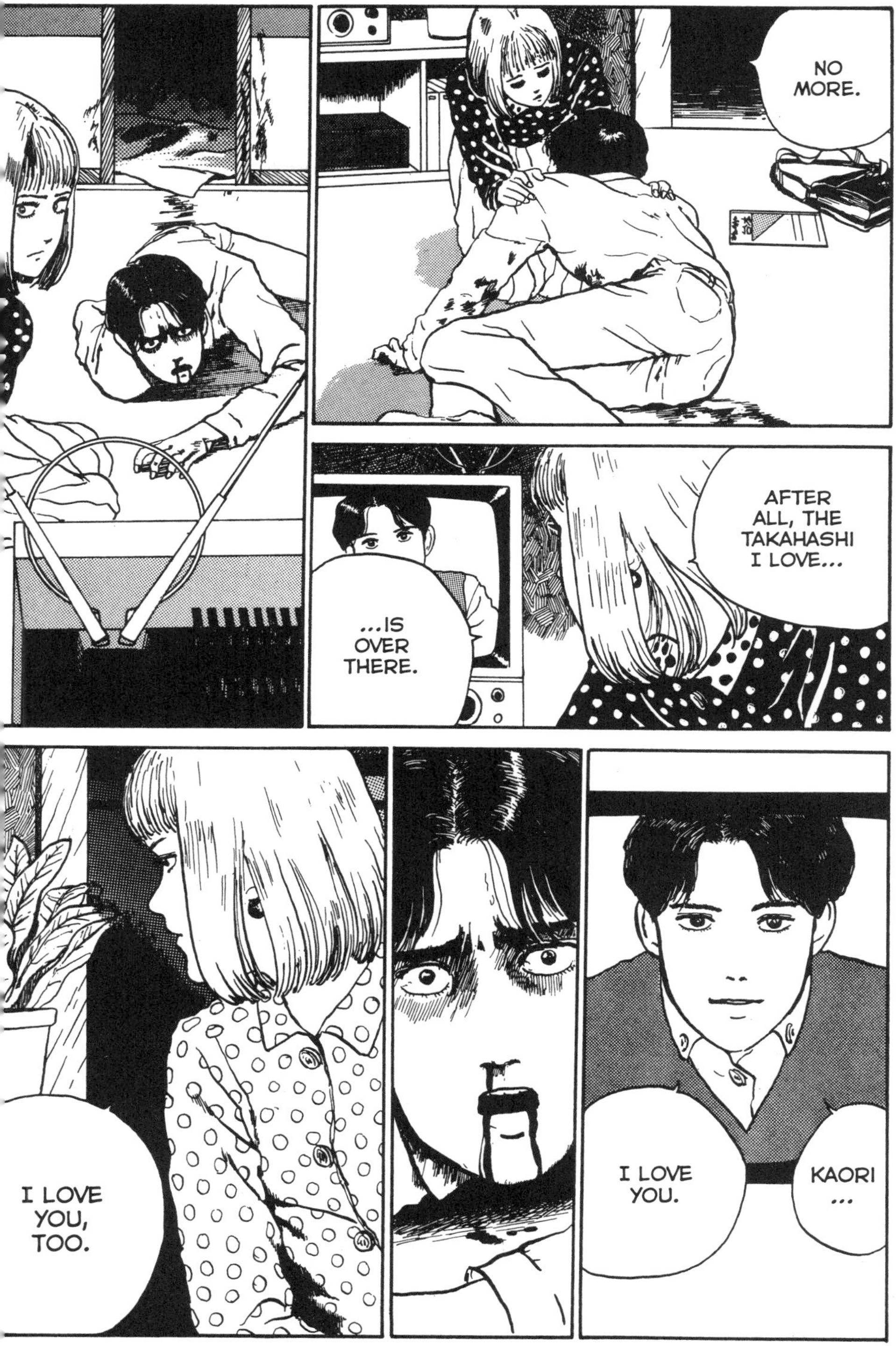
NO MORE.
AFTER ALL, THE TAKAHASHI I LOVE...
...IS OVER THERE.
KAORI ...
I LOVE YOU.
I LOVE YOU, TOO.

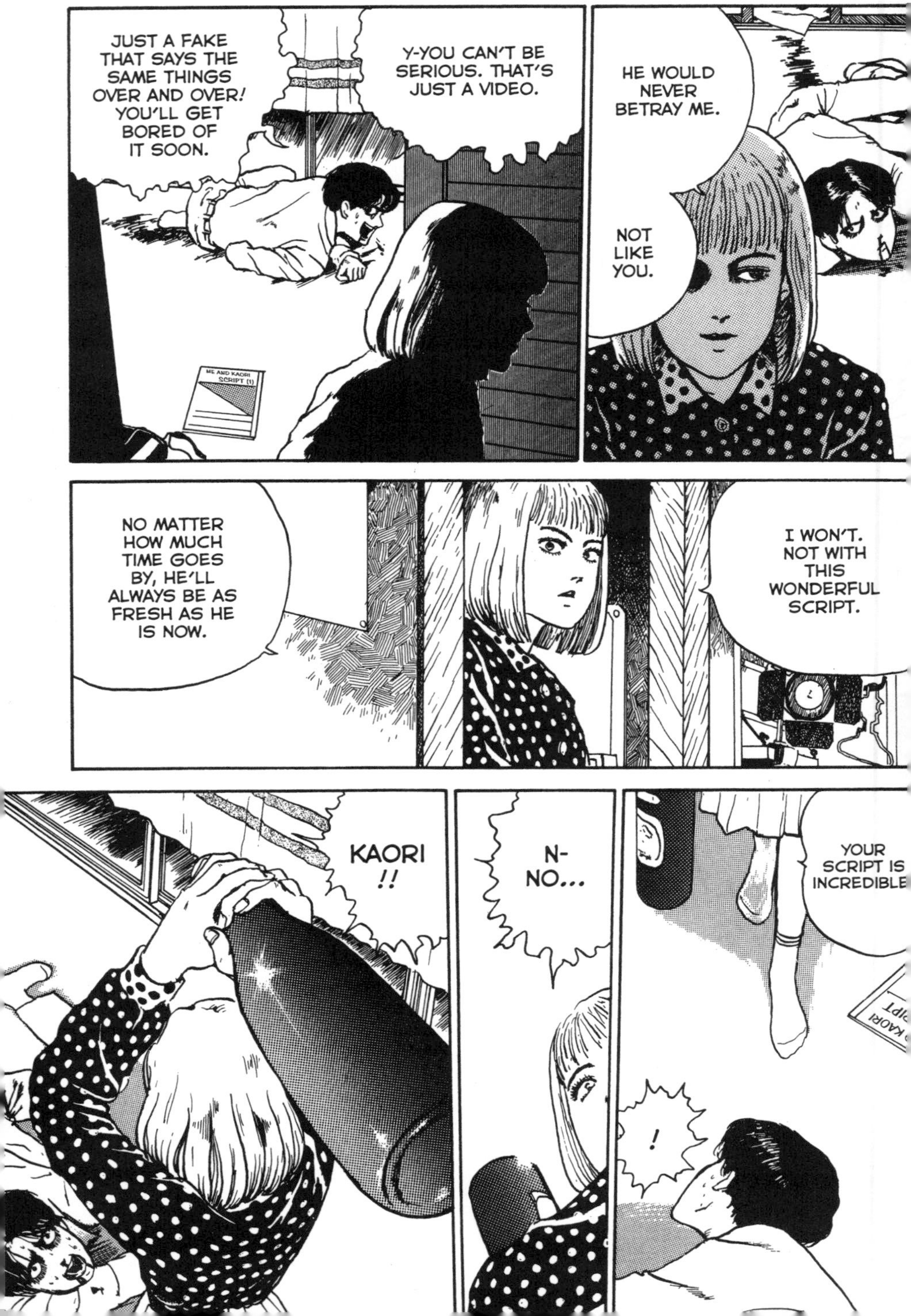
HE WOULD NEVER BETRAY ME.
NOT LIKE YOU.
Y-YOU CAN'T BE SERIOUS. THAT'S JUST A VIDEO.
JUST A FAKE THAT SAYS THE SAME THINGS OVER AND OVER! YOU'LL GET BORED OF IT SOON.
ME AND KAORI SCRIPT (1)
I WON'T. NOT WITH THIS WONDERFUL SCRIPT.
NO MATTER HOW MUCH TIME GOES BY, HE'LL ALWAYS BE AS FRESH AS HE IS NOW.
YOUR SCRIPT IS INCREDIBLE
!
N- NO...
KAORI !!

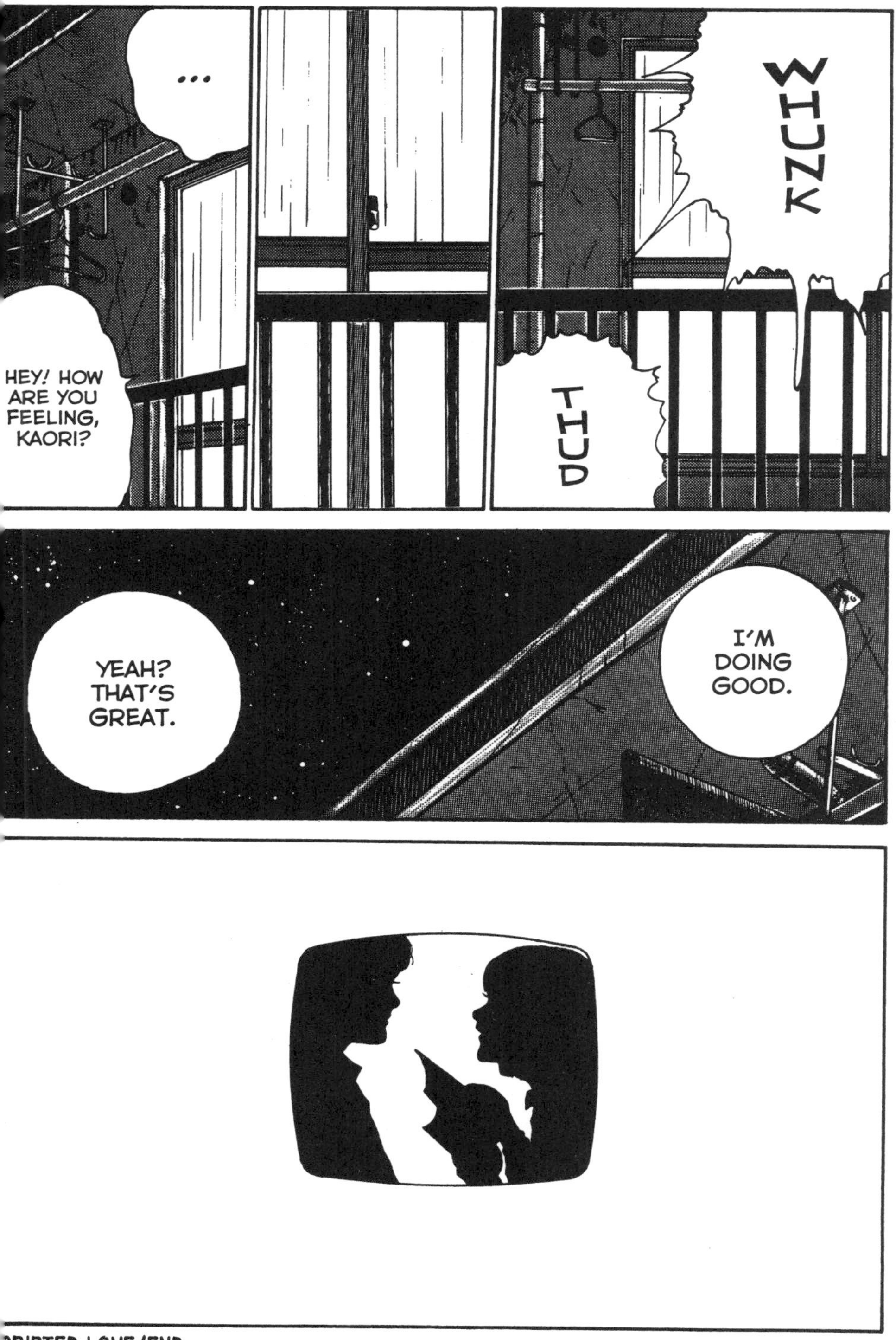
WHUNK
THUD
...
HEY! HOW ARE YOU FEELING, KAORI?
I'M DOING GOOD.
YEAH? THAT'S GREAT.

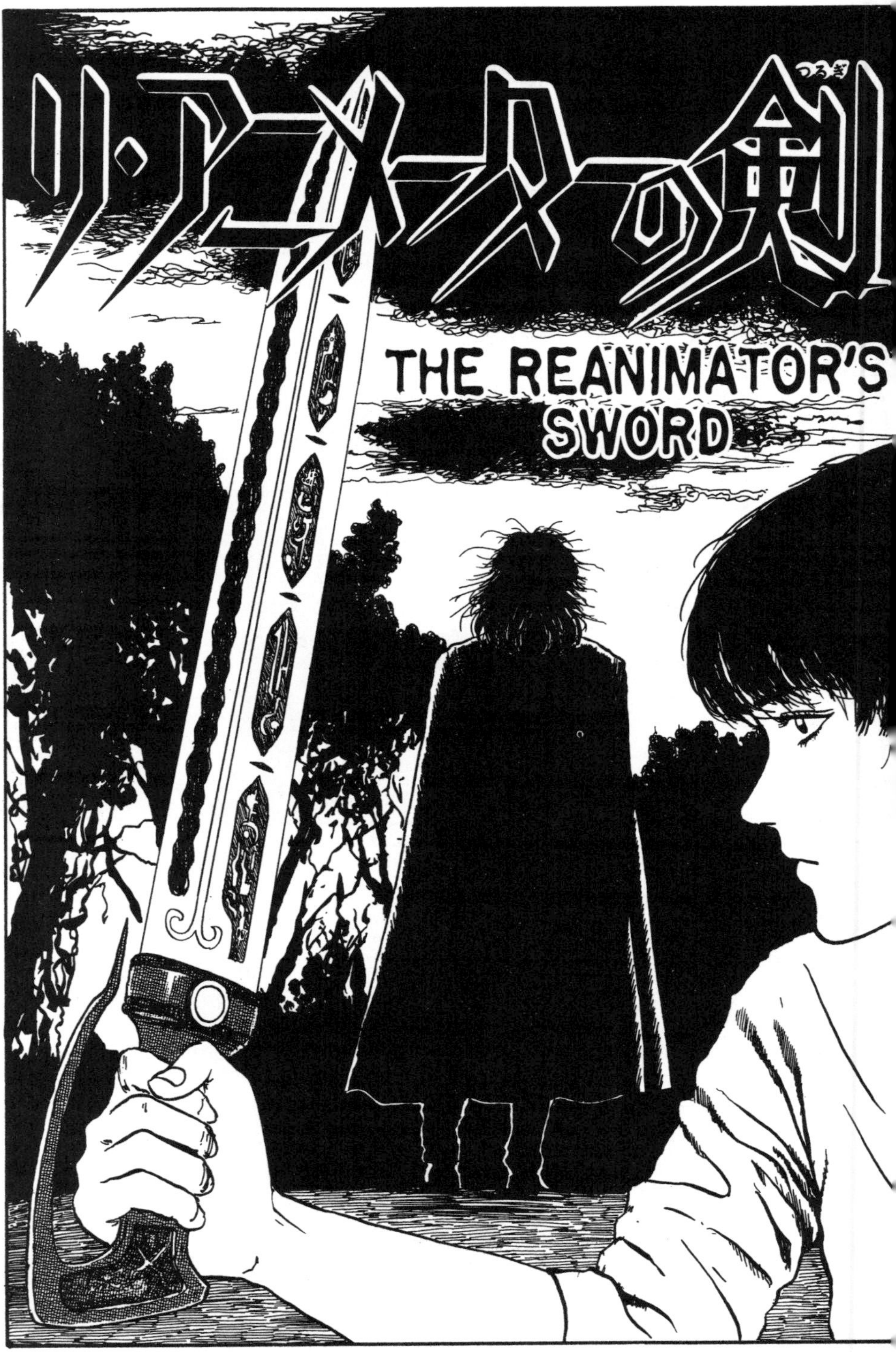

リ・アニメーターの剣
つるぎ
THE REANIMATOR'S SWORD

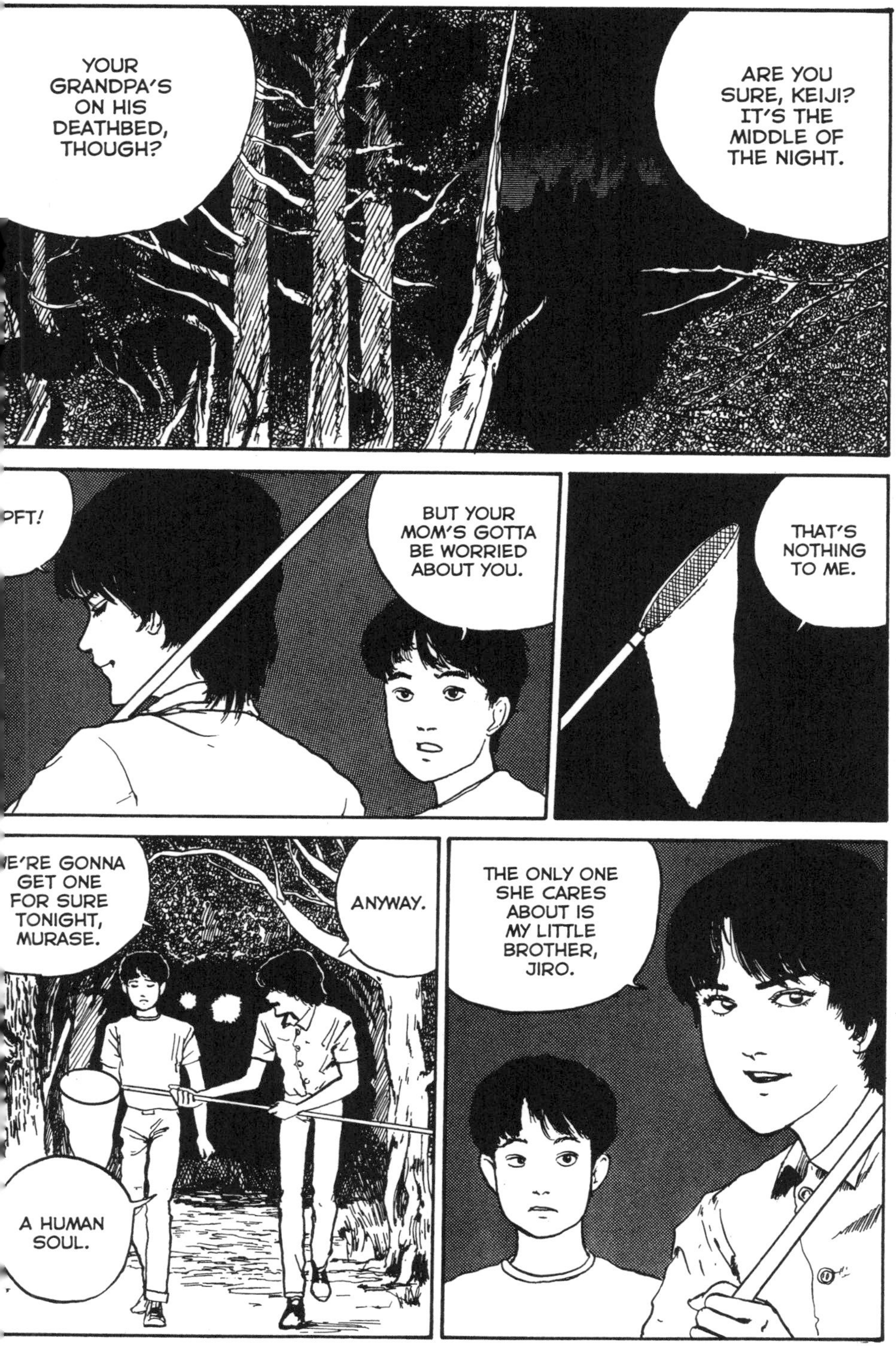
ARE YOU SURE, KEIJI? IT'S THE MIDDLE OF THE NIGHT.
YOUR GRANDPA'S ON HIS DEATHBED, THOUGH?
THAT'S NOTHING TO ME.
BUT YOUR MOM'S GOTTA BE WORRIED ABOUT YOU.
PFT!
THE ONLY ONE SHE CARES ABOUT IS MY LITTLE BROTHER, JIRO.
ANYWAY.
E'RE GONNA GET ONE FOR SURE TONIGHT, MURASE.
A HUMAN SOUL.

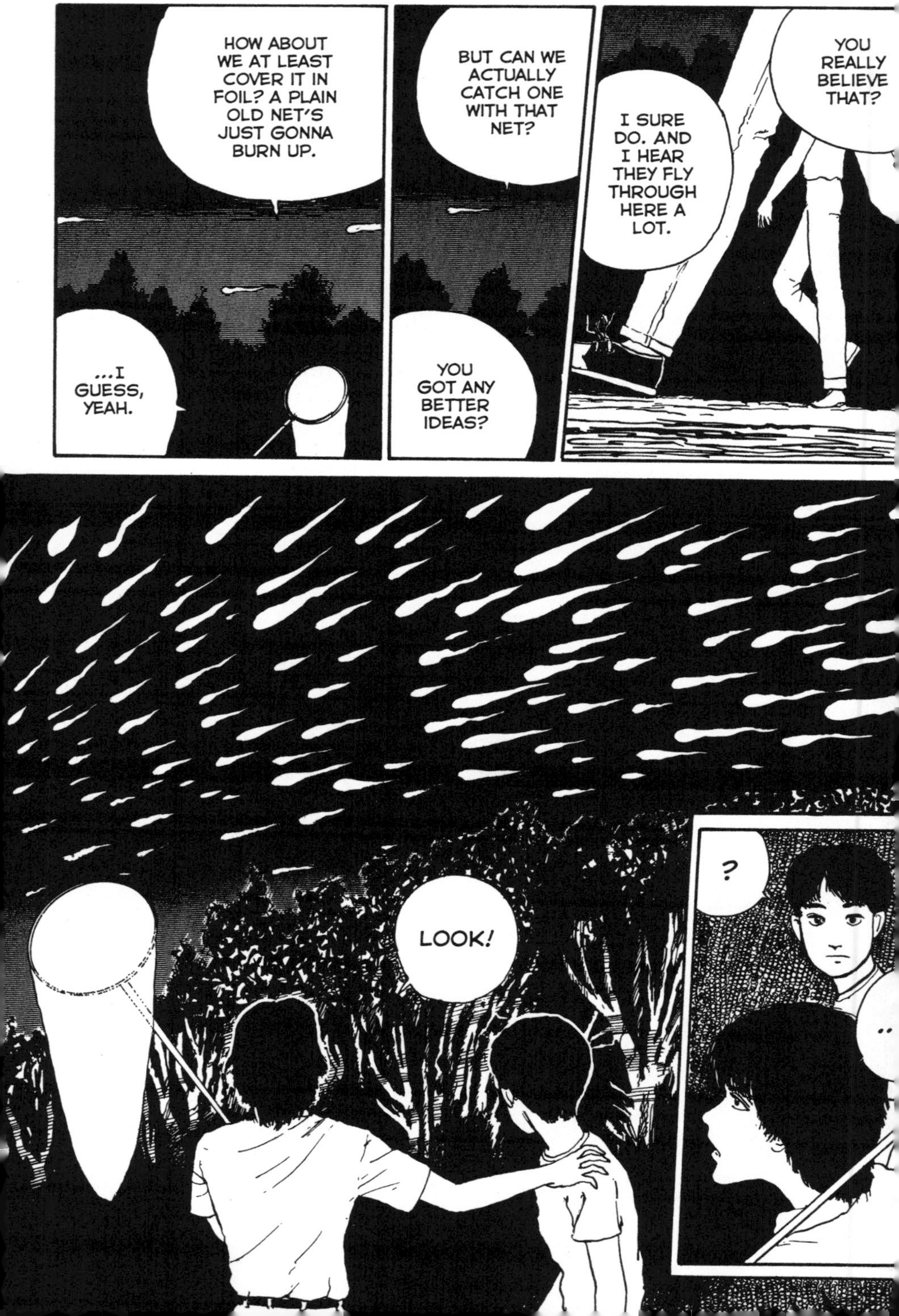
YOU REALLY BELIEVE THAT?
I SURE DO. AND I HEAR THEY FLY THROUGH HERE A LOT.
BUT CAN WE ACTUALLY CATCH ONE WITH THAT NET?
YOU GOT ANY BETTER IDEAS?
HOW ABOUT WE AT LEAST COVER IT IN FOIL? A PLAIN OLD NET'S JUST GONNA BURN UP.
...I GUESS, YEAH.
?
...
LOOK!

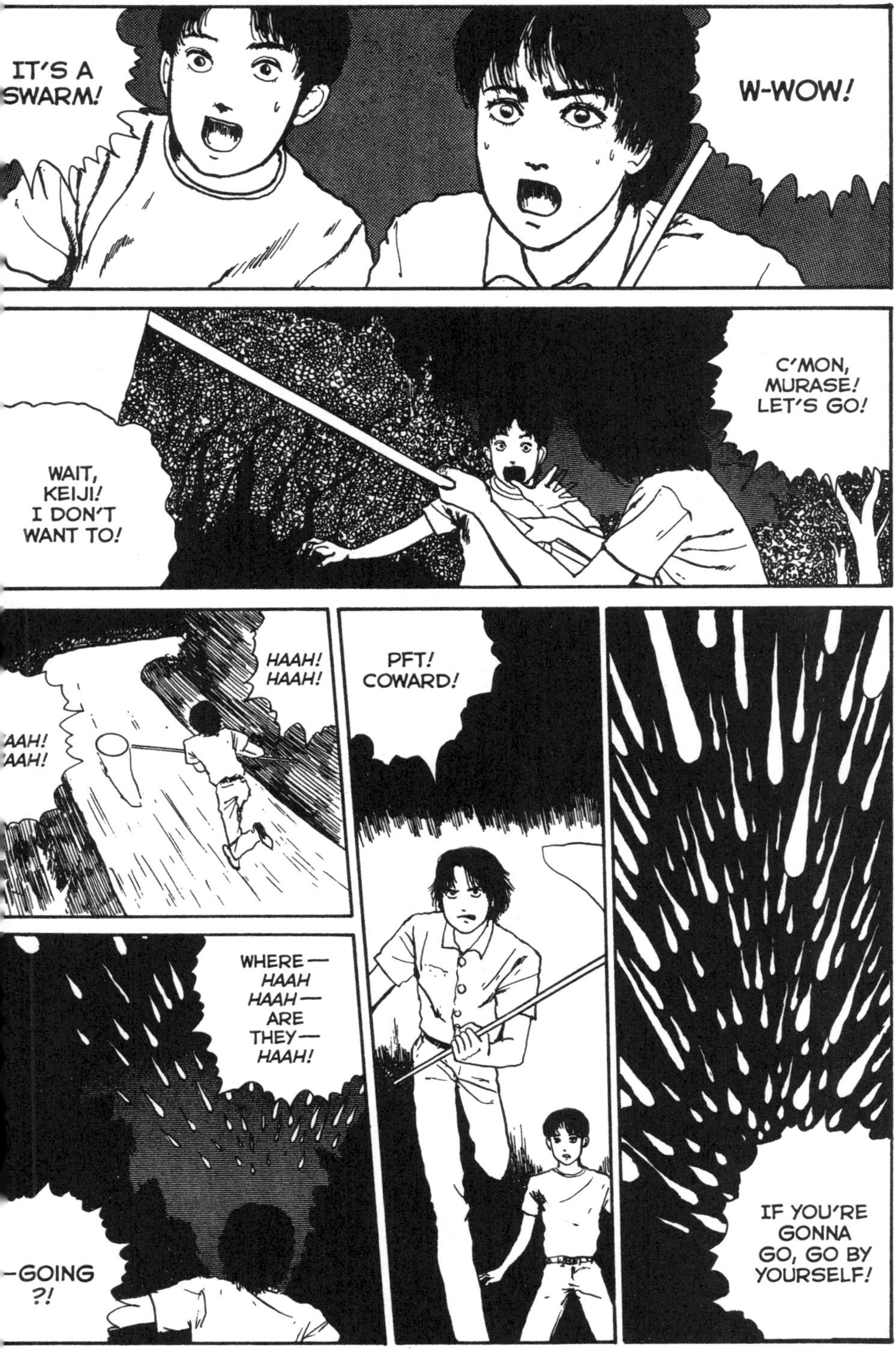
W-WOW!
IT'S A SWARM!
C'MON, MURASE! LET'S GO!
WAIT, KEIJI! I DON'T WANT TO!
IF YOU'RE GONNA GO, GO BY YOURSELF!
PFT! COWARD!
HAAH! HAAH!
AAH! AAH!
WHERE— HAAH HAAH— ARE THEY— HAAH!
—GOING ?!

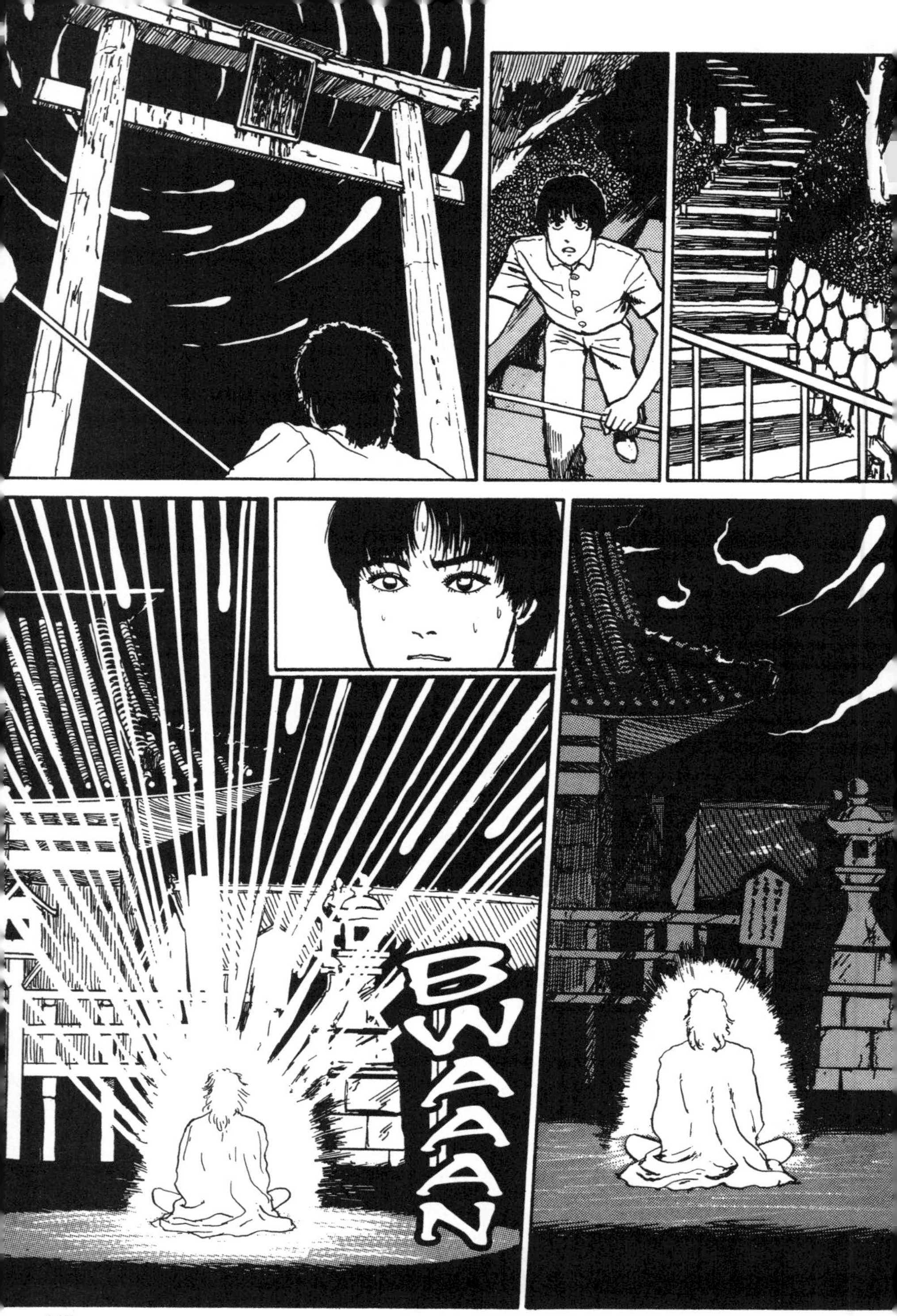
BWAAAN

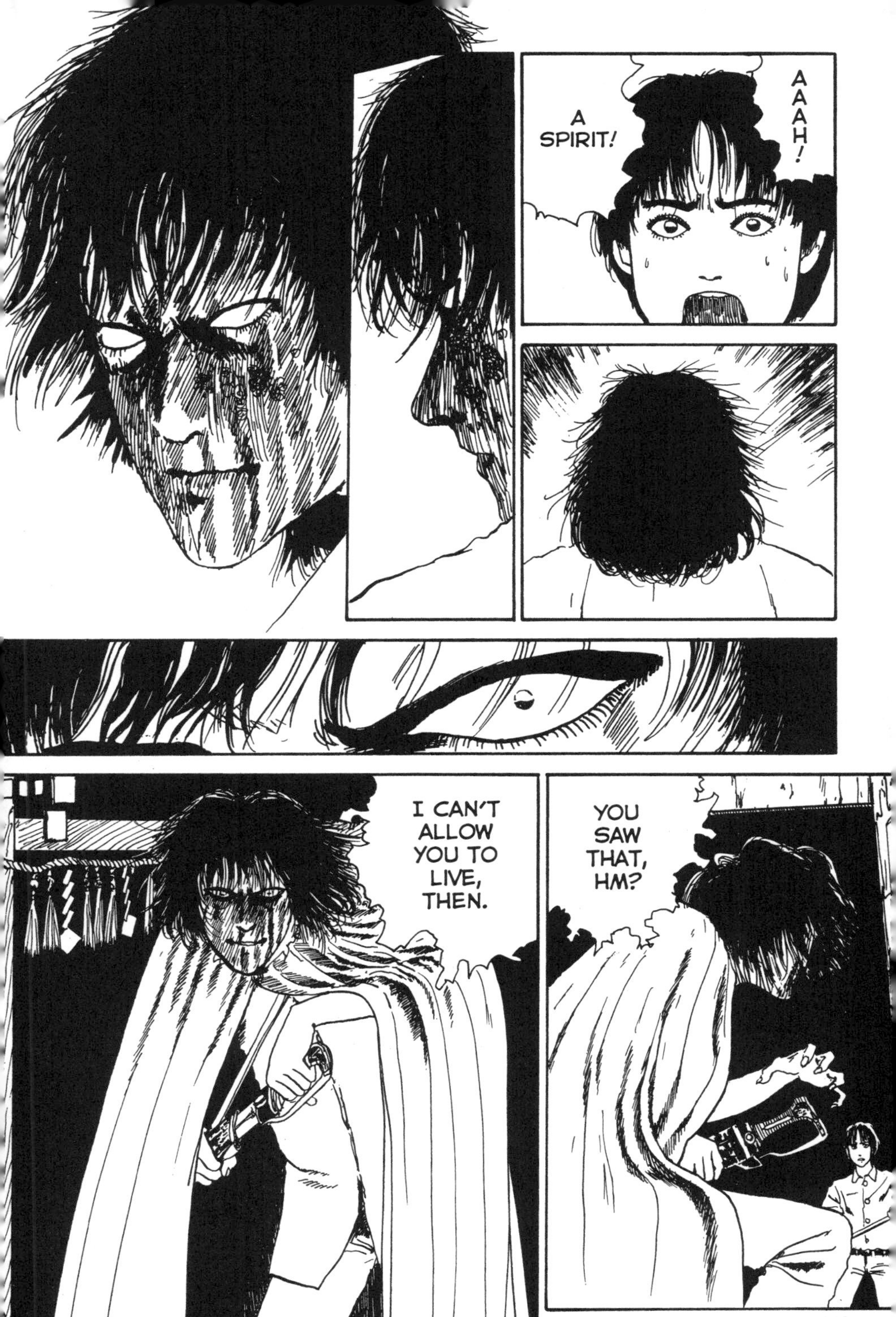
AAAH!
A SPIRIT!
YOU SAW THAT, HM?
I CAN'T ALLOW YOU TO LIVE, THEN.

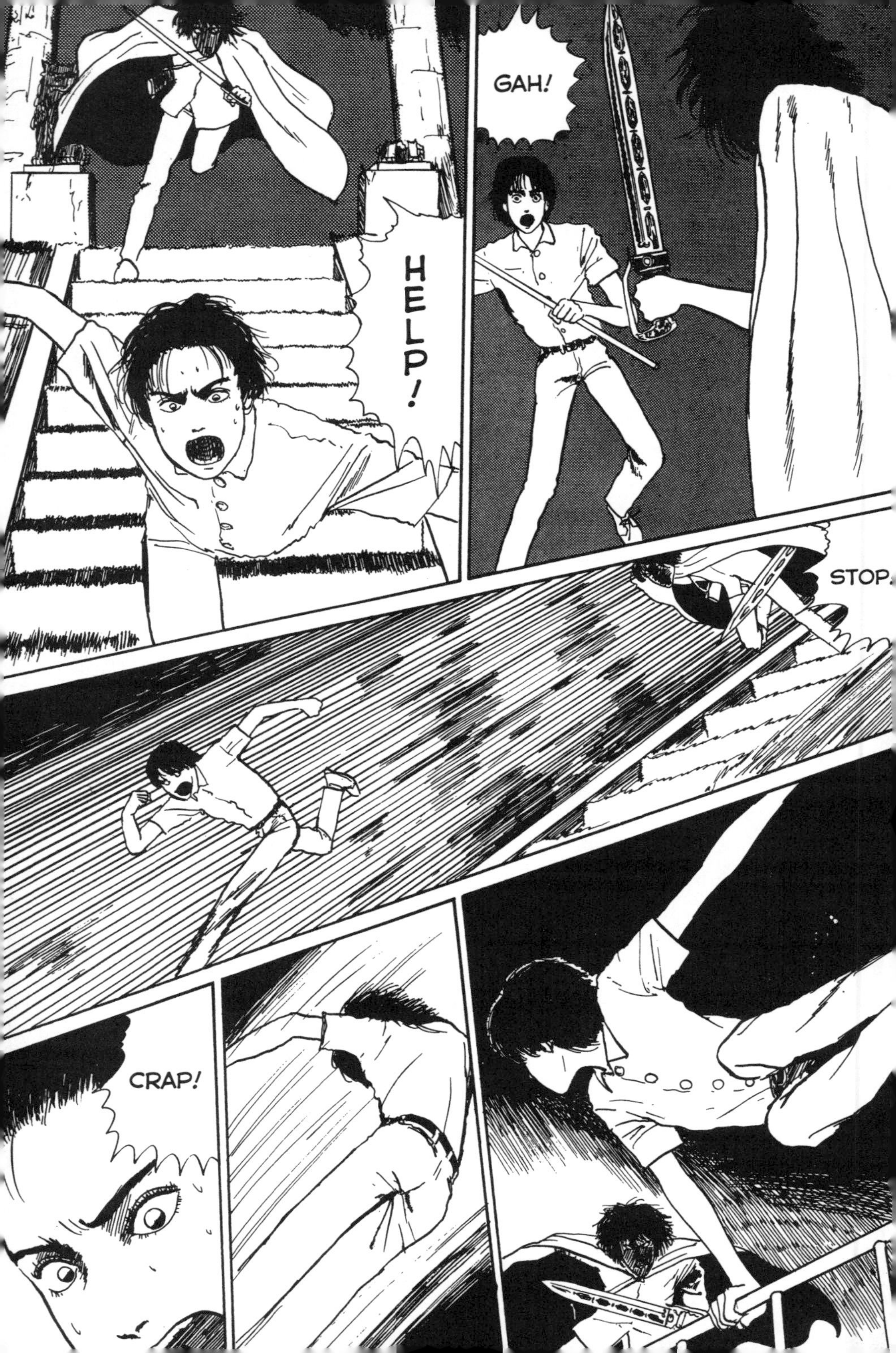
GAH!
HELP!
STOP.
CRAP!

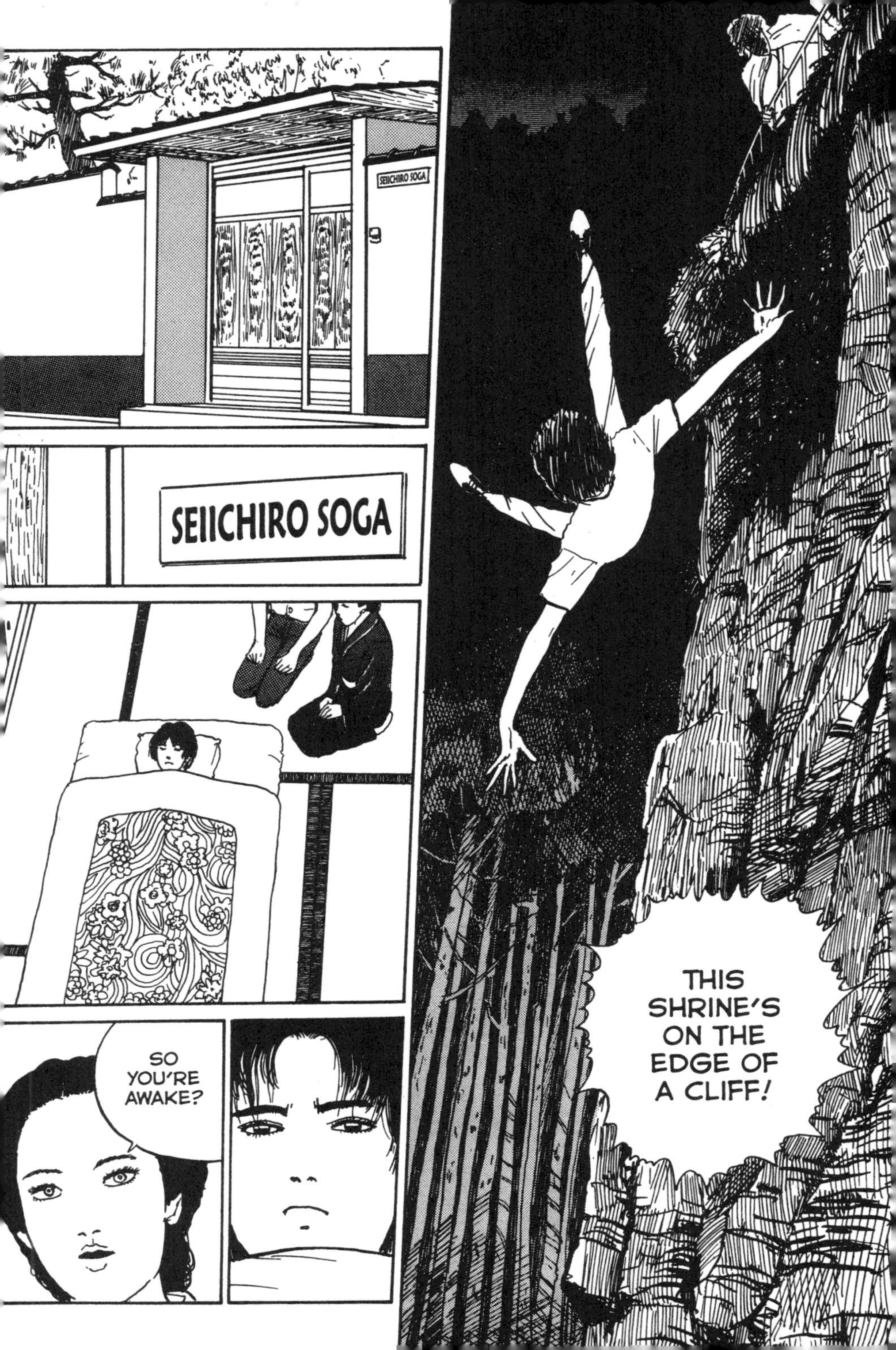
THIS SHRINE'S ON THE EDGE OF A CLIFF!
SEIICHIRO SOGA
SEIICHIRO SOGA
SO YOU'RE AWAKE?

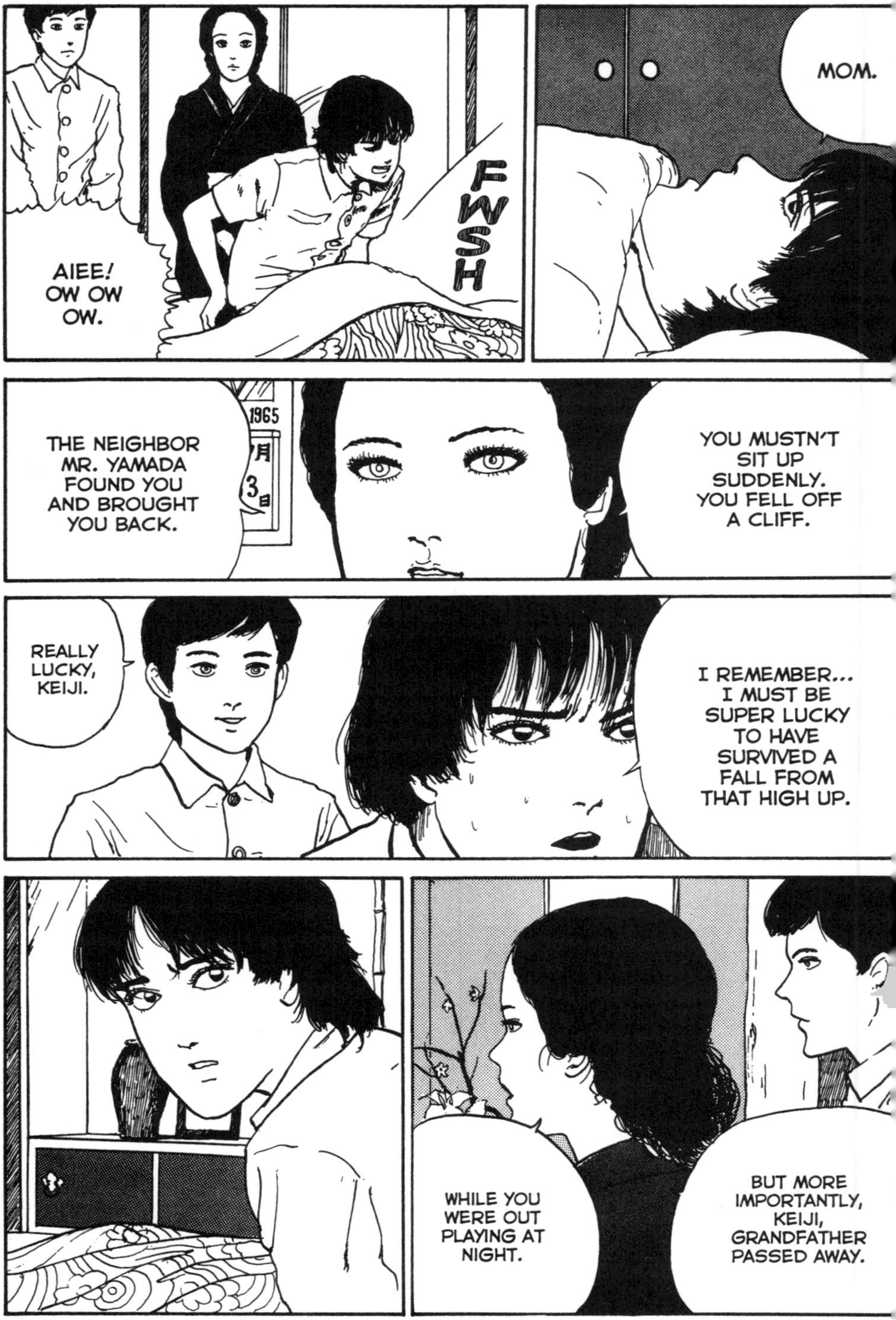
MOM.
FWSH
AIEE! OW OW OW.
YOU MUSTN'T SIT UP SUDDENLY. YOU FELL OFF A CLIFF.
1965
THE NEIGHBOR MR. YAMADA FOUND YOU AND BROUGHT YOU BACK.
I REMEMBER... I MUST BE SUPER LUCKY TO HAVE SURVIVED A FALL FROM THAT HIGH UP.
REALLY LUCKY, KEIJI.
BUT MORE IMPORTANTLY, KEIJI, GRANDFATHER PASSED AWAY.
WHILE YOU WERE OUT PLAYING AT NIGHT.

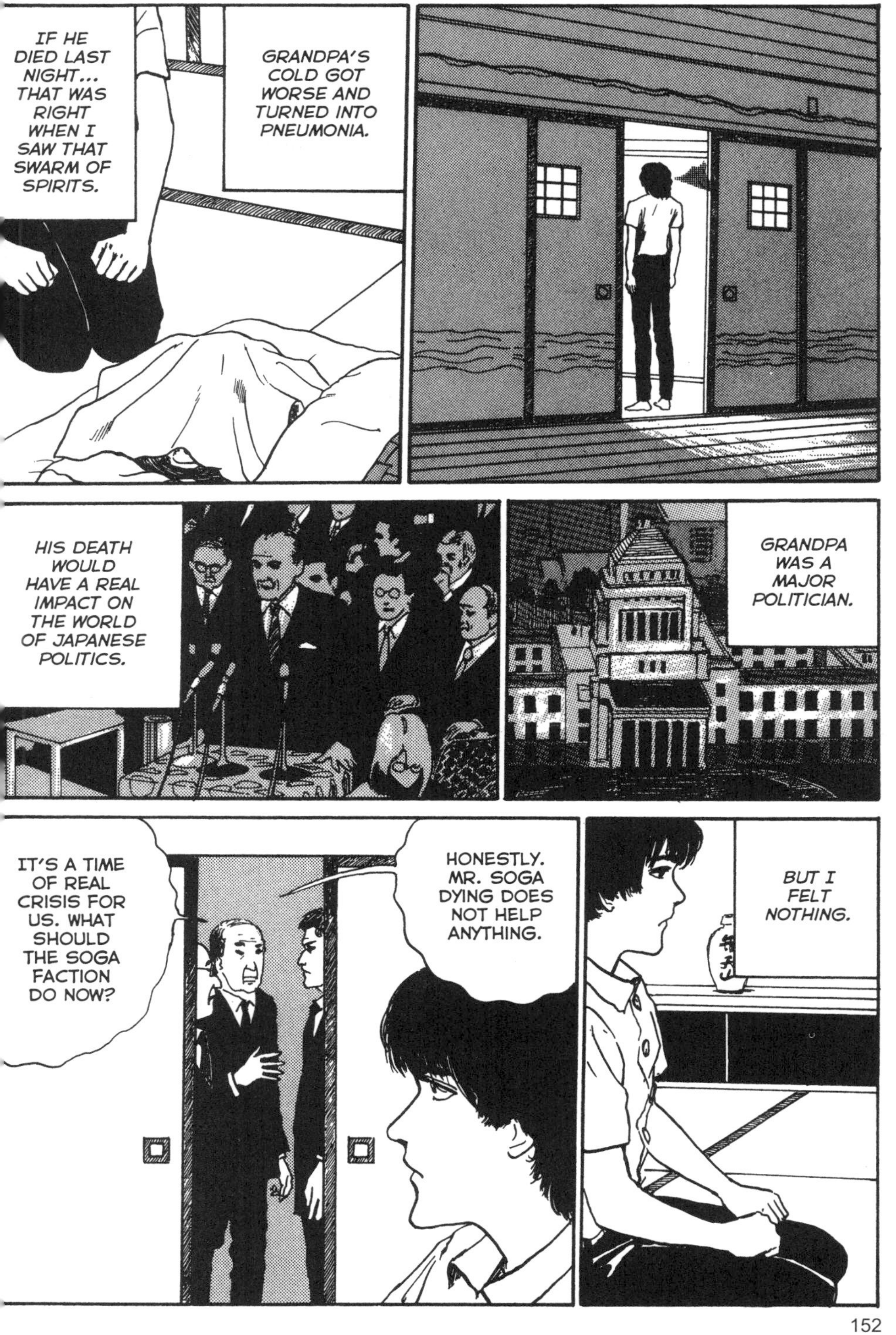
GRANDPA'S COLD GOT WORSE AND TURNED INTO PNEUMONIA.
IF HE DIED LAST NIGHT... THAT WAS RIGHT WHEN I SAW THAT SWARM OF SPIRITS.
GRANDPA WAS A MAJOR POLITICIAN.
HIS DEATH WOULD HAVE A REAL IMPACT ON THE WORLD OF JAPANESE POLITICS.
BUT I FELT NOTHING.
HONESTLY. MR. SOGA DYING DOES NOT HELP ANYTHING.
IT'S A TIME OF REAL CRISIS FOR US. WHAT SHOULD THE SOGA FACTION DO NOW?

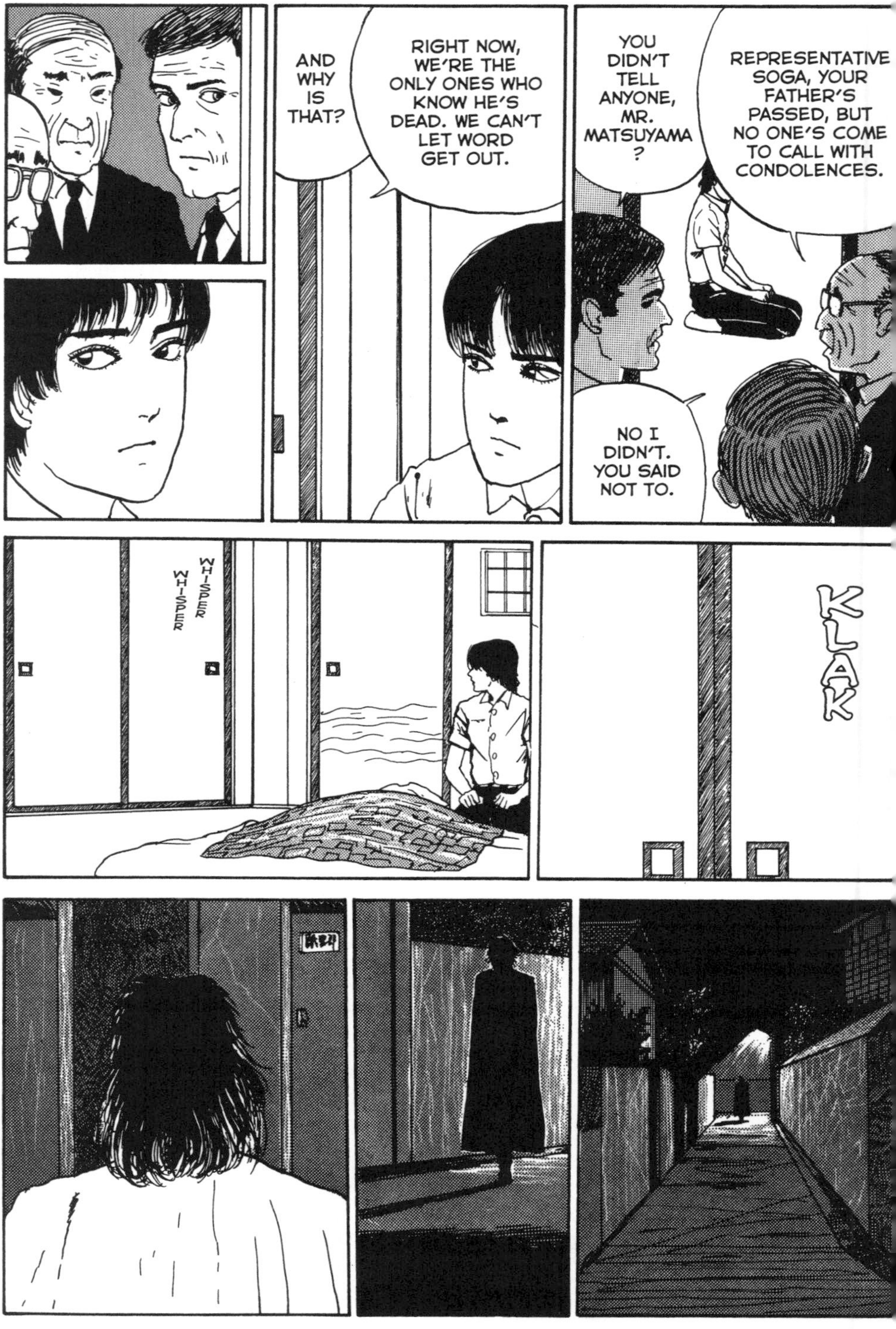
REPRESENTATIVE SOGA, YOUR FATHER'S PASSED, BUT NO ONE'S COME TO CALL WITH CONDOLENCES.
YOU DIDN'T TELL ANYONE, MR. MATSUYAMA?
NO I DIDN'T. YOU SAID NOT TO.
RIGHT NOW, WE'RE THE ONLY ONES WHO KNOW HE'S DEAD. WE CAN'T LET WORD GET OUT.
AND WHY IS THAT?
KLAK
WHISPER WHISPER

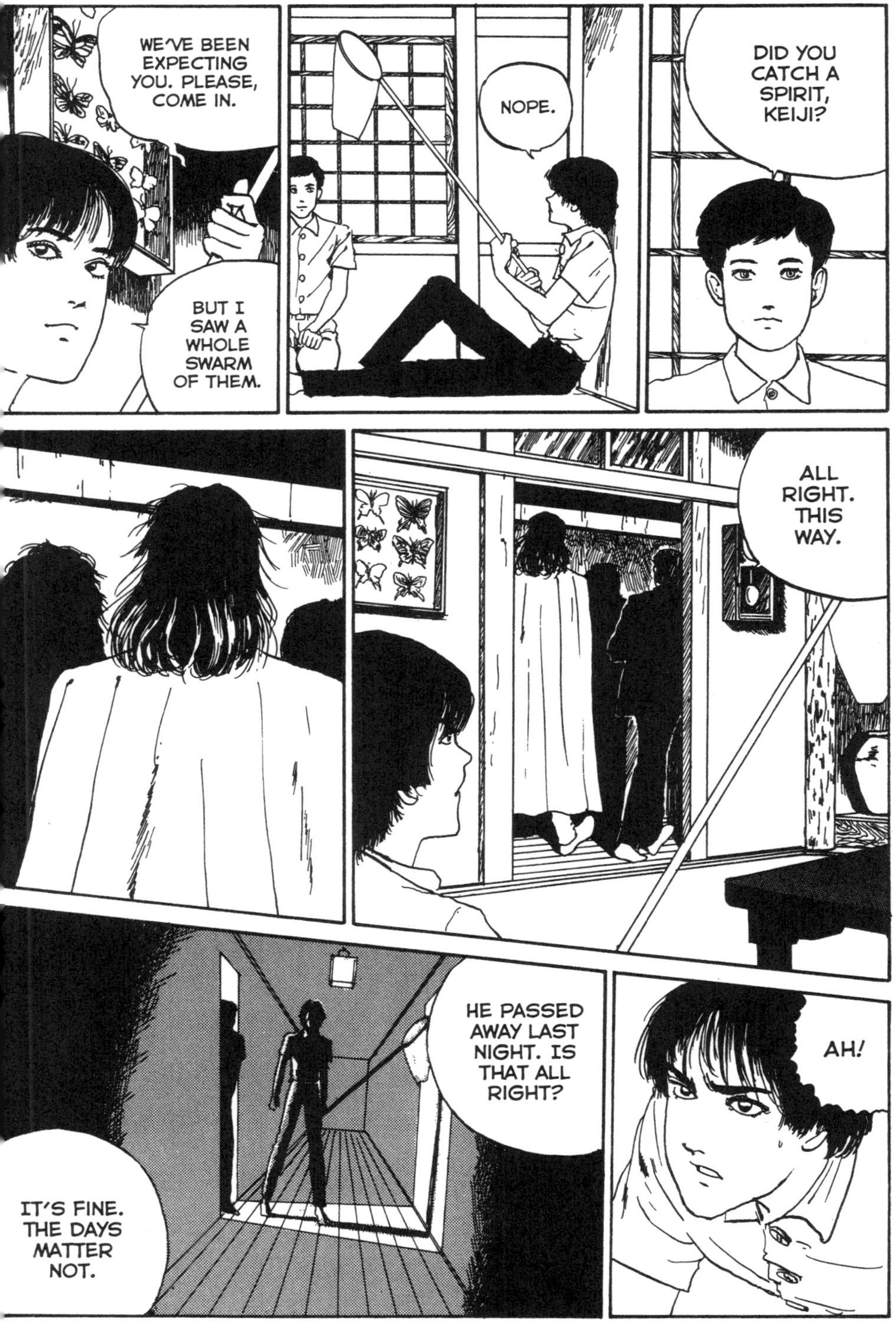
DID YOU CATCH A SPIRIT, KEIJI?
NOPE.
WE'VE BEEN EXPECTING YOU. PLEASE, COME IN.
BUT I SAW A WHOLE SWARM OF THEM.
ALL RIGHT. THIS WAY.
AH!
HE PASSED AWAY LAST NIGHT. IS THAT ALL RIGHT?
IT'S FINE. THE DAYS MATTER NOT.

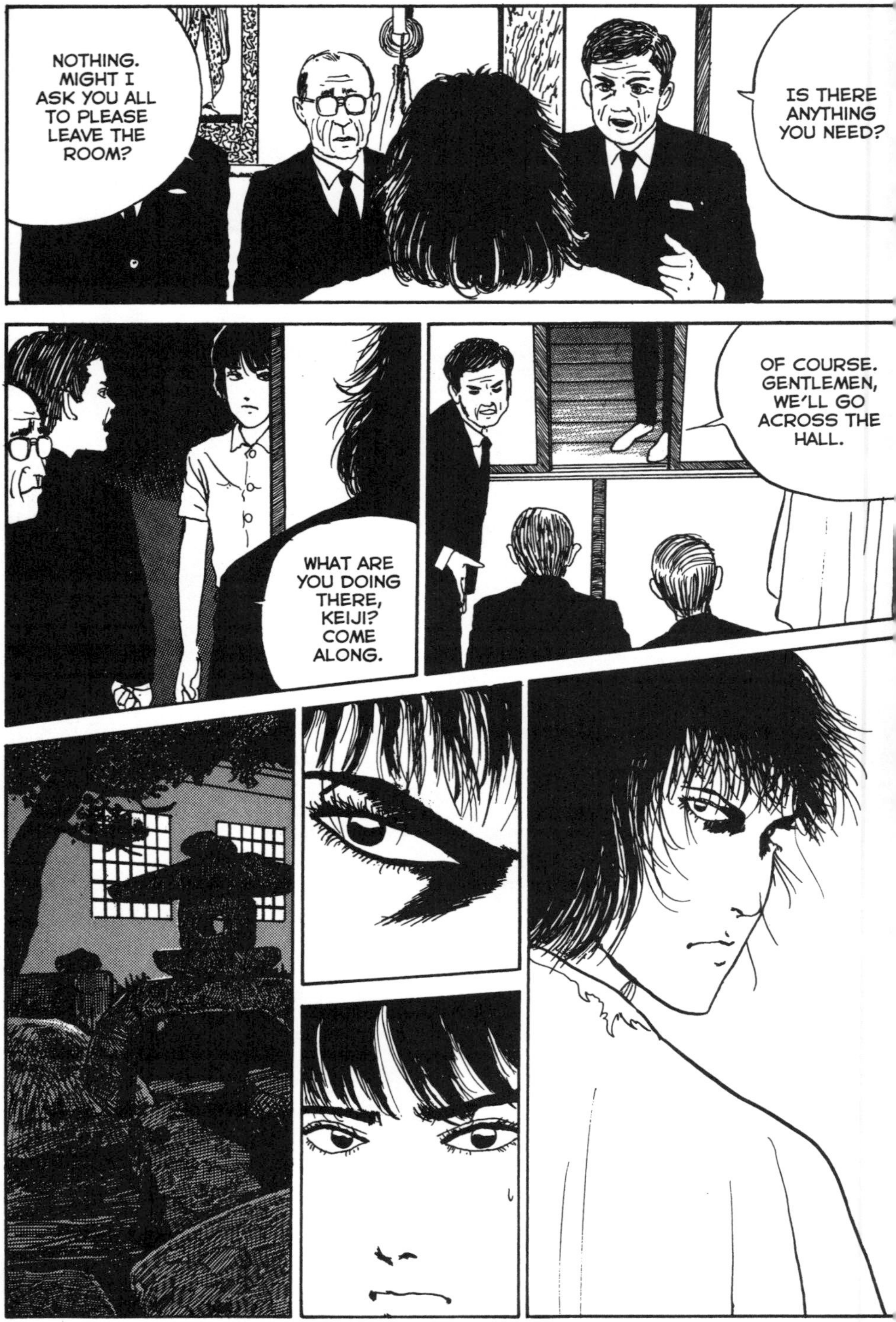
IS THERE ANYTHING YOU NEED?
NOTHING. MIGHT I ASK YOU ALL TO PLEASE LEAVE THE ROOM?
OF COURSE. GENTLEMEN, WE'LL GO ACROSS THE HALL.
WHAT ARE YOU DOING THERE, KEIJI? COME ALONG.

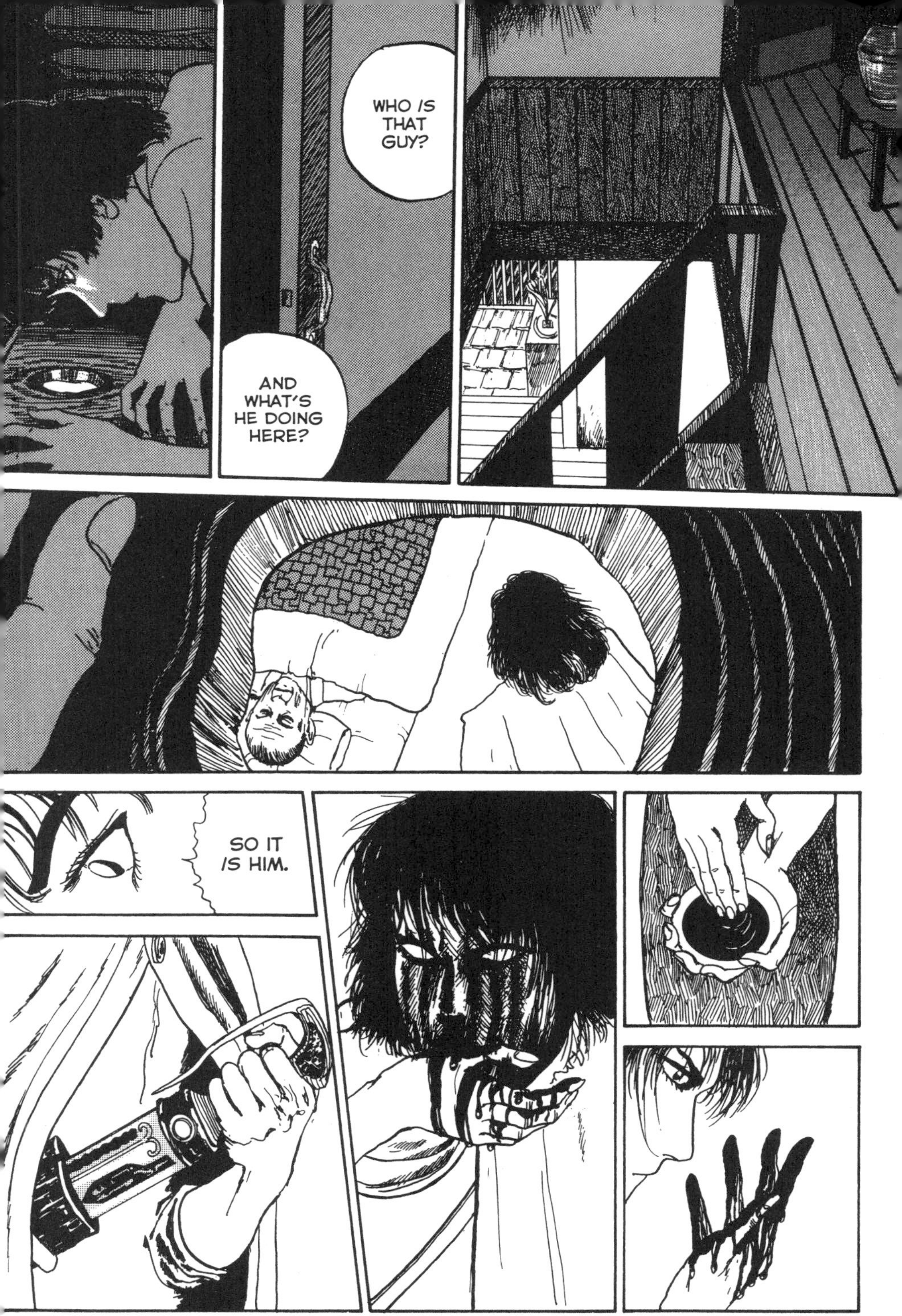
WHO IS THAT GUY?
AND WHAT'S HE DOING HERE?
SO IT IS HIM.

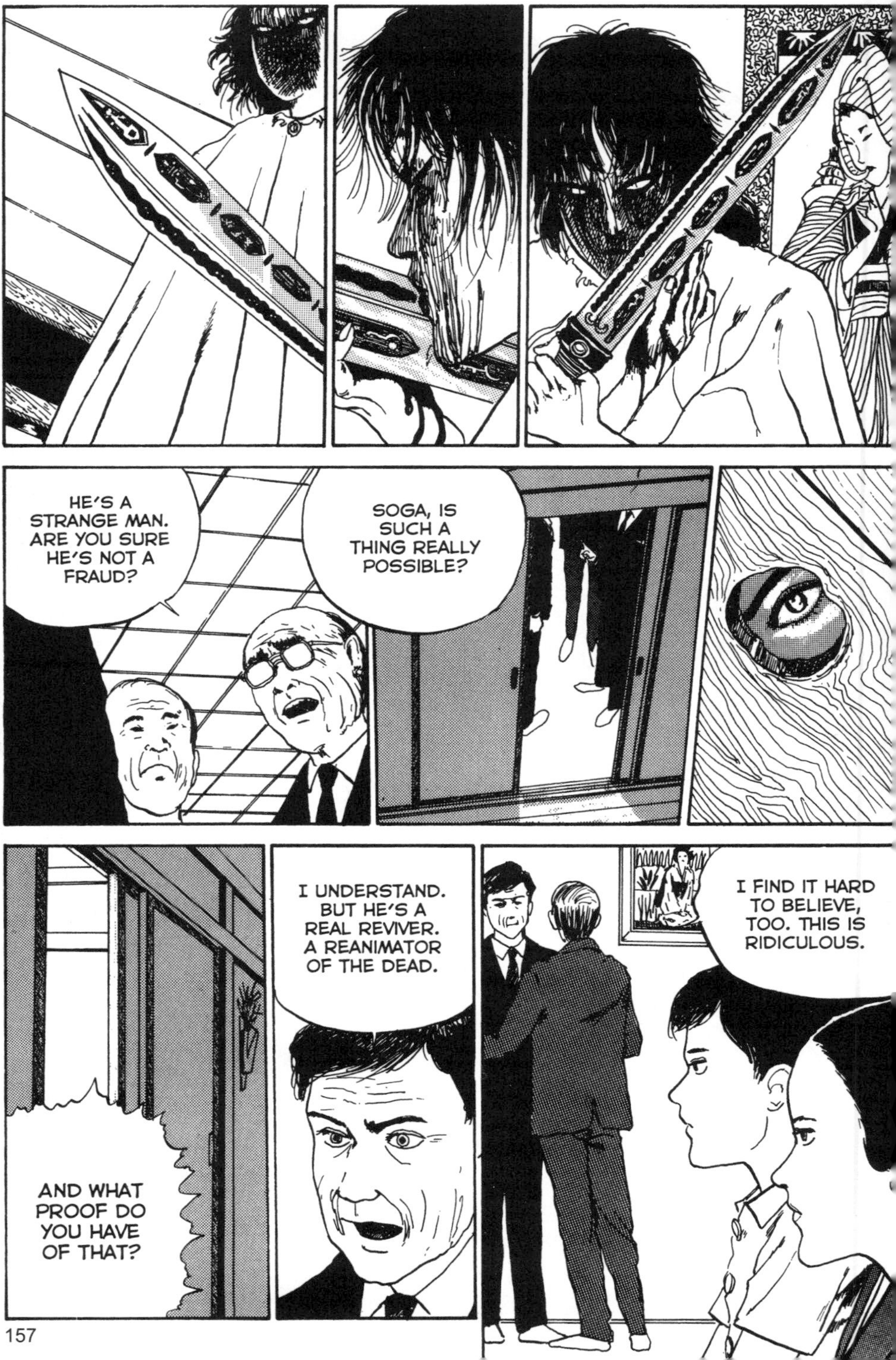
SOGA, IS SUCH A THING REALLY POSSIBLE?
HE'S A STRANGE MAN. ARE YOU SURE HE'S NOT A FRAUD?
I FIND IT HARD TO BELIEVE, TOO. THIS IS RIDICULOUS.
I UNDERSTAND. BUT HE'S A REAL REVIVER. A REANIMATOR OF THE DEAD.
AND WHAT PROOF DO YOU HAVE OF THAT?

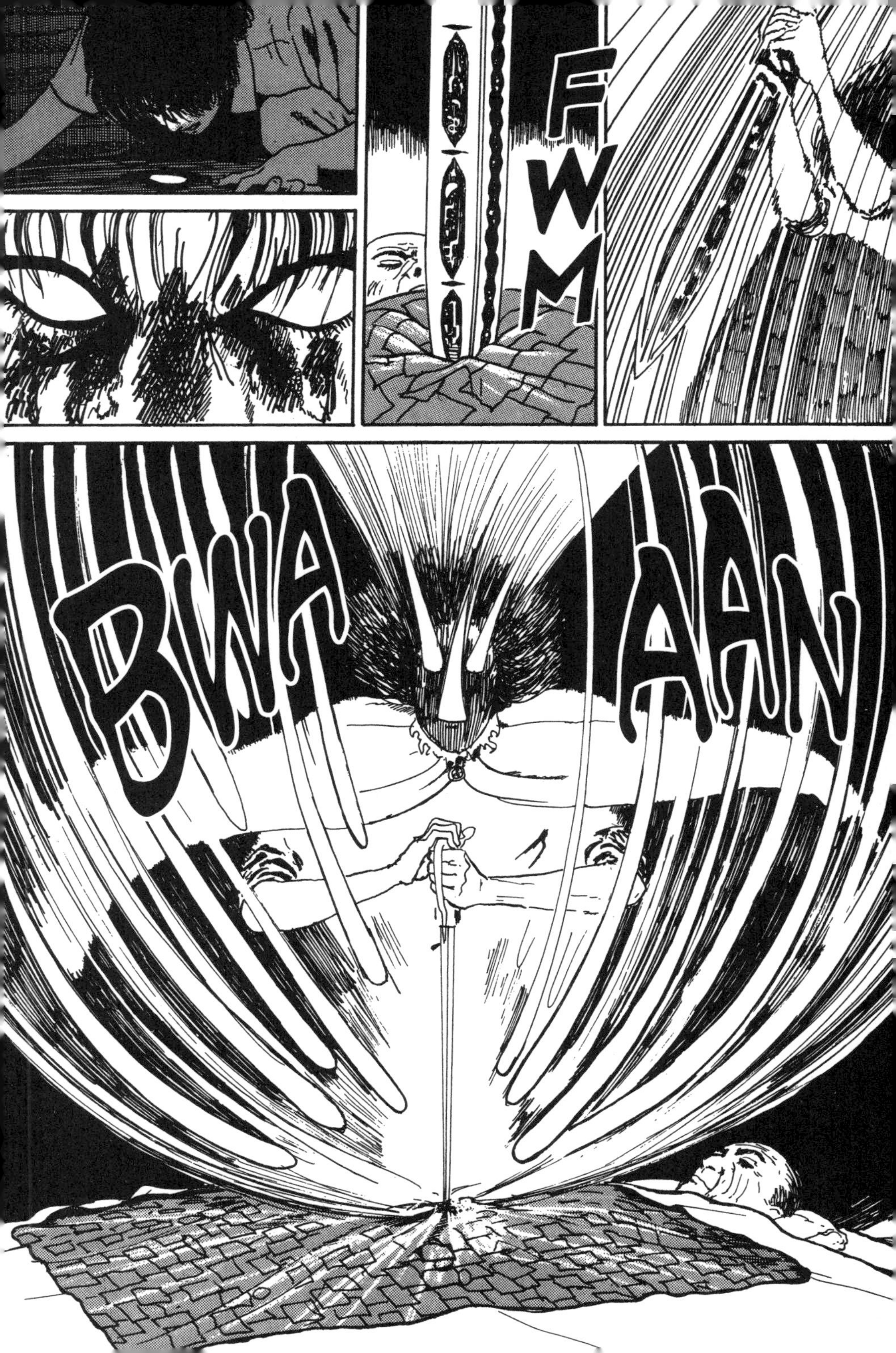
FWM
BWAAAN

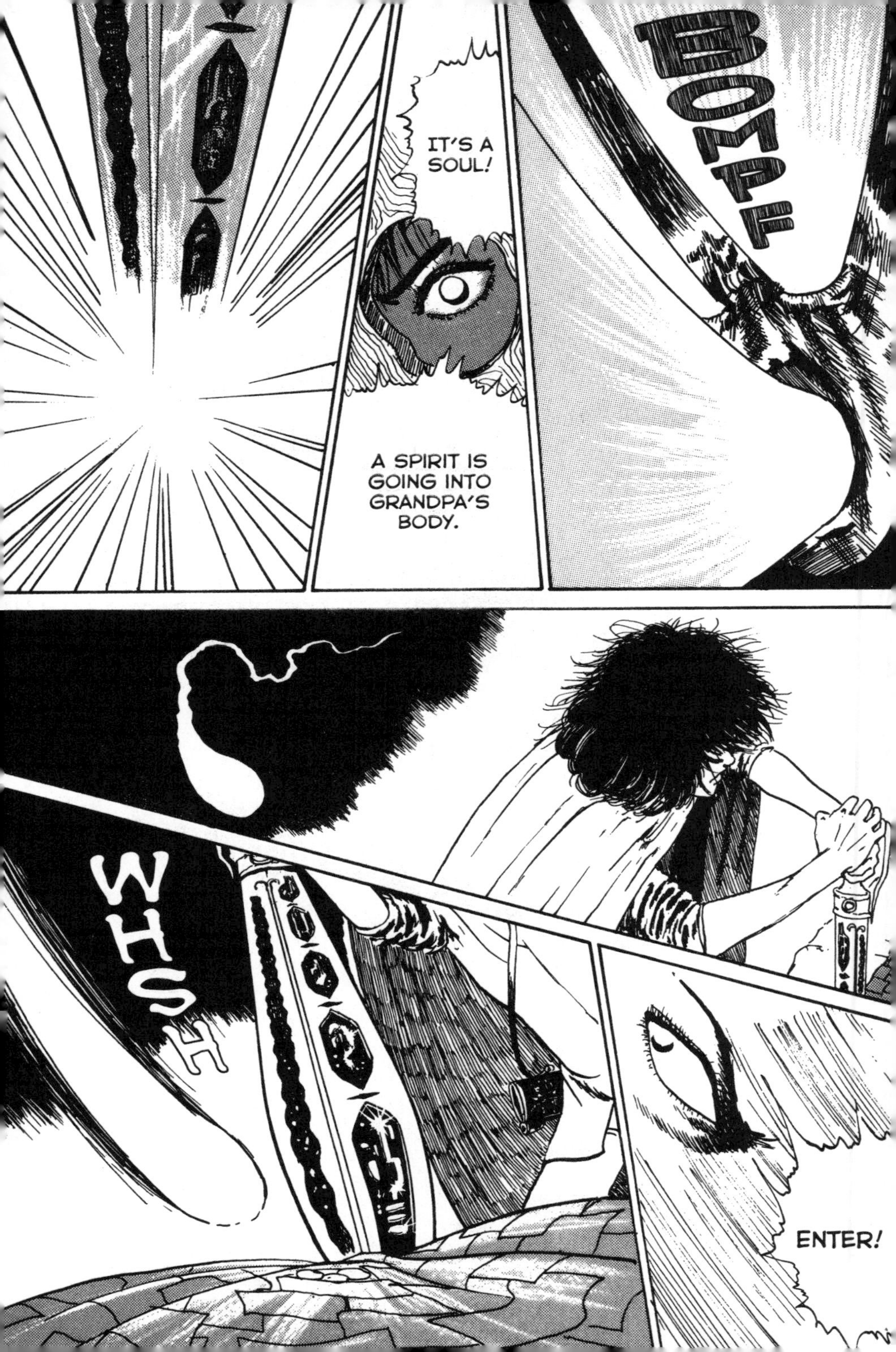
BOMPF
IT'S A SOUL!
A SPIRIT IS GOING INTO GRANDPA'S BODY.
ENTER!
WHSH

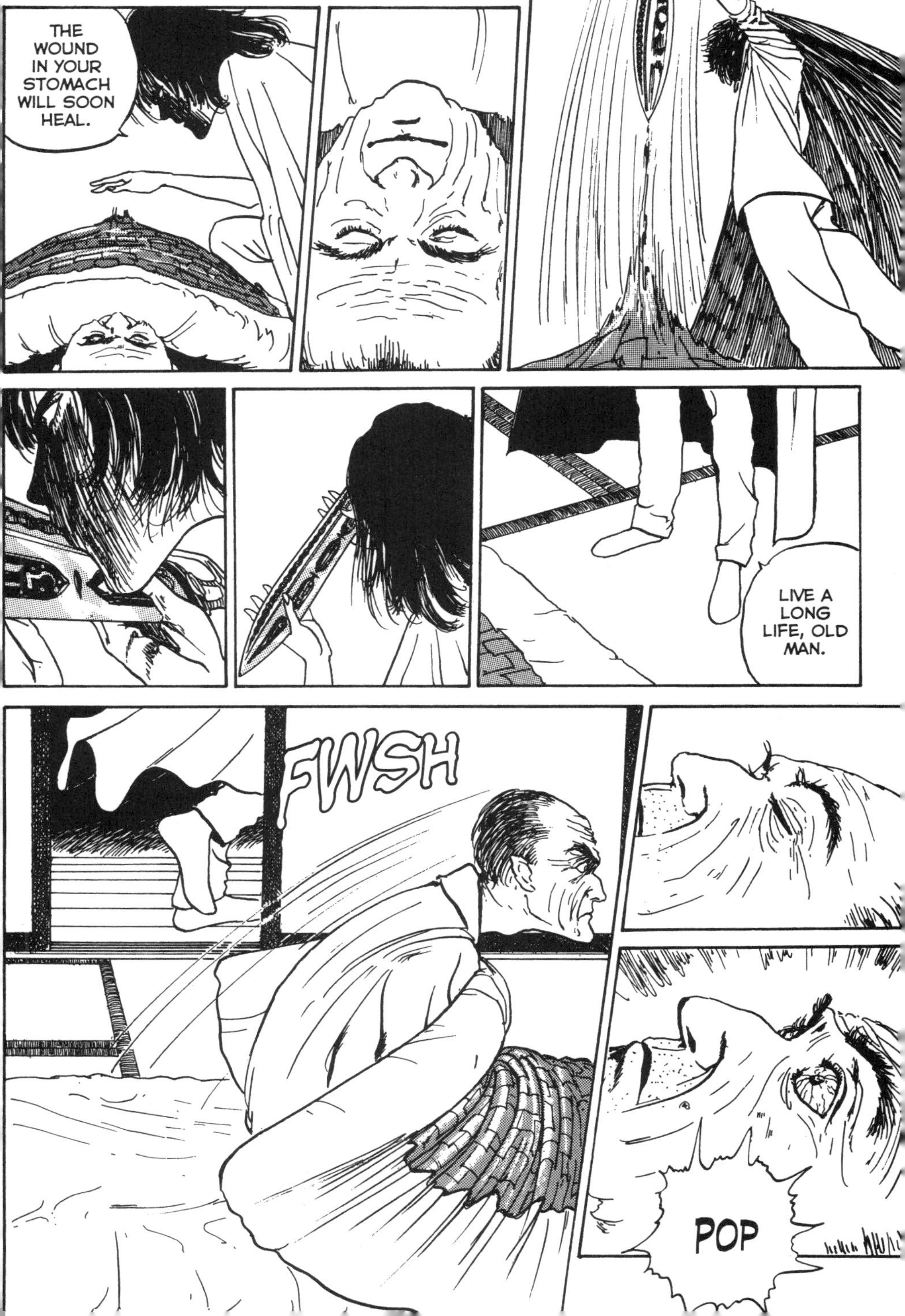
THE WOUND IN YOUR STOMACH WILL SOON HEAL.
LIVE A LONG LIFE, OLD MAN.
POP
FWSH

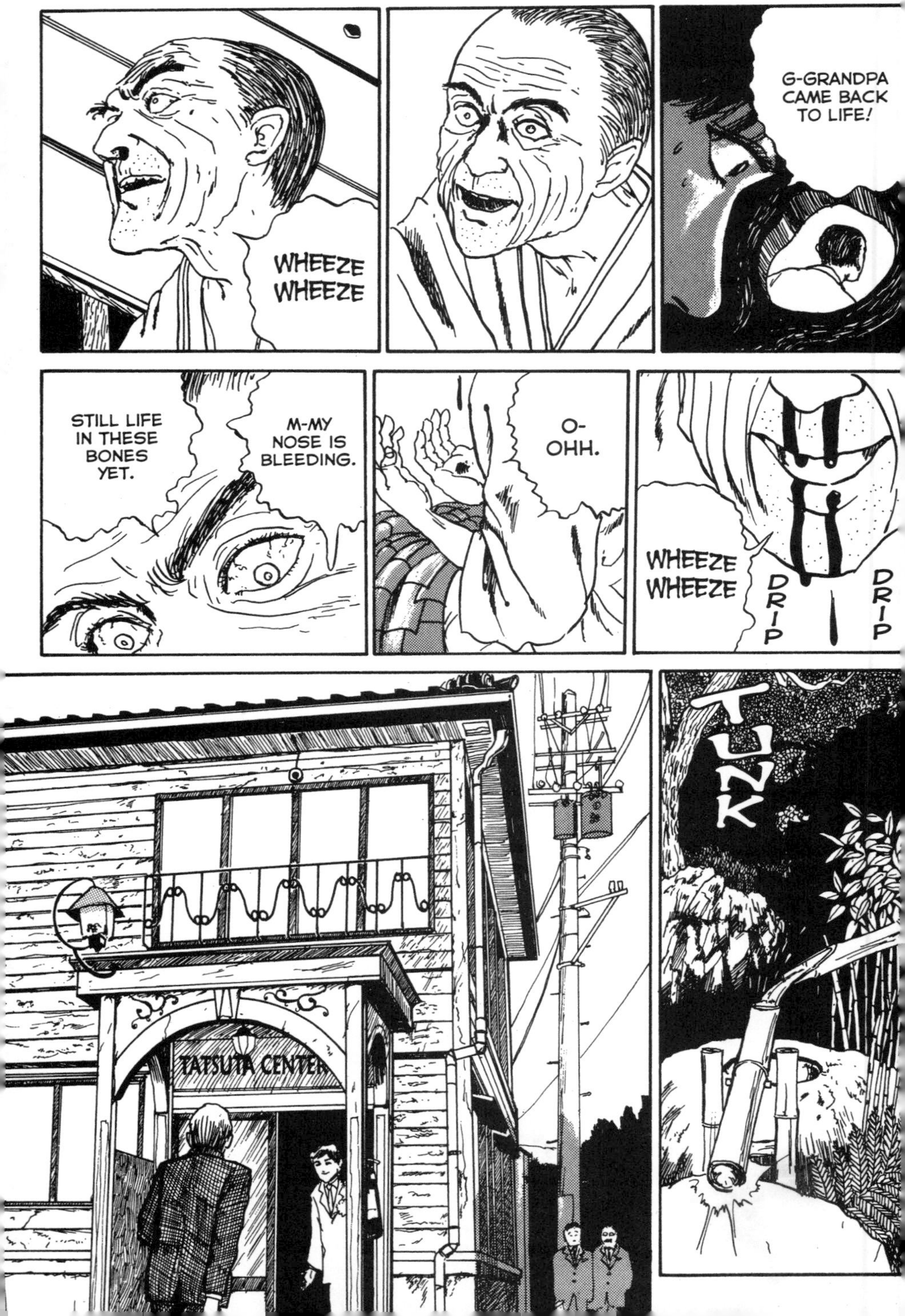
G-GRANDPA CAME BACK TO LIFE!
WHEEZE WHEEZE
DRIP DRIP
WHEEZE WHEEZE
O-OHH.
M-MY NOSE IS BLEEDING.
STILL LIFE IN THESE BONES YET.
TUNK
TATSUTA CENTER

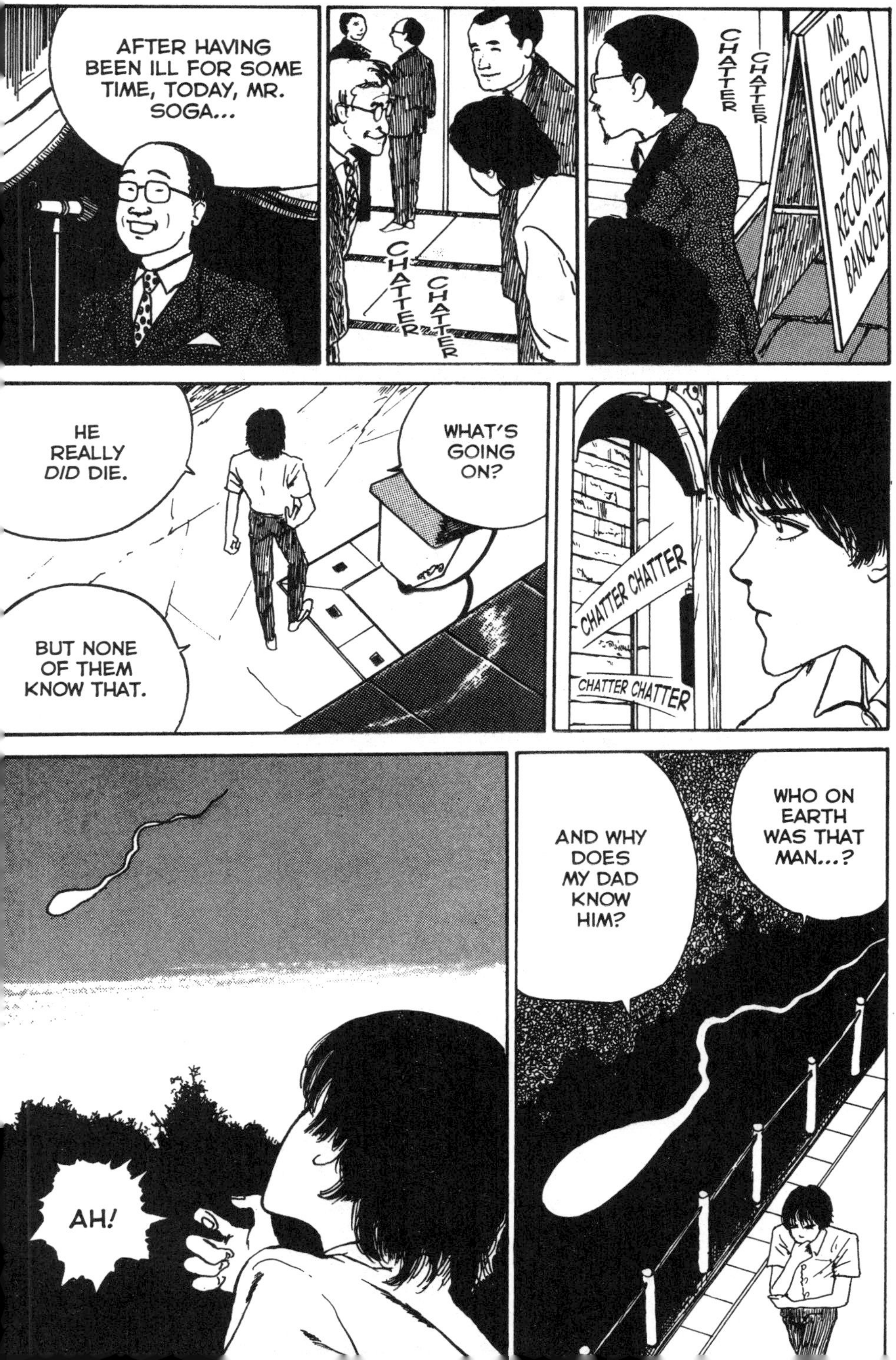
MR. SEIICHIRO SOGA RECOVERY BANQUET
CHATTER
CHATTER
CHATTER
CHATTER
AFTER HAVING BEEN ILL FOR SOME TIME, TODAY, MR. SOGA...
CHATTER CHATTER
CHATTER CHATTER
WHAT'S GOING ON?
HE REALLY *DID* DIE.
BUT NONE OF THEM KNOW THAT.
WHO ON EARTH WAS THAT MAN...?
AND WHY DOES MY DAD KNOW HIM?
AH!

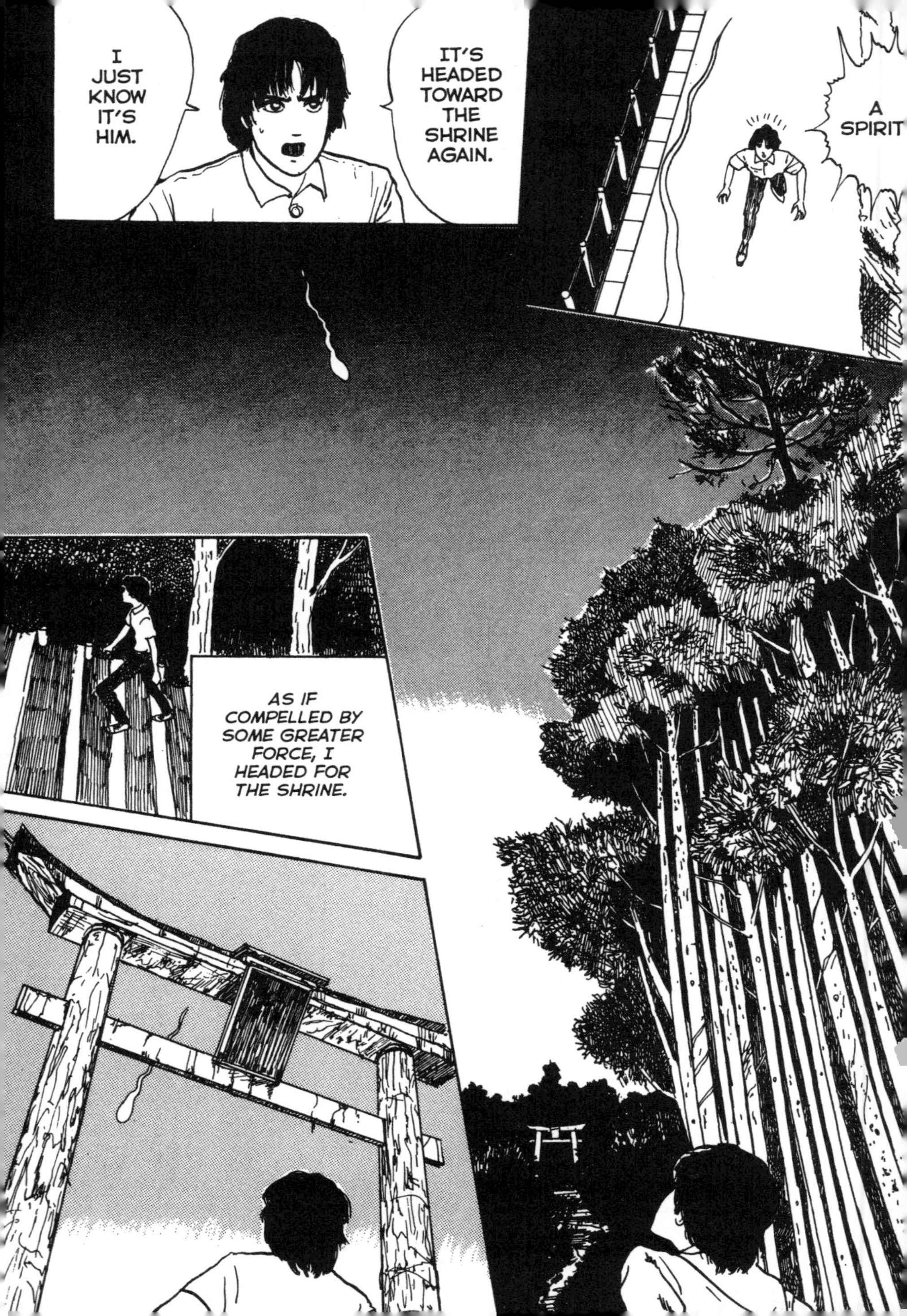
A SPIRIT
IT'S HEADED TOWARD THE SHRINE AGAIN.
I JUST KNOW IT'S HIM.
AS IF COMPELLED BY SOME GREATER FORCE, I HEADED FOR THE SHRINE.

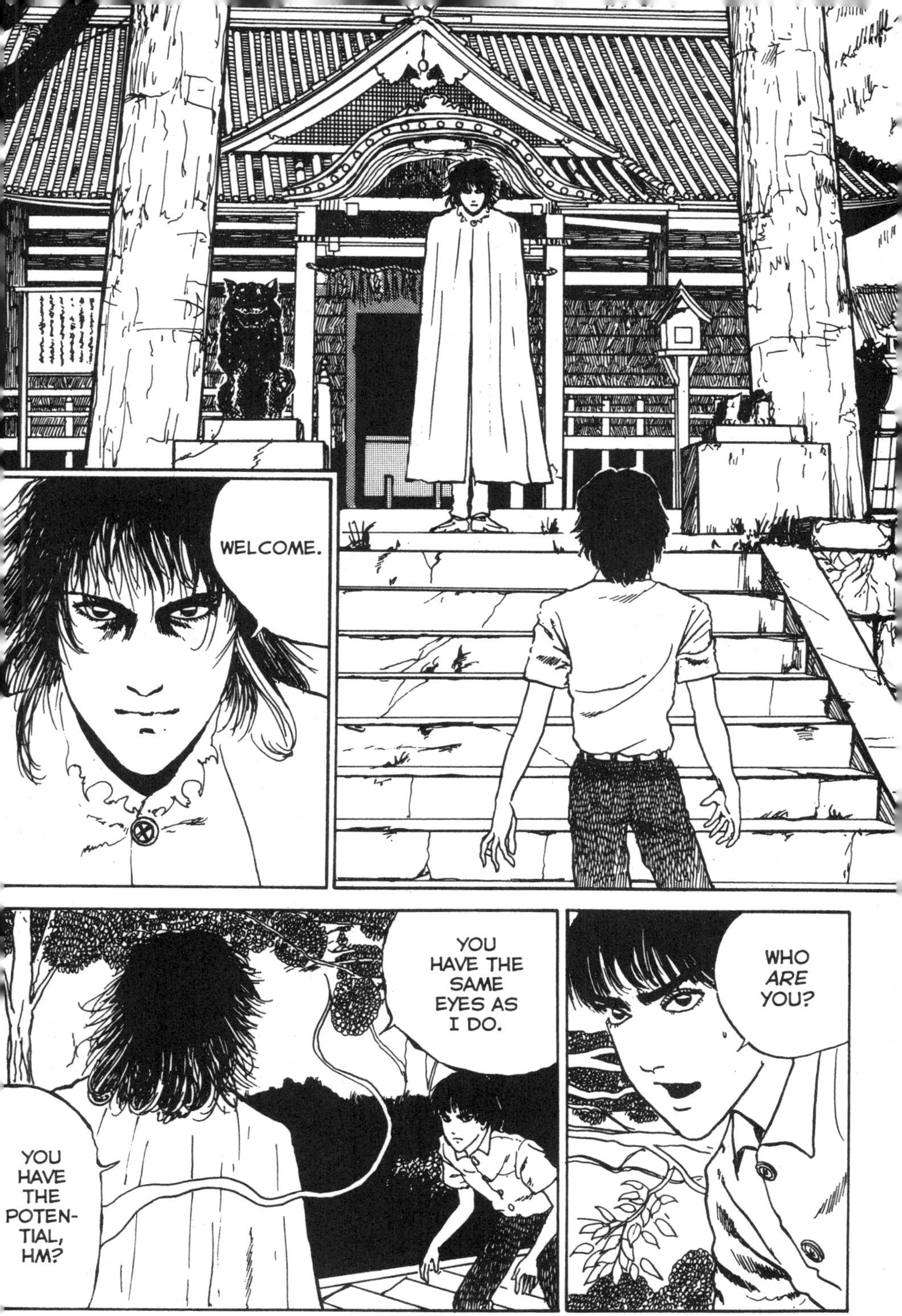
WELCOME.
WHO *ARE* YOU?
YOU HAVE THE SAME EYES AS I DO.
YOU HAVE THE POTEN-TIAL, HM?

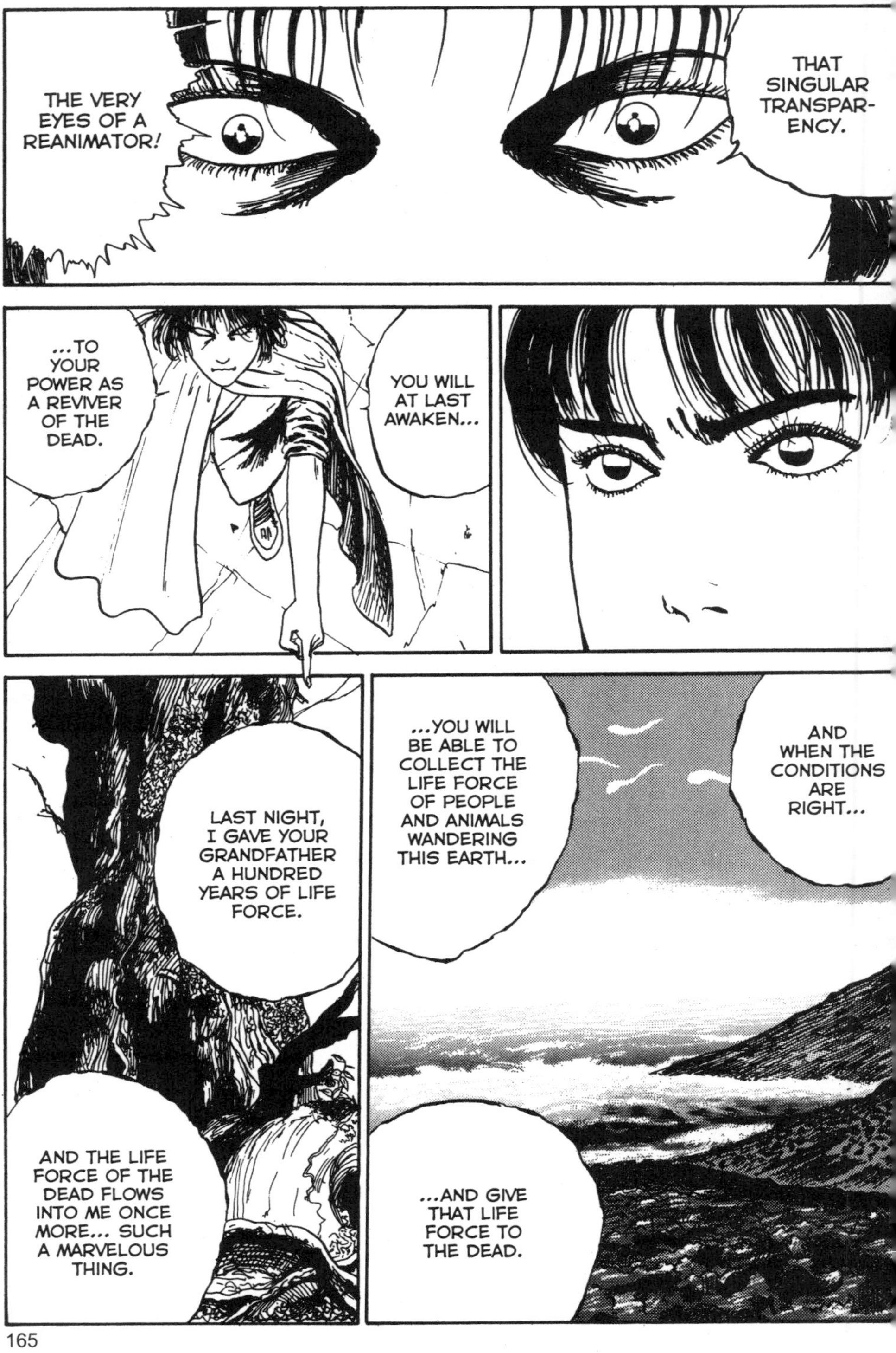
THAT SINGULAR TRANSPAR-ENCY.
THE VERY EYES OF A REANIMATOR!
YOU WILL AT LAST AWAKEN...
...TO YOUR POWER AS A REVIVER OF THE DEAD.
AND WHEN THE CONDITIONS ARE RIGHT...
...YOU WILL BE ABLE TO COLLECT THE LIFE FORCE OF PEOPLE AND ANIMALS WANDERING THIS EARTH...
...AND GIVE THAT LIFE FORCE TO THE DEAD.
LAST NIGHT, I GAVE YOUR GRANDFATHER A HUNDRED YEARS OF LIFE FORCE.
AND THE LIFE FORCE OF THE DEAD FLOWS INTO ME ONCE MORE... SUCH A MARVELOUS THING.

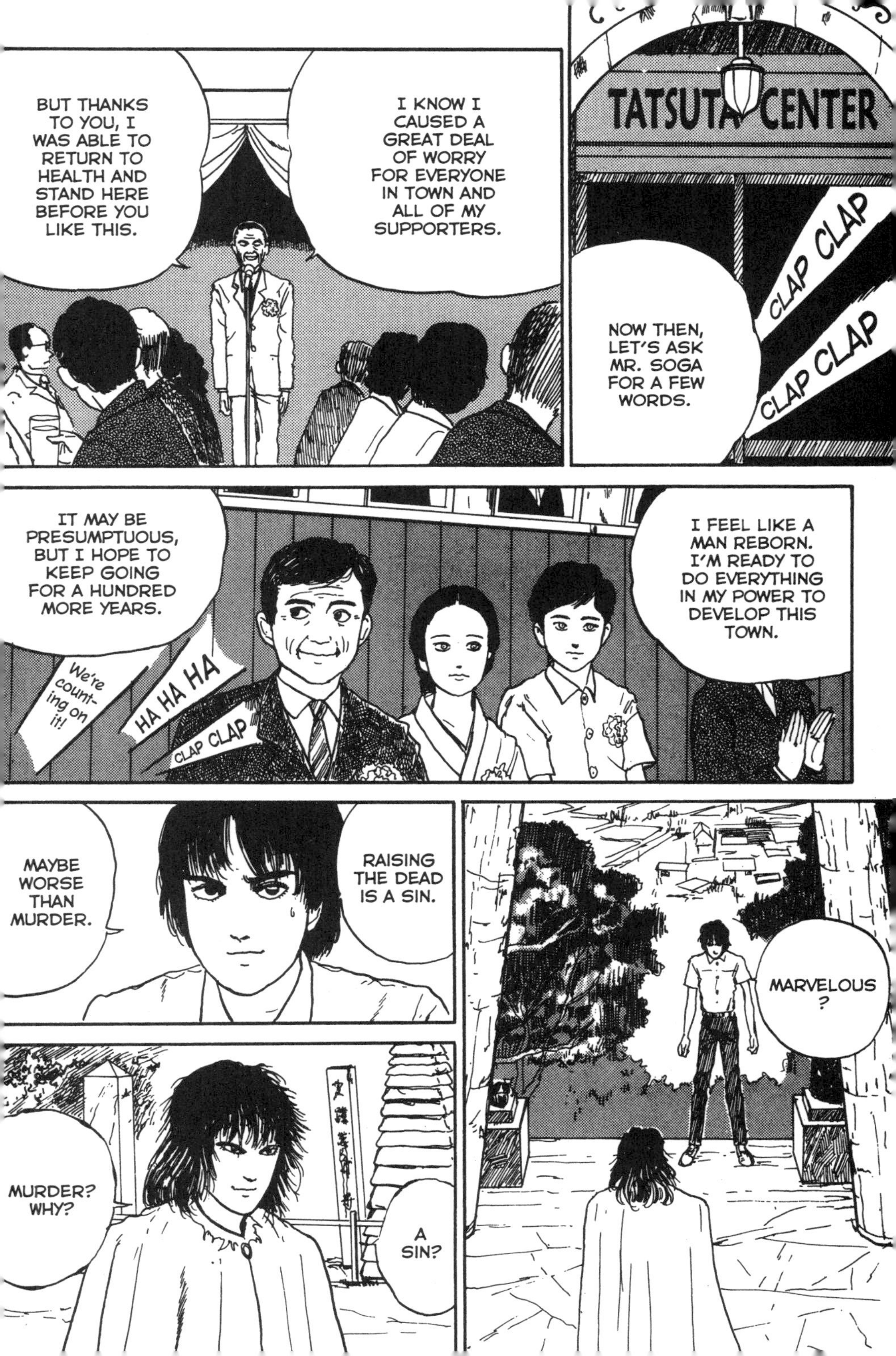
TATSUTA CENTER
NOW THEN, LET'S ASK MR. SOGA FOR A FEW WORDS.
CLAP CLAP
CLAP CLAP
I KNOW I CAUSED A GREAT DEAL OF WORRY FOR EVERYONE IN TOWN AND ALL OF MY SUPPORTERS.
BUT THANKS TO YOU, I WAS ABLE TO RETURN TO HEALTH AND STAND HERE BEFORE YOU LIKE THIS.
I FEEL LIKE A MAN REBORN. I'M READY TO DO EVERYTHING IN MY POWER TO DEVELOP THIS TOWN.
IT MAY BE PRESUMPTUOUS, BUT I HOPE TO KEEP GOING FOR A HUNDRED MORE YEARS.
HA HA HA
We're counting on it!
CLAP CLAP
MARVELOUS?
RAISING THE DEAD IS A SIN.
MAYBE WORSE THAN MURDER.
A SIN?
MURDER? WHY?

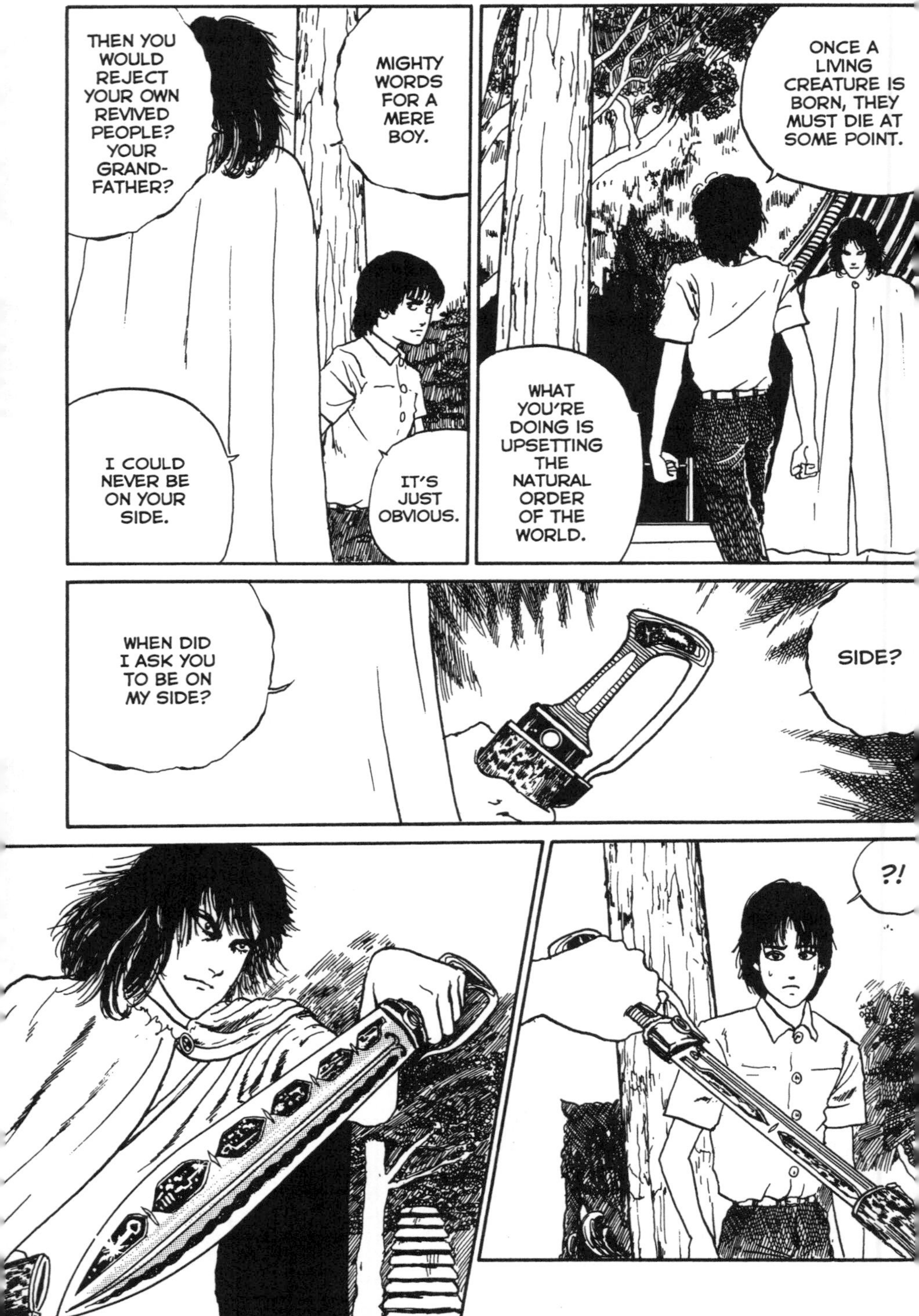
ONCE A LIVING CREATURE IS BORN, THEY MUST DIE AT SOME POINT.
WHAT YOU'RE DOING IS UPSETTING THE NATURAL ORDER OF THE WORLD.
MIGHTY WORDS FOR A MERE BOY.
THEN YOU WOULD REJECT YOUR OWN REVIVED PEOPLE? YOUR GRAND-FATHER?
IT'S JUST OBVIOUS.
I COULD NEVER BE ON YOUR SIDE.
SIDE?
WHEN DID I ASK YOU TO BE ON MY SIDE?
?!

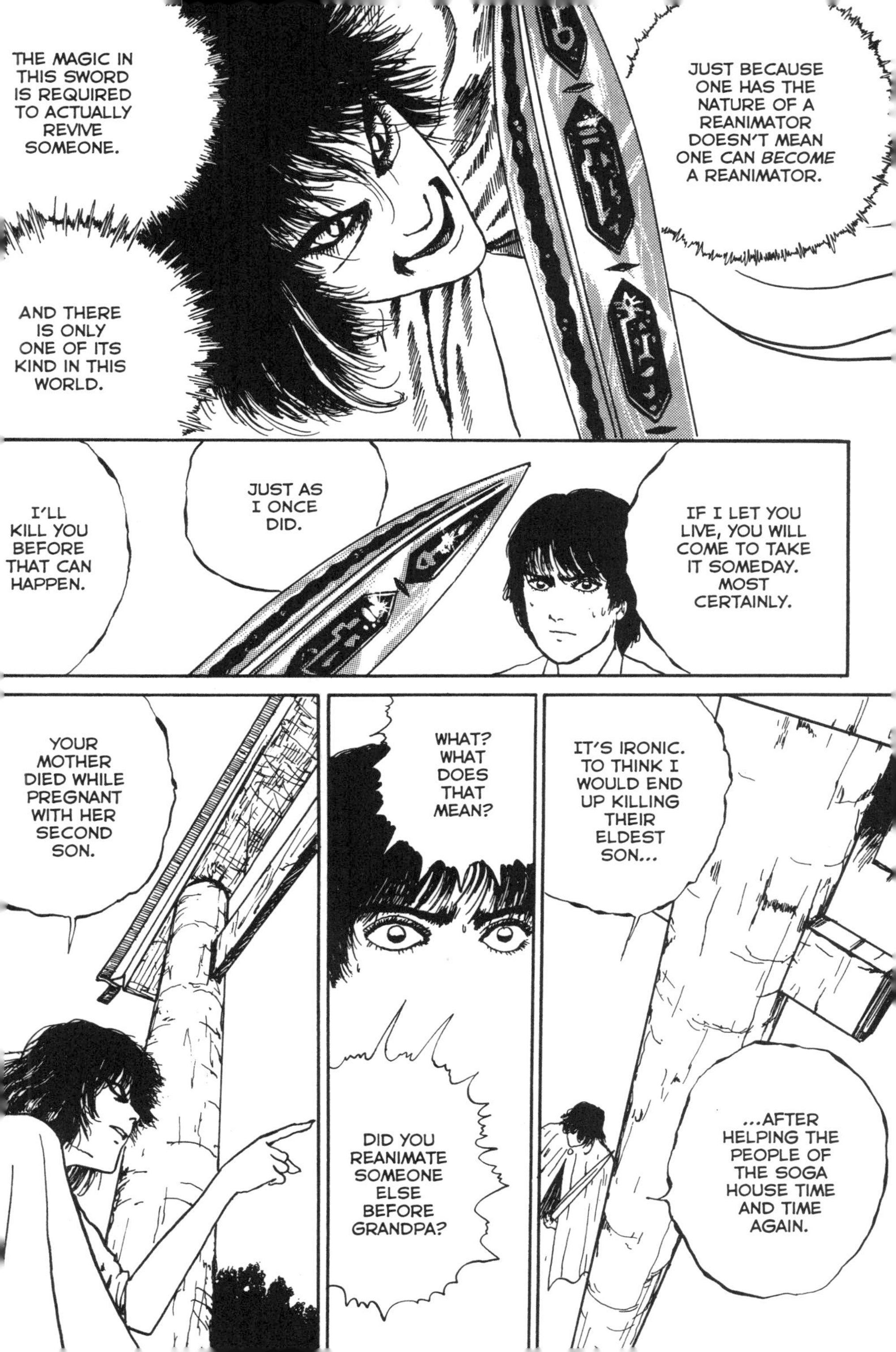

JUST BECAUSE ONE HAS THE NATURE OF A REANIMATOR DOESN'T MEAN ONE CAN *BECOME* A REANIMATOR.
THE MAGIC IN THIS SWORD IS REQUIRED TO ACTUALLY REVIVE SOMEONE.
AND THERE IS ONLY ONE OF ITS KIND IN THIS WORLD.
IF I LET YOU LIVE, YOU WILL COME TO TAKE IT SOMEDAY. MOST CERTAINLY.
JUST AS I ONCE DID.
I'LL KILL YOU BEFORE THAT CAN HAPPEN.
IT'S IRONIC. TO THINK I WOULD END UP KILLING THEIR ELDEST SON...
...AFTER HELPING THE PEOPLE OF THE SOGA HOUSE TIME AND TIME AGAIN.
WHAT? WHAT DOES THAT MEAN?
DID YOU REANIMATE SOMEONE ELSE BEFORE GRANDPA?
YOUR MOTHER DIED WHILE PREGNANT WITH HER SECOND SON.

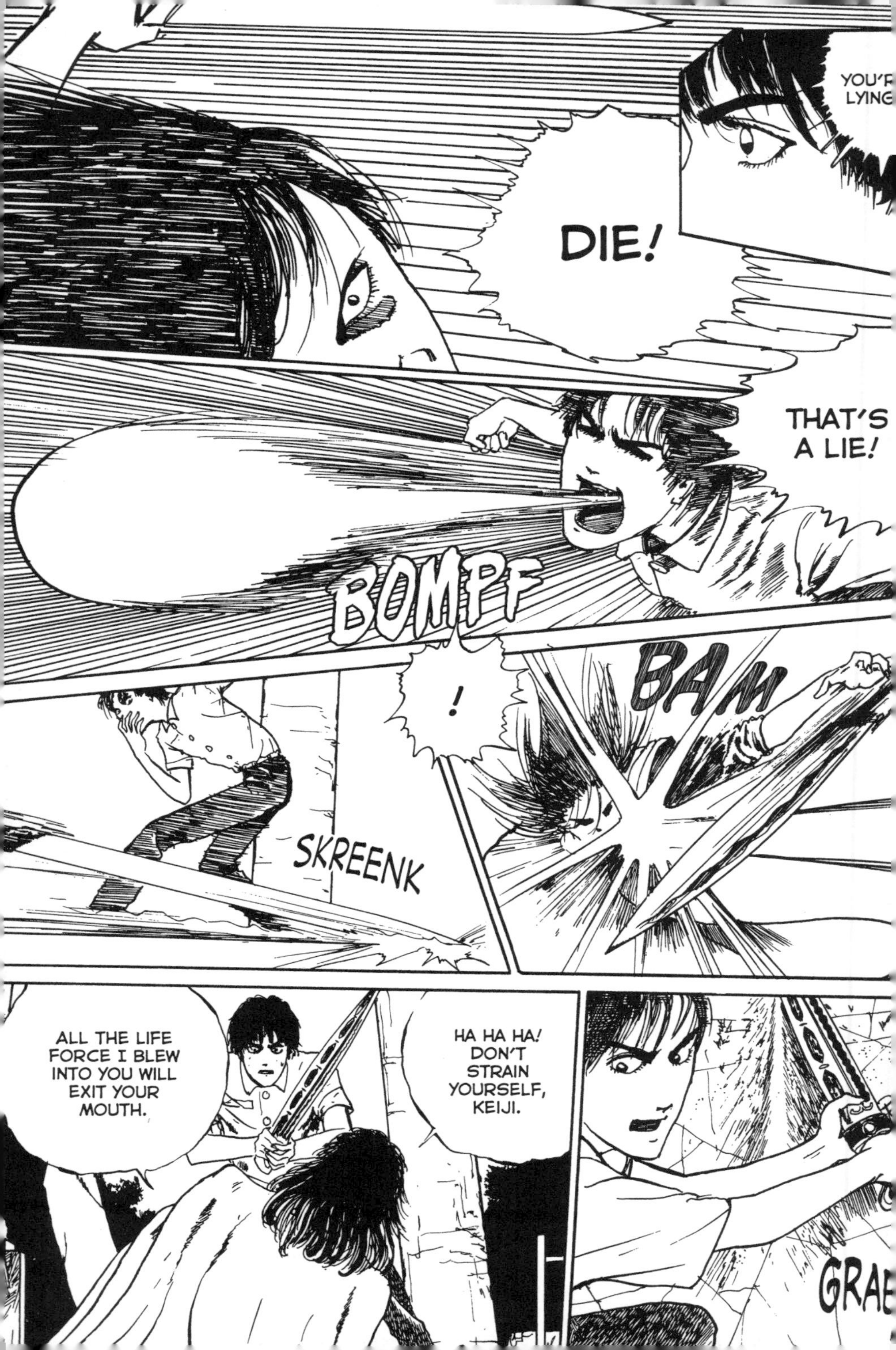
YOU'R
LYING
DIE!
THAT'S A LIE!
BOMPF
BAM
!
SKREENK
GRAB
HA HA HA! DON'T STRAIN YOURSELF, KEIJI.
ALL THE LIFE FORCE I BLEW INTO YOU WILL EXIT YOUR MOUTH.

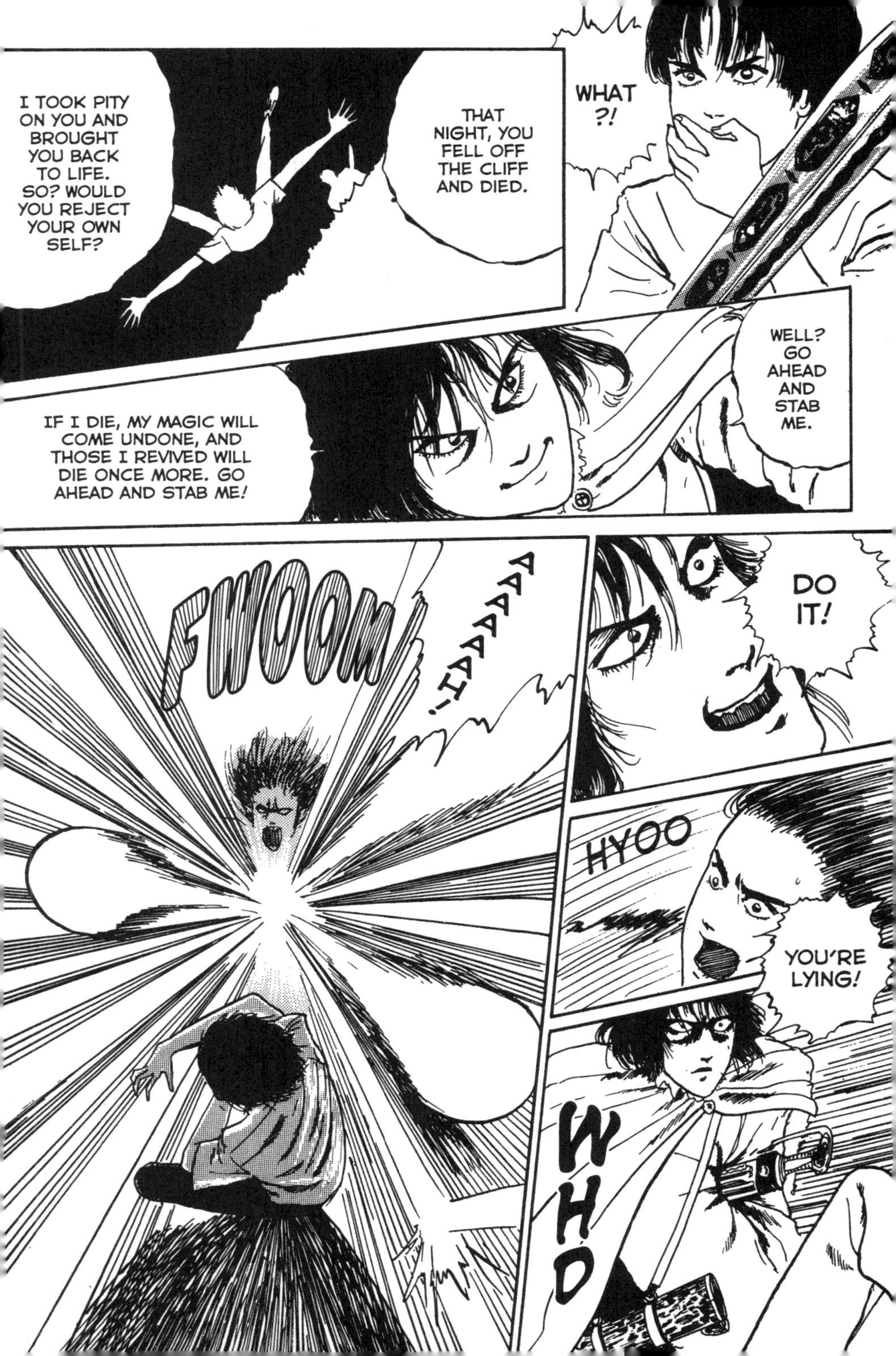
WHAT ?!
THAT NIGHT, YOU FELL OFF THE CLIFF AND DIED.
I TOOK PITY ON YOU AND BROUGHT YOU BACK TO LIFE. SO? WOULD YOU REJECT YOUR OWN SELF?
WELL? GO AHEAD AND STAB ME.
IF I DIE, MY MAGIC WILL COME UNDONE, AND THOSE I REVIVED WILL DIE ONCE MORE. GO AHEAD AND STAB ME!
DO IT!
HYOO
YOU'RE LYING!
WHOD
FWOOM
AAAAAAAH!

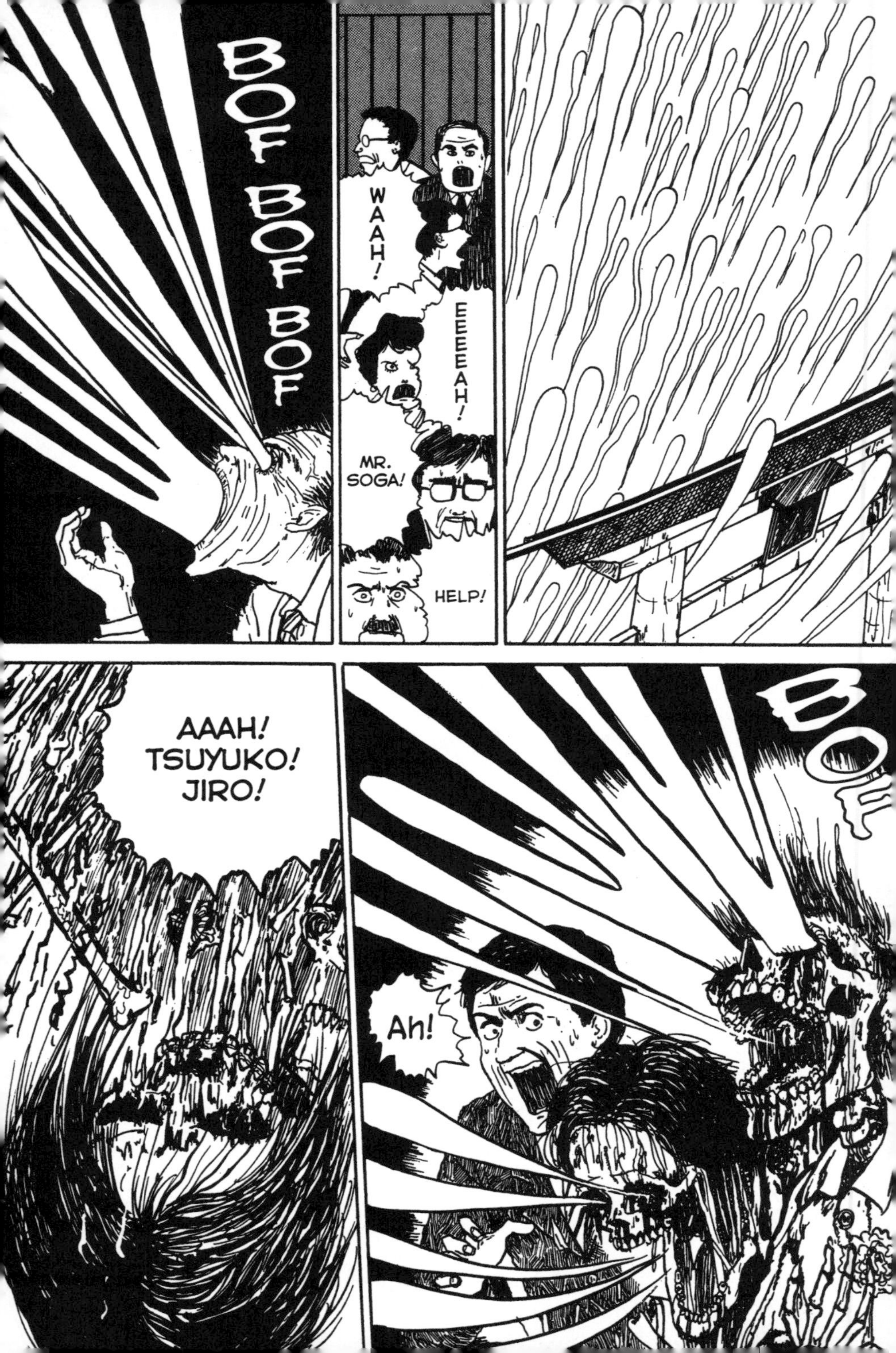

WAAAH!
EEEEAH!
MR. SOGA!
HELP!
BOF BOF BOF BOF
BOF
Ah!
AAAH! TSUYUKO! JIRO!

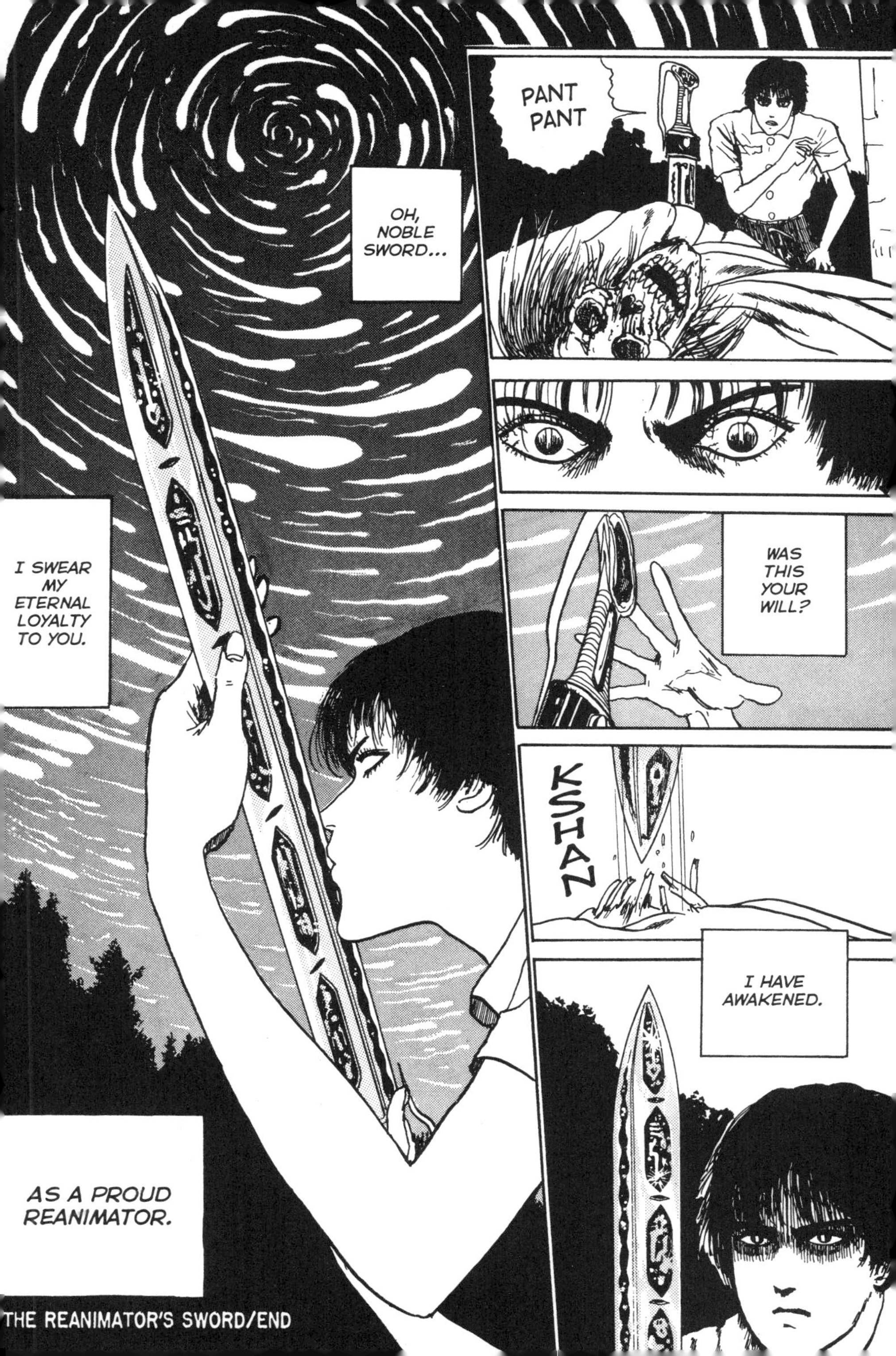
PANT PANT
OH, NOBLE SWORD...
WAS THIS YOUR WILL?
KSHAN
I HAVE AWAKENED.
I SWEAR MY ETERNAL LOYALTY TO YOU.
AS A PROUD REANIMATOR.

THE REANIMATOR'S SWORD/END

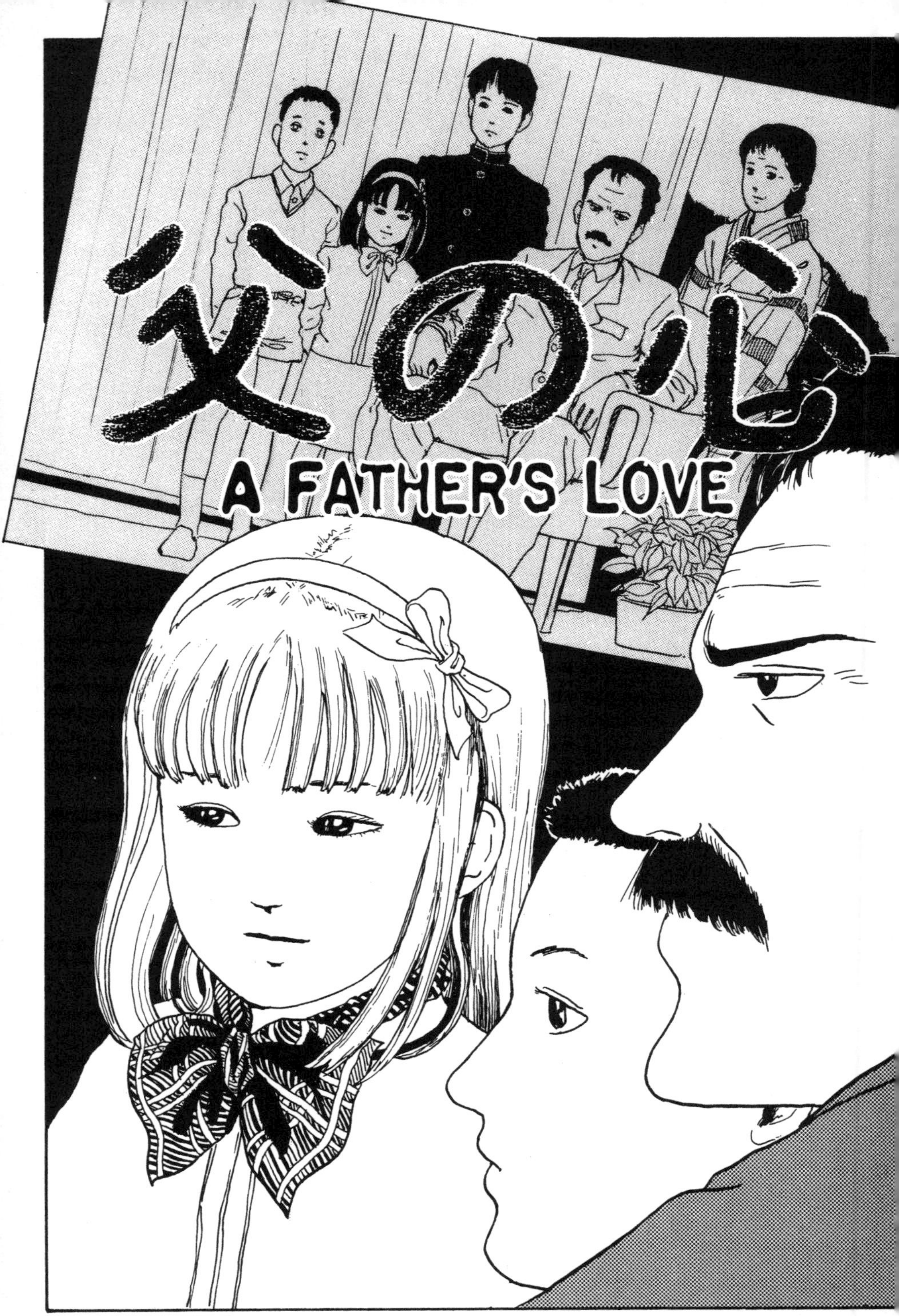
父の心
A FATHER'S LOVE

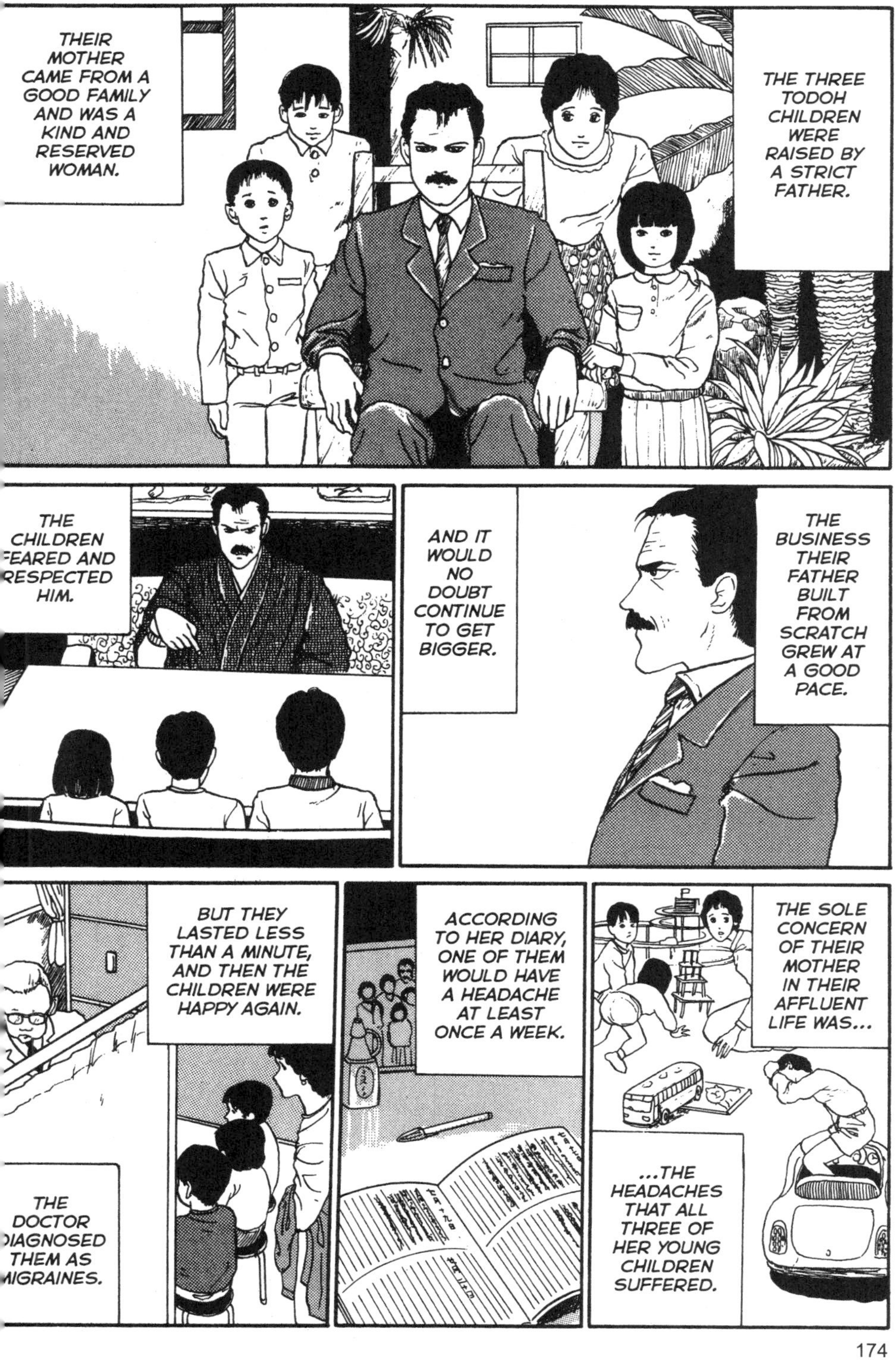
THE THREE TODOH CHILDREN WERE RAISED BY A STRICT FATHER.
THEIR MOTHER CAME FROM A GOOD FAMILY AND WAS A KIND AND RESERVED WOMAN.
THE BUSINESS THEIR FATHER BUILT FROM SCRATCH GREW AT A GOOD PACE.
AND IT WOULD NO DOUBT CONTINUE TO GET BIGGER.
THE CHILDREN EARED AND RESPECTED HIM.
THE SOLE CONCERN OF THEIR MOTHER IN THEIR AFFLUENT LIFE WAS...
...THE HEADACHES THAT ALL THREE OF HER YOUNG CHILDREN SUFFERED.
ACCORDING TO HER DIARY, ONE OF THEM WOULD HAVE A HEADACHE AT LEAST ONCE A WEEK.
BUT THEY LASTED LESS THAN A MINUTE, AND THEN THE CHILDREN WERE HAPPY AGAIN.
THE DOCTOR IAGNOSED THEM AS IGRAINES.

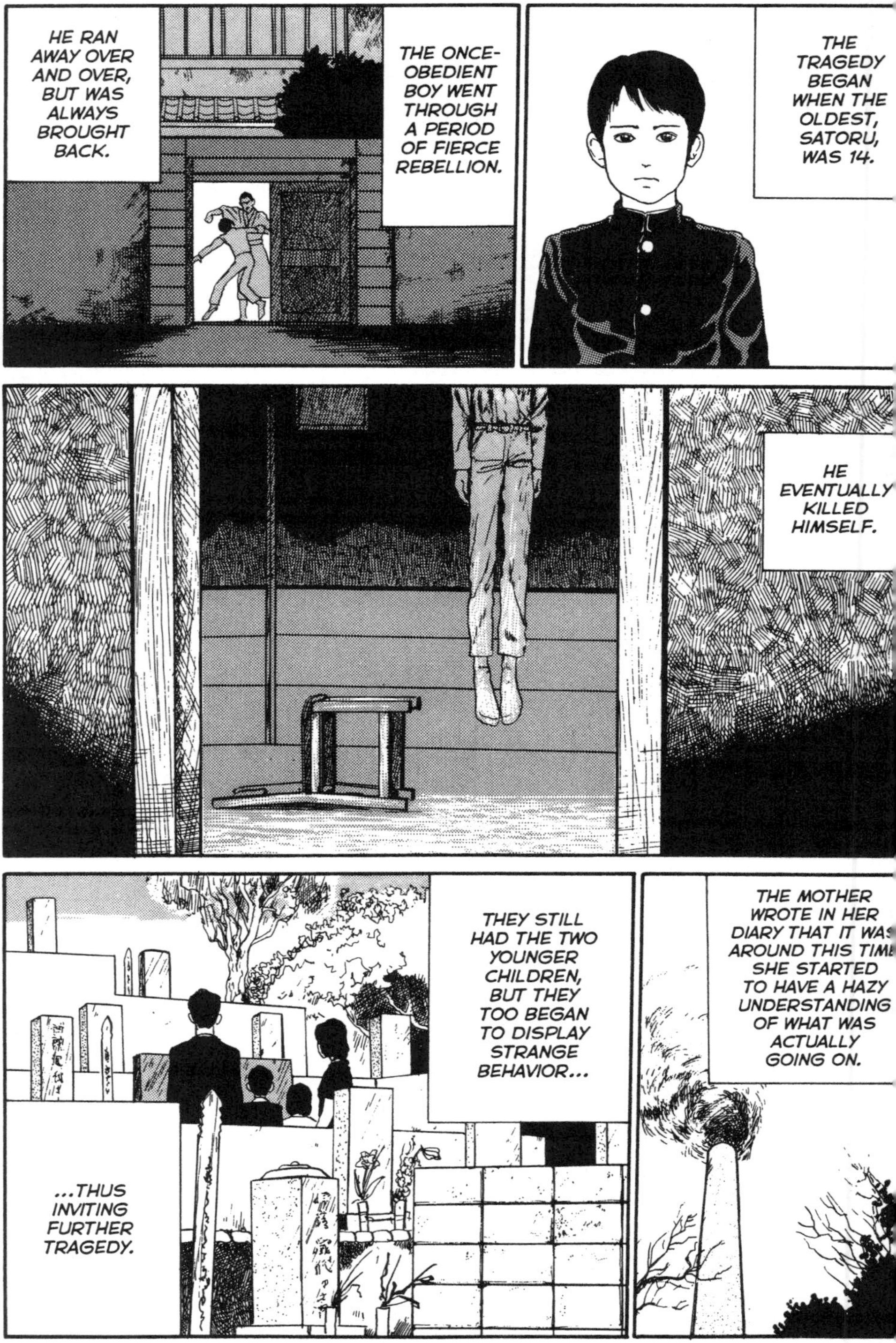
THE TRAGEDY BEGAN WHEN THE OLDEST, SATORU, WAS 14.
THE ONCE-OBEDIENT BOY WENT THROUGH A PERIOD OF FIERCE REBELLION.
HE RAN AWAY OVER AND OVER, BUT WAS ALWAYS BROUGHT BACK.
HE EVENTUALLY KILLED HIMSELF.
THE MOTHER WROTE IN HER DIARY THAT IT WAS AROUND THIS TIME SHE STARTED TO HAVE A HAZY UNDERSTANDING OF WHAT WAS ACTUALLY GOING ON.
THEY STILL HAD THE TWO YOUNGER CHILDREN, BUT THEY TOO BEGAN TO DISPLAY STRANGE BEHAVIOR...
...THUS INVITING FURTHER TRAGEDY.

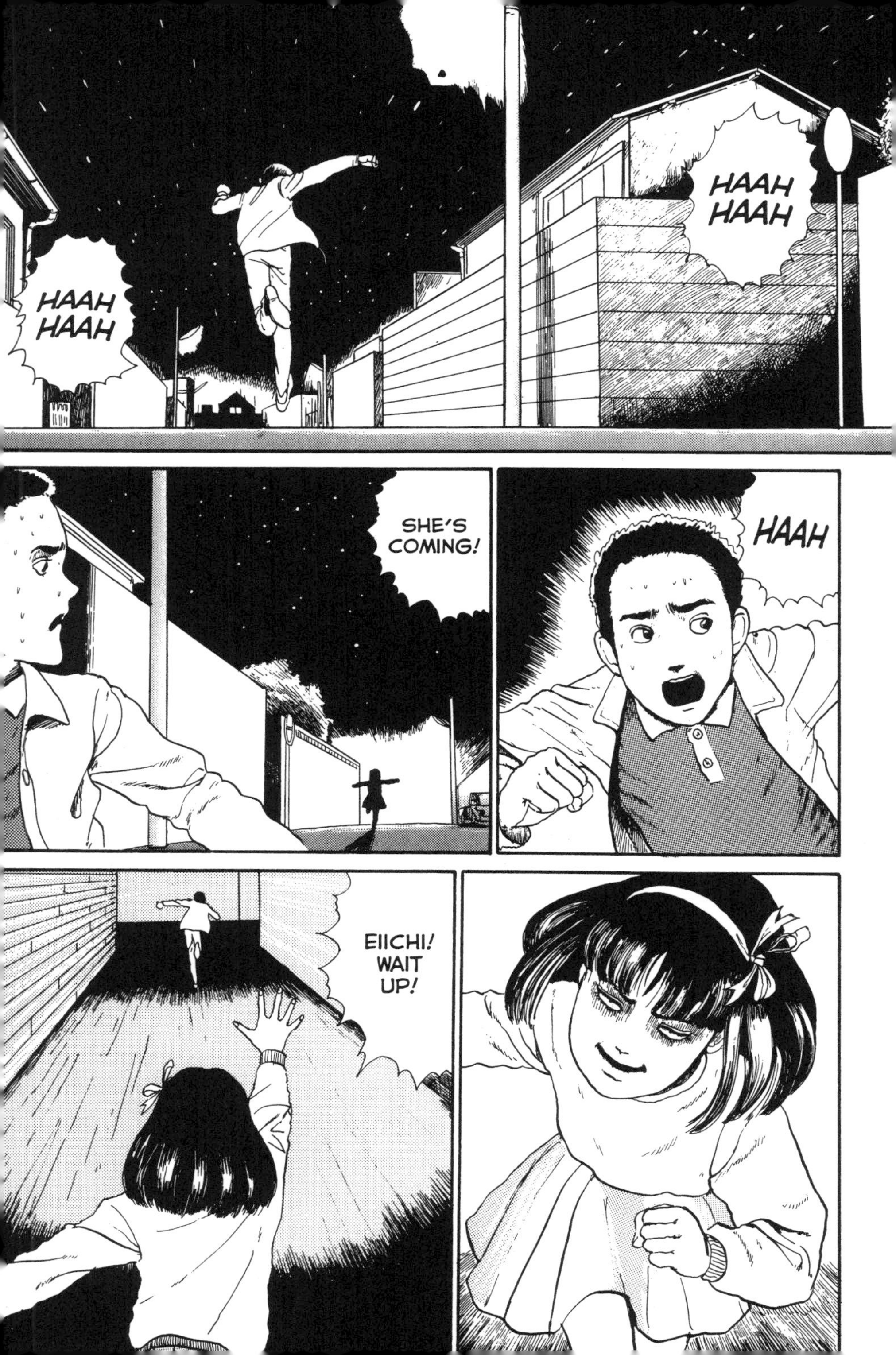
HAAH HAAH
HAAH HAAH
HAAH
SHE'S COMING!
EIICHI! WAIT UP!

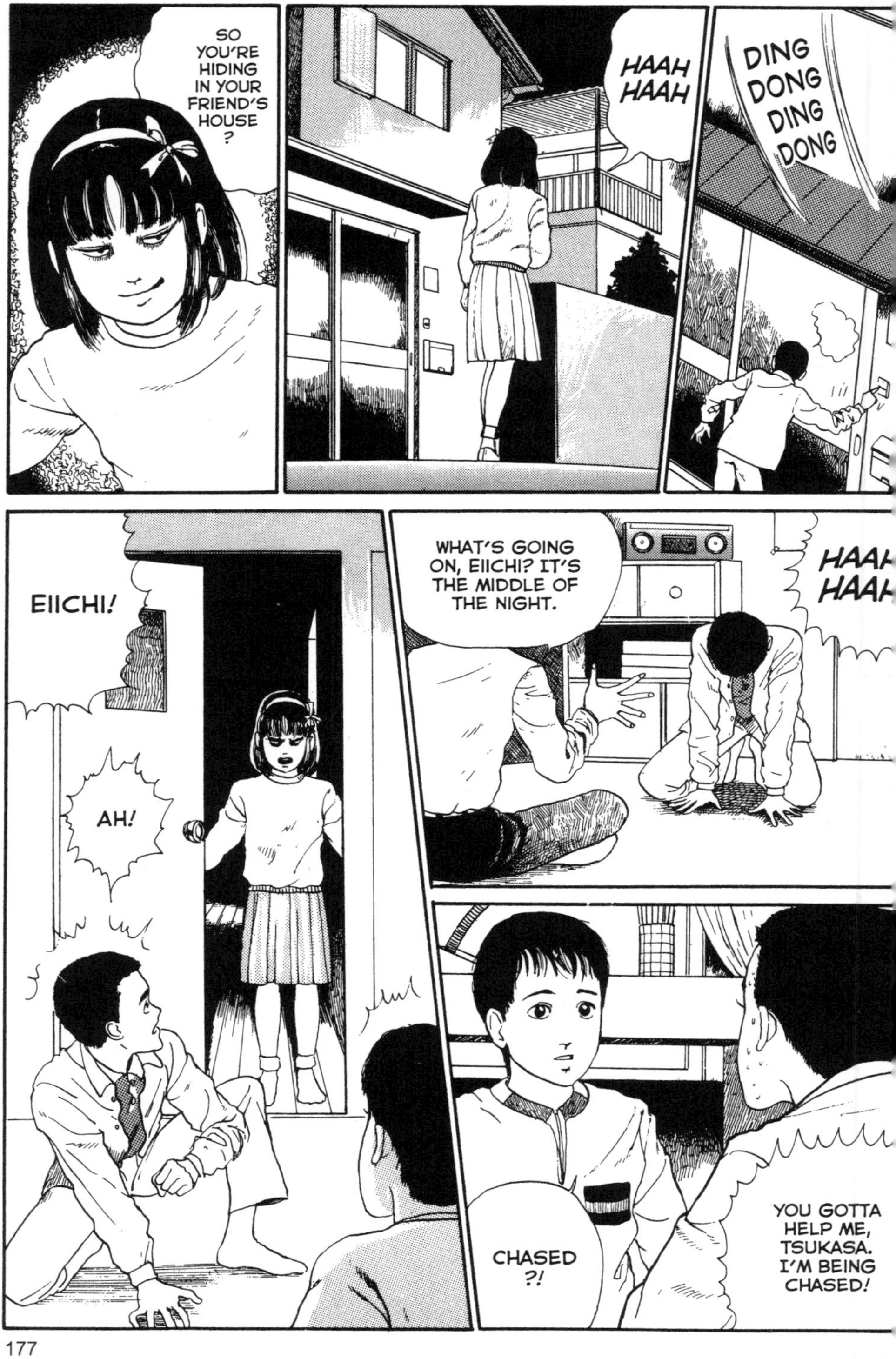
DING DONG DING DONG
HAAH HAAH
SO YOU'RE HIDING IN YOUR FRIEND'S HOUSE?
HAAH HAAH
WHAT'S GOING ON, EIICHI? IT'S THE MIDDLE OF THE NIGHT.
YOU GOTTA HELP ME, TSUKASA. I'M BEING CHASED!
CHASED?!
EIICHI!
AH!

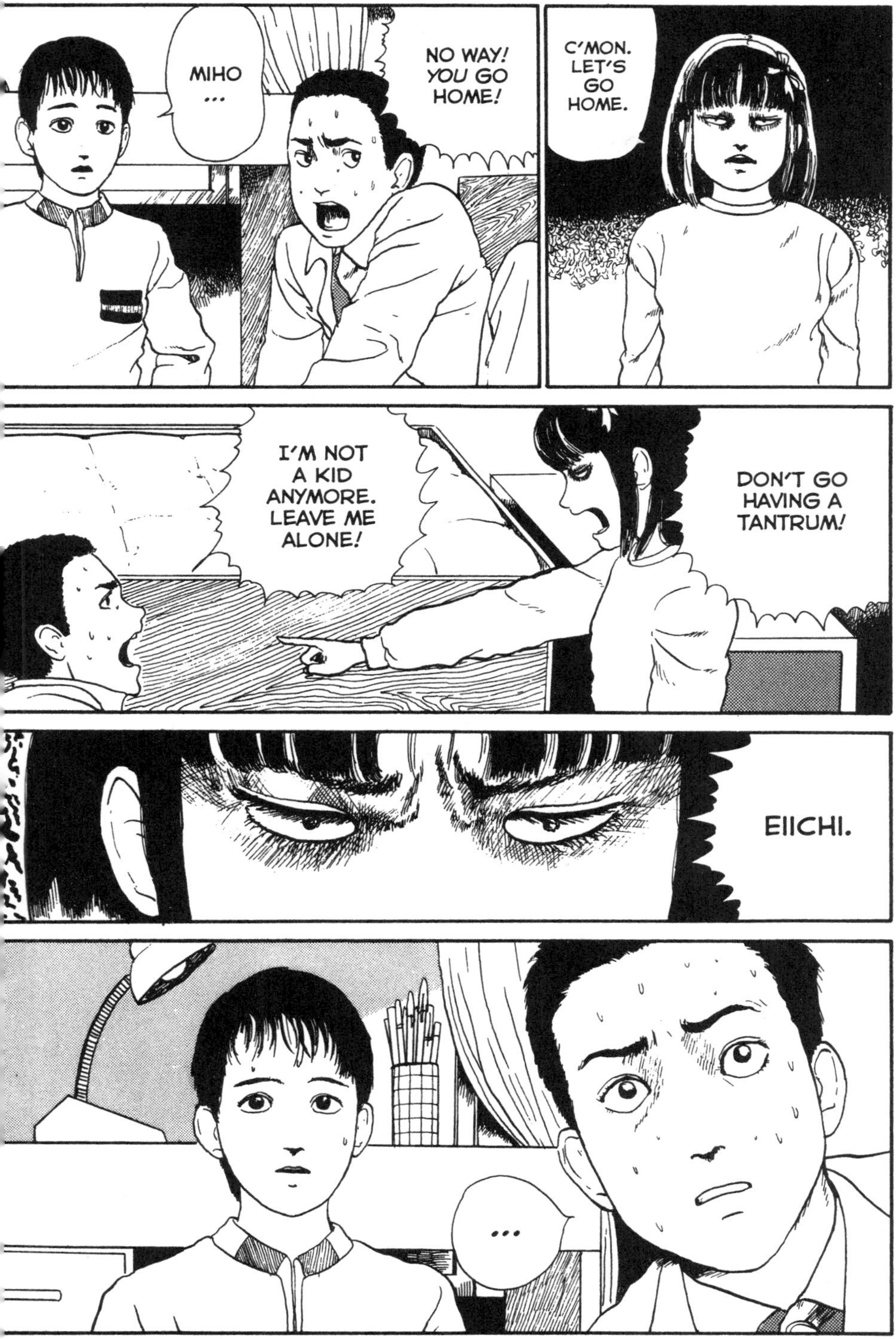
C'MON. LET'S GO HOME.
NO WAY! *YOU* GO HOME!
MIHO ...
DON'T GO HAVING A TANTRUM!
I'M NOT A KID ANYMORE. LEAVE ME ALONE!
EIICHI.
...

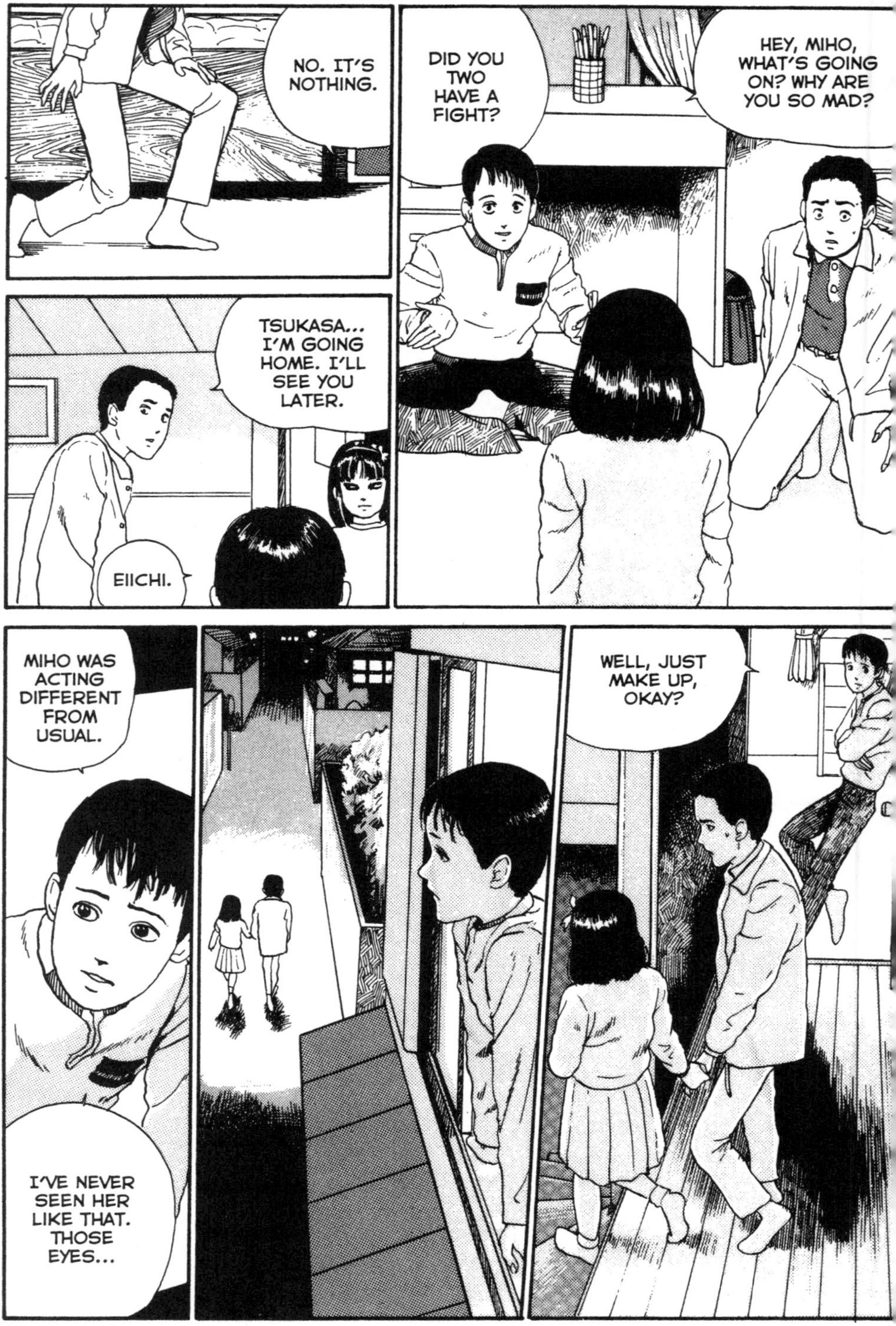
HEY, MIHO, WHAT'S GOING ON? WHY ARE YOU SO MAD?
DID YOU TWO HAVE A FIGHT?
NO. IT'S NOTHING.
TSUKASA... I'M GOING HOME. I'LL SEE YOU LATER.
EIICHI.
WELL, JUST MAKE UP, OKAY?
MIHO WAS ACTING DIFFERENT FROM USUAL.
I'VE NEVER SEEN HER LIKE THAT. THOSE EYES...

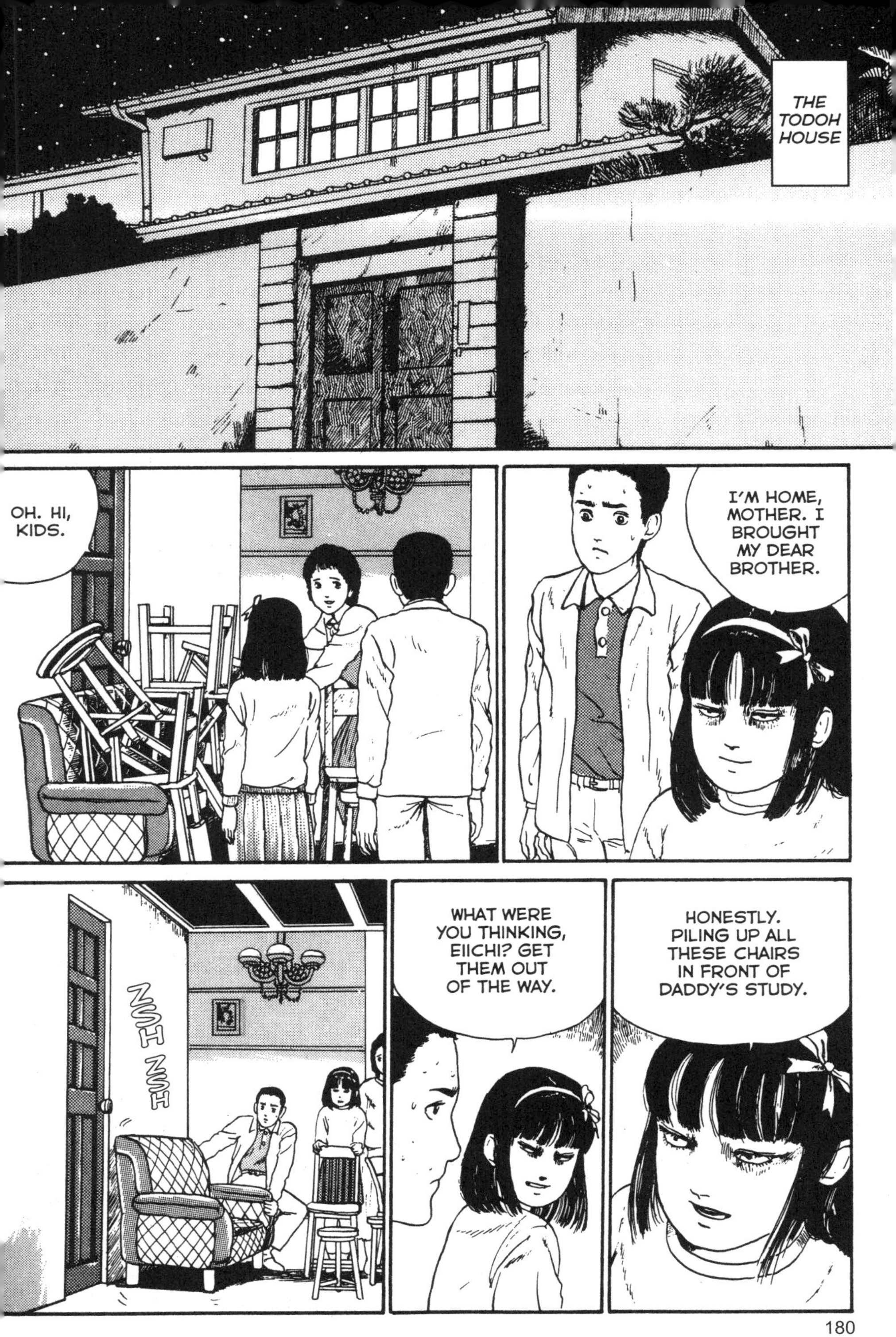
THE TODOH HOUSE
I'M HOME, MOTHER. I BROUGHT MY DEAR BROTHER.
OH. HI, KIDS.
HONESTLY. PILING UP ALL THESE CHAIRS IN FRONT OF DADDY'S STUDY.
WHAT WERE YOU THINKING, EIICHI? GET THEM OUT OF THE WAY.
ZSH ZSH

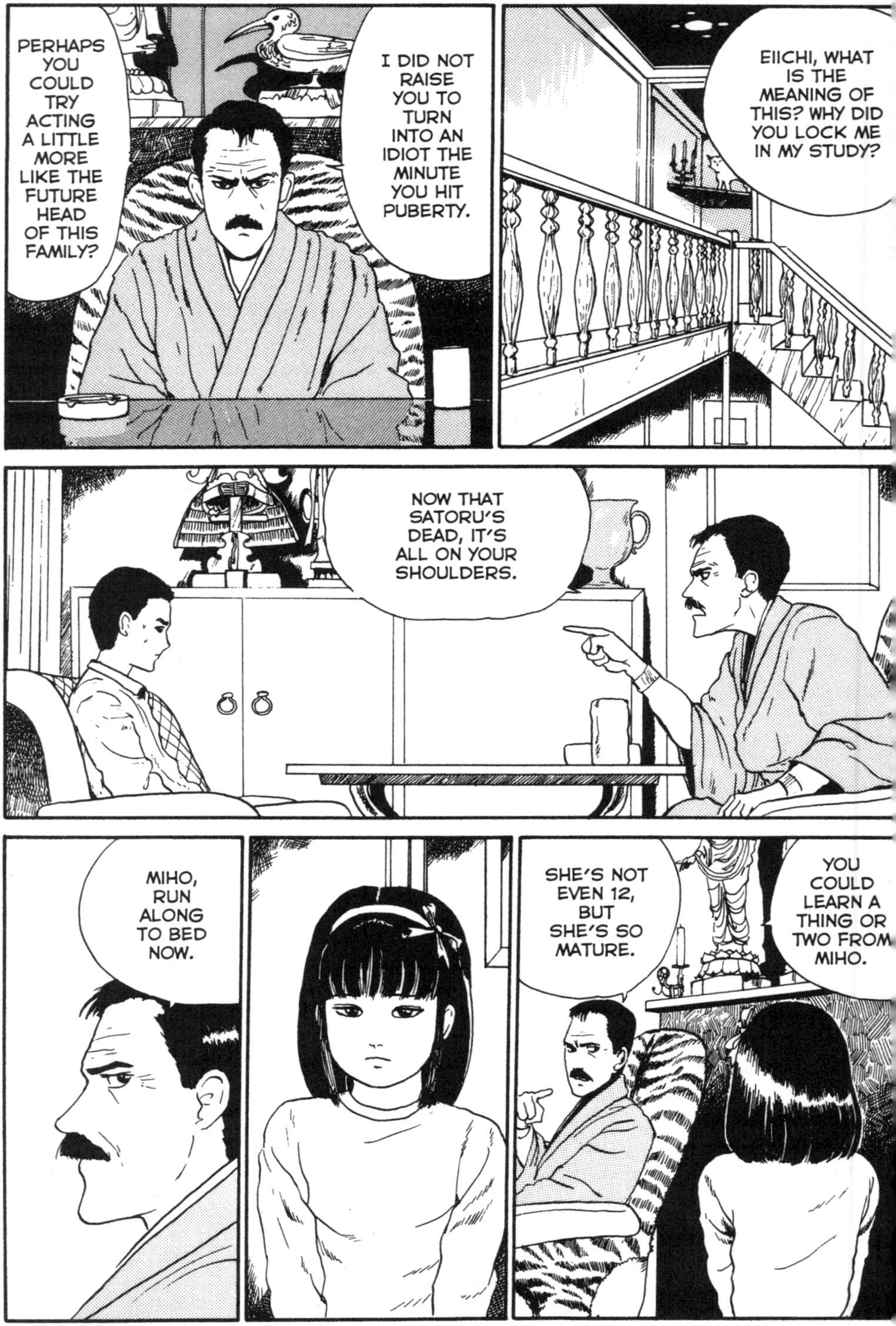
EIICHI, WHAT IS THE MEANING OF THIS? WHY DID YOU LOCK ME IN MY STUDY?
I DID NOT RAISE YOU TO TURN INTO AN IDIOT THE MINUTE YOU HIT PUBERTY.
PERHAPS YOU COULD TRY ACTING A LITTLE MORE LIKE THE FUTURE HEAD OF THIS FAMILY?
NOW THAT SATORU'S DEAD, IT'S ALL ON YOUR SHOULDERS.
YOU COULD LEARN A THING OR TWO FROM MIHO.
SHE'S NOT EVEN 12, BUT SHE'S SO MATURE.
MIHO, RUN ALONG TO BED NOW.

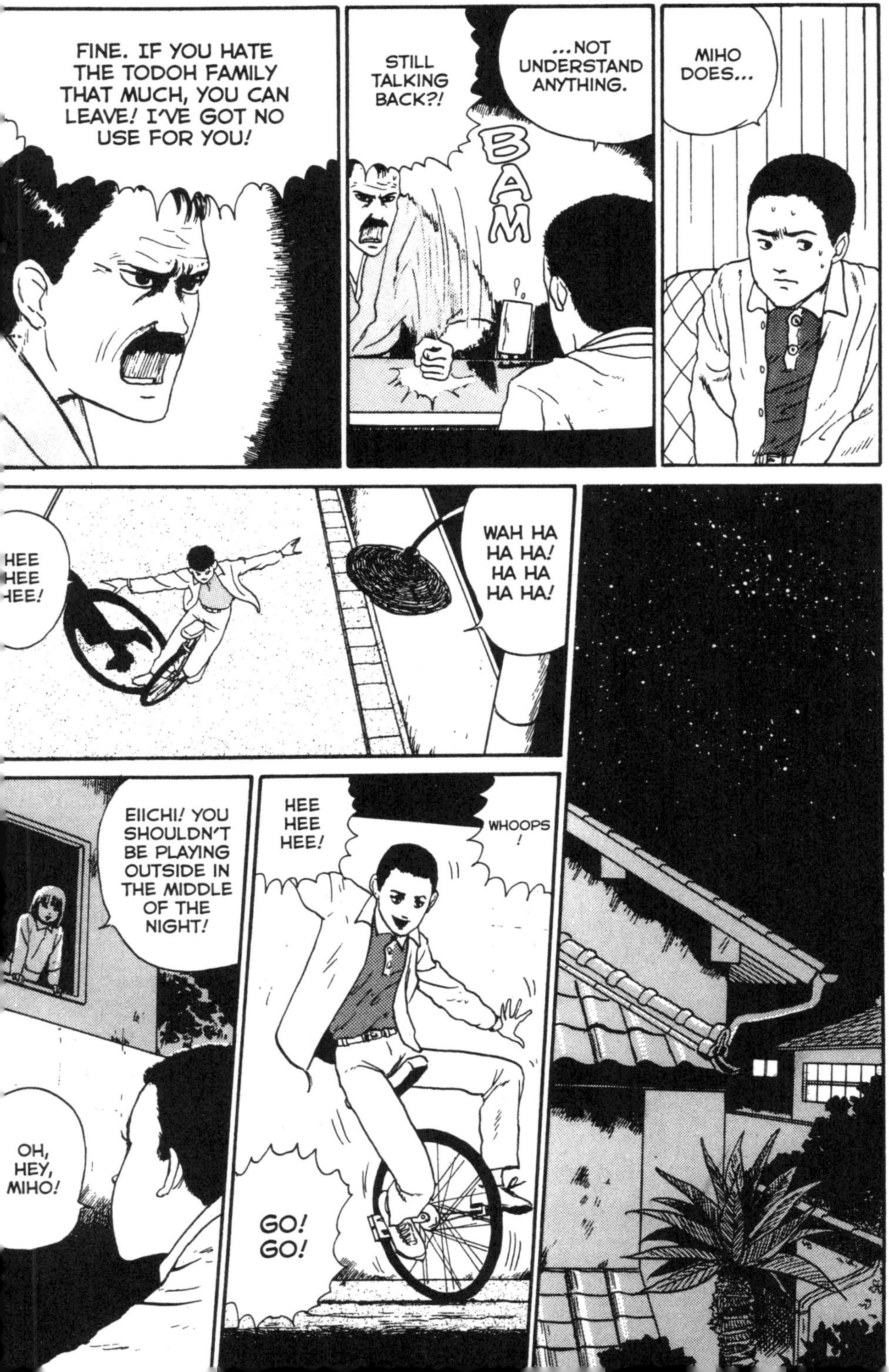
MIHO DOES...
...NOT UNDERSTAND ANYTHING.
STILL TALKING BACK?!
BAM
FINE. IF YOU HATE THE TODOH FAMILY THAT MUCH, YOU CAN LEAVE! I'VE GOT NO USE FOR YOU!
WAH HA HA HA! HA HA HA HA!
HEE HEE HEE!
WHOOPS!
HEE HEE HEE!
GO! GO!
EIICHI! YOU SHOULDN'T BE PLAYING OUTSIDE IN THE MIDDLE OF THE NIGHT!
OH, HEY, MIHO!

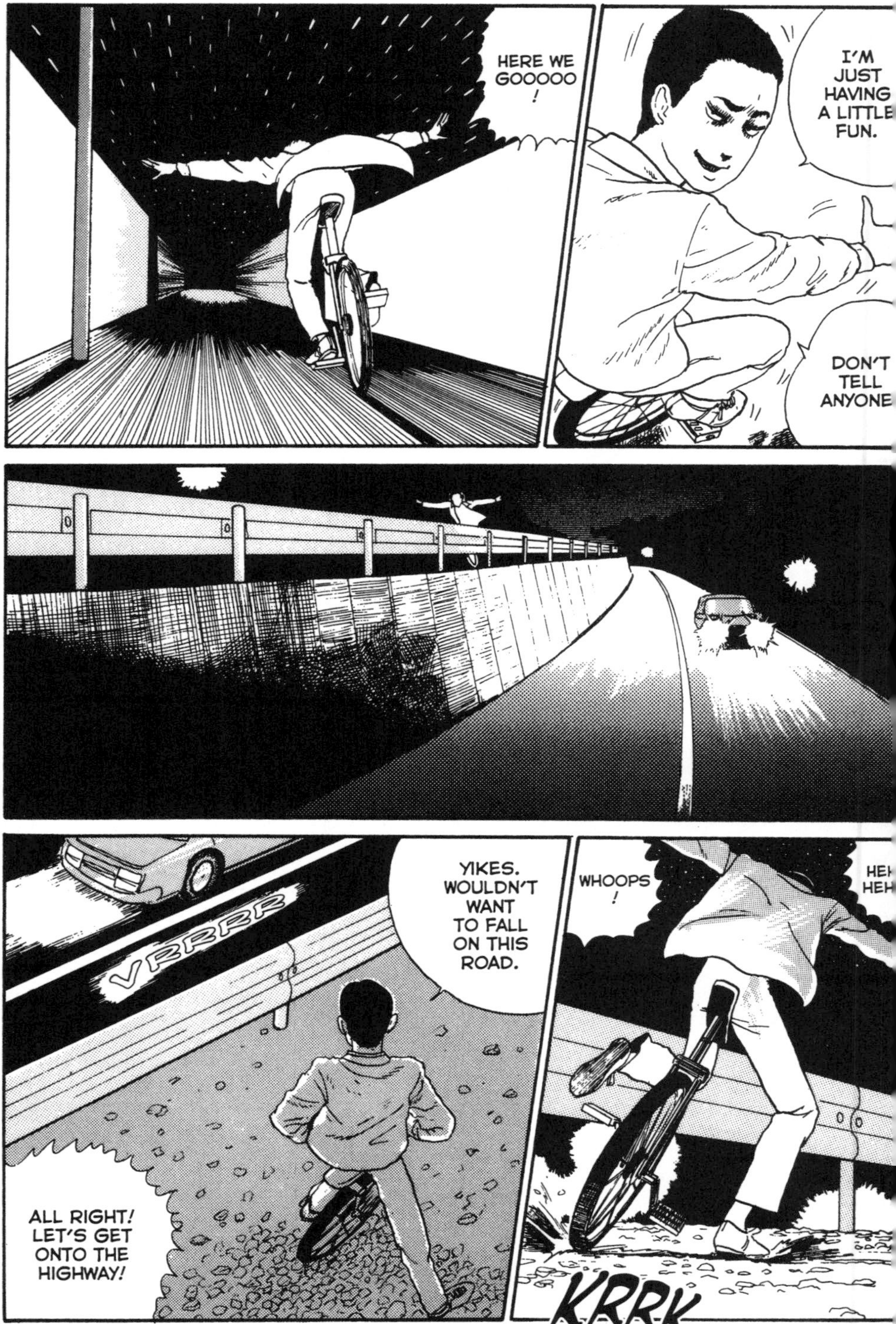
I'M JUST HAVING A LITTLE FUN.
DON'T TELL ANYONE
HERE WE GOOOOO!
WHOOPS!
KRRK
YIKES. WOULDN'T WANT TO FALL ON THIS ROAD.
VRRRR
ALL RIGHT! LET'S GET ONTO THE HIGHWAY!

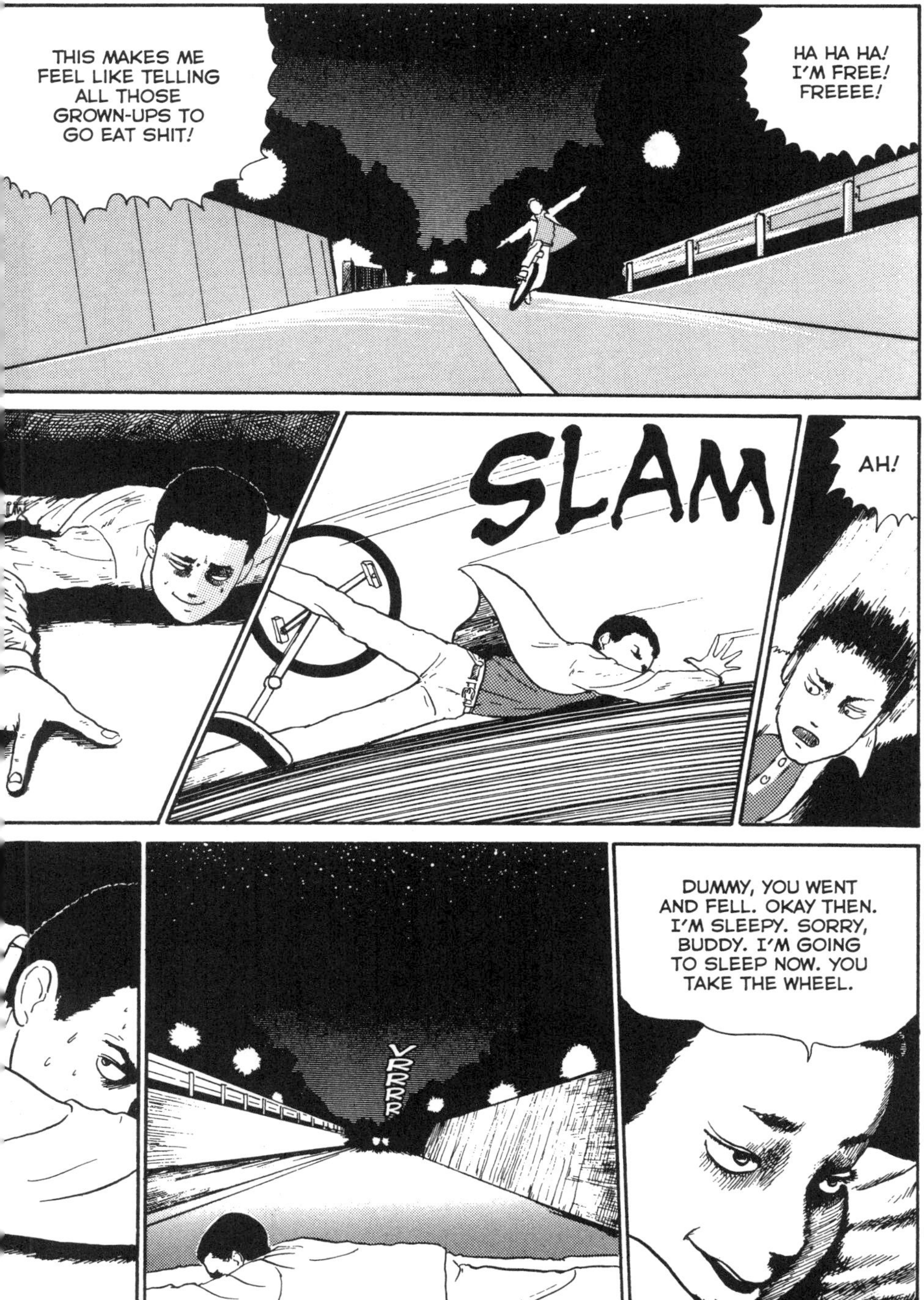
HA HA HA! I'M FREE! FREEEE!
THIS MAKES ME FEEL LIKE TELLING ALL THOSE GROWN-UPS TO GO EAT SHIT!
AH!
SLAM
DUMMY, YOU WENT AND FELL. OKAY THEN. I'M SLEEPY. SORRY, BUDDY. I'M GOING TO SLEEP NOW. YOU TAKE THE WHEEL.
VRRRR

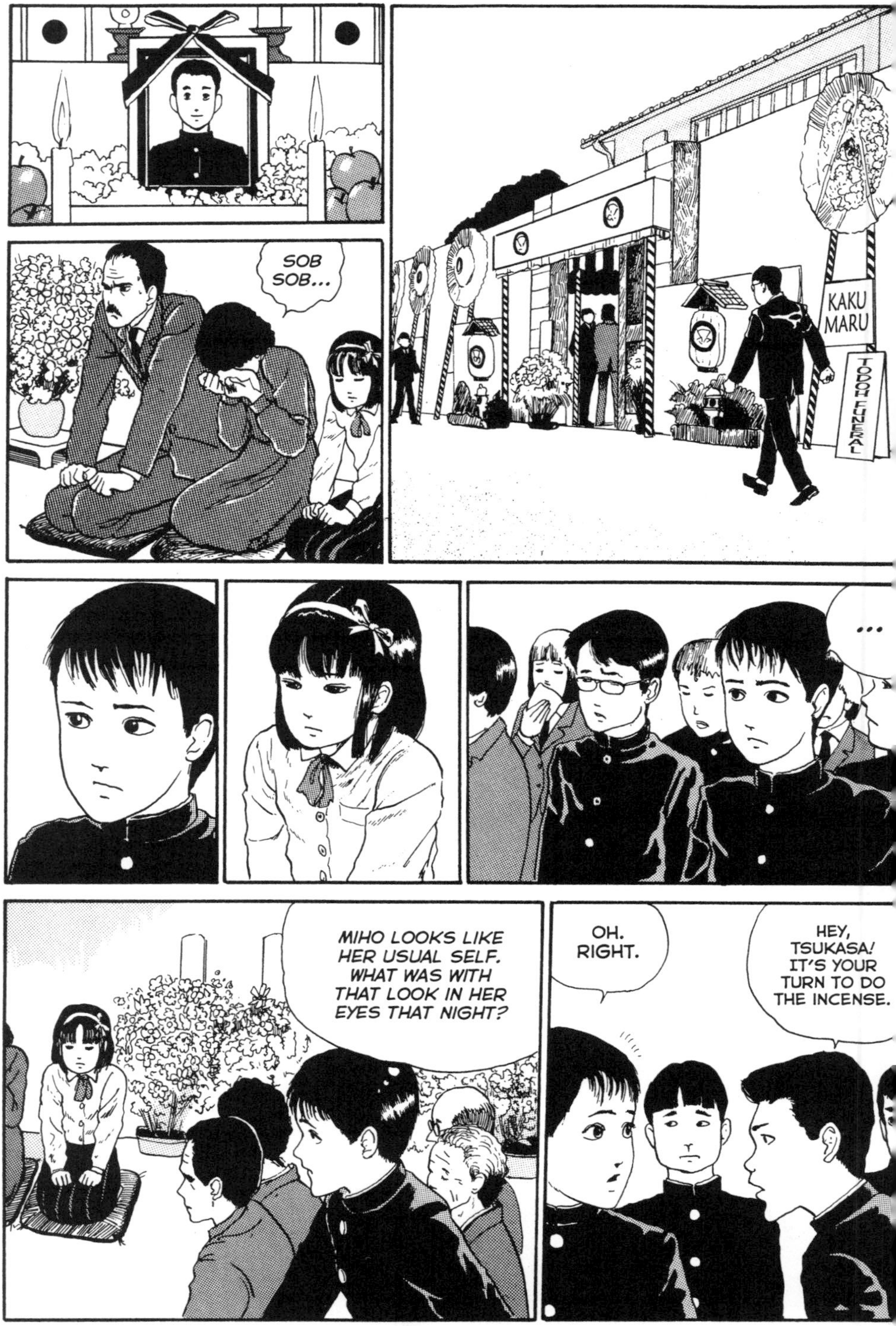
KAKU MARU
TODOH FUNERAL
SOB SOB...
...
HEY, TSUKASA! IT'S YOUR TURN TO DO THE INCENSE.
OH. RIGHT.
MIHO LOOKS LIKE HER USUAL SELF. WHAT WAS WITH THAT LOOK IN HER EYES THAT NIGHT?

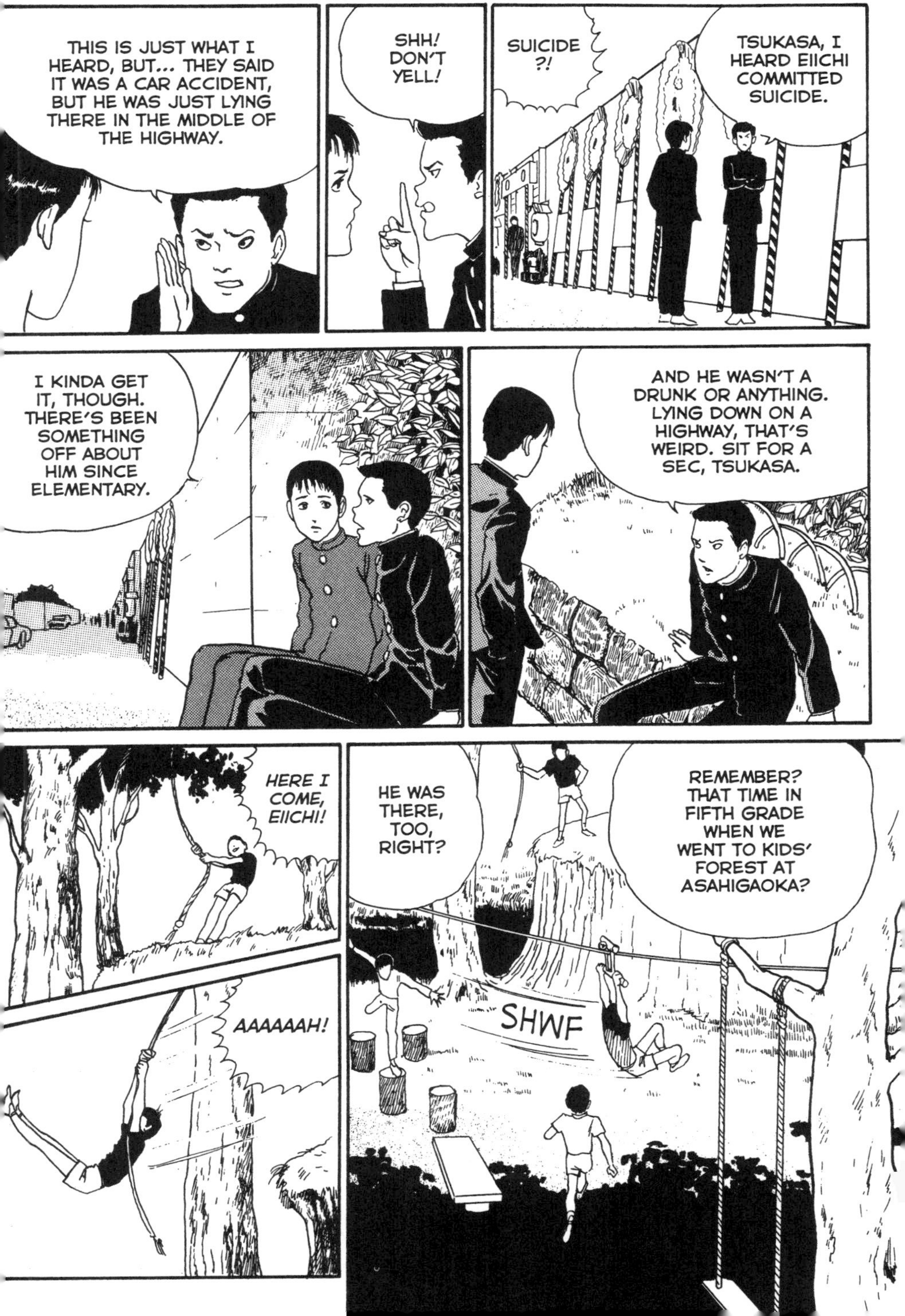
TSUKASA, I HEARD EIICHI COMMITTED SUICIDE.
SUICIDE?!
SHH! DON'T YELL!
THIS IS JUST WHAT I HEARD, BUT... THEY SAID IT WAS A CAR ACCIDENT, BUT HE WAS JUST LYING THERE IN THE MIDDLE OF THE HIGHWAY.
AND HE WASN'T A DRUNK OR ANYTHING. LYING DOWN ON A HIGHWAY, THAT'S WEIRD. SIT FOR A SEC, TSUKASA.
I KINDA GET IT, THOUGH. THERE'S BEEN SOMETHING OFF ABOUT HIM SINCE ELEMENTARY.
REMEMBER? THAT TIME IN FIFTH GRADE WHEN WE WENT TO KIDS' FOREST AT ASAHIGAOKA?
HE WAS THERE, TOO, RIGHT?
SHWF
HERE I COME, EIICHI!
AAAAAAH!

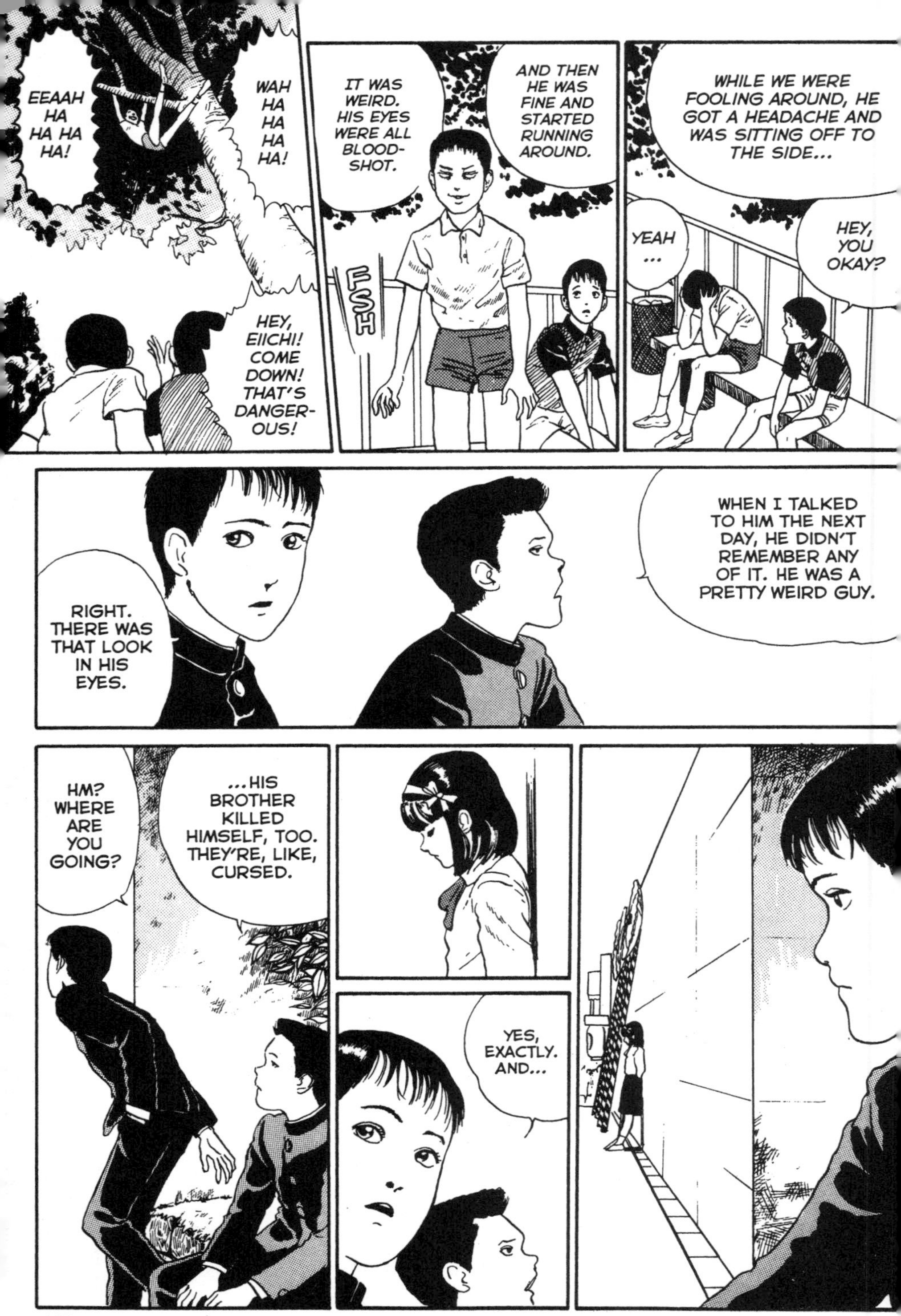
WHILE WE WERE FOOLING AROUND, HE GOT A HEADACHE AND WAS SITTING OFF TO THE SIDE...
HEY, YOU OKAY?
YEAH ...
AND THEN HE WAS FINE AND STARTED RUNNING AROUND.
IT WAS WEIRD. HIS EYES WERE ALL BLOOD-SHOT.
FSH
WAH HA HA HA HA!
EEAAH HA HA HA HA!
HEY, EIICHI! COME DOWN! THAT'S DANGER-OUS!
WHEN I TALKED TO HIM THE NEXT DAY, HE DIDN'T REMEMBER ANY OF IT. HE WAS A PRETTY WEIRD GUY.
RIGHT. THERE WAS THAT LOOK IN HIS EYES.
YES, EXACTLY. AND...
...HIS BROTHER KILLED HIMSELF, TOO. THEY'RE, LIKE, CURSED.
HM? WHERE ARE YOU GOING?

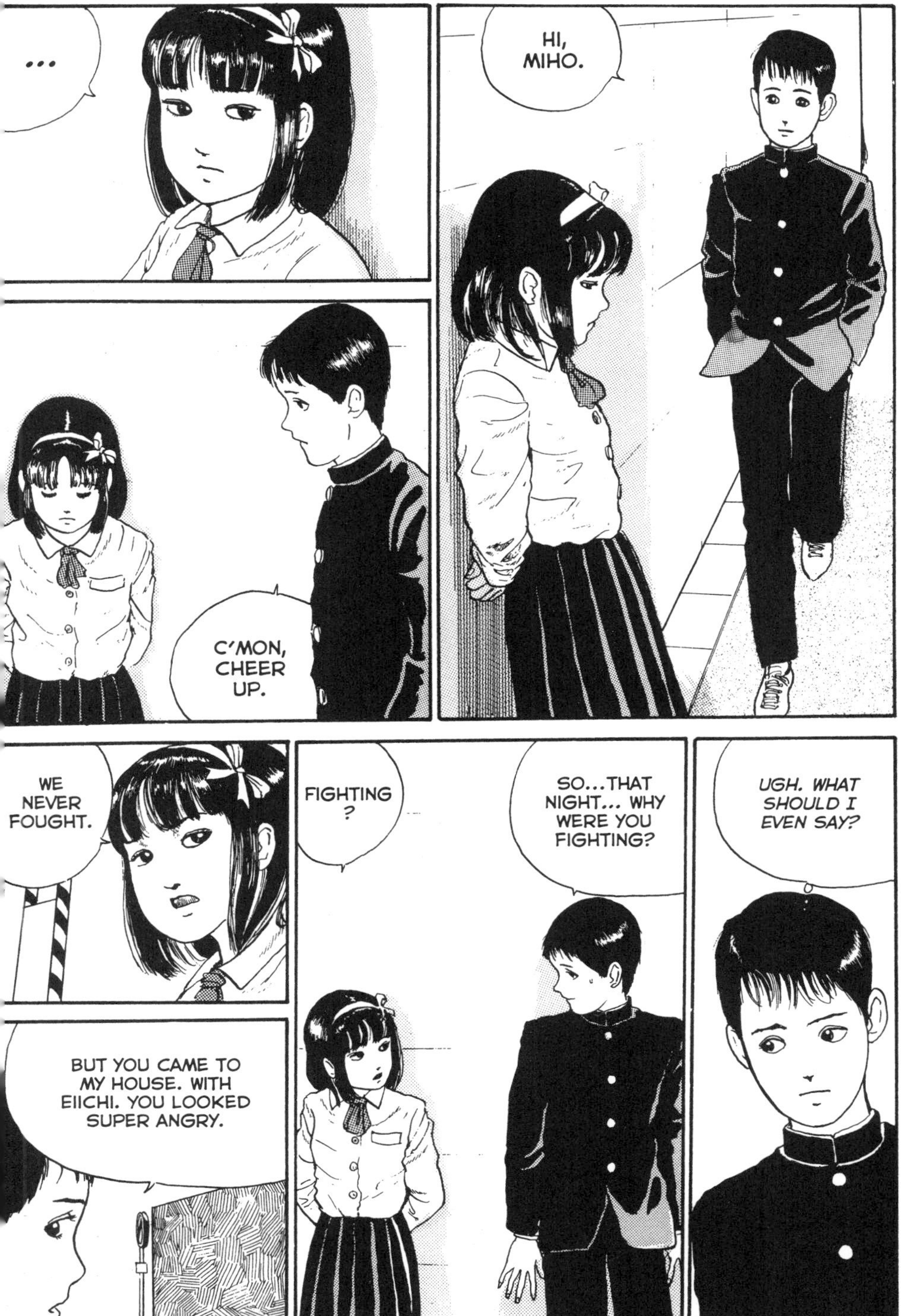
HI, MIHO.
...
C'MON, CHEER UP.
UGH. WHAT SHOULD I EVEN SAY?
SO...THAT NIGHT... WHY WERE YOU FIGHTING?
FIGHTING ?
WE NEVER FOUGHT.
BUT YOU CAME TO MY HOUSE. WITH EIICHI. YOU LOOKED SUPER ANGRY.

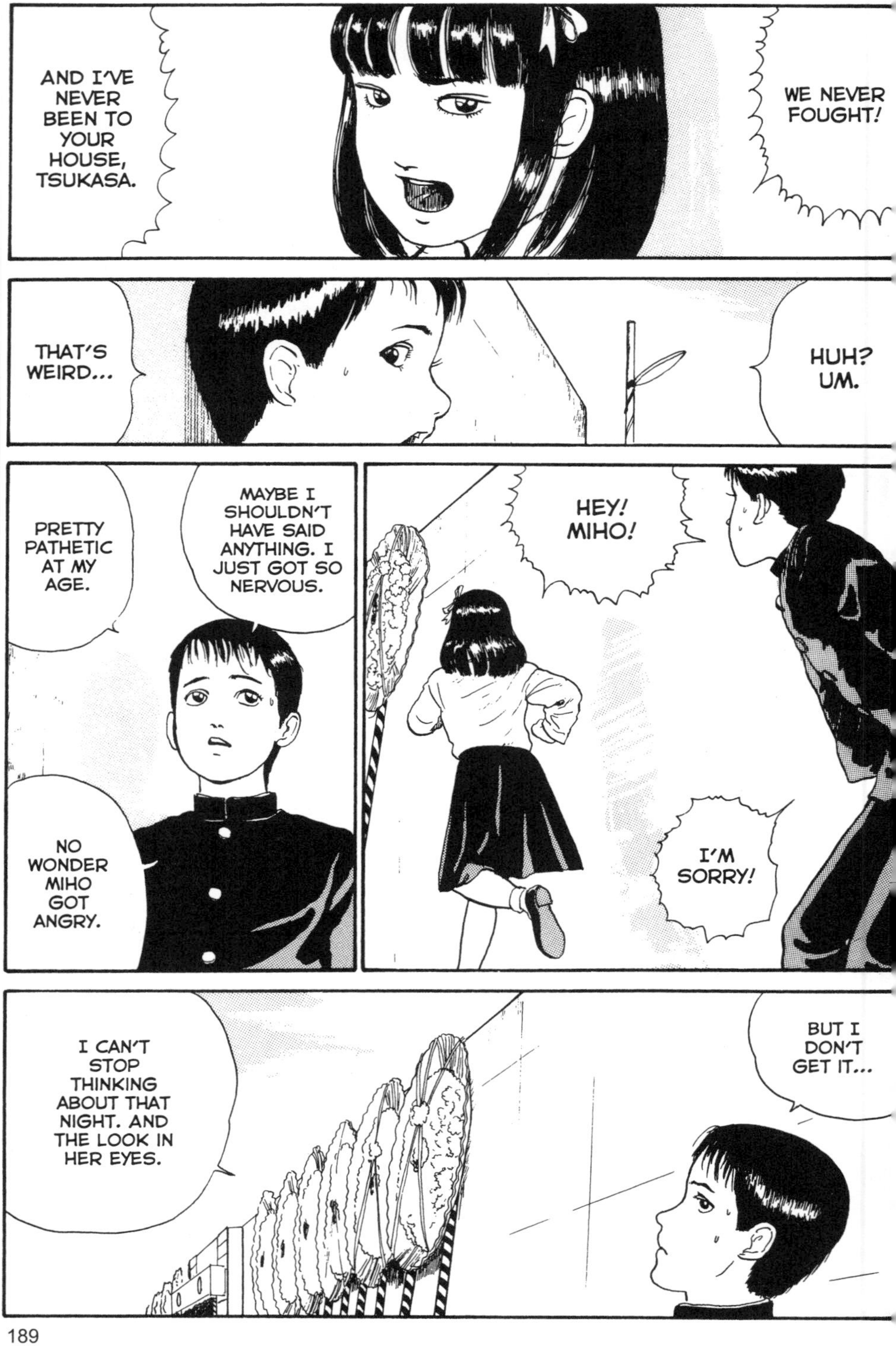
WE NEVER FOUGHT!
AND I'VE NEVER BEEN TO YOUR HOUSE, TSUKASA.
HUH? UM.
THAT'S WEIRD...
HEY! MIHO!
I'M SORRY!
MAYBE I SHOULDN'T HAVE SAID ANYTHING. I JUST GOT SO NERVOUS.
PRETTY PATHETIC AT MY AGE.
NO WONDER MIHO GOT ANGRY.
BUT I DON'T GET IT...
I CAN'T STOP THINKING ABOUT THAT NIGHT. AND THE LOOK IN HER EYES.

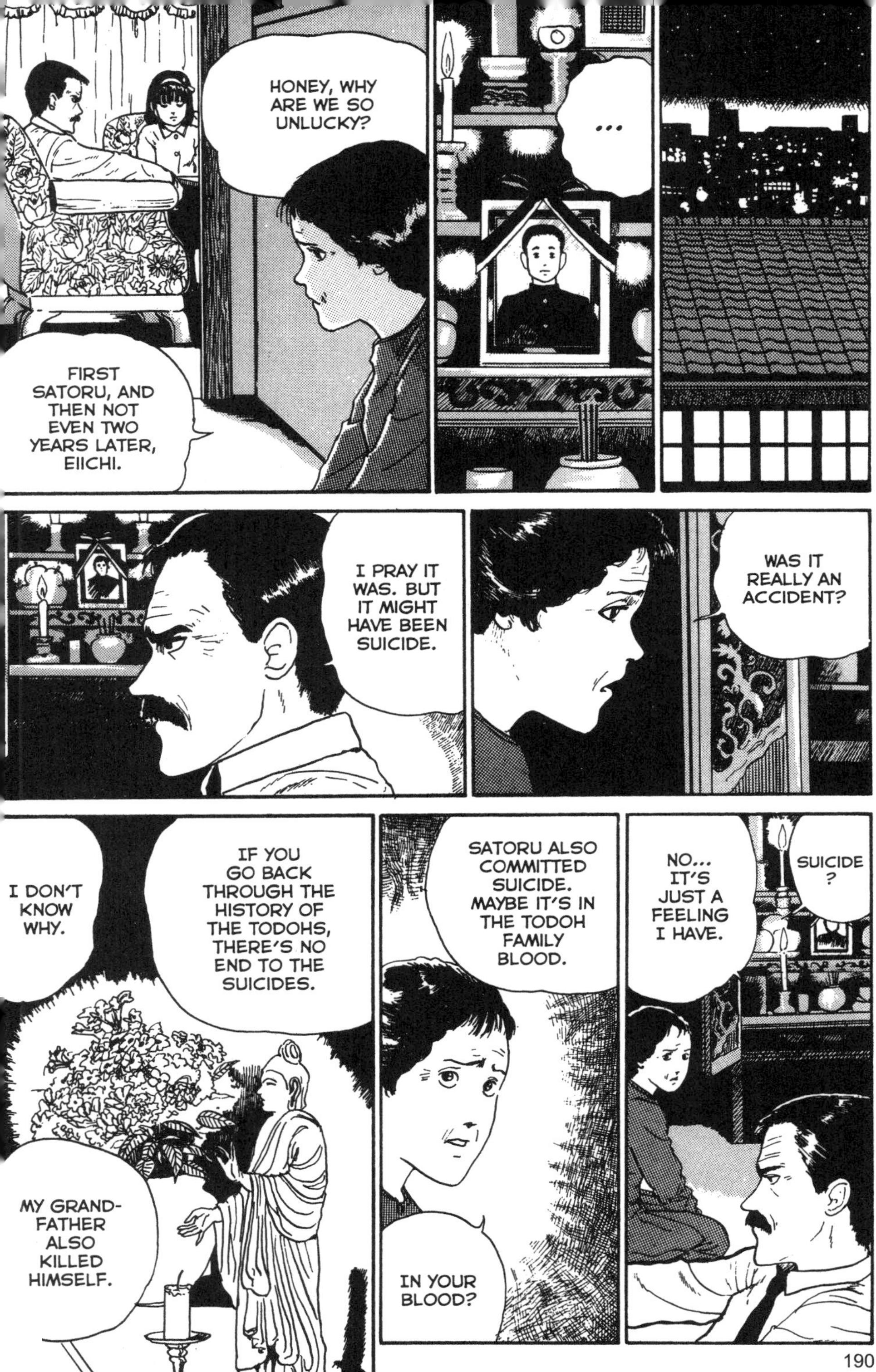
...
HONEY, WHY ARE WE SO UNLUCKY?
FIRST SATORU, AND THEN NOT EVEN TWO YEARS LATER, EIICHI.
WAS IT REALLY AN ACCIDENT?
I PRAY IT WAS. BUT IT MIGHT HAVE BEEN SUICIDE.
SUICIDE ?
NO... IT'S JUST A FEELING I HAVE.
SATORU ALSO COMMITTED SUICIDE. MAYBE IT'S IN THE TODOH FAMILY BLOOD.
IN YOUR BLOOD?
IF YOU GO BACK THROUGH THE HISTORY OF THE TODOHS, THERE'S NO END TO THE SUICIDES.
I DON'T KNOW WHY.
MY GRAND-FATHER ALSO KILLED HIMSELF.

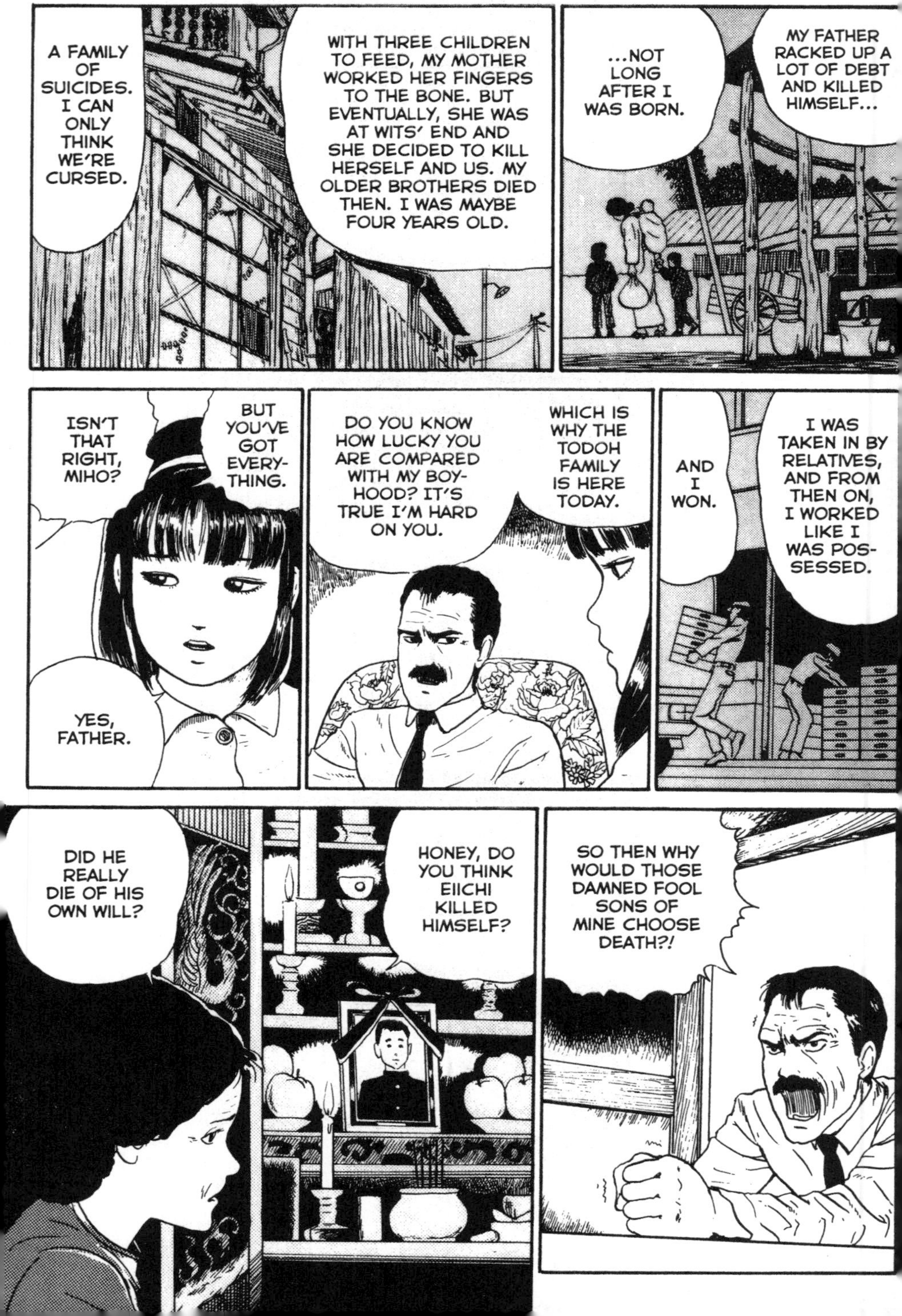
MY FATHER RACKED UP A LOT OF DEBT AND KILLED HIMSELF...
...NOT LONG AFTER I WAS BORN.
WITH THREE CHILDREN TO FEED, MY MOTHER WORKED HER FINGERS TO THE BONE. BUT EVENTUALLY, SHE WAS AT WITS' END AND SHE DECIDED TO KILL HERSELF AND US. MY OLDER BROTHERS DIED THEN. I WAS MAYBE FOUR YEARS OLD.
A FAMILY OF SUICIDES. I CAN ONLY THINK WE'RE CURSED.
I WAS TAKEN IN BY RELATIVES, AND FROM THEN ON, I WORKED LIKE I WAS POSSESSED.
AND I WON.
WHICH IS WHY THE TODOH FAMILY IS HERE TODAY.
DO YOU KNOW HOW LUCKY YOU ARE COMPARED WITH MY BOYHOOD? IT'S TRUE I'M HARD ON YOU.
BUT YOU'VE GOT EVERYTHING.
ISN'T THAT RIGHT, MIHO?
YES, FATHER.
SO THEN WHY WOULD THOSE DAMNED FOOL SONS OF MINE CHOOSE DEATH?!
HONEY, DO YOU THINK EIICHI KILLED HIMSELF?
DID HE REALLY DIE OF HIS OWN WILL?

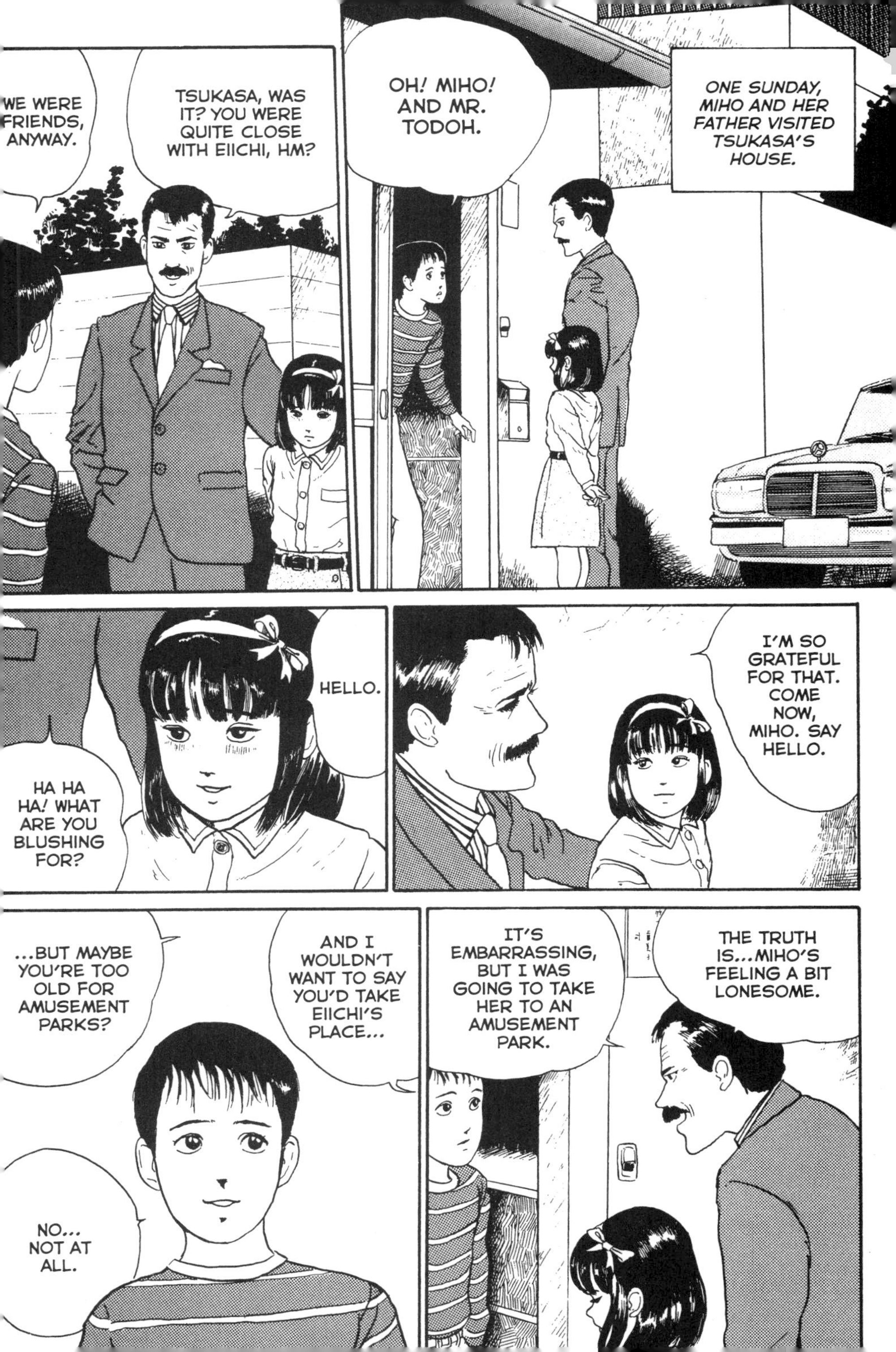
ONE SUNDAY, MIHO AND HER FATHER VISITED TSUKASA'S HOUSE.
OH! MIHO! AND MR. TODOH.
TSUKASA, WAS IT? YOU WERE QUITE CLOSE WITH EIICHI, HM?
WE WERE FRIENDS, ANYWAY.
I'M SO GRATEFUL FOR THAT. COME NOW, MIHO. SAY HELLO.
HELLO.
HA HA HA! WHAT ARE YOU BLUSHING FOR?
THE TRUTH IS...MIHO'S FEELING A BIT LONESOME.
IT'S EMBARRASSING, BUT I WAS GOING TO TAKE HER TO AN AMUSEMENT PARK.
AND I WOULDN'T WANT TO SAY YOU'D TAKE EIICHI'S PLACE...
...BUT MAYBE YOU'RE TOO OLD FOR AMUSEMENT PARKS?
NO... NOT AT ALL.

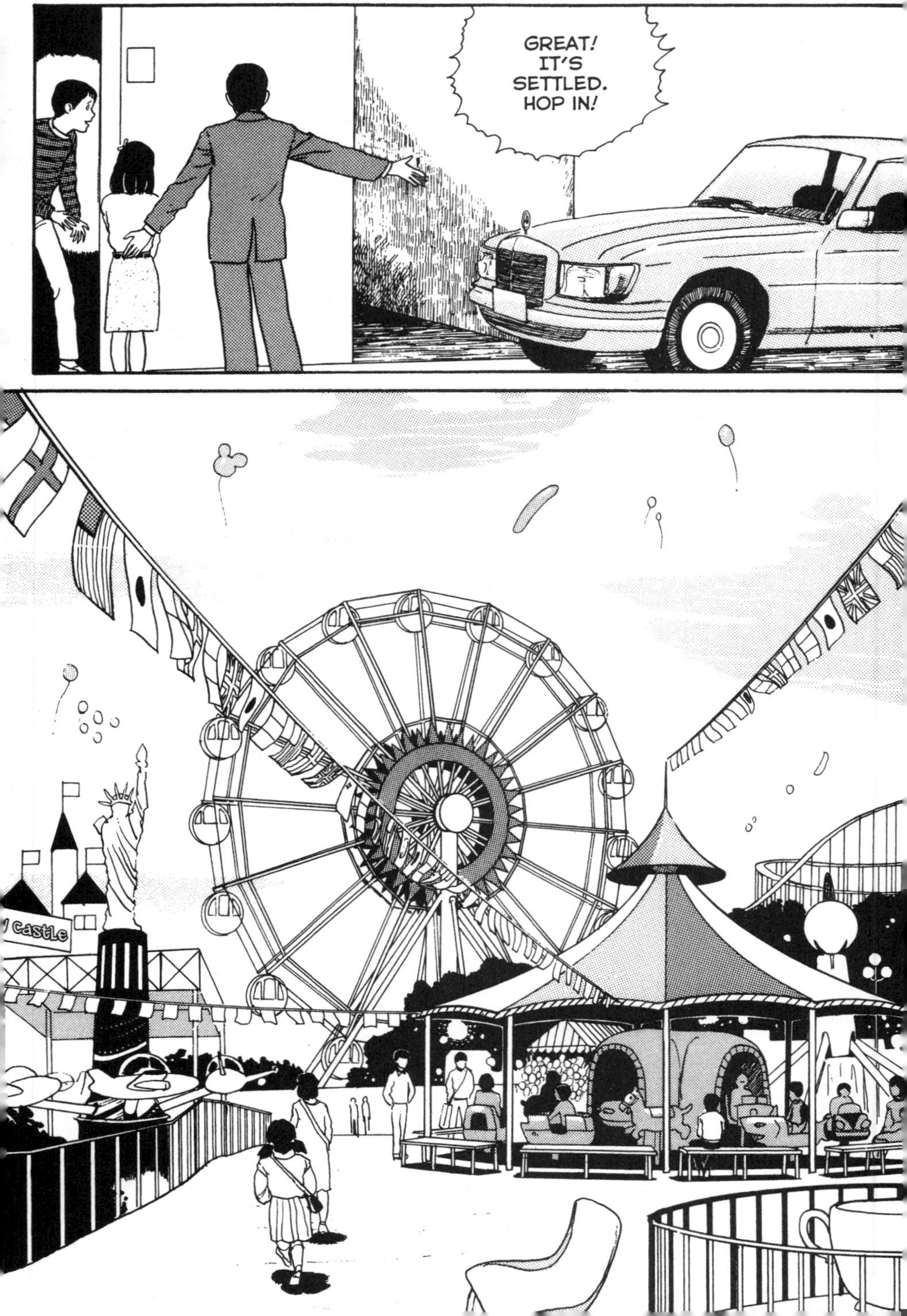
GREAT! IT'S SETTLED. HOP IN!
castle

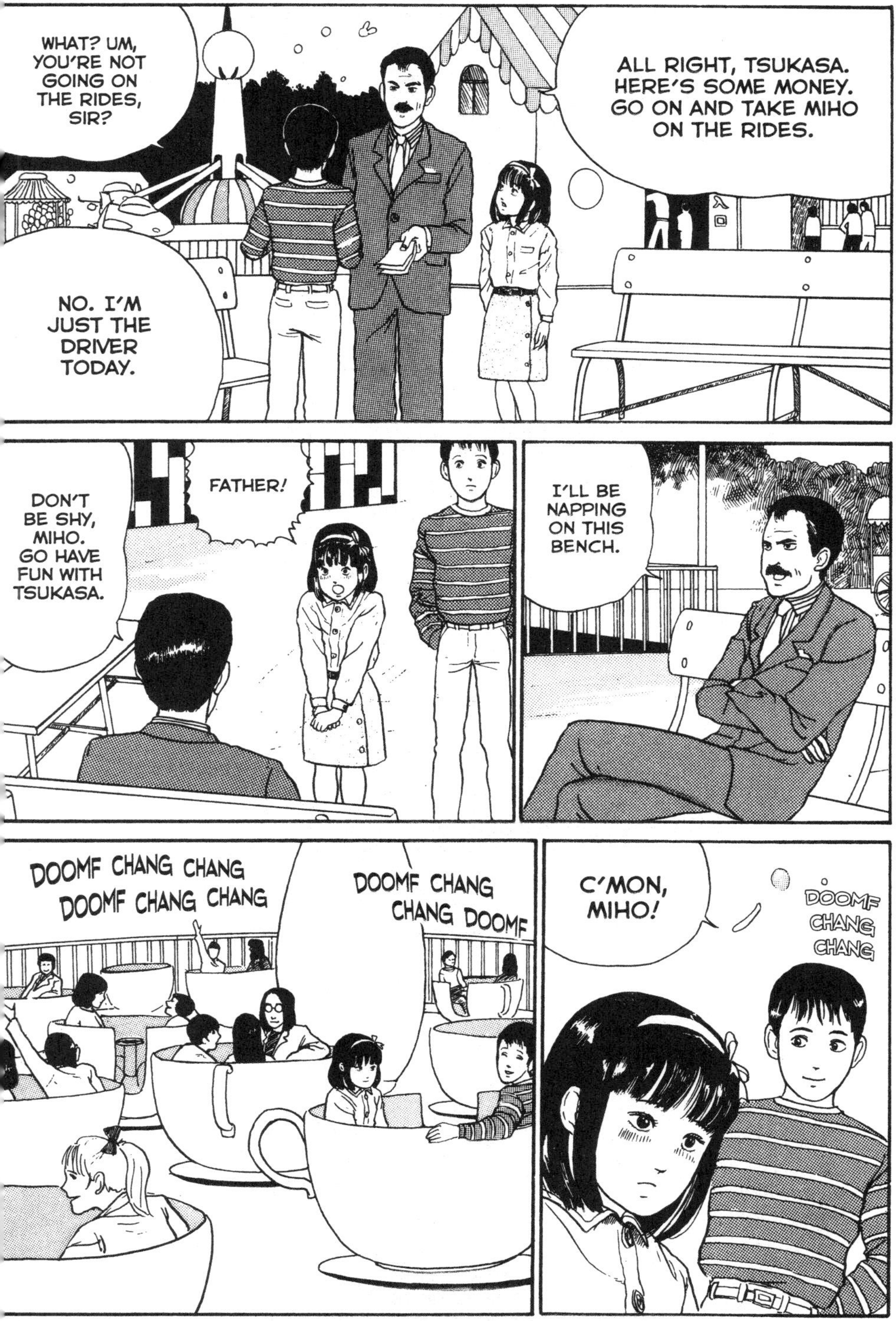
ALL RIGHT, TSUKASA. HERE'S SOME MONEY. GO ON AND TAKE MIHO ON THE RIDES.
WHAT? UM, YOU'RE NOT GOING ON THE RIDES, SIR?
NO. I'M JUST THE DRIVER TODAY.
I'LL BE NAPPING ON THIS BENCH.
FATHER!
DON'T BE SHY, MIHO. GO HAVE FUN WITH TSUKASA.
C'MON, MIHO!
DOOMF CHANG CHANG
DOOMF CHANG CHANG DOOMF
DOOMF CHANG CHANG DOOMF CHANG CHANG

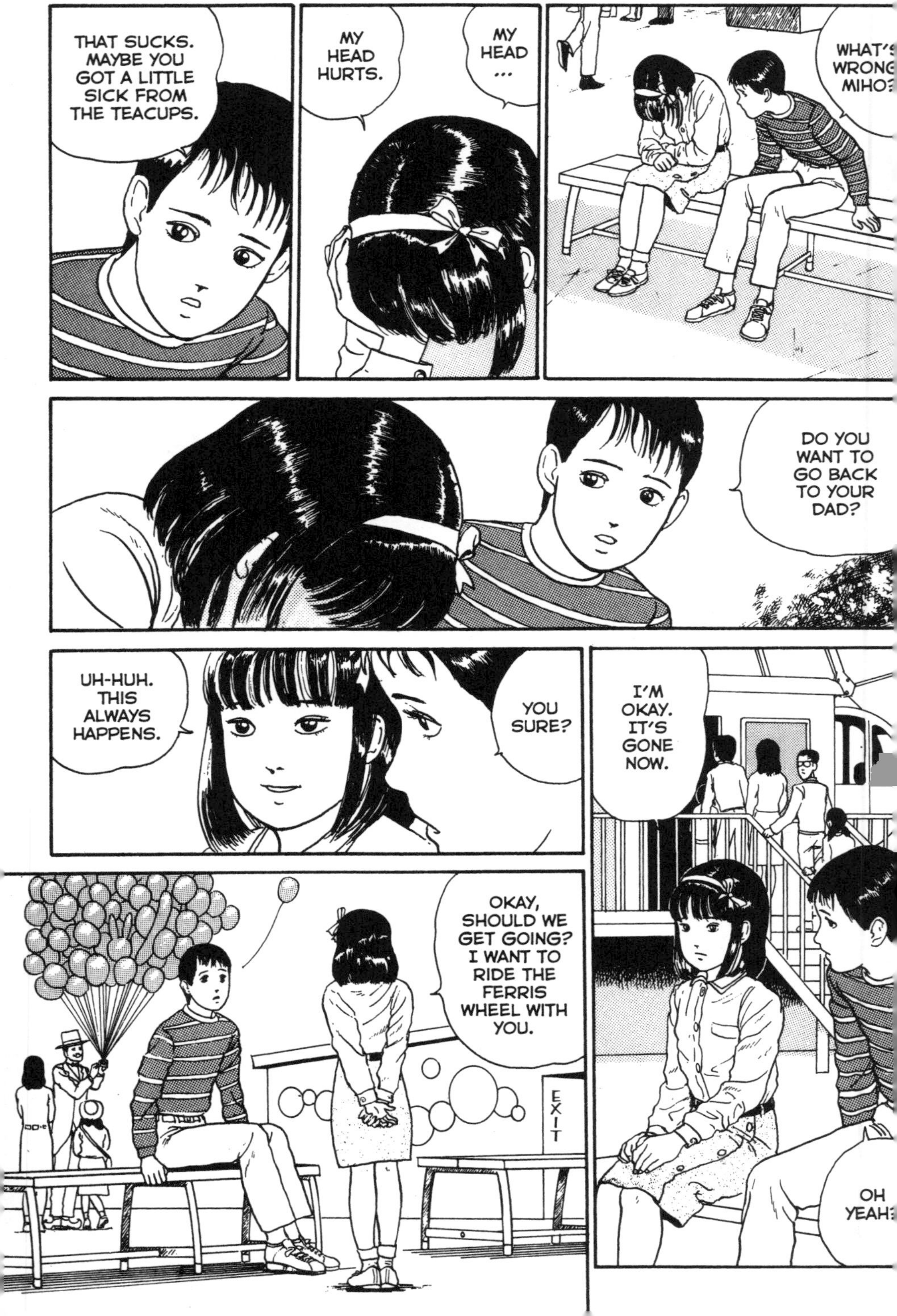

WHAT'S WRONG MIHO?
MY HEAD ...
MY HEAD HURTS.
THAT SUCKS. MAYBE YOU GOT A LITTLE SICK FROM THE TEACUPS.
DO YOU WANT TO GO BACK TO YOUR DAD?
I'M OKAY. IT'S GONE NOW.
OH YEAH?
YOU SURE?
UH-HUH. THIS ALWAYS HAPPENS.
OKAY, SHOULD WE GET GOING? I WANT TO RIDE THE FERRIS WHEEL WITH YOU.
EXIT

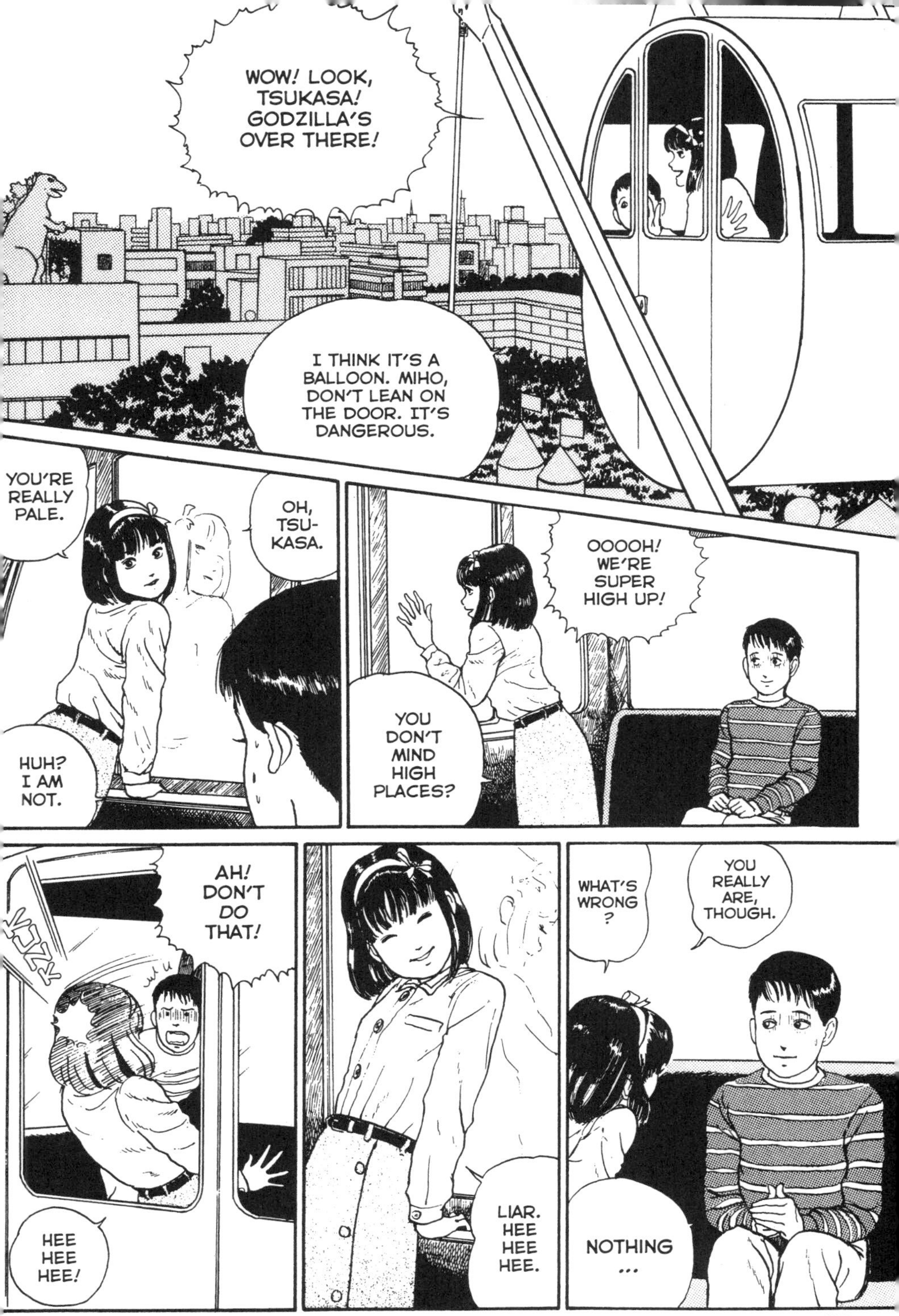
WOW! LOOK, TSUKASA! GODZILLA'S OVER THERE!
I THINK IT'S A BALLOON. MIHO, DON'T LEAN ON THE DOOR. IT'S DANGEROUS.
OOOOH! WE'RE SUPER HIGH UP!
YOU DON'T MIND HIGH PLACES?
OH, TSU-KASA.
YOU'RE REALLY PALE.
HUH? I AM NOT.
YOU REALLY ARE, THOUGH.
WHAT'S WRONG?
NOTHING...
LIAR. HEE HEE HEE.
AH! DON'T DO THAT!
HEE HEE HEE!

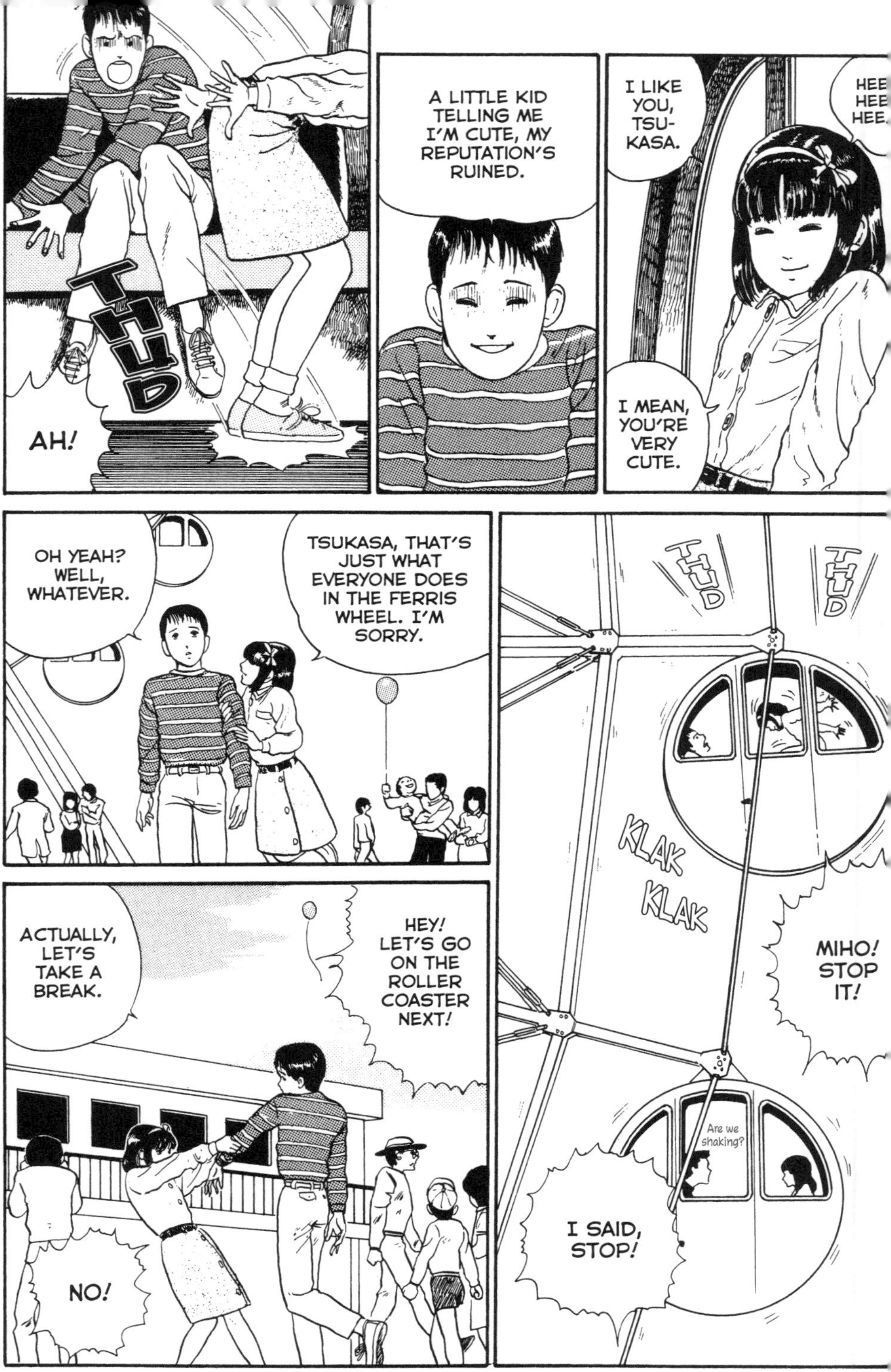
HEE HEE HEE.
I LIKE YOU, TSUKASA.
I MEAN, YOU'RE VERY CUTE.
A LITTLE KID TELLING ME I'M CUTE, MY REPUTATION'S RUINED.
THUD
AH!
THUD
THUD
KLAK
KLAK
MIHO! STOP IT!
Are we shaking?
I SAID, STOP!
TSUKASA, THAT'S JUST WHAT EVERYONE DOES IN THE FERRIS WHEEL. I'M SORRY.
OH YEAH? WELL, WHATEVER.
HEY! LET'S GO ON THE ROLLER COASTER NEXT!
ACTUALLY, LET'S TAKE A BREAK.
NO!

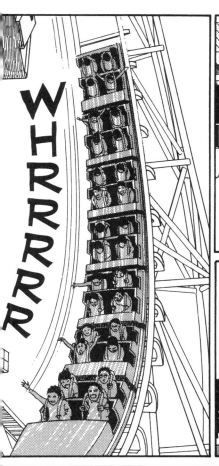

WHRRRRRR

I'LL TELL DADDY!

HE GAVE YOU MONEY, DIDN'T HE?!

AAAAAH

KRRRRR

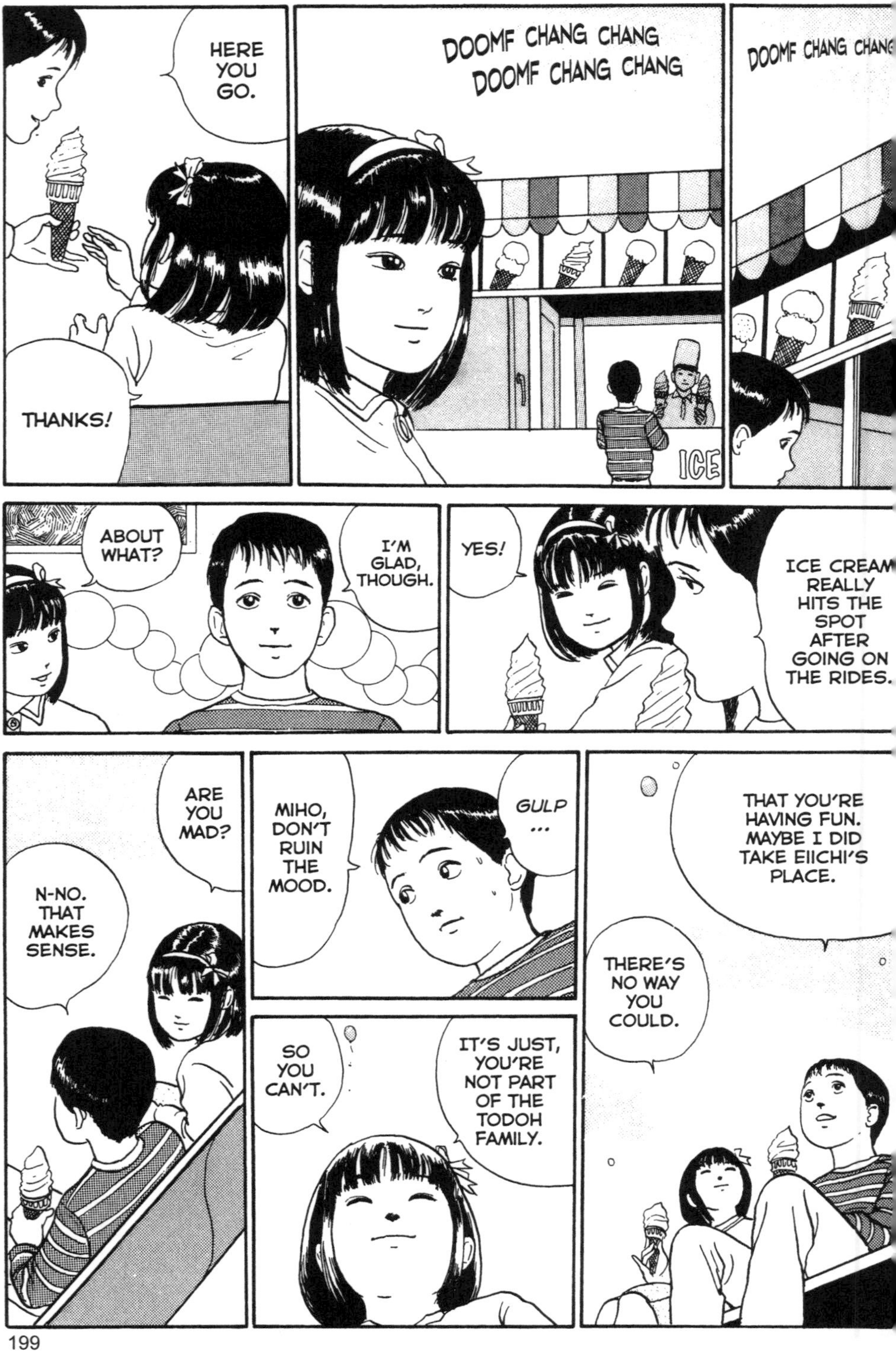
DOOMF CHANG CHANG
DOOMF CHANG CHANG
DOOMF CHANG CHANG
ICE
HERE YOU GO.
THANKS!
ICE CREAM REALLY HITS THE SPOT AFTER GOING ON THE RIDES.
YES!
I'M GLAD, THOUGH.
ABOUT WHAT?
THAT YOU'RE HAVING FUN. MAYBE I DID TAKE EIICHI'S PLACE.
THERE'S NO WAY YOU COULD.
GULP ...
MIHO, DON'T RUIN THE MOOD.
IT'S JUST, YOU'RE NOT PART OF THE TODOH FAMILY.
SO YOU CAN'T.
ARE YOU MAD?
N-NO. THAT MAKES SENSE.

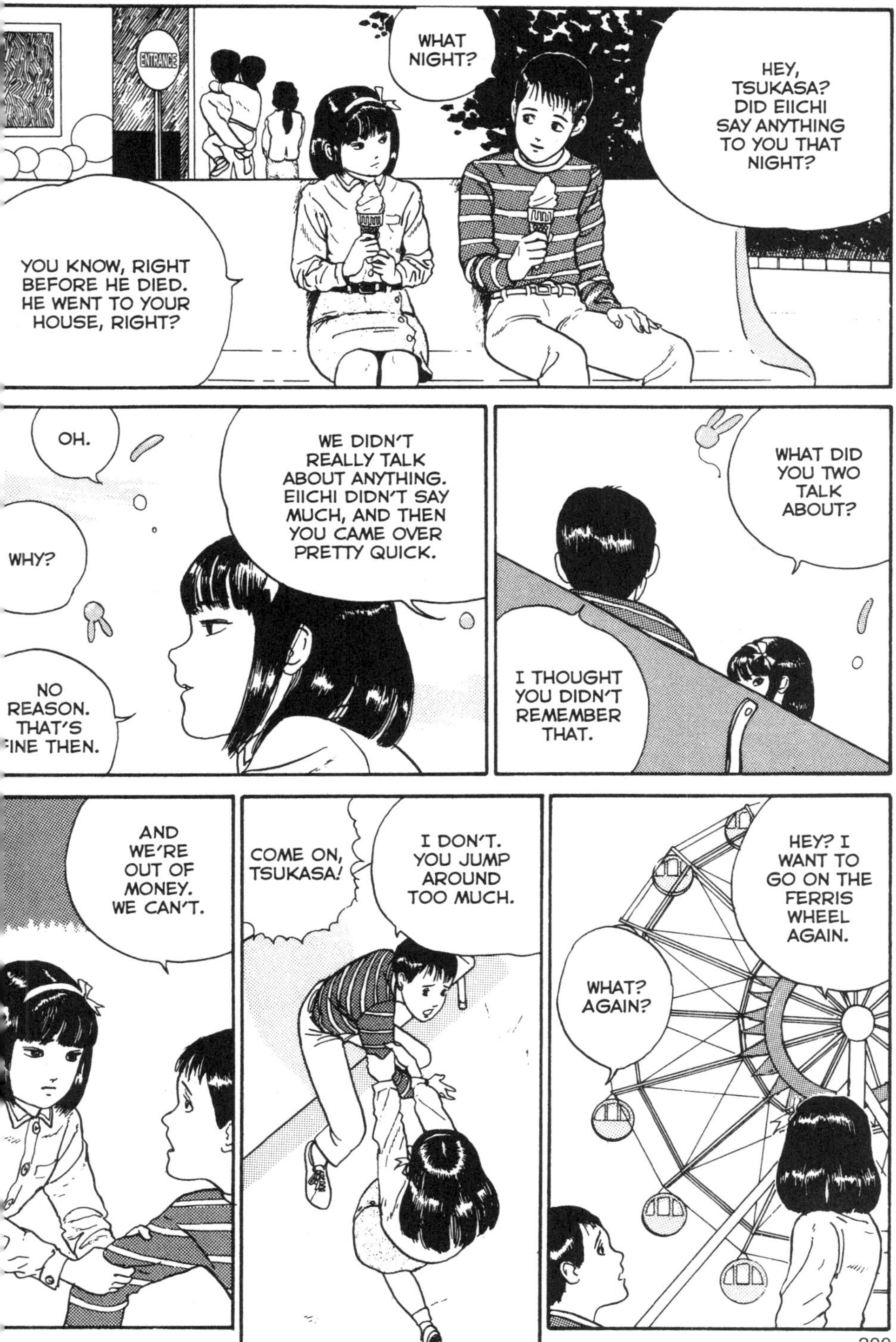

ENTRANCE
HEY, TSUKASA? DID EIICHI SAY ANYTHING TO YOU THAT NIGHT?
WHAT NIGHT?
YOU KNOW, RIGHT BEFORE HE DIED. HE WENT TO YOUR HOUSE, RIGHT?
WHAT DID YOU TWO TALK ABOUT?
I THOUGHT YOU DIDN'T REMEMBER THAT.
WE DIDN'T REALLY TALK ABOUT ANYTHING. EIICHI DIDN'T SAY MUCH, AND THEN YOU CAME OVER PRETTY QUICK.
OH.
WHY?
NO REASON. THAT'S FINE THEN.
HEY? I WANT TO GO ON THE FERRIS WHEEL AGAIN.
WHAT? AGAIN?
I DON'T. YOU JUMP AROUND TOO MUCH.
COME ON, TSUKASA!
AND WE'RE OUT OF MONEY. WE CAN'T.

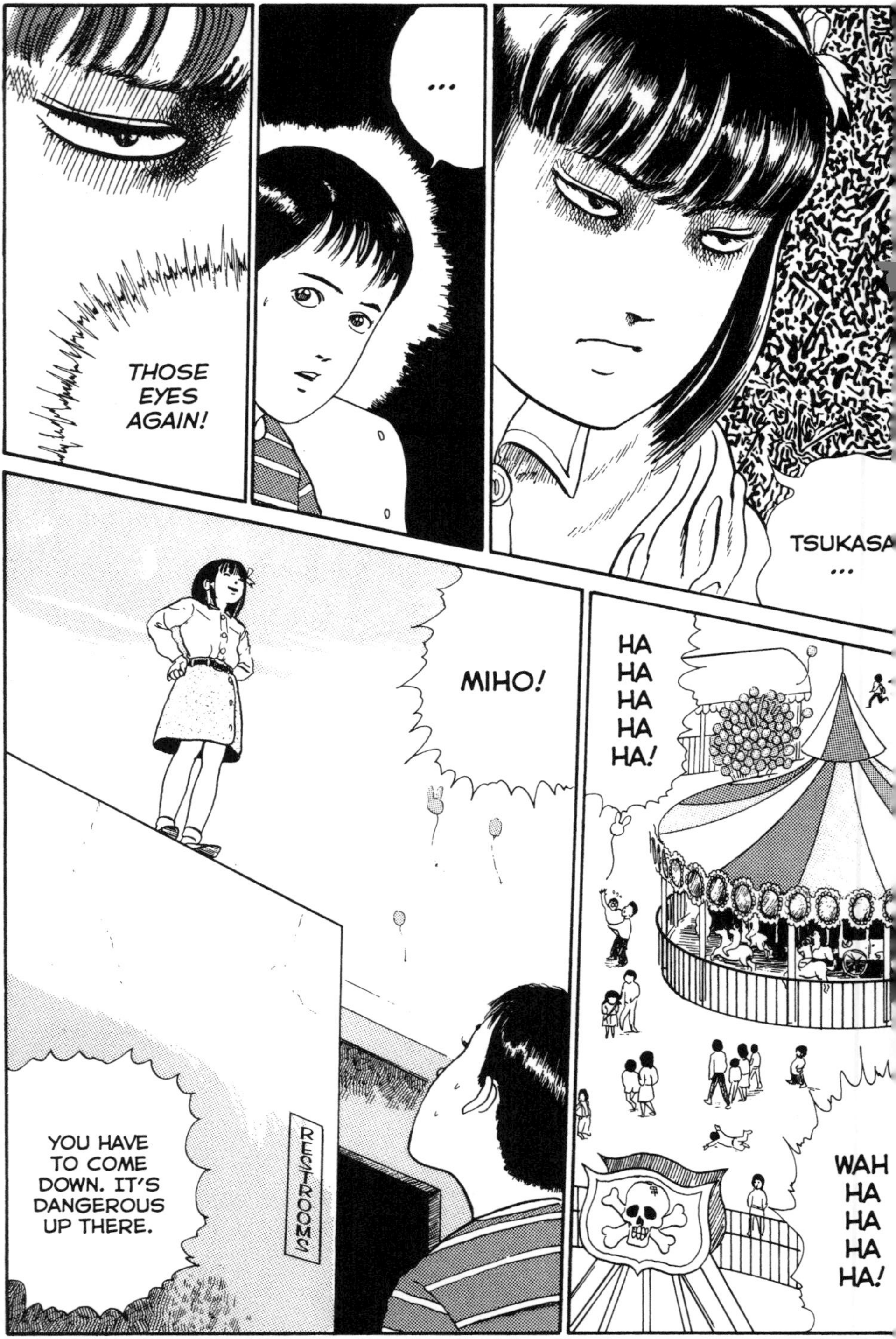
TSUKASA ...
...
THOSE EYES AGAIN!
HA HA HA HA HA!
WAH HA HA HA HA!
MIHO!
RESTROOMS
YOU HAVE TO COME DOWN. IT'S DANGEROUS UP THERE.

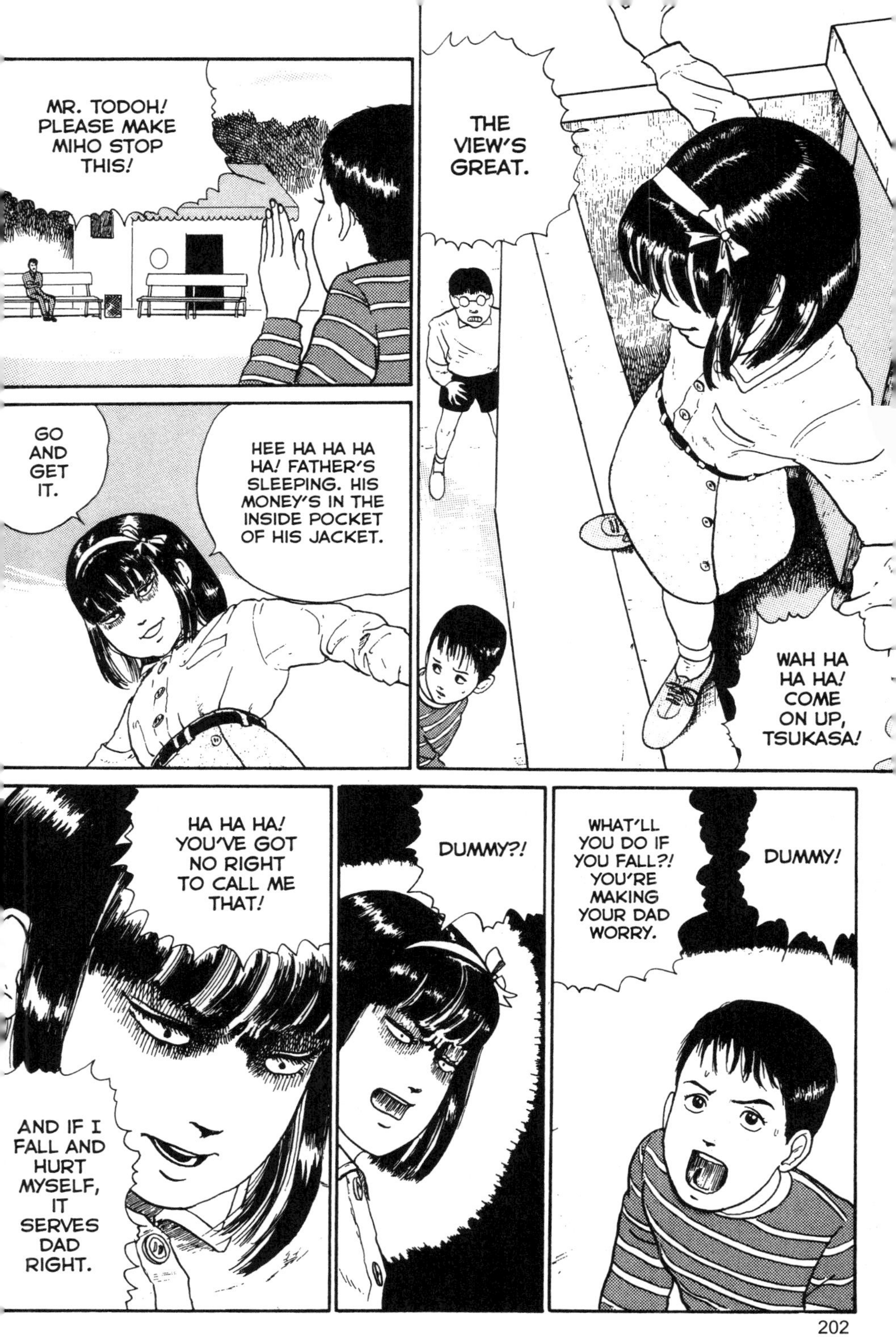
THE VIEW'S GREAT.
WAH HA HA HA! COME ON UP, TSUKASA!
MR. TODOH! PLEASE MAKE MIHO STOP THIS!
HEE HA HA HA HA! FATHER'S SLEEPING. HIS MONEY'S IN THE INSIDE POCKET OF HIS JACKET.
GO AND GET IT.
DUMMY!
WHAT'LL YOU DO IF YOU FALL?! YOU'RE MAKING YOUR DAD WORRY.
DUMMY?!
HA HA HA! YOU'VE GOT NO RIGHT TO CALL ME THAT!
AND IF I FALL AND HURT MYSELF, IT SERVES DAD RIGHT.

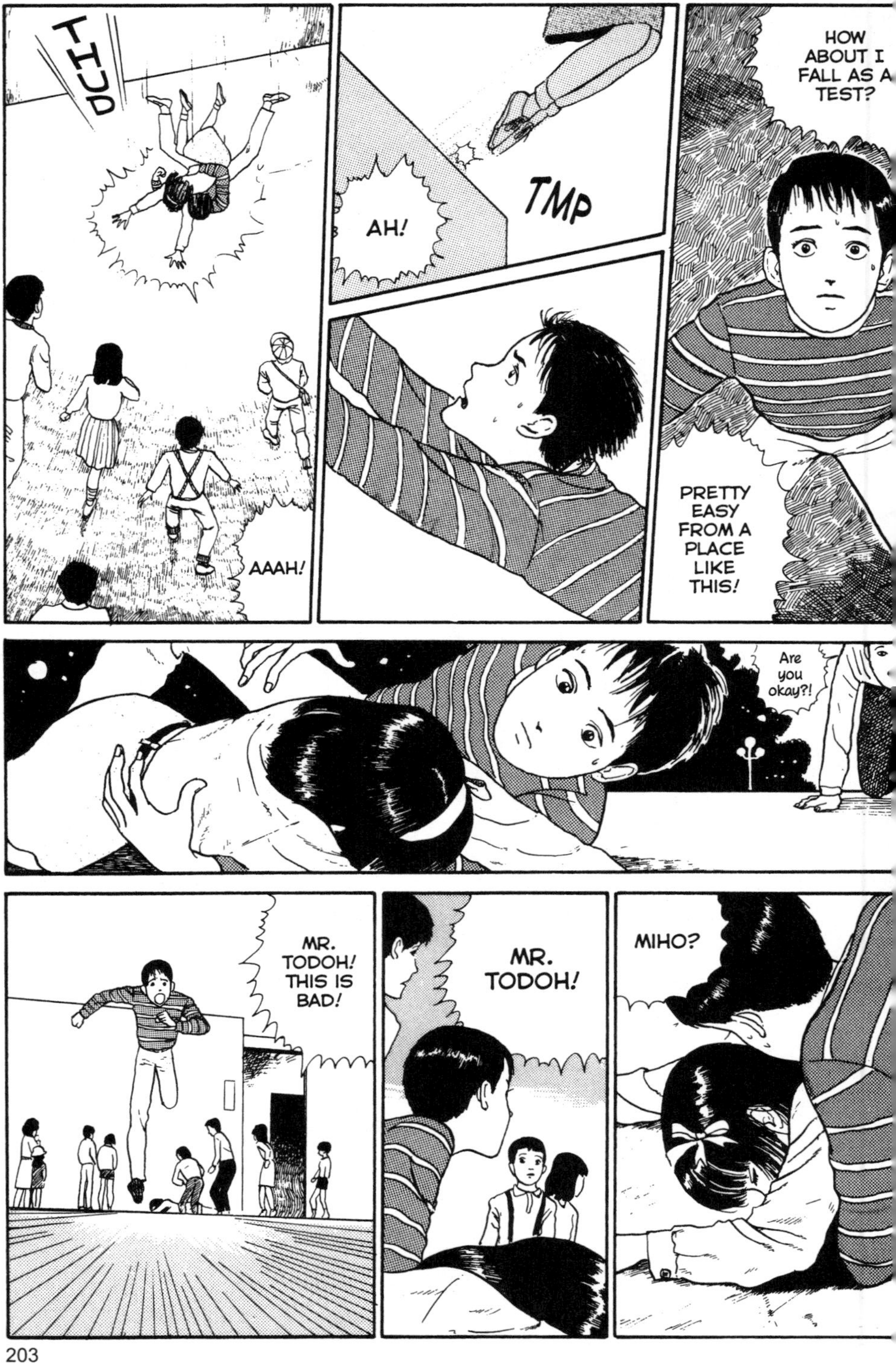
HOW ABOUT I FALL AS A TEST?
PRETTY EASY FROM A PLACE LIKE THIS!
TMP
AH!
THUD
AAAH!
Are you okay?!
MIHO?
MR. TODOH!
MR. TODOH! THIS IS BAD!

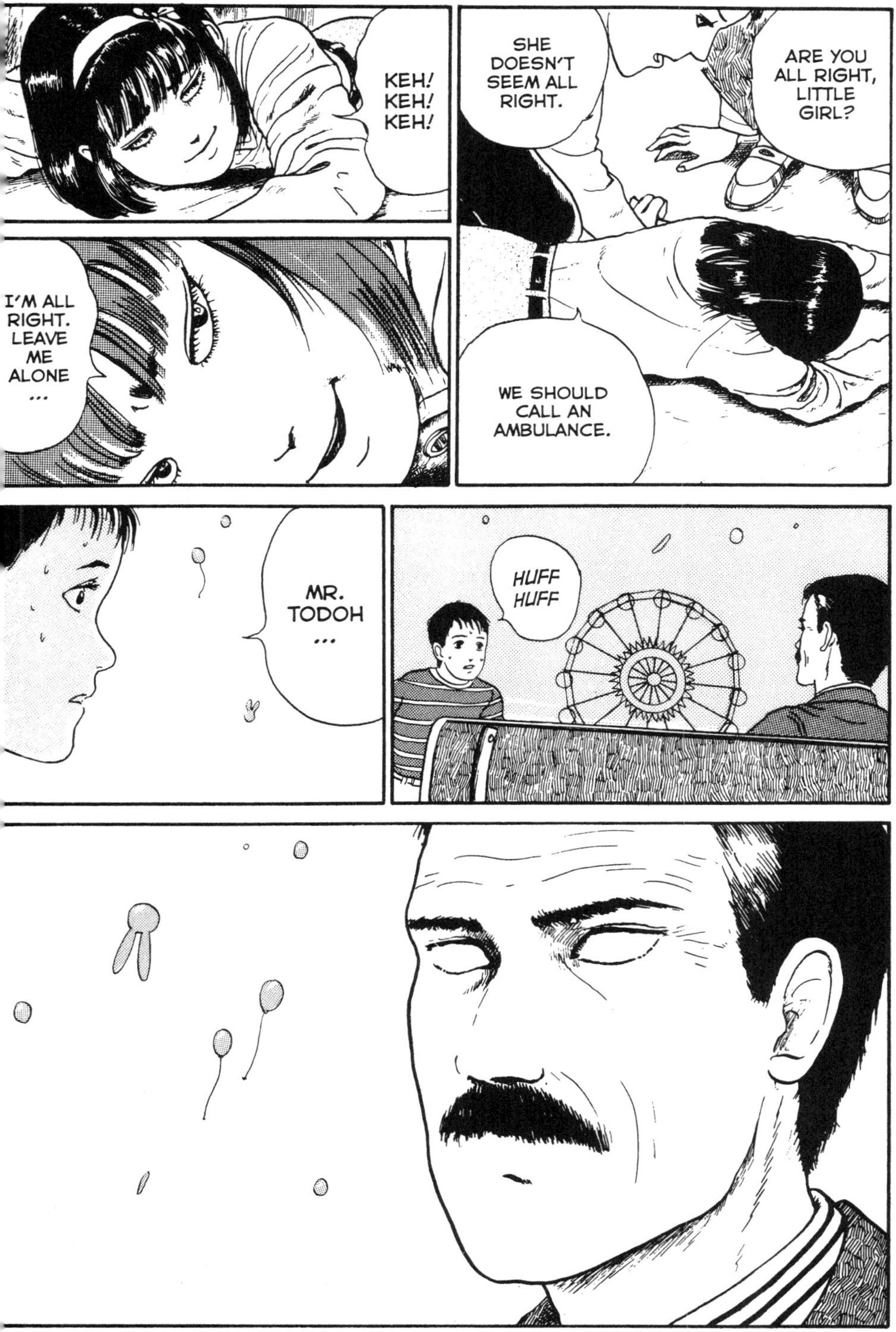
ARE YOU ALL RIGHT, LITTLE GIRL?
SHE DOESN'T SEEM ALL RIGHT.
WE SHOULD CALL AN AMBULANCE.
KEH! KEH! KEH!
I'M ALL RIGHT. LEAVE ME ALONE ...
HUFF HUFF
MR. TODOH ...

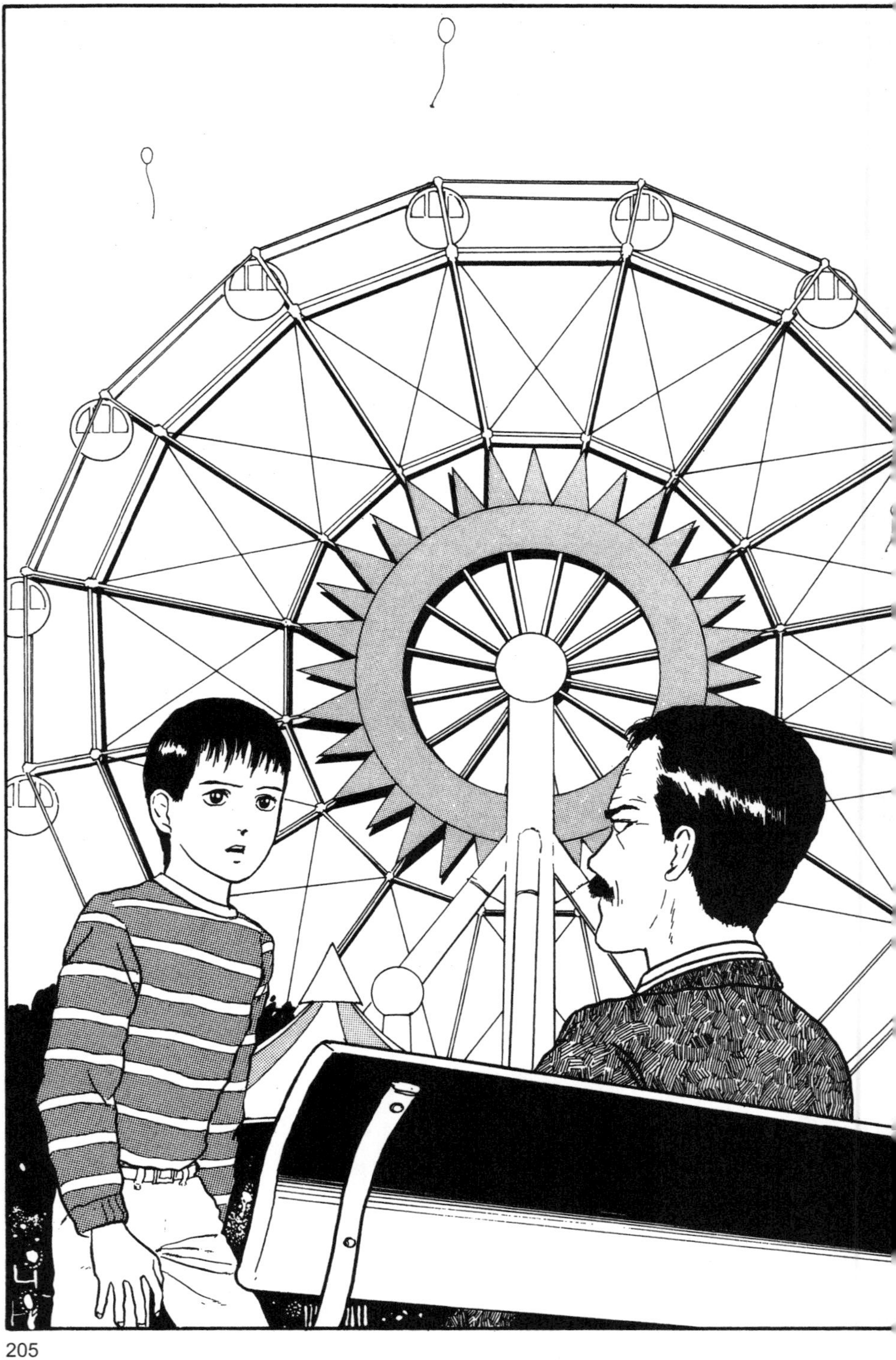

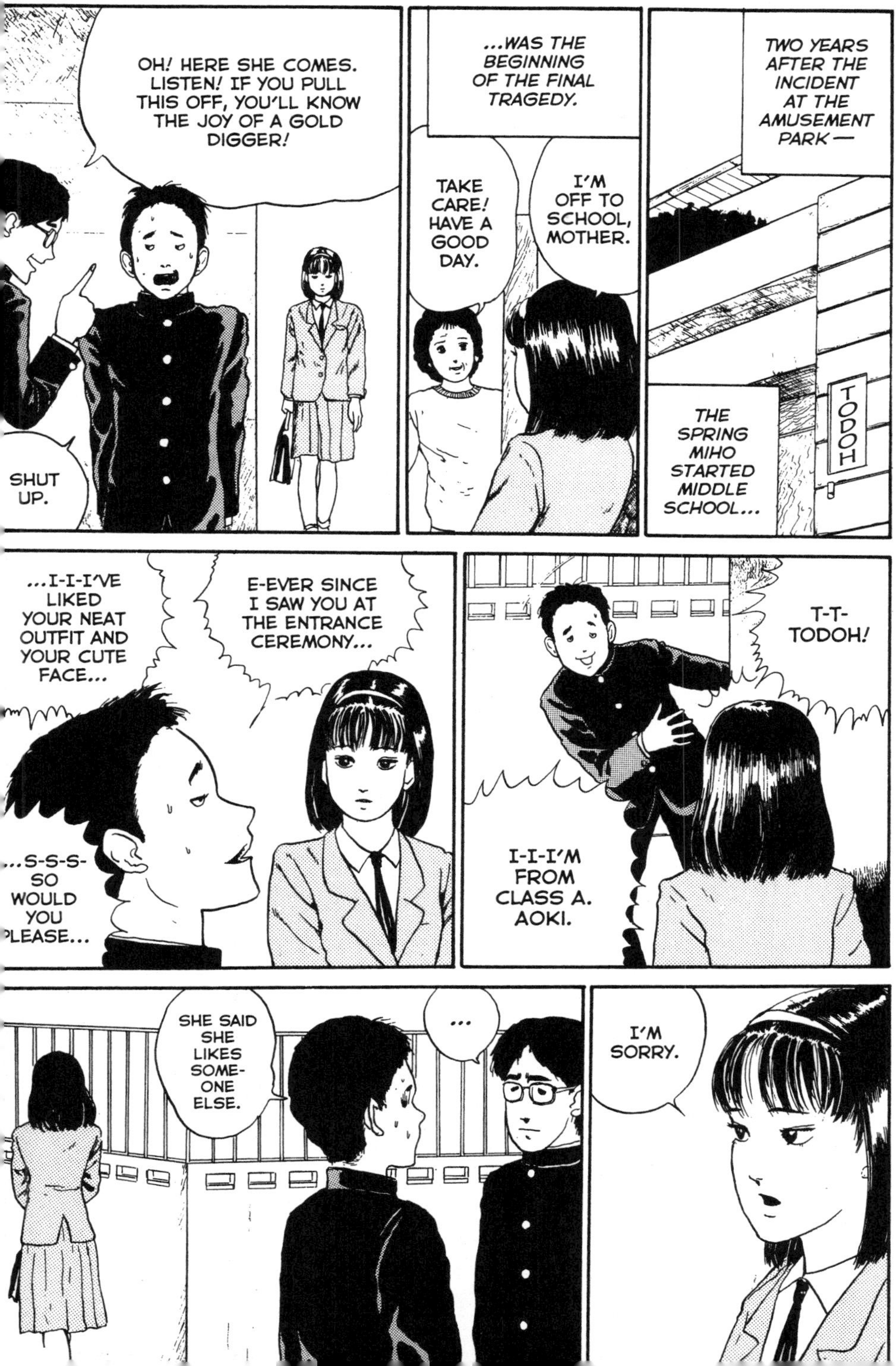
TWO YEARS AFTER THE INCIDENT AT THE AMUSEMENT PARK—
THE SPRING MIHO STARTED MIDDLE SCHOOL...
TODOH
...WAS THE BEGINNING OF THE FINAL TRAGEDY.
I'M OFF TO SCHOOL, MOTHER.
TAKE CARE! HAVE A GOOD DAY.
OH! HERE SHE COMES. LISTEN! IF YOU PULL THIS OFF, YOU'LL KNOW THE JOY OF A GOLD DIGGER!
SHUT UP.
T-T-TODOH!
I-I-I'M FROM CLASS A. AOKI.
E-EVER SINCE I SAW YOU AT THE ENTRANCE CEREMONY...
...I-I-I'VE LIKED YOUR NEAT OUTFIT AND YOUR CUTE FACE...
...S-S-S-SO WOULD YOU LEASE...
I'M SORRY.
...
SHE SAID SHE LIKES SOME-ONE ELSE.

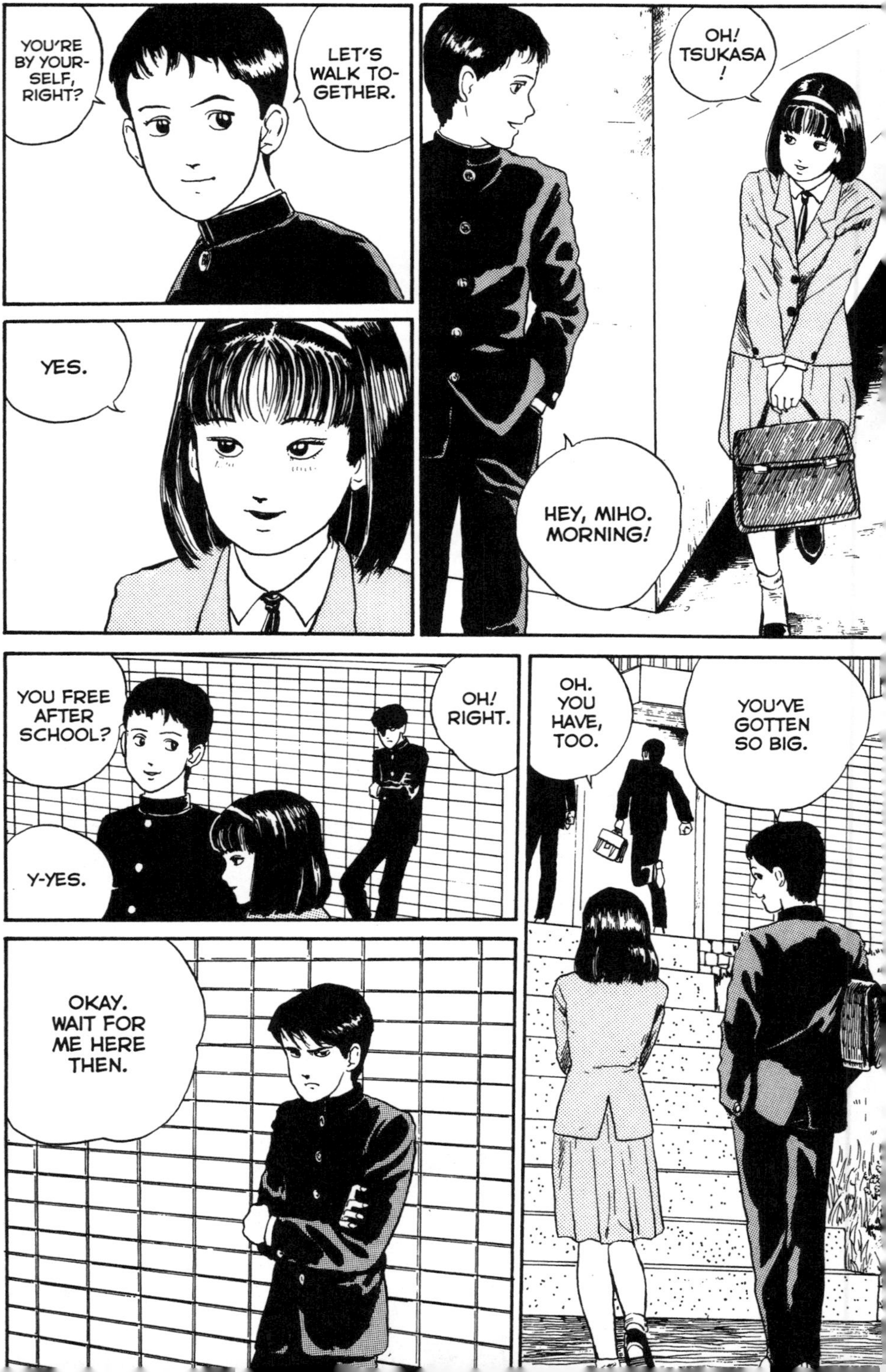
OH! TSUKASA!
HEY, MIHO. MORNING!
LET'S WALK TO-GETHER.
YOU'RE BY YOUR-SELF, RIGHT?
YES.
YOU'VE GOTTEN SO BIG.
OH. YOU HAVE, TOO.
OH! RIGHT.
YOU FREE AFTER SCHOOL?
Y-YES.
OKAY. WAIT FOR ME HERE THEN.

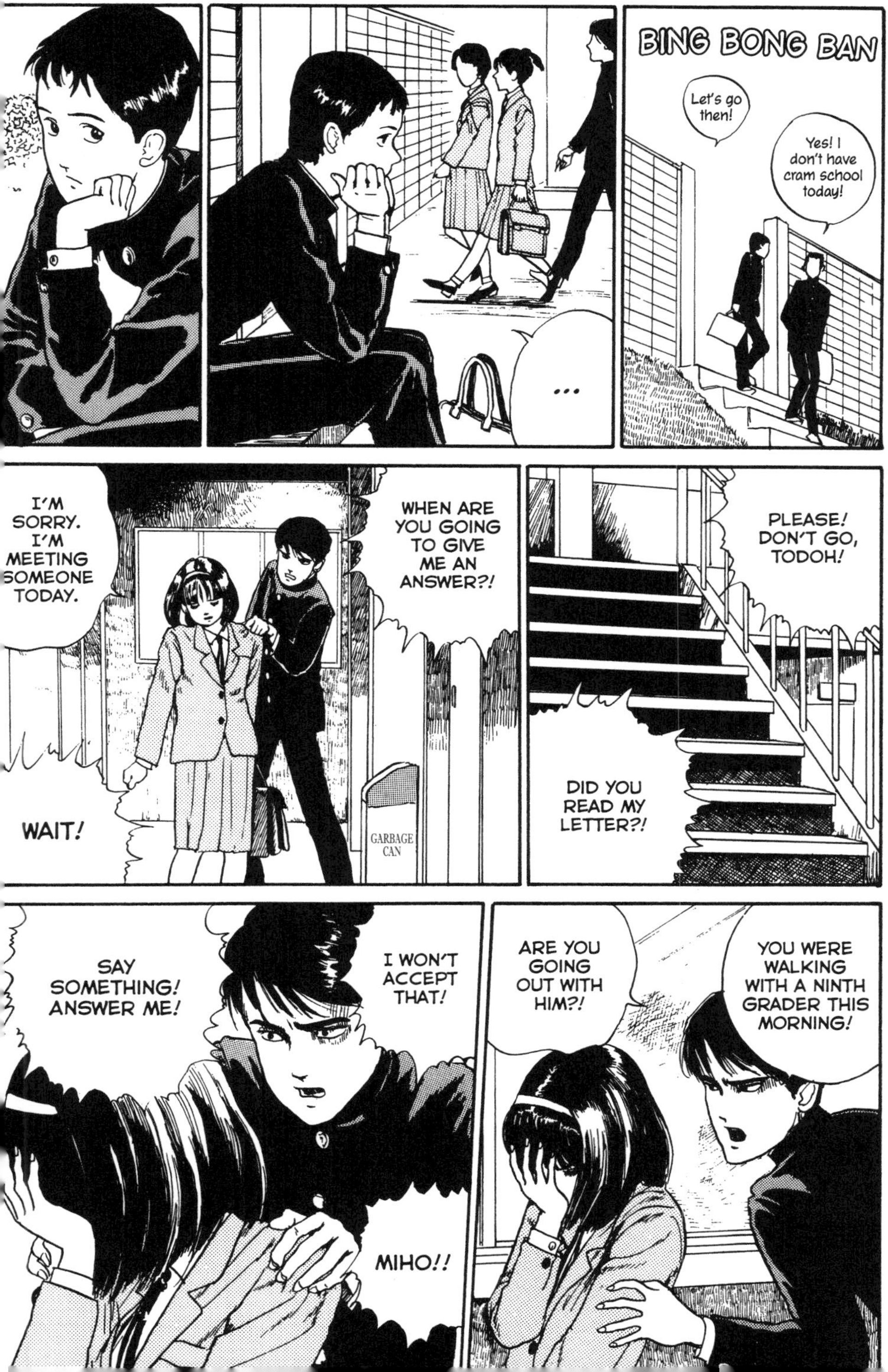
BING BONG BAN
Let's go then!
Yes! I don't have cram school today!
...
PLEASE! DON'T GO, TODOH!
DID YOU READ MY LETTER?!
WHEN ARE YOU GOING TO GIVE ME AN ANSWER?!
I'M SORRY. I'M MEETING SOMEONE TODAY.
WAIT!
GARBAGE CAN
YOU WERE WALKING WITH A NINTH GRADER THIS MORNING!
ARE YOU GOING OUT WITH HIM?!
I WON'T ACCEPT THAT!
SAY SOMETHING! ANSWER ME!
MIHO!!

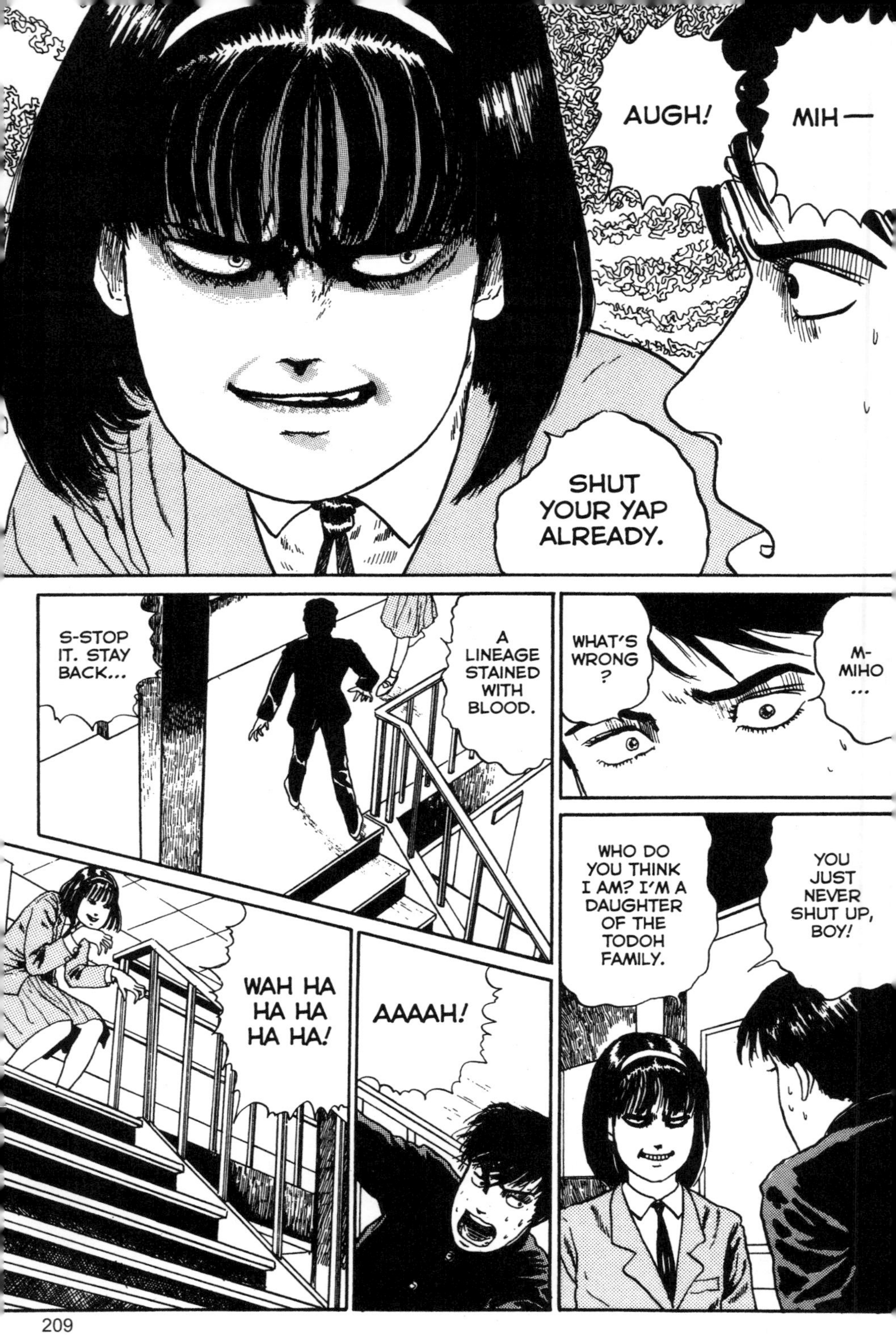
MIH—
AUGH!
SHUT YOUR YAP ALREADY.
M-MIHO...
WHAT'S WRONG?
YOU JUST NEVER SHUT UP, BOY!
WHO DO YOU THINK I AM? I'M A DAUGHTER OF THE TODOH FAMILY.
A LINEAGE STAINED WITH BLOOD.
S-STOP IT. STAY BACK...
AAAAH!
WAH HA HA HA HA HA!

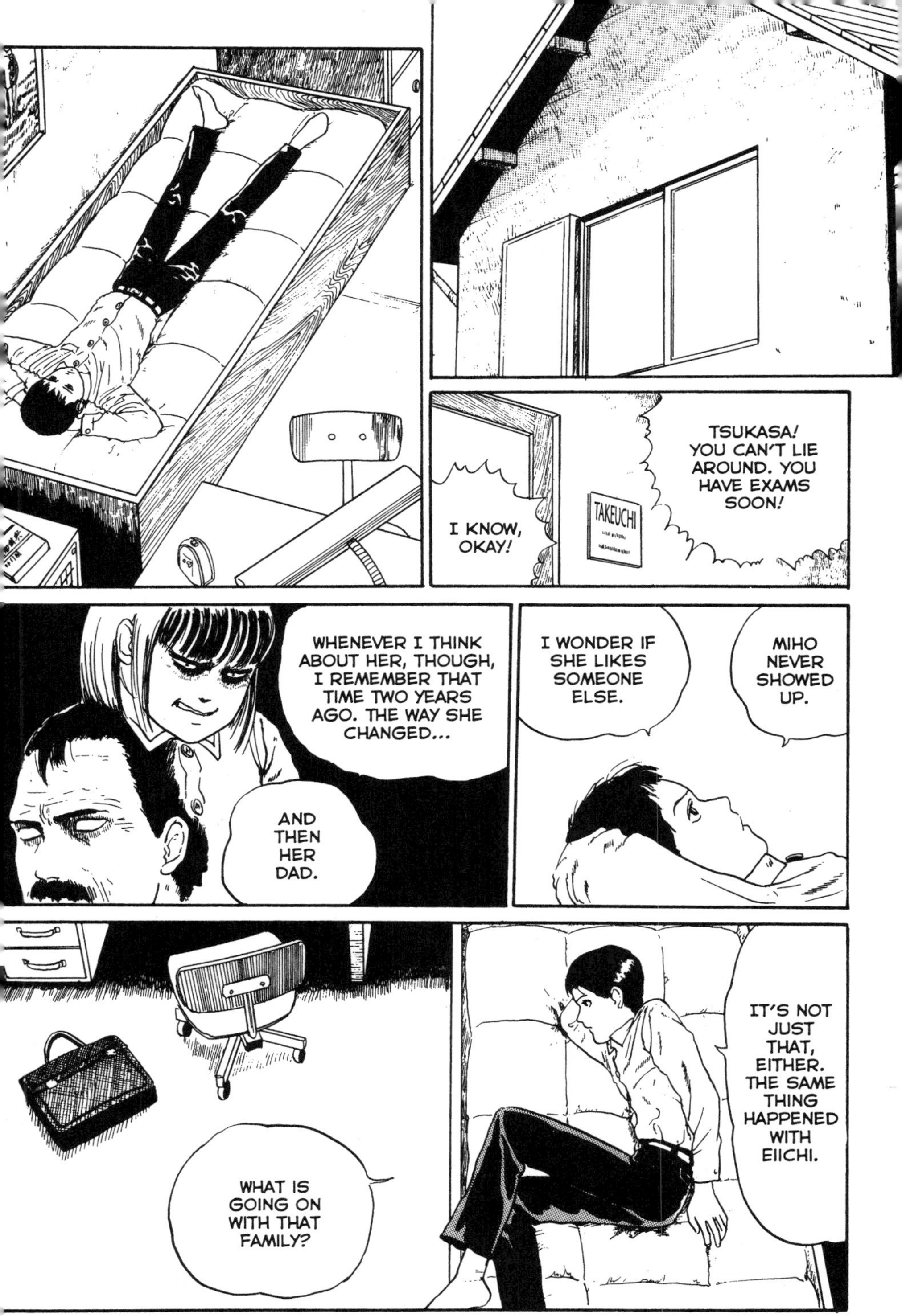
TSUKASA! YOU CAN'T LIE AROUND. YOU HAVE EXAMS SOON!
TAKEUCHI
I KNOW, OKAY!
MIHO NEVER SHOWED UP.
I WONDER IF SHE LIKES SOMEONE ELSE.
WHENEVER I THINK ABOUT HER, THOUGH, I REMEMBER THAT TIME TWO YEARS AGO. THE WAY SHE CHANGED...
AND THEN HER DAD.
IT'S NOT JUST THAT, EITHER. THE SAME THING HAPPENED WITH EIICHI.
WHAT IS GOING ON WITH THAT FAMILY?

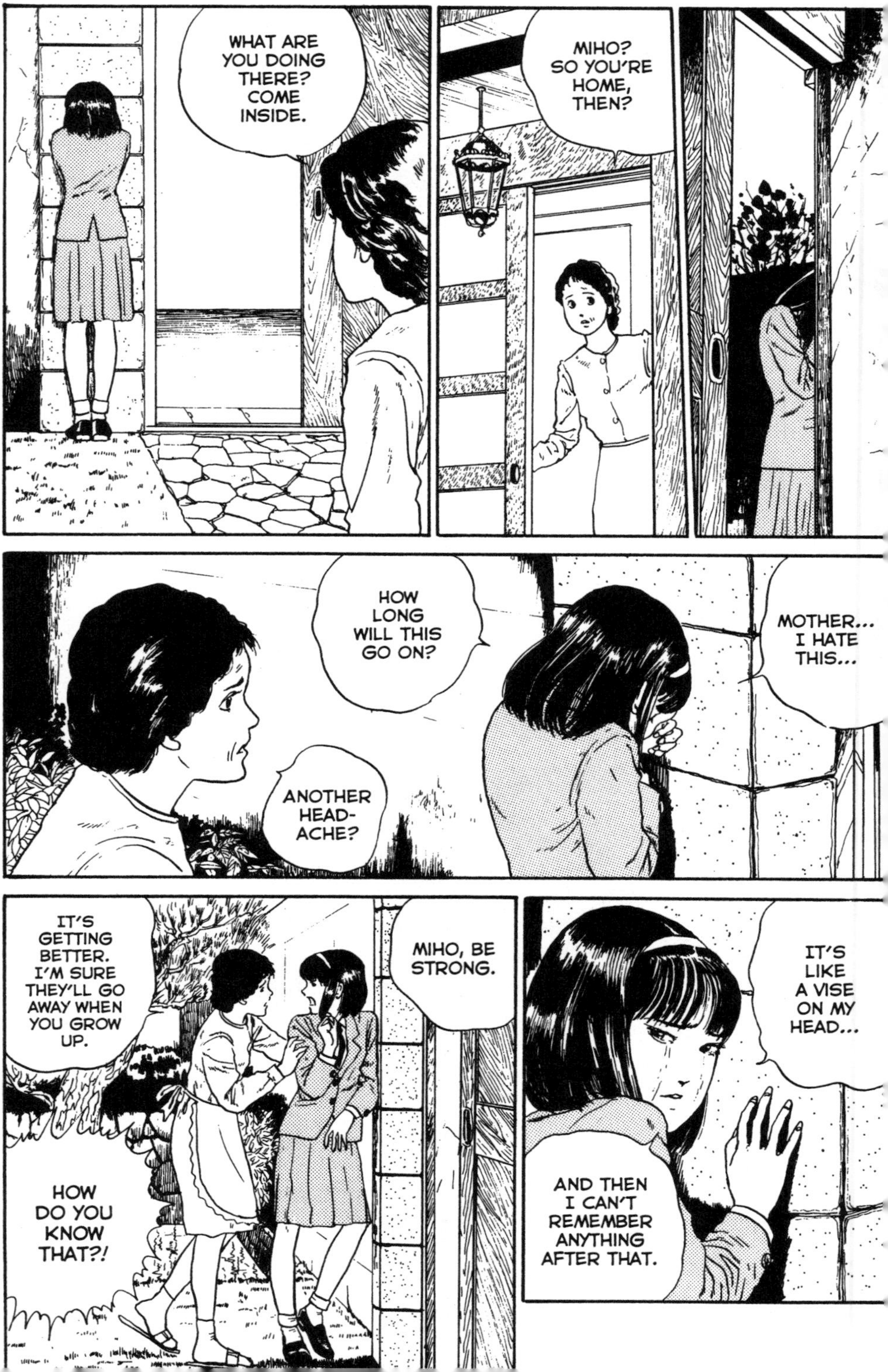
MIHO? SO YOU'RE HOME, THEN?
WHAT ARE YOU DOING THERE? COME INSIDE.
MOTHER... I HATE THIS...
HOW LONG WILL THIS GO ON?
ANOTHER HEAD-ACHE?
IT'S LIKE A VISE ON MY HEAD...
AND THEN I CAN'T REMEMBER ANYTHING AFTER THAT.
MIHO, BE STRONG.
IT'S GETTING BETTER. I'M SURE THEY'LL GO AWAY WHEN YOU GROW UP.
HOW DO YOU KNOW THAT?!

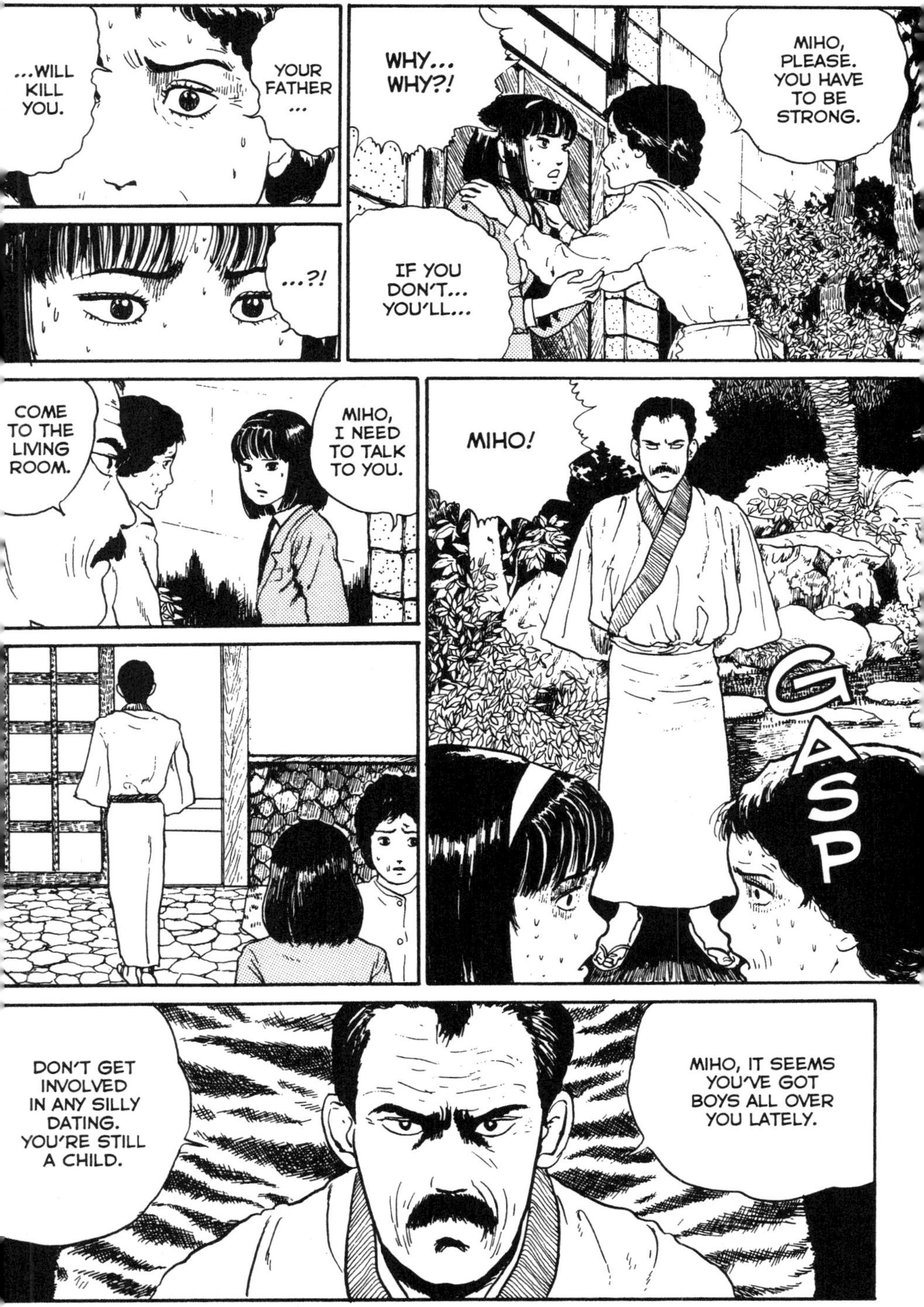
MIHO, PLEASE. YOU HAVE TO BE STRONG.
WHY... WHY?!
IF YOU DON'T... YOU'LL...
YOUR FATHER ...
...WILL KILL YOU.
...?!
MIHO!
GASP
MIHO, I NEED TO TALK TO YOU.
COME TO THE LIVING ROOM.
MIHO, IT SEEMS YOU'VE GOT BOYS ALL OVER YOU LATELY.
DON'T GET INVOLVED IN ANY SILLY DATING. YOU'RE STILL A CHILD.

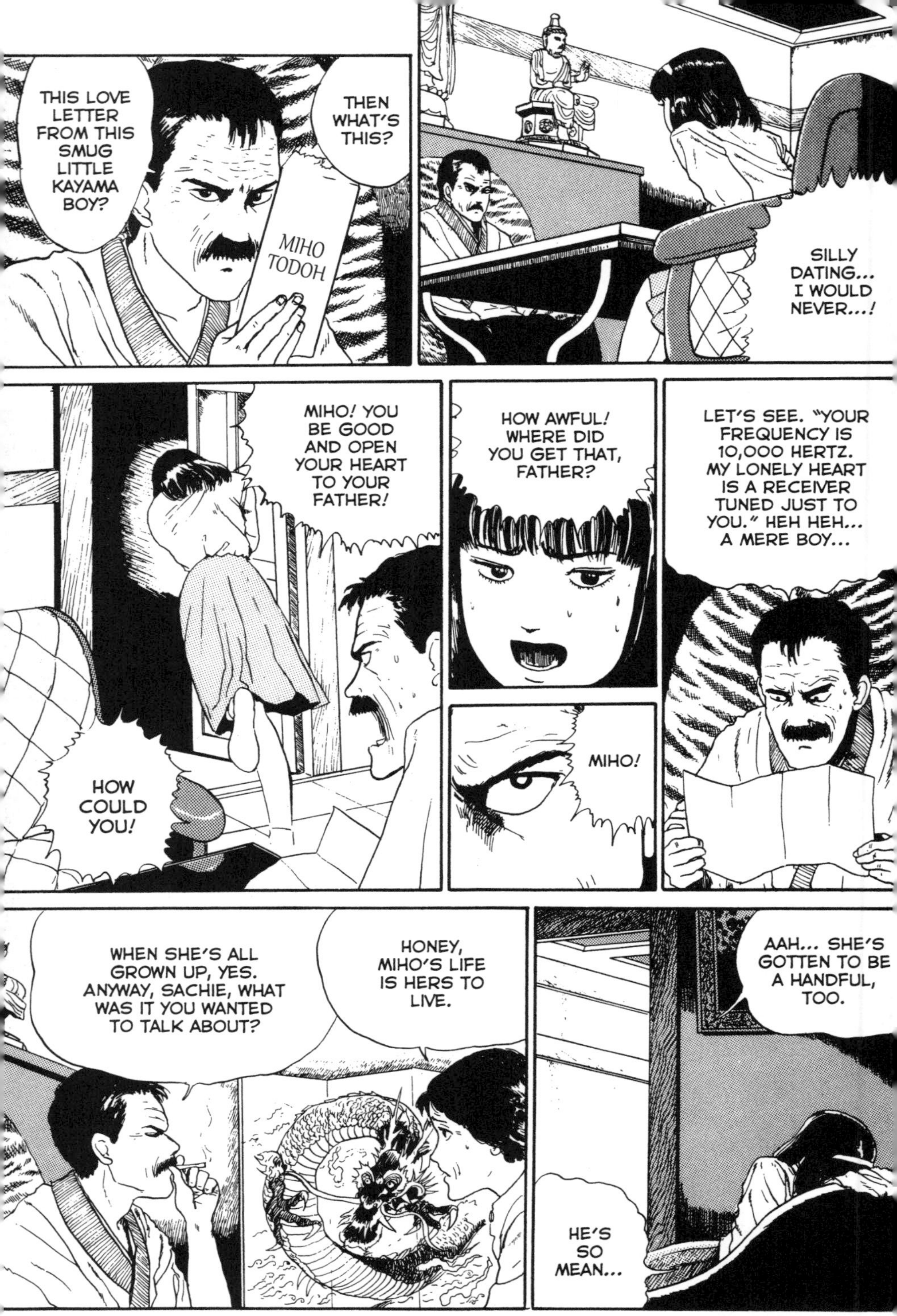
SILLY DATING... I WOULD NEVER...!
THEN WHAT'S THIS?
THIS LOVE LETTER FROM THIS SMUG LITTLE KAYAMA BOY?
MIHO TODOH
LET'S SEE. "YOUR FREQUENCY IS 10,000 HERTZ. MY LONELY HEART IS A RECEIVER TUNED JUST TO YOU." HEH HEH... A MERE BOY...
HOW AWFUL! WHERE DID YOU GET THAT, FATHER?
MIHO!
MIHO! YOU BE GOOD AND OPEN YOUR HEART TO YOUR FATHER!
HOW COULD YOU!
AAH... SHE'S GOTTEN TO BE A HANDFUL, TOO.
HE'S SO MEAN...
HONEY, MIHO'S LIFE IS HERS TO LIVE.
WHEN SHE'S ALL GROWN UP, YES. ANYWAY, SACHIE, WHAT WAS IT YOU WANTED TO TALK ABOUT?

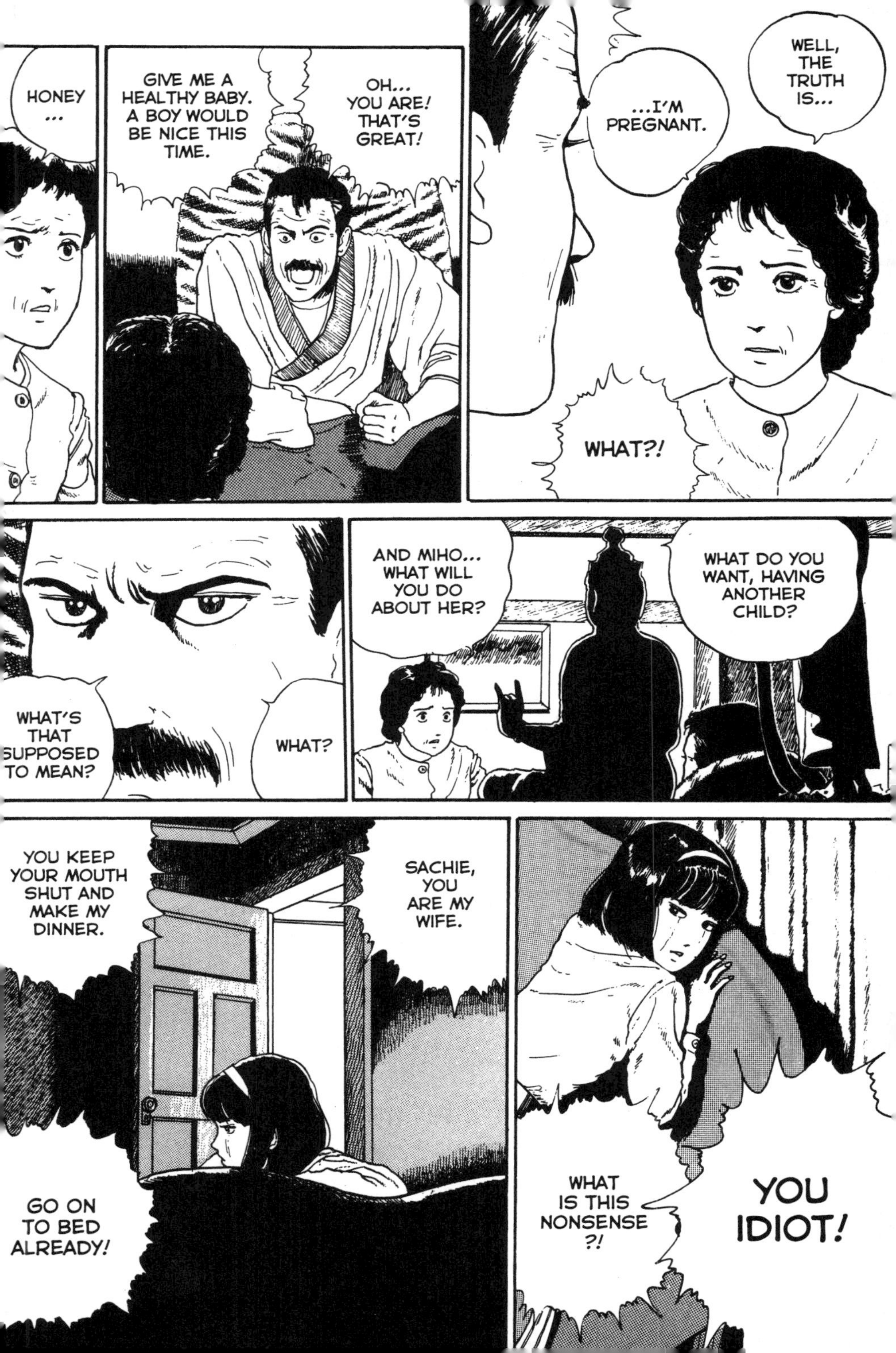
WELL, THE TRUTH IS...
...I'M PREGNANT.
WHAT?!
OH... YOU ARE! THAT'S GREAT!
GIVE ME A HEALTHY BABY. A BOY WOULD BE NICE THIS TIME.
HONEY ...
WHAT DO YOU WANT, HAVING ANOTHER CHILD?
AND MIHO... WHAT WILL YOU DO ABOUT HER?
WHAT?
WHAT'S THAT SUPPOSED TO MEAN?
YOU IDIOT!
WHAT IS THIS NONSENSE ?!
SACHIE, YOU ARE MY WIFE.
YOU KEEP YOUR MOUTH SHUT AND MAKE MY DINNER.
GO ON TO BED ALREADY!

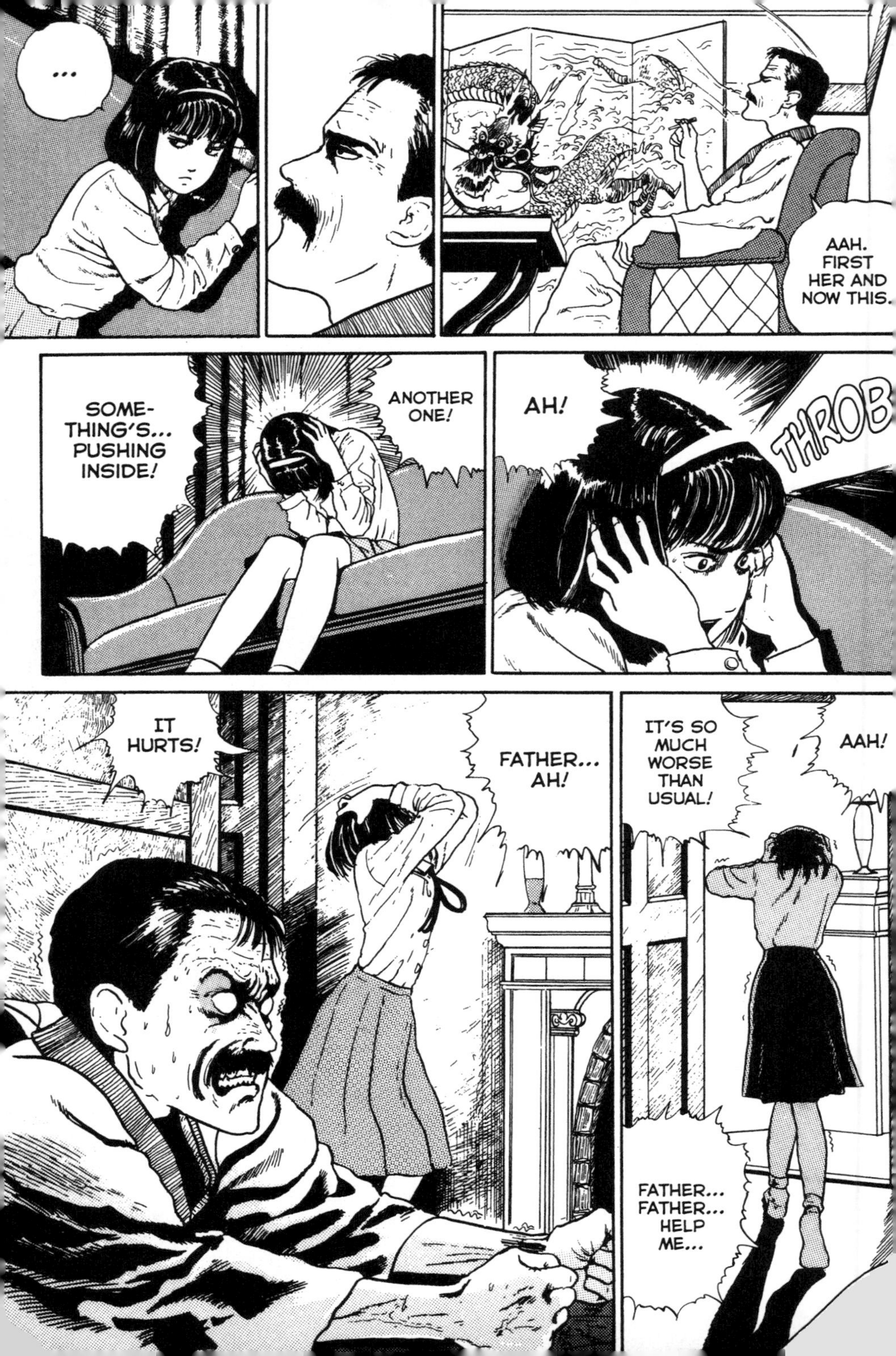
AAH. FIRST HER AND NOW THIS.
...
AH!
THROB
ANOTHER ONE!
SOME-THING'S... PUSHING INSIDE!
AAH!
IT'S SO MUCH WORSE THAN USUAL!
FATHER... FATHER... HELP ME...
FATHER... AH!
IT HURTS!

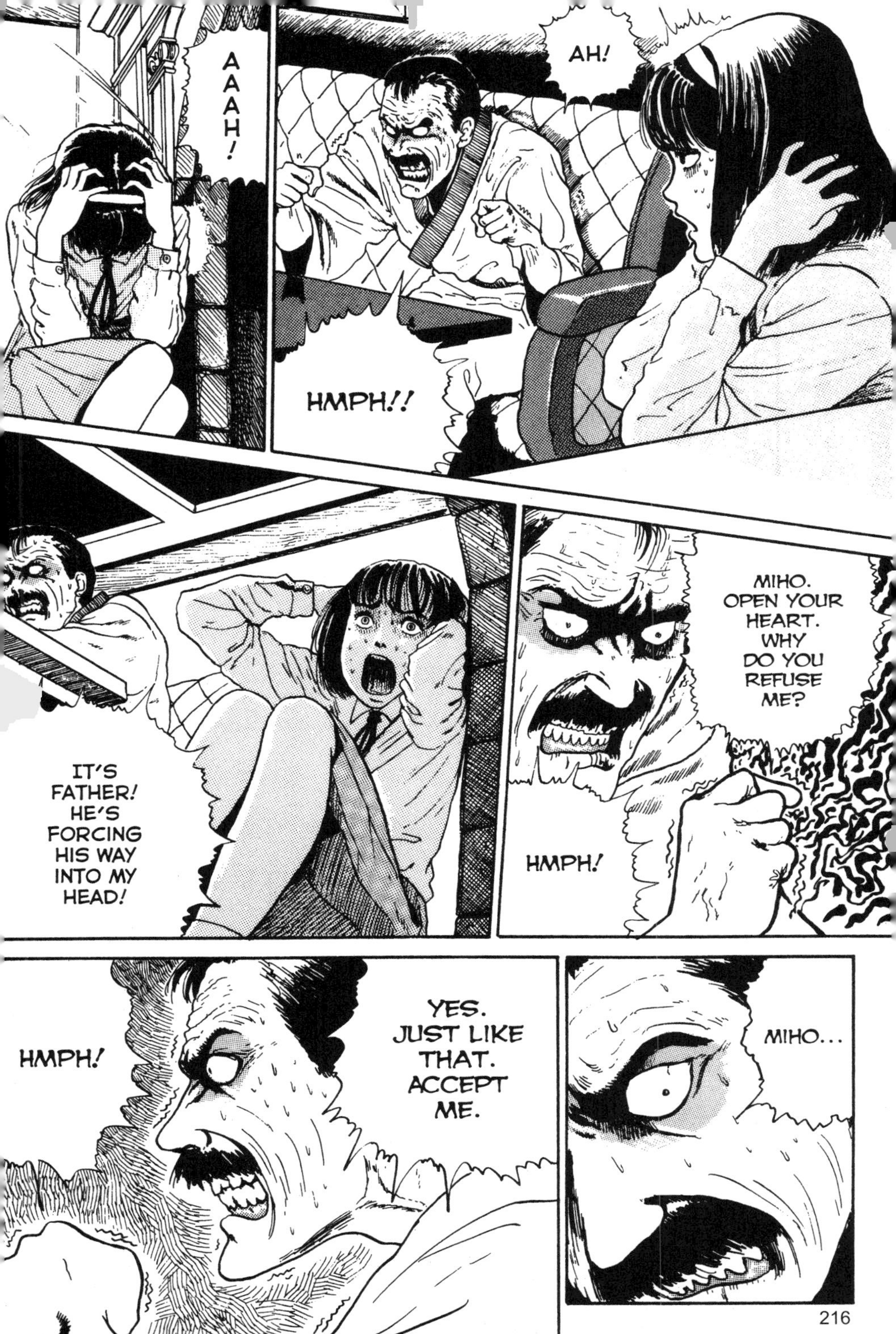
AH!
HMPH!!
AAAH!
MIHO. OPEN YOUR HEART. WHY DO YOU REFUSE ME?
HMPH!
IT'S FATHER! HE'S FORCING HIS WAY INTO MY HEAD!
MIHO...
YES. JUST LIKE THAT. ACCEPT ME.
HMPH!

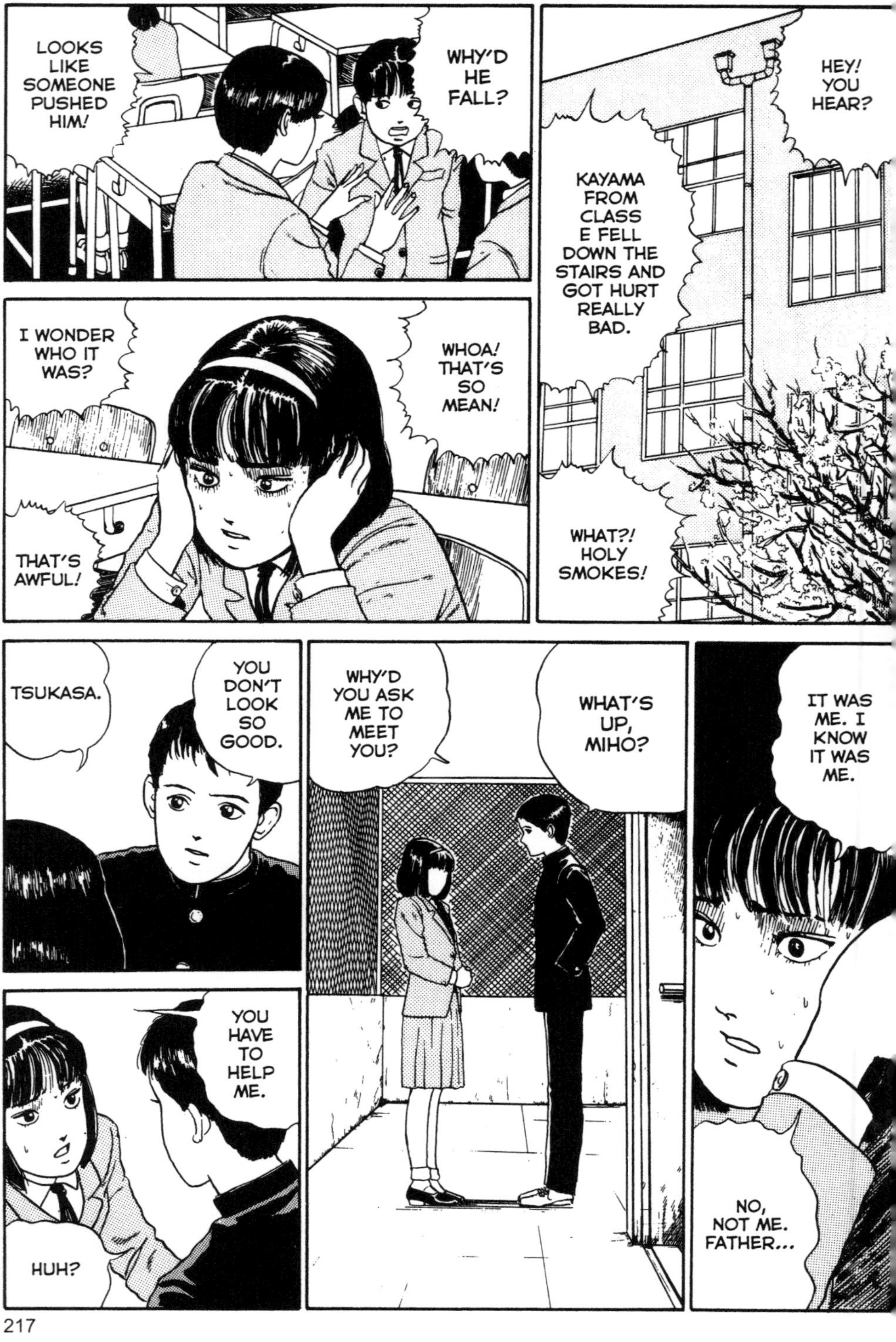
HEY! YOU HEAR?
KAYAMA FROM CLASS E FELL DOWN THE STAIRS AND GOT HURT REALLY BAD.
WHAT?! HOLY SMOKES!
WHY'D HE FALL?
LOOKS LIKE SOMEONE PUSHED HIM!
WHOA! THAT'S SO MEAN!
I WONDER WHO IT WAS?
THAT'S AWFUL!
IT WAS ME. I KNOW IT WAS ME.
NO, NOT ME. FATHER...
WHAT'S UP, MIHO?
WHY'D YOU ASK ME TO MEET YOU?
YOU DON'T LOOK SO GOOD.
TSUKASA.
YOU HAVE TO HELP ME.
HUH?

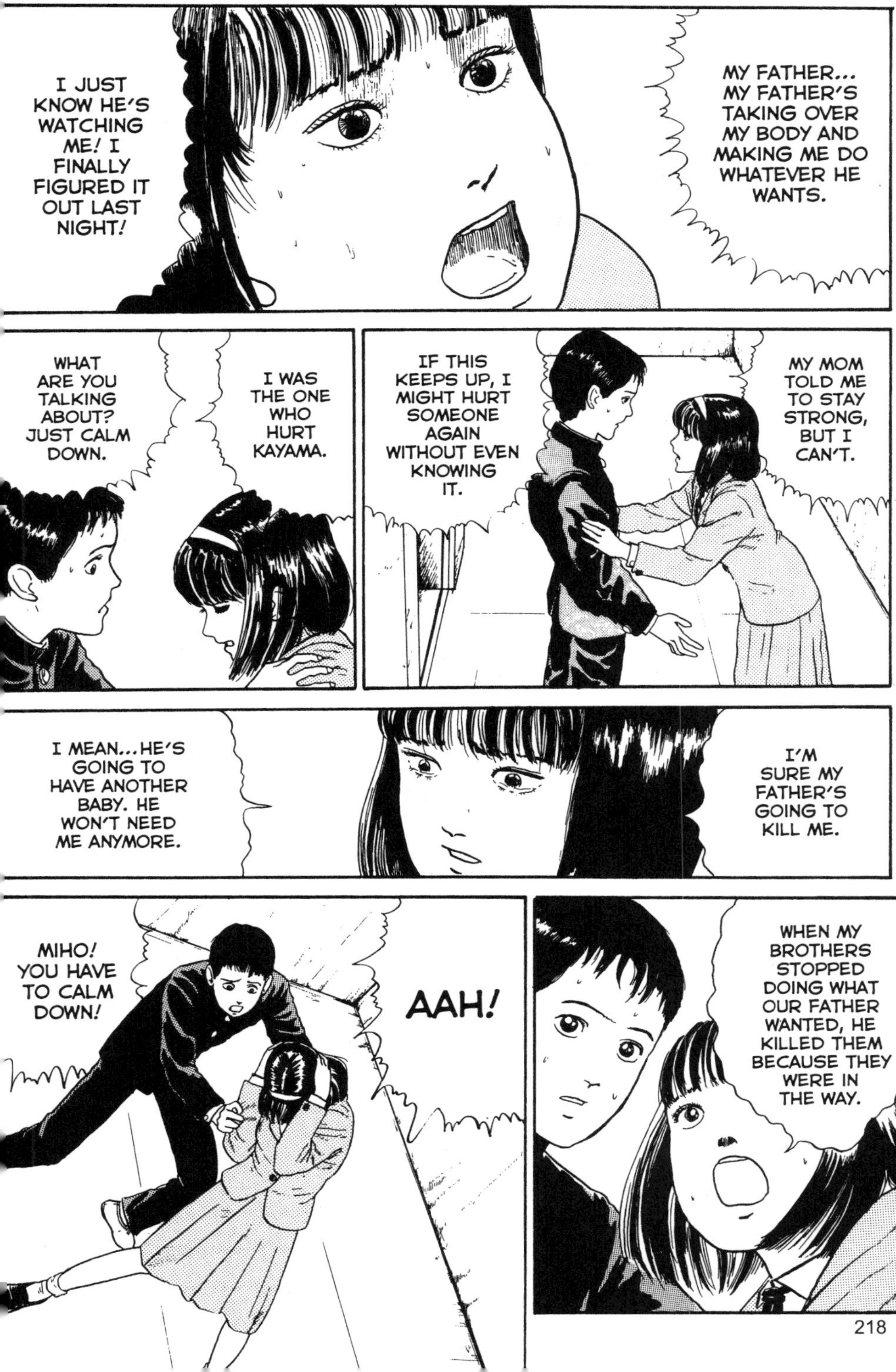
MY FATHER... MY FATHER'S TAKING OVER MY BODY AND MAKING ME DO WHATEVER HE WANTS.
I JUST KNOW HE'S WATCHING ME! I FINALLY FIGURED IT OUT LAST NIGHT!
MY MOM TOLD ME TO STAY STRONG, BUT I CAN'T.
IF THIS KEEPS UP, I MIGHT HURT SOMEONE AGAIN WITHOUT EVEN KNOWING IT.
I WAS THE ONE WHO HURT KAYAMA.
WHAT ARE YOU TALKING ABOUT? JUST CALM DOWN.
I'M SURE MY FATHER'S GOING TO KILL ME.
I MEAN...HE'S GOING TO HAVE ANOTHER BABY. HE WON'T NEED ME ANYMORE.
WHEN MY BROTHERS STOPPED DOING WHAT OUR FATHER WANTED, HE KILLED THEM BECAUSE THEY WERE IN THE WAY.
AAH!
MIHO! YOU HAVE TO CALM DOWN!

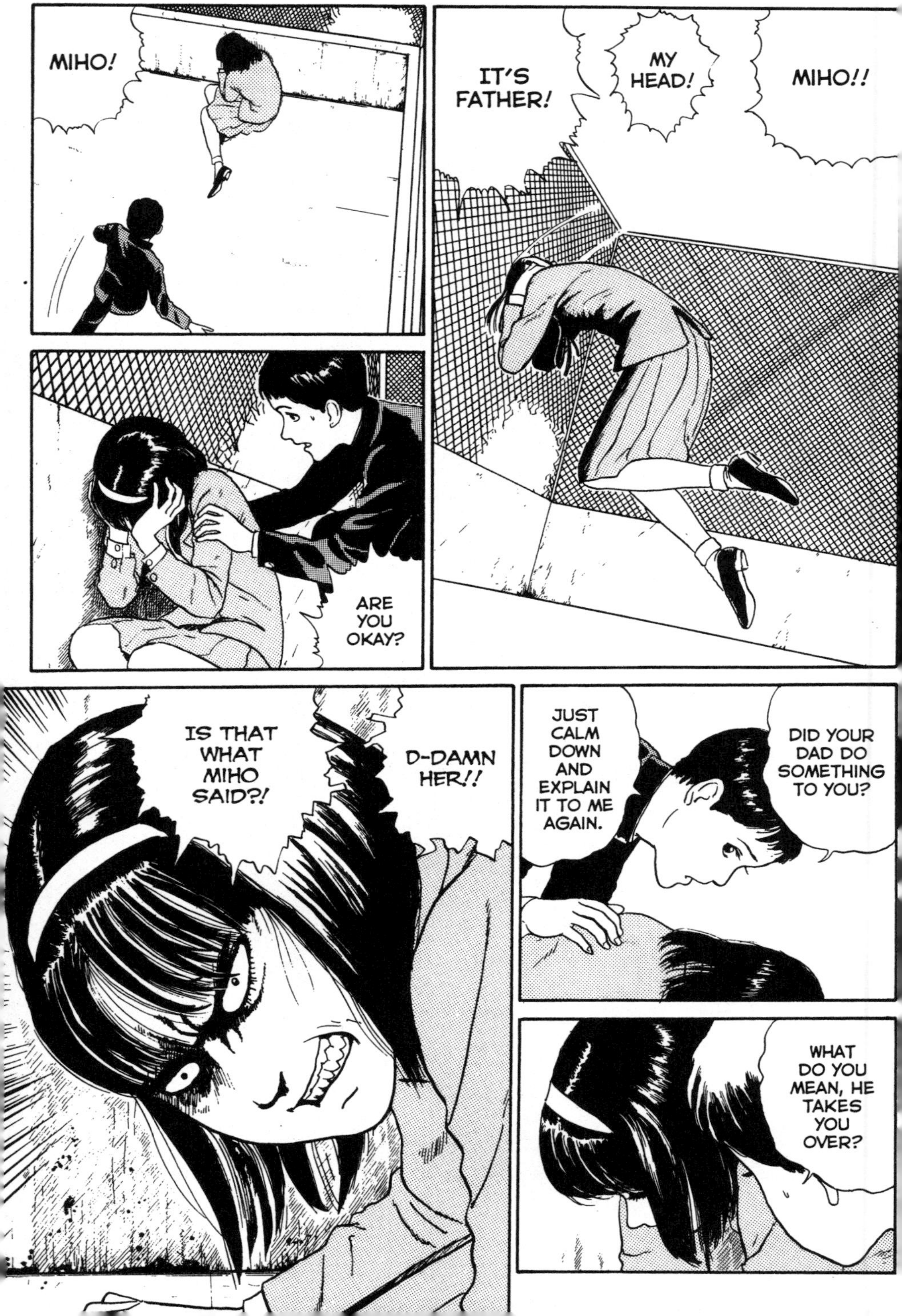
MIHO!!
MY HEAD!
IT'S FATHER!
MIHO!
ARE YOU OKAY?
DID YOUR DAD DO SOMETHING TO YOU?
JUST CALM DOWN AND EXPLAIN IT TO ME AGAIN.
WHAT DO YOU MEAN, HE TAKES YOU OVER?
D-DAMN HER!!
IS THAT WHAT MIHO SAID?!

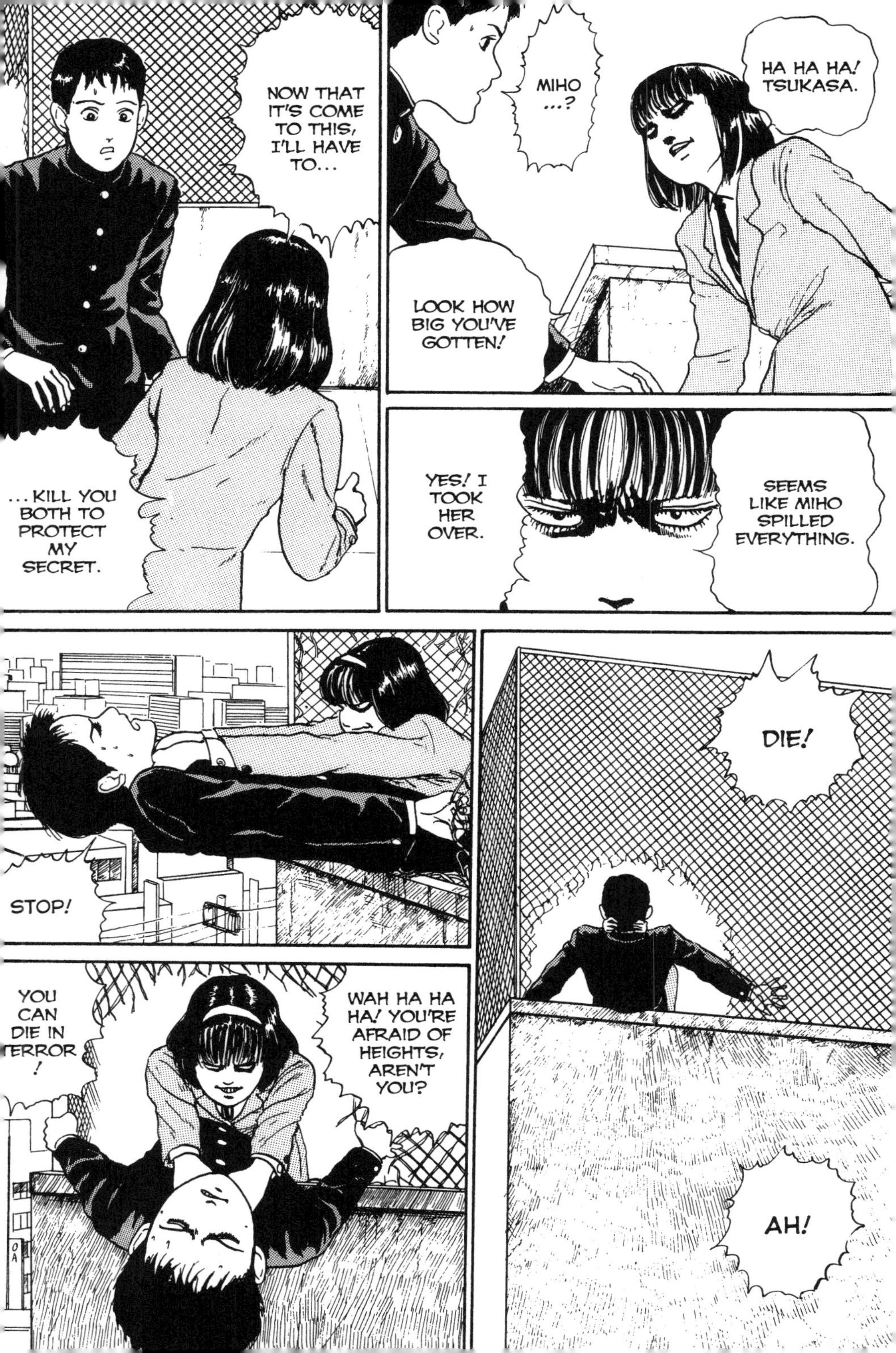
HA HA HA! TSUKASA.
MIHO ...?
LOOK HOW BIG YOU'VE GOTTEN!
SEEMS LIKE MIHO SPILLED EVERYTHING.
YES! I TOOK HER OVER.
NOW THAT IT'S COME TO THIS, I'LL HAVE TO...
...KILL YOU BOTH TO PROTECT MY SECRET.
DIE!
AH!
STOP!
WAH HA HA HA! YOU'RE AFRAID OF HEIGHTS, AREN'T YOU?
YOU CAN DIE IN TERROR!

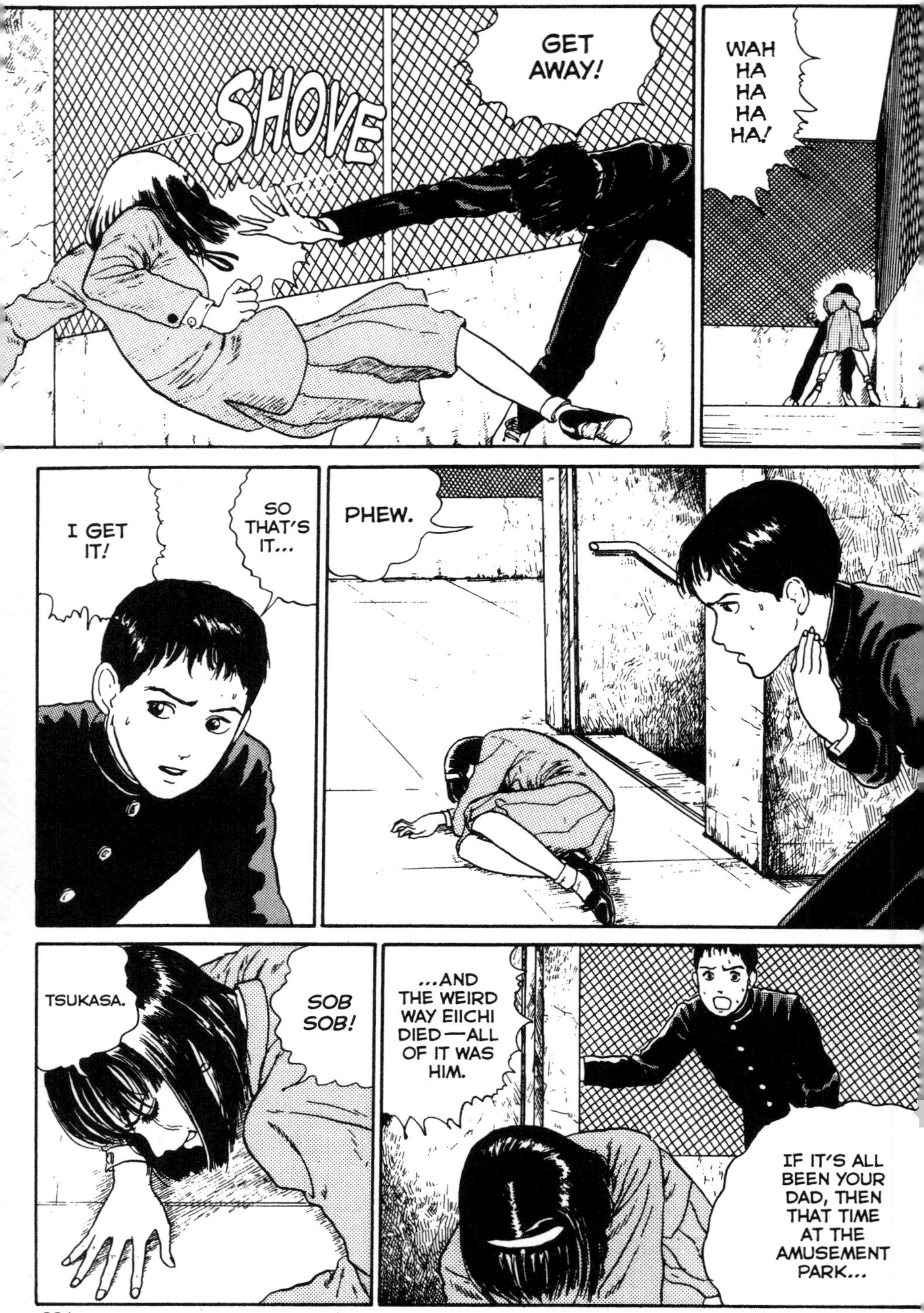
WAH HA HA HA HA!
GET AWAY!
SHOVE
PHEW.
SO THAT'S IT...
I GET IT!
IF IT'S ALL BEEN YOUR DAD, THEN THAT TIME AT THE AMUSEMENT PARK...
...AND THE WEIRD WAY EIICHI DIED—ALL OF IT WAS HIM.
SOB SOB!
TSUKASA.

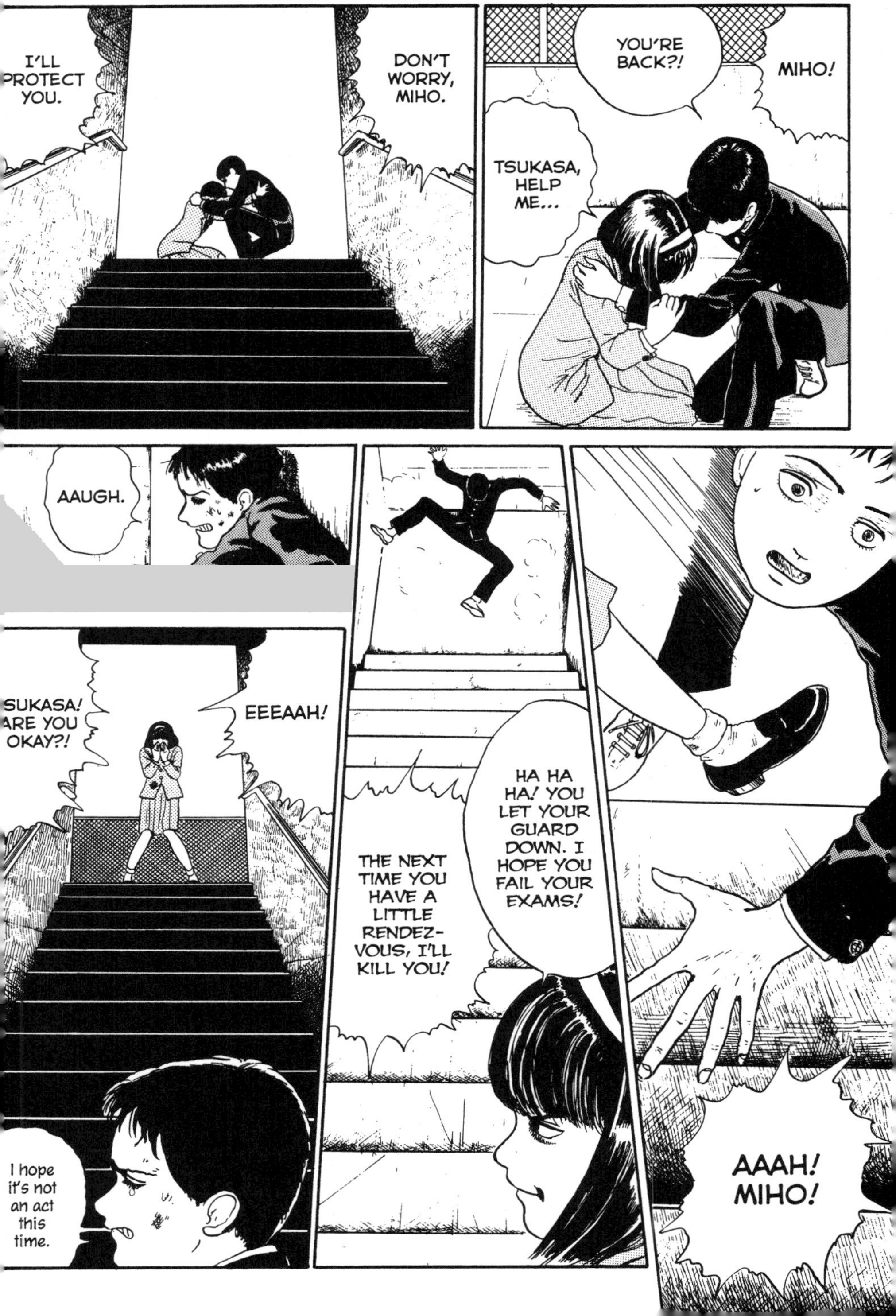
MIHO!
YOU'RE BACK?!
TSUKASA, HELP ME...
DON'T WORRY, MIHO.
I'LL PROTECT YOU.
AAAH! MIHO!
HA HA HA! YOU LET YOUR GUARD DOWN. I HOPE YOU FAIL YOUR EXAMS!
THE NEXT TIME YOU HAVE A LITTLE RENDEZ-VOUS, I'LL KILL YOU!
AAUGH.
EEEAAH!
SUKASA! ARE YOU OKAY?!
I hope it's not an act this time.

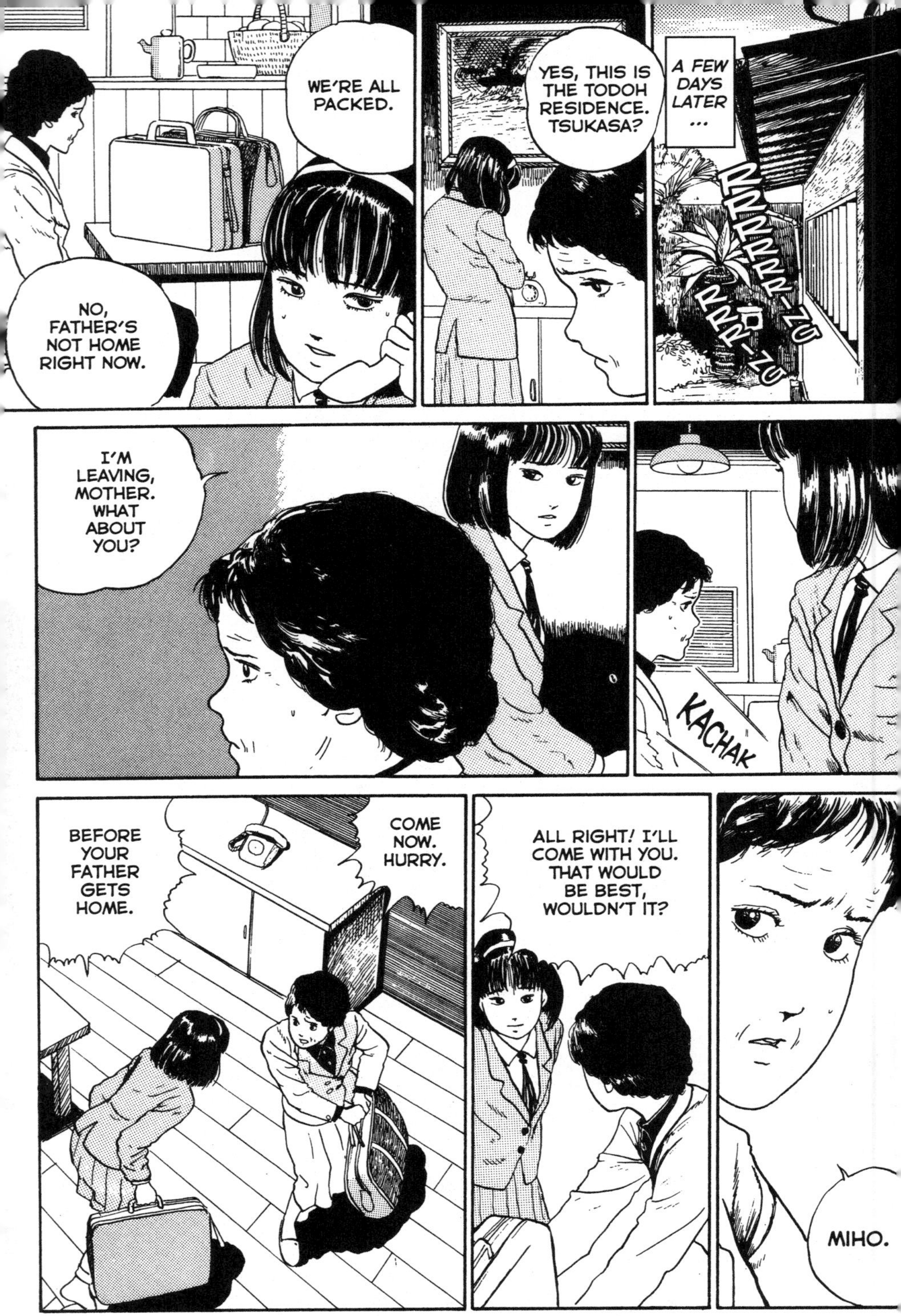
A FEW DAYS LATER ...
RRRRRR-ZU
RRR-ZU
YES, THIS IS THE TODOH RESIDENCE. TSUKASA?
WE'RE ALL PACKED.
NO, FATHER'S NOT HOME RIGHT NOW.
KACHAK
I'M LEAVING, MOTHER. WHAT ABOUT YOU?
MIHO.
ALL RIGHT! I'LL COME WITH YOU. THAT WOULD BE BEST, WOULDN'T IT?
COME NOW. HURRY.
BEFORE YOUR FATHER GETS HOME.

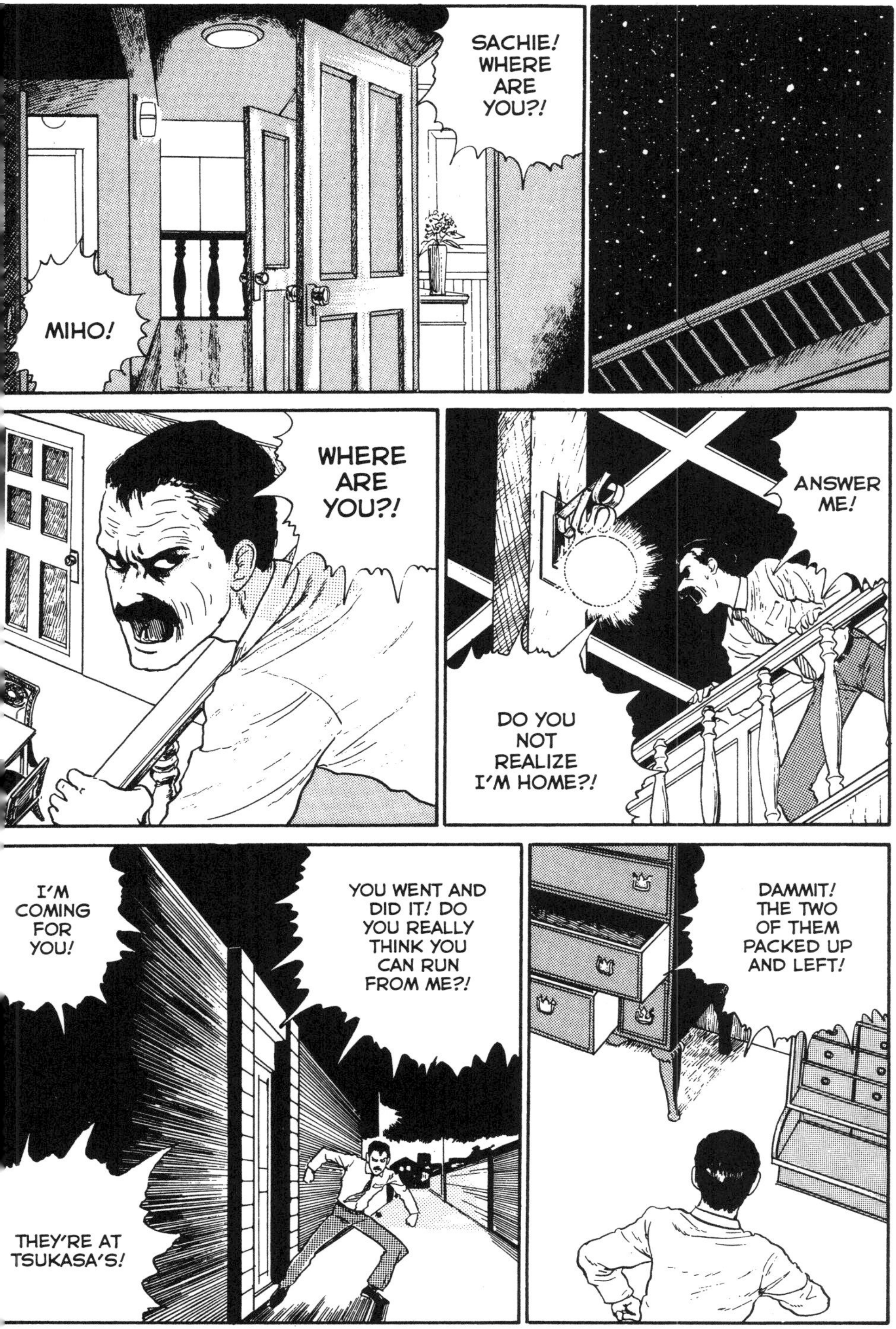
SACHIE! WHERE ARE YOU?!
MIHO!
ANSWER ME!
DO YOU NOT REALIZE I'M HOME?!
WHERE ARE YOU?!
DAMMIT! THE TWO OF THEM PACKED UP AND LEFT!
YOU WENT AND DID IT! DO YOU REALLY THINK YOU CAN RUN FROM ME?!
I'M COMING FOR YOU!
THEY'RE AT TSUKASA'S!

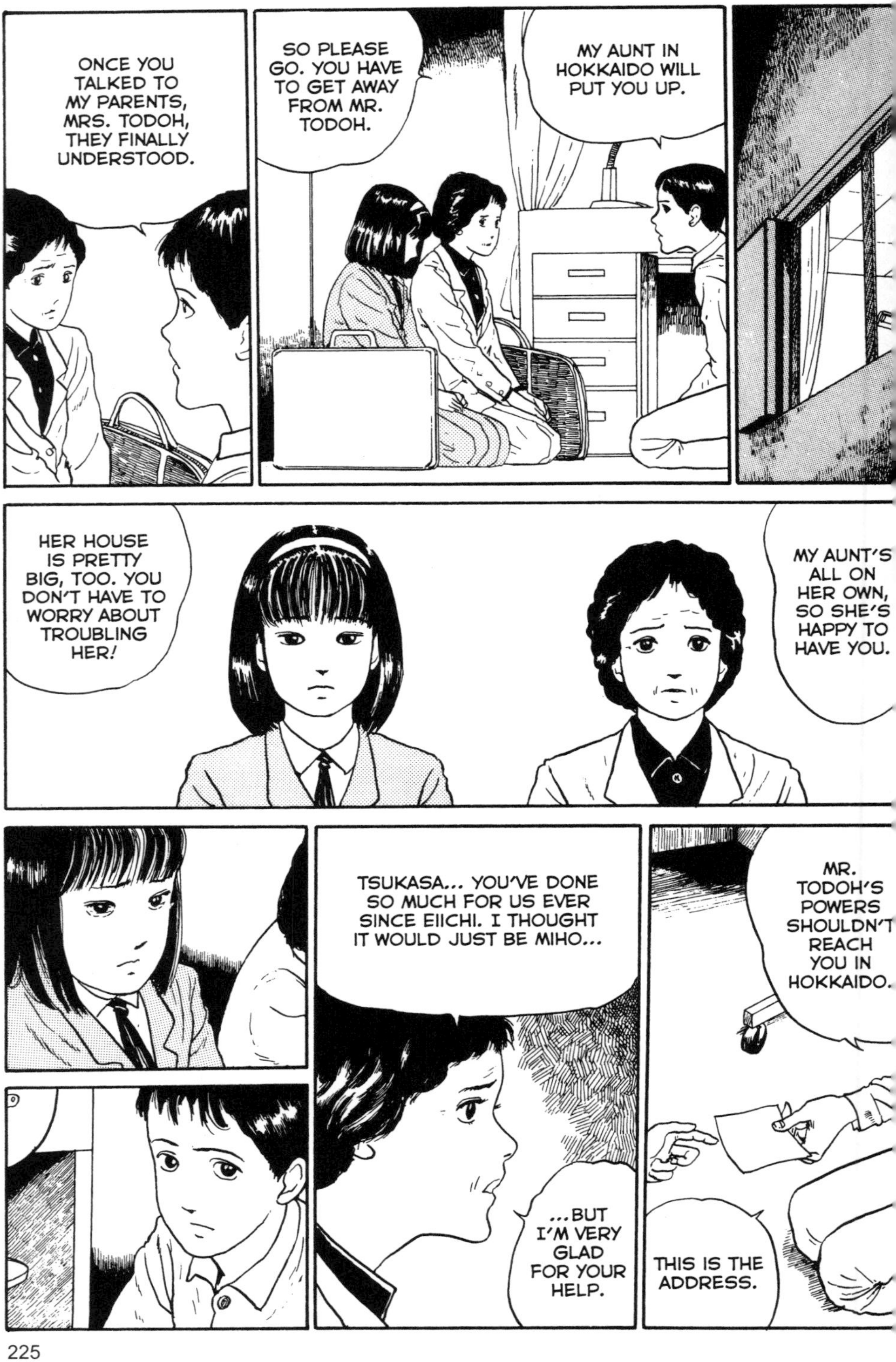
MY AUNT IN HOKKAIDO WILL PUT YOU UP.
SO PLEASE GO. YOU HAVE TO GET AWAY FROM MR. TODOH.
ONCE YOU TALKED TO MY PARENTS, MRS. TODOH, THEY FINALLY UNDERSTOOD.
MY AUNT'S ALL ON HER OWN, SO SHE'S HAPPY TO HAVE YOU.
HER HOUSE IS PRETTY BIG, TOO. YOU DON'T HAVE TO WORRY ABOUT TROUBLING HER!
MR. TODOH'S POWERS SHOULDN'T REACH YOU IN HOKKAIDO.
THIS IS THE ADDRESS.
TSUKASA... YOU'VE DONE SO MUCH FOR US EVER SINCE EIICHI. I THOUGHT IT WOULD JUST BE MIHO...
...BUT I'M VERY GLAD FOR YOUR HELP.

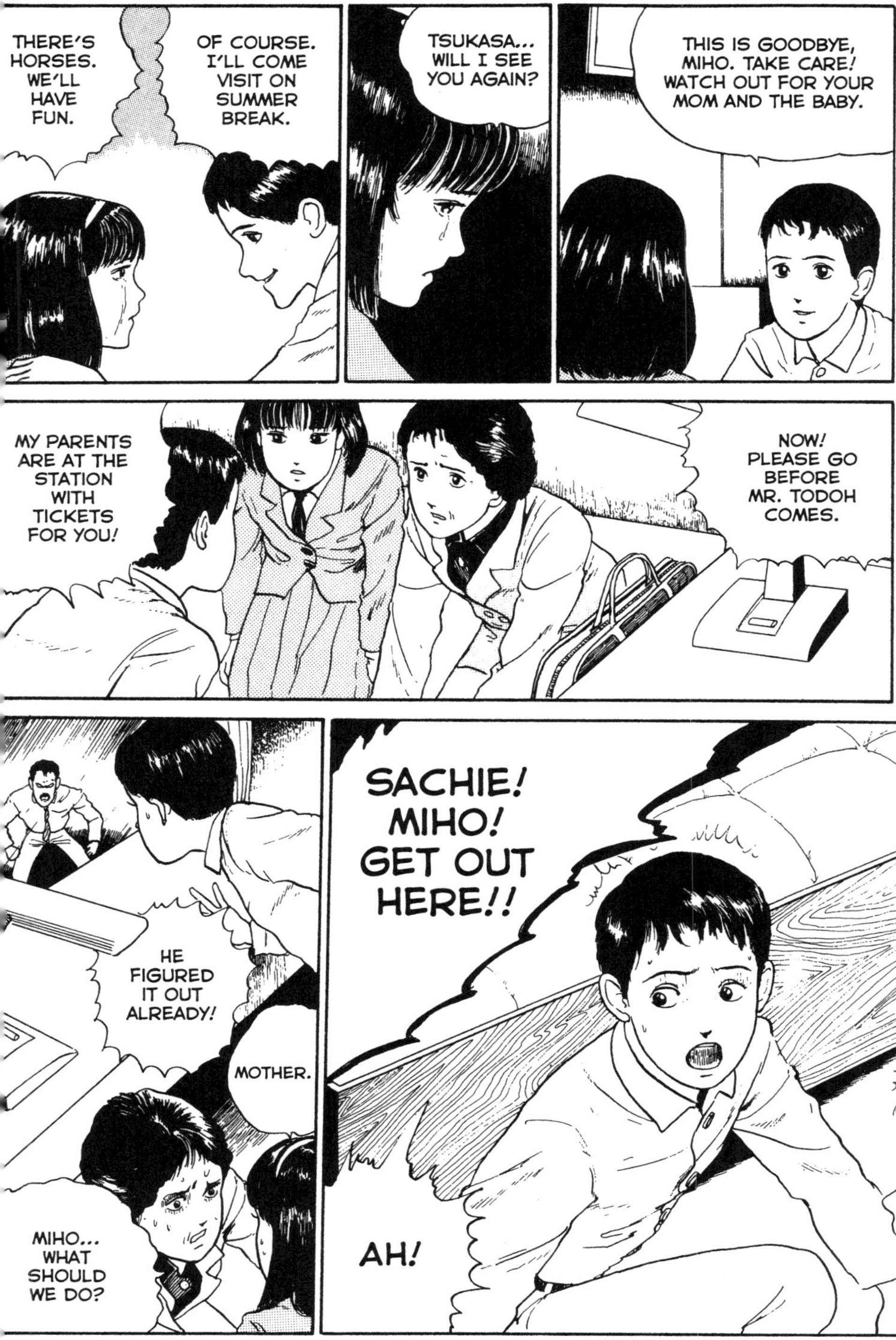
THIS IS GOODBYE, MIHO. TAKE CARE! WATCH OUT FOR YOUR MOM AND THE BABY.
TSUKASA... WILL I SEE YOU AGAIN?
OF COURSE. I'LL COME VISIT ON SUMMER BREAK.
THERE'S HORSES. WE'LL HAVE FUN.
NOW! PLEASE GO BEFORE MR. TODOH COMES.
MY PARENTS ARE AT THE STATION WITH TICKETS FOR YOU!
SACHIE! MIHO! GET OUT HERE!!
AH!
HE FIGURED IT OUT ALREADY!
MOTHER.
MIHO... WHAT SHOULD WE DO?

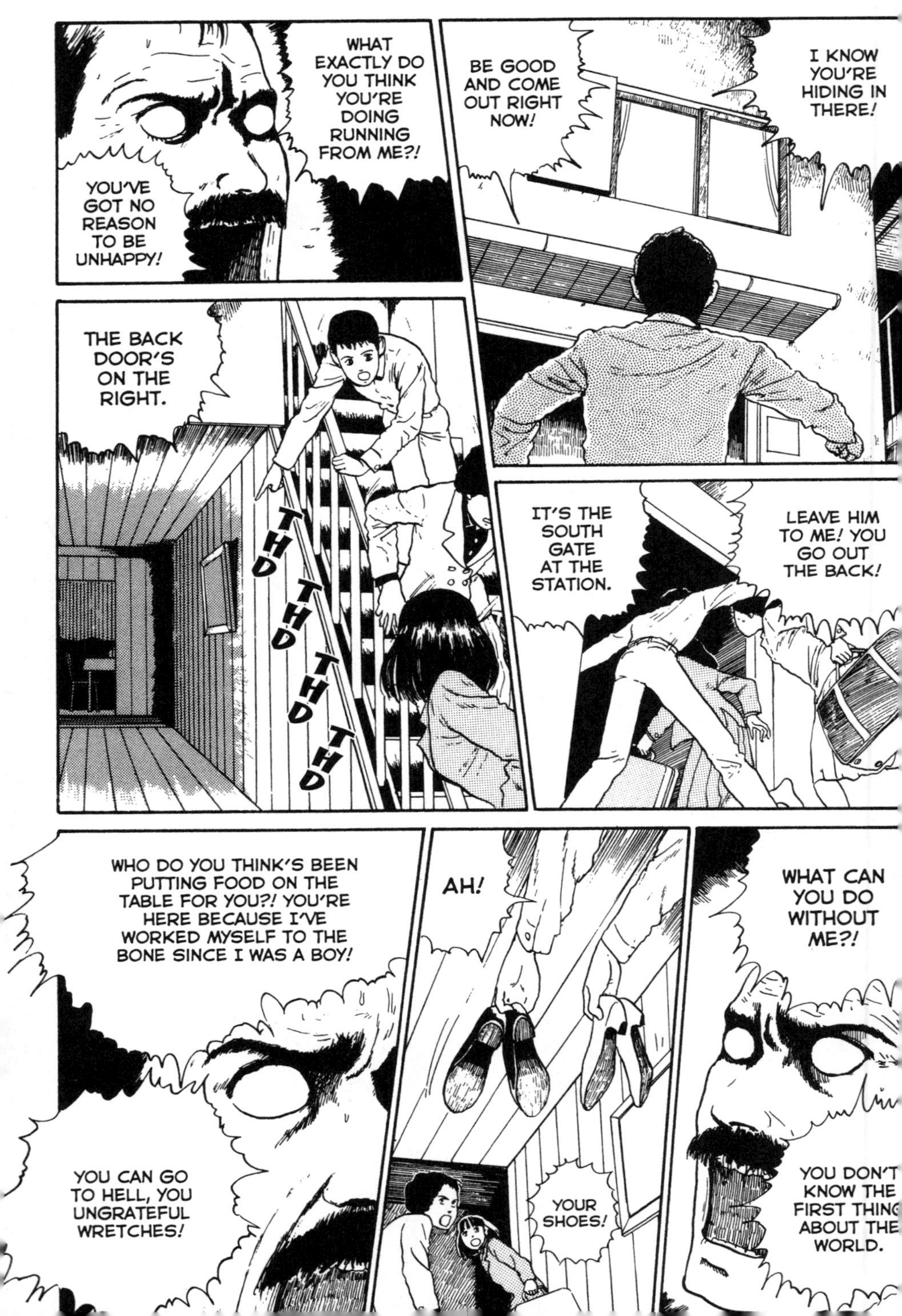
I KNOW YOU'RE HIDING IN THERE!
BE GOOD AND COME OUT RIGHT NOW!
WHAT EXACTLY DO YOU THINK YOU'RE DOING RUNNING FROM ME?!
YOU'VE GOT NO REASON TO BE UNHAPPY!
LEAVE HIM TO ME! YOU GO OUT THE BACK!
IT'S THE SOUTH GATE AT THE STATION.
THE BACK DOOR'S ON THE RIGHT.
THD
THD
THD
THD
WHAT CAN YOU DO WITHOUT ME?!
YOU DON'T KNOW THE FIRST THING ABOUT THE WORLD.
AH!
YOUR SHOES!
WHO DO YOU THINK'S BEEN PUTTING FOOD ON THE TABLE FOR YOU?! YOU'RE HERE BECAUSE I'VE WORKED MYSELF TO THE BONE SINCE I WAS A BOY!
YOU CAN GO TO HELL, YOU UNGRATEFUL WRETCHES!

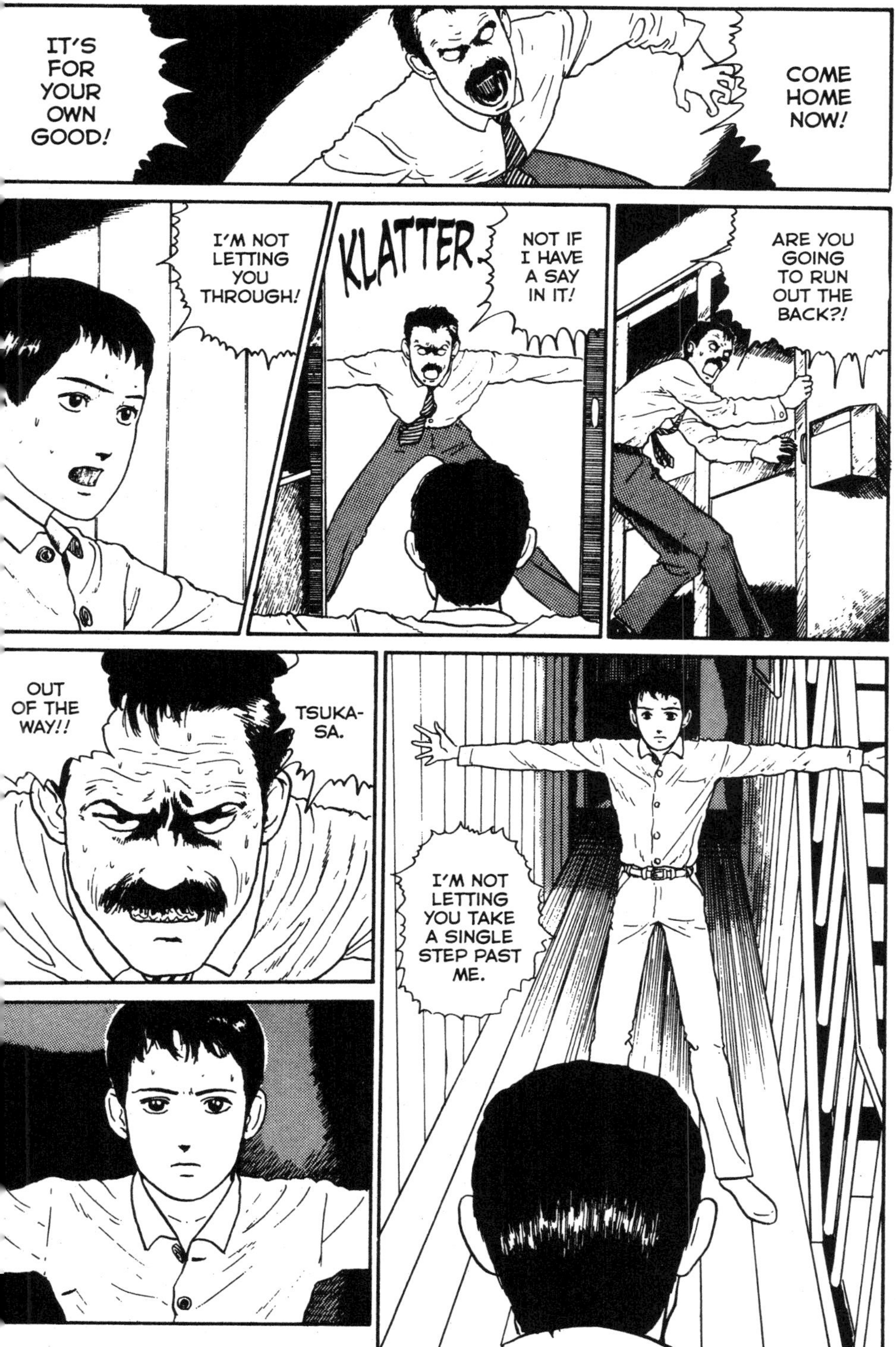
COME HOME NOW!
IT'S FOR YOUR OWN GOOD!
ARE YOU GOING TO RUN OUT THE BACK?!
NOT IF I HAVE A SAY IN IT!
KLATTER
I'M NOT LETTING YOU THROUGH!
I'M NOT LETTING YOU TAKE A SINGLE STEP PAST ME.
TSUKA-SA.
OUT OF THE WAY!!

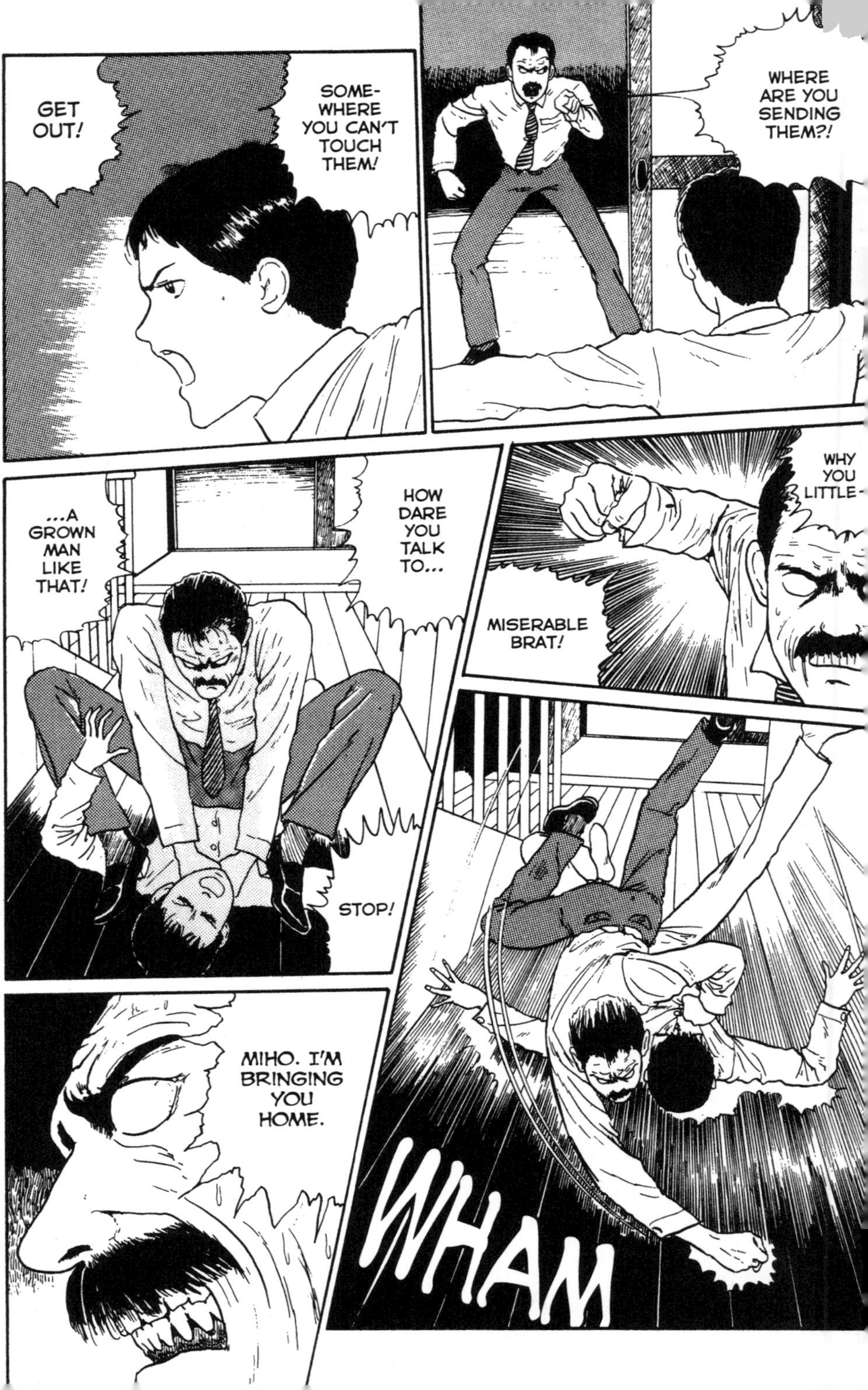
WHERE ARE YOU SENDING THEM?!
SOME-WHERE YOU CAN'T TOUCH THEM!
GET OUT!
WHY YOU LITTLE-
MISERABLE BRAT!
WHAM
HOW DARE YOU TALK TO...
...A GROWN MAN LIKE THAT!
STOP!
MIHO. I'M BRINGING YOU HOME.

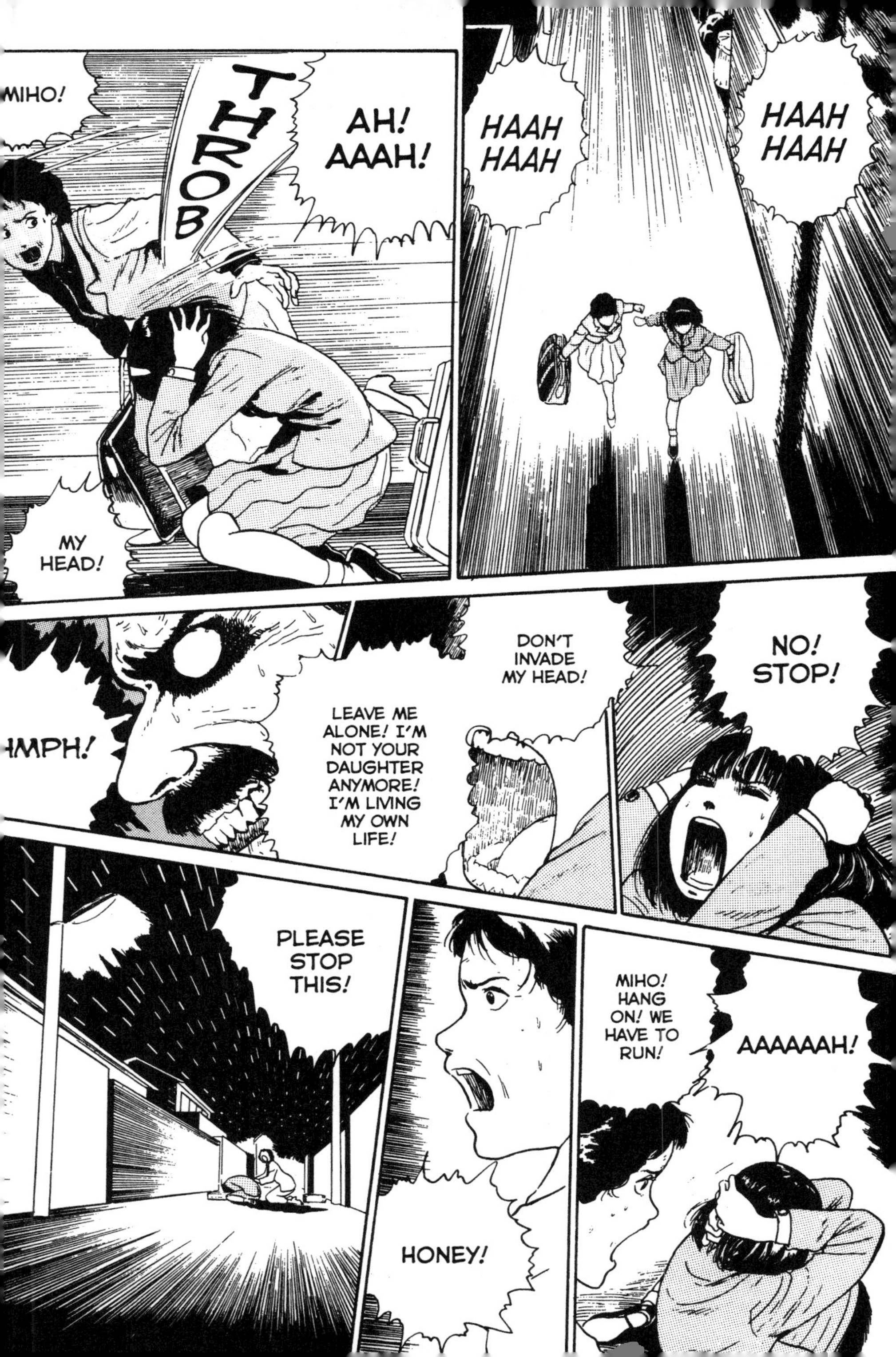
HAAH HAAH
HAAH HAAH
AH! AAAH!
THROB
MIHO!
MY HEAD!
NO! STOP!
DON'T INVADE MY HEAD!
LEAVE ME ALONE! I'M NOT YOUR DAUGHTER ANYMORE! I'M LIVING MY OWN LIFE!
MPH!
AAAAAAH!
MIHO! HANG ON! WE HAVE TO RUN!
HONEY!
PLEASE STOP THIS!

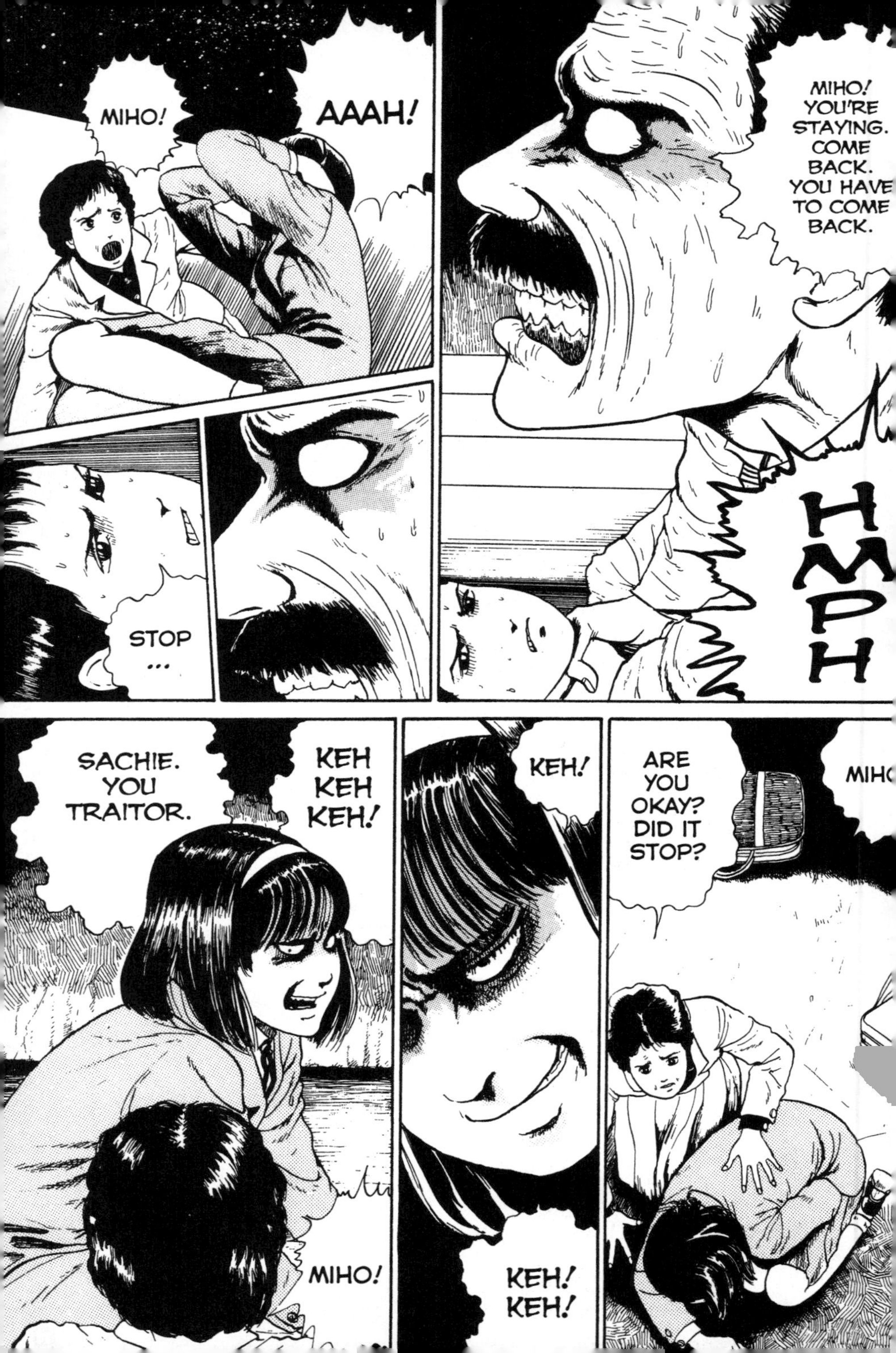
MIHO! YOU'RE STAYING. COME BACK. YOU HAVE TO COME BACK.
HMPH
AAAH!
MIHO!
STOP ...
MIH
ARE YOU OKAY? DID IT STOP?
KEH!
KEH! KEH!
KEH KEH KEH!
SACHIE. YOU TRAITOR.
MIHO!

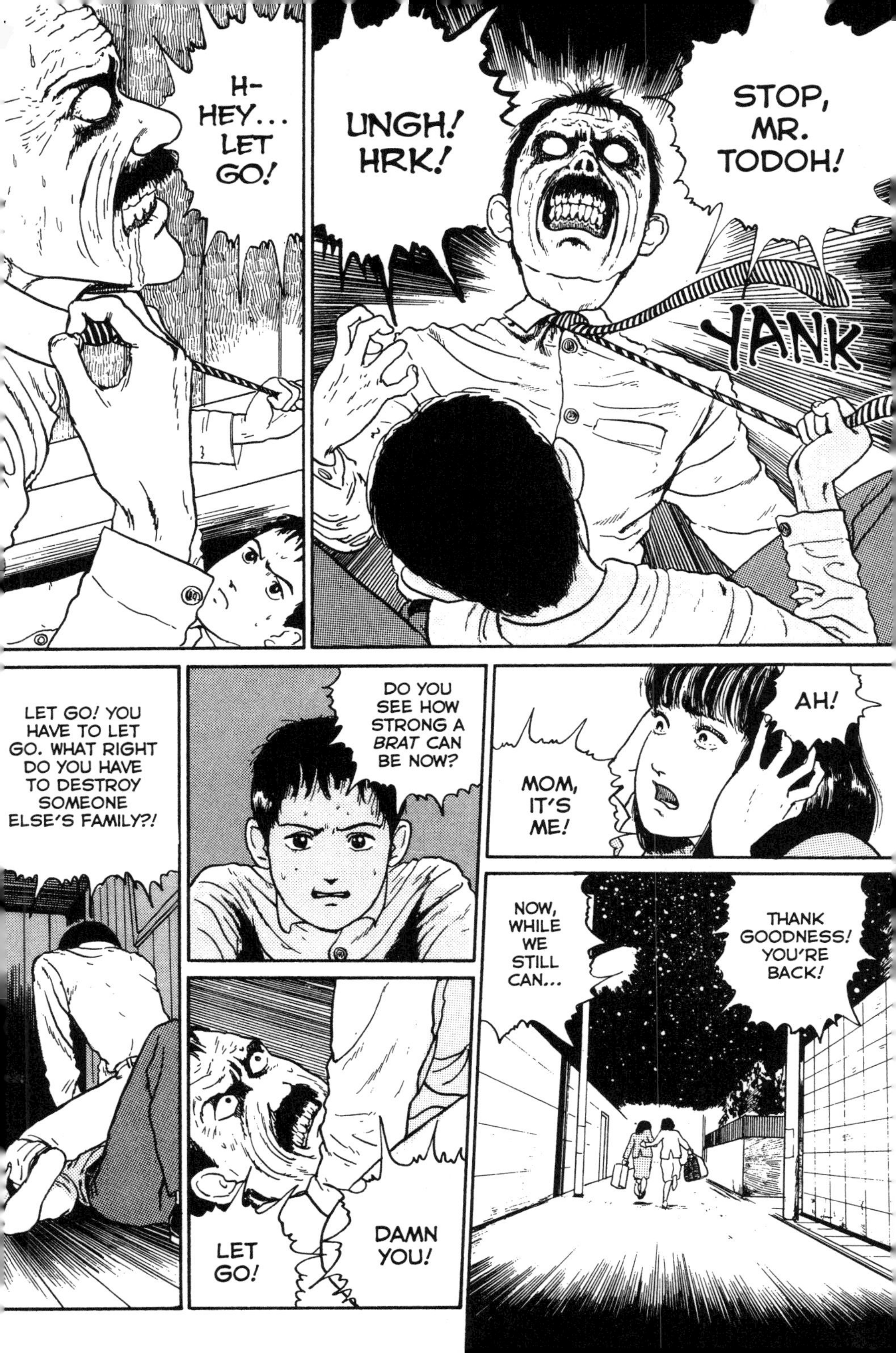

STOP, MR. TODOH!
UNGH! HRK!
YANK
H- HEY... LET GO!
AH!
MOM, IT'S ME!
THANK GOODNESS! YOU'RE BACK!
NOW, WHILE WE STILL CAN...
DO YOU SEE HOW STRONG A *BRAT* CAN BE NOW?
DAMN YOU!
LET GO!
LET GO! YOU HAVE TO LET GO. WHAT RIGHT DO YOU HAVE TO DESTROY SOMEONE ELSE'S FAMILY?!

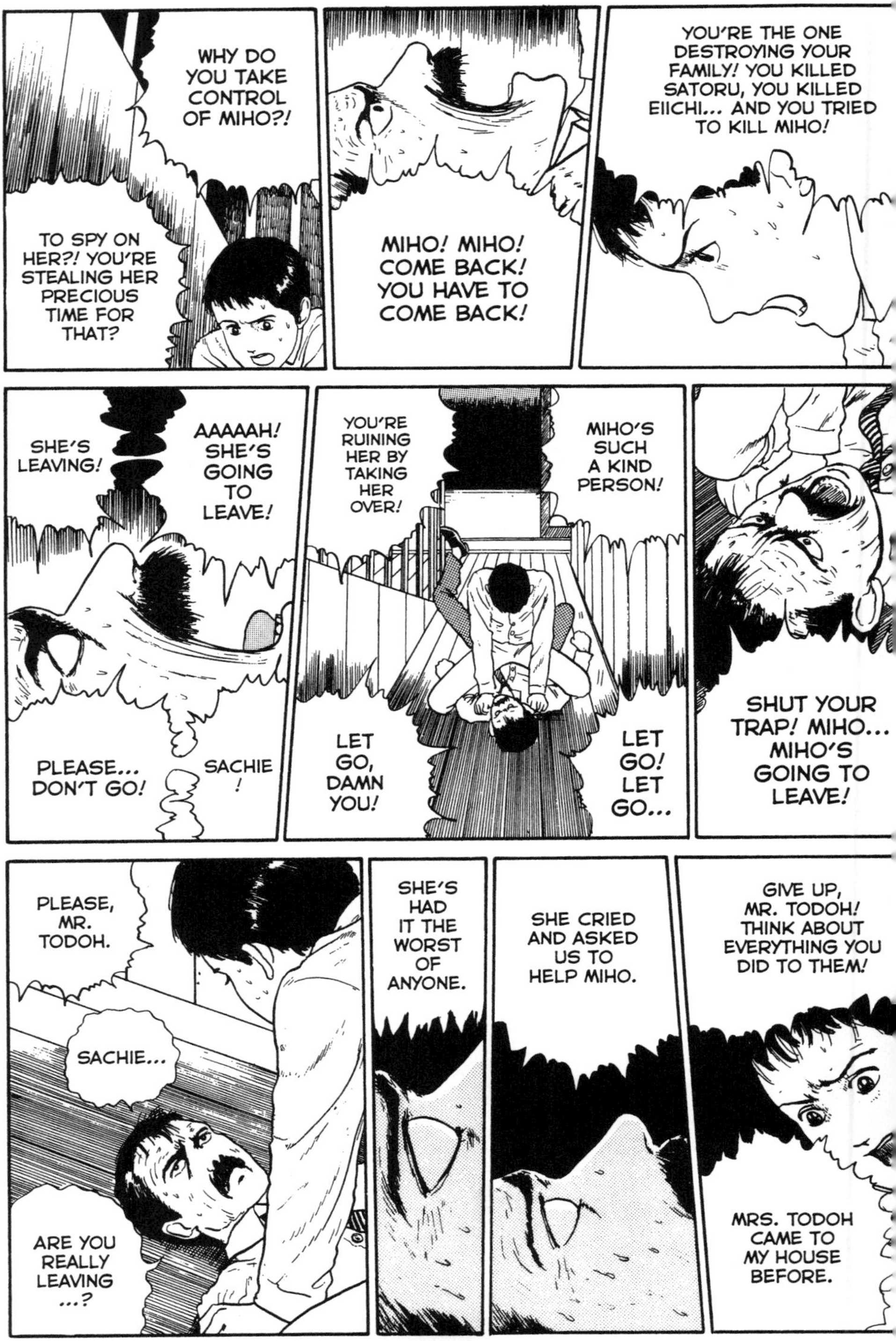
YOU'RE THE ONE DESTROYING YOUR FAMILY! YOU KILLED SATORU, YOU KILLED EIICHI... AND YOU TRIED TO KILL MIHO!
MIHO! MIHO! COME BACK! YOU HAVE TO COME BACK!
WHY DO YOU TAKE CONTROL OF MIHO?!
TO SPY ON HER?! YOU'RE STEALING HER PRECIOUS TIME FOR THAT?
SHUT YOUR TRAP! MIHO... MIHO'S GOING TO LEAVE!
MIHO'S SUCH A KIND PERSON!
YOU'RE RUINING HER BY TAKING HER OVER!
LET GO! LET GO...
LET GO, DAMN YOU!
AAAAAH! SHE'S GOING TO LEAVE!
SHE'S LEAVING!
SACHIE!
PLEASE... DON'T GO!
GIVE UP, MR. TODOH! THINK ABOUT EVERYTHING YOU DID TO THEM!
MRS. TODOH CAME TO MY HOUSE BEFORE.
SHE CRIED AND ASKED US TO HELP MIHO.
SHE'S HAD IT THE WORST OF ANYONE.
PLEASE, MR. TODOH.
SACHIE...
ARE YOU REALLY LEAVING...?

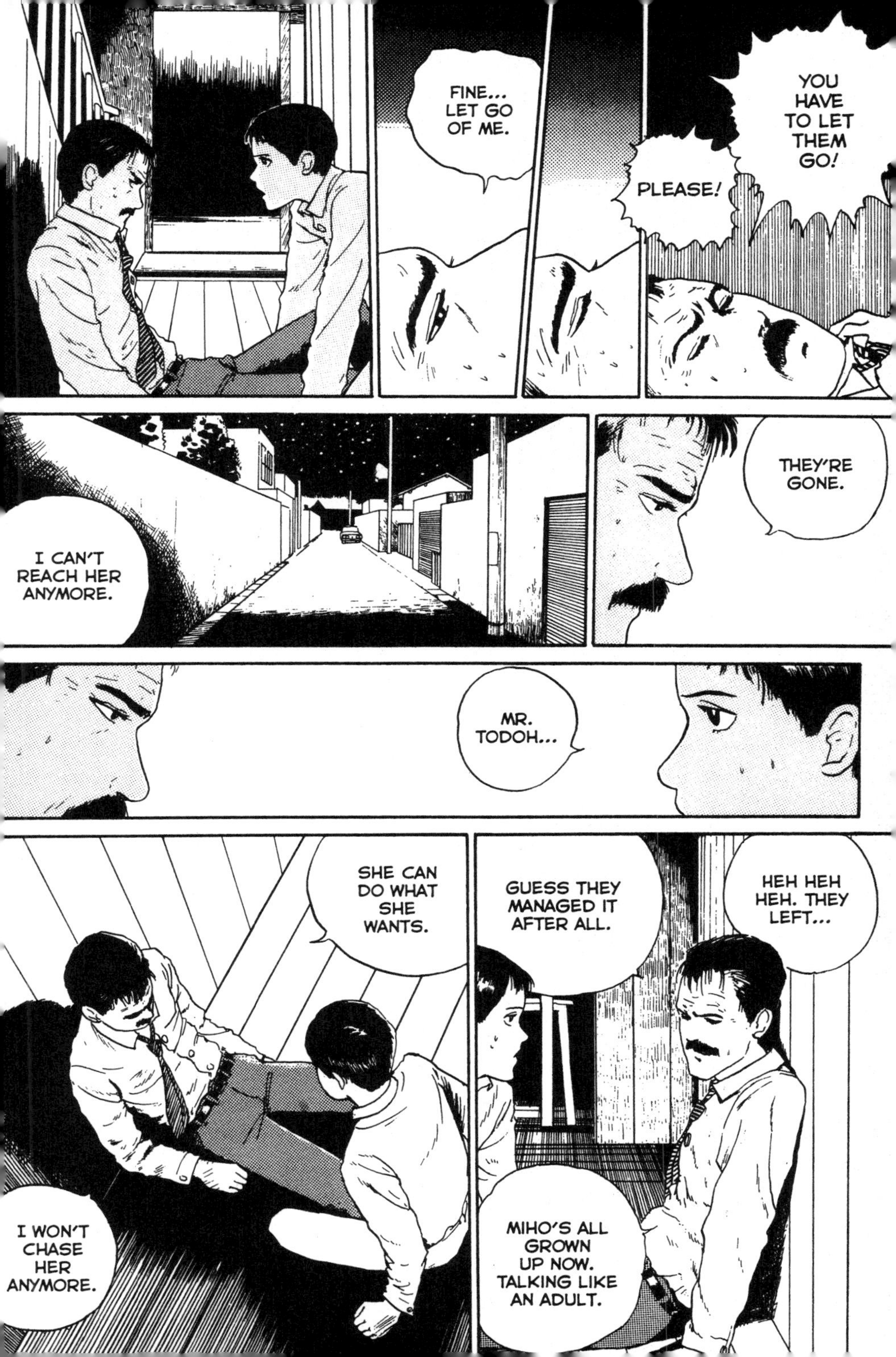
YOU HAVE TO LET THEM GO!
PLEASE!
FINE... LET GO OF ME.
THEY'RE GONE.
I CAN'T REACH HER ANYMORE.
MR. TODOH...
HEH HEH HEH. THEY LEFT...
GUESS THEY MANAGED IT AFTER ALL.
MIHO'S ALL GROWN UP NOW. TALKING LIKE AN ADULT.
SHE CAN DO WHAT SHE WANTS.
I WON'T CHASE HER ANYMORE.

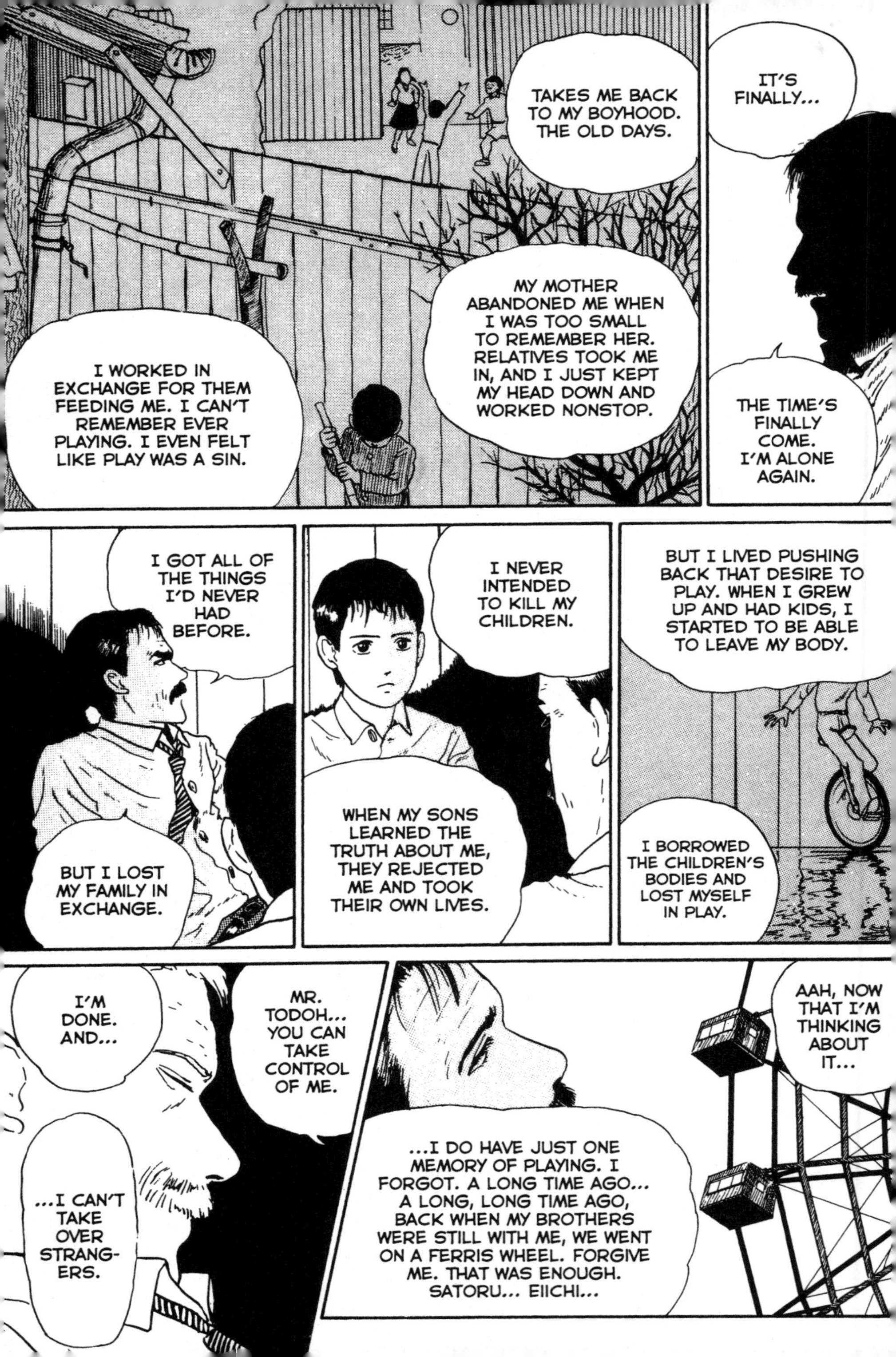
IT'S FINALLY...
THE TIME'S FINALLY COME. I'M ALONE AGAIN.
TAKES ME BACK TO MY BOYHOOD. THE OLD DAYS.
MY MOTHER ABANDONED ME WHEN I WAS TOO SMALL TO REMEMBER HER. RELATIVES TOOK ME IN, AND I JUST KEPT MY HEAD DOWN AND WORKED NONSTOP.
I WORKED IN EXCHANGE FOR THEM FEEDING ME. I CAN'T REMEMBER EVER PLAYING. I EVEN FELT LIKE PLAY WAS A SIN.
BUT I LIVED PUSHING BACK THAT DESIRE TO PLAY. WHEN I GREW UP AND HAD KIDS, I STARTED TO BE ABLE TO LEAVE MY BODY.
I BORROWED THE CHILDREN'S BODIES AND LOST MYSELF IN PLAY.
I NEVER INTENDED TO KILL MY CHILDREN.
WHEN MY SONS LEARNED THE TRUTH ABOUT ME, THEY REJECTED ME AND TOOK THEIR OWN LIVES.
I GOT ALL OF THE THINGS I'D NEVER HAD BEFORE.
BUT I LOST MY FAMILY IN EXCHANGE.
AAH, NOW THAT I'M THINKING ABOUT IT...
...I DO HAVE JUST ONE MEMORY OF PLAYING. I FORGOT. A LONG TIME AGO... A LONG, LONG TIME AGO, BACK WHEN MY BROTHERS WERE STILL WITH ME, WE WENT ON A FERRIS WHEEL. FORGIVE ME. THAT WAS ENOUGH. SATORU... EIICHI...
MR. TODOH... YOU CAN TAKE CONTROL OF ME.
I'M DONE. AND...
...I CAN'T TAKE OVER STRANGERS.

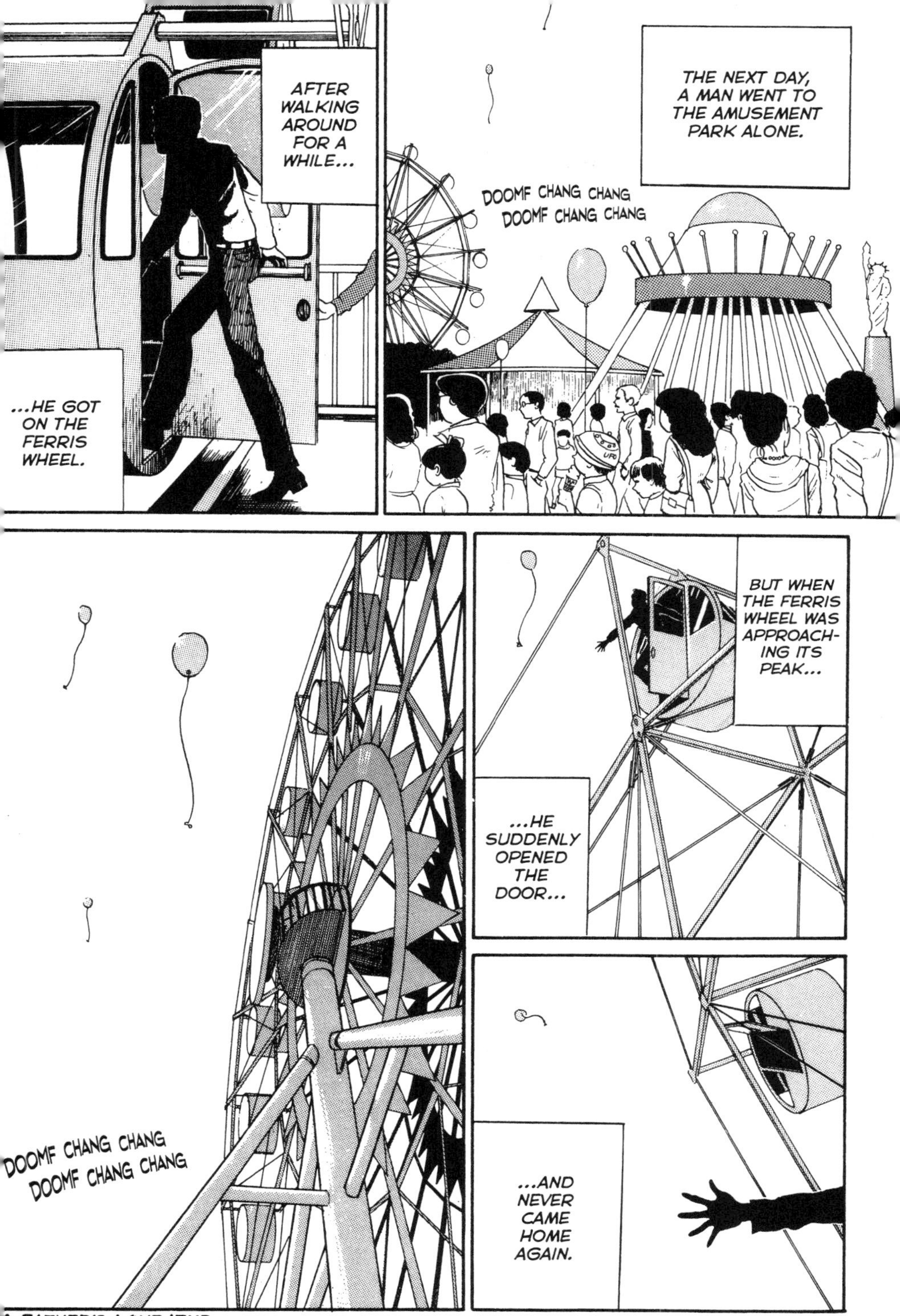
THE NEXT DAY, A MAN WENT TO THE AMUSEMENT PARK ALONE.
DOOMF CHANG CHANG
DOOMF CHANG CHANG
AFTER WALKING AROUND FOR A WHILE...
...HE GOT ON THE FERRIS WHEEL.
BUT WHEN THE FERRIS WHEEL WAS APPROACHING ITS PEAK...
...HE SUDDENLY OPENED THE DOOR...
...AND NEVER CAME HOME AGAIN.
DOOMF CHANG CHANG
DOOMF CHANG CHANG

A FATHER'S LOVE/END

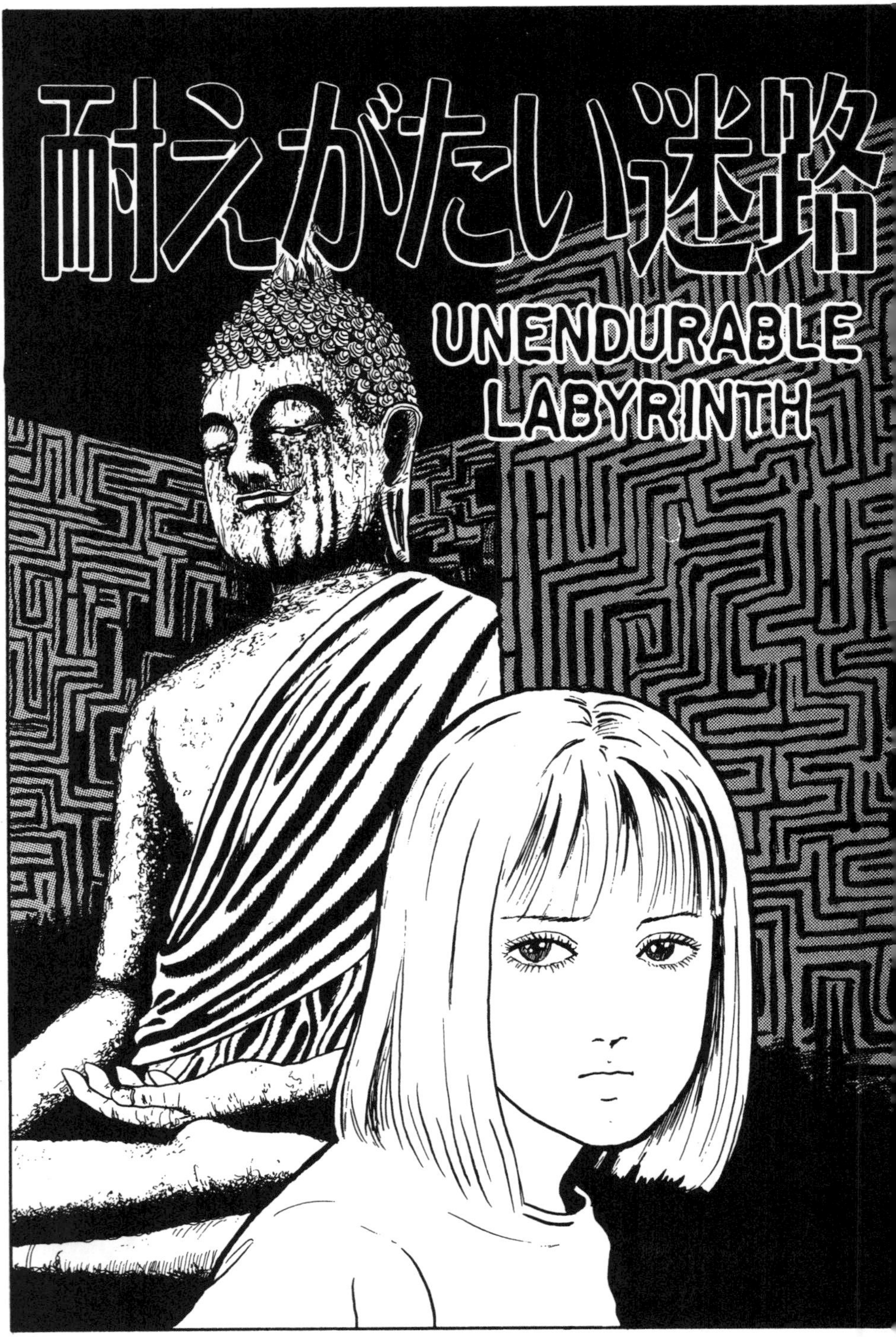
耐えがたい迷路
UNENDURABLE
LABYRINTH

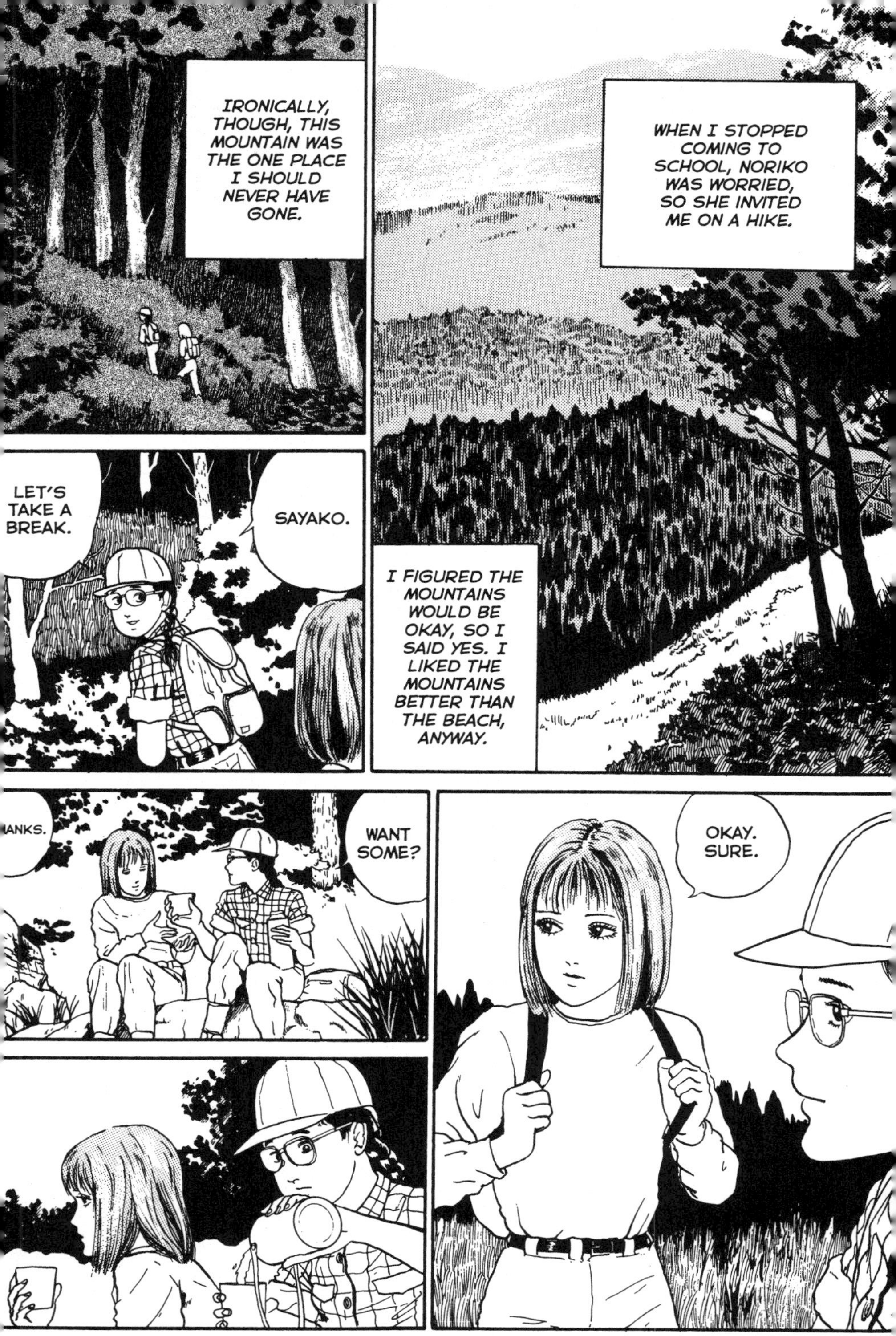
WHEN I STOPPED COMING TO SCHOOL, NORIKO WAS WORRIED, SO SHE INVITED ME ON A HIKE.
I FIGURED THE MOUNTAINS WOULD BE OKAY, SO I SAID YES. I LIKED THE MOUNTAINS BETTER THAN THE BEACH, ANYWAY.
IRONICALLY, THOUGH, THIS MOUNTAIN WAS THE ONE PLACE I SHOULD NEVER HAVE GONE.
SAYAKO.
LET'S TAKE A BREAK.
OKAY. SURE.
WANT SOME?
ANKS.

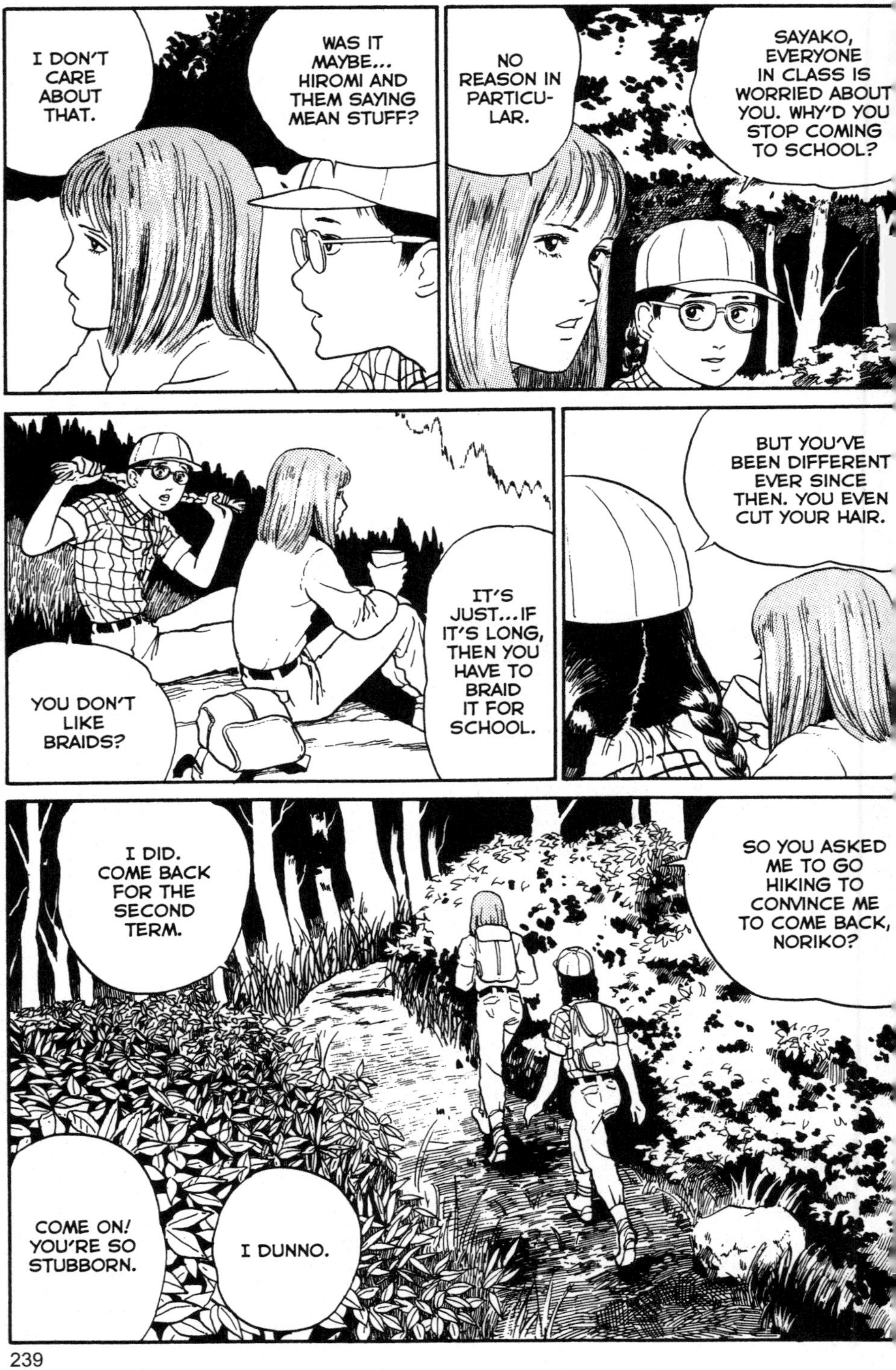
SAYAKO, EVERYONE IN CLASS IS WORRIED ABOUT YOU. WHY'D YOU STOP COMING TO SCHOOL?
NO REASON IN PARTICU-LAR.
WAS IT MAYBE... HIROMI AND THEM SAYING MEAN STUFF?
I DON'T CARE ABOUT THAT.
BUT YOU'VE BEEN DIFFERENT EVER SINCE THEN. YOU EVEN CUT YOUR HAIR.
IT'S JUST...IF IT'S LONG, THEN YOU HAVE TO BRAID IT FOR SCHOOL.
YOU DON'T LIKE BRAIDS?
SO YOU ASKED ME TO GO HIKING TO CONVINCE ME TO COME BACK, NORIKO?
I DID. COME BACK FOR THE SECOND TERM.
I DUNNO.
COME ON! YOU'RE SO STUBBORN.

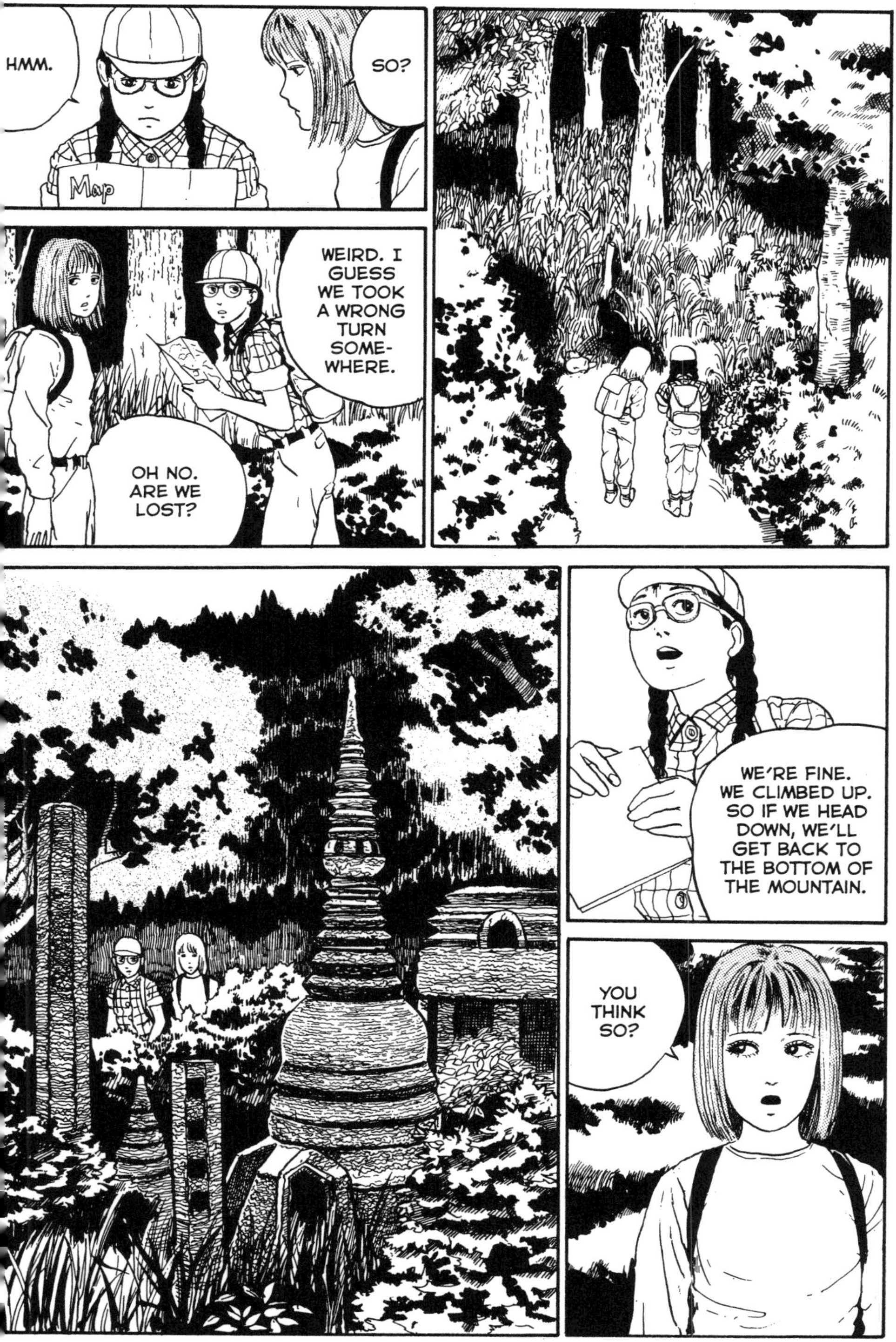
SO?
HMM.
WEIRD. I GUESS WE TOOK A WRONG TURN SOME-WHERE.
OH NO. ARE WE LOST?
WE'RE FINE. WE CLIMBED UP. SO IF WE HEAD DOWN, WE'LL GET BACK TO THE BOTTOM OF THE MOUNTAIN.
YOU THINK SO?

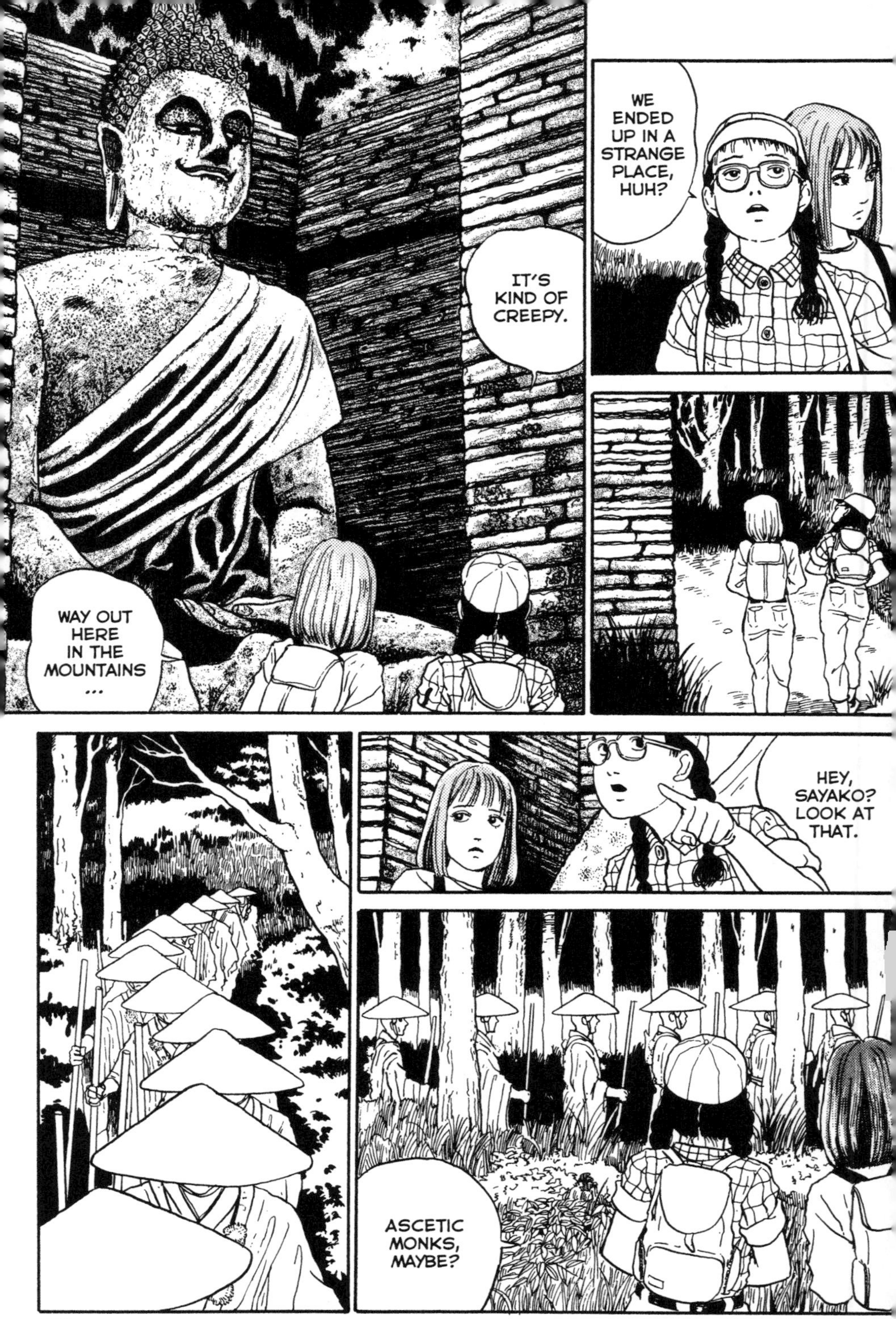
WE ENDED UP IN A STRANGE PLACE, HUH?
IT'S KIND OF CREEPY.
WAY OUT HERE IN THE MOUNTAINS ...
HEY, SAYAKO? LOOK AT THAT.
ASCETIC MONKS, MAYBE?

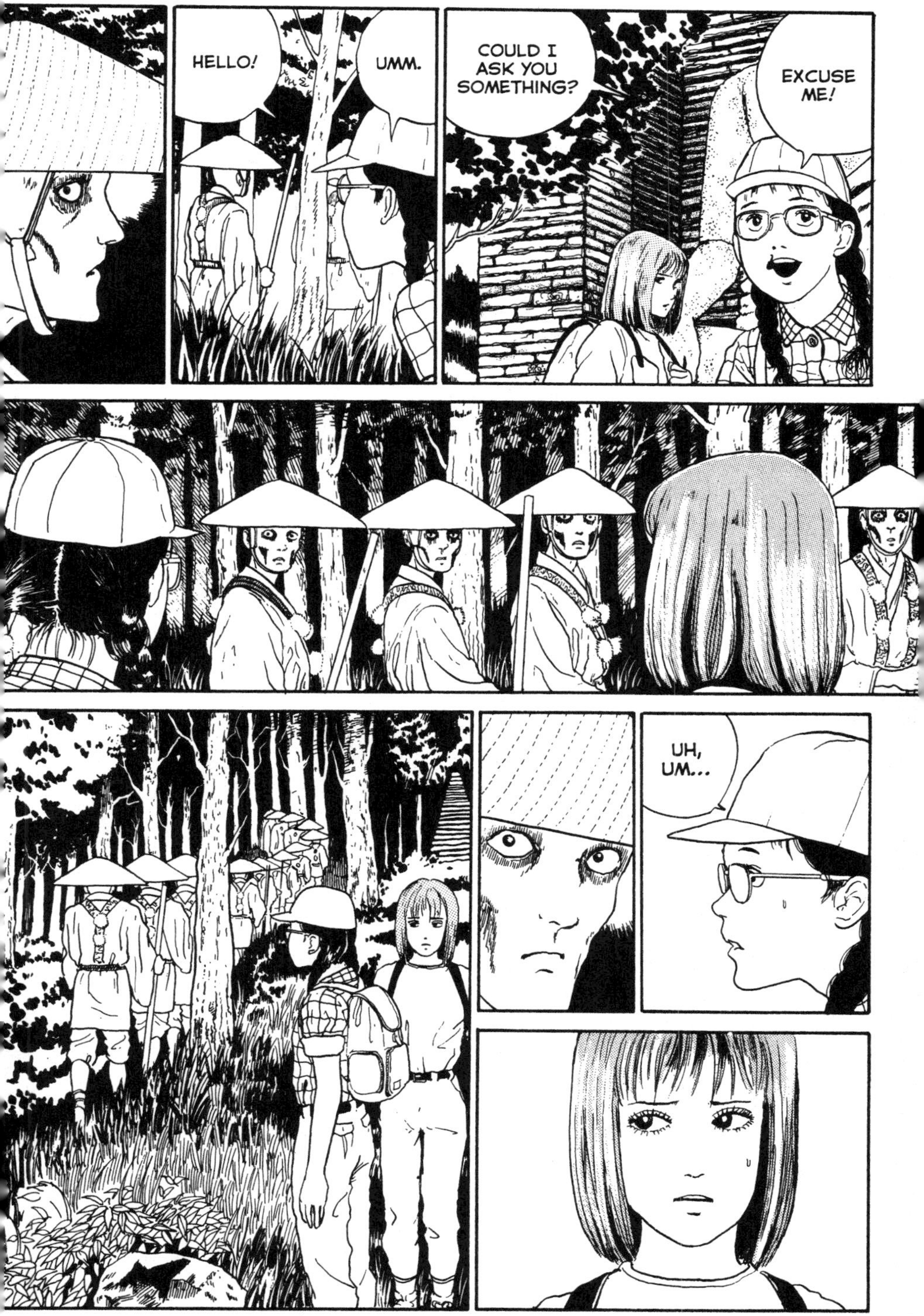
EXCUSE ME!
COULD I ASK YOU SOMETHING?
UMM.
HELLO!
UH, UM...

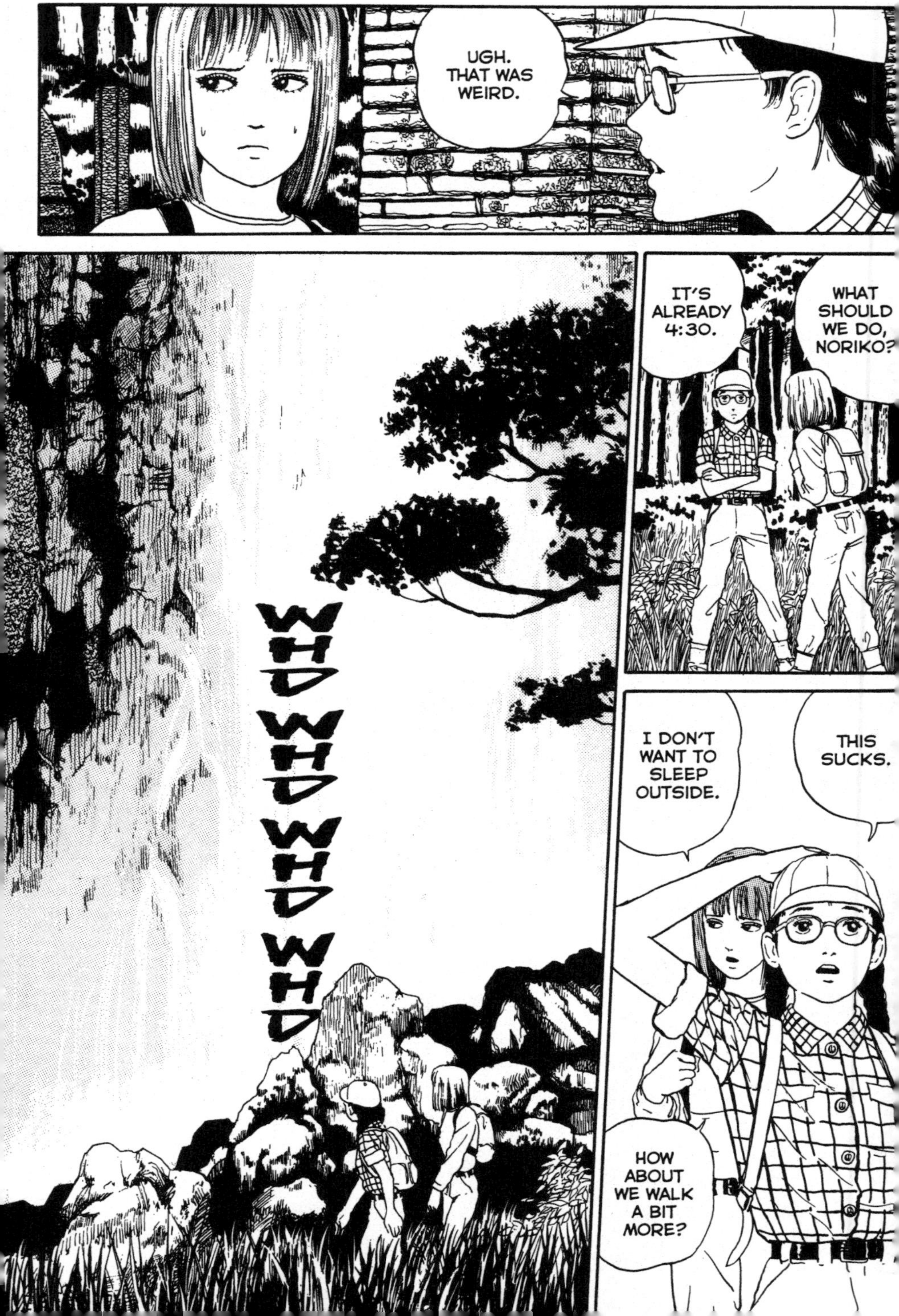
UGH. THAT WAS WEIRD.
WHAT SHOULD WE DO, NORIKO?
IT'S ALREADY 4:30.
THIS SUCKS.
I DON'T WANT TO SLEEP OUTSIDE.
HOW ABOUT WE WALK A BIT MORE?
WHD WHD WHD WHD

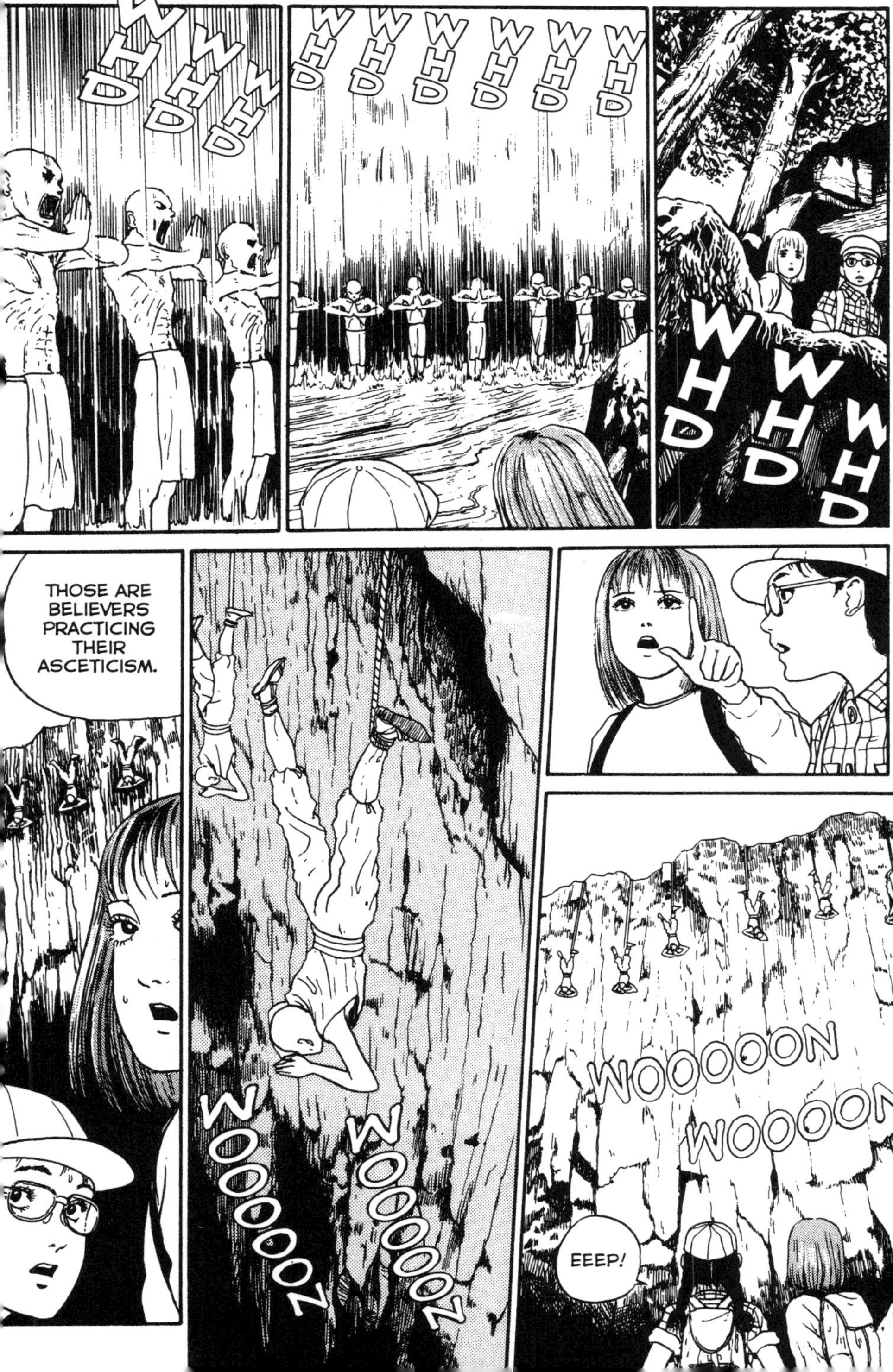
WHD
WHD
WHD
WHD
WHD
WHD
WHD
WHD
WHD
WHD
WHD
WHD
WOOOOON
WOOOON
EEEP!
WOOOOOZ
WOOOOOZ
THOSE ARE BELIEVERS PRACTICING THEIR ASCETICISM.

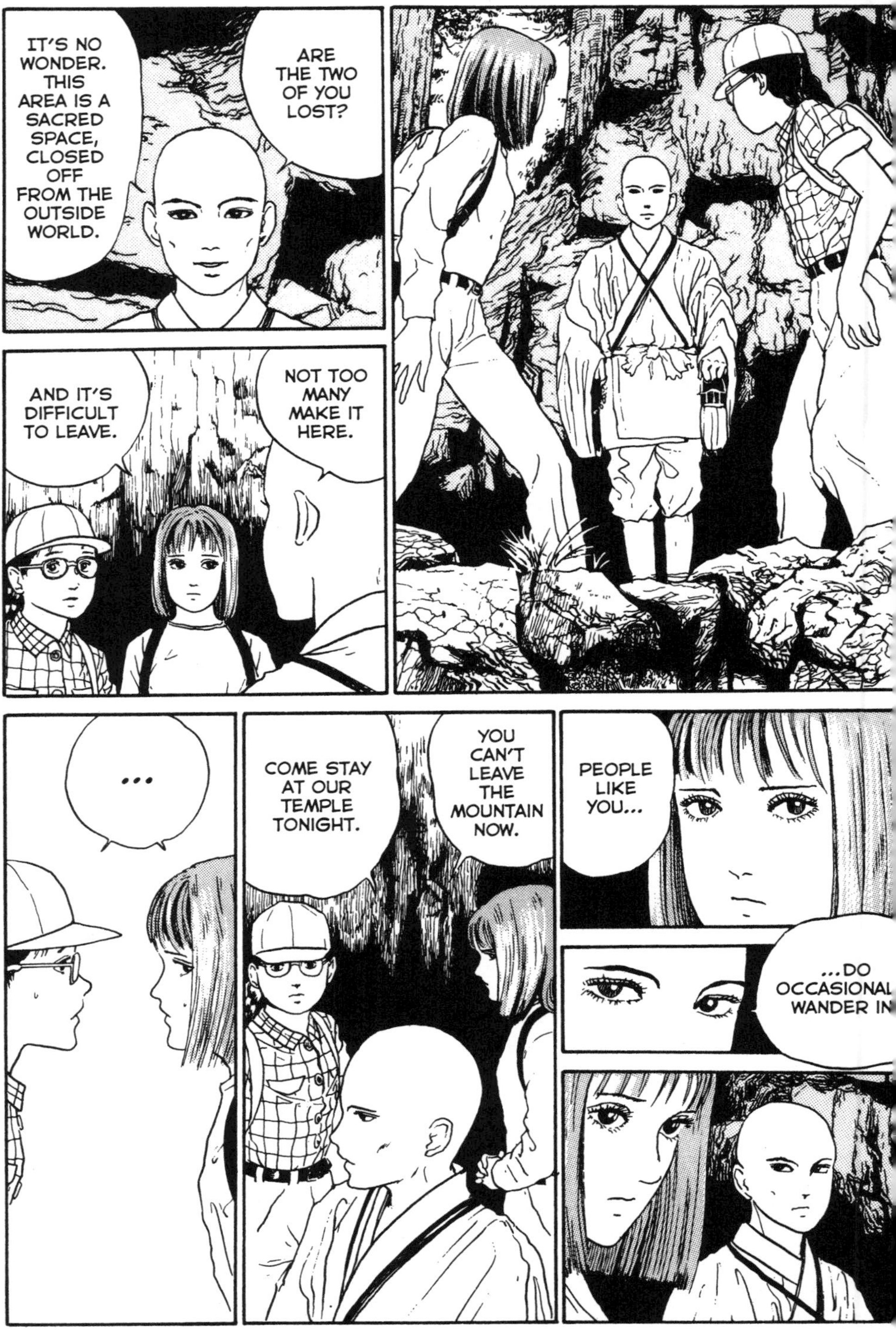
ARE THE TWO OF YOU LOST?
IT'S NO WONDER. THIS AREA IS A SACRED SPACE, CLOSED OFF FROM THE OUTSIDE WORLD.
NOT TOO MANY MAKE IT HERE.
AND IT'S DIFFICULT TO LEAVE.
PEOPLE LIKE YOU...
...DO OCCASIONAL WANDER IN
YOU CAN'T LEAVE THE MOUNTAIN NOW.
COME STAY AT OUR TEMPLE TONIGHT.
...

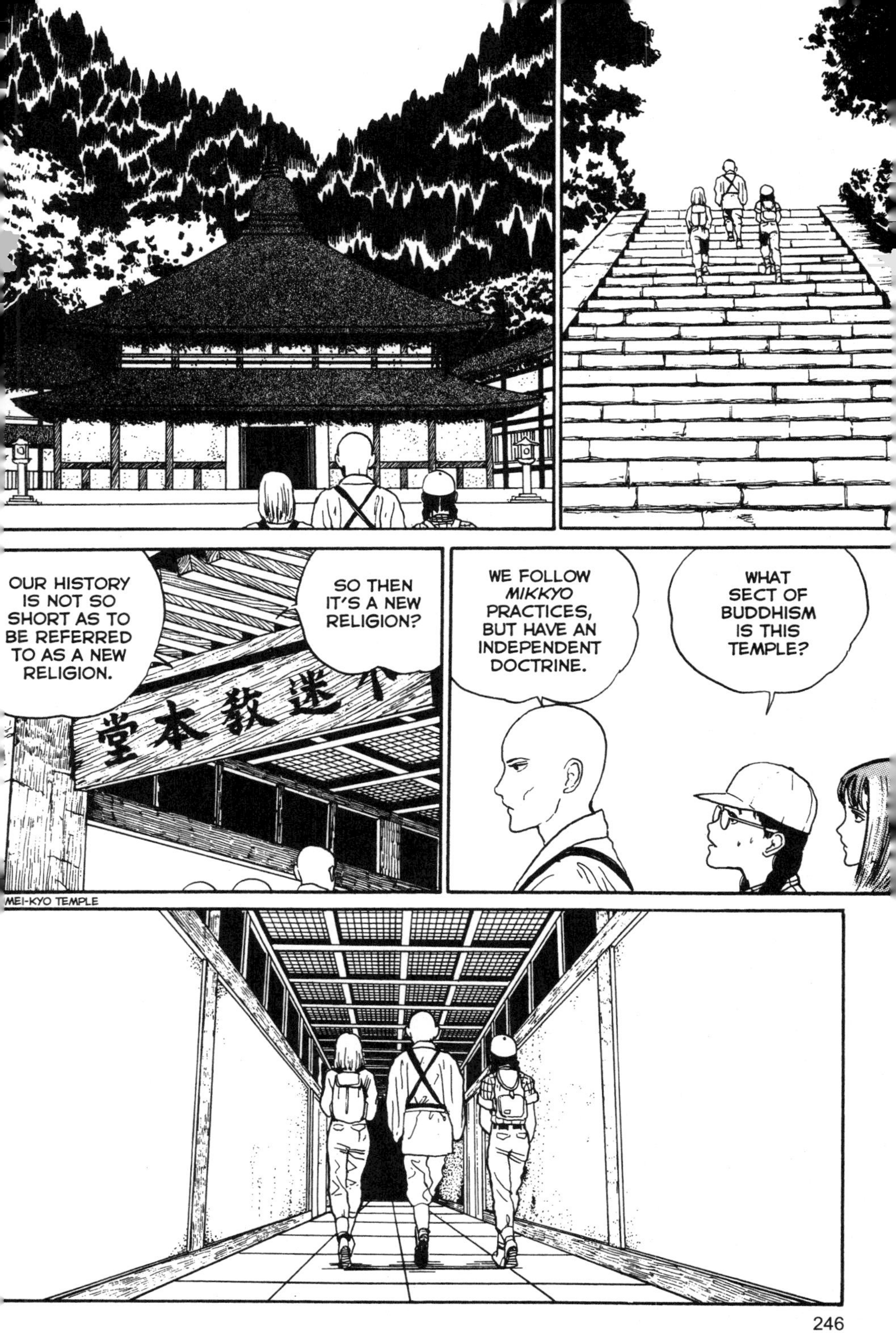
WHAT SECT OF BUDDHISM IS THIS TEMPLE?
WE FOLLOW *MIKKYO* PRACTICES, BUT HAVE AN INDEPENDENT DOCTRINE.
SO THEN IT'S A NEW RELIGION?
OUR HISTORY IS NOT SO SHORT AS TO BE REFERRED TO AS A NEW RELIGION.
MEI-KYO TEMPLE

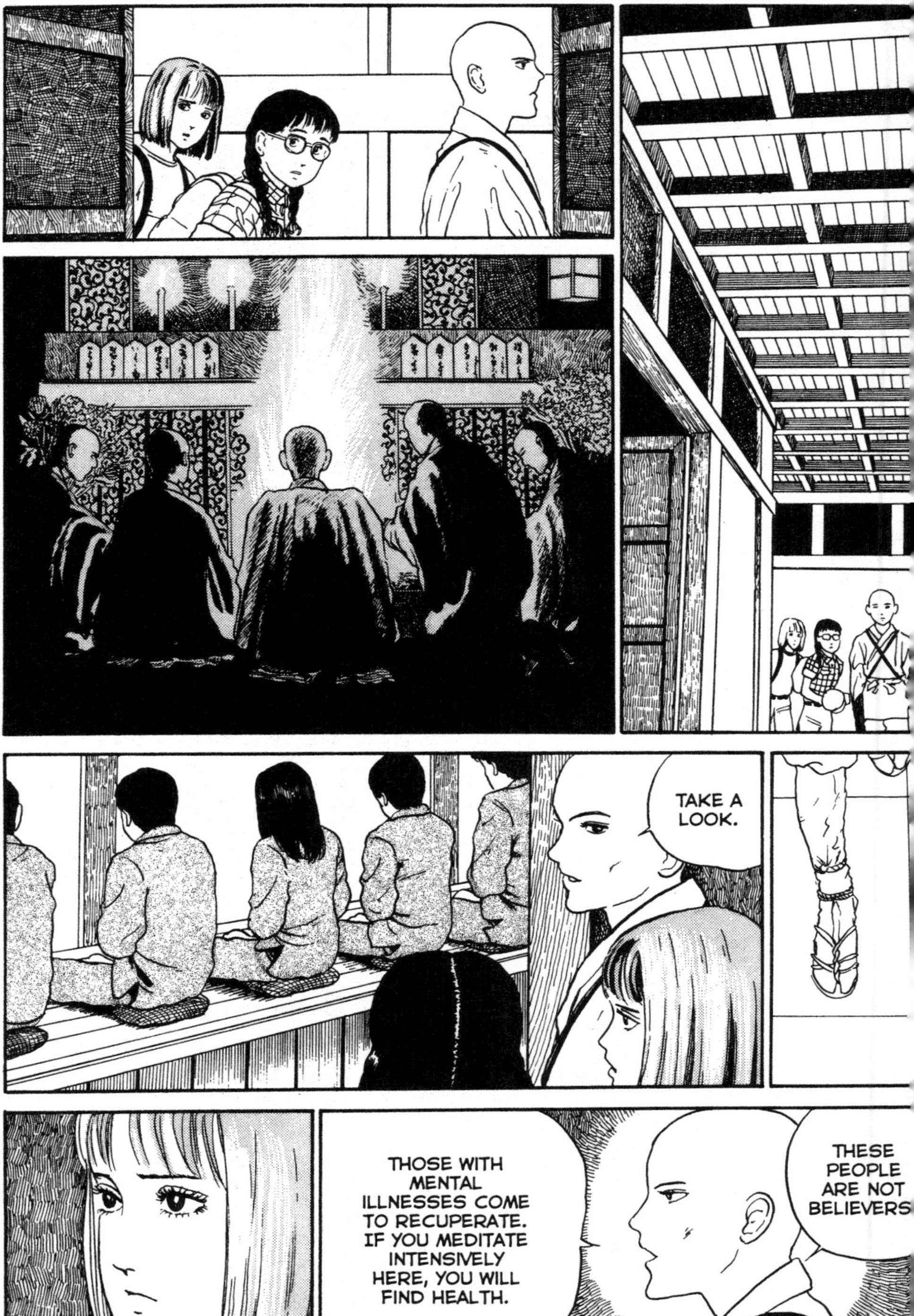
TAKE A LOOK.
THESE PEOPLE ARE NOT BELIEVERS
THOSE WITH MENTAL ILLNESSES COME TO RECUPERATE. IF YOU MEDITATE INTENSIVELY HERE, YOU WILL FIND HEALTH.

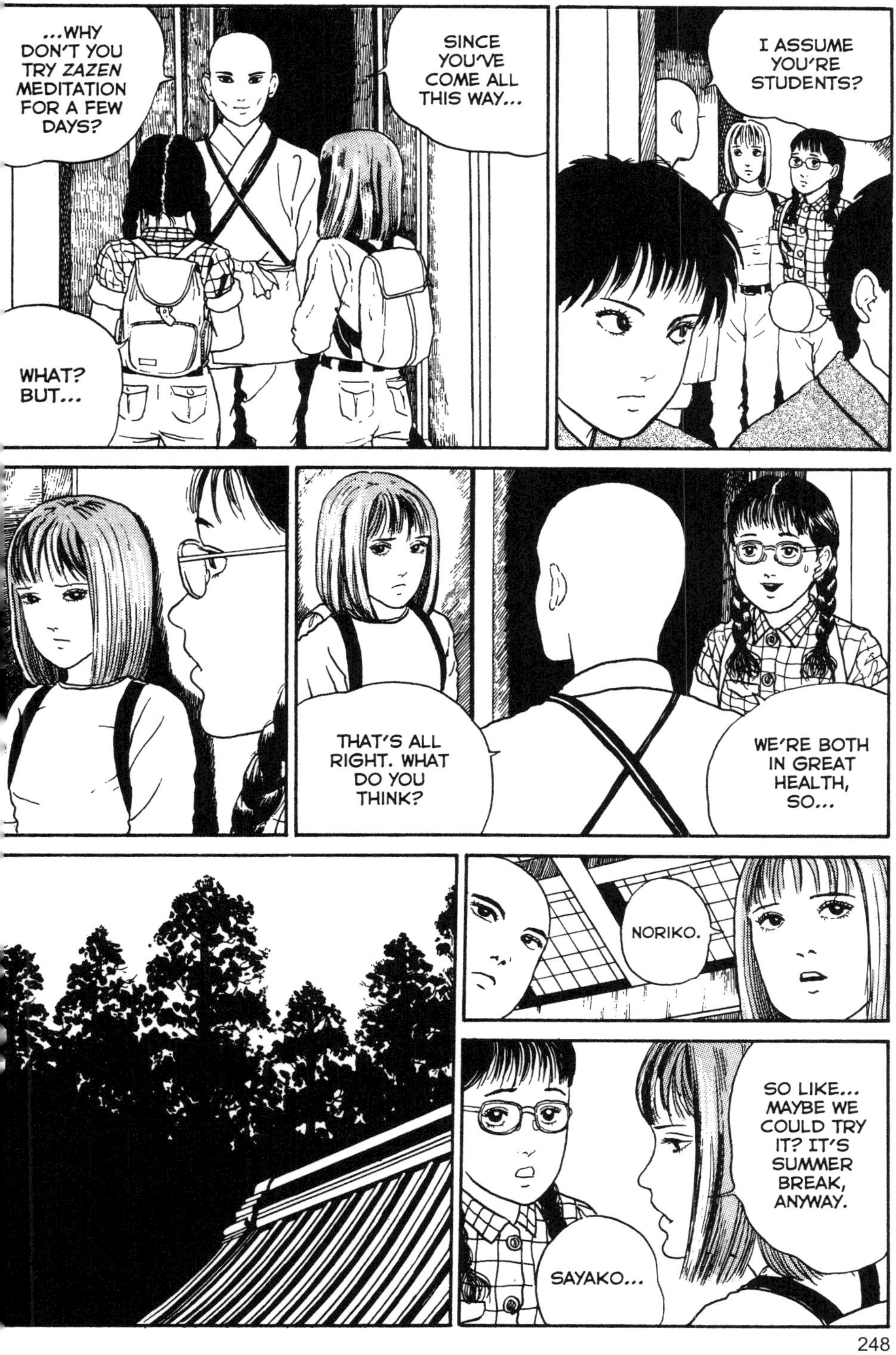
I ASSUME YOU'RE STUDENTS?
SINCE YOU'VE COME ALL THIS WAY...
...WHY DON'T YOU TRY *ZAZEN* MEDITATION FOR A FEW DAYS?
WHAT? BUT...
WE'RE BOTH IN GREAT HEALTH, SO...
THAT'S ALL RIGHT. WHAT DO YOU THINK?
NORIKO.
SO LIKE... MAYBE WE COULD TRY IT? IT'S SUMMER BREAK, ANYWAY.
SAYAKO...

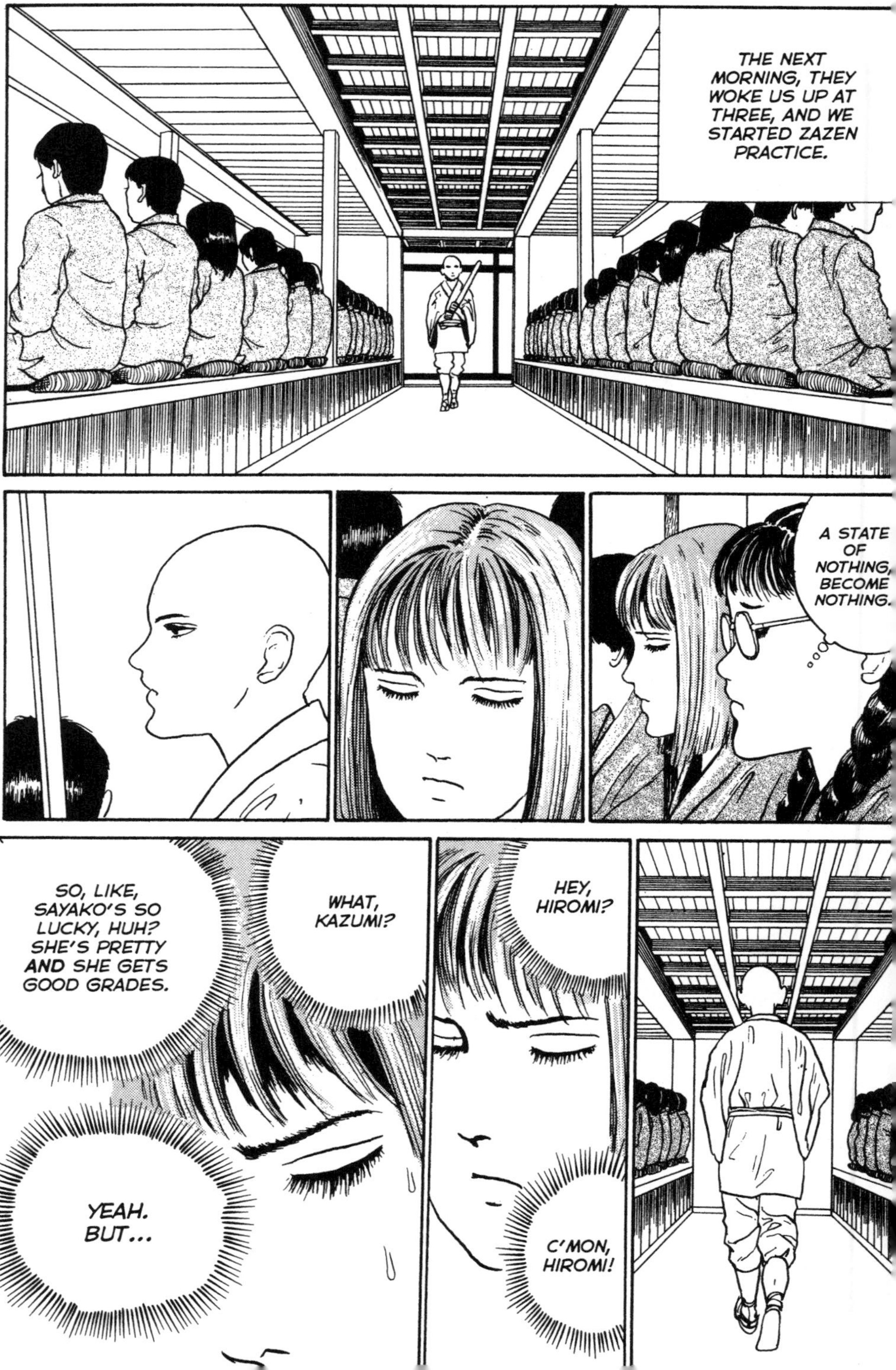
THE NEXT MORNING, THEY WOKE US UP AT THREE, AND WE STARTED ZAZEN PRACTICE.
A STATE OF NOTHING, BECOME NOTHING.
HEY, HIROMI?
C'MON, HIROMI!
WHAT, KAZUMI?
SO, LIKE, SAYAKO'S SO LUCKY, HUH? SHE'S PRETTY **AND** SHE GETS GOOD GRADES.
YEAH. BUT...

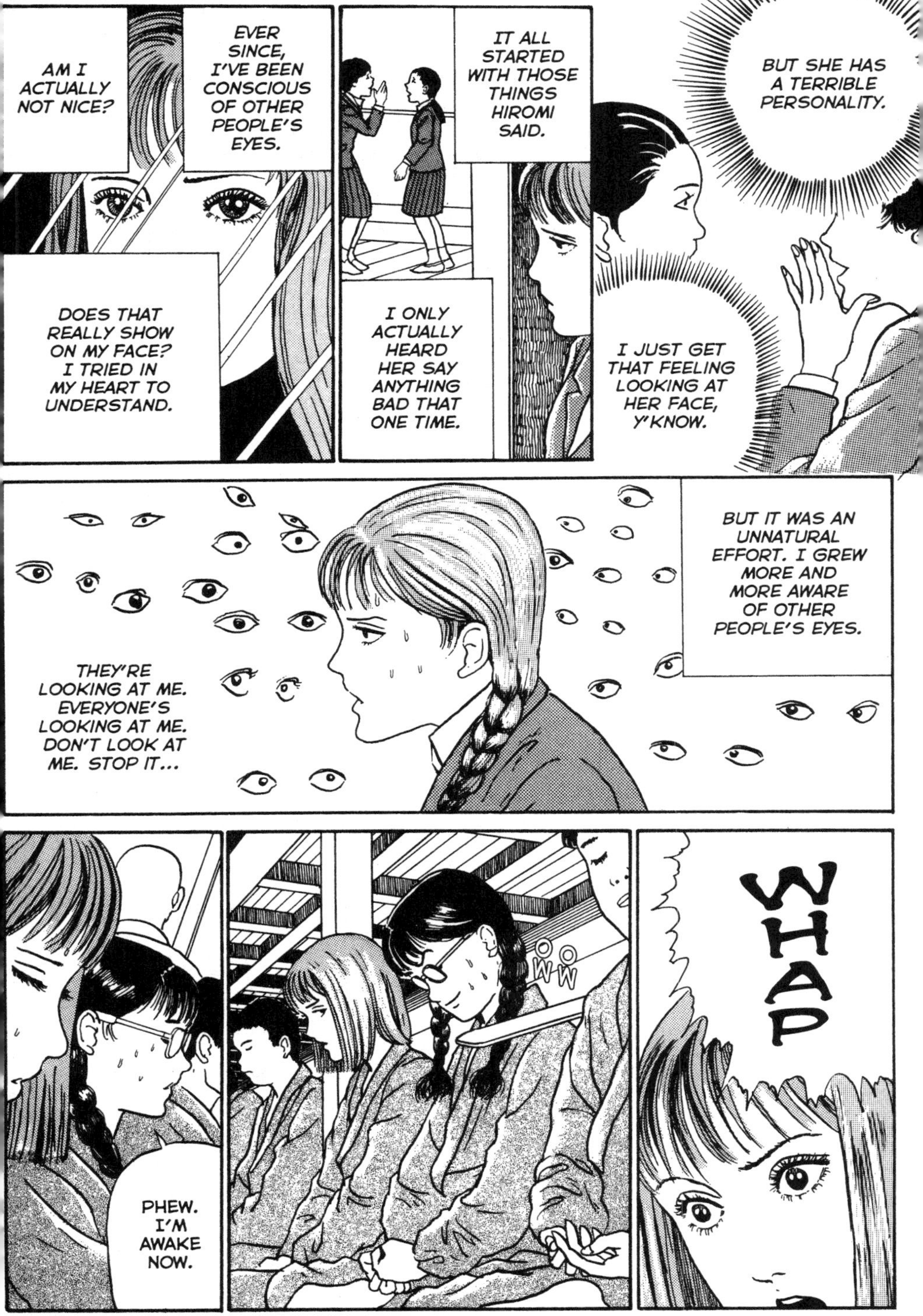
BUT SHE HAS A TERRIBLE PERSONALITY.
I JUST GET THAT FEELING LOOKING AT HER FACE, Y'KNOW.
IT ALL STARTED WITH THOSE THINGS HIROMI SAID.
I ONLY ACTUALLY HEARD HER SAY ANYTHING BAD THAT ONE TIME.
EVER SINCE, I'VE BEEN CONSCIOUS OF OTHER PEOPLE'S EYES.
AM I ACTUALLY NOT NICE?
DOES THAT REALLY SHOW ON MY FACE? I TRIED IN MY HEART TO UNDERSTAND.
BUT IT WAS AN UNNATURAL EFFORT. I GREW MORE AND MORE AWARE OF OTHER PEOPLE'S EYES.
THEY'RE LOOKING AT ME. EVERYONE'S LOOKING AT ME. DON'T LOOK AT ME. STOP IT...
WHAP
OWW
PHEW. I'M AWAKE NOW.

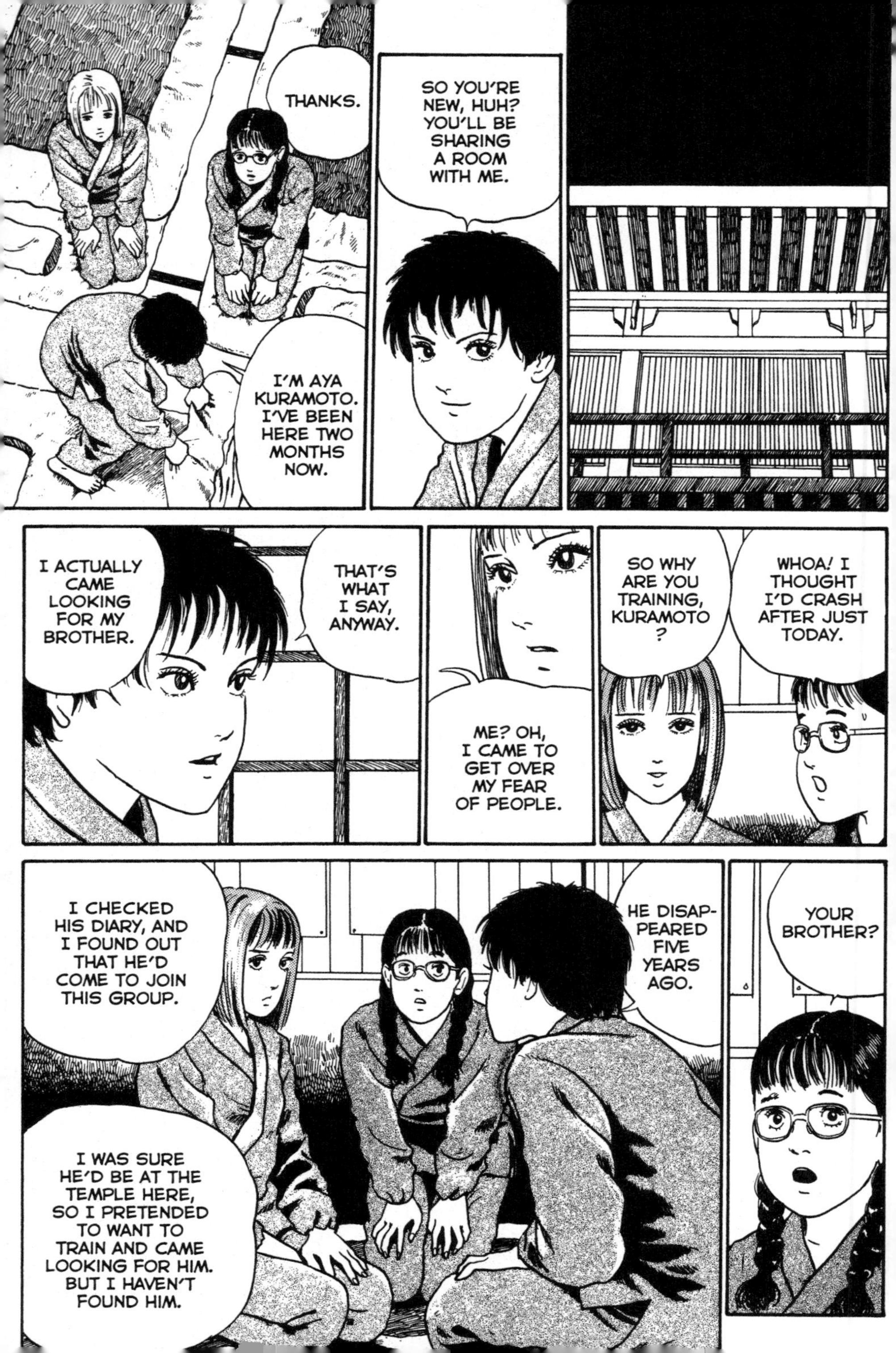
SO YOU'RE NEW, HUH? YOU'LL BE SHARING A ROOM WITH ME.
THANKS.
I'M AYA KURAMOTO. I'VE BEEN HERE TWO MONTHS NOW.
WHOA! I THOUGHT I'D CRASH AFTER JUST TODAY.
SO WHY ARE YOU TRAINING, KURAMOTO?
ME? OH, I CAME TO GET OVER MY FEAR OF PEOPLE.
THAT'S WHAT I SAY, ANYWAY.
I ACTUALLY CAME LOOKING FOR MY BROTHER.
YOUR BROTHER?
HE DISAP-PEARED FIVE YEARS AGO.
I CHECKED HIS DIARY, AND I FOUND OUT THAT HE'D COME TO JOIN THIS GROUP.
I WAS SURE HE'D BE AT THE TEMPLE HERE, SO I PRETENDED TO WANT TO TRAIN AND CAME LOOKING FOR HIM. BUT I HAVEN'T FOUND HIM.

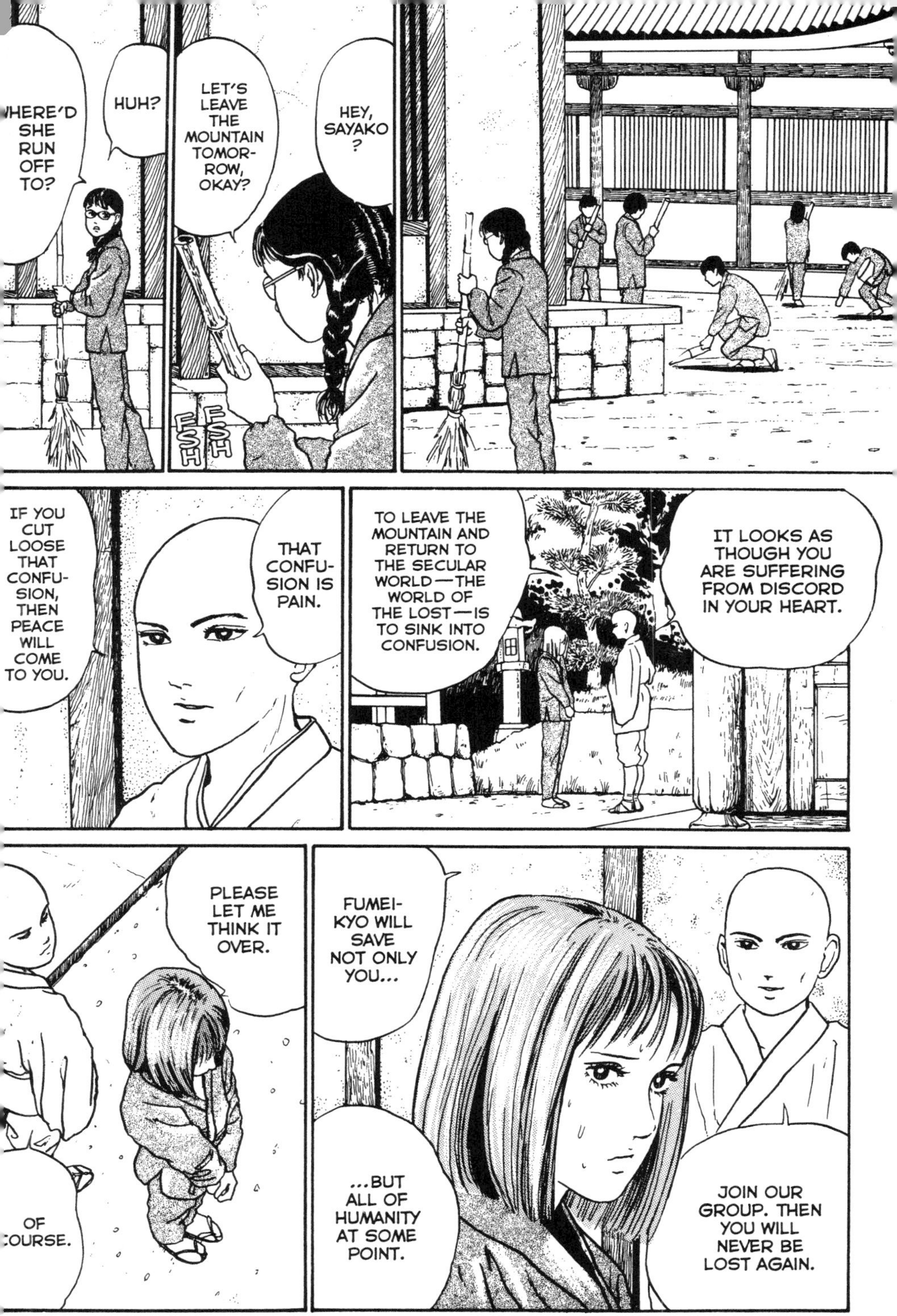

HEY, SAYAKO?
LET'S LEAVE THE MOUNTAIN TOMORROW, OKAY?
FSH FSH
HUH?
HERE'D SHE RUN OFF TO?
IT LOOKS AS THOUGH YOU ARE SUFFERING FROM DISCORD IN YOUR HEART.
TO LEAVE THE MOUNTAIN AND RETURN TO THE SECULAR WORLD—THE WORLD OF THE LOST—IS TO SINK INTO CONFUSION.
THAT CONFUSION IS PAIN.
IF YOU CUT LOOSE THAT CONFUSION, THEN PEACE WILL COME TO YOU.
FUMEIKYO WILL SAVE NOT ONLY YOU...
...BUT ALL OF HUMANITY AT SOME POINT.
JOIN OUR GROUP. THEN YOU WILL NEVER BE LOST AGAIN.
PLEASE LET ME THINK IT OVER.
OF COURSE.

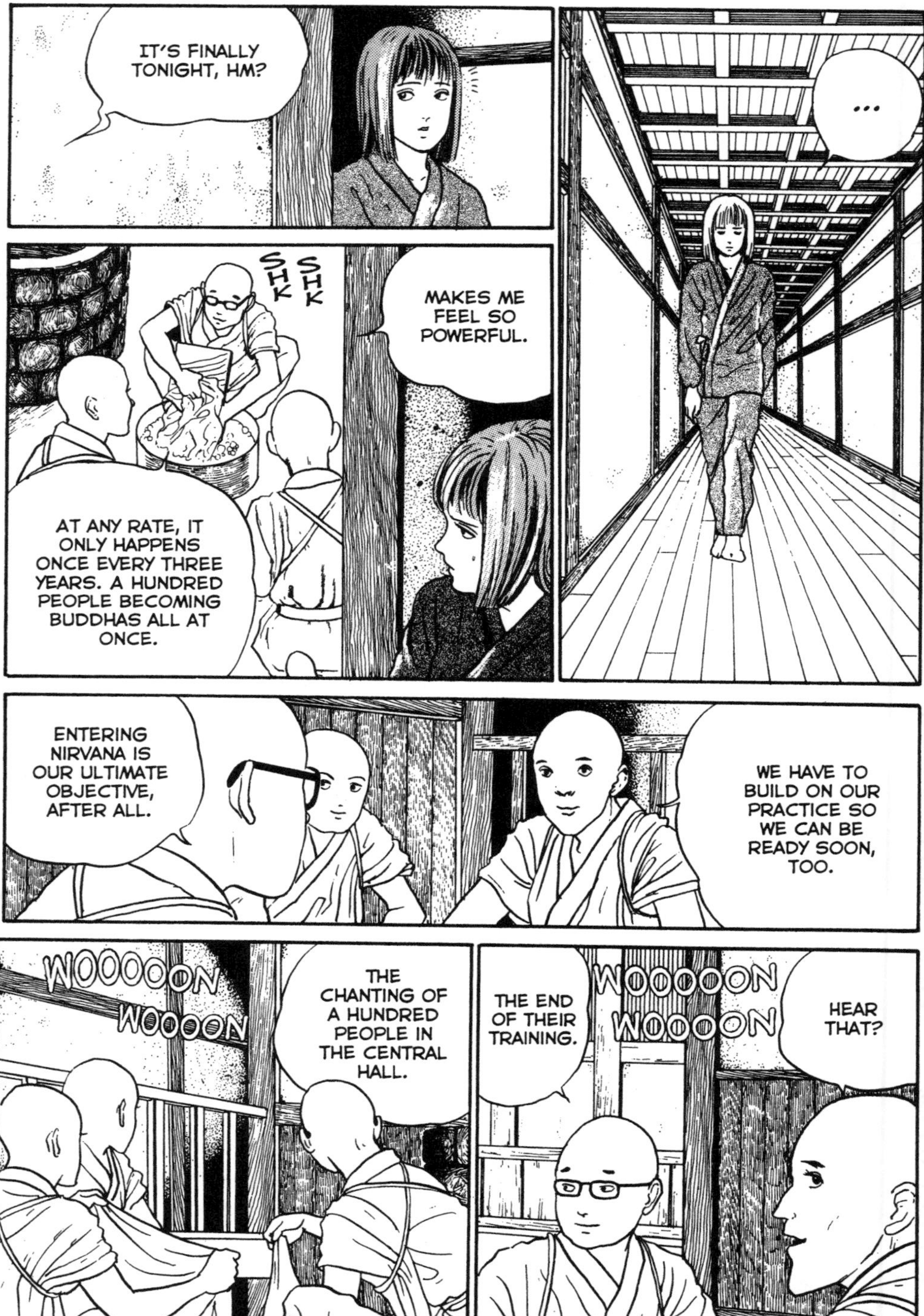
...
IT'S FINALLY TONIGHT, HM?
MAKES ME FEEL SO POWERFUL.
SHK SHK
AT ANY RATE, IT ONLY HAPPENS ONCE EVERY THREE YEARS. A HUNDRED PEOPLE BECOMING BUDDHAS ALL AT ONCE.
WE HAVE TO BUILD ON OUR PRACTICE SO WE CAN BE READY SOON, TOO.
ENTERING NIRVANA IS OUR ULTIMATE OBJECTIVE, AFTER ALL.
HEAR THAT?
WOOOOON WOOOON
THE END OF THEIR TRAINING.
THE CHANTING OF A HUNDRED PEOPLE IN THE CENTRAL HALL.
WOOOOON WOOOON

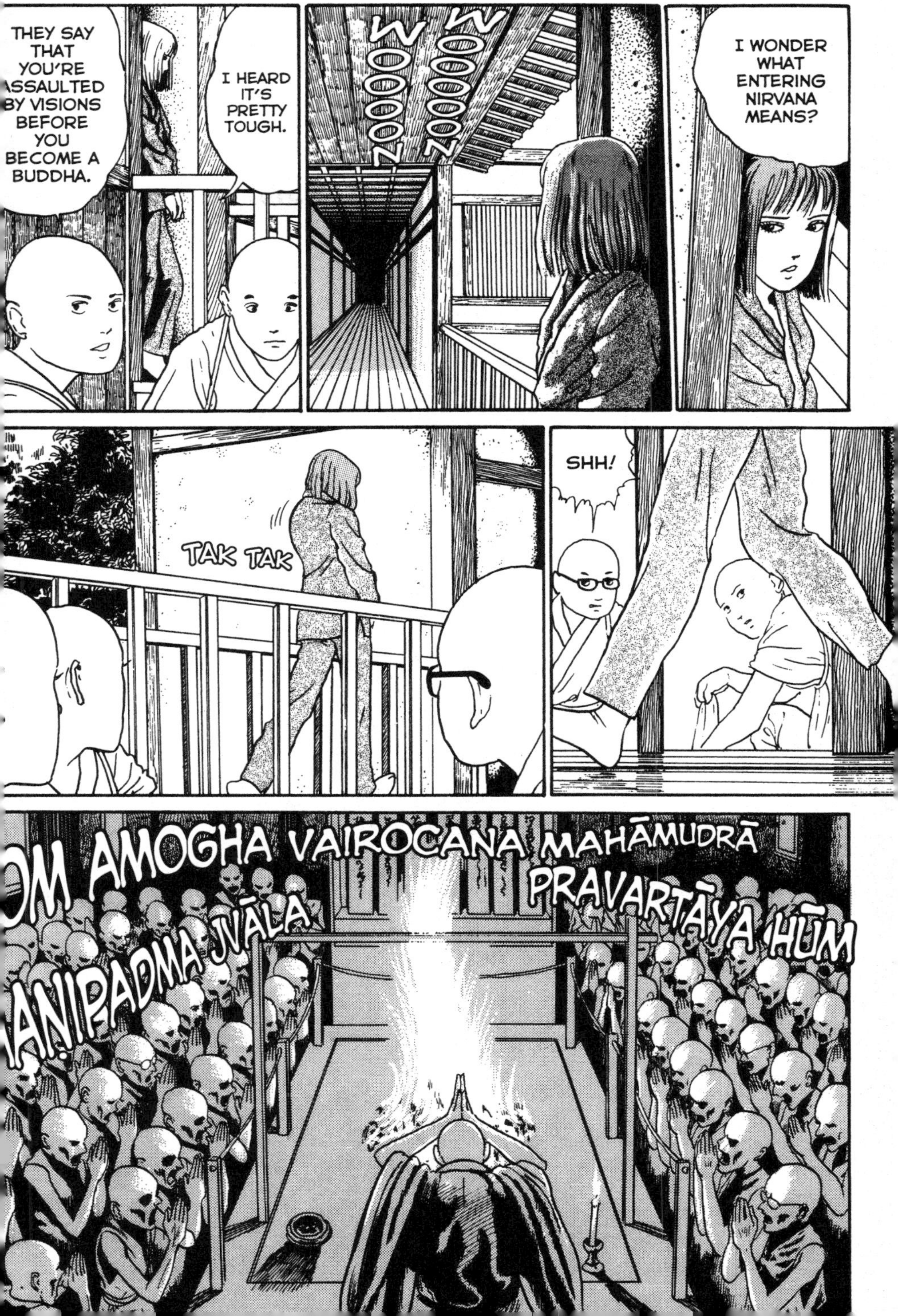
I WONDER WHAT ENTERING NIRVANA MEANS?
WOOOOON
WOOOOON
I HEARD IT'S PRETTY TOUGH.
THEY SAY THAT YOU'RE ASSAULTED BY VISIONS BEFORE YOU BECOME A BUDDHA.
SHH!
TAK TAK
OM AMOGHA VAIROCANA MAHĀMUDRĀ
PRAVARTĀYA HŪM
AṆIPADMA JVĀLA

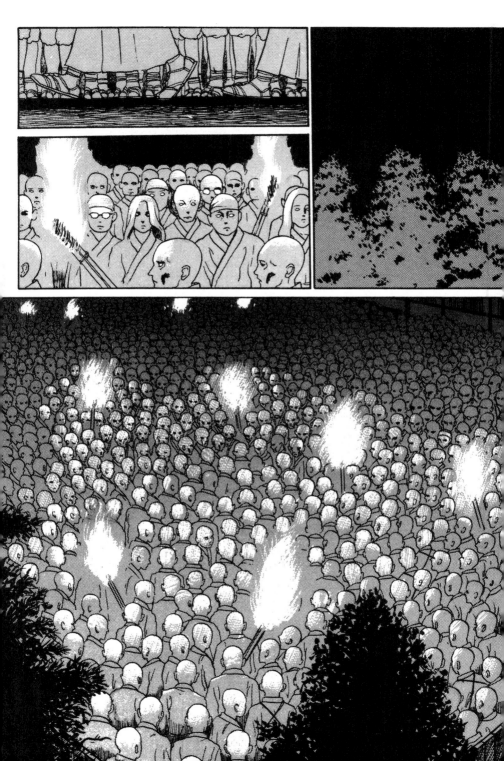

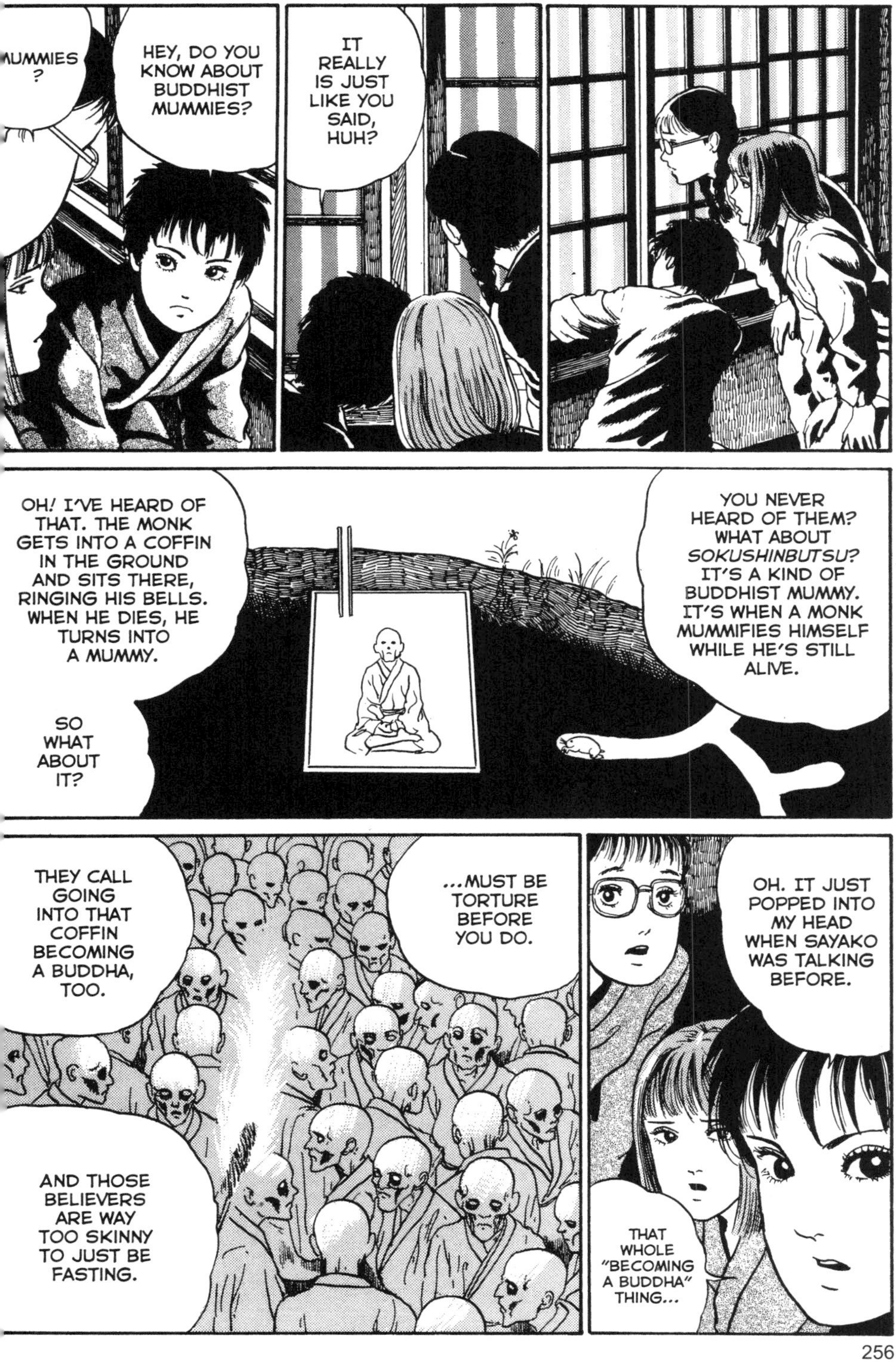
IT REALLY IS JUST LIKE YOU SAID, HUH?
HEY, DO YOU KNOW ABOUT BUDDHIST MUMMIES?
MUMMIES?
YOU NEVER HEARD OF THEM? WHAT ABOUT *SOKUSHINBUTSU?* IT'S A KIND OF BUDDHIST MUMMY. IT'S WHEN A MONK MUMMIFIES HIMSELF WHILE HE'S STILL ALIVE.
OH! I'VE HEARD OF THAT. THE MONK GETS INTO A COFFIN IN THE GROUND AND SITS THERE, RINGING HIS BELLS. WHEN HE DIES, HE TURNS INTO A MUMMY.
SO WHAT ABOUT IT?
OH. IT JUST POPPED INTO MY HEAD WHEN SAYAKO WAS TALKING BEFORE.
THAT WHOLE "BECOMING A BUDDHA" THING...
...MUST BE TORTURE BEFORE YOU DO.
THEY CALL GOING INTO THAT COFFIN BECOMING A BUDDHA, TOO.
AND THOSE BELIEVERS ARE WAY TOO SKINNY TO JUST BE FASTING.

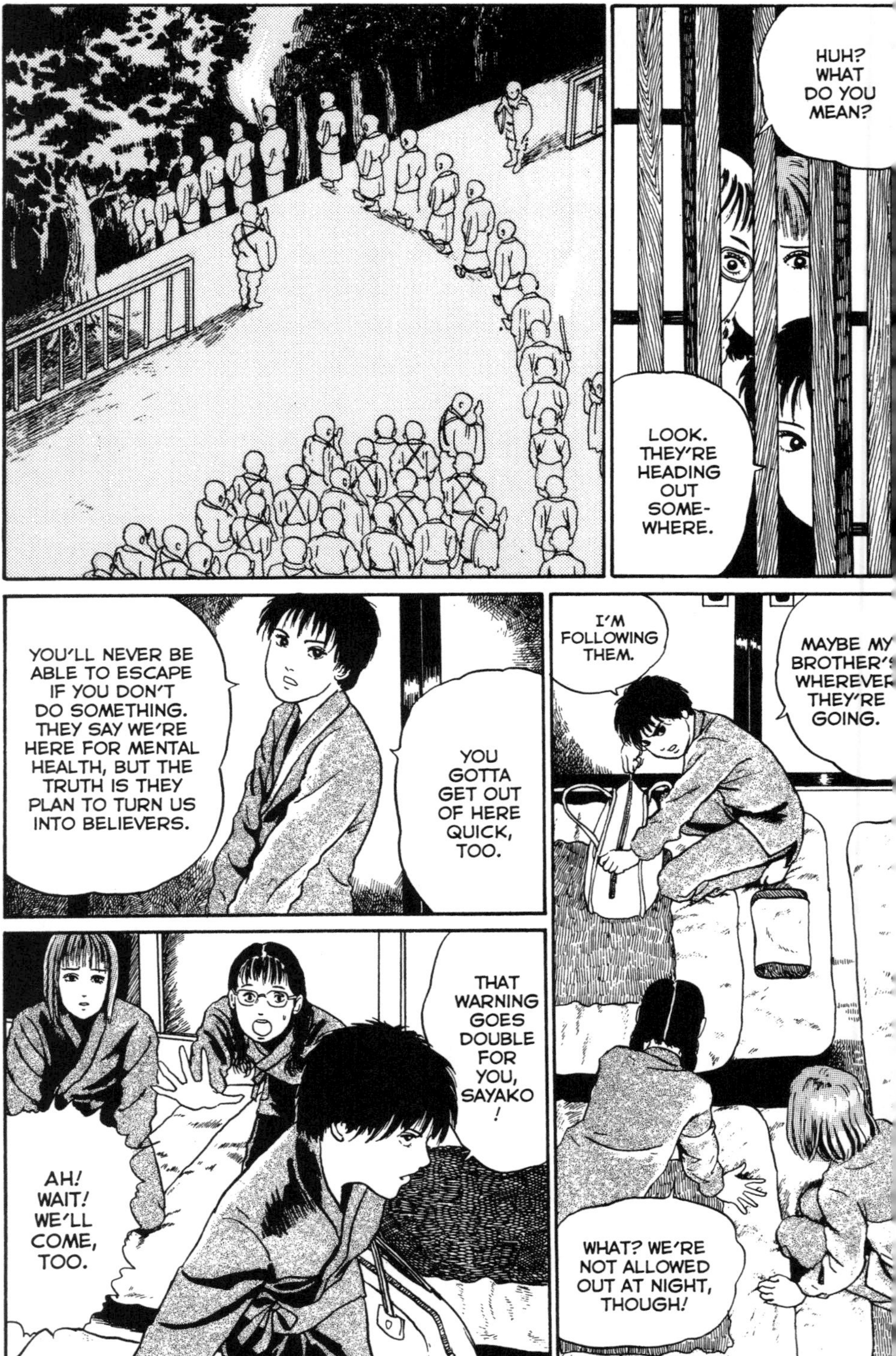
HUH? WHAT DO YOU MEAN?
LOOK. THEY'RE HEADING OUT SOME-WHERE.
MAYBE MY BROTHER'S WHEREVER THEY'RE GOING.
I'M FOLLOWING THEM.
WHAT? WE'RE NOT ALLOWED OUT AT NIGHT, THOUGH!
YOU'LL NEVER BE ABLE TO ESCAPE IF YOU DON'T DO SOMETHING. THEY SAY WE'RE HERE FOR MENTAL HEALTH, BUT THE TRUTH IS THEY PLAN TO TURN US INTO BELIEVERS.
YOU GOTTA GET OUT OF HERE QUICK, TOO.
THAT WARNING GOES DOUBLE FOR YOU, SAYAKO!
AH! WAIT! WE'LL COME, TOO.

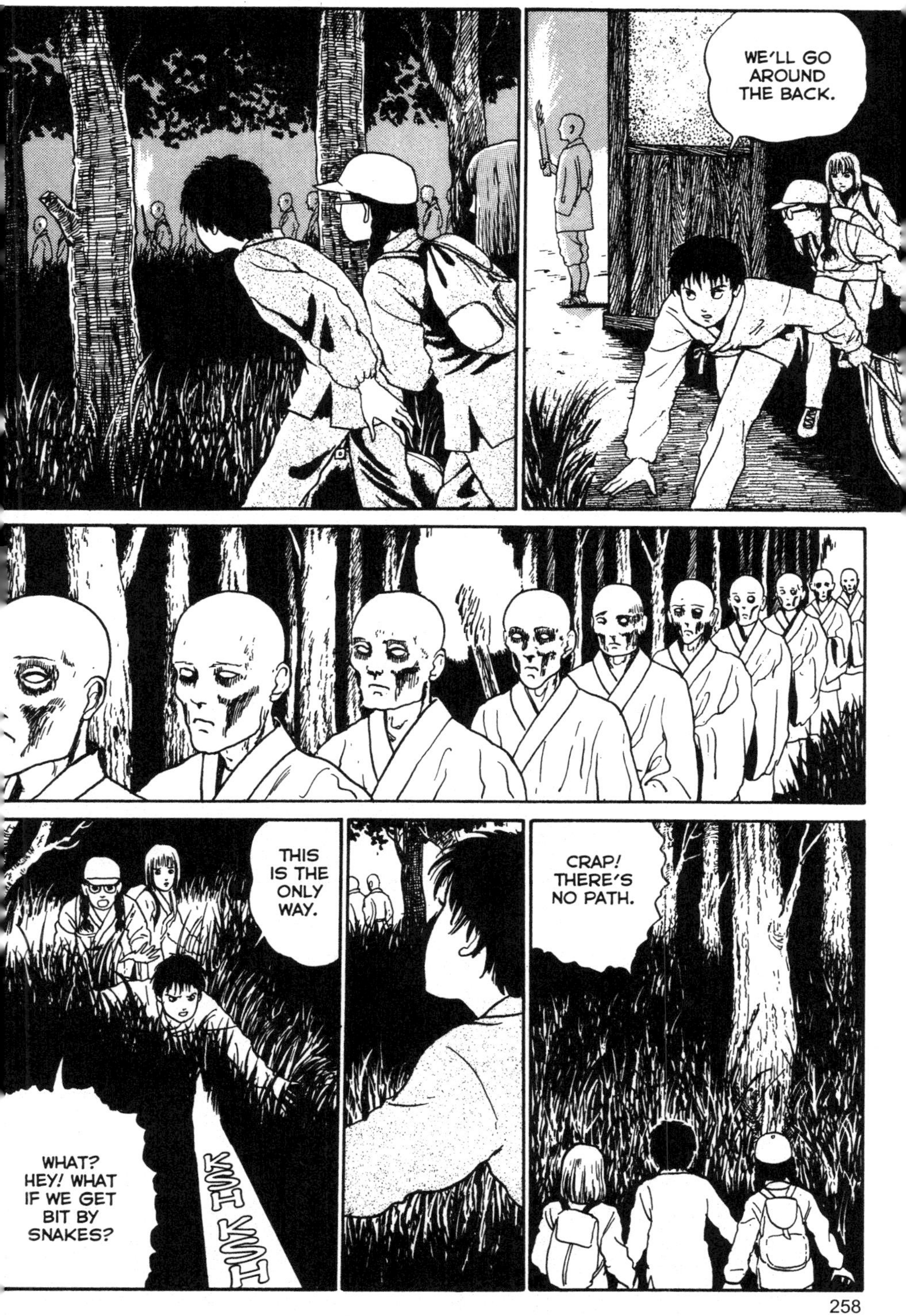
WE'LL GO AROUND THE BACK.
CRAP! THERE'S NO PATH.
THIS IS THE ONLY WAY.
WHAT? HEY! WHAT IF WE GET BIT BY SNAKES?
KSH KSH

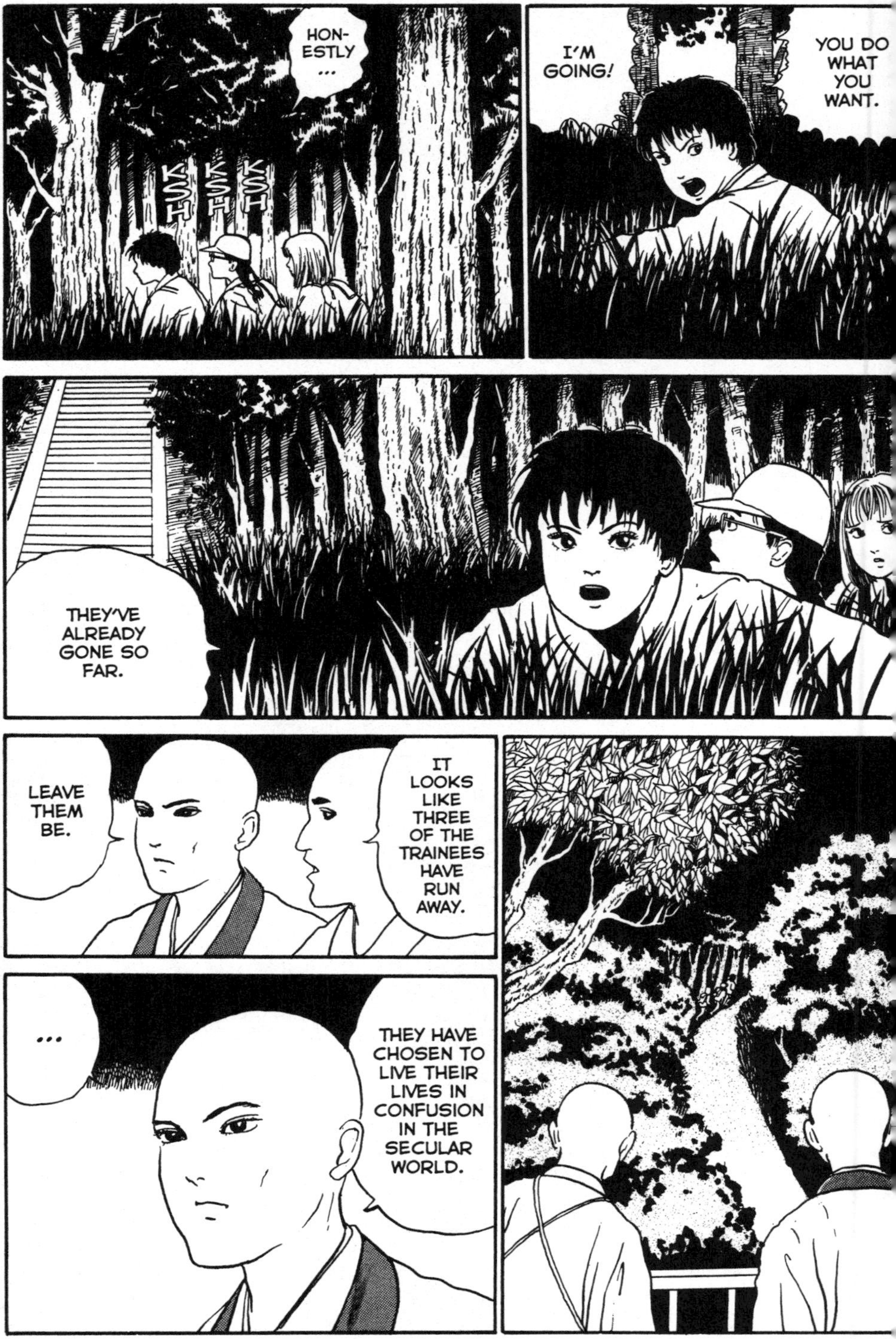
YOU DO WHAT YOU WANT.
I'M GOING!
HON-ESTLY ...
KSH KSH KSH
THEY'VE ALREADY GONE SO FAR.
IT LOOKS LIKE THREE OF THE TRAINEES HAVE RUN AWAY.
LEAVE THEM BE.
THEY HAVE CHOSEN TO LIVE THEIR LIVES IN CONFUSION IN THE SECULAR WORLD.
...

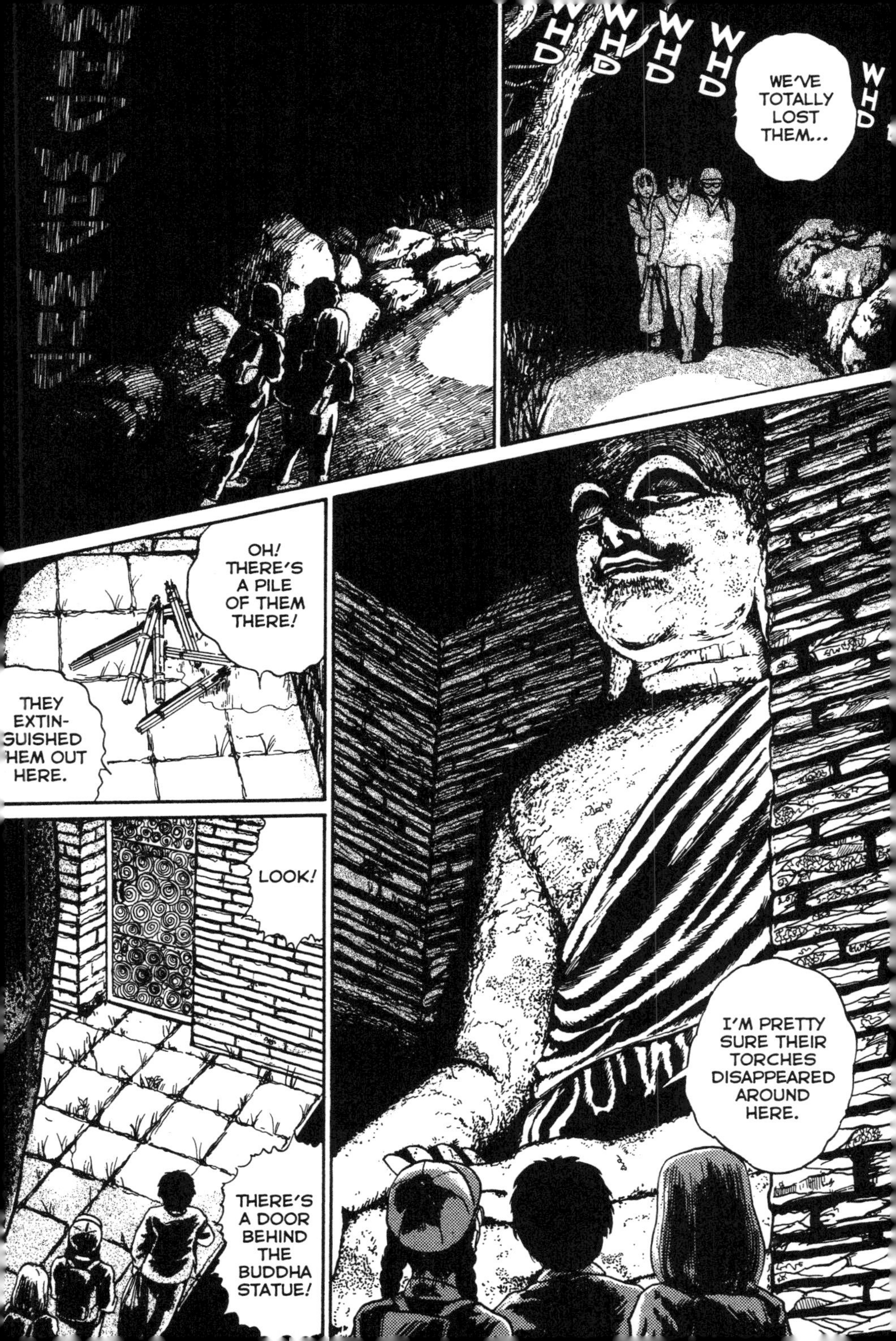

WHD
WHD
WHD
WHD
WE'VE TOTALLY LOST THEM...
WHD
I'M PRETTY SURE THEIR TORCHES DISAPPEARED AROUND HERE.
OH! THERE'S A PILE OF THEM THERE!
THEY EXTIN-GUISHED HEM OUT HERE.
LOOK!
THERE'S A DOOR BEHIND THE BUDDHA STATUE!

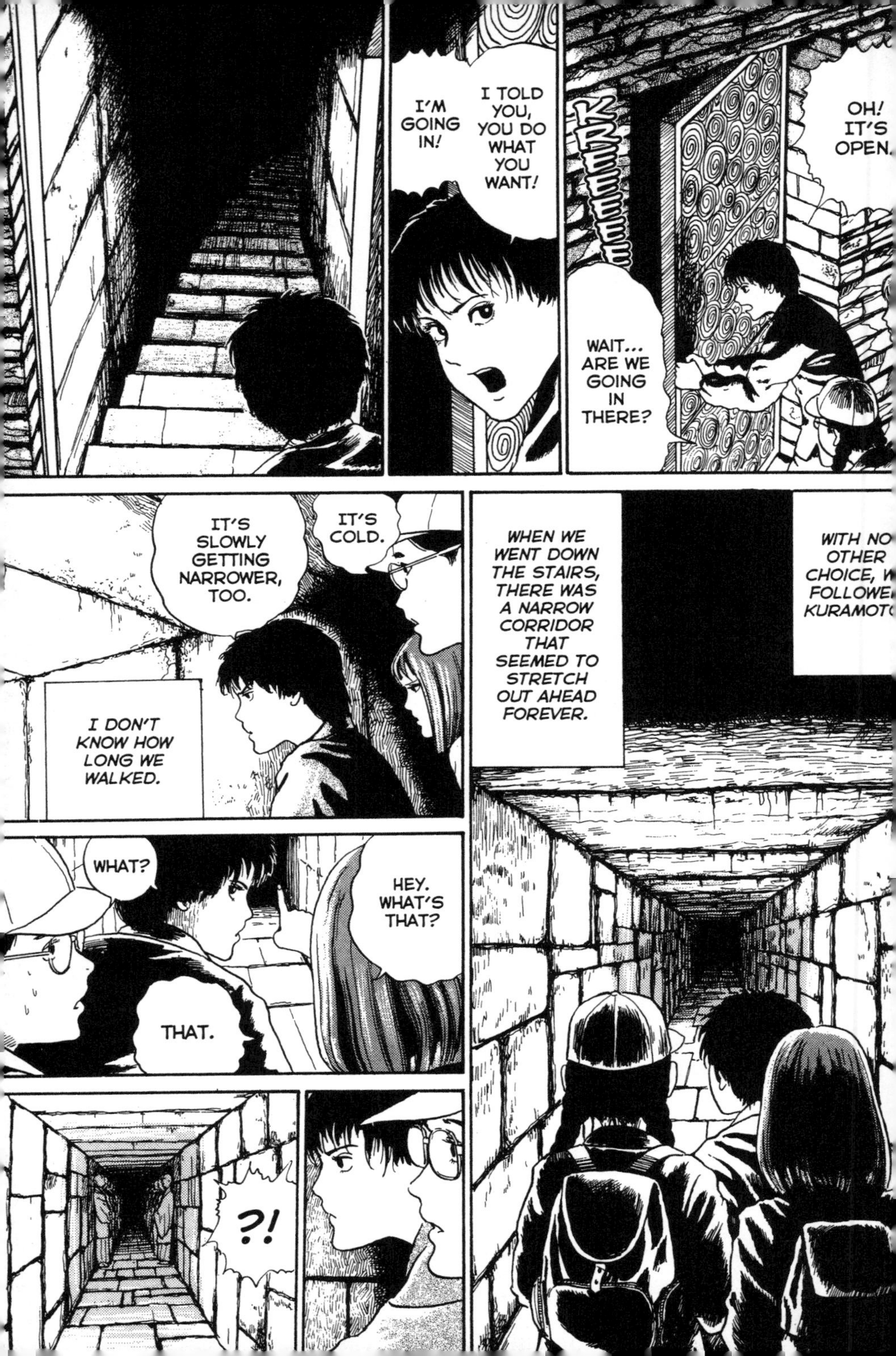
OH! IT'S OPEN.
KREEEEE
WAIT... ARE WE GOING IN THERE?
I TOLD YOU, YOU DO WHAT YOU WANT!
I'M GOING IN!
WITH NO OTHER CHOICE, W FOLLOWE KURAMOT
WHEN WE WENT DOWN THE STAIRS, THERE WAS A NARROW CORRIDOR THAT SEEMED TO STRETCH OUT AHEAD FOREVER.
IT'S COLD.
IT'S SLOWLY GETTING NARROWER, TOO.
I DON'T KNOW HOW LONG WE WALKED.
HEY. WHAT'S THAT?
WHAT?
THAT.
?!

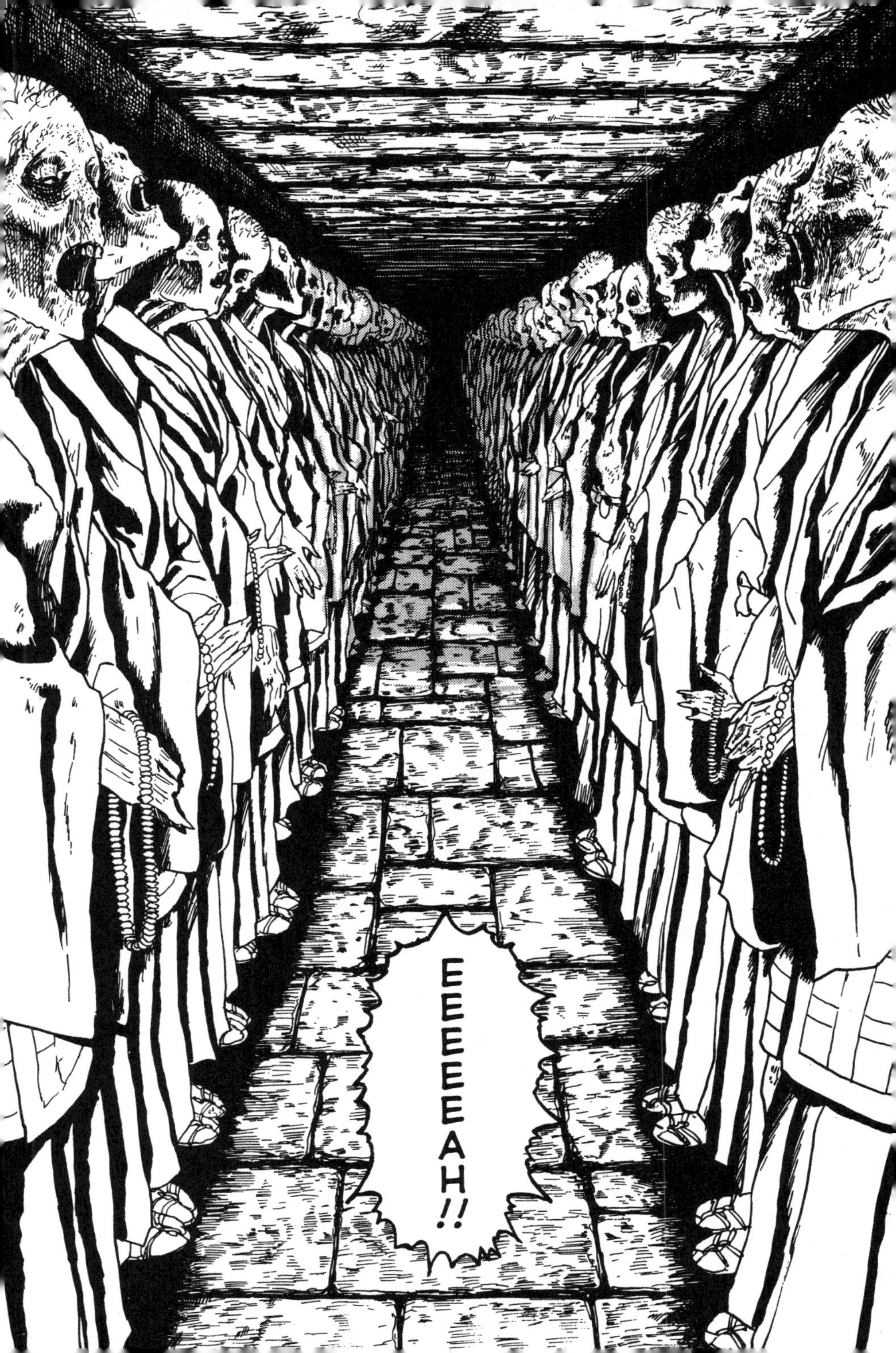
EEEEEEAH!!

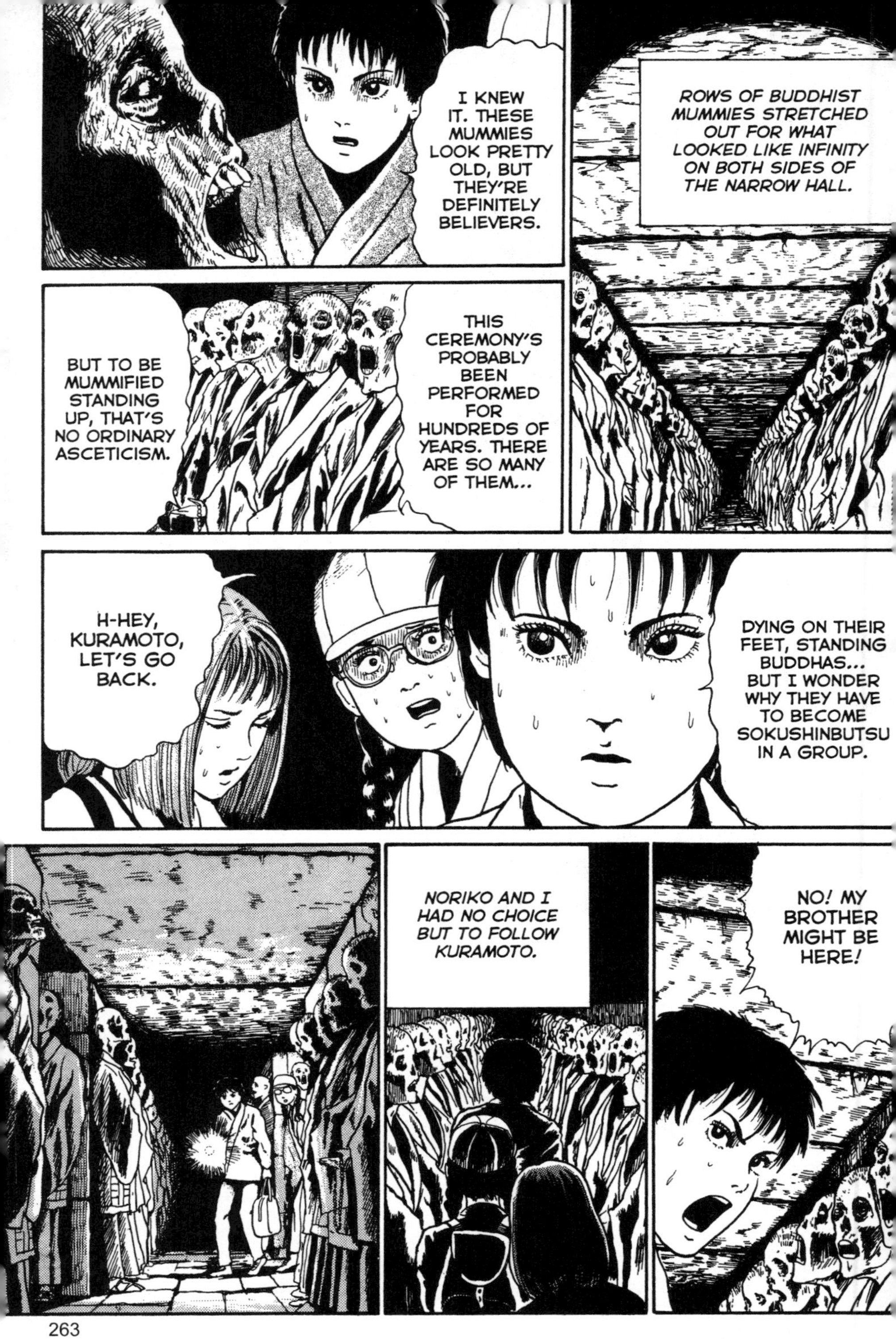
ROWS OF BUDDHIST MUMMIES STRETCHED OUT FOR WHAT LOOKED LIKE INFINITY ON BOTH SIDES OF THE NARROW HALL.
I KNEW IT. THESE MUMMIES LOOK PRETTY OLD, BUT THEY'RE DEFINITELY BELIEVERS.
THIS CEREMONY'S PROBABLY BEEN PERFORMED FOR HUNDREDS OF YEARS. THERE ARE SO MANY OF THEM...
BUT TO BE MUMMIFIED STANDING UP, THAT'S NO ORDINARY ASCETICISM.
DYING ON THEIR FEET, STANDING BUDDHAS... BUT I WONDER WHY THEY HAVE TO BECOME SOKUSHINBUTSU IN A GROUP.
H-HEY, KURAMOTO, LET'S GO BACK.
NO! MY BROTHER MIGHT BE HERE!
NORIKO AND I HAD NO CHOICE BUT TO FOLLOW KURAMOTO.

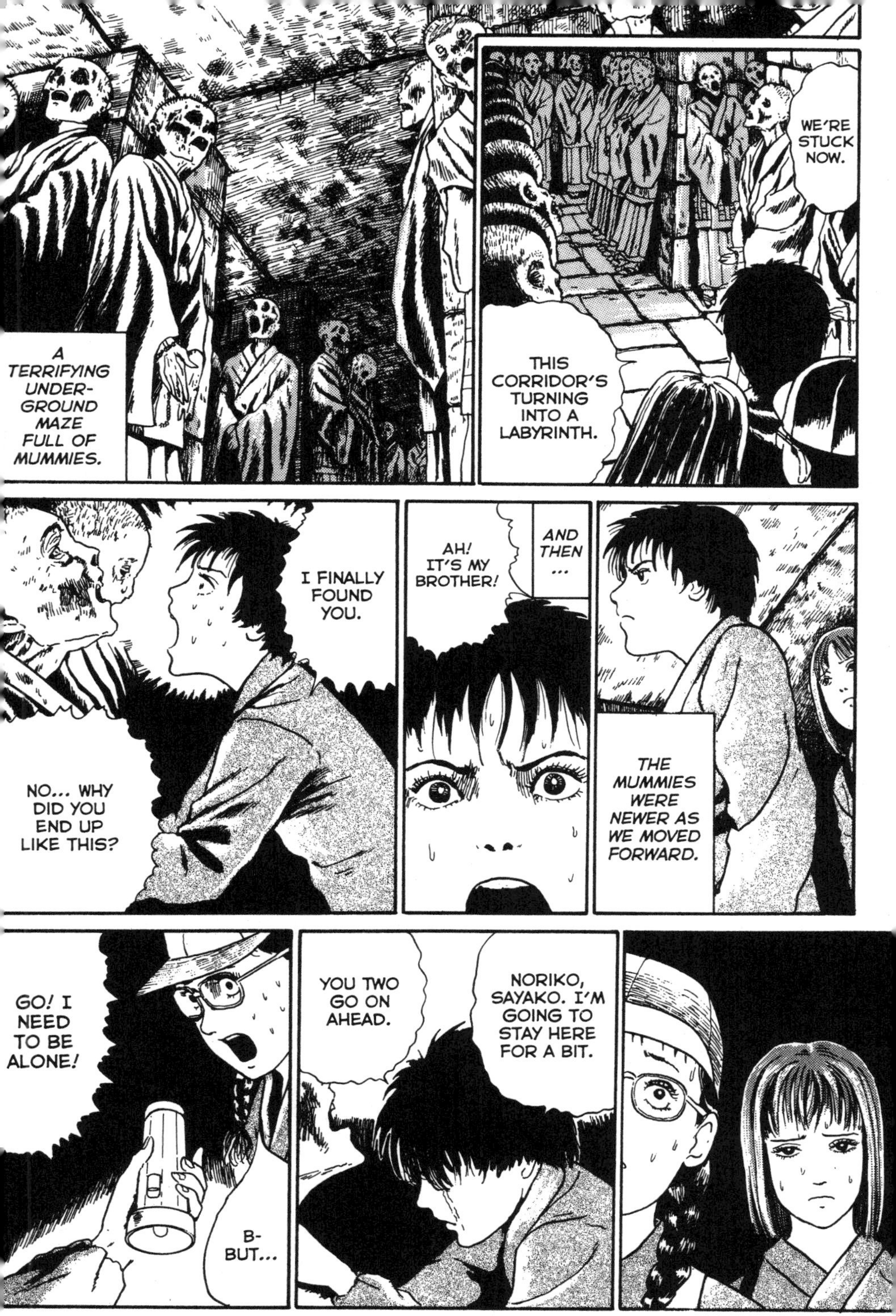
WE'RE STUCK NOW.
THIS CORRIDOR'S TURNING INTO A LABYRINTH.
A TERRIFYING UNDER-GROUND MAZE FULL OF MUMMIES.
THE MUMMIES WERE NEWER AS WE MOVED FORWARD.
AND THEN ...
AH! IT'S MY BROTHER!
I FINALLY FOUND YOU.
NO... WHY DID YOU END UP LIKE THIS?
NORIKO, SAYAKO. I'M GOING TO STAY HERE FOR A BIT.
YOU TWO GO ON AHEAD.
GO! I NEED TO BE ALONE!
B-BUT...

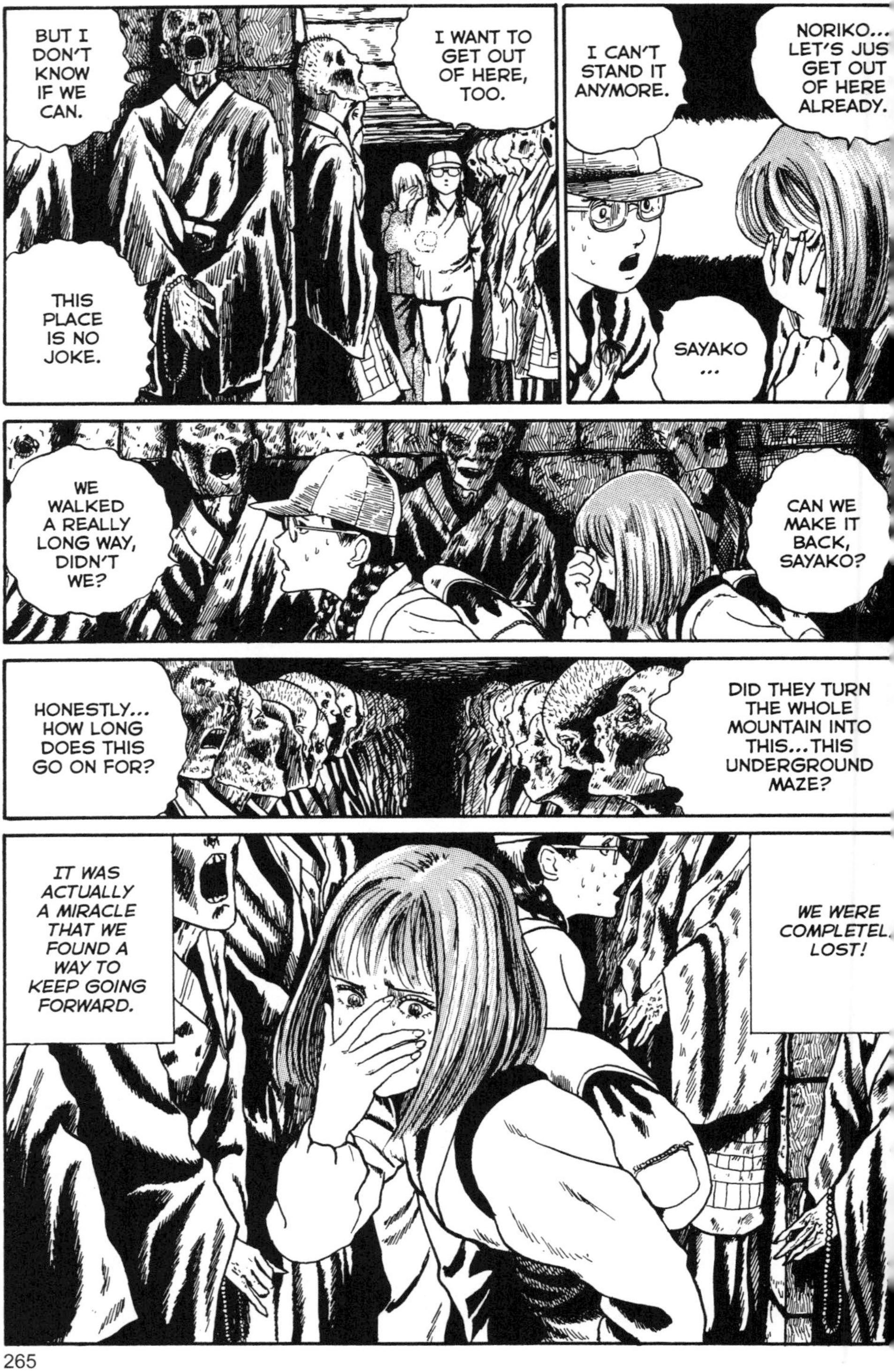
NORIKO... LET'S JUS GET OUT OF HERE ALREADY.
I CAN'T STAND IT ANYMORE.
SAYAKO ...
I WANT TO GET OUT OF HERE, TOO.
BUT I DON'T KNOW IF WE CAN.
THIS PLACE IS NO JOKE.
CAN WE MAKE IT BACK, SAYAKO?
WE WALKED A REALLY LONG WAY, DIDN'T WE?
DID THEY TURN THE WHOLE MOUNTAIN INTO THIS...THIS UNDERGROUND MAZE?
HONESTLY... HOW LONG DOES THIS GO ON FOR?
WE WERE COMPLETEL LOST!
IT WAS ACTUALLY A MIRACLE THAT WE FOUND A WAY TO KEEP GOING FORWARD.

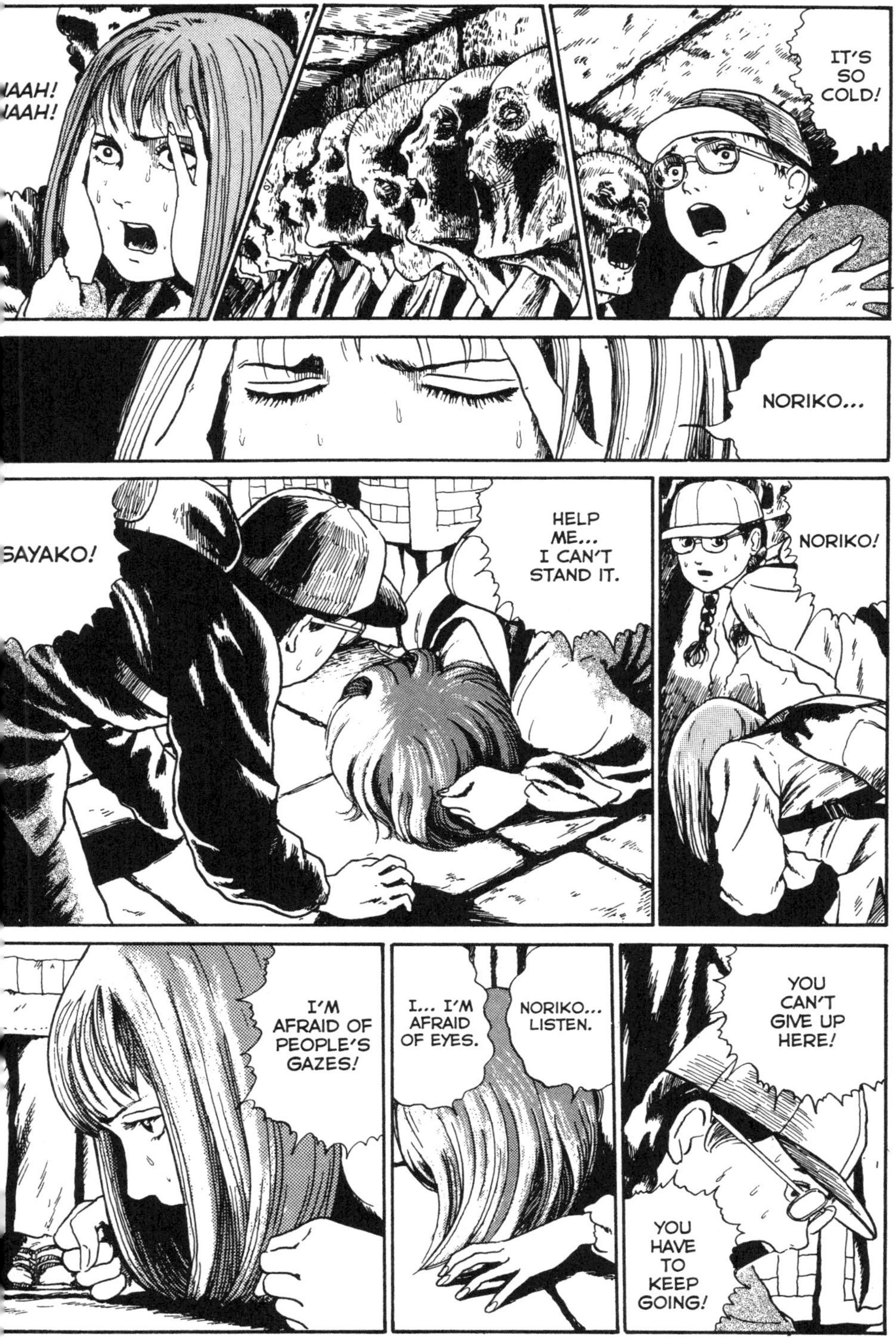
IT'S SO COLD!
AAH! AAH!
NORIKO...
NORIKO!
HELP ME... I CAN'T STAND IT.
SAYAKO!
YOU CAN'T GIVE UP HERE!
YOU HAVE TO KEEP GOING!
NORIKO... LISTEN.
I... I'M AFRAID OF EYES.
I'M AFRAID OF PEOPLE'S GAZES!

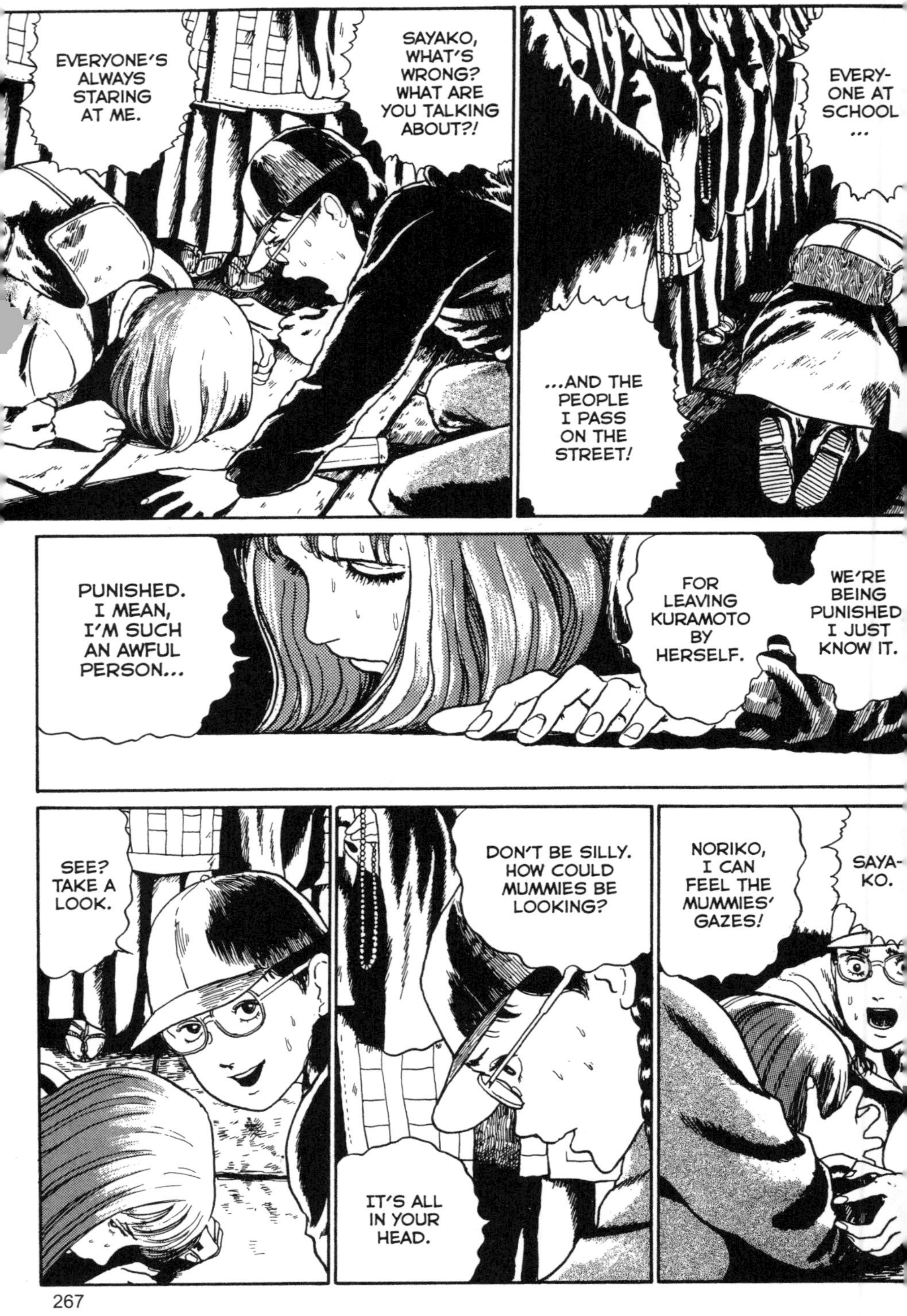
EVERY-ONE AT SCHOOL ...
...AND THE PEOPLE I PASS ON THE STREET!
SAYAKO, WHAT'S WRONG? WHAT ARE YOU TALKING ABOUT?!
EVERYONE'S ALWAYS STARING AT ME.
WE'RE BEING PUNISHED I JUST KNOW IT.
FOR LEAVING KURAMOTO BY HERSELF.
PUNISHED. I MEAN, I'M SUCH AN AWFUL PERSON...
SAYA-KO.
NORIKO, I CAN FEEL THE MUMMIES' GAZES!
DON'T BE SILLY. HOW COULD MUMMIES BE LOOKING?
IT'S ALL IN YOUR HEAD.
SEE? TAKE A LOOK.

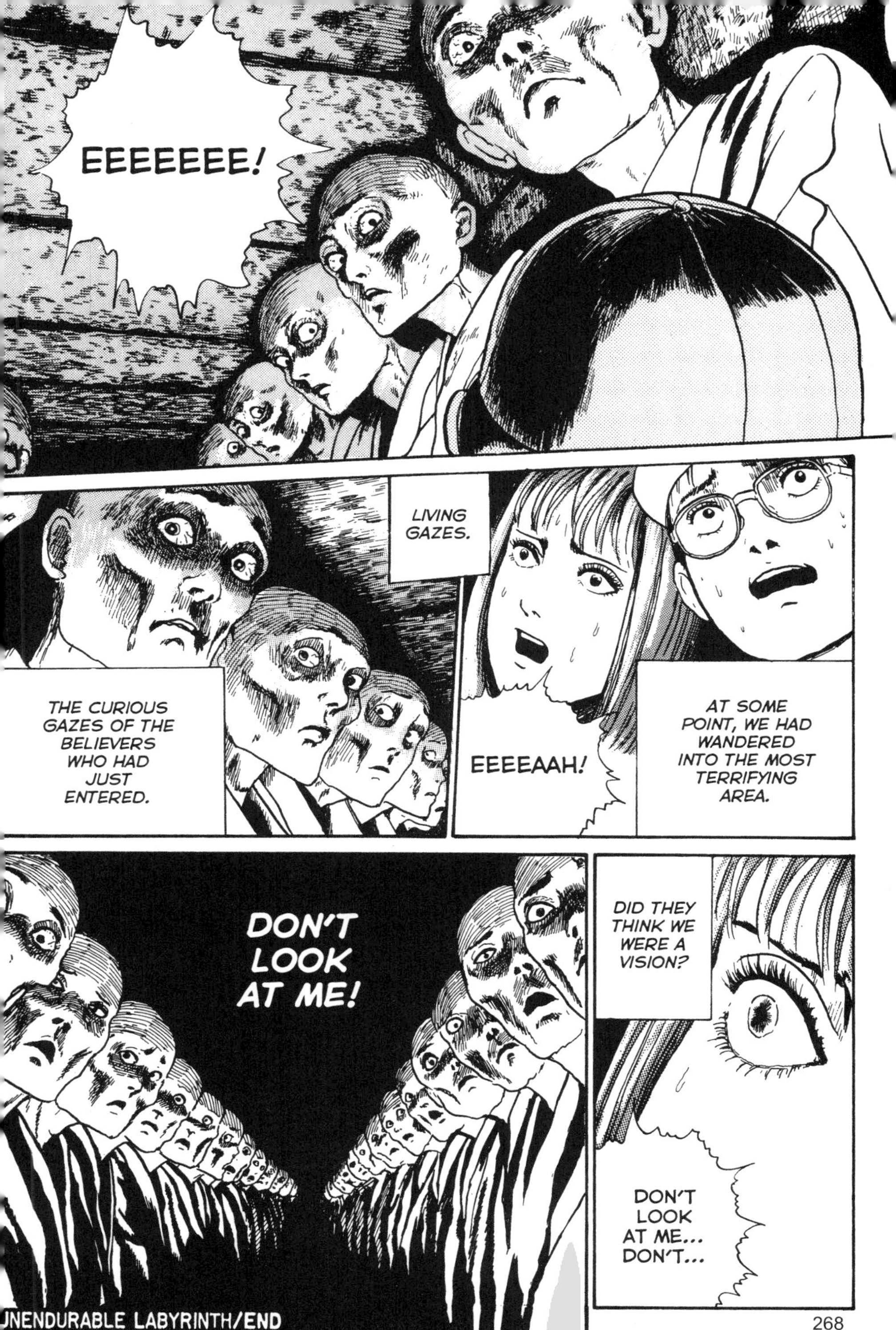
EEEEEEE!
AT SOME POINT, WE HAD WANDERED INTO THE MOST TERRIFYING AREA.
EEEEAAH!
LIVING GAZES.
THE CURIOUS GAZES OF THE BELIEVERS WHO HAD JUST ENTERED.
DID THEY THINK WE WERE A VISION?
DON'T LOOK AT ME... DON'T...
DON'T LOOK AT ME!

UNENDURABLE LABYRINTH/END

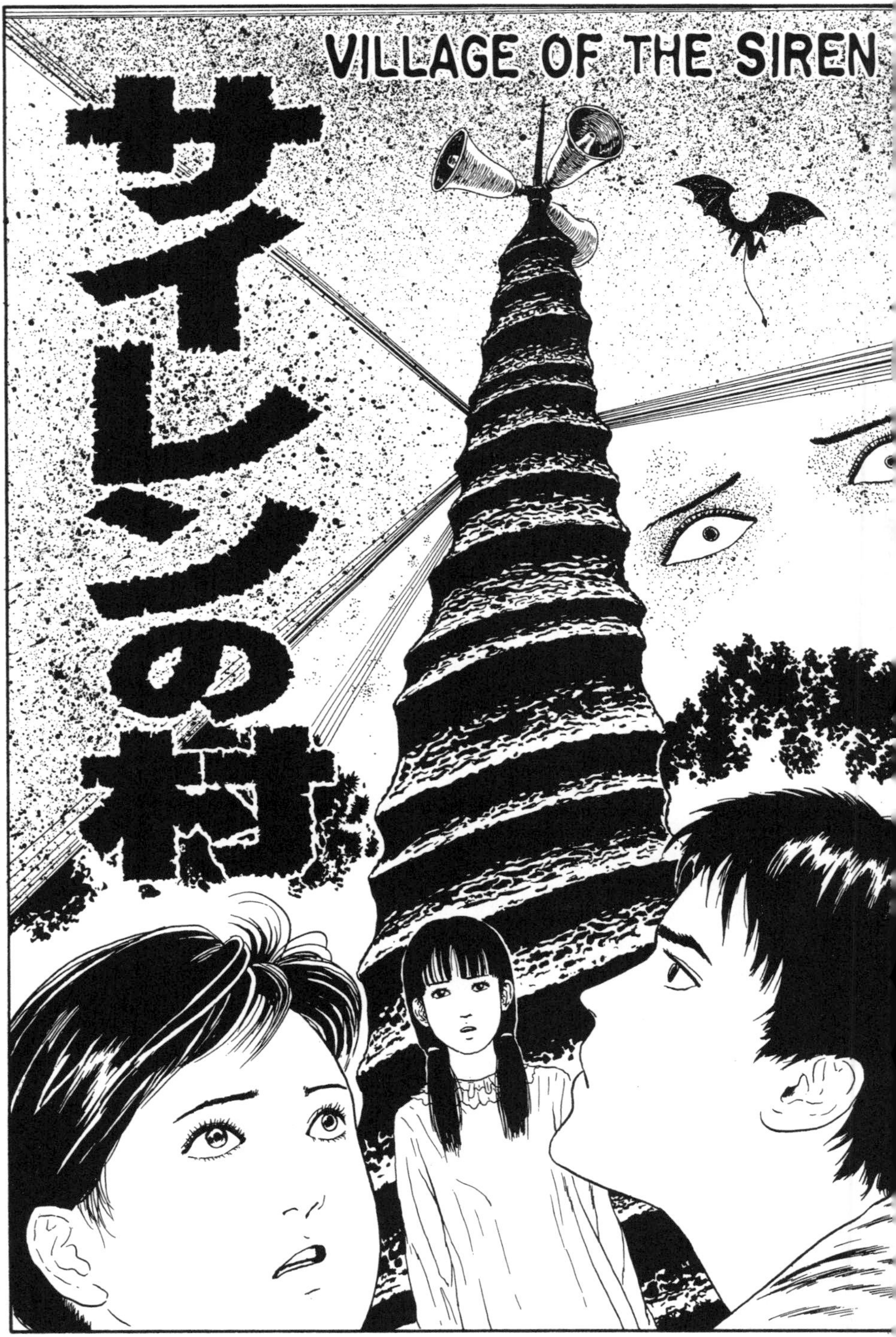
VILLAGE OF THE SIREN
サイレンの村

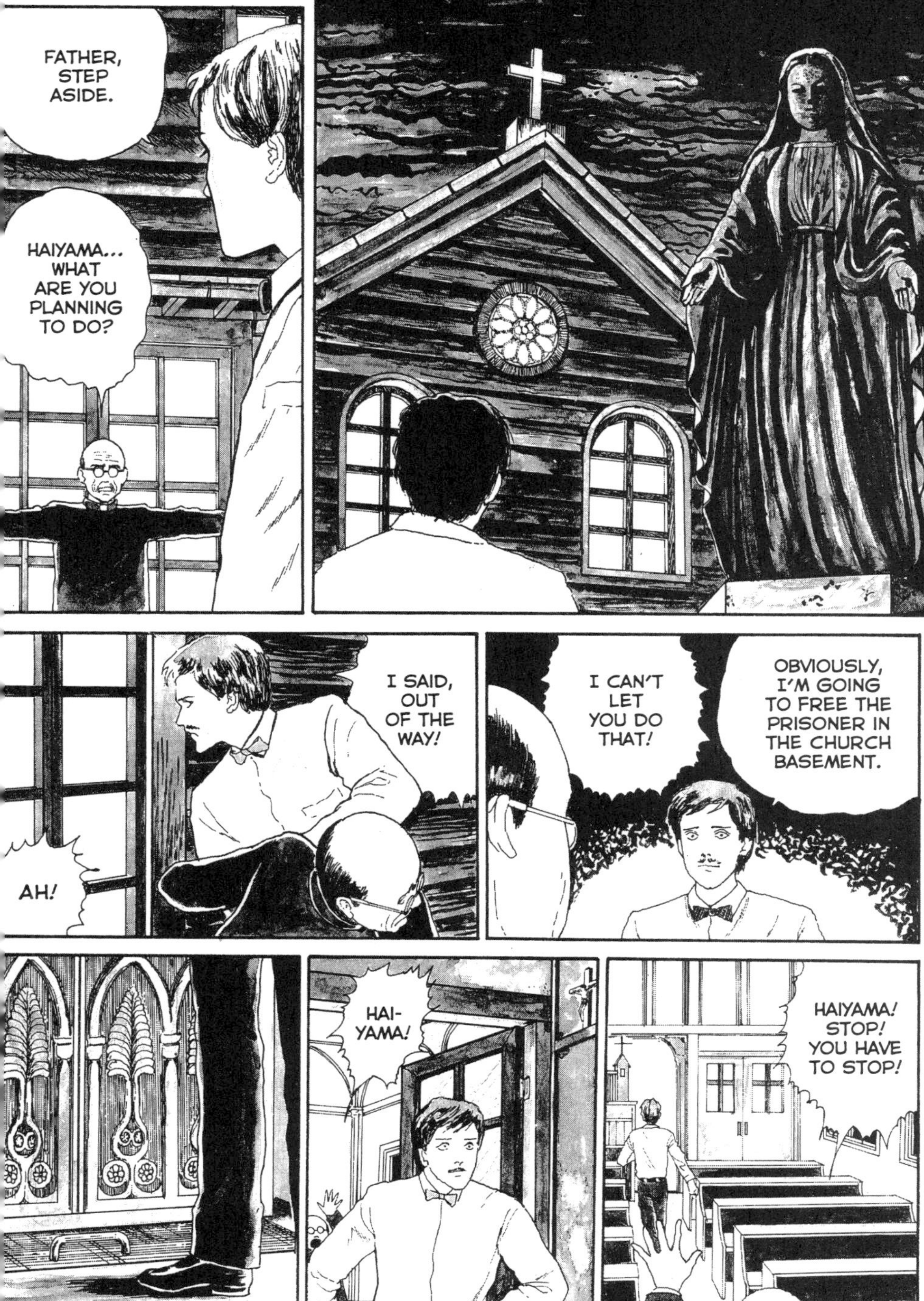
FATHER, STEP ASIDE.
HAIYAMA... WHAT ARE YOU PLANNING TO DO?
OBVIOUSLY, I'M GOING TO FREE THE PRISONER IN THE CHURCH BASEMENT.
I CAN'T LET YOU DO THAT!
I SAID, OUT OF THE WAY!
AH!
HAIYAMA! STOP! YOU HAVE TO STOP!
HAI-YAMA!

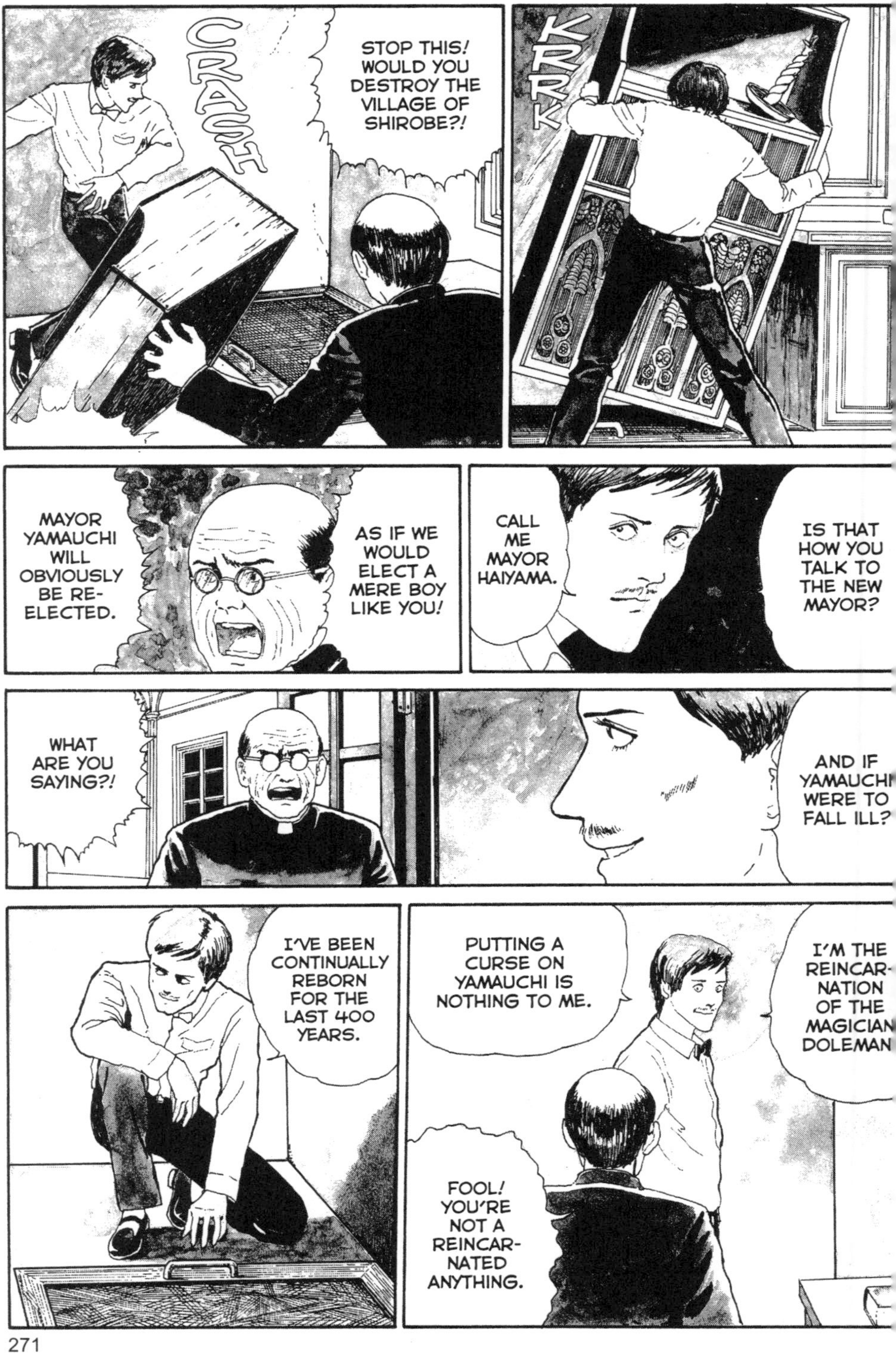

KRRK
CRASH
STOP THIS! WOULD YOU DESTROY THE VILLAGE OF SHIROBE?!
IS THAT HOW YOU TALK TO THE NEW MAYOR?
CALL ME MAYOR HAIYAMA.
AS IF WE WOULD ELECT A MERE BOY LIKE YOU!
MAYOR YAMAUCHI WILL OBVIOUSLY BE RE-ELECTED.
AND IF YAMAUCHI WERE TO FALL ILL?
WHAT ARE YOU SAYING?!
I'M THE REINCARNATION OF THE MAGICIAN DOLEMAN
PUTTING A CURSE ON YAMAUCHI IS NOTHING TO ME.
FOOL! YOU'RE NOT A REINCARNATED ANYTHING.
I'VE BEEN CONTINUALLY REBORN FOR THE LAST 400 YEARS.

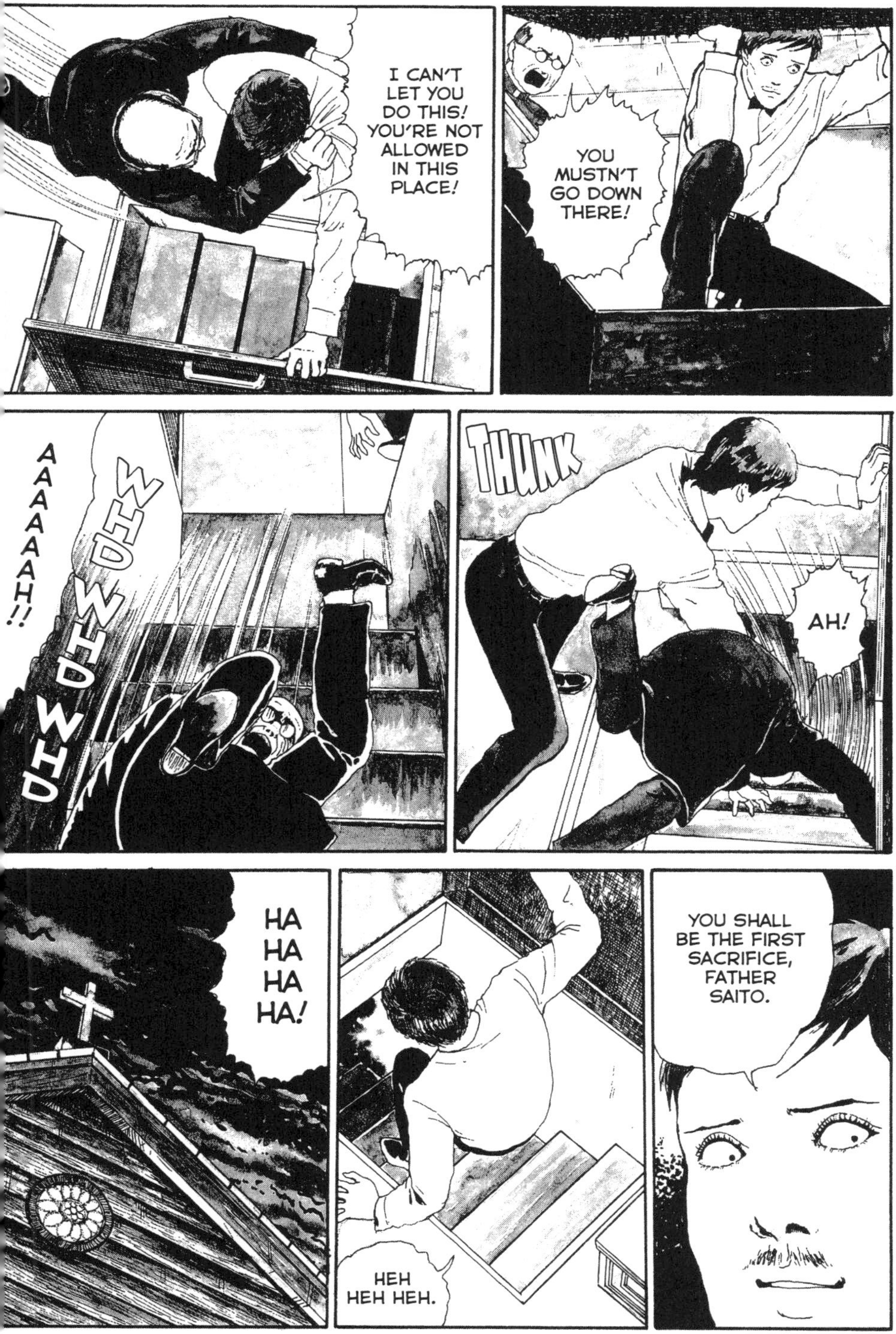
YOU MUSTN'T GO DOWN THERE!
I CAN'T LET YOU DO THIS! YOU'RE NOT ALLOWED IN THIS PLACE!
THUNK
AH!
WHD WHD WHD WHD
AAAAAAAH!!
YOU SHALL BE THE FIRST SACRIFICE, FATHER SAITO.
HEH HEH HEH.
HA HA HA HA!

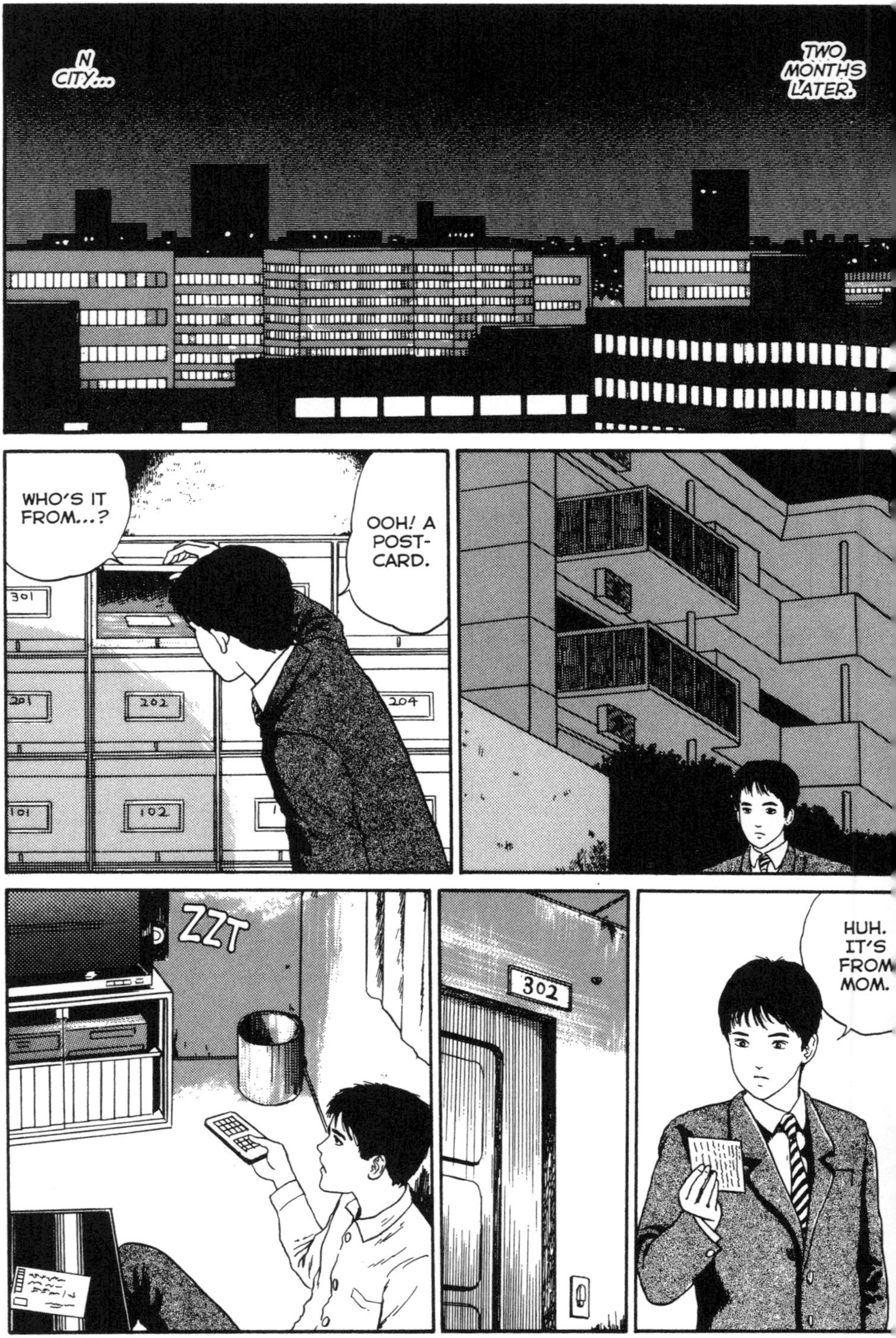
TWO MONTHS LATER.
N CITY...
OOH! A POST-CARD.
WHO'S IT FROM...?
HUH. IT'S FROM MOM.
302
ZZT

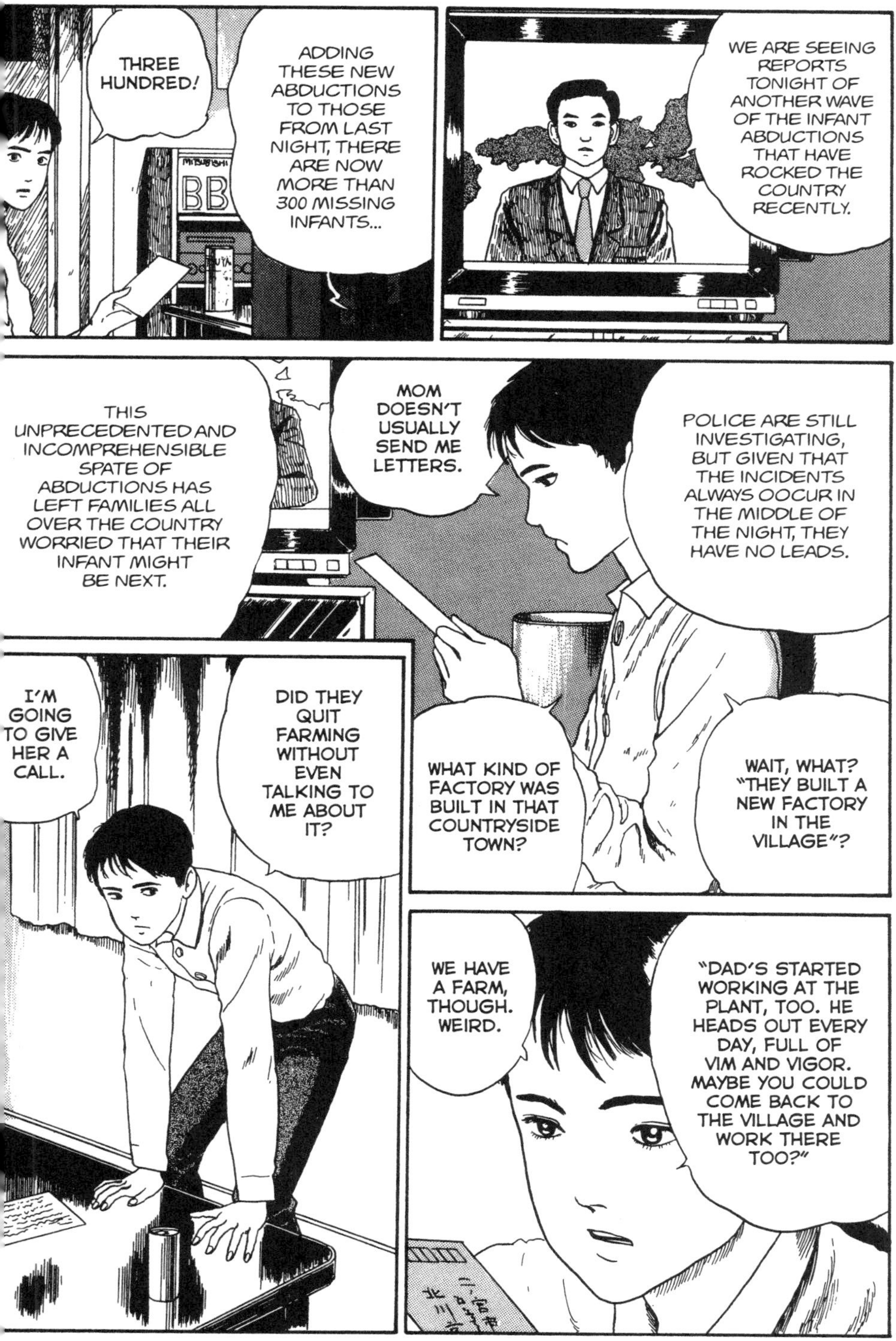
WE ARE SEEING REPORTS TONIGHT OF ANOTHER WAVE OF THE INFANT ABDUCTIONS THAT HAVE ROCKED THE COUNTRY RECENTLY.
ADDING THESE NEW ABDUCTIONS TO THOSE FROM LAST NIGHT, THERE ARE NOW MORE THAN 300 MISSING INFANTS...
THREE HUNDRED!
POLICE ARE STILL INVESTIGATING, BUT GIVEN THAT THE INCIDENTS ALWAYS OOCUR IN THE MIDDLE OF THE NIGHT, THEY HAVE NO LEADS.
MOM DOESN'T USUALLY SEND ME LETTERS.
THIS UNPRECEDENTED AND INCOMPREHENSIBLE SPATE OF ABDUCTIONS HAS LEFT FAMILIES ALL OVER THE COUNTRY WORRIED THAT THEIR INFANT MIGHT BE NEXT.
WAIT, WHAT? "THEY BUILT A NEW FACTORY IN THE VILLAGE"?
WHAT KIND OF FACTORY WAS BUILT IN THAT COUNTRYSIDE TOWN?
"DAD'S STARTED WORKING AT THE PLANT, TOO. HE HEADS OUT EVERY DAY, FULL OF VIM AND VIGOR. MAYBE YOU COULD COME BACK TO THE VILLAGE AND WORK THERE TOO?"
WE HAVE A FARM, THOUGH. WEIRD.
DID THEY QUIT FARMING WITHOUT EVEN TALKING TO ME ABOUT IT?
I'M GOING TO GIVE HER A CALL.

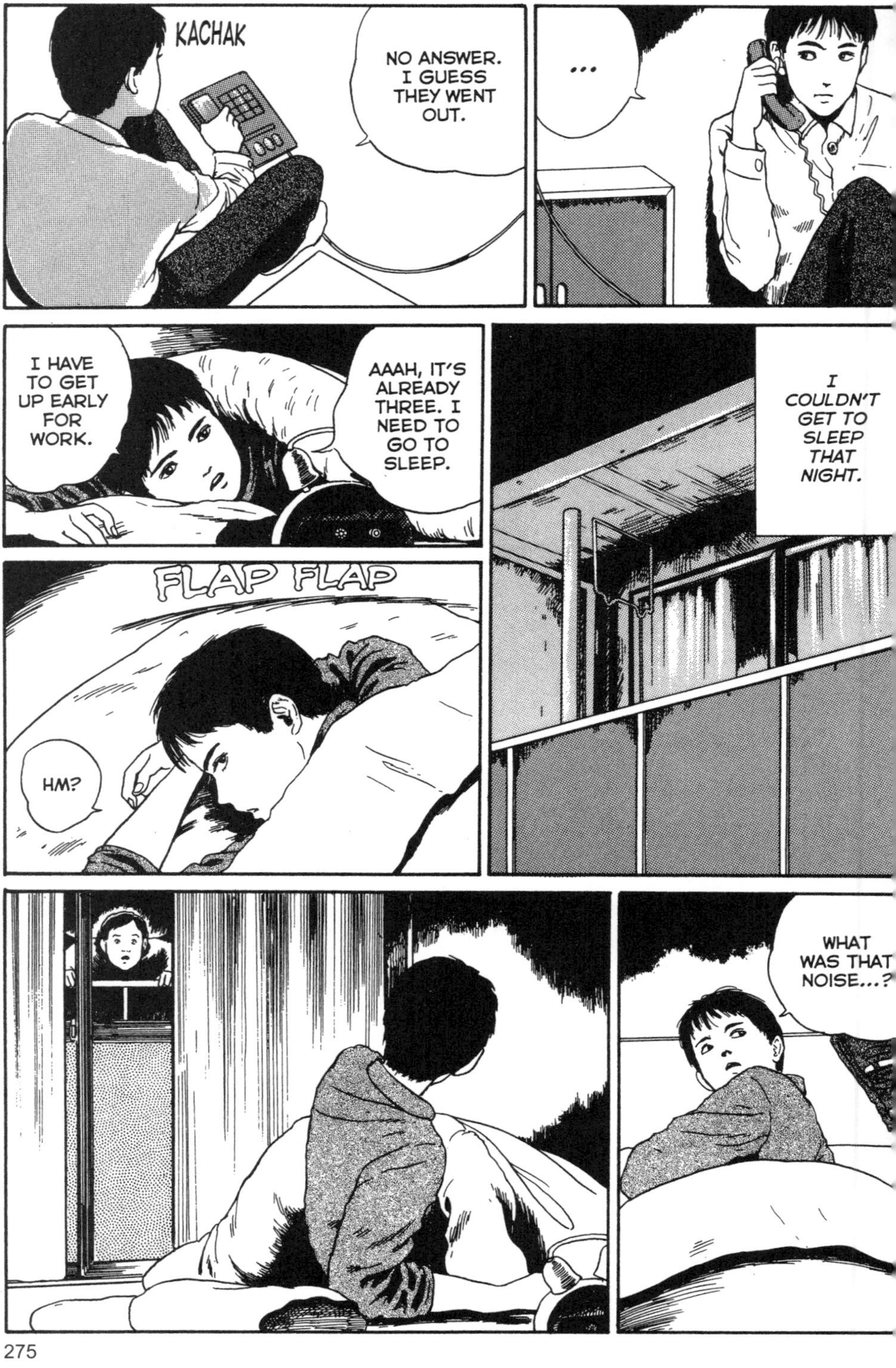
...
NO ANSWER. I GUESS THEY WENT OUT.
KACHAK
I COULDN'T GET TO SLEEP THAT NIGHT.
AAAH, IT'S ALREADY THREE. I NEED TO GO TO SLEEP.
I HAVE TO GET UP EARLY FOR WORK.
FLAP FLAP
HM?
WHAT WAS THAT NOISE...?

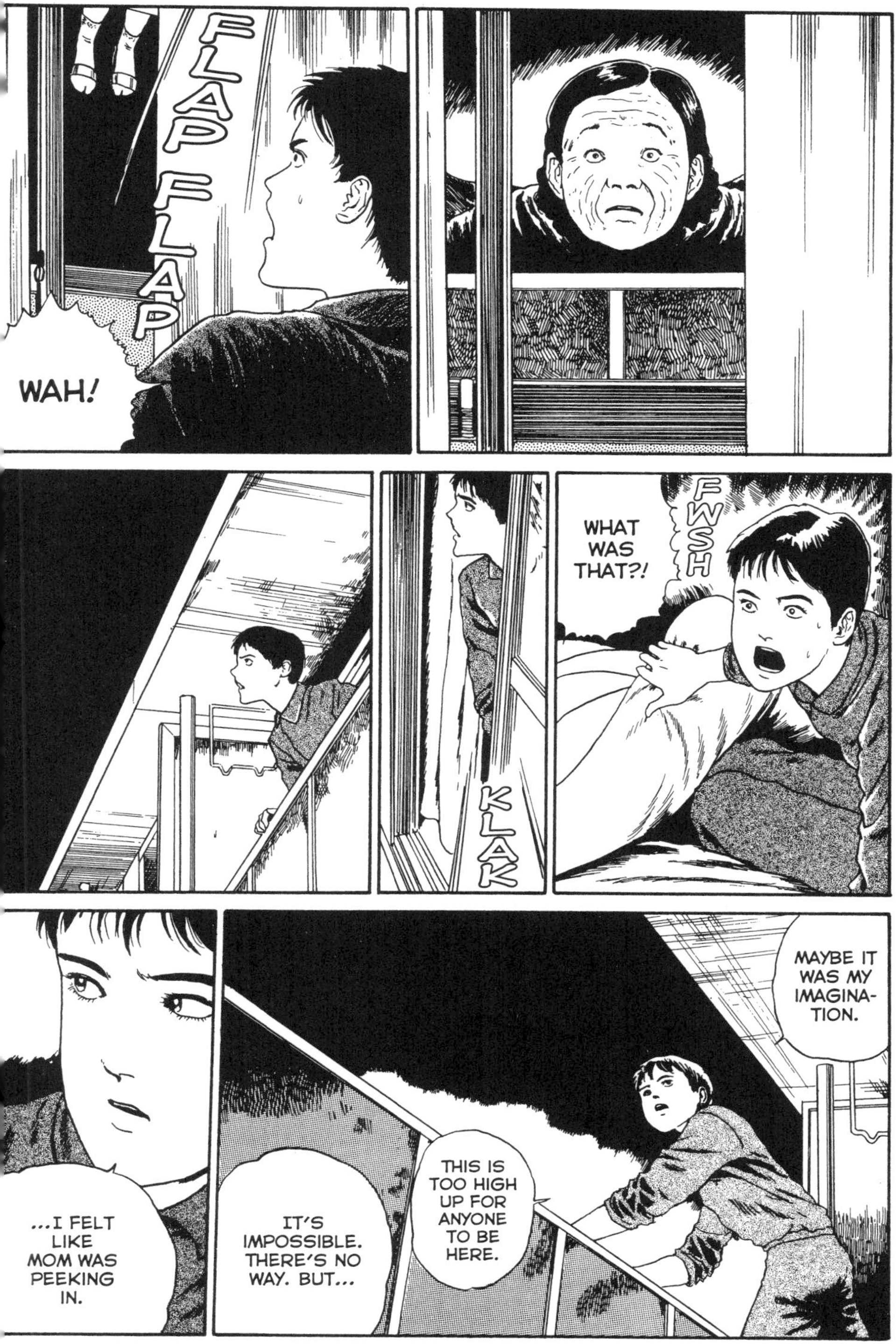
FLAP FLAP FLAP
WAH!
FWSH
WHAT WAS THAT?!
KLAK
MAYBE IT WAS MY IMAGINATION.
THIS IS TOO HIGH UP FOR ANYONE TO BE HERE.
IT'S IMPOSSIBLE. THERE'S NO WAY. BUT...
...I FELT LIKE MOM WAS PEEKING IN.

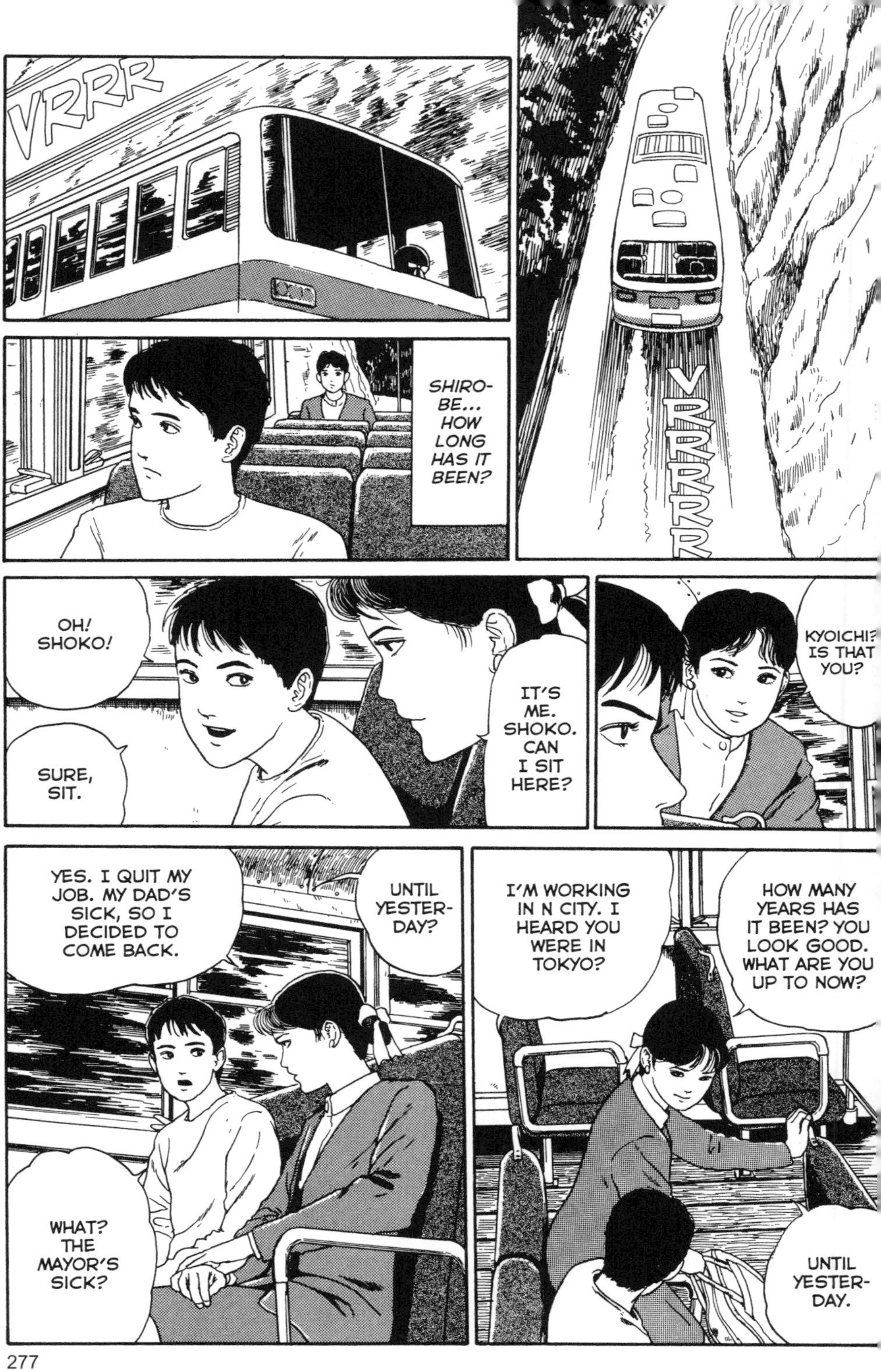
VRRRRR
VRRR
SHIRO-BE... HOW LONG HAS IT BEEN?
KYOICHI? IS THAT YOU?
IT'S ME. SHOKO. CAN I SIT HERE?
OH! SHOKO!
SURE, SIT.
HOW MANY YEARS HAS IT BEEN? YOU LOOK GOOD. WHAT ARE YOU UP TO NOW?
I'M WORKING IN N CITY. I HEARD YOU WERE IN TOKYO?
UNTIL YESTERDAY.
UNTIL YESTERDAY?
YES. I QUIT MY JOB. MY DAD'S SICK, SO I DECIDED TO COME BACK.
WHAT? THE MAYOR'S SICK?

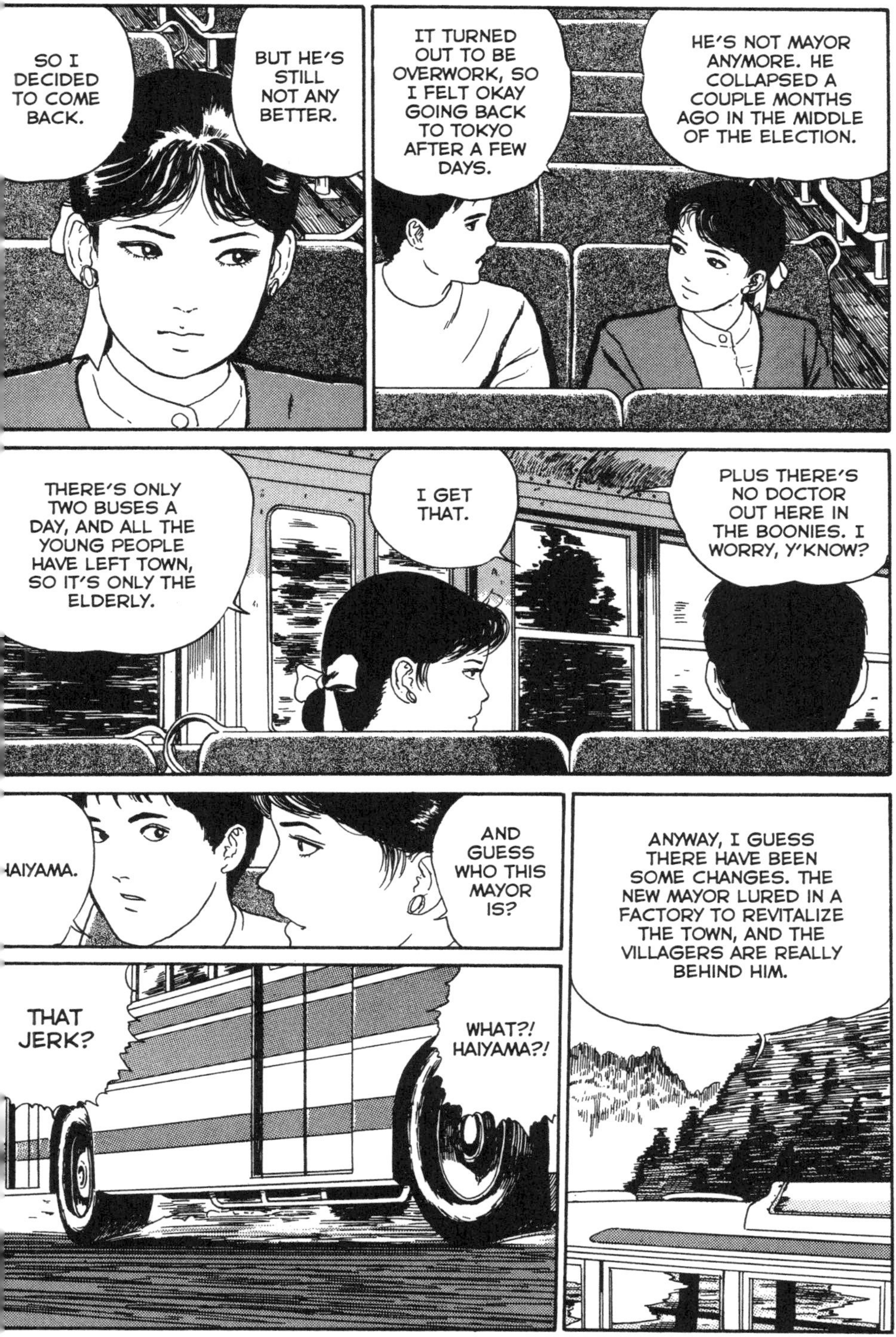
HE'S NOT MAYOR ANYMORE. HE COLLAPSED A COUPLE MONTHS AGO IN THE MIDDLE OF THE ELECTION.
IT TURNED OUT TO BE OVERWORK, SO I FELT OKAY GOING BACK TO TOKYO AFTER A FEW DAYS.
BUT HE'S STILL NOT ANY BETTER.
SO I DECIDED TO COME BACK.
PLUS THERE'S NO DOCTOR OUT HERE IN THE BOONIES. I WORRY, Y'KNOW?
I GET THAT.
THERE'S ONLY TWO BUSES A DAY, AND ALL THE YOUNG PEOPLE HAVE LEFT TOWN, SO IT'S ONLY THE ELDERLY.
ANYWAY, I GUESS THERE HAVE BEEN SOME CHANGES. THE NEW MAYOR LURED IN A FACTORY TO REVITALIZE THE TOWN, AND THE VILLAGERS ARE REALLY BEHIND HIM.
AND GUESS WHO THIS MAYOR IS?
AIYAMA.
WHAT?! HAIYAMA?!
THAT JERK?

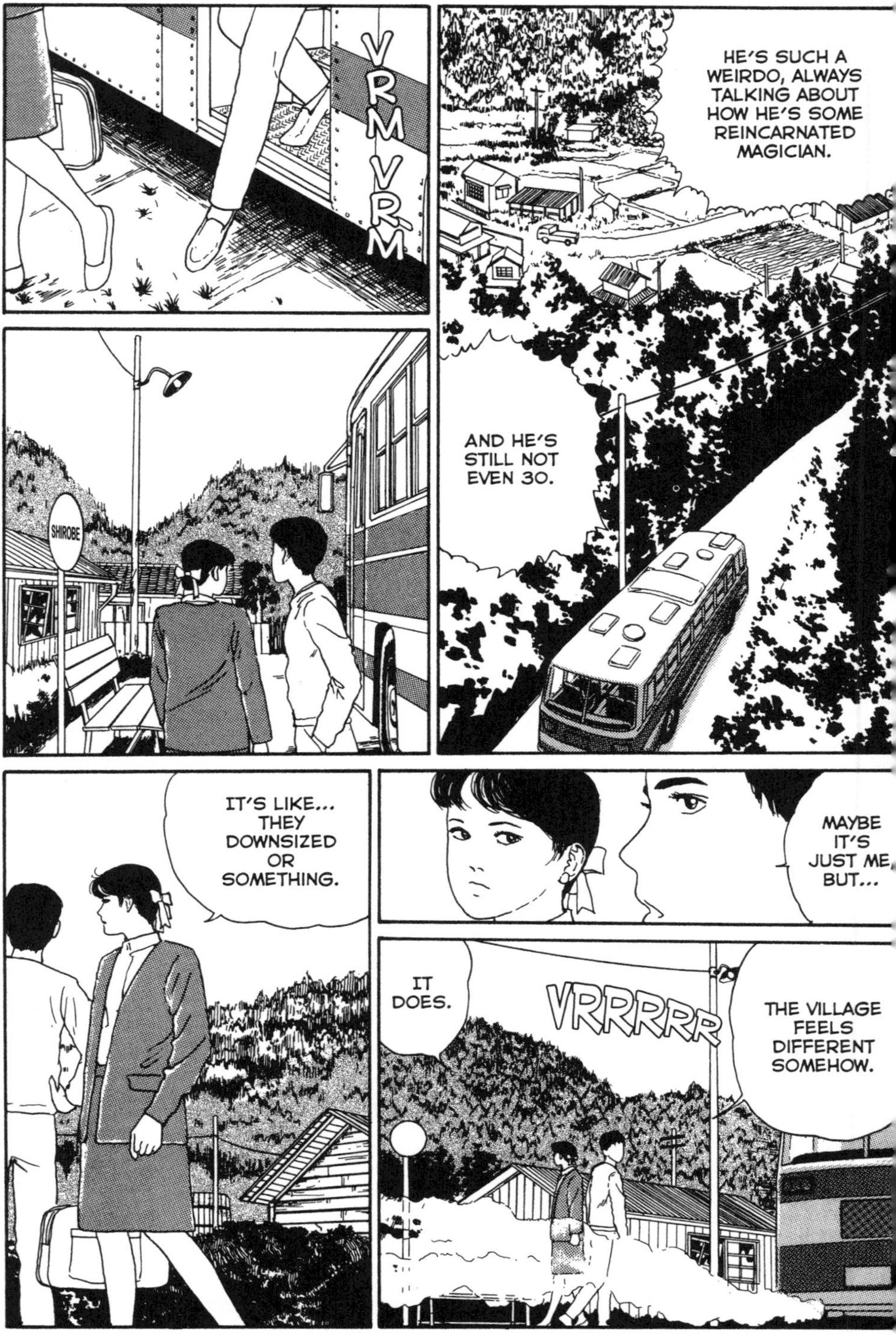
HE'S SUCH A WEIRDO, ALWAYS TALKING ABOUT HOW HE'S SOME REINCARNATED MAGICIAN.
AND HE'S STILL NOT EVEN 30.
VRM VRM VRM
SHIROBE
MAYBE IT'S JUST ME BUT...
THE VILLAGE FEELS DIFFERENT SOMEHOW.
VRRRRR
IT DOES.
IT'S LIKE... THEY DOWNSIZED OR SOMETHING.

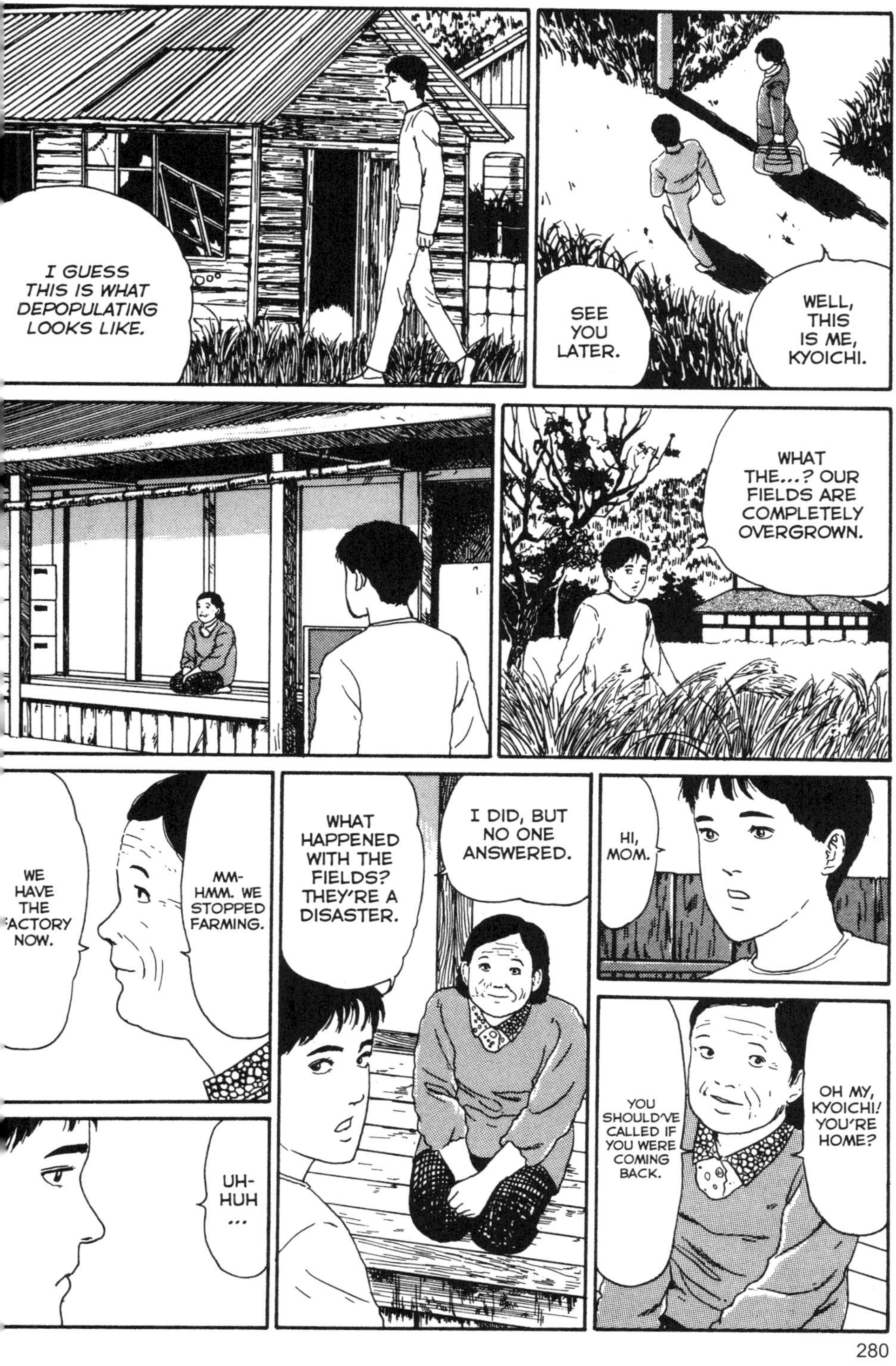
WELL, THIS IS ME, KYOICHI.
SEE YOU LATER.
I GUESS THIS IS WHAT DEPOPULATING LOOKS LIKE.
WHAT THE...? OUR FIELDS ARE COMPLETELY OVERGROWN.
HI, MOM.
OH MY, KYOICHI! YOU'RE HOME?
YOU SHOULD'VE CALLED IF YOU WERE COMING BACK.
I DID, BUT NO ONE ANSWERED.
WHAT HAPPENED WITH THE FIELDS? THEY'RE A DISASTER.
MM-HMM. WE STOPPED FARMING.
WE HAVE THE FACTORY NOW.
UH-HUH...

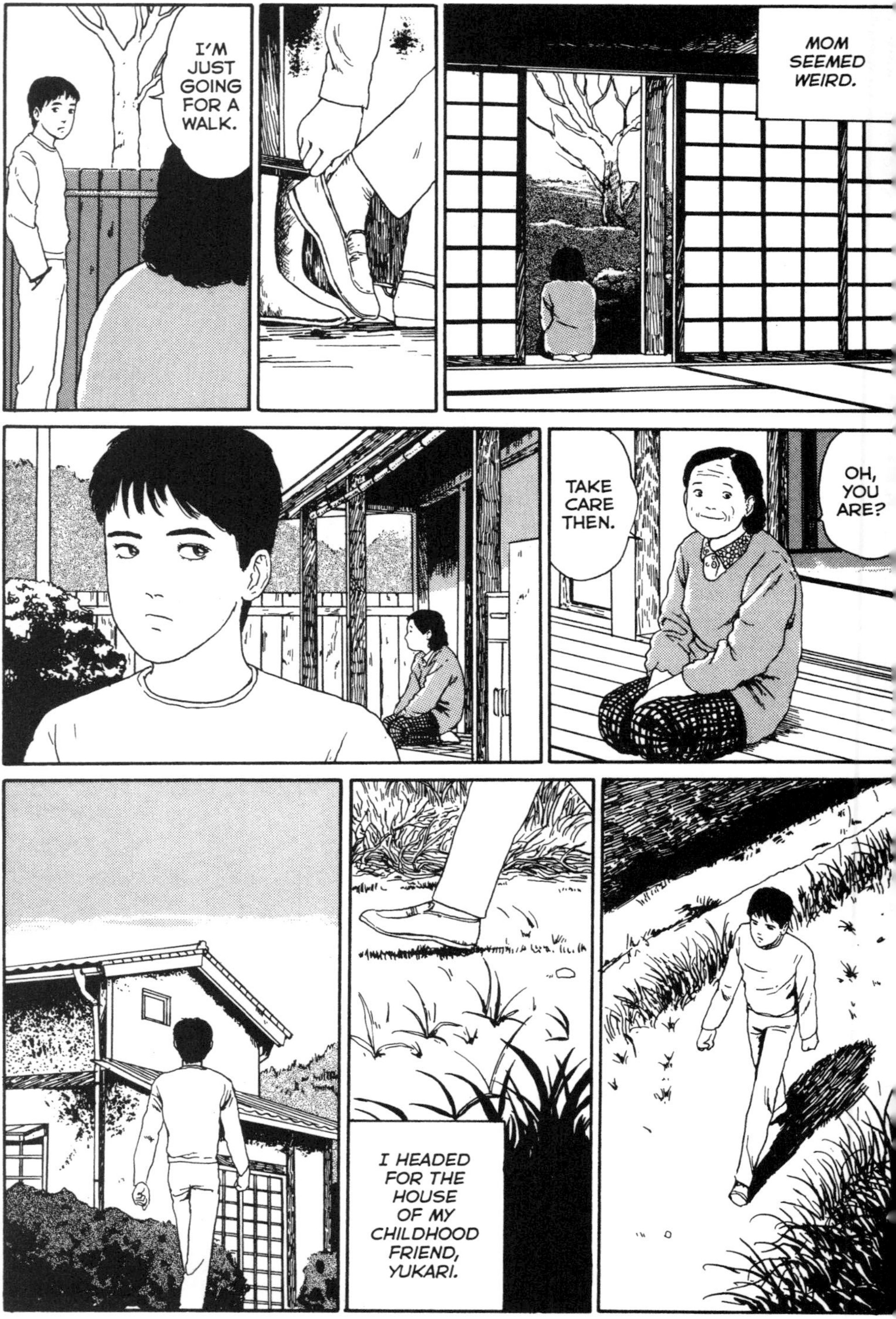
MOM SEEMED WEIRD.
I'M JUST GOING FOR A WALK.
OH, YOU ARE?
TAKE CARE THEN.
I HEADED FOR THE HOUSE OF MY CHILDHOOD FRIEND, YUKARI.

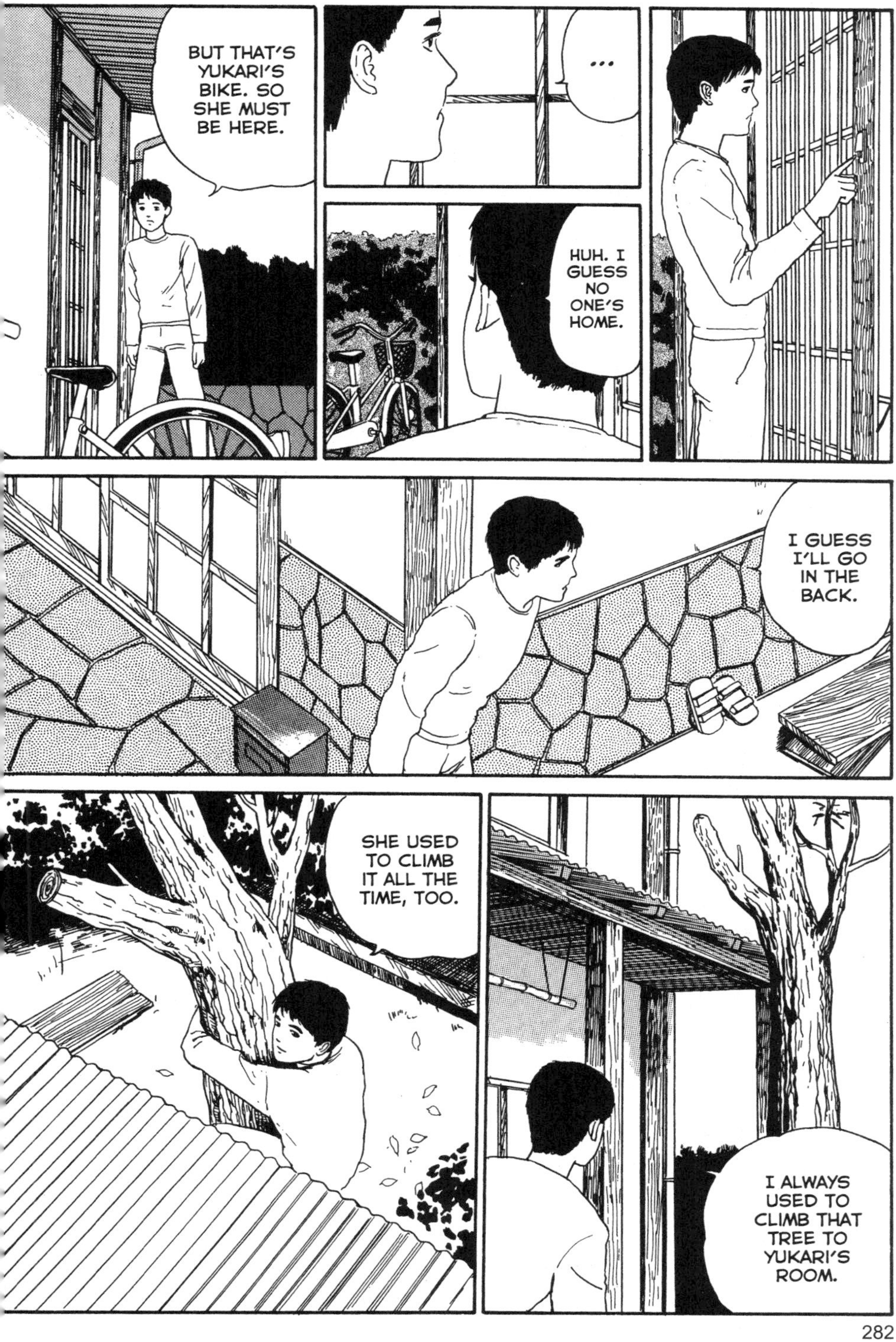
...
HUH. I GUESS NO ONE'S HOME.
BUT THAT'S YUKARI'S BIKE. SO SHE MUST BE HERE.
I GUESS I'LL GO IN THE BACK.
I ALWAYS USED TO CLIMB THAT TREE TO YUKARI'S ROOM.
SHE USED TO CLIMB IT ALL THE TIME, TOO.

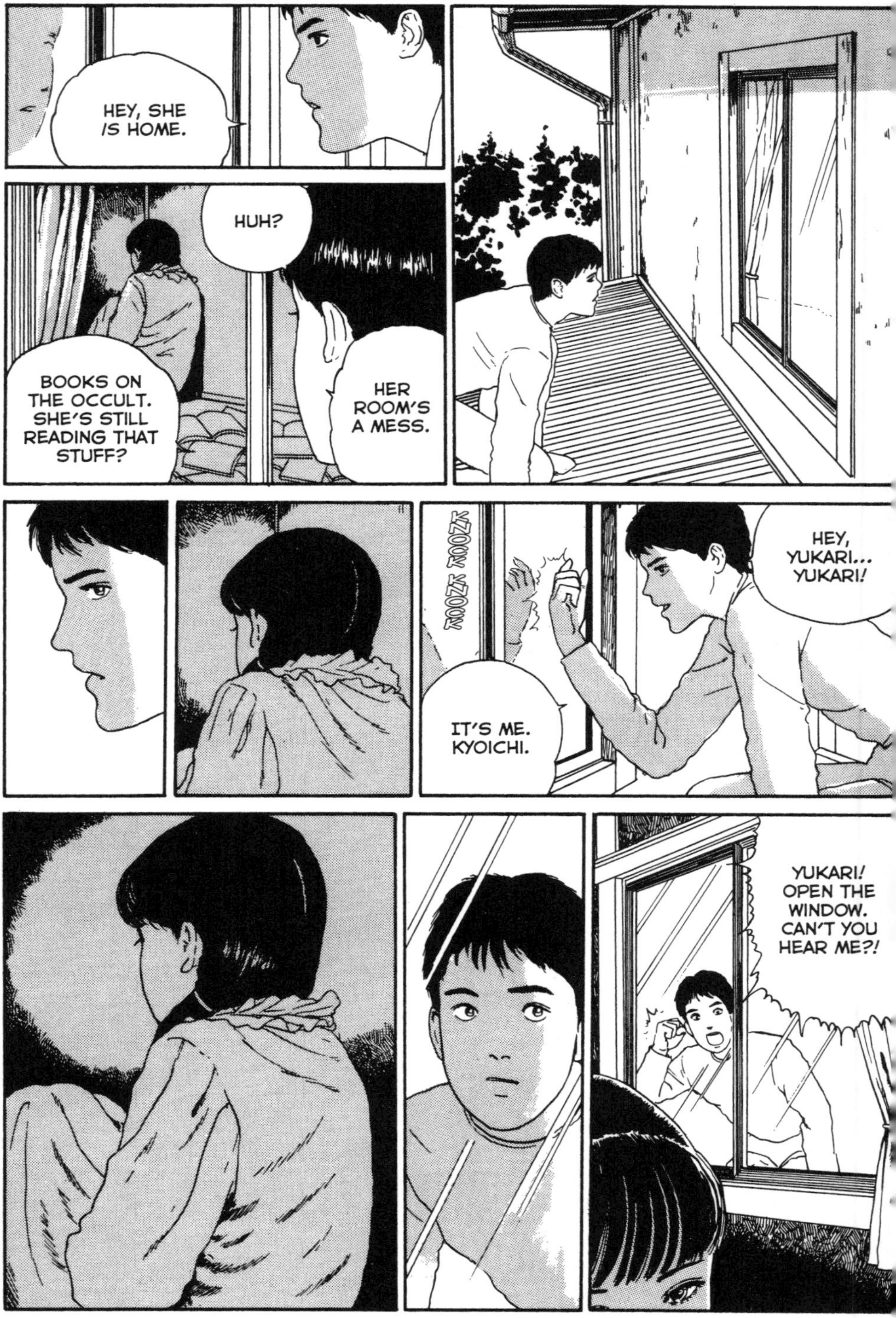
HEY, SHE IS HOME.
HUH?
HER ROOM'S A MESS.
BOOKS ON THE OCCULT. SHE'S STILL READING THAT STUFF?
HEY, YUKARI... YUKARI!
KNOCK KNOCK
IT'S ME. KYOICHI.
YUKARI! OPEN THE WINDOW. CAN'T YOU HEAR ME?!

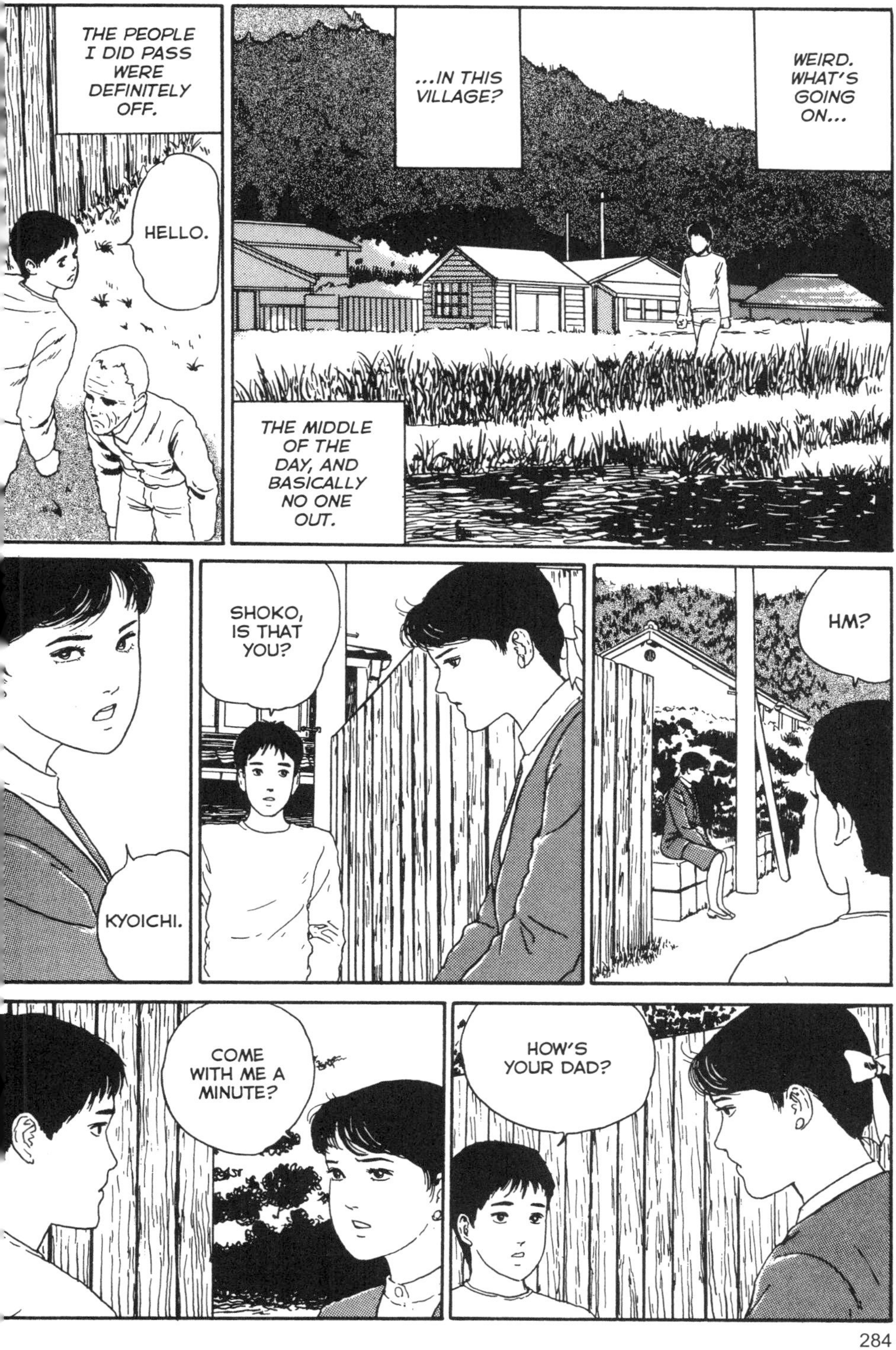
WEIRD. WHAT'S GOING ON...
...IN THIS VILLAGE?
THE MIDDLE OF THE DAY, AND BASICALLY NO ONE OUT.
THE PEOPLE I DID PASS WERE DEFINITELY OFF.
HELLO.
HM?
SHOKO, IS THAT YOU?
KYOICHI.
HOW'S YOUR DAD?
COME WITH ME A MINUTE?

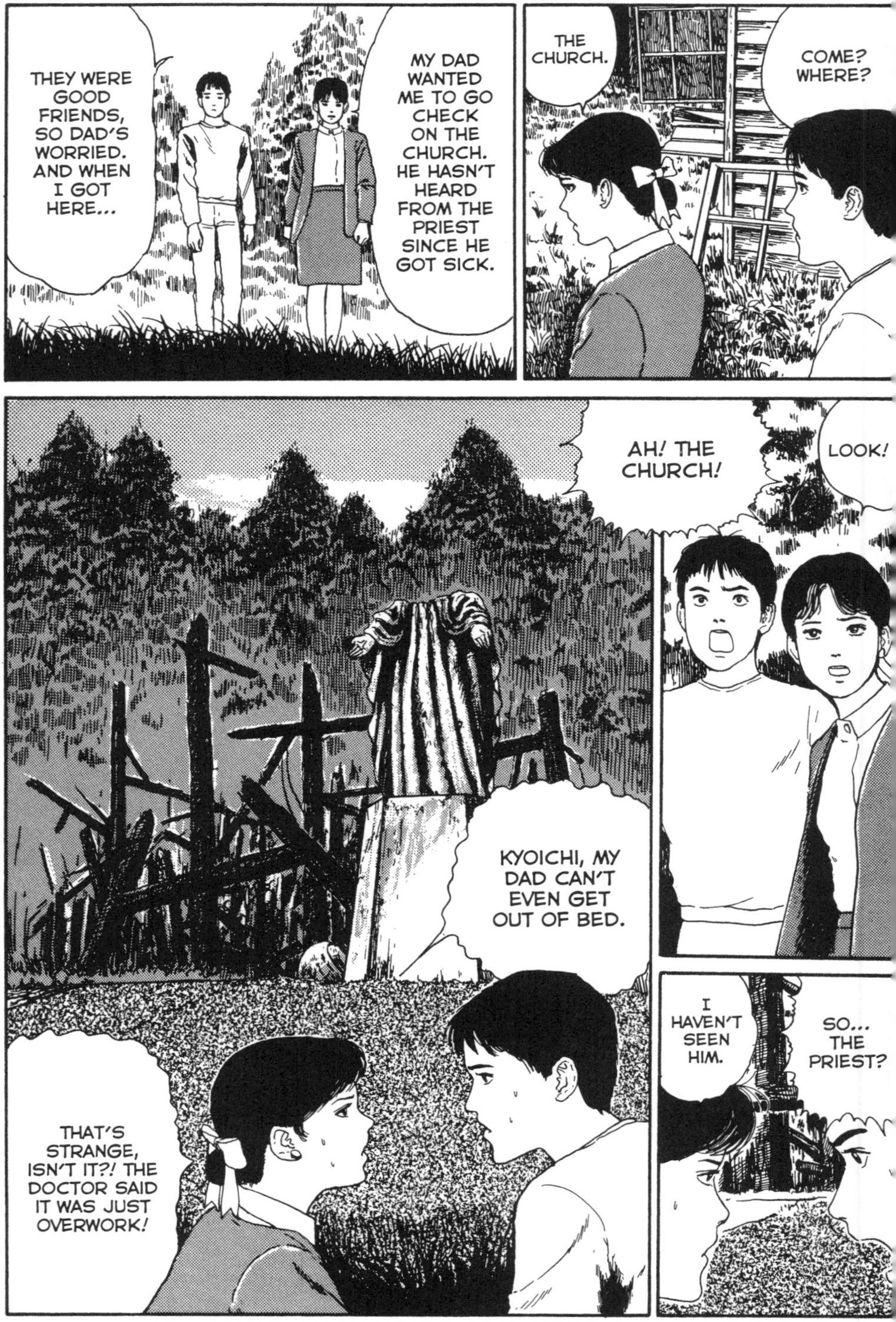
COME? WHERE?
THE CHURCH.
MY DAD WANTED ME TO GO CHECK ON THE CHURCH. HE HASN'T HEARD FROM THE PRIEST SINCE HE GOT SICK.
THEY WERE GOOD FRIENDS, SO DAD'S WORRIED. AND WHEN I GOT HERE...
LOOK!
AH! THE CHURCH!
SO... THE PRIEST?
I HAVEN'T SEEN HIM.
KYOICHI, MY DAD CAN'T EVEN GET OUT OF BED.
THAT'S STRANGE, ISN'T IT?! THE DOCTOR SAID IT WAS JUST OVERWORK!

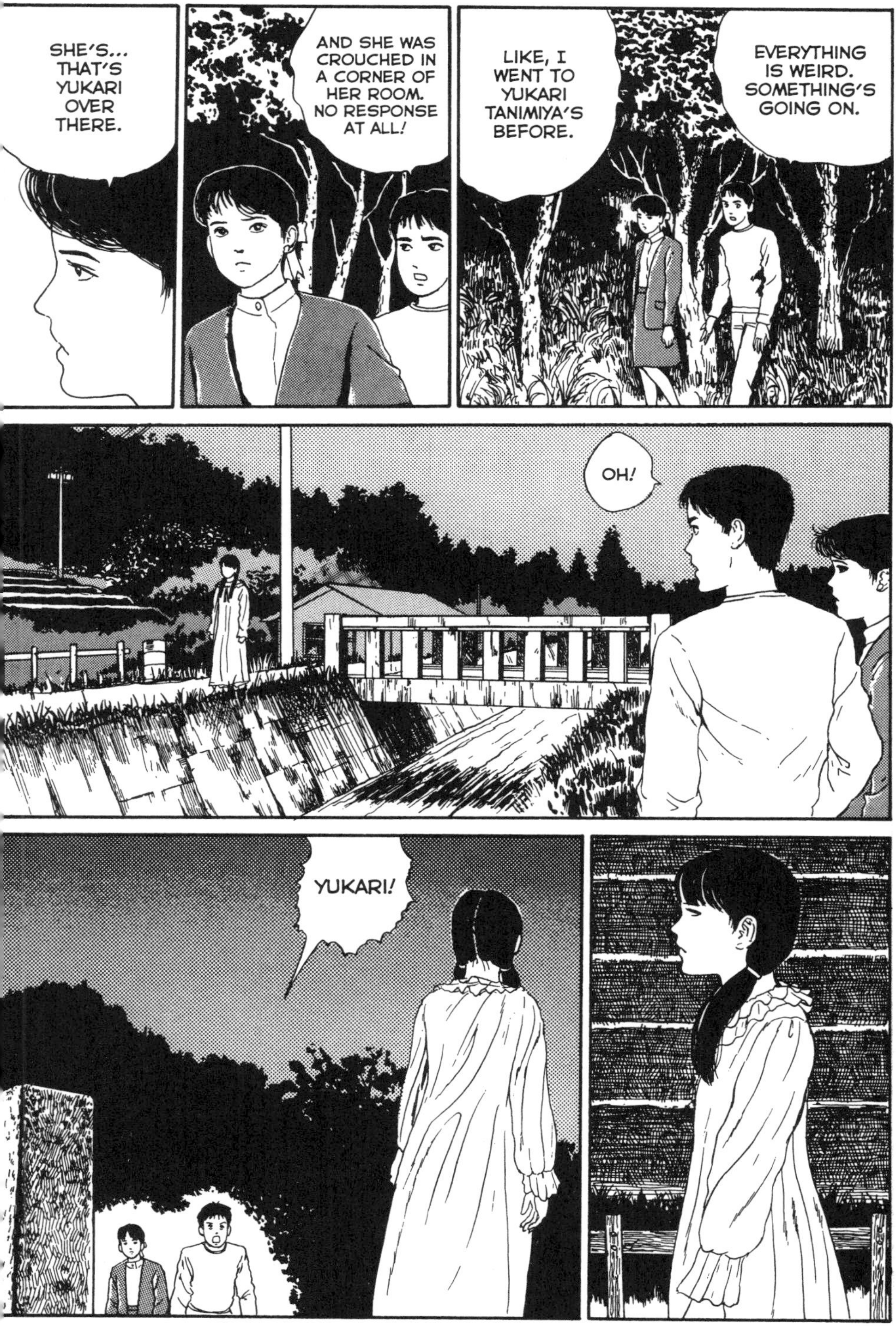
EVERYTHING IS WEIRD. SOMETHING'S GOING ON.
LIKE, I WENT TO YUKARI TANIMIYA'S BEFORE.
AND SHE WAS CROUCHED IN A CORNER OF HER ROOM. NO RESPONSE AT ALL!
SHE'S... THAT'S YUKARI OVER THERE.
OH!
YUKARI!

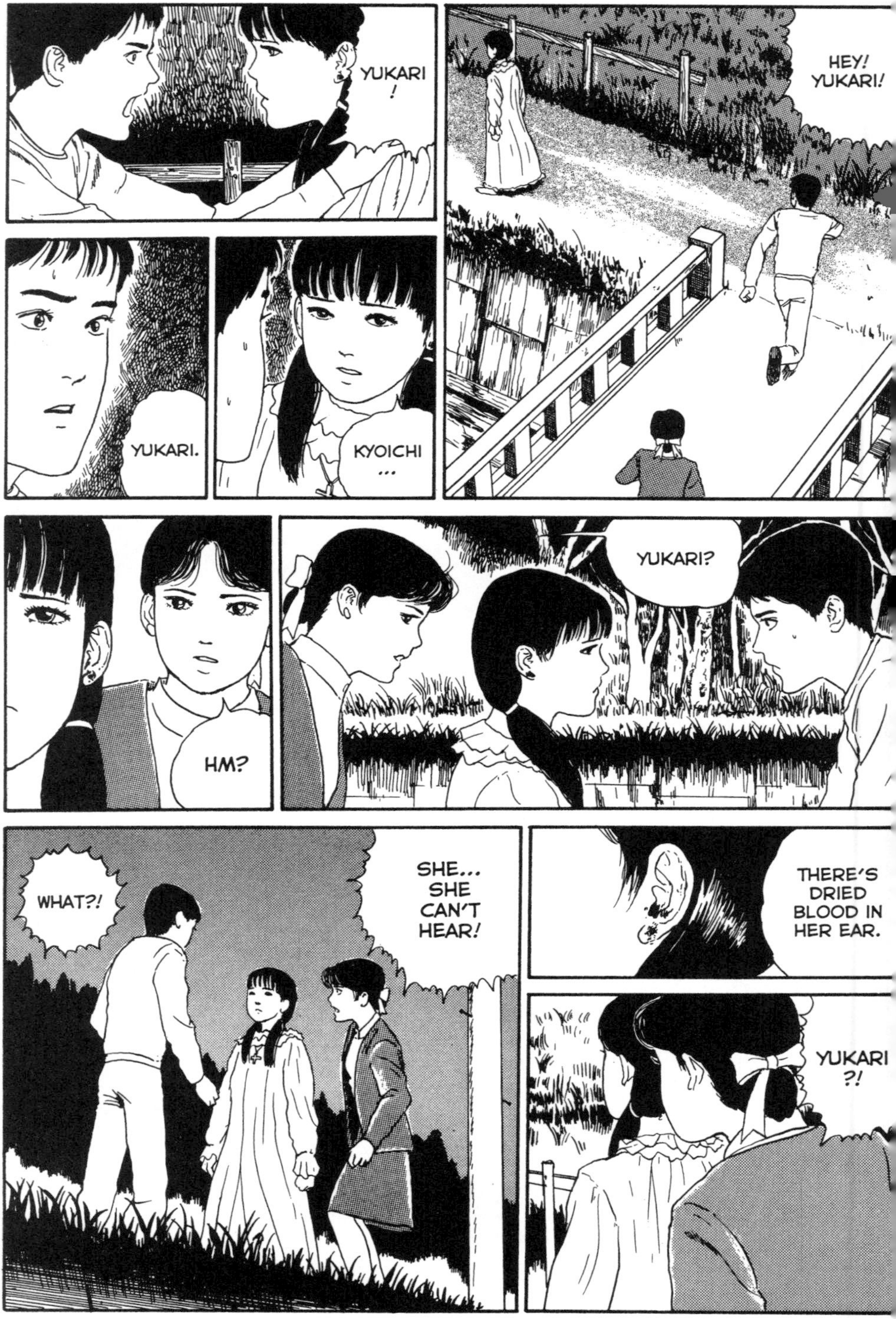
HEY! YUKARI!
YUKARI!
KYOICHI...
YUKARI.
YUKARI?
HM?
THERE'S DRIED BLOOD IN HER EAR.
YUKARI?!
SHE... SHE CAN'T HEAR!
WHAT?!

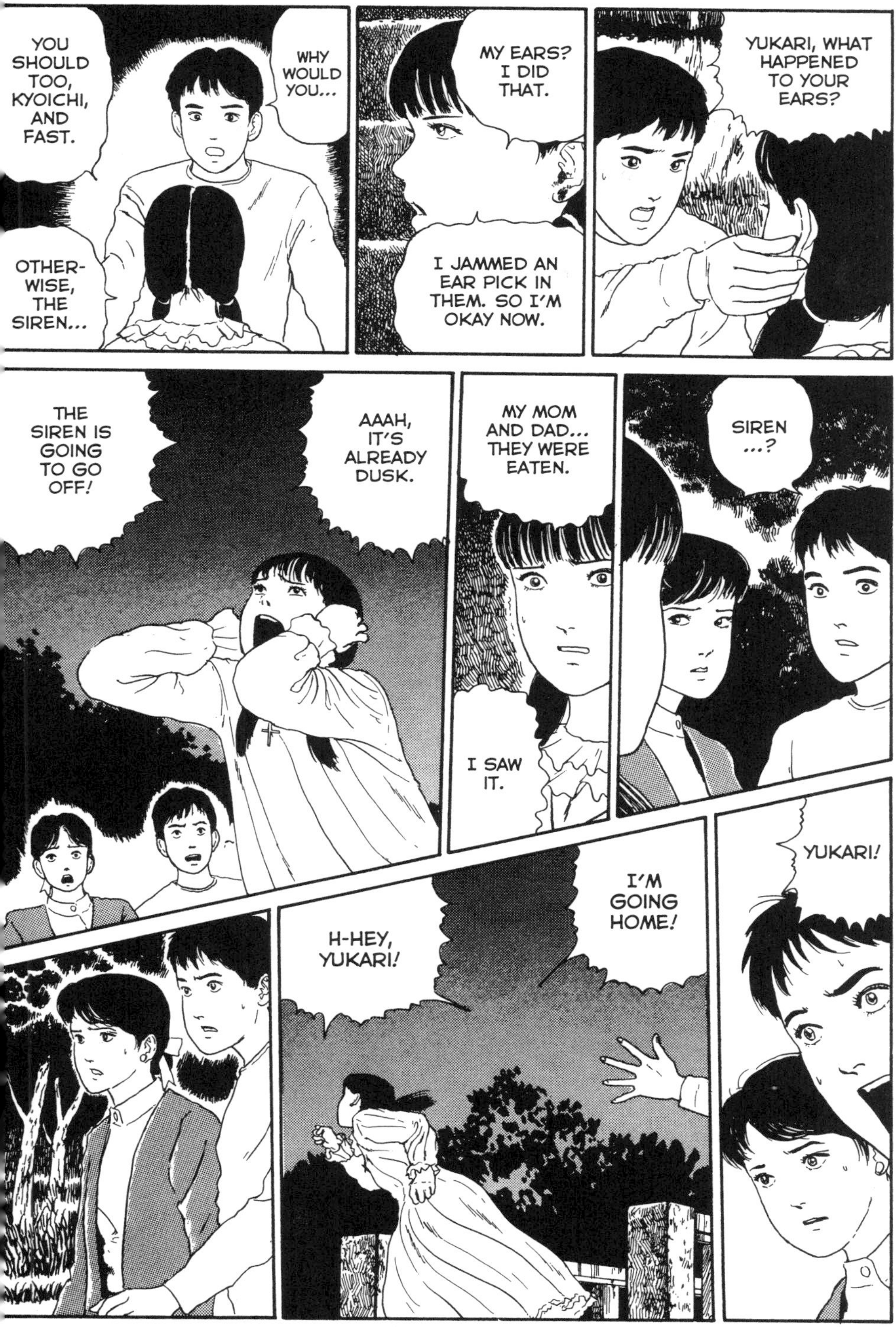
YUKARI, WHAT HAPPENED TO YOUR EARS?
MY EARS? I DID THAT.
I JAMMED AN EAR PICK IN THEM. SO I'M OKAY NOW.
WHY WOULD YOU...
YOU SHOULD TOO, KYOICHI, AND FAST.
OTHER-WISE, THE SIREN...
SIREN ...?
MY MOM AND DAD... THEY WERE EATEN.
I SAW IT.
AAAH, IT'S ALREADY DUSK.
THE SIREN IS GOING TO GO OFF!
YUKARI!
I'M GOING HOME!
H-HEY, YUKARI!

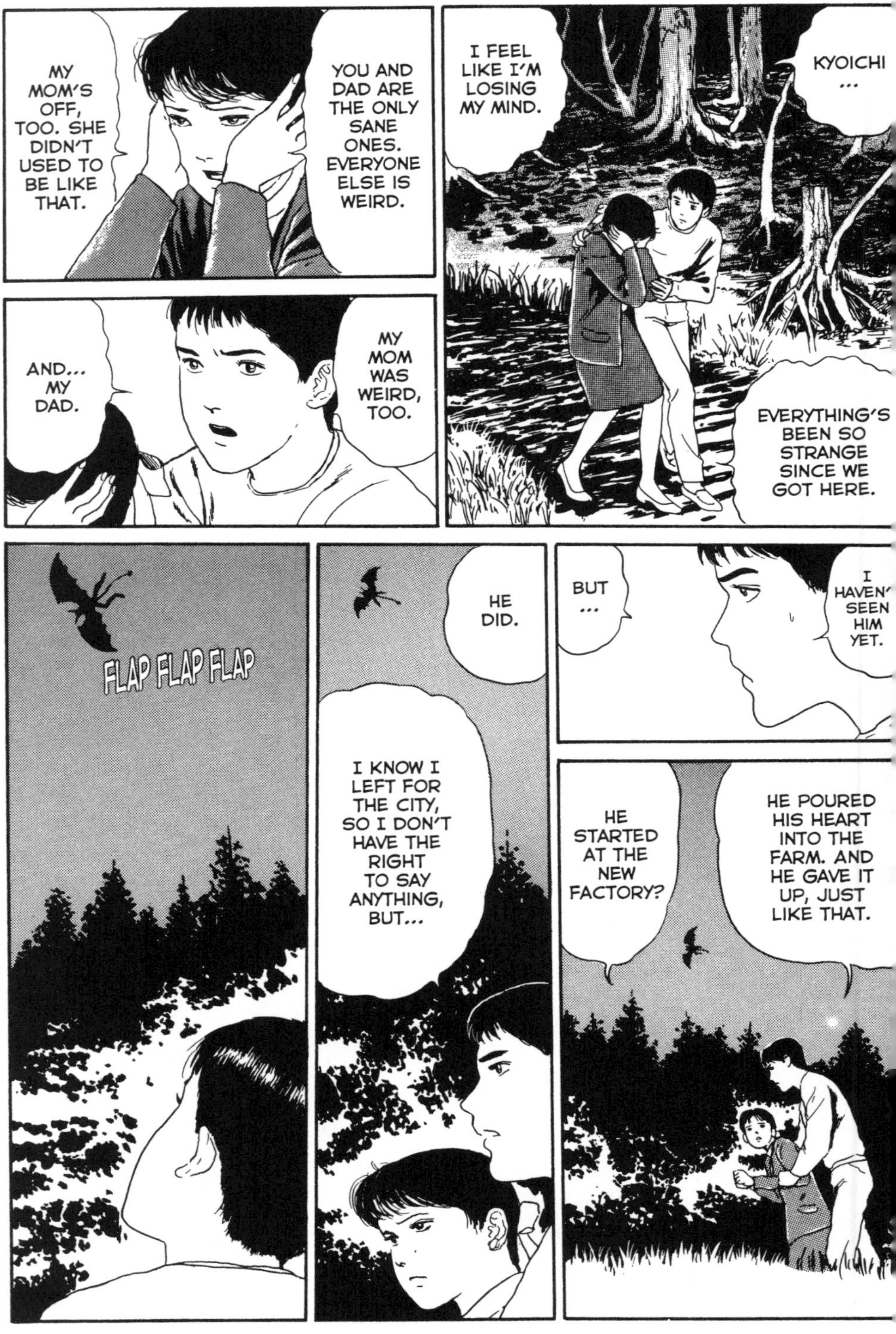
KYOICHI ...
I FEEL LIKE I'M LOSING MY MIND.
EVERYTHING'S BEEN SO STRANGE SINCE WE GOT HERE.
YOU AND DAD ARE THE ONLY SANE ONES. EVERYONE ELSE IS WEIRD.
MY MOM'S OFF, TOO. SHE DIDN'T USED TO BE LIKE THAT.
MY MOM WAS WEIRD, TOO.
AND... MY DAD.
I HAVEN' SEEN HIM YET.
BUT ...
HE POURED HIS HEART INTO THE FARM. AND HE GAVE IT UP, JUST LIKE THAT.
HE STARTED AT THE NEW FACTORY?
HE DID.
I KNOW I LEFT FOR THE CITY, SO I DON'T HAVE THE RIGHT TO SAY ANYTHING, BUT...
FLAP FLAP FLAP

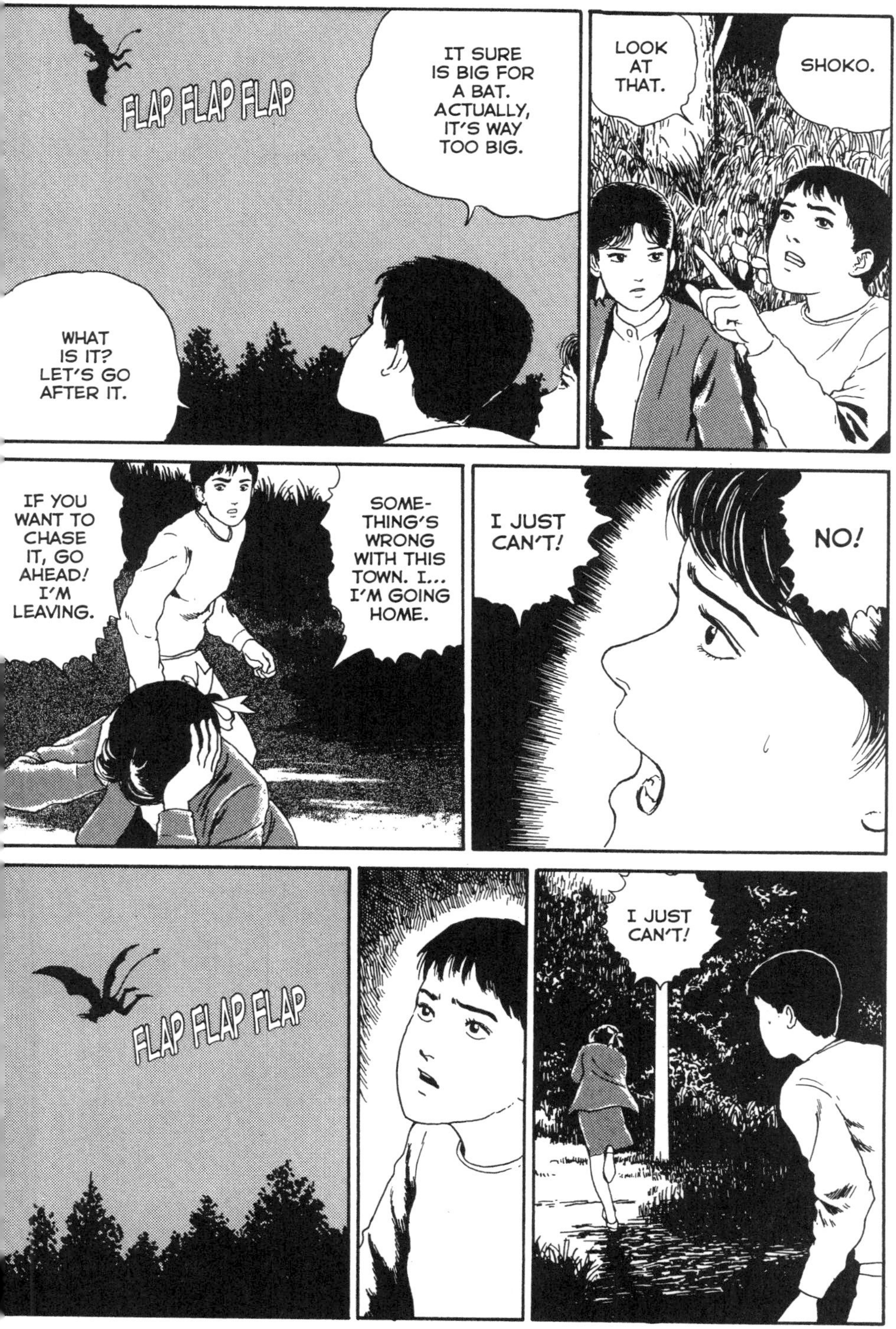
SHOKO.
LOOK AT THAT.
IT SURE IS BIG FOR A BAT. ACTUALLY, IT'S WAY TOO BIG.
FLAP FLAP FLAP
WHAT IS IT? LET'S GO AFTER IT.
NO!
I JUST CAN'T!
SOME-THING'S WRONG WITH THIS TOWN. I... I'M GOING HOME.
IF YOU WANT TO CHASE IT, GO AHEAD! I'M LEAVING.
I JUST CAN'T!
FLAP FLAP FLAP

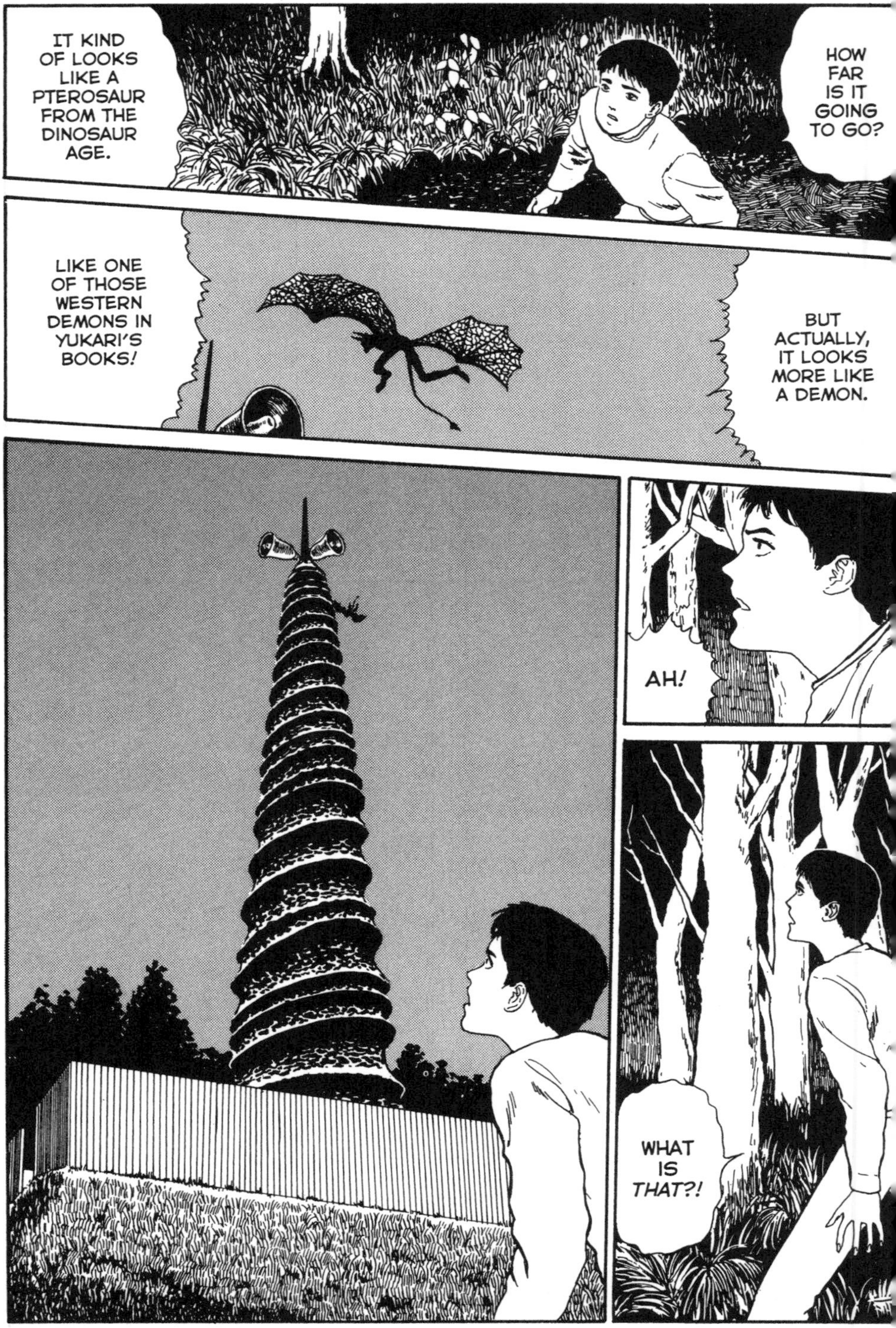
HOW FAR IS IT GOING TO GO?
IT KIND OF LOOKS LIKE A PTEROSAUR FROM THE DINOSAUR AGE.
BUT ACTUALLY, IT LOOKS MORE LIKE A DEMON.
LIKE ONE OF THOSE WESTERN DEMONS IN YUKARI'S BOOKS!
AH!
WHAT IS *THAT?!*

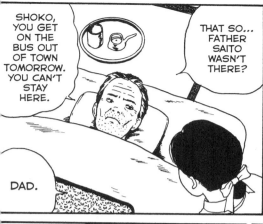

THAT SO... FATHER SAITO WASN'T THERE?
SHOKO, YOU GET ON THE BUS OUT OF TOWN TOMORROW. YOU CAN'T STAY HERE.
DAD.
THINGS HAVE BEEN ODD EVER SINCE HAIYAMA BECAME MAYOR.
HE'S LIKELY THE ONE WHO BURNED THE CHURCH DOWN. HE COULD HAVE BROKEN THE SEAL IN THE BASEMENT.
THE SEAL IN THE BASE-MENT?
ACCORDING TO THE OLD CHURCH RECORDS, ABOUT 400 YEARS AGO, A MAGICIAN CALLED DOLEMAN CAME TO THIS VILLAGE WITH A GROUP OF MISSIONARIES.
THIS DOLEMAN USED BLACK MAGIC TO SUMMON THREE DEMONS TO WORK EVIL FOR HIM.
THEY SET HOUSES ON FIRE, ATE PEOPLE, AND CONTROLLED THE VILLAGERS WITH THEIR TERRIFYING VOICES.
UNABLE TO ENDURE IT ANY LONGER, THE PEOPLE GOT HELP FROM THE MISSIONARIES TO DEFEAT DOLEMAN AND DESTROY TWO OF THE DEMONS. THEY LOCKED THE LAST ONE UP IN THE CHURCH BASEMENT.

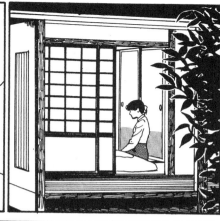

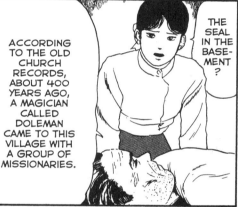

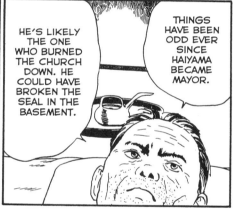

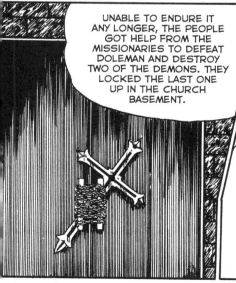

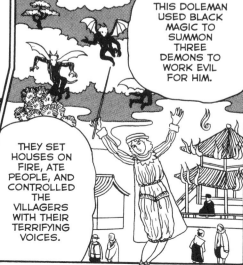

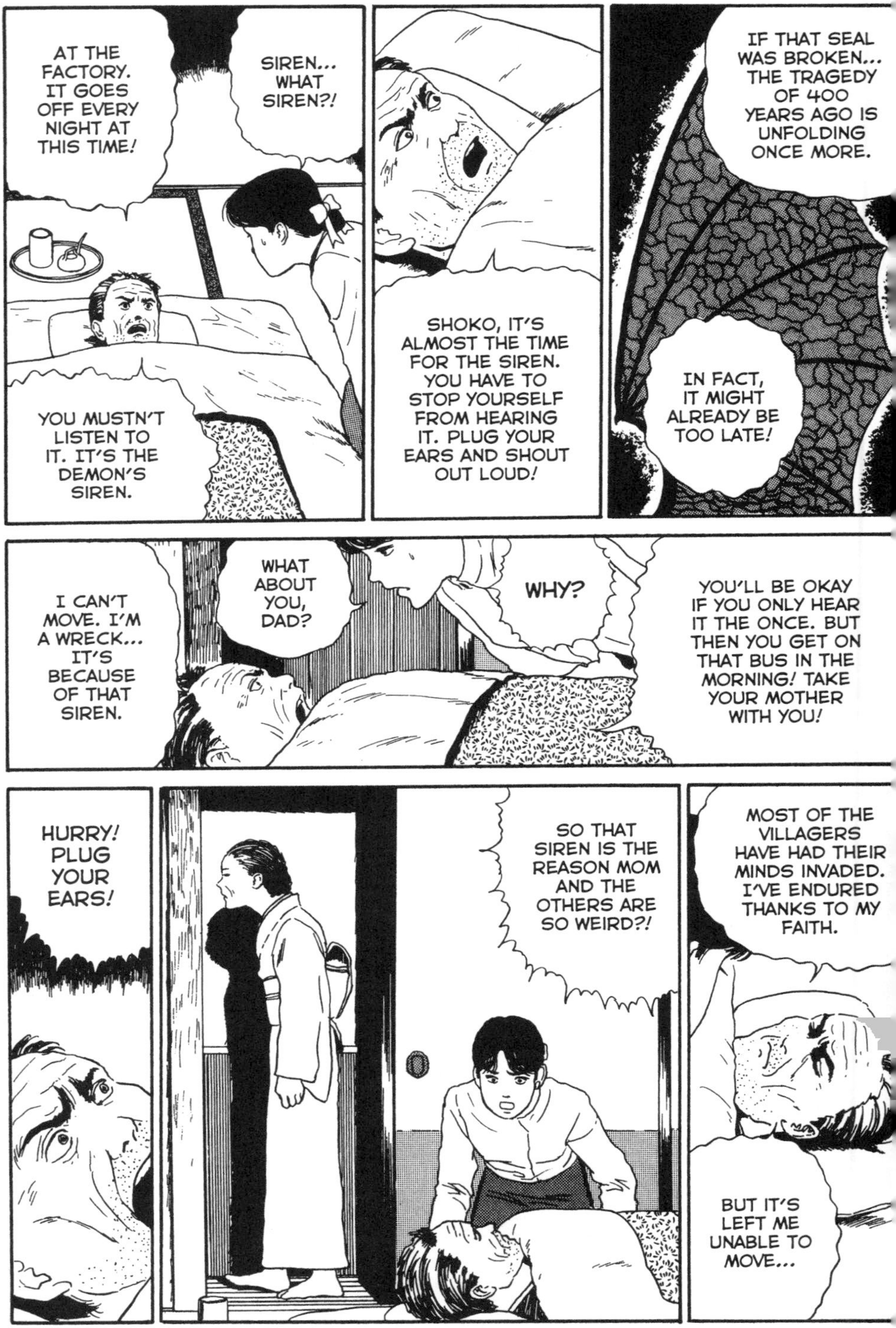
IF THAT SEAL WAS BROKEN... THE TRAGEDY OF 400 YEARS AGO IS UNFOLDING ONCE MORE.
IN FACT, IT MIGHT ALREADY BE TOO LATE!
SHOKO, IT'S ALMOST THE TIME FOR THE SIREN. YOU HAVE TO STOP YOURSELF FROM HEARING IT. PLUG YOUR EARS AND SHOUT OUT LOUD!
SIREN... WHAT SIREN?!
AT THE FACTORY. IT GOES OFF EVERY NIGHT AT THIS TIME!
YOU MUSTN'T LISTEN TO IT. IT'S THE DEMON'S SIREN.
YOU'LL BE OKAY IF YOU ONLY HEAR IT THE ONCE. BUT THEN YOU GET ON THAT BUS IN THE MORNING! TAKE YOUR MOTHER WITH YOU!
WHY?
WHAT ABOUT YOU, DAD?
I CAN'T MOVE. I'M A WRECK... IT'S BECAUSE OF THAT SIREN.
MOST OF THE VILLAGERS HAVE HAD THEIR MINDS INVADED. I'VE ENDURED THANKS TO MY FAITH.
BUT IT'S LEFT ME UNABLE TO MOVE...
SO THAT SIREN IS THE REASON MOM AND THE OTHERS ARE SO WEIRD?!
HURRY! PLUG YOUR EARS!

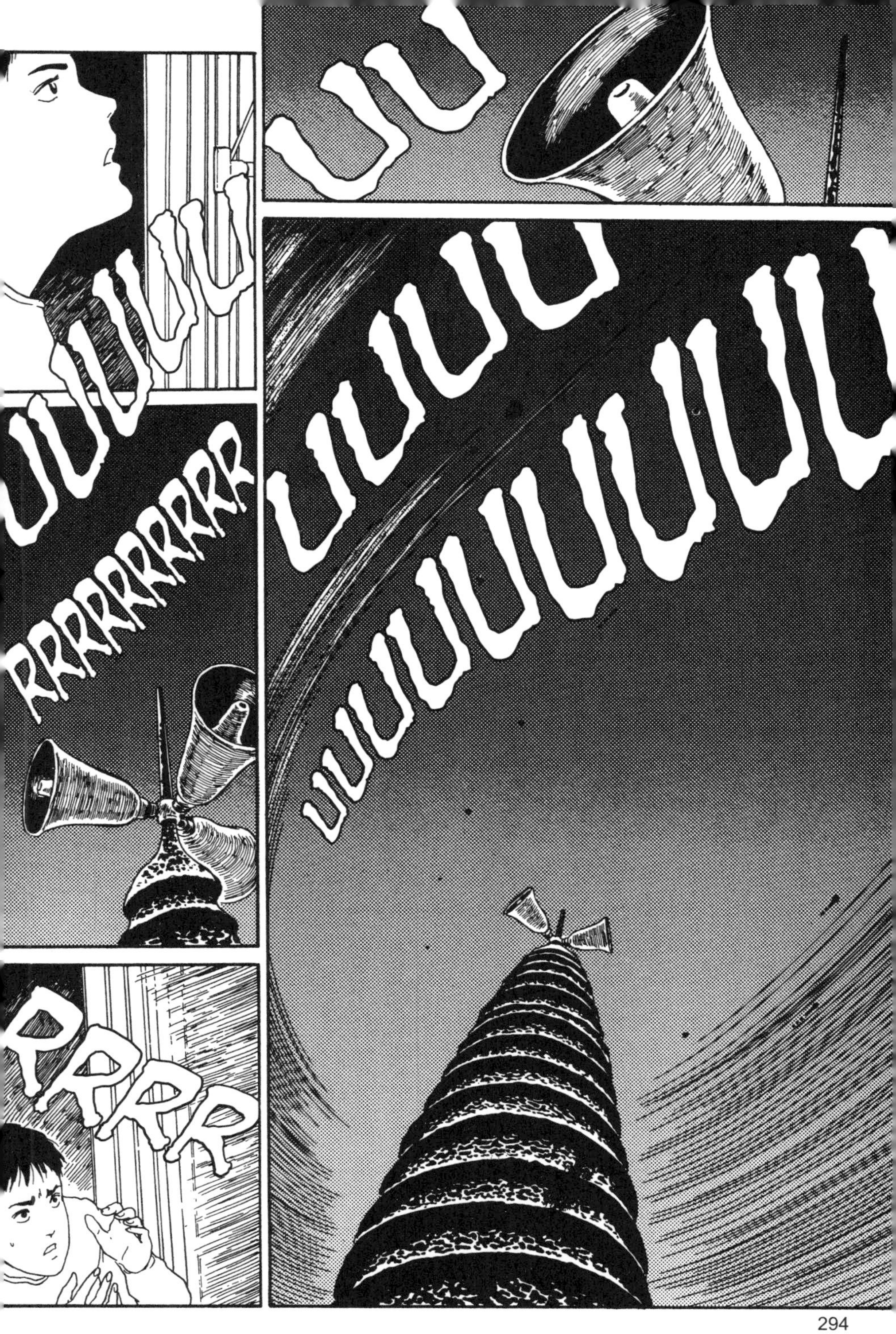
UU
UUUUU
UUUUUUUUUUUUU
UUUUU
UUUU
RRRRRRRRR
RRRR

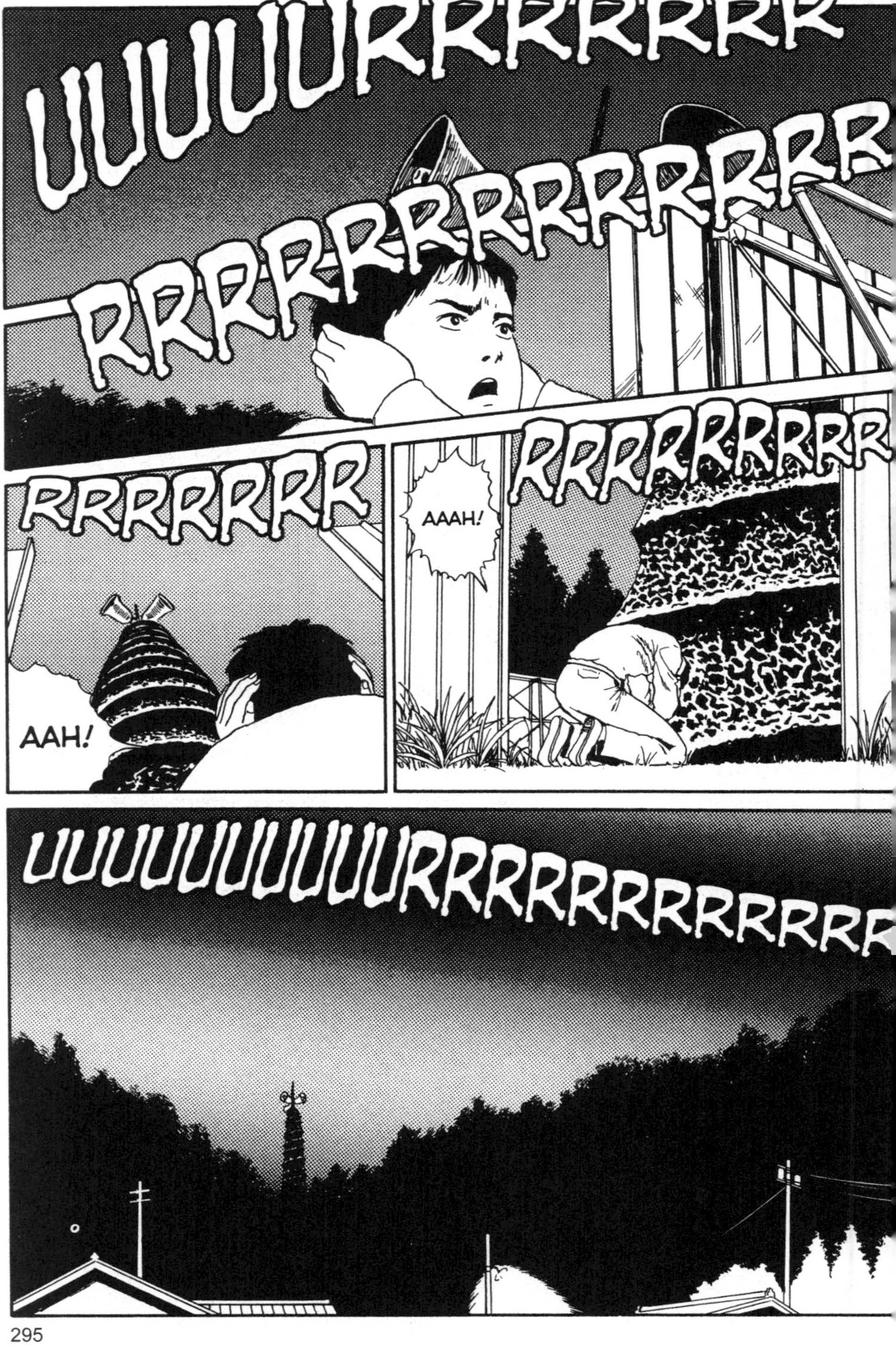

UUUUURRRRRRRR
RRRRRRRRRRRRRR
RRRRRRRRR
AAAH!
RRRRRRRR
AAH!
UUUUUUUUUURRRRRRRRRRRR

UUUUUURRRRRRR

MOM! WHERE ARE YOU GOING?!

RRRRRRRRR

RRRRRR

UUUUUUU

UUUURRRRRRRRR

DEAD END

296

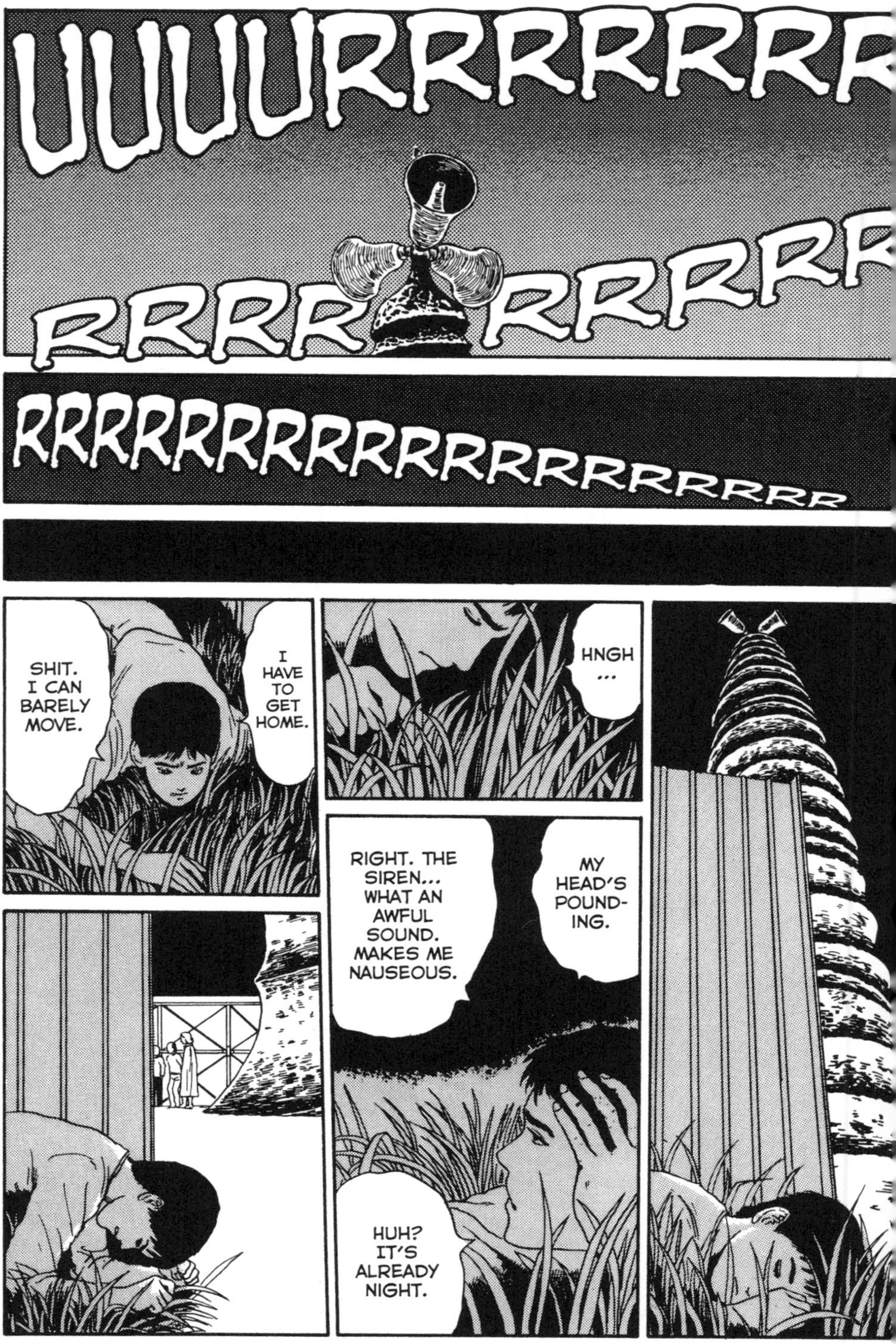
UUUURRRRRRRRR
RRRRRRRRR RRRR
RRRRRRRRRRRRRRRRRRR
HNGH ...
I HAVE TO GET HOME.
SHIT. I CAN BARELY MOVE.
MY HEAD'S POUND-ING.
RIGHT. THE SIREN... WHAT AN AWFUL SOUND. MAKES ME NAUSEOUS.
HUH? IT'S ALREADY NIGHT.

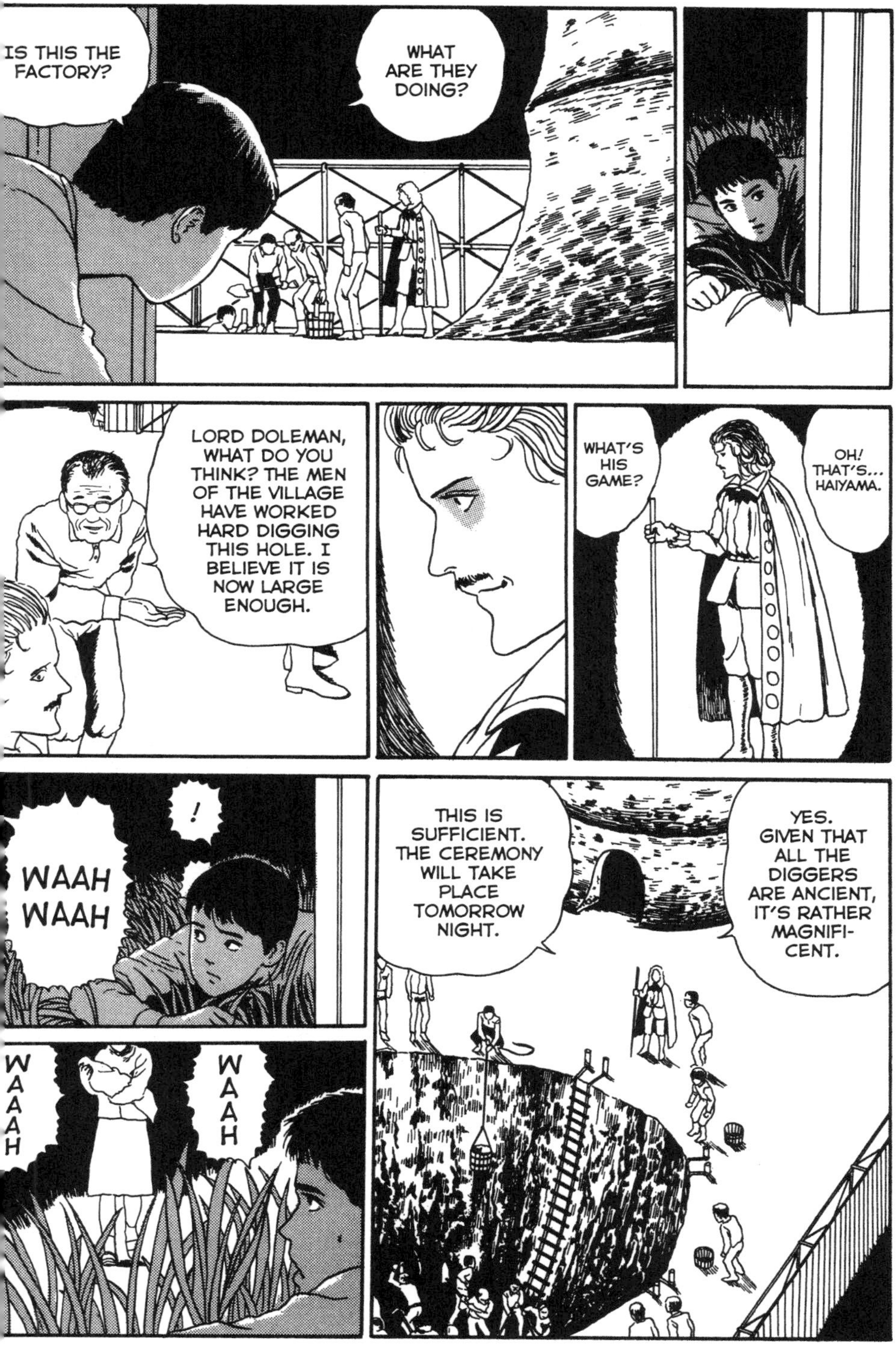
WHAT ARE THEY DOING?
IS THIS THE FACTORY?
OH! THAT'S... HAIYAMA.
WHAT'S HIS GAME?
LORD DOLEMAN, WHAT DO YOU THINK? THE MEN OF THE VILLAGE HAVE WORKED HARD DIGGING THIS HOLE. I BELIEVE IT IS NOW LARGE ENOUGH.
YES. GIVEN THAT ALL THE DIGGERS ARE ANCIENT, IT'S RATHER MAGNIFI-CENT.
THIS IS SUFFICIENT. THE CEREMONY WILL TAKE PLACE TOMORROW NIGHT.
!
WAAH WAAH
WAAH
WAAAAH

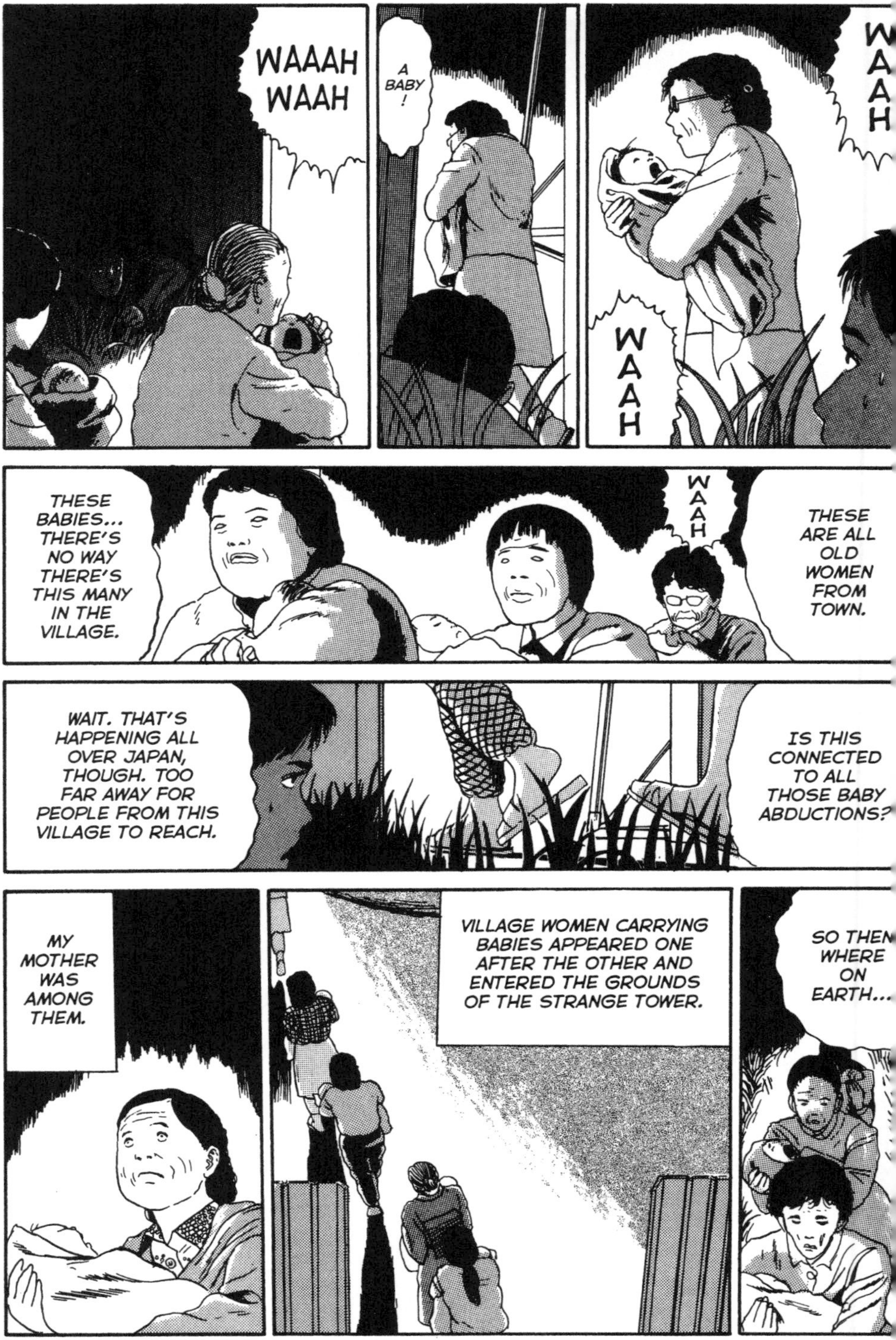
WAAH
WAAH
A BABY!
WAAAH WAAH
THESE ARE ALL OLD WOMEN FROM TOWN.
WAAH
THESE BABIES... THERE'S NO WAY THERE'S THIS MANY IN THE VILLAGE.
IS THIS CONNECTED TO ALL THOSE BABY ABDUCTIONS?
WAIT. THAT'S HAPPENING ALL OVER JAPAN, THOUGH. TOO FAR AWAY FOR PEOPLE FROM THIS VILLAGE TO REACH.
SO THEN WHERE ON EARTH...
VILLAGE WOMEN CARRYING BABIES APPEARED ONE AFTER THE OTHER AND ENTERED THE GROUNDS OF THE STRANGE TOWER.
MY MOTHER WAS AMONG THEM.

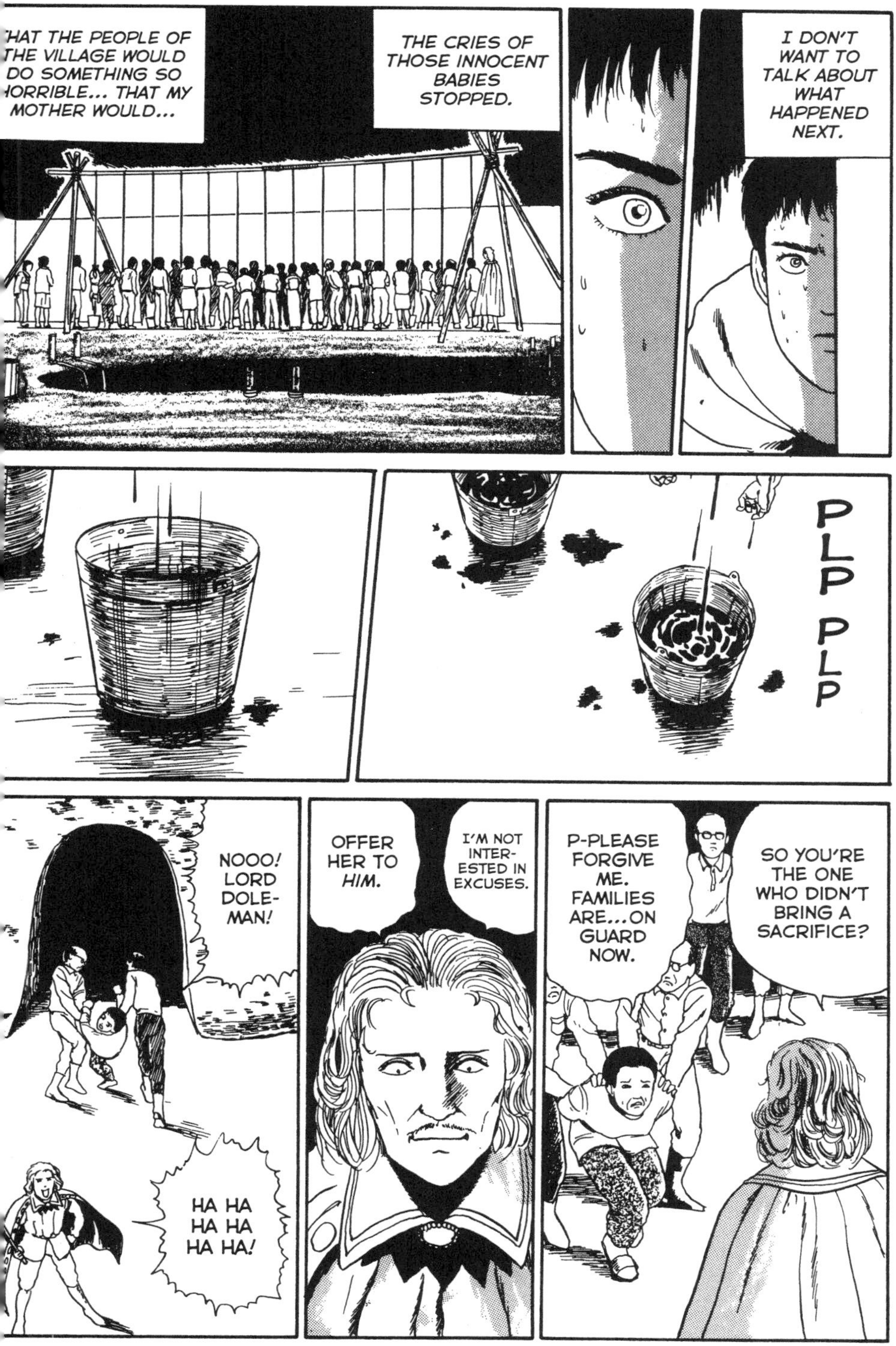
I DON'T WANT TO TALK ABOUT WHAT HAPPENED NEXT.
THE CRIES OF THOSE INNOCENT BABIES STOPPED.
HAT THE PEOPLE OF THE VILLAGE WOULD DO SOMETHING SO HORRIBLE... THAT MY MOTHER WOULD...
PLP PLP PLP
SO YOU'RE THE ONE WHO DIDN'T BRING A SACRIFICE?
P-PLEASE FORGIVE ME. FAMILIES ARE...ON GUARD NOW.
I'M NOT INTER-ESTED IN EXCUSES.
OFFER HER TO *HIM*.
NOOO! LORD DOLE-MAN!
HA HA HA HA HA HA!

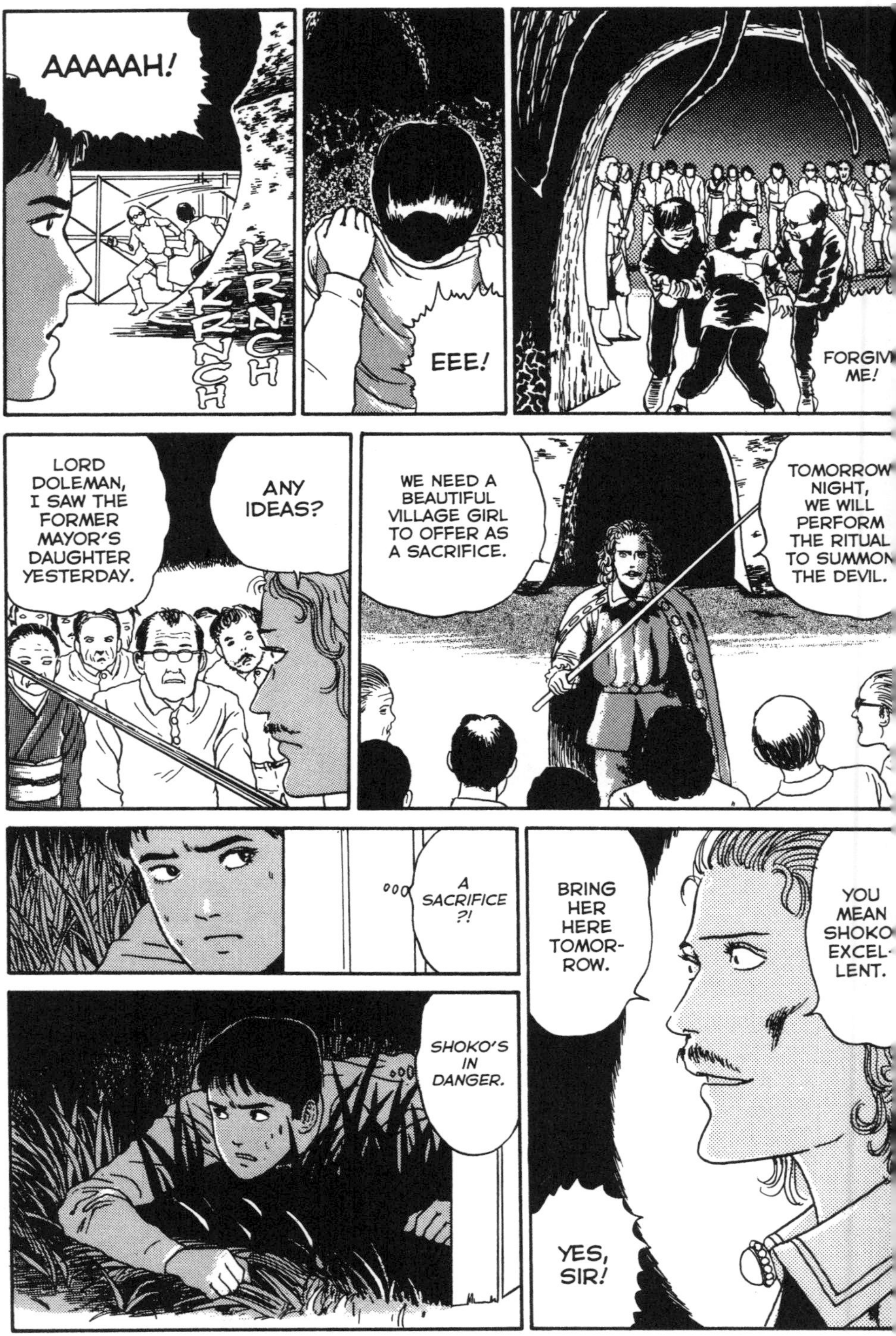
FORGIV ME!
EEE!
AAAAAH!
KRNCH KRNCH
TOMORROW NIGHT, WE WILL PERFORM THE RITUAL TO SUMMON THE DEVIL.
WE NEED A BEAUTIFUL VILLAGE GIRL TO OFFER AS A SACRIFICE.
ANY IDEAS?
LORD DOLEMAN, I SAW THE FORMER MAYOR'S DAUGHTER YESTERDAY.
YOU MEAN SHOKO EXCEL-LENT.
BRING HER HERE TOMOR-ROW.
YES, SIR!
A SACRIFICE?!
SHOKO'S IN DANGER.

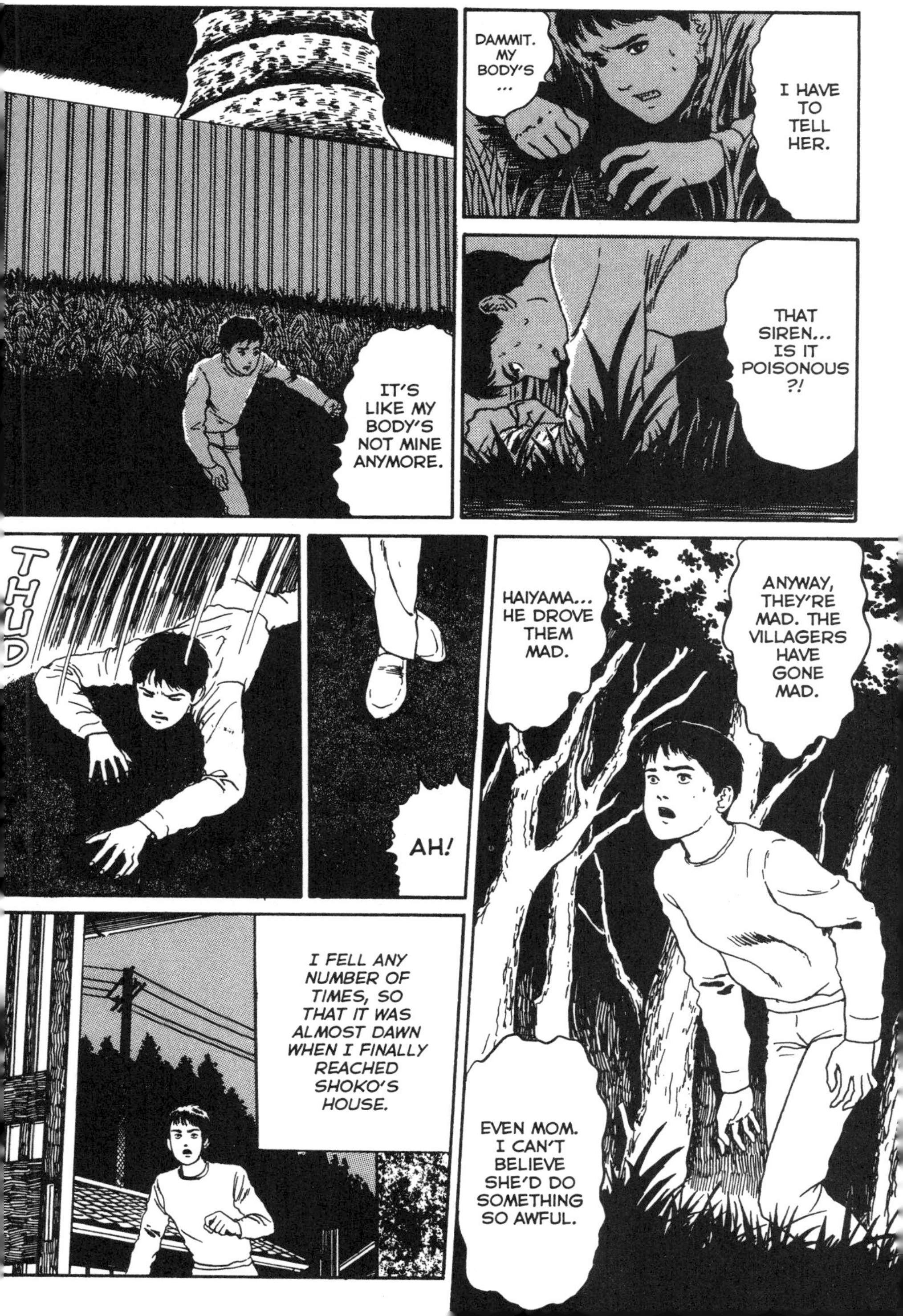
DAMMIT. MY BODY'S ...
I HAVE TO TELL HER.
THAT SIREN... IS IT POISONOUS?!
IT'S LIKE MY BODY'S NOT MINE ANYMORE.
ANYWAY, THEY'RE MAD. THE VILLAGERS HAVE GONE MAD.
HAIYAMA... HE DROVE THEM MAD.
EVEN MOM. I CAN'T BELIEVE SHE'D DO SOMETHING SO AWFUL.
AH!
THUD
I FELL ANY NUMBER OF TIMES, SO THAT IT WAS ALMOST DAWN WHEN I FINALLY REACHED SHOKO'S HOUSE.

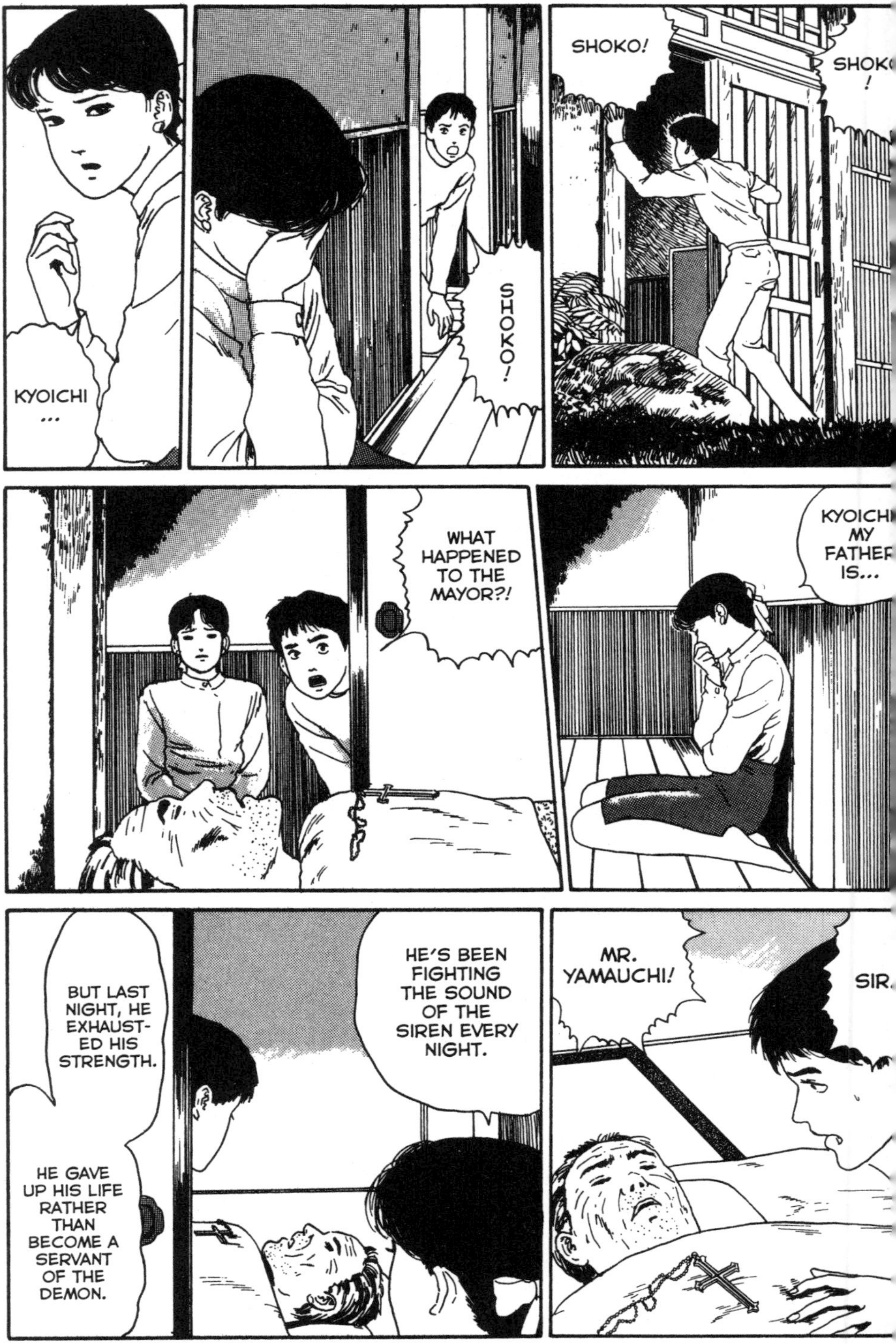
SHOK!
SHOKO!
SHOKO!
KYOICHI ...
KYOICH MY FATHER IS...
WHAT HAPPENED TO THE MAYOR?!
SIR.
MR. YAMAUCHI!
HE'S BEEN FIGHTING THE SOUND OF THE SIREN EVERY NIGHT.
BUT LAST NIGHT, HE EXHAUST-ED HIS STRENGTH.
HE GAVE UP HIS LIFE RATHER THAN BECOME A SERVANT OF THE DEMON.

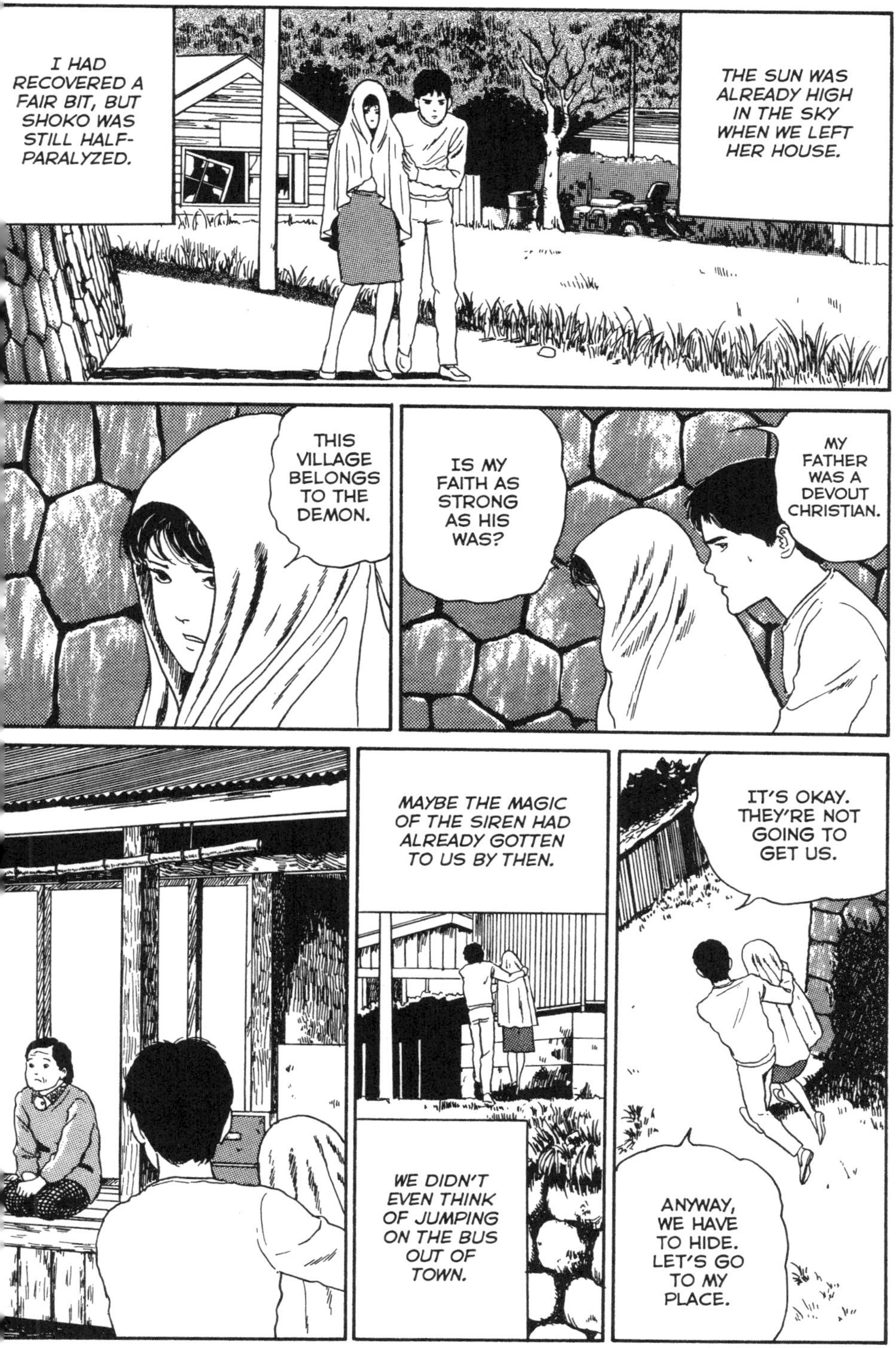
THE SUN WAS ALREADY HIGH IN THE SKY WHEN WE LEFT HER HOUSE.
I HAD RECOVERED A FAIR BIT, BUT SHOKO WAS STILL HALF-PARALYZED.
MY FATHER WAS A DEVOUT CHRISTIAN.
IS MY FAITH AS STRONG AS HIS WAS?
THIS VILLAGE BELONGS TO THE DEMON.
IT'S OKAY. THEY'RE NOT GOING TO GET US.
ANYWAY, WE HAVE TO HIDE. LET'S GO TO MY PLACE.
MAYBE THE MAGIC OF THE SIREN HAD ALREADY GOTTEN TO US BY THEN.
WE DIDN'T EVEN THINK OF JUMPING ON THE BUS OUT OF TOWN.

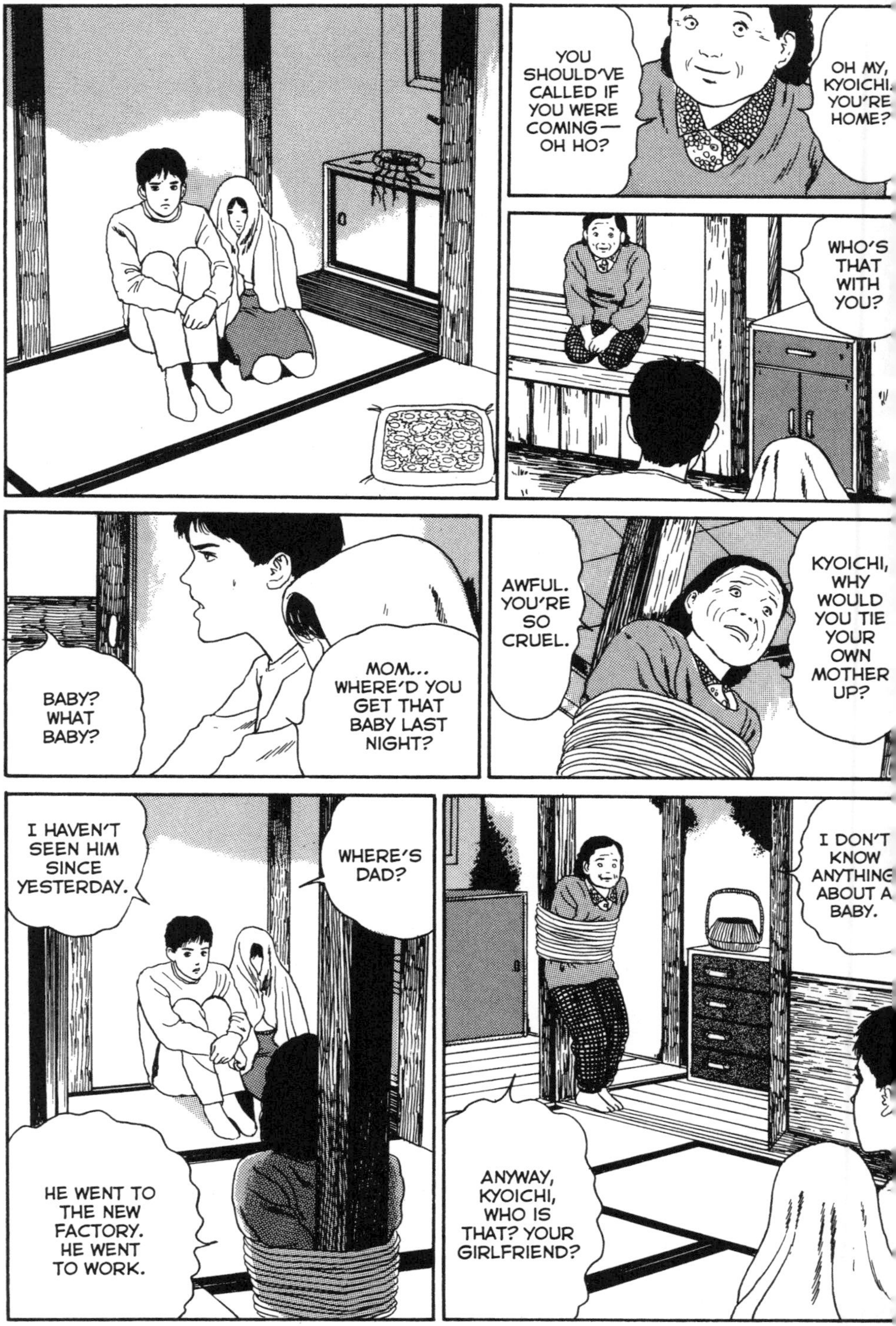
OH MY, KYOICHI. YOU'RE HOME?
YOU SHOULD'VE CALLED IF YOU WERE COMING— OH HO?
WHO'S THAT WITH YOU?
KYOICHI, WHY WOULD YOU TIE YOUR OWN MOTHER UP?
AWFUL. YOU'RE SO CRUEL.
MOM... WHERE'D YOU GET THAT BABY LAST NIGHT?
BABY? WHAT BABY?
I DON'T KNOW ANYTHING ABOUT A BABY.
ANYWAY, KYOICHI, WHO IS THAT? YOUR GIRLFRIEND?
WHERE'S DAD?
I HAVEN'T SEEN HIM SINCE YESTERDAY.
HE WENT TO THE NEW FACTORY. HE WENT TO WORK.

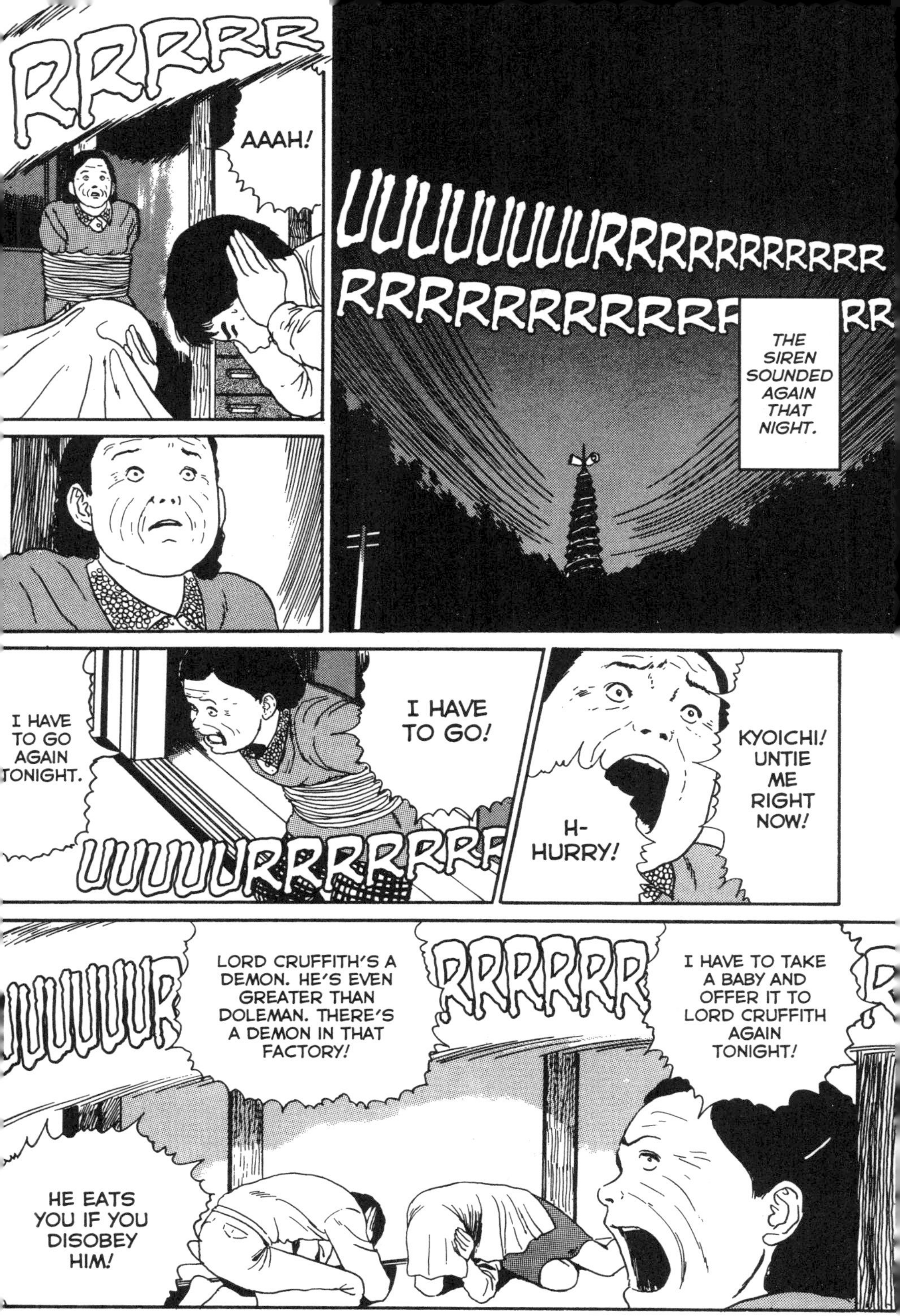
UUUUUUUUURRRRRRRRRRRRRRRRRRRRRRRR
THE SIREN SOUNDED AGAIN THAT NIGHT.
RRRRR
AAAH!
KYOICHI! UNTIE ME RIGHT NOW!
H- HURRY!
I HAVE TO GO!
I HAVE TO GO AGAIN TONIGHT.
UUUUURRRRRR
I HAVE TO TAKE A BABY AND OFFER IT TO LORD CRUFFITH AGAIN TONIGHT!
RRRRRR
LORD CRUFFITH'S A DEMON. HE'S EVEN GREATER THAN DOLEMAN. THERE'S A DEMON IN THAT FACTORY!
UUUUUUR
HE EATS YOU IF YOU DISOBEY HIM!

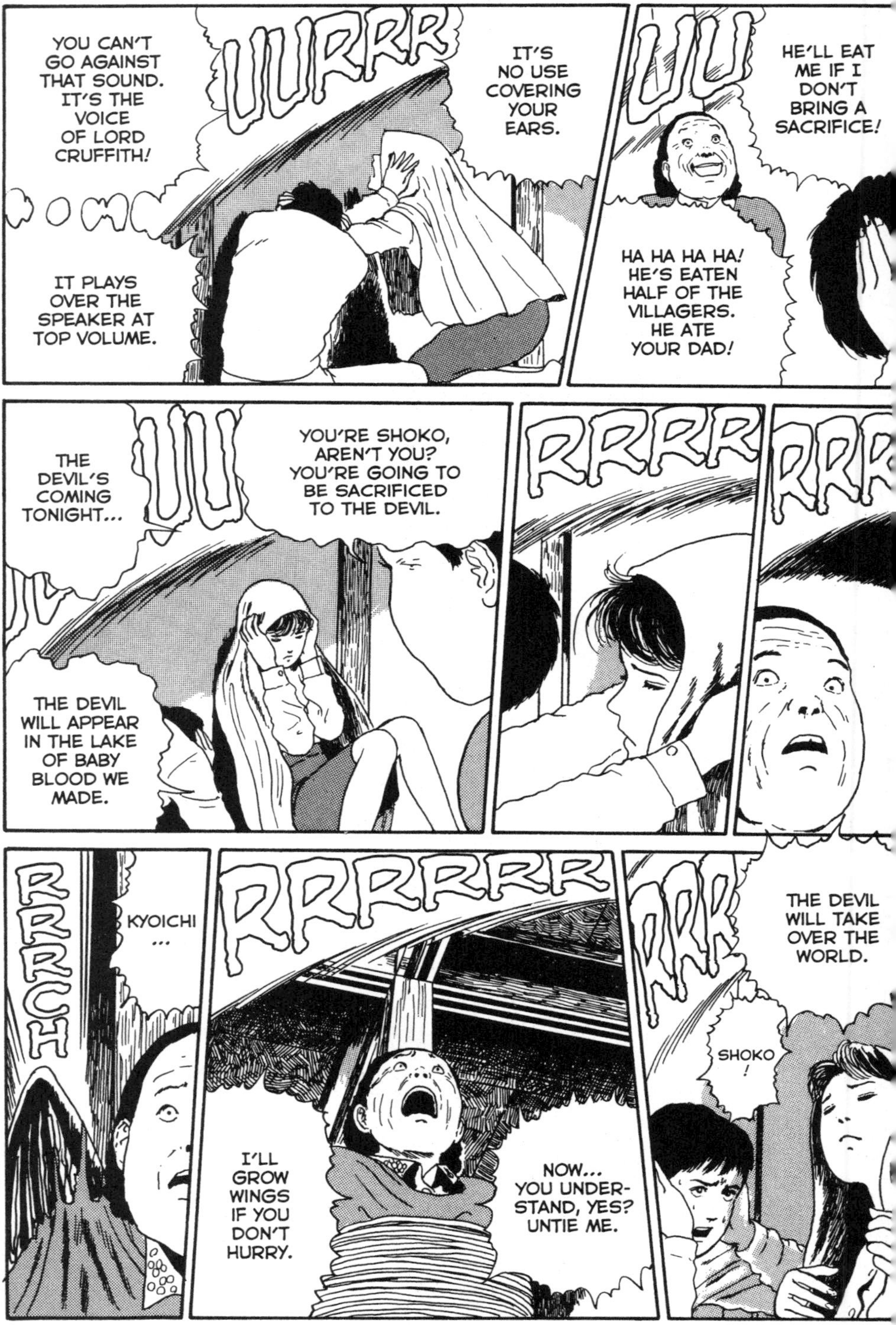
UU
HE'LL EAT ME IF I DON'T BRING A SACRIFICE!
HA HA HA HA! HE'S EATEN HALF OF THE VILLAGERS. HE ATE YOUR DAD!
UURRR
IT'S NO USE COVERING YOUR EARS.
YOU CAN'T GO AGAINST THAT SOUND. IT'S THE VOICE OF LORD CRUFFITH!
IT PLAYS OVER THE SPEAKER AT TOP VOLUME.
RRR
RRRR
UU
YOU'RE SHOKO, AREN'T YOU? YOU'RE GOING TO BE SACRIFICED TO THE DEVIL.
THE DEVIL'S COMING TONIGHT...
THE DEVIL WILL APPEAR IN THE LAKE OF BABY BLOOD WE MADE.
RRK
THE DEVIL WILL TAKE OVER THE WORLD.
SHOKO!
RRRRRR
NOW... YOU UNDERSTAND, YES? UNTIE ME.
I'LL GROW WINGS IF YOU DON'T HURRY.
RRRCH
KYOICHI ...

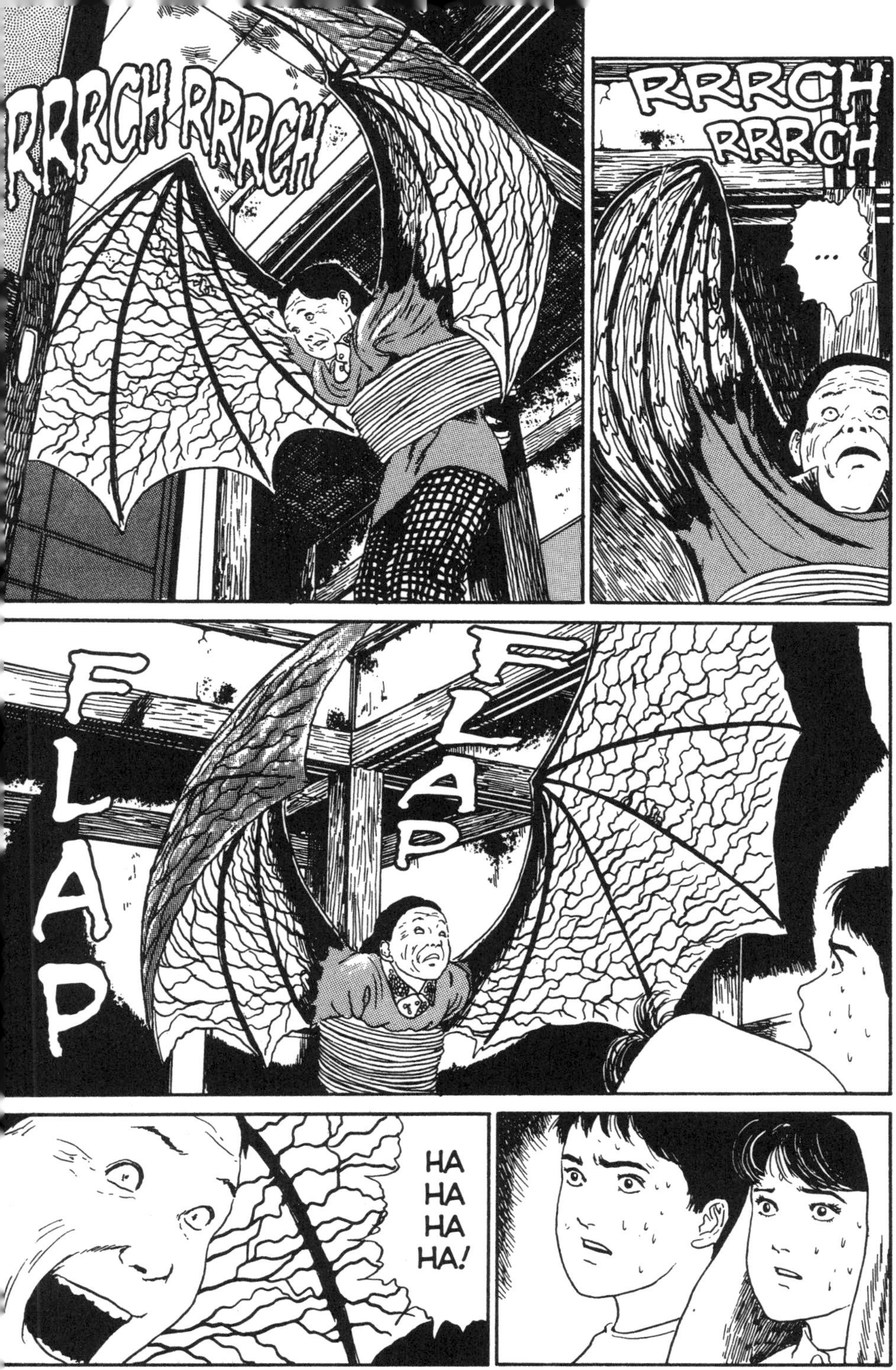
RRRCH
RRRCH
...
RRRCH RRRCH
FLAP
FLAP
HA
HA
HA
HA!

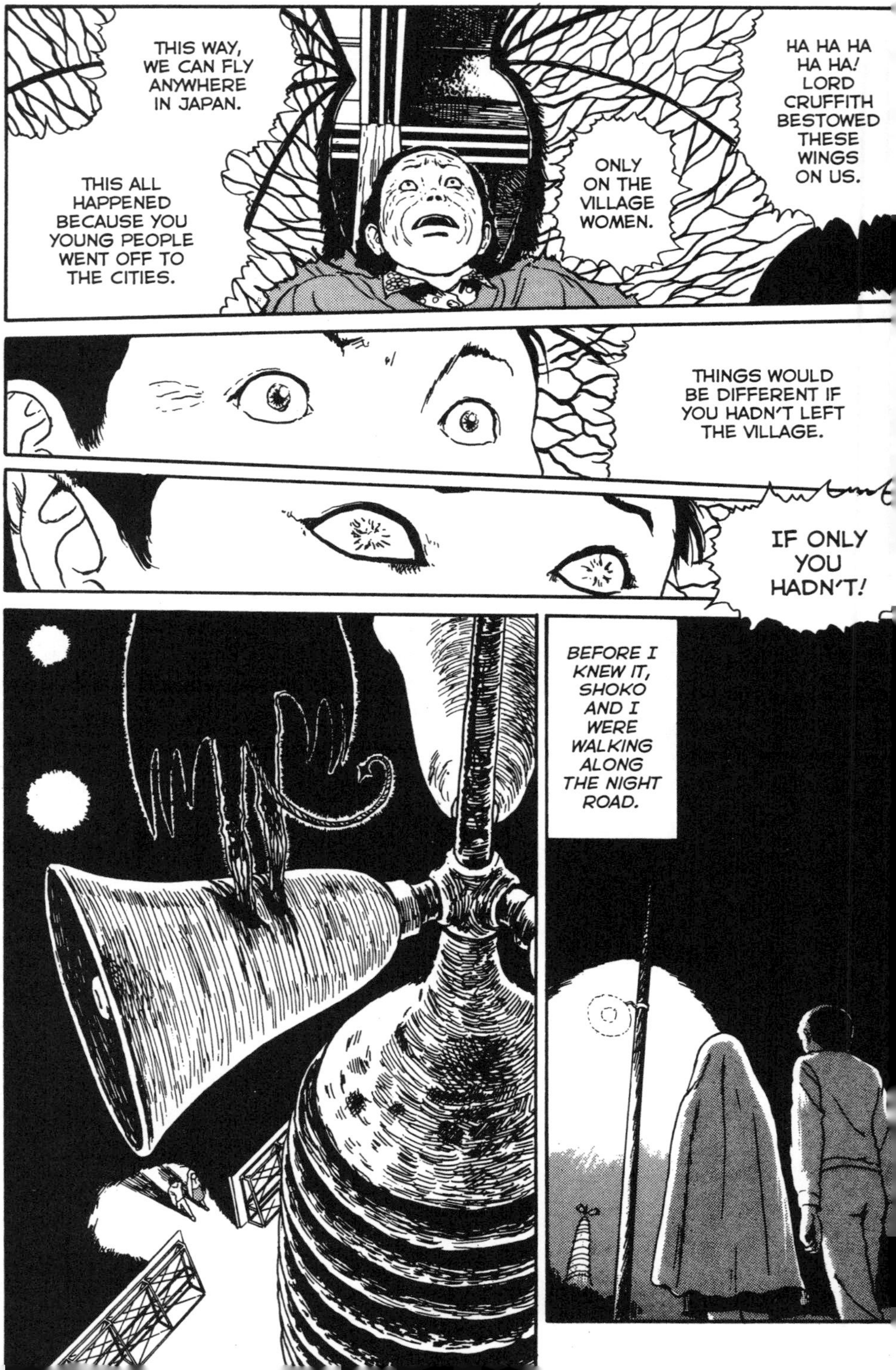
HA HA HA HA HA! LORD CRUFFITH BESTOWED THESE WINGS ON US.
ONLY ON THE VILLAGE WOMEN.
THIS WAY, WE CAN FLY ANYWHERE IN JAPAN.
THIS ALL HAPPENED BECAUSE YOU YOUNG PEOPLE WENT OFF TO THE CITIES.
THINGS WOULD BE DIFFERENT IF YOU HADN'T LEFT THE VILLAGE.
IF ONLY YOU HADN'T!
BEFORE I KNEW IT, SHOKO AND I WERE WALKING ALONG THE NIGHT ROAD.

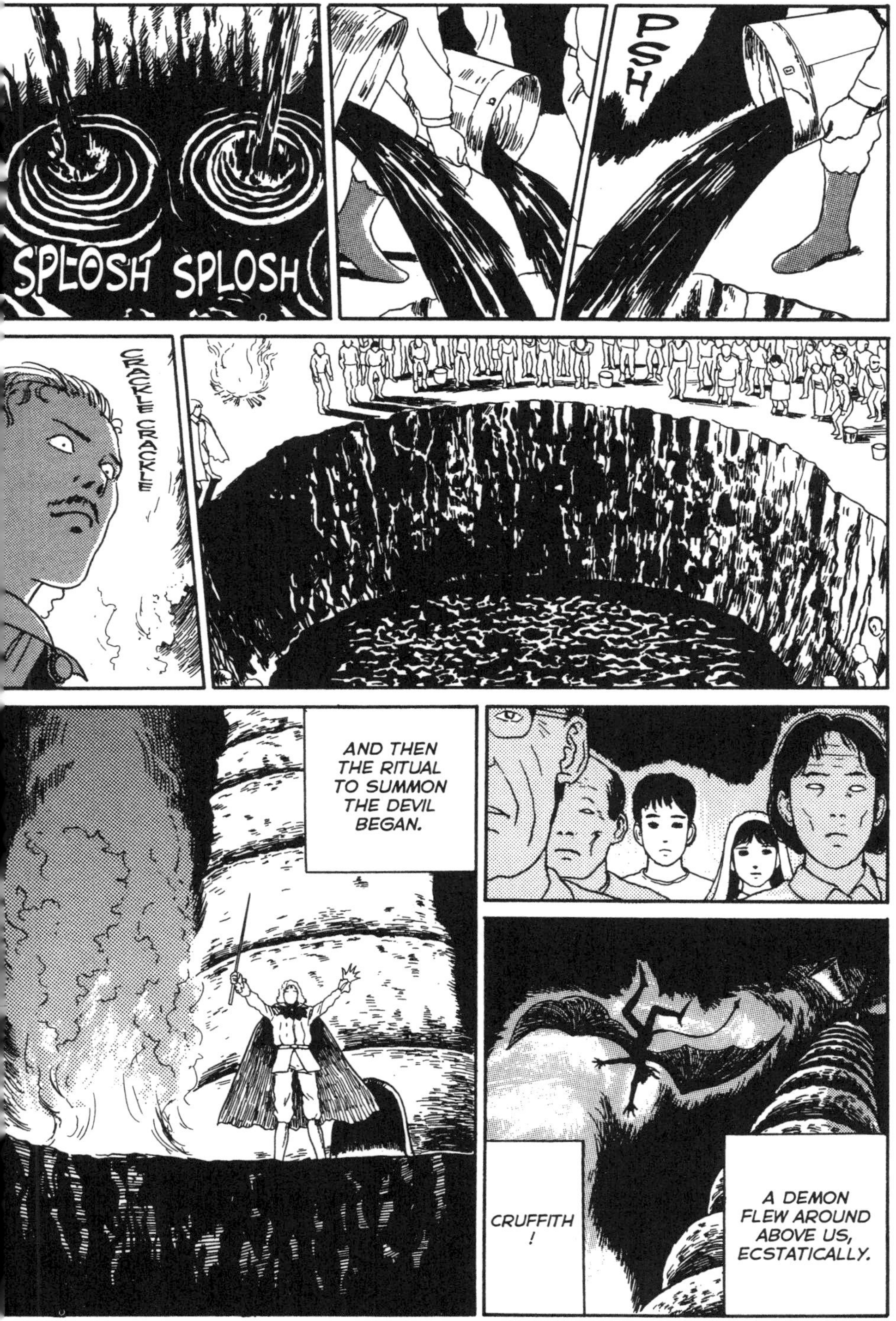
PSH
SPLOSH SPLOSH
CRACKLE CRACKLE
A DEMON FLEW AROUND ABOVE US, ECSTATICALLY.
CRUFFITH !
AND THEN THE RITUAL TO SUMMON THE DEVIL BEGAN.

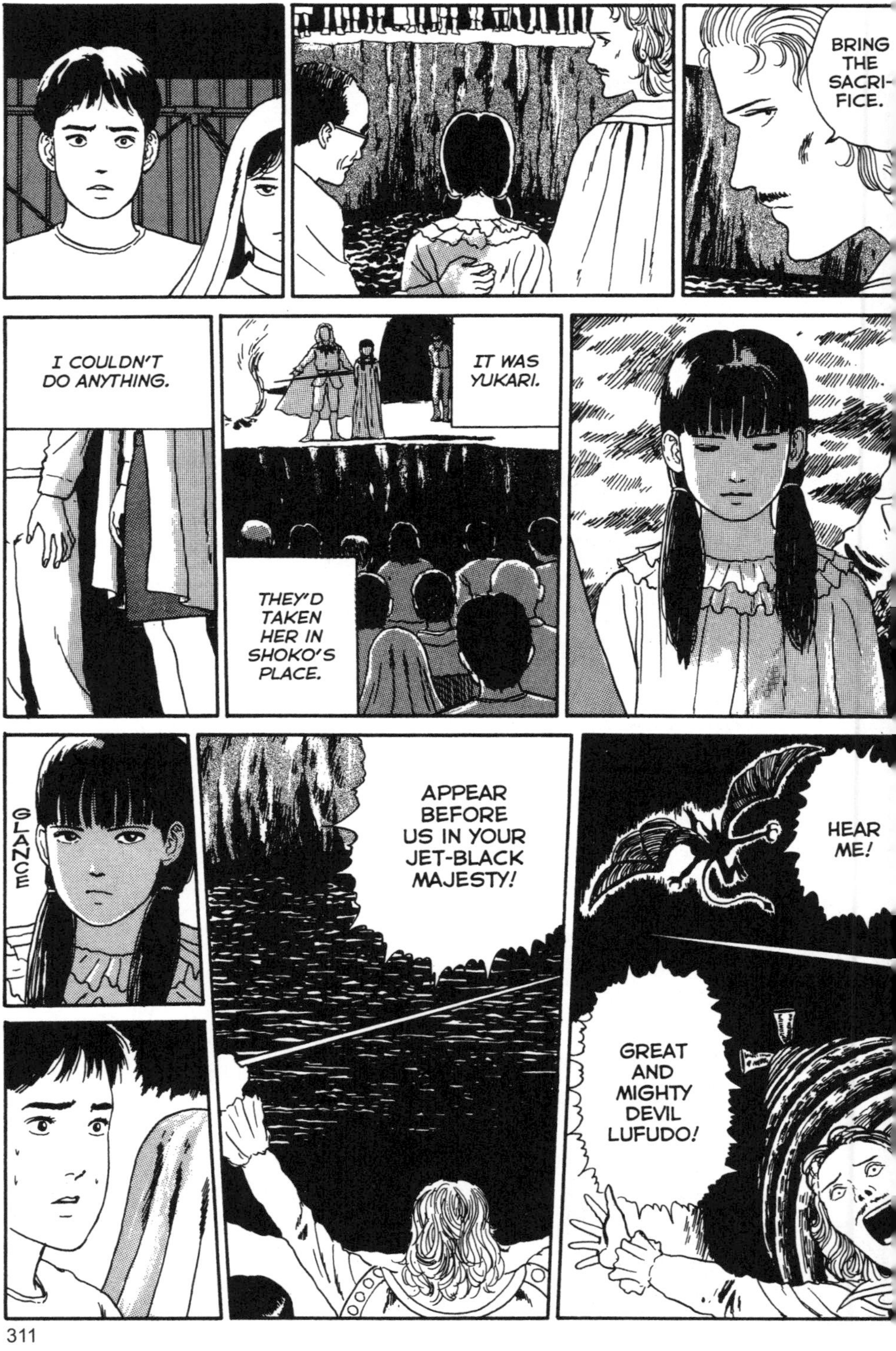
BRING THE SACRIFICE.
IT WAS YUKARI.
THEY'D TAKEN HER IN SHOKO'S PLACE.
I COULDN'T DO ANYTHING.
HEAR ME!
GREAT AND MIGHTY DEVIL LUFUDO!
APPEAR BEFORE US IN YOUR JET-BLACK MAJESTY!
GLANCE

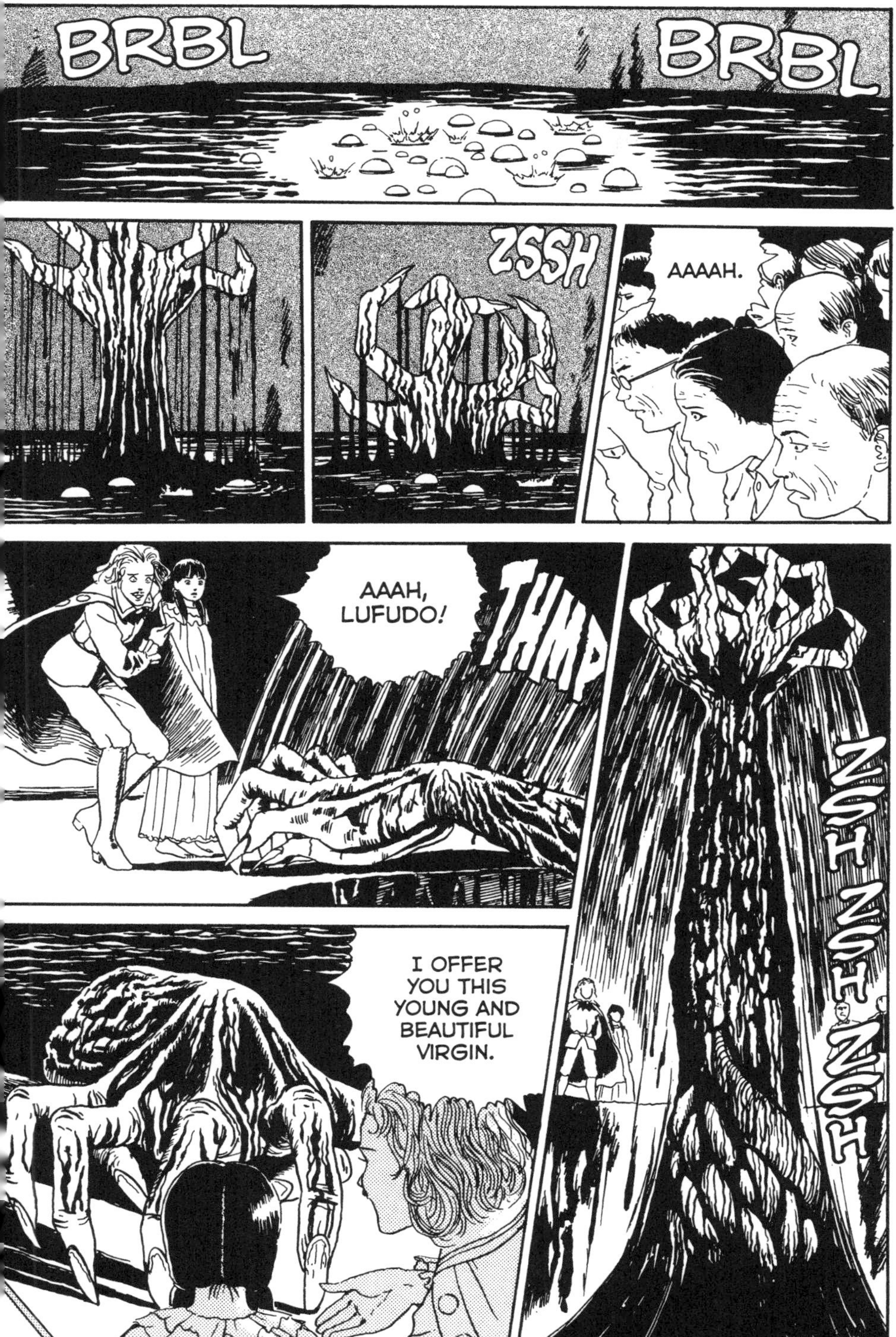
BRBL BRBL
AAAAH.
ZSSH
ZSH ZSH ZSH
THMP
AAAH, LUFUDO!
I OFFER YOU THIS YOUNG AND BEAUTIFUL VIRGIN.

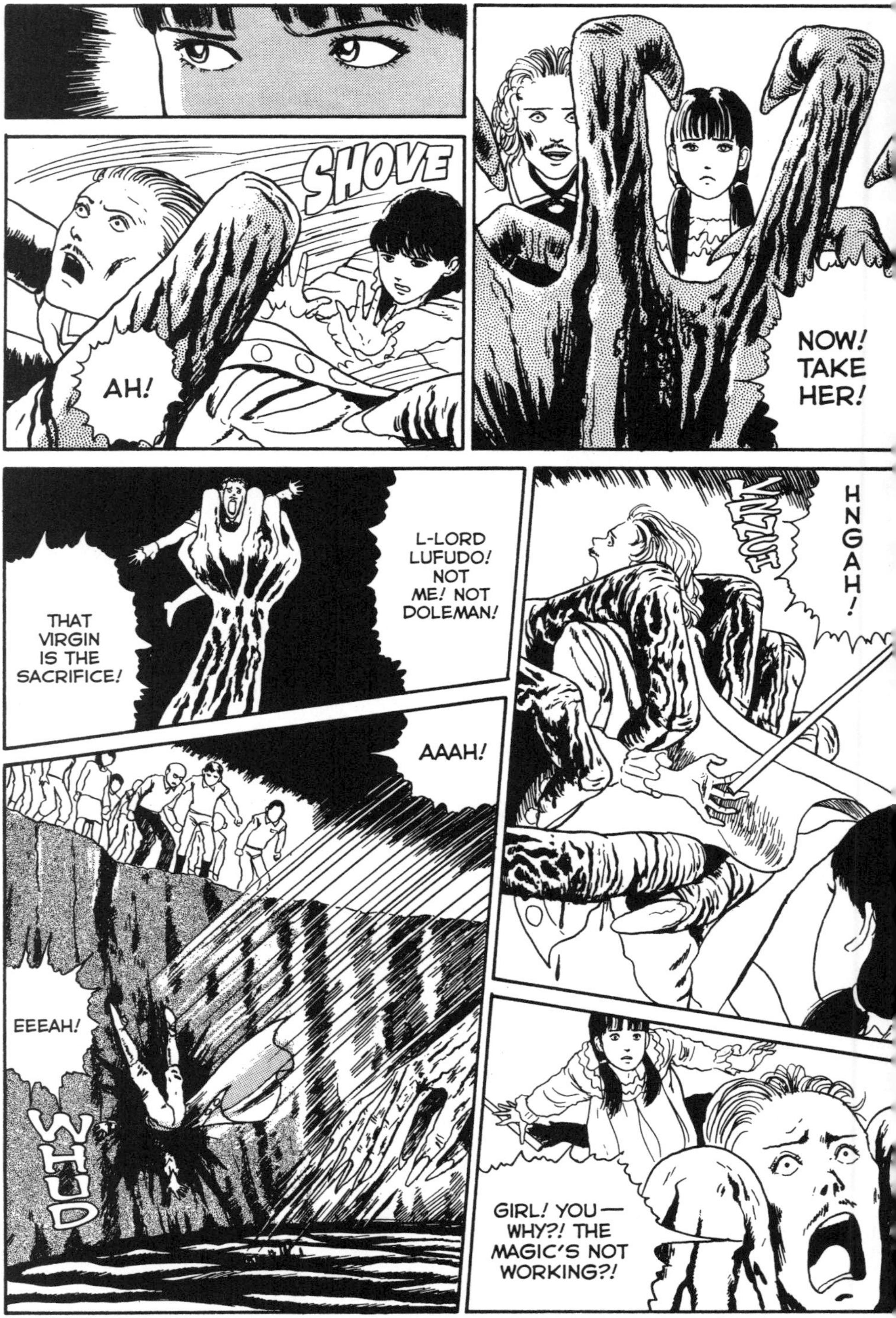
NOW! TAKE HER!
SHOVE
AH!
HNGAH!
L-LORD LUFUDO! NOT ME! NOT DOLEMAN!
THAT VIRGIN IS THE SACRIFICE!
AAAH!
EEEAH!
WHUD
GIRL! YOU— WHY?! THE MAGIC'S NOT WORKING?!

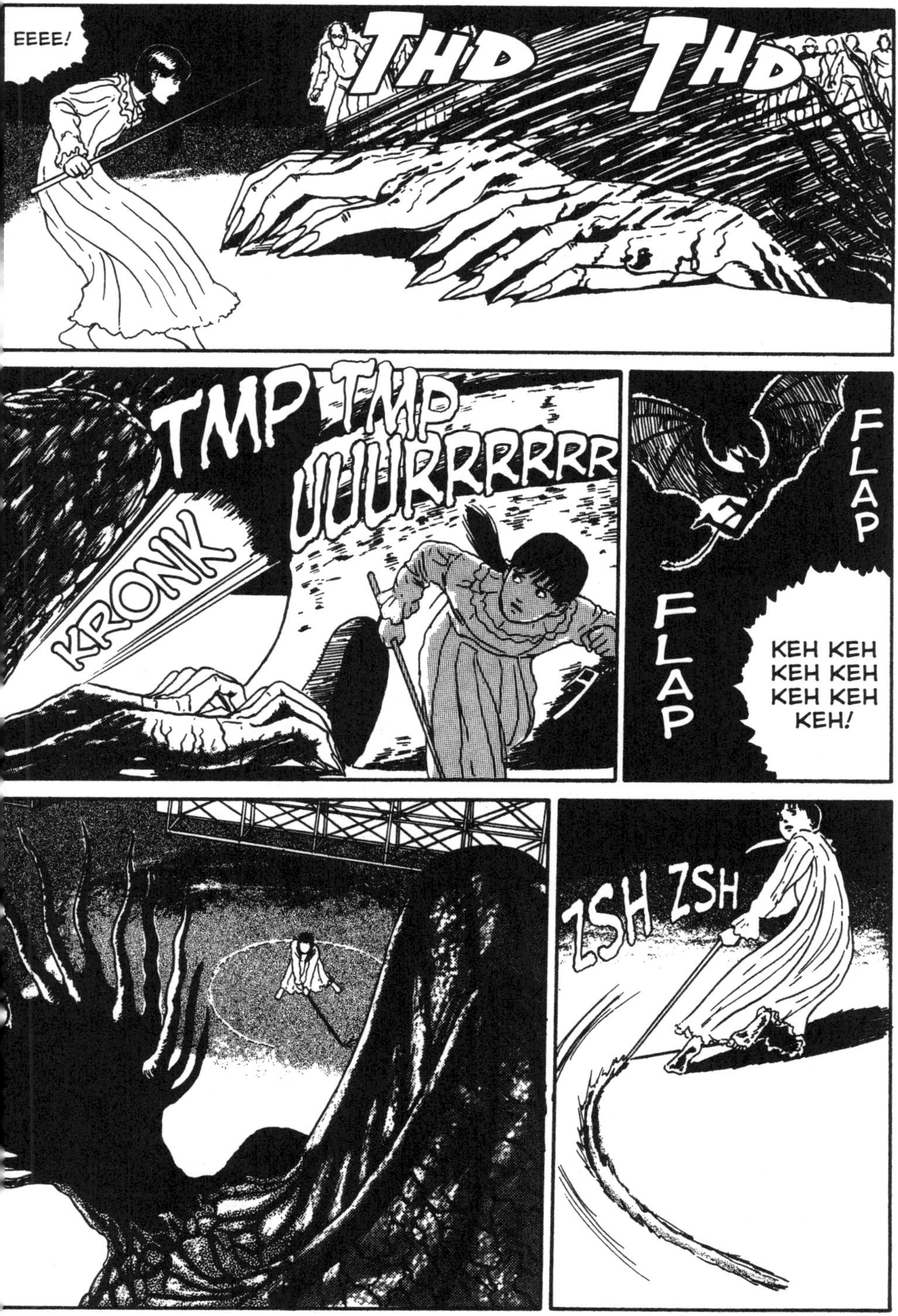
THD THD
EEEE!
FLAP
FLAP
KEH KEH KEH KEH KEH KEH KEH!
TMP TMP
UUURRRRRR
KRONK
ZSH ZSH

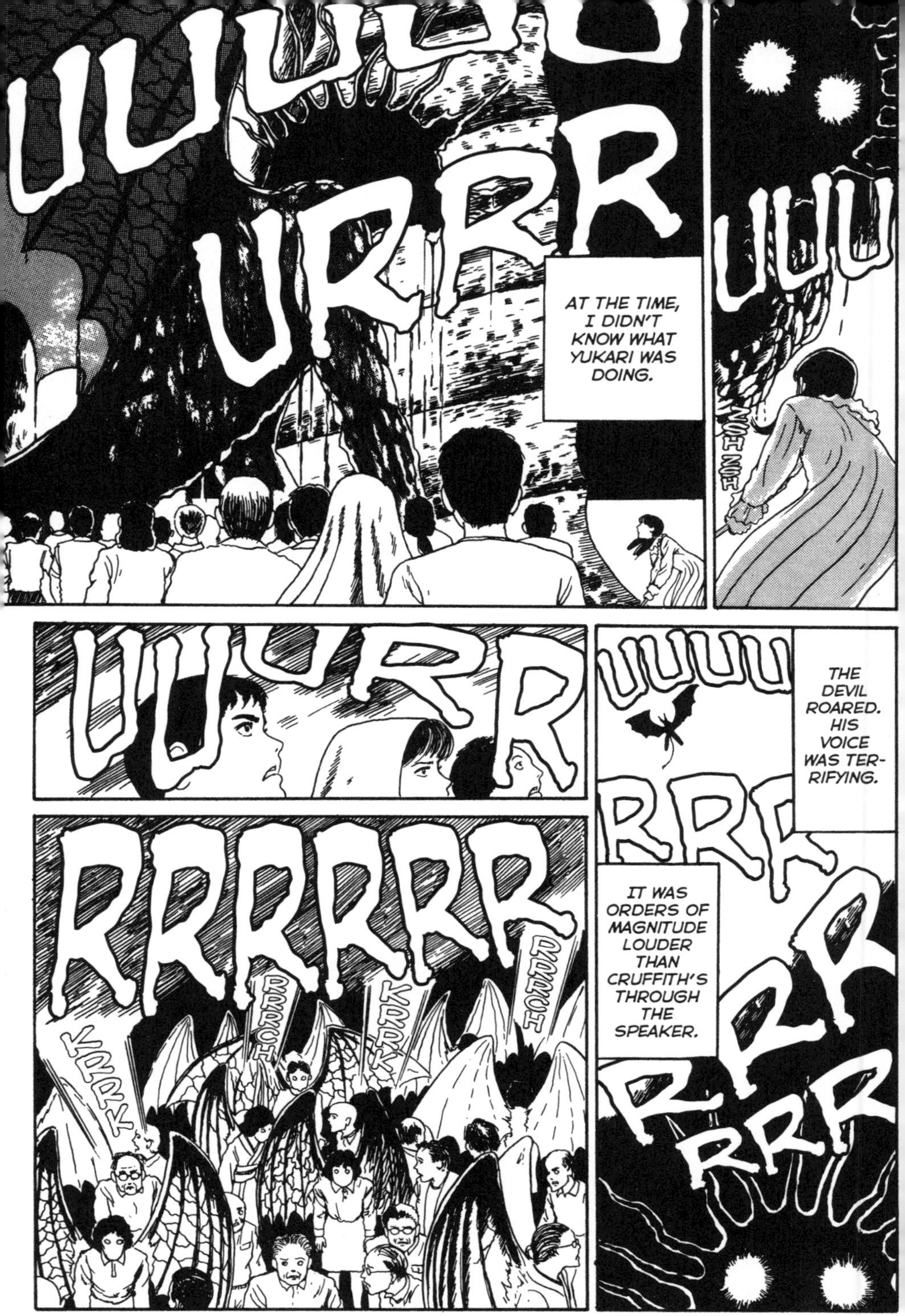
UUU
ZSH ZSH
UUUUU
URRR
AT THE TIME, I DIDN'T KNOW WHAT YUKARI WAS DOING.
UUUU
THE DEVIL ROARED. HIS VOICE WAS TERRIFYING.
RRRRRR
IT WAS ORDERS OF MAGNITUDE LOUDER THAN CRUFFITH'S THROUGH THE SPEAKER.
RRR
RRR
UURRR
RRRRRR
KRRK
RRRCH
KRRK
RRRCH

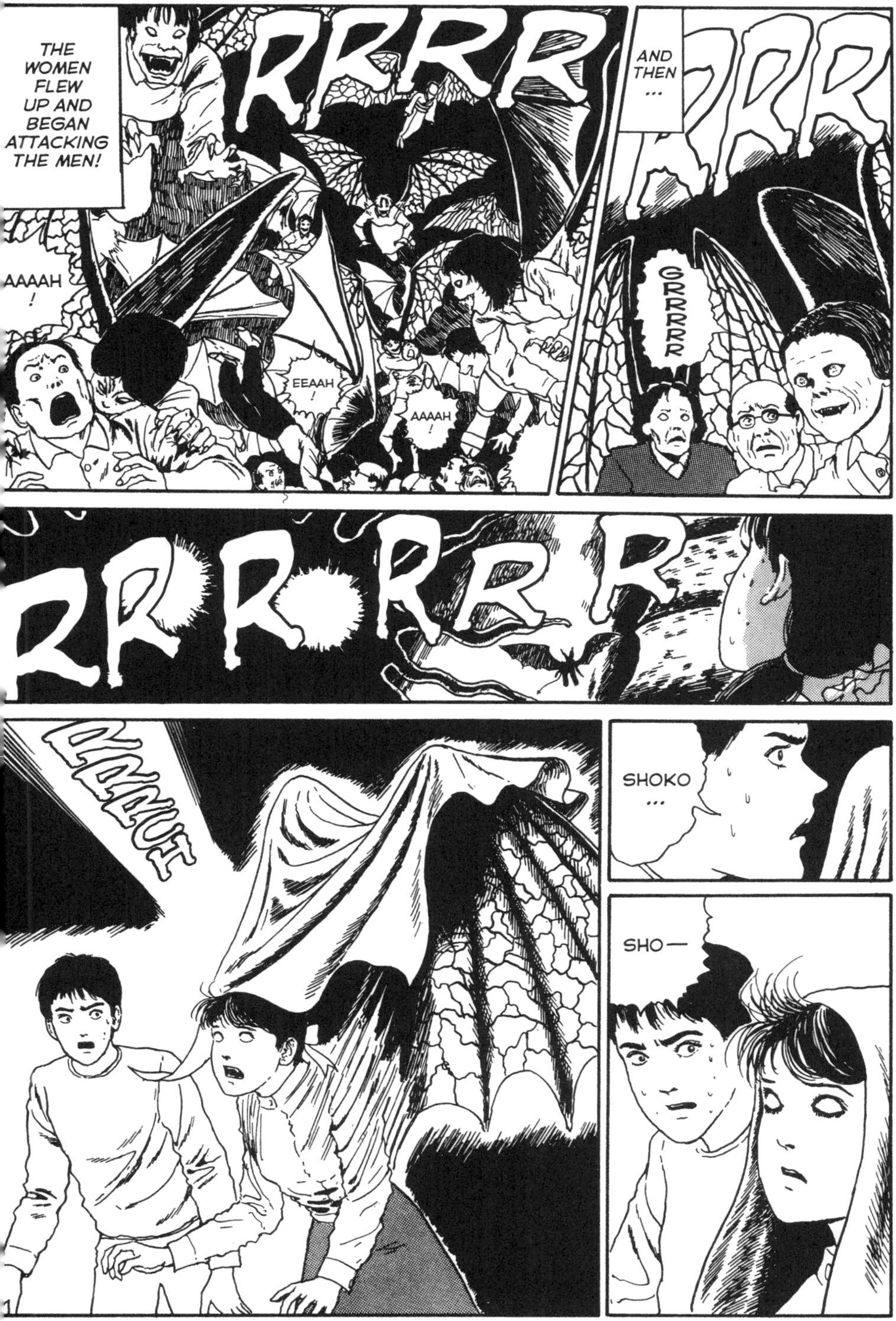
AND THEN ...
RRRR
GRRRRR
THE WOMEN FLEW UP AND BEGAN ATTACKING THE MEN!
RRRR
AAAAH!
EEAAH!
AAAAH!
RRRRRR
SHOKO ...
SHO—

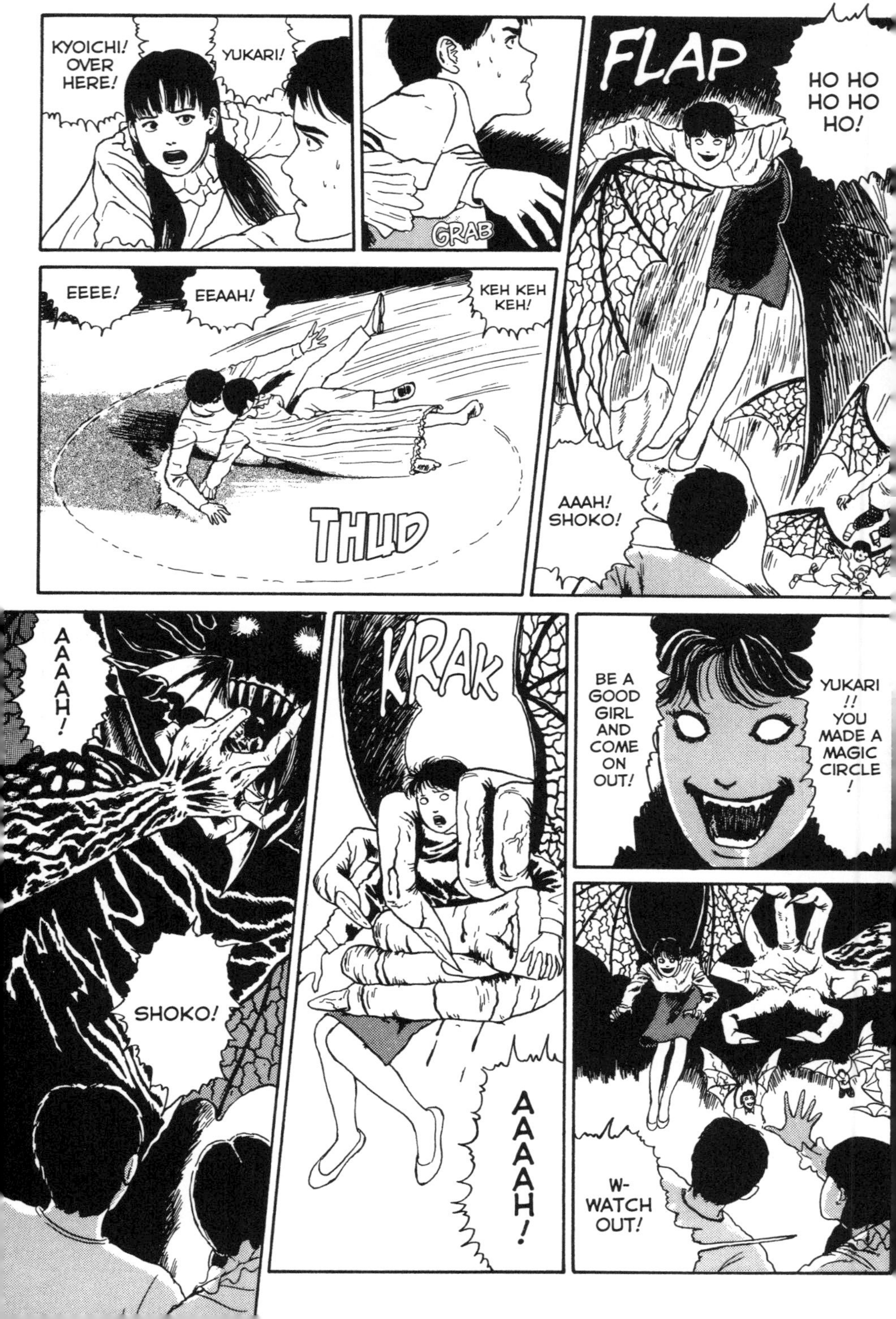

FLAP
HO HO HO HO HO!
AAAH! SHOKO!
GRAB
YUKARI!
KYOICHI! OVER HERE!
KEH KEH KEH!
EEAAH!
EEEE!
THUD
YUKARI!! YOU MADE A MAGIC CIRCLE!
BE A GOOD GIRL AND COME ON OUT!
W-WATCH OUT!
KRAK
AAAAH!
AAAAH!
SHOKO!

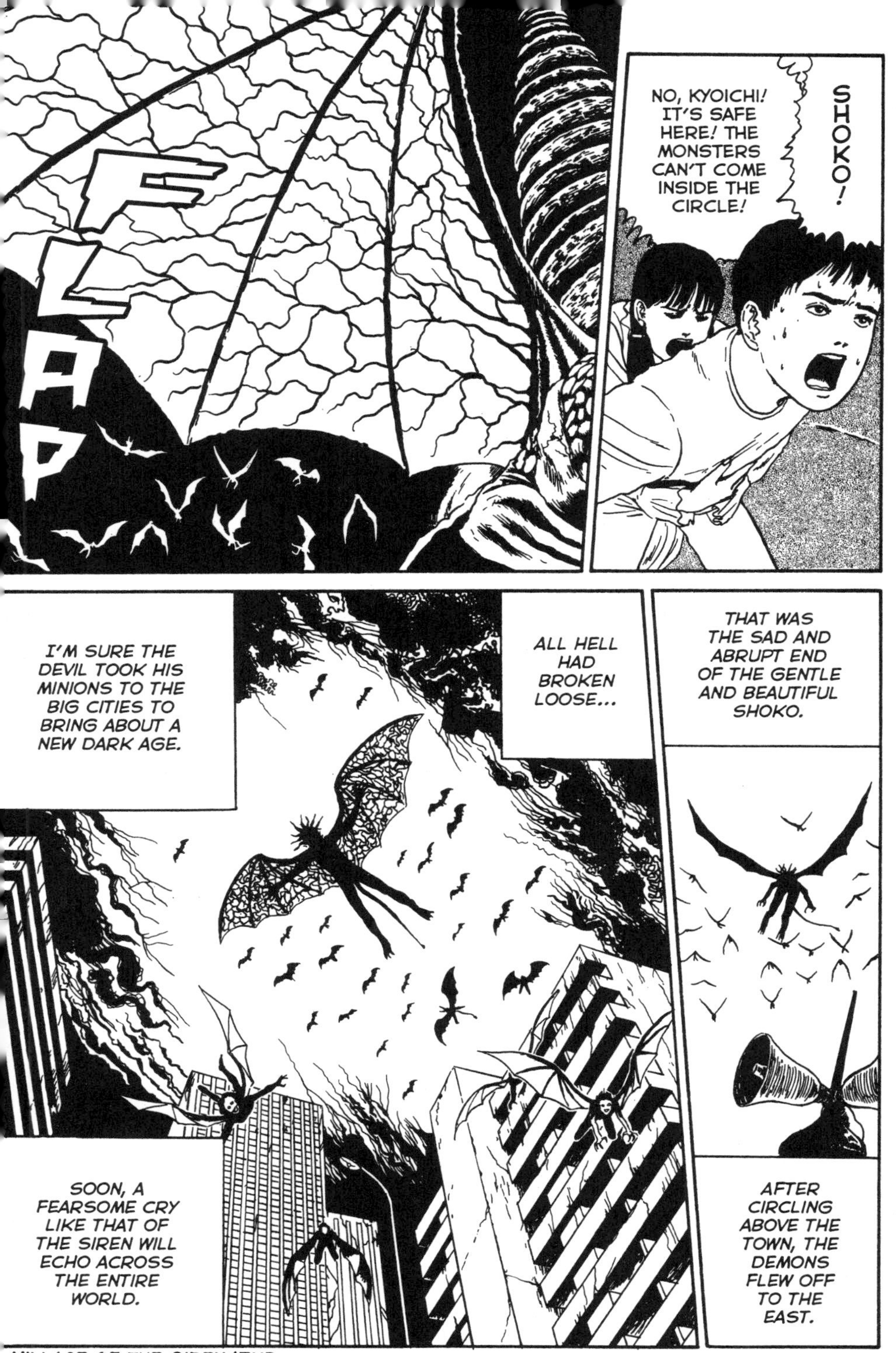
SHOKO!
NO, KYOICHI! IT'S SAFE HERE! THE MONSTERS CAN'T COME INSIDE THE CIRCLE!
FLAP
THAT WAS THE SAD AND ABRUPT END OF THE GENTLE AND BEAUTIFUL SHOKO.
AFTER CIRCLING ABOVE THE TOWN, THE DEMONS FLEW OFF TO THE EAST.
ALL HELL HAD BROKEN LOOSE...
I'M SURE THE DEVIL TOOK HIS MINIONS TO THE BIG CITIES TO BRING ABOUT A NEW DARK AGE.
SOON, A FEARSOME CRY LIKE THAT OF THE SIREN WILL ECHO ACROSS THE ENTIRE WORLD.

VILLAGE OF THE SIREN/END

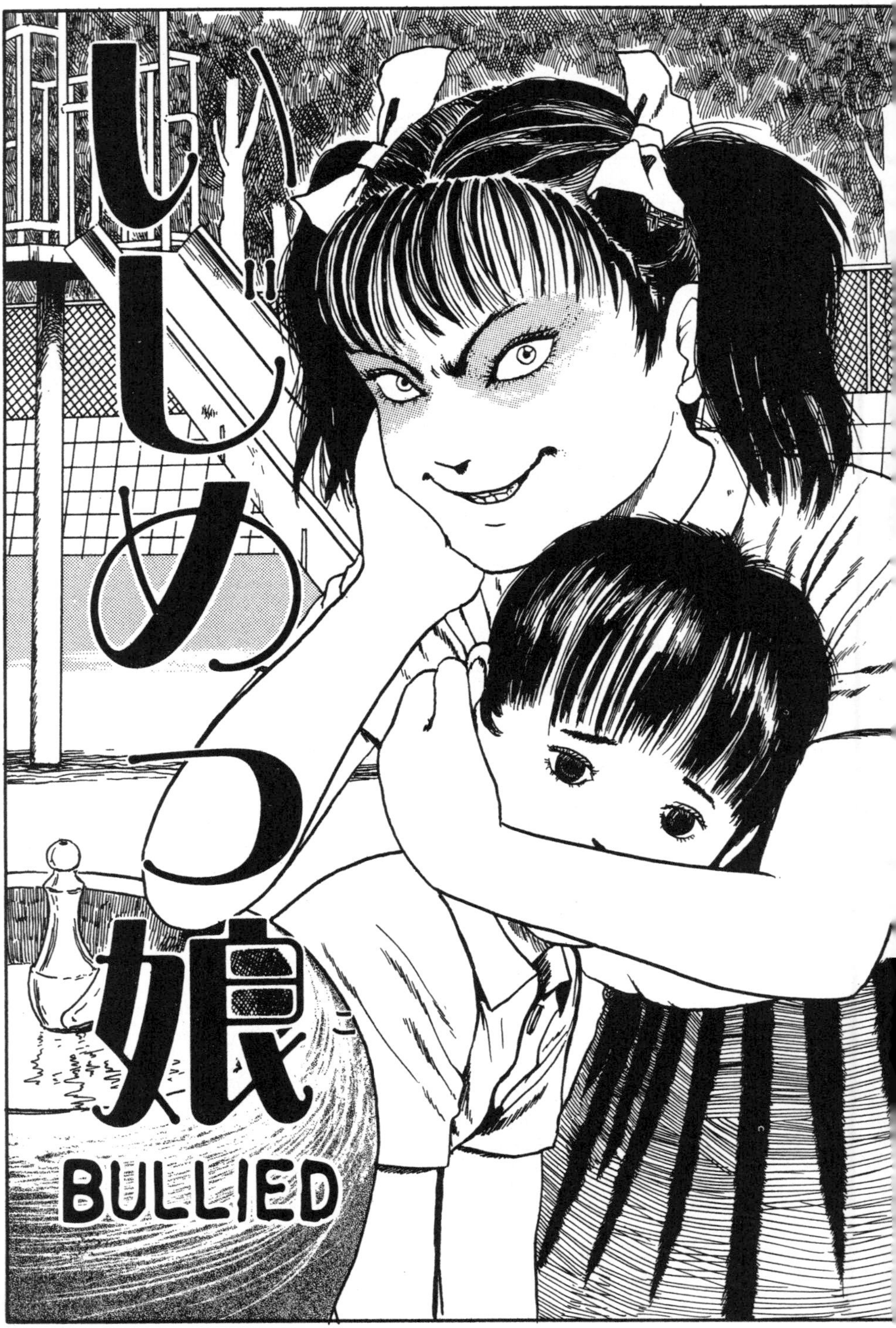
いじめっ娘
BULLIED

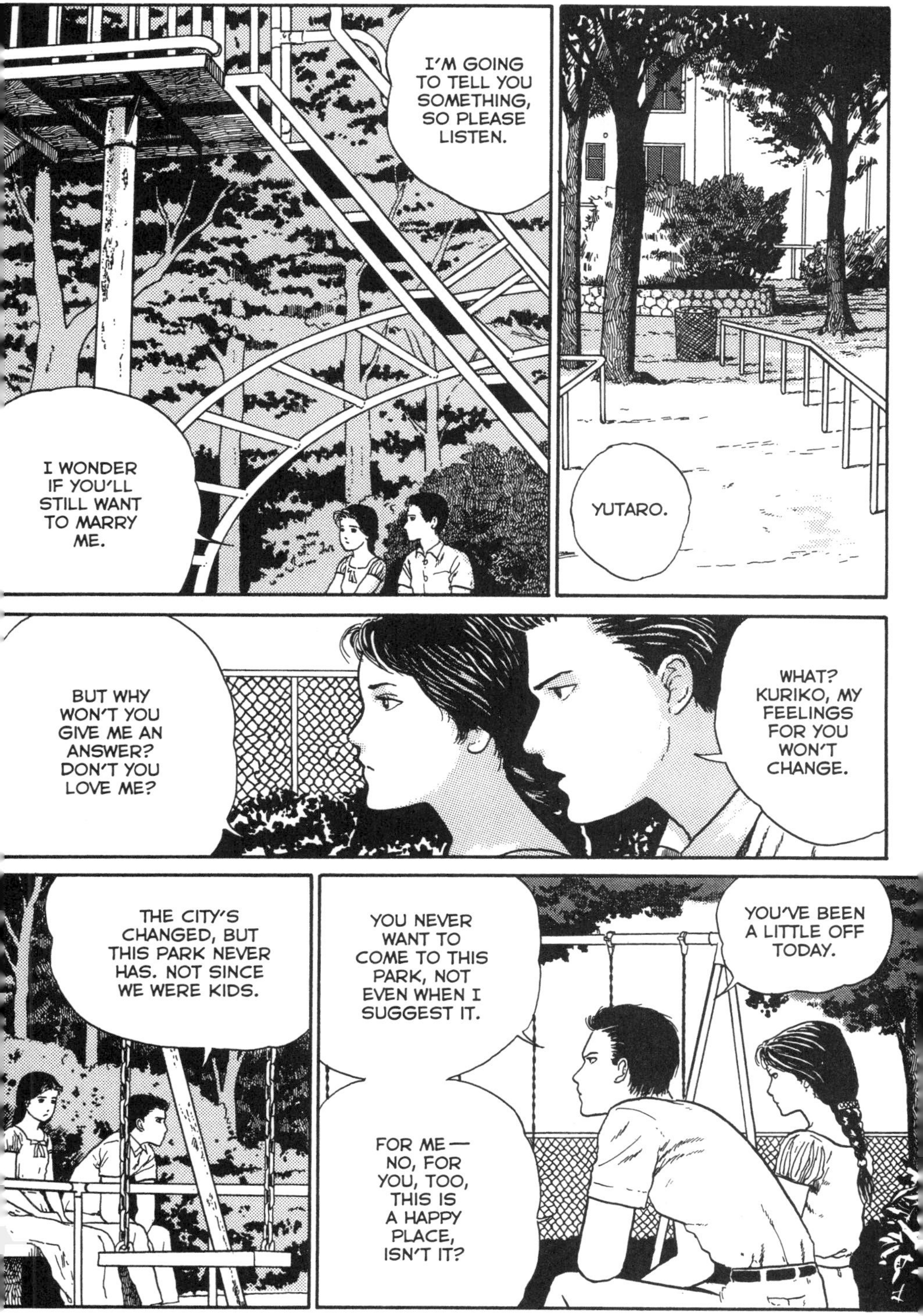
YUTARO.
I'M GOING TO TELL YOU SOMETHING, SO PLEASE LISTEN.
I WONDER IF YOU'LL STILL WANT TO MARRY ME.
WHAT? KURIKO, MY FEELINGS FOR YOU WON'T CHANGE.
BUT WHY WON'T YOU GIVE ME AN ANSWER? DON'T YOU LOVE ME?
YOU'VE BEEN A LITTLE OFF TODAY.
YOU NEVER WANT TO COME TO THIS PARK, NOT EVEN WHEN I SUGGEST IT.
FOR ME— NO, FOR YOU, TOO, THIS IS A HAPPY PLACE, ISN'T IT?
THE CITY'S CHANGED, BUT THIS PARK NEVER HAS. NOT SINCE WE WERE KIDS.

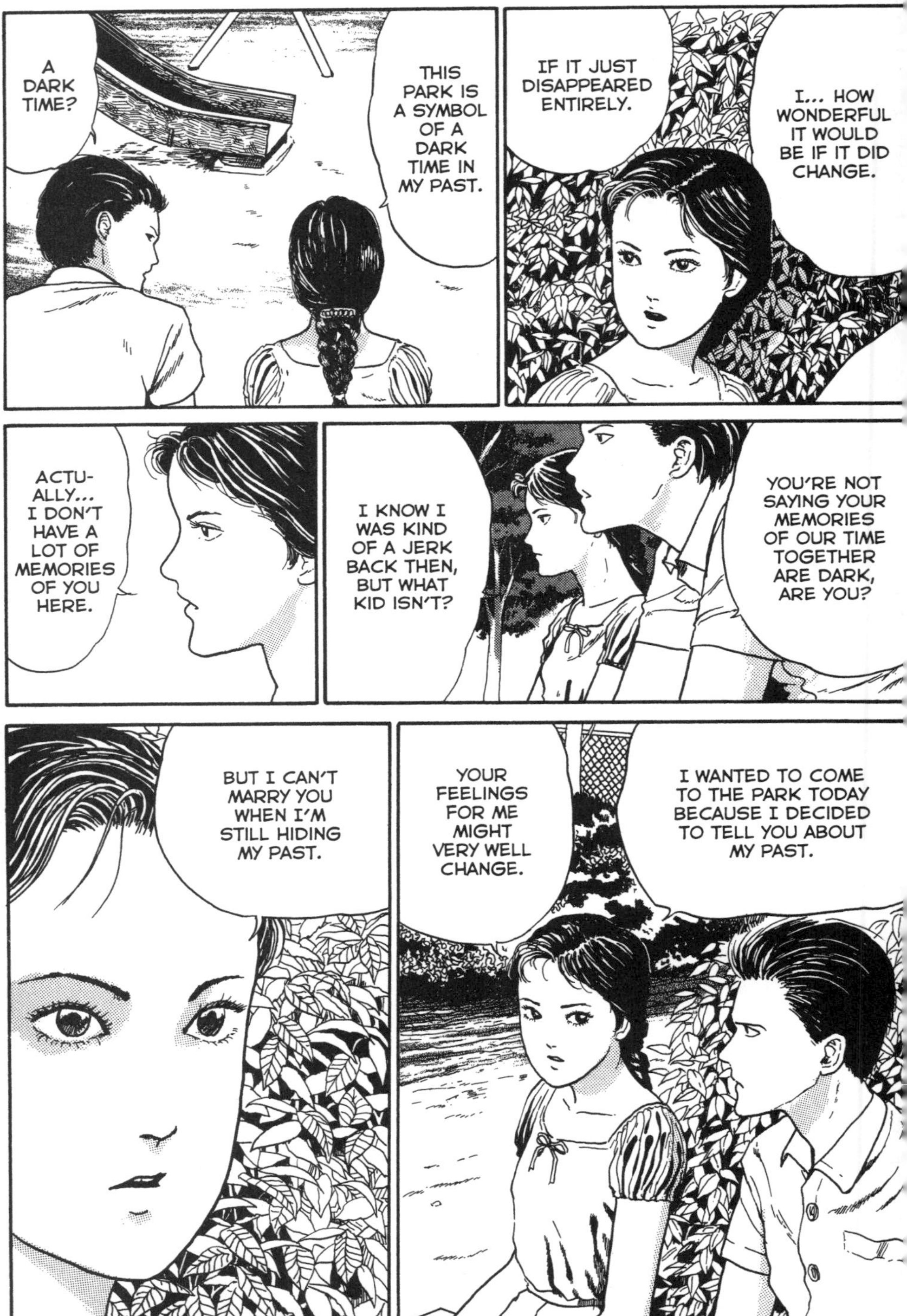
I... HOW WONDERFUL IT WOULD BE IF IT DID CHANGE.
IF IT JUST DISAPPEARED ENTIRELY.
THIS PARK IS A SYMBOL OF A DARK TIME IN MY PAST.
A DARK TIME?
YOU'RE NOT SAYING YOUR MEMORIES OF OUR TIME TOGETHER ARE DARK, ARE YOU?
I KNOW I WAS KIND OF A JERK BACK THEN, BUT WHAT KID ISN'T?
ACTU- ALLY... I DON'T HAVE A LOT OF MEMORIES OF YOU HERE.
I WANTED TO COME TO THE PARK TODAY BECAUSE I DECIDED TO TELL YOU ABOUT MY PAST.
YOUR FEELINGS FOR ME MIGHT VERY WELL CHANGE.
BUT I CAN'T MARRY YOU WHEN I'M STILL HIDING MY PAST.

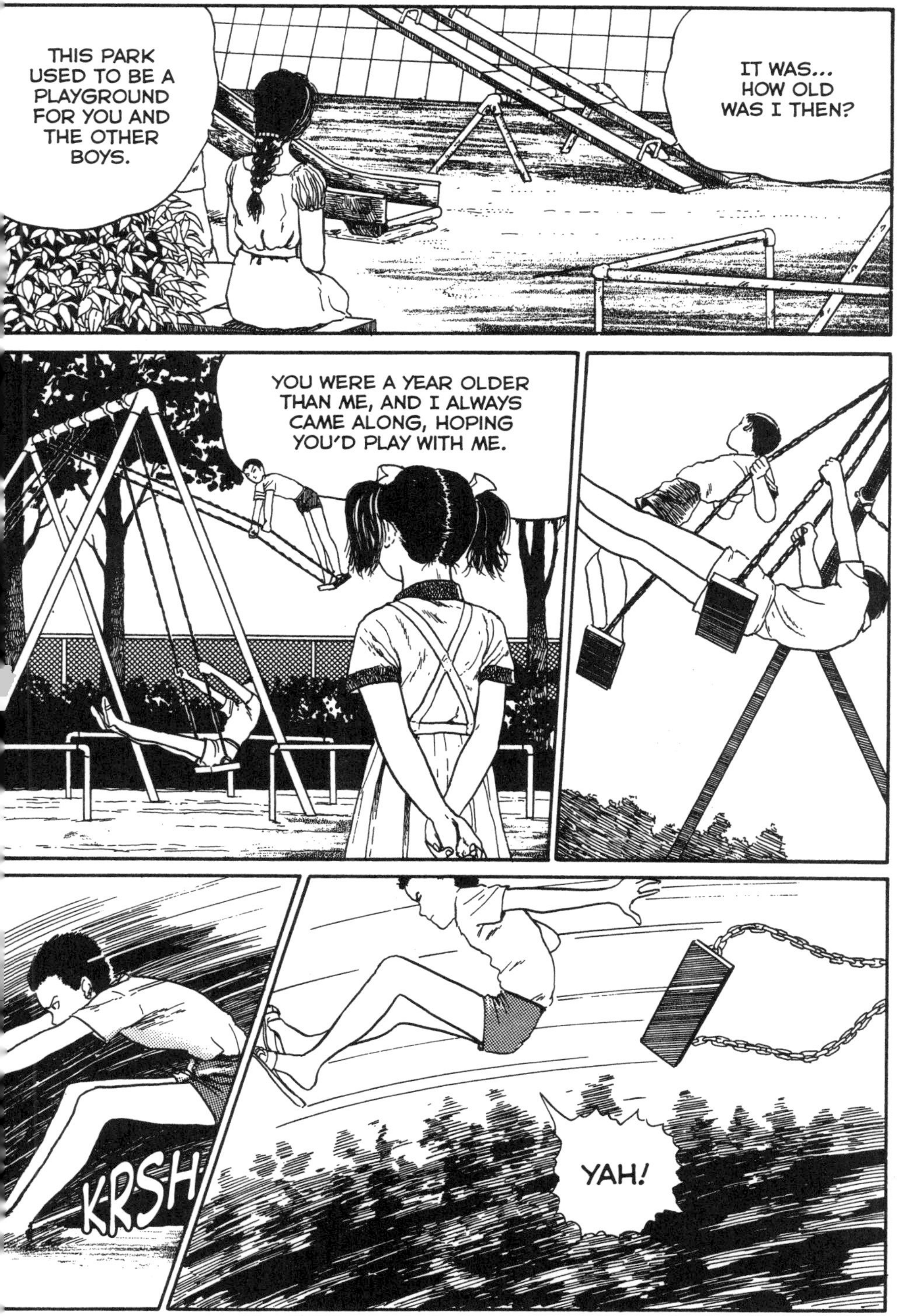
IT WAS... HOW OLD WAS I THEN?
THIS PARK USED TO BE A PLAYGROUND FOR YOU AND THE OTHER BOYS.
YOU WERE A YEAR OLDER THAN ME, AND I ALWAYS CAME ALONG, HOPING YOU'D PLAY WITH ME.
YAH!
KRSH

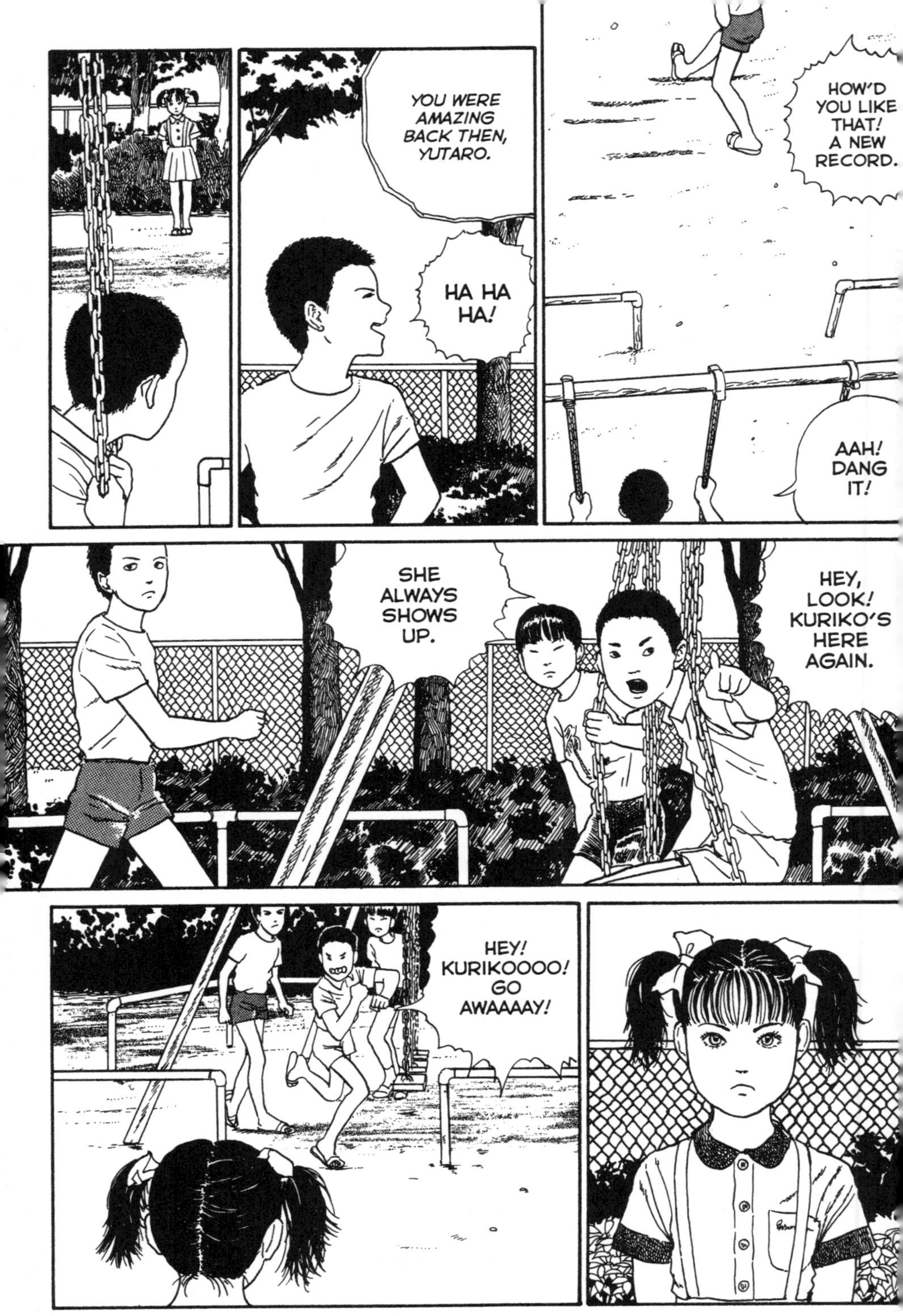
HOW'D YOU LIKE THAT! A NEW RECORD.
AAH! DANG IT!
YOU WERE AMAZING BACK THEN, YUTARO.
HA HA HA!
HEY, LOOK! KURIKO'S HERE AGAIN.
SHE ALWAYS SHOWS UP.
HEY! KURIKOOOO! GO AWAAAAY!

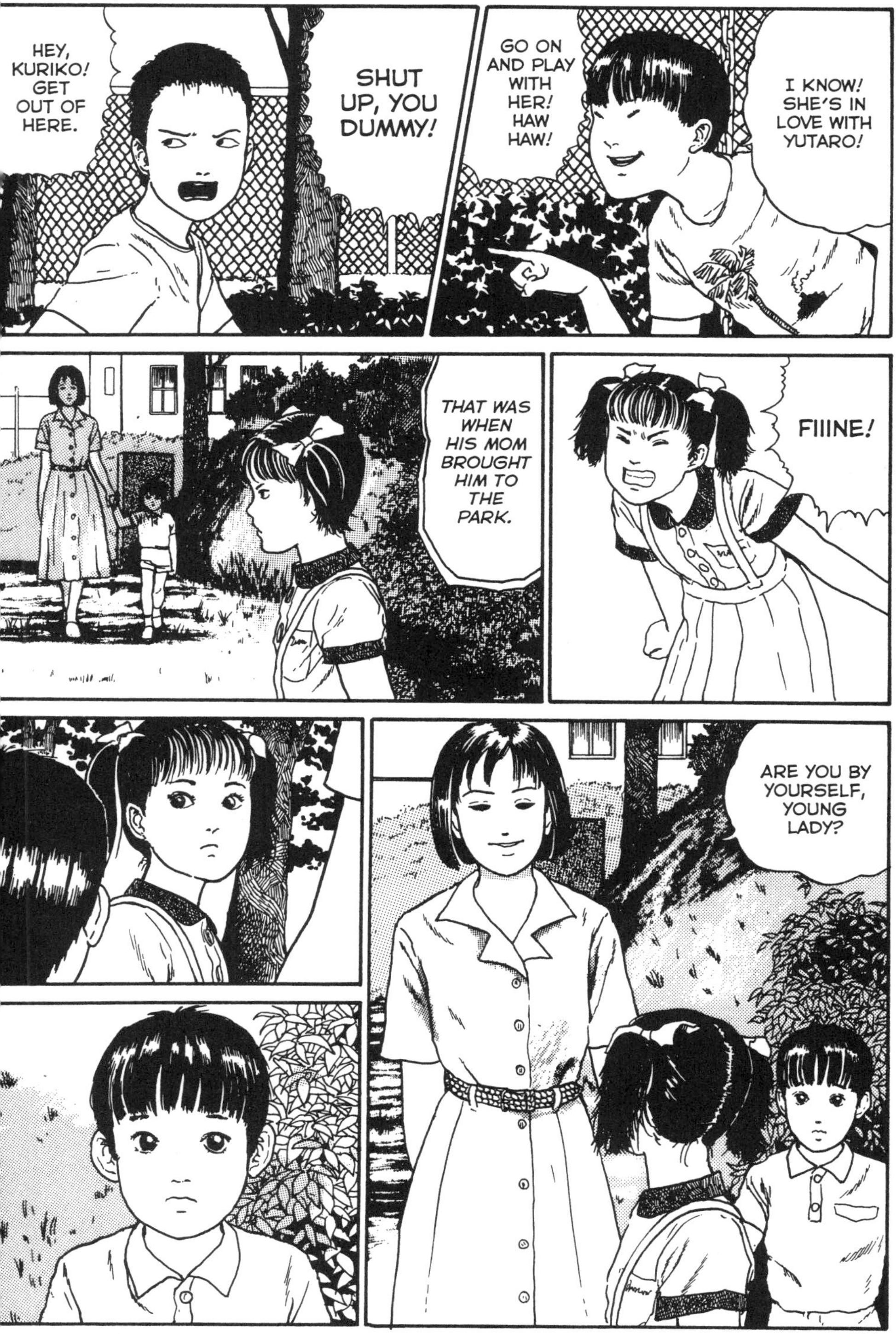
I KNOW! SHE'S IN LOVE WITH YUTARO!
GO ON AND PLAY WITH HER! HAW HAW!
SHUT UP, YOU DUMMY!
HEY, KURIKO! GET OUT OF HERE.
FIIINE!
THAT WAS WHEN HIS MOM BROUGHT HIM TO THE PARK.
ARE YOU BY YOURSELF, YOUNG LADY?

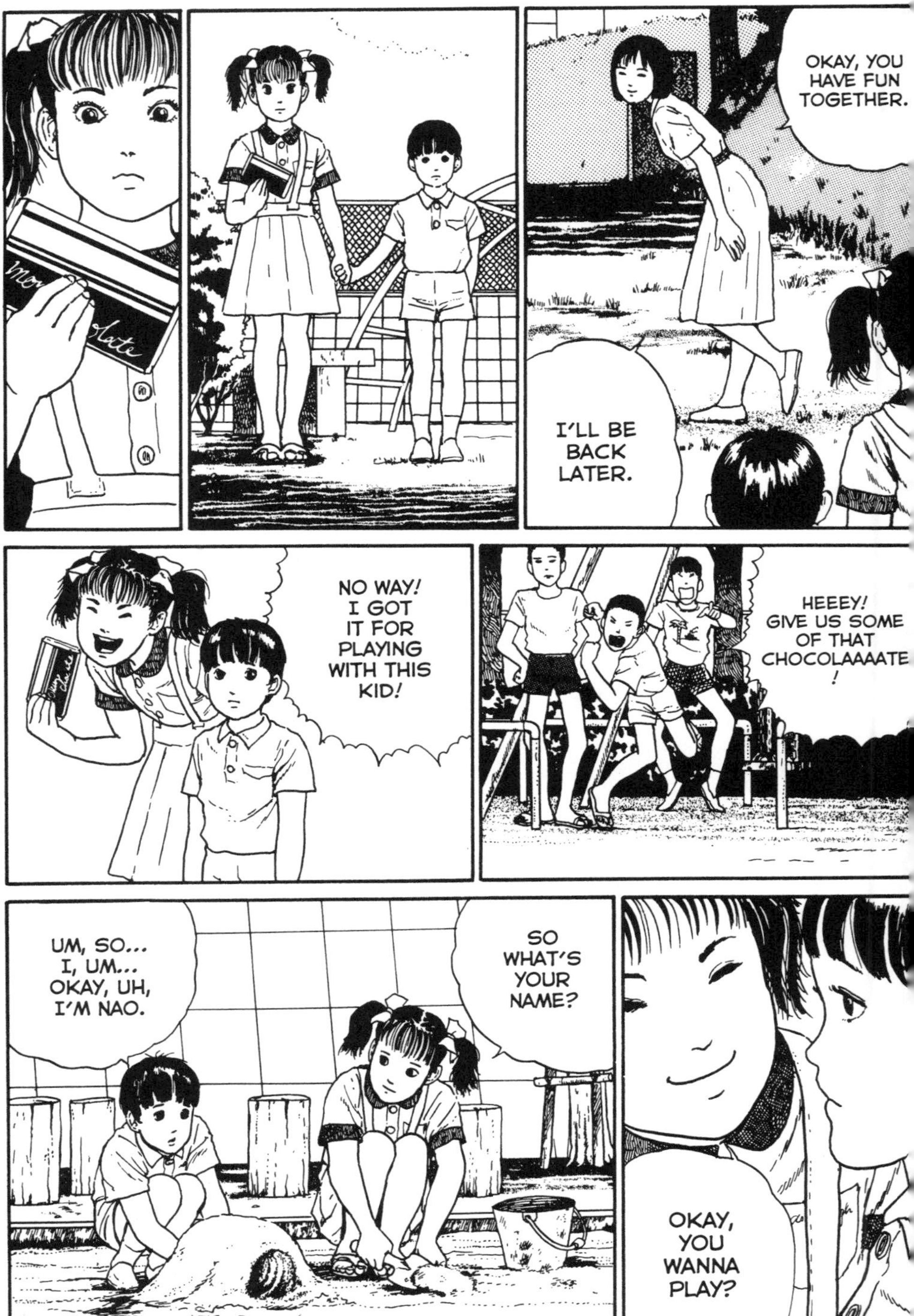
OKAY, YOU HAVE FUN TOGETHER.
I'LL BE BACK LATER.
HEEEY! GIVE US SOME OF THAT CHOCOLAAAATE!
NO WAY! I GOT IT FOR PLAYING WITH THIS KID!
OKAY, YOU WANNA PLAY?
SO WHAT'S YOUR NAME?
UM, SO... I, UM... OKAY, UH, I'M NAO.

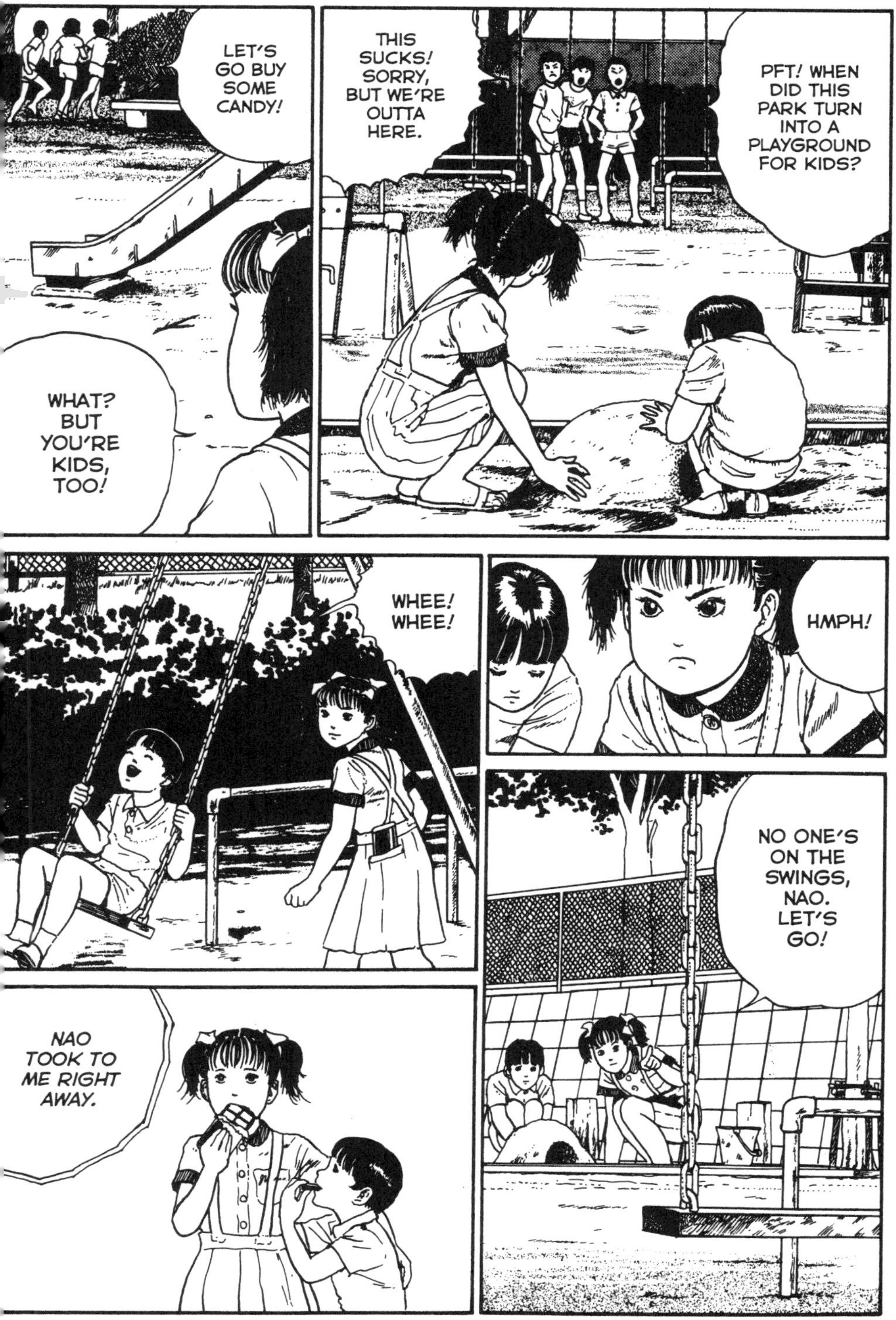
PFT! WHEN DID THIS PARK TURN INTO A PLAYGROUND FOR KIDS?
THIS SUCKS! SORRY, BUT WE'RE OUTTA HERE.
LET'S GO BUY SOME CANDY!
WHAT? BUT YOU'RE KIDS, TOO!
HMPH!
NO ONE'S ON THE SWINGS, NAO. LET'S GO!
WHEE! WHEE!
NAO TOOK TO ME RIGHT AWAY.

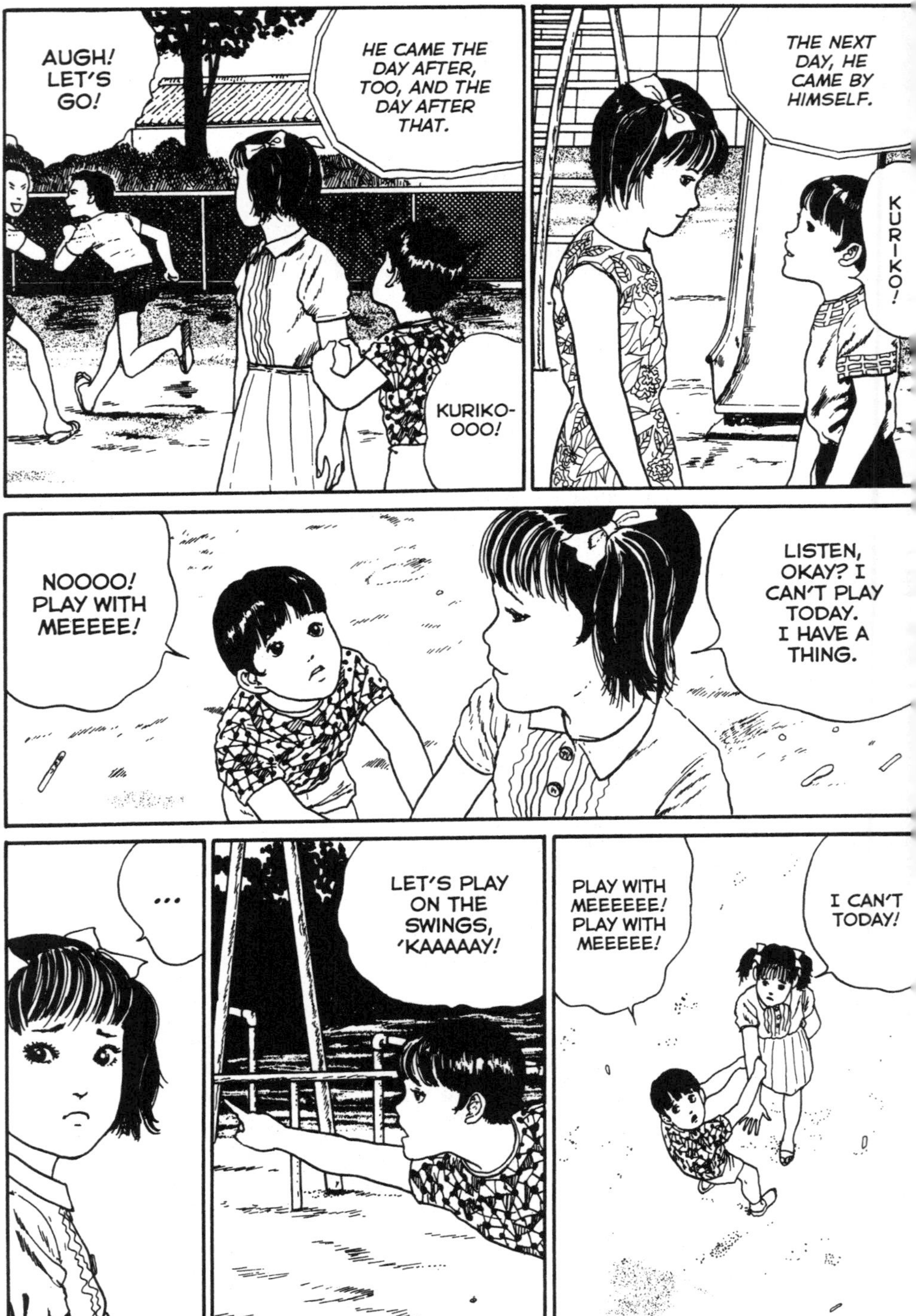
THE NEXT DAY, HE CAME BY HIMSELF.
KURIKO!
HE CAME THE DAY AFTER, TOO, AND THE DAY AFTER THAT.
KURIKO-OOO!
AUGH! LET'S GO!
LISTEN, OKAY? I CAN'T PLAY TODAY. I HAVE A THING.
NOOOO! PLAY WITH MEEEEE!
I CAN'T TODAY!
PLAY WITH MEEEEEE! PLAY WITH MEEEEE!
LET'S PLAY ON THE SWINGS, 'KAAAAAY!
...

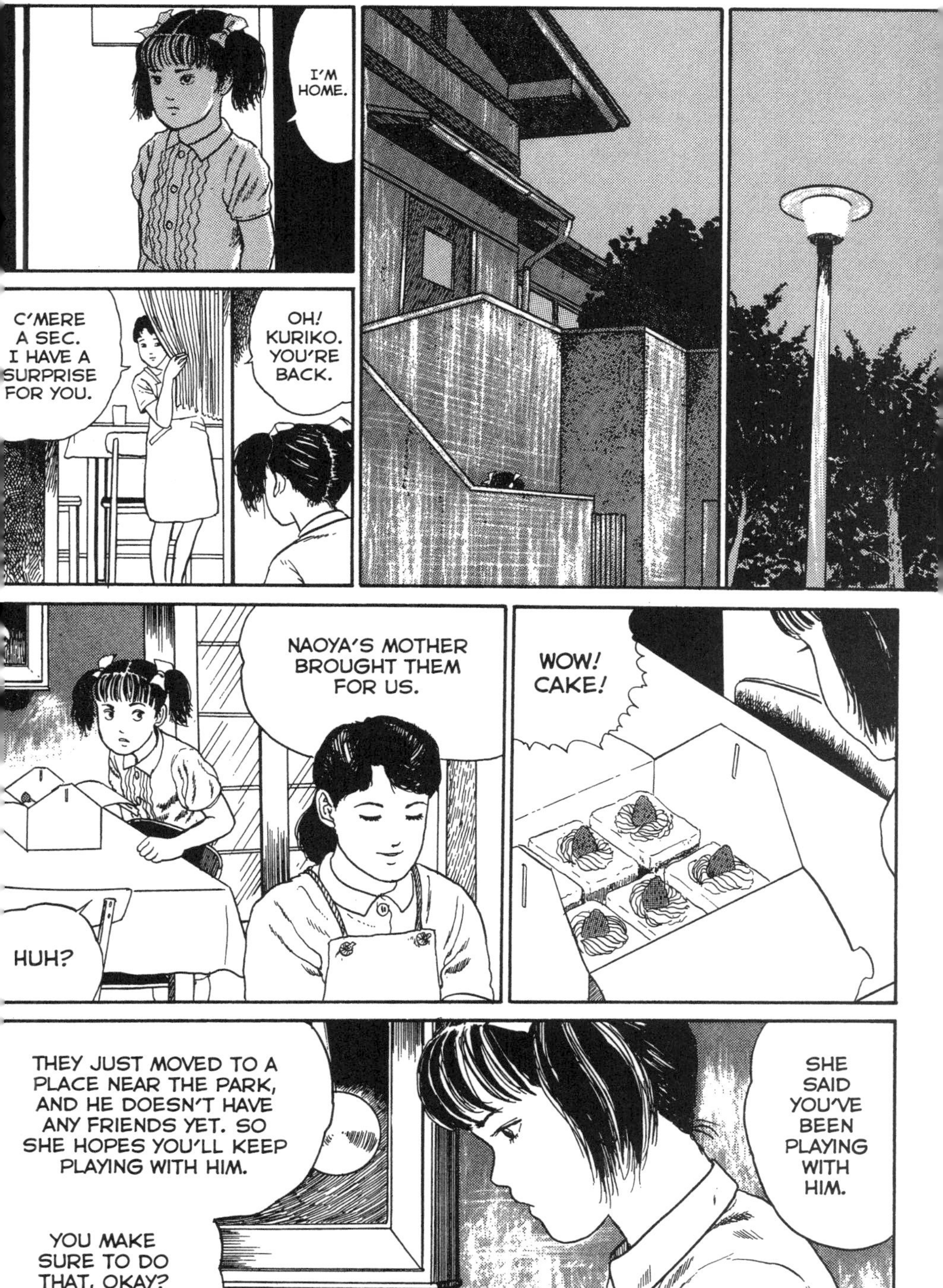
I'M HOME.
OH! KURIKO. YOU'RE BACK.
C'MERE A SEC. I HAVE A SURPRISE FOR YOU.
WOW! CAKE!
NAOYA'S MOTHER BROUGHT THEM FOR US.
HUH?
SHE SAID YOU'VE BEEN PLAYING WITH HIM.
THEY JUST MOVED TO A PLACE NEAR THE PARK, AND HE DOESN'T HAVE ANY FRIENDS YET. SO SHE HOPES YOU'LL KEEP PLAYING WITH HIM.
YOU MAKE SURE TO DO THAT, OKAY?

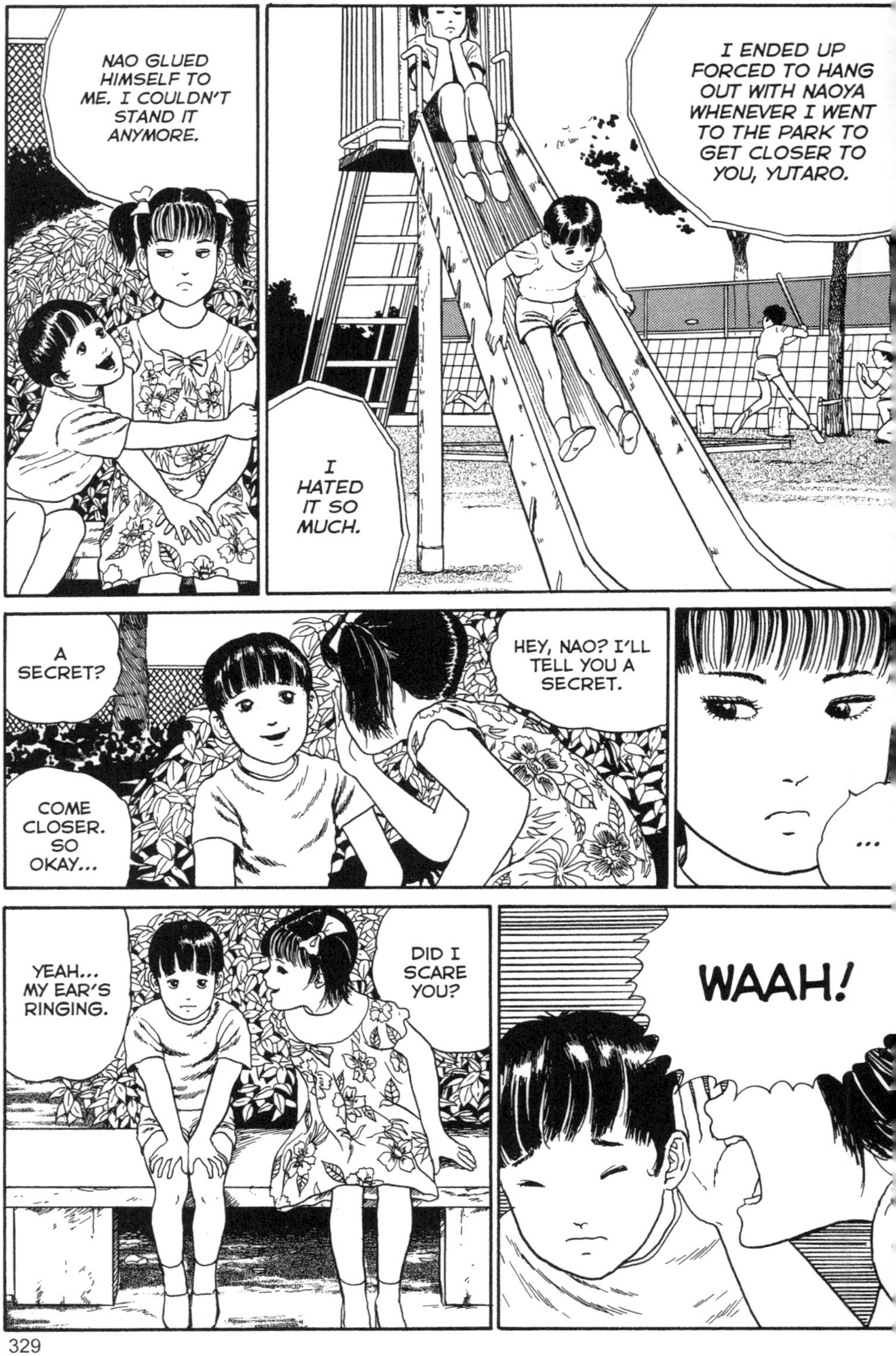
I ENDED UP FORCED TO HANG OUT WITH NAOYA WHENEVER I WENT TO THE PARK TO GET CLOSER TO YOU, YUTARO.
I HATED IT SO MUCH.
NAO GLUED HIMSELF TO ME. I COULDN'T STAND IT ANYMORE.
...
HEY, NAO? I'LL TELL YOU A SECRET.
A SECRET?
COME CLOSER. SO OKAY...
WAAH!
DID I SCARE YOU?
YEAH... MY EAR'S RINGING.

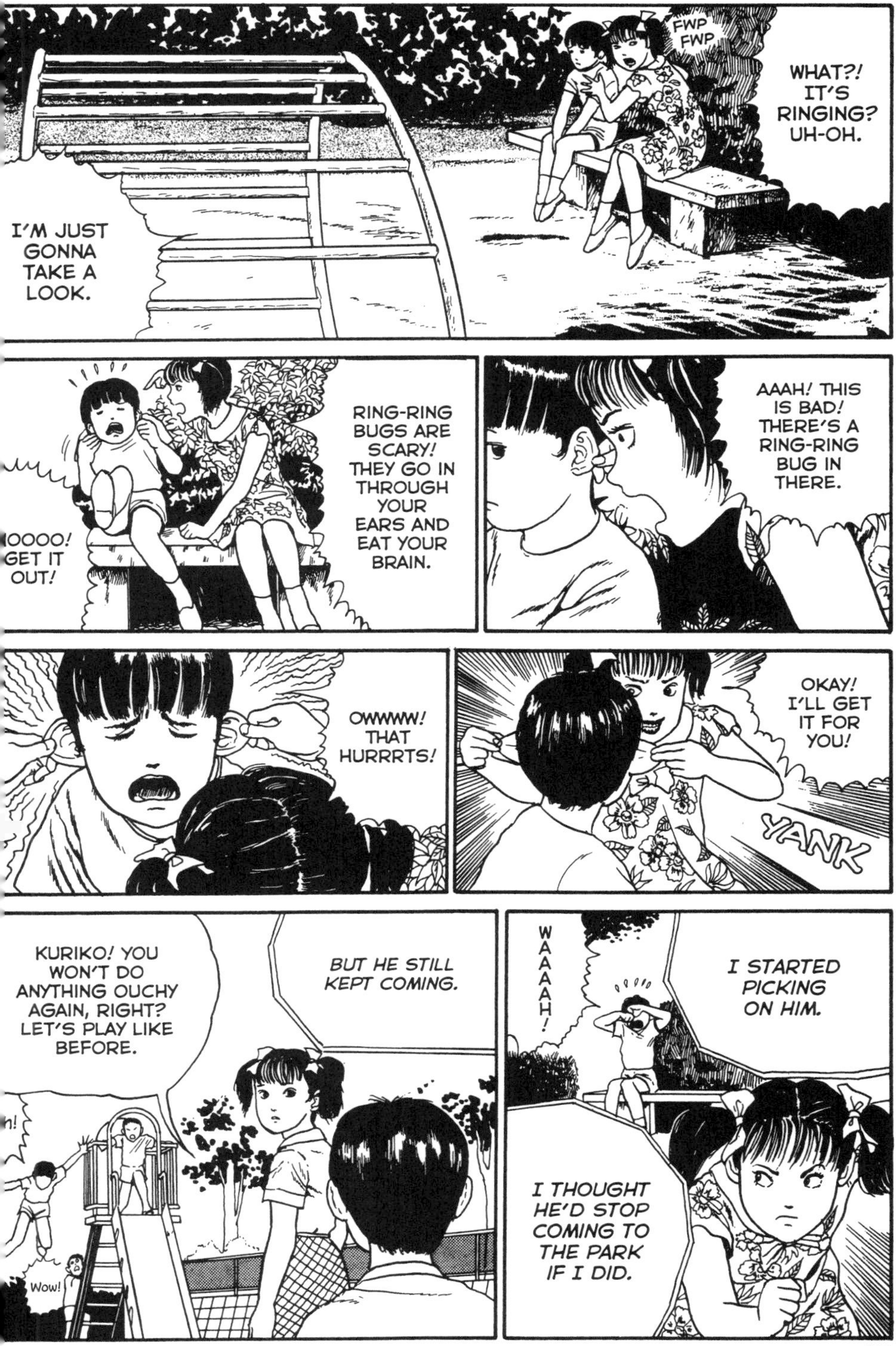
FWP FWP
WHAT?! IT'S RINGING? UH-OH.
I'M JUST GONNA TAKE A LOOK.
AAAH! THIS IS BAD! THERE'S A RING-RING BUG IN THERE.
RING-RING BUGS ARE SCARY! THEY GO IN THROUGH YOUR EARS AND EAT YOUR BRAIN.
OOOO! GET IT OUT!
OKAY! I'LL GET IT FOR YOU!
YANK
OWWWW! THAT HURRRTS!
WAAAAH!
I STARTED PICKING ON HIM.
I THOUGHT HE'D STOP COMING TO THE PARK IF I DID.
BUT HE STILL KEPT COMING.
KURIKO! YOU WON'T DO ANYTHING OUCHY AGAIN, RIGHT? LET'S PLAY LIKE BEFORE.
Wow!

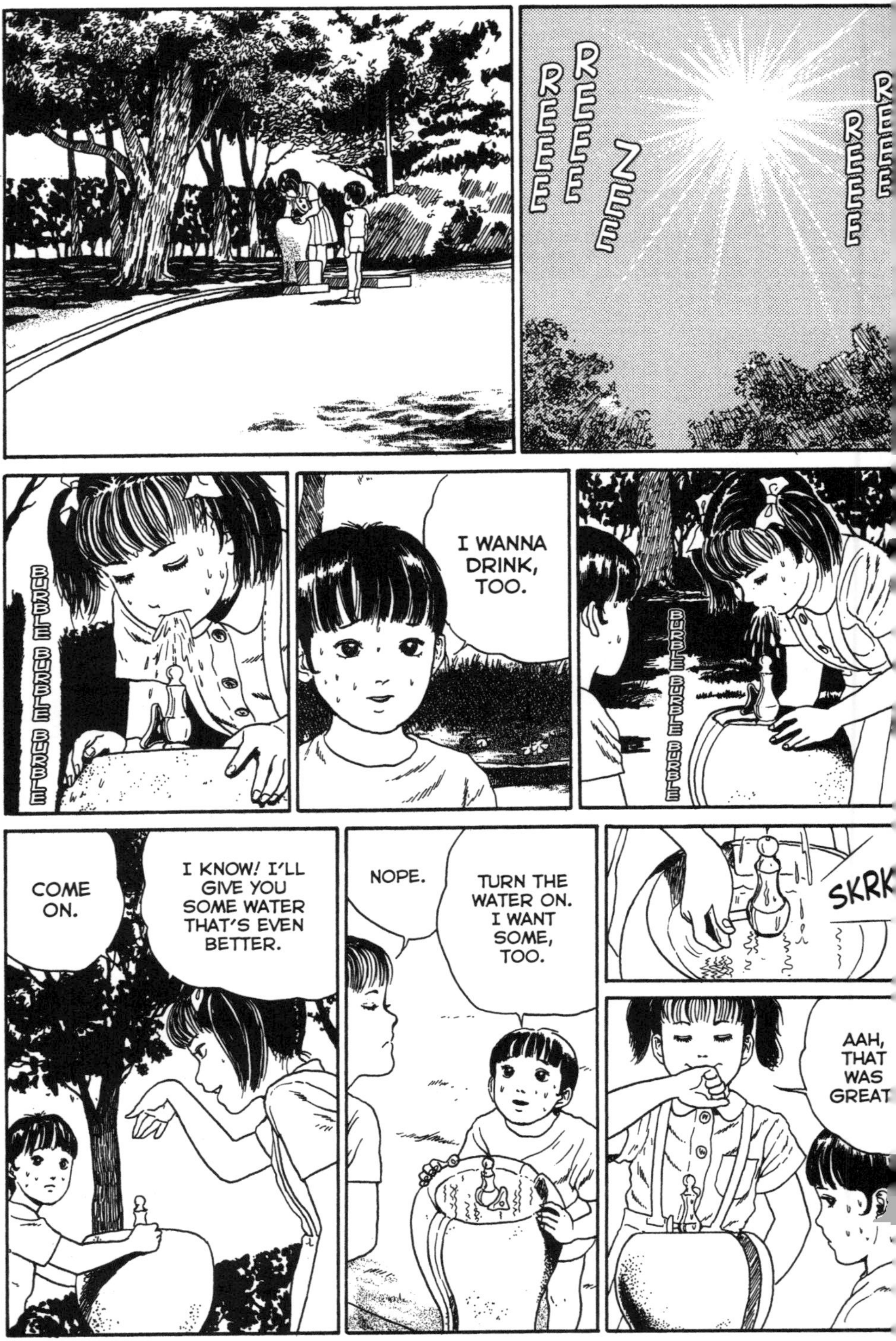
REEEE
REEEE
ZEE
REEEE
REEEE
BURBLE BURBLE BURBLE
I WANNA DRINK, TOO.
BURBLE BURBLE BURBLE
SKRK
AAH, THAT WAS GREAT
TURN THE WATER ON. I WANT SOME, TOO.
NOPE.
I KNOW! I'LL GIVE YOU SOME WATER THAT'S EVEN BETTER.
COME ON.

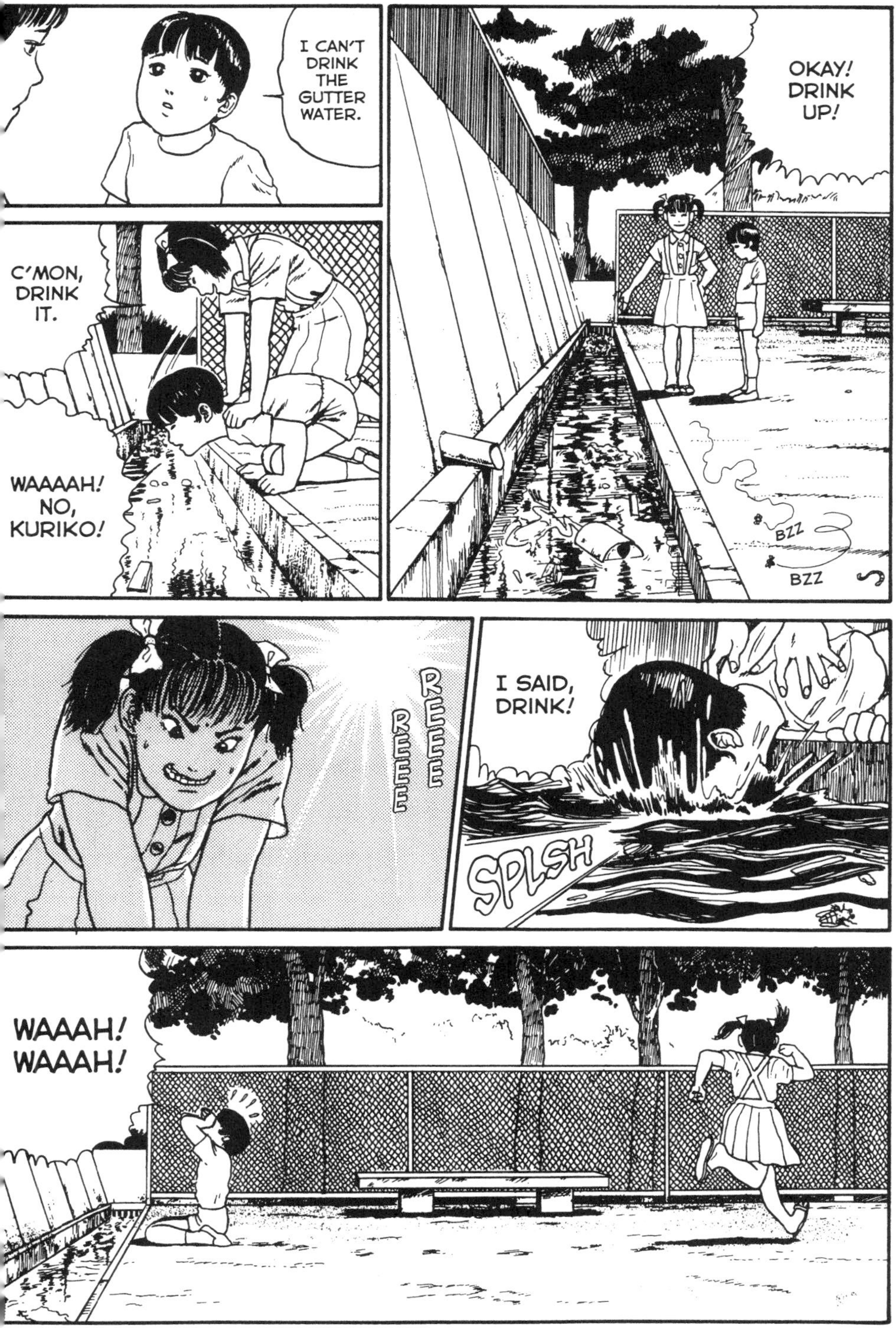
OKAY! DRINK UP!
BZZ
BZZ
I CAN'T DRINK THE GUTTER WATER.
C'MON, DRINK IT.
WAAAAH! NO, KURIKO!
I SAID, DRINK!
SPLSH
REEEE
REEEE
WAAAH! WAAAH!

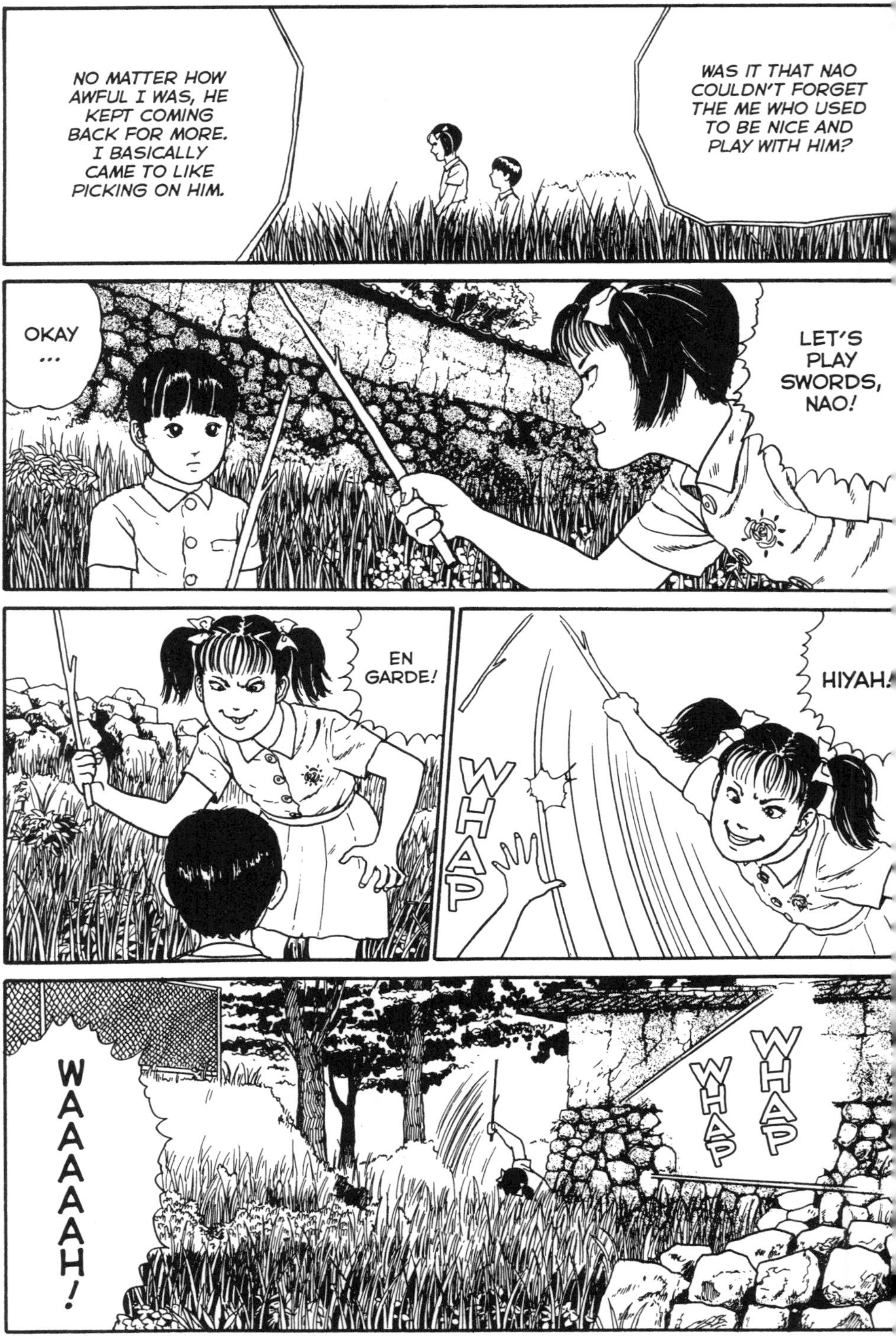
WAS IT THAT NAO COULDN'T FORGET THE ME WHO USED TO BE NICE AND PLAY WITH HIM?
NO MATTER HOW AWFUL I WAS, HE KEPT COMING BACK FOR MORE. I BASICALLY CAME TO LIKE PICKING ON HIM.
LET'S PLAY SWORDS, NAO!
OKAY ...
HIYAH!
WHAP
EN GARDE!
WHAP
WHAP
WAAAAAAH!

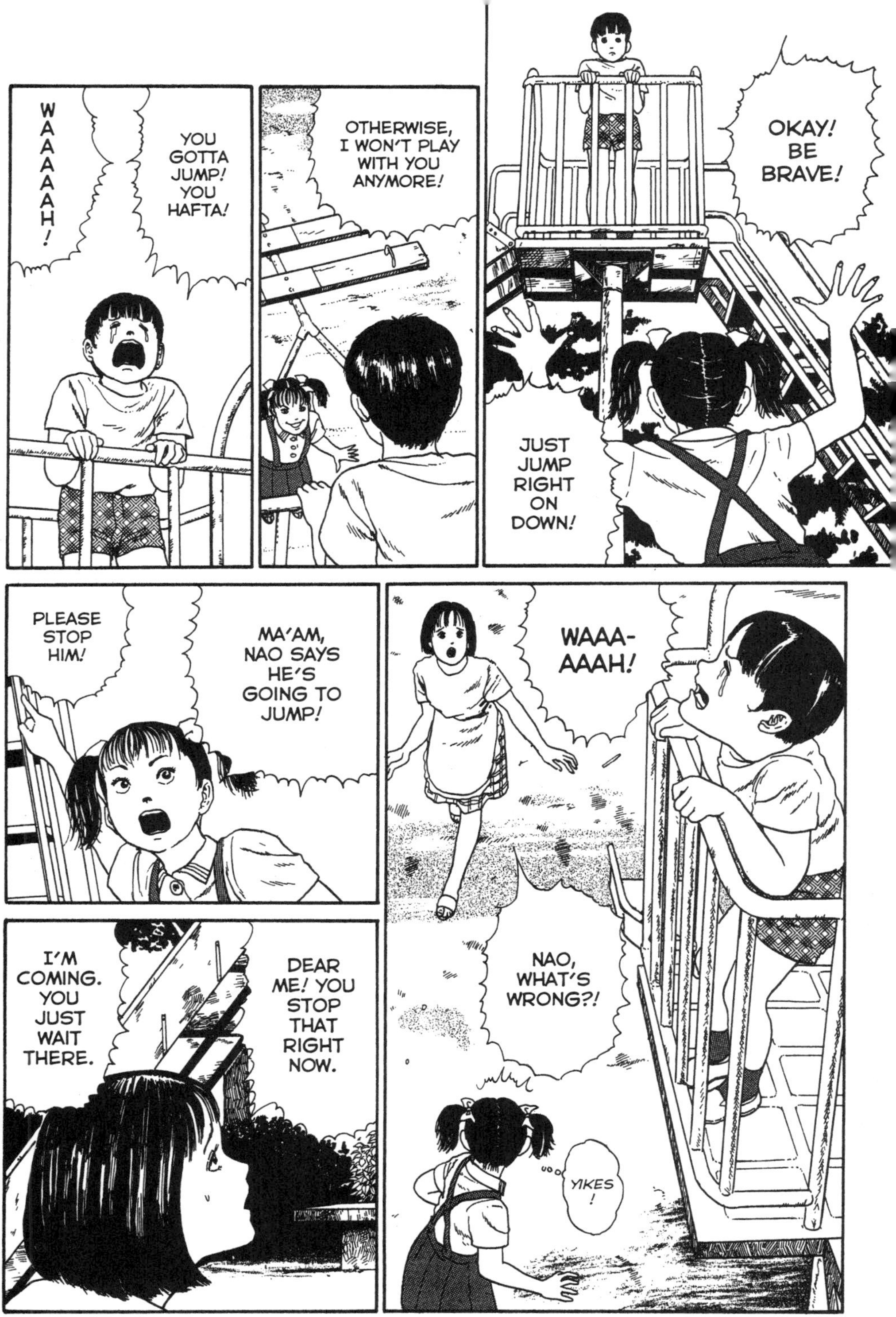
OKAY! BE BRAVE!
JUST JUMP RIGHT ON DOWN!
OTHERWISE, I WON'T PLAY WITH YOU ANYMORE!
YOU GOTTA JUMP! YOU HAFTA!
WAAAAAAH!
WAAA-AAAH!
NAO, WHAT'S WRONG?!
YIKES!
MA'AM, NAO SAYS HE'S GOING TO JUMP!
PLEASE STOP HIM!
DEAR ME! YOU STOP THAT RIGHT NOW.
I'M COMING. YOU JUST WAIT THERE.

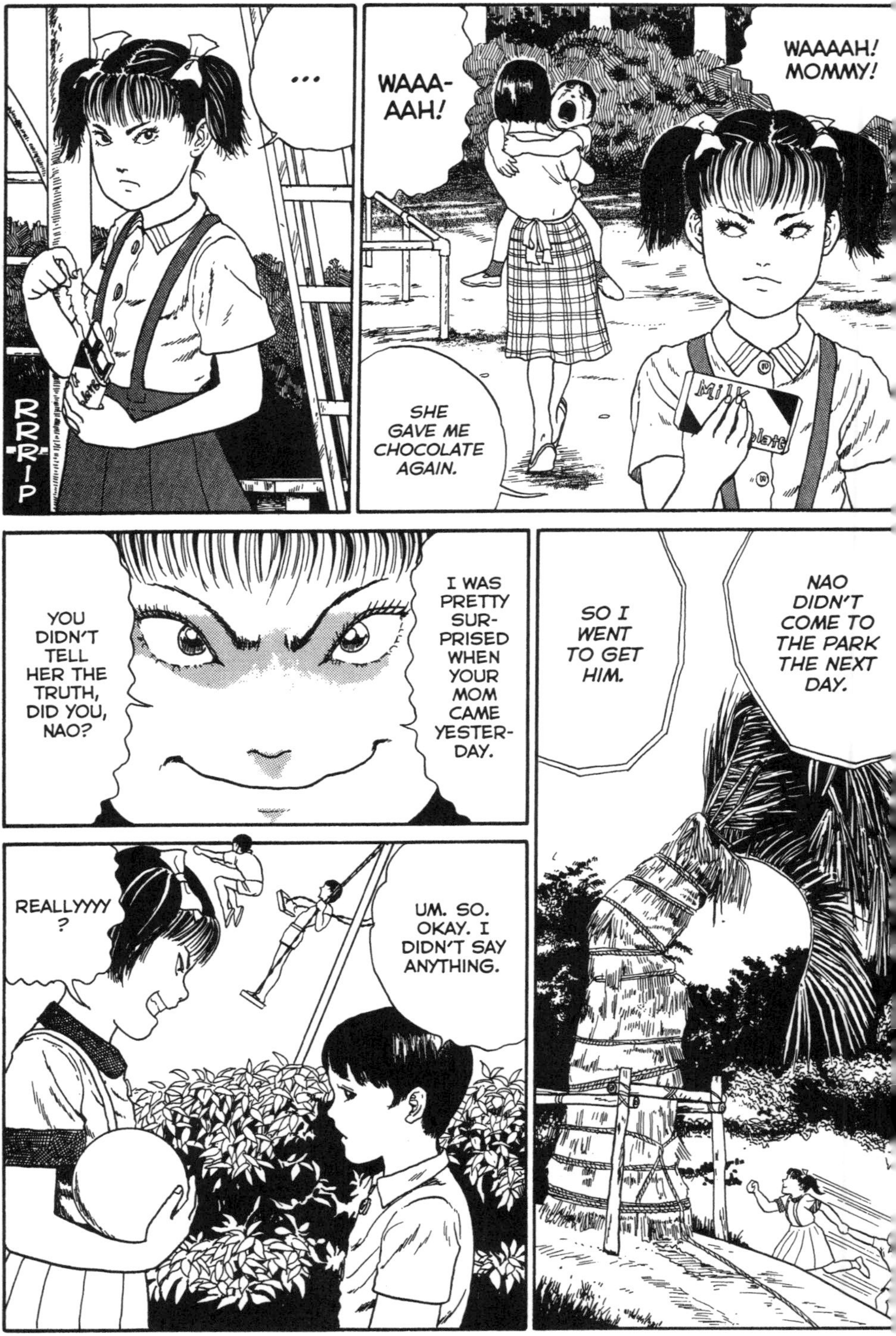
WAAAAH! MOMMY!
WAAA-AAH!
SHE GAVE ME CHOCOLATE AGAIN.
...
RRRIP
NAO DIDN'T COME TO THE PARK THE NEXT DAY.
SO I WENT TO GET HIM.
I WAS PRETTY SURPRISED WHEN YOUR MOM CAME YESTERDAY.
YOU DIDN'T TELL HER THE TRUTH, DID YOU, NAO?
UM. SO. OKAY. I DIDN'T SAY ANYTHING.
REALLYYYY?

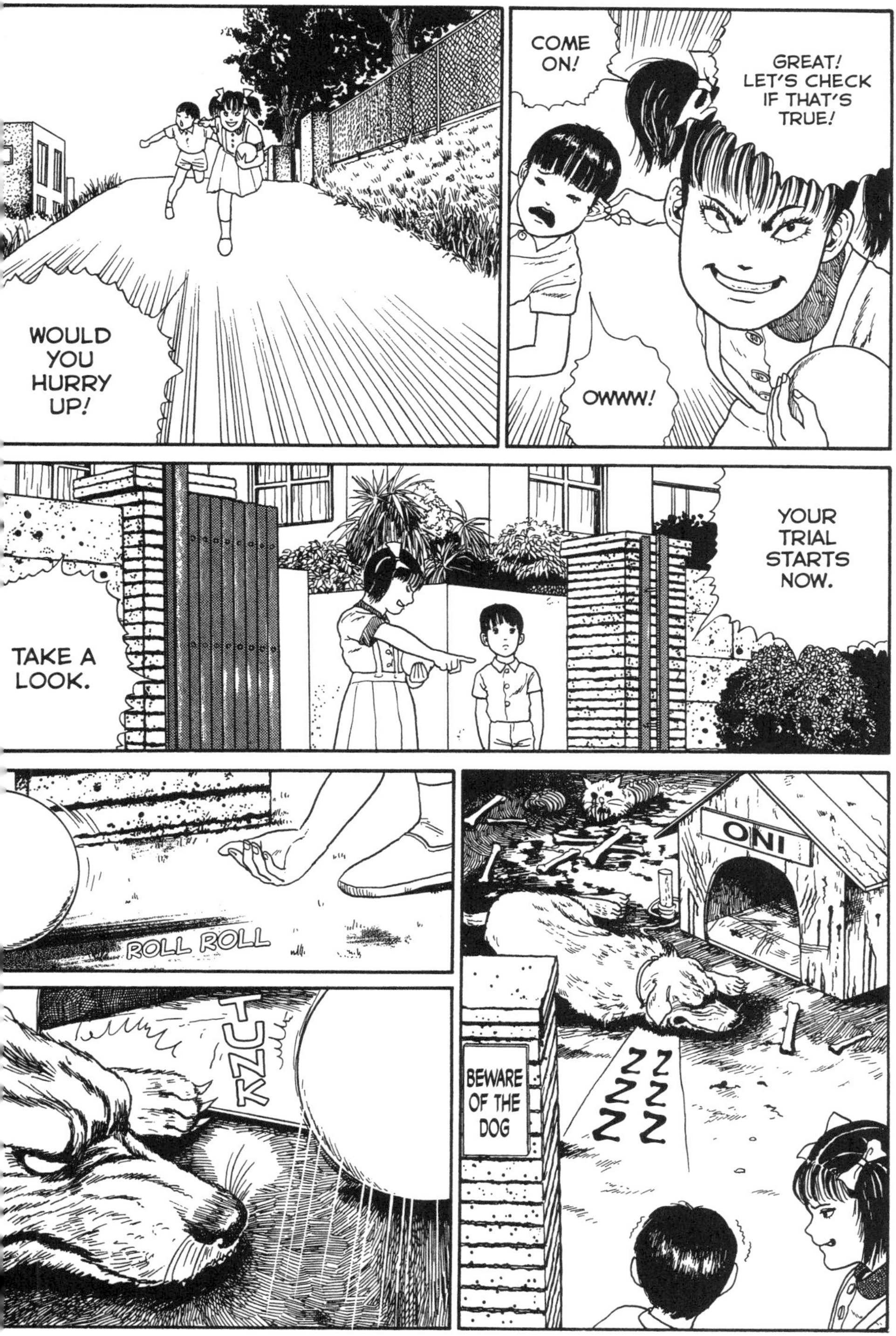
GREAT! LET'S CHECK IF THAT'S TRUE!
COME ON!
OWWW!
WOULD YOU HURRY UP!
YOUR TRIAL STARTS NOW.
TAKE A LOOK.
ONI
ZZZ
ZZZ
BEWARE OF THE DOG
ROLL ROLL
TUNK

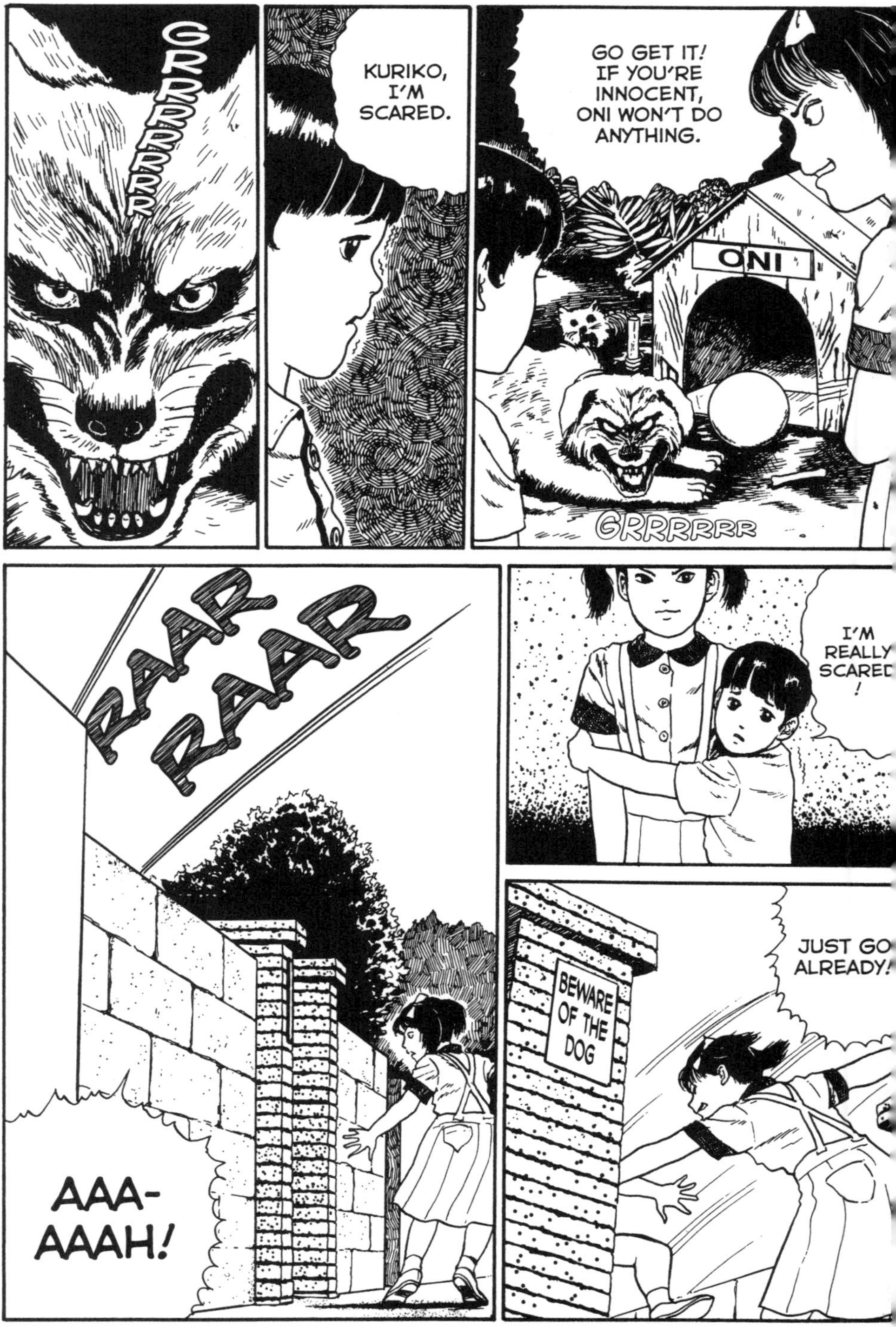
GO GET IT! IF YOU'RE INNOCENT, ONI WON'T DO ANYTHING.
ONI
GRRRRRR
KURIKO, I'M SCARED.
GRRRRRRRR
I'M REALLY SCARED!
JUST GO ALREADY!
BEWARE OF THE DOG
RAAR RAAR
AAA-AAAH!

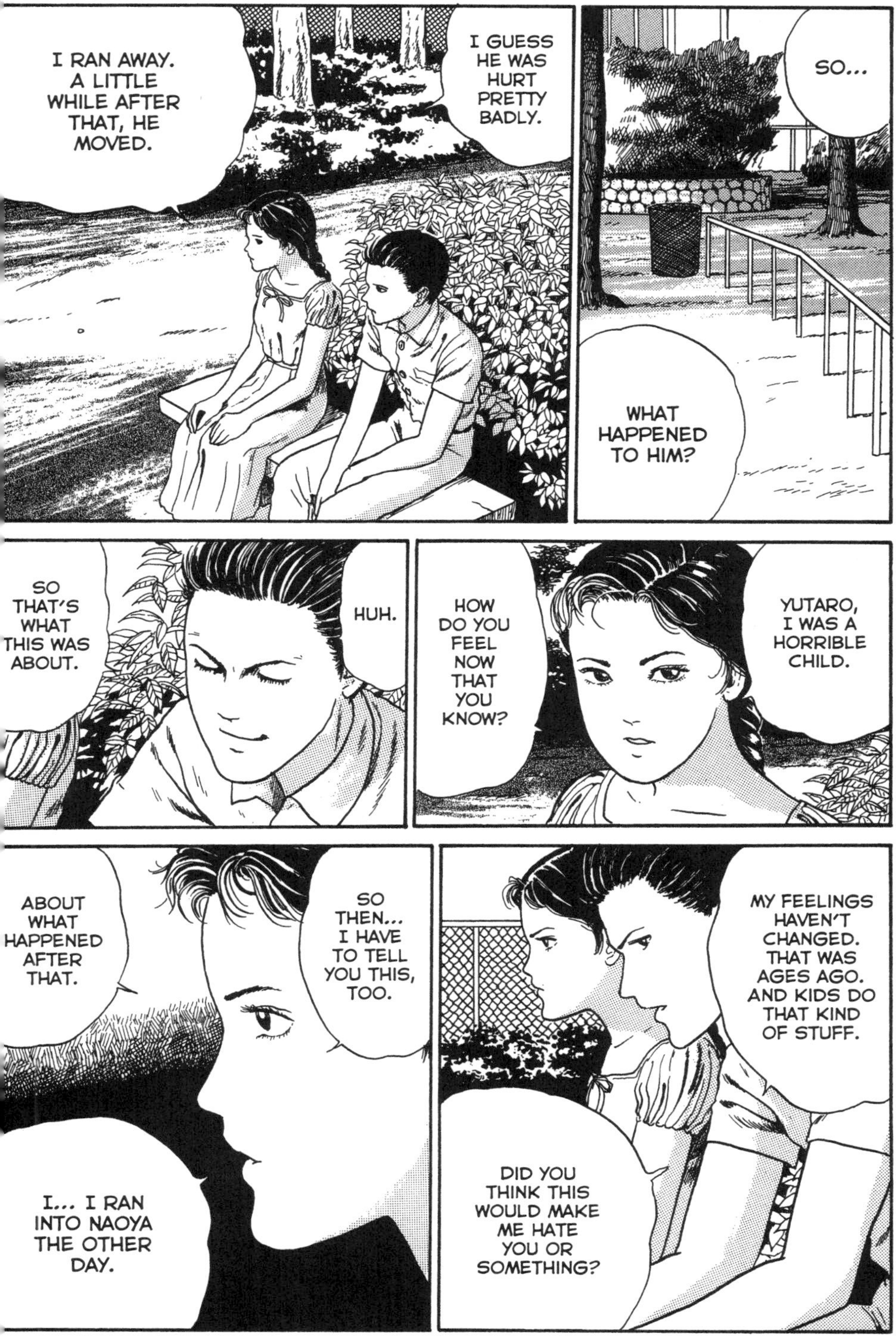
SO...
WHAT HAPPENED TO HIM?
I GUESS HE WAS HURT PRETTY BADLY.
I RAN AWAY. A LITTLE WHILE AFTER THAT, HE MOVED.
YUTARO, I WAS A HORRIBLE CHILD.
HOW DO YOU FEEL NOW THAT YOU KNOW?
HUH.
SO THAT'S WHAT THIS WAS ABOUT.
MY FEELINGS HAVEN'T CHANGED. THAT WAS AGES AGO. AND KIDS DO THAT KIND OF STUFF.
DID YOU THINK THIS WOULD MAKE ME HATE YOU OR SOMETHING?
SO THEN... I HAVE TO TELL YOU THIS, TOO.
ABOUT WHAT HAPPENED AFTER THAT.
I... I RAN INTO NAOYA THE OTHER DAY.

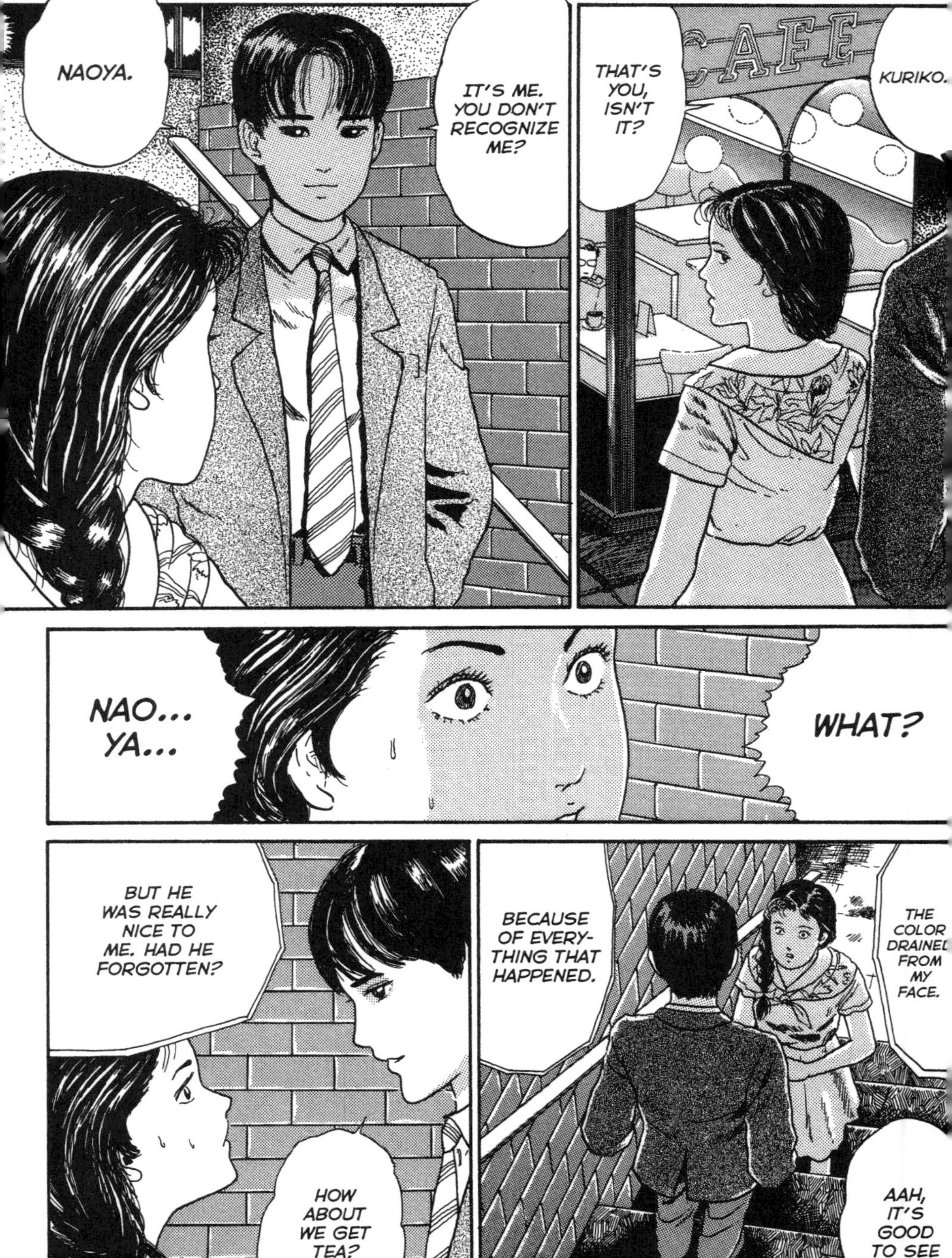
KURIKO.
THAT'S YOU, ISN'T IT?
IT'S ME. YOU DON'T RECOGNIZE ME?
NAOYA.
WHAT?
NAO... YA...
THE COLOR DRAINED FROM MY FACE.
BECAUSE OF EVERY-THING THAT HAPPENED.
AAH, IT'S GOOD TO SEE YOU.
BUT HE WAS REALLY NICE TO ME. HAD HE FORGOTTEN?
HOW ABOUT WE GET TEA?

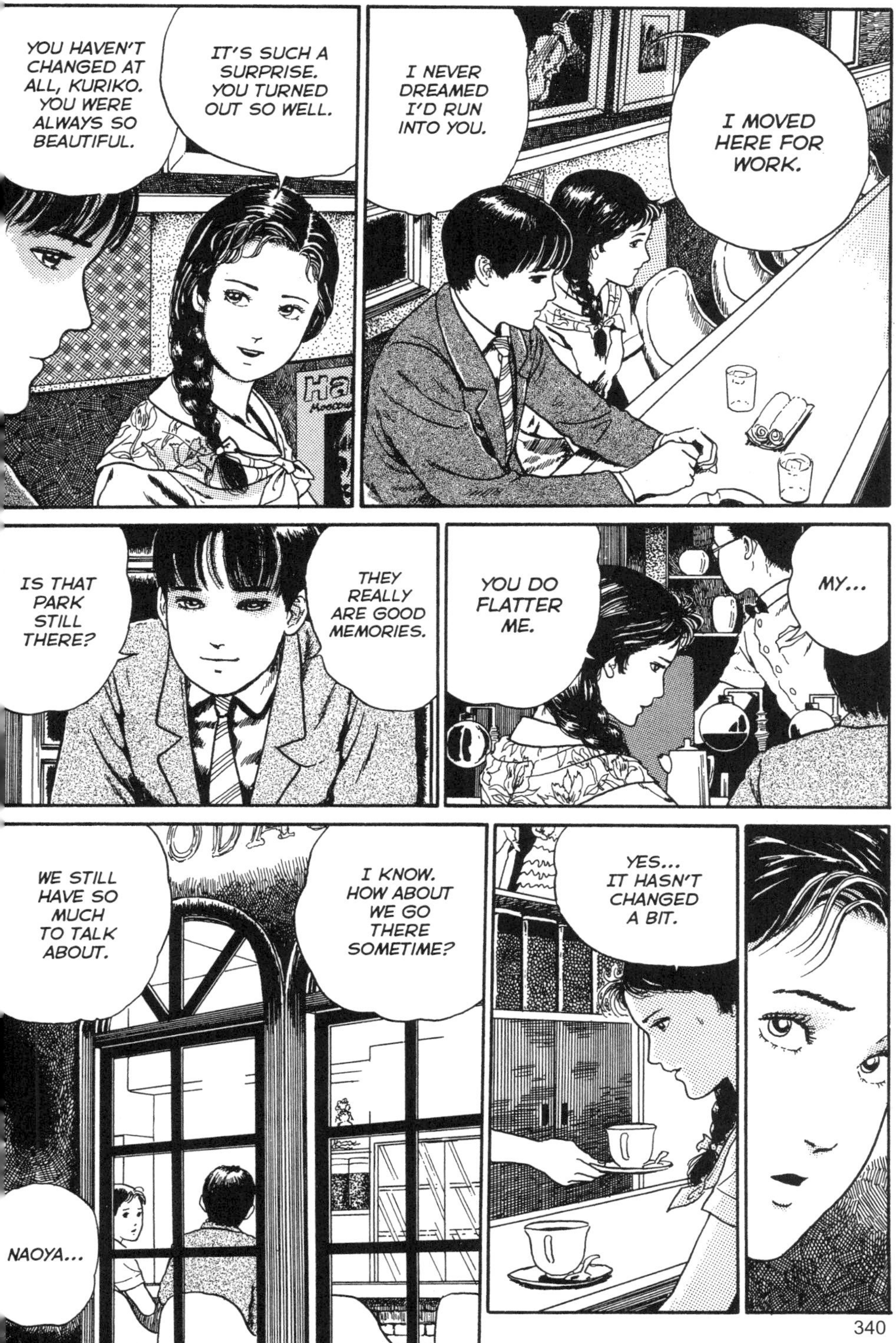
I MOVED HERE FOR WORK.
I NEVER DREAMED I'D RUN INTO YOU.
IT'S SUCH A SURPRISE. YOU TURNED OUT SO WELL.
YOU HAVEN'T CHANGED AT ALL, KURIKO. YOU WERE ALWAYS SO BEAUTIFUL.
MY...
YOU DO FLATTER ME.
THEY REALLY ARE GOOD MEMORIES.
IS THAT PARK STILL THERE?
YES... IT HASN'T CHANGED A BIT.
I KNOW. HOW ABOUT WE GO THERE SOMETIME?
WE STILL HAVE SO MUCH TO TALK ABOUT.
NAOYA...

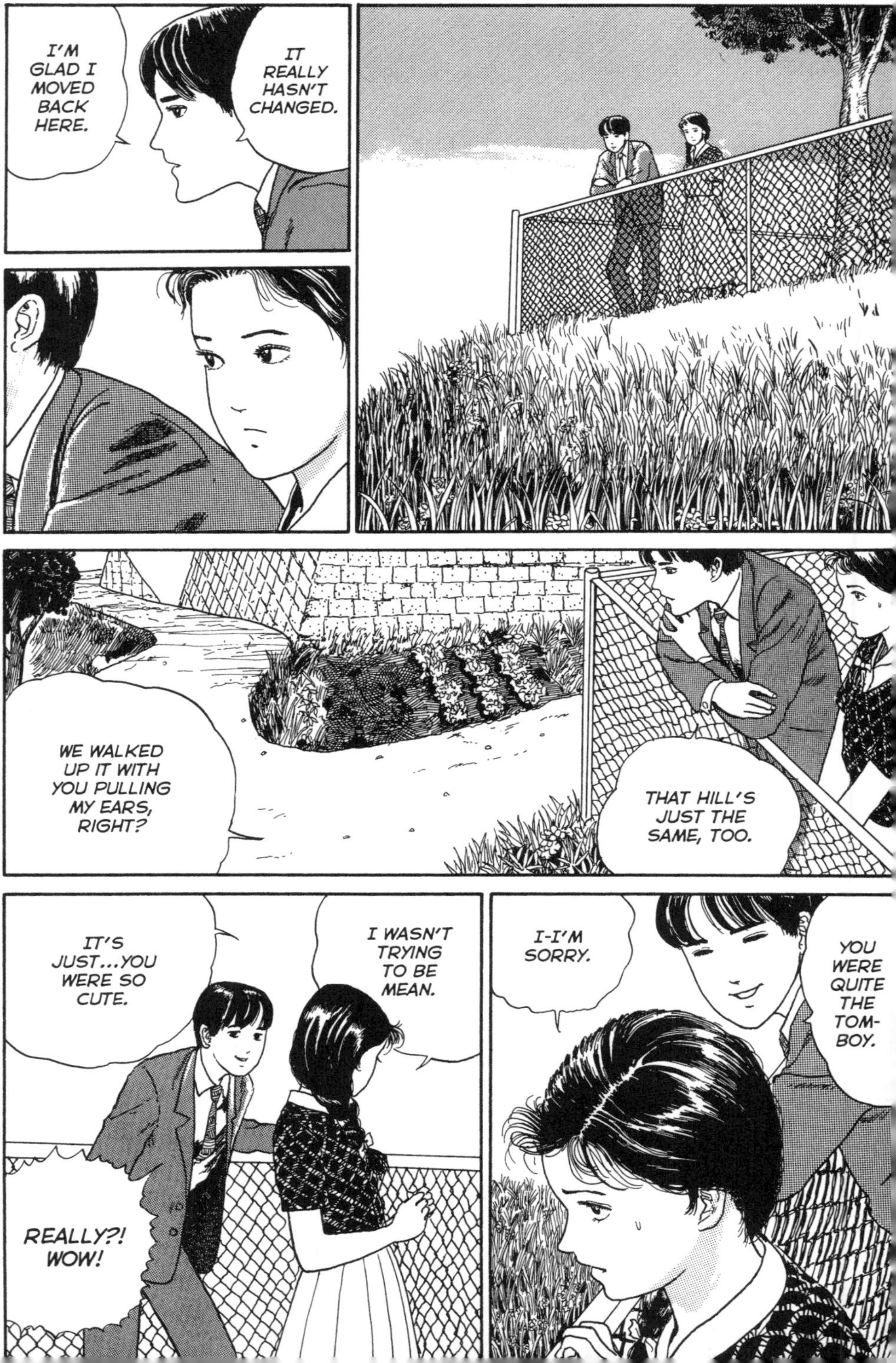
IT REALLY HASN'T CHANGED.
I'M GLAD I MOVED BACK HERE.
THAT HILL'S JUST THE SAME, TOO.
WE WALKED UP IT WITH YOU PULLING MY EARS, RIGHT?
YOU WERE QUITE THE TOM-BOY.
I-I'M SORRY.
I WASN'T TRYING TO BE MEAN.
IT'S JUST...YOU WERE SO CUTE.
REALLY?! WOW!

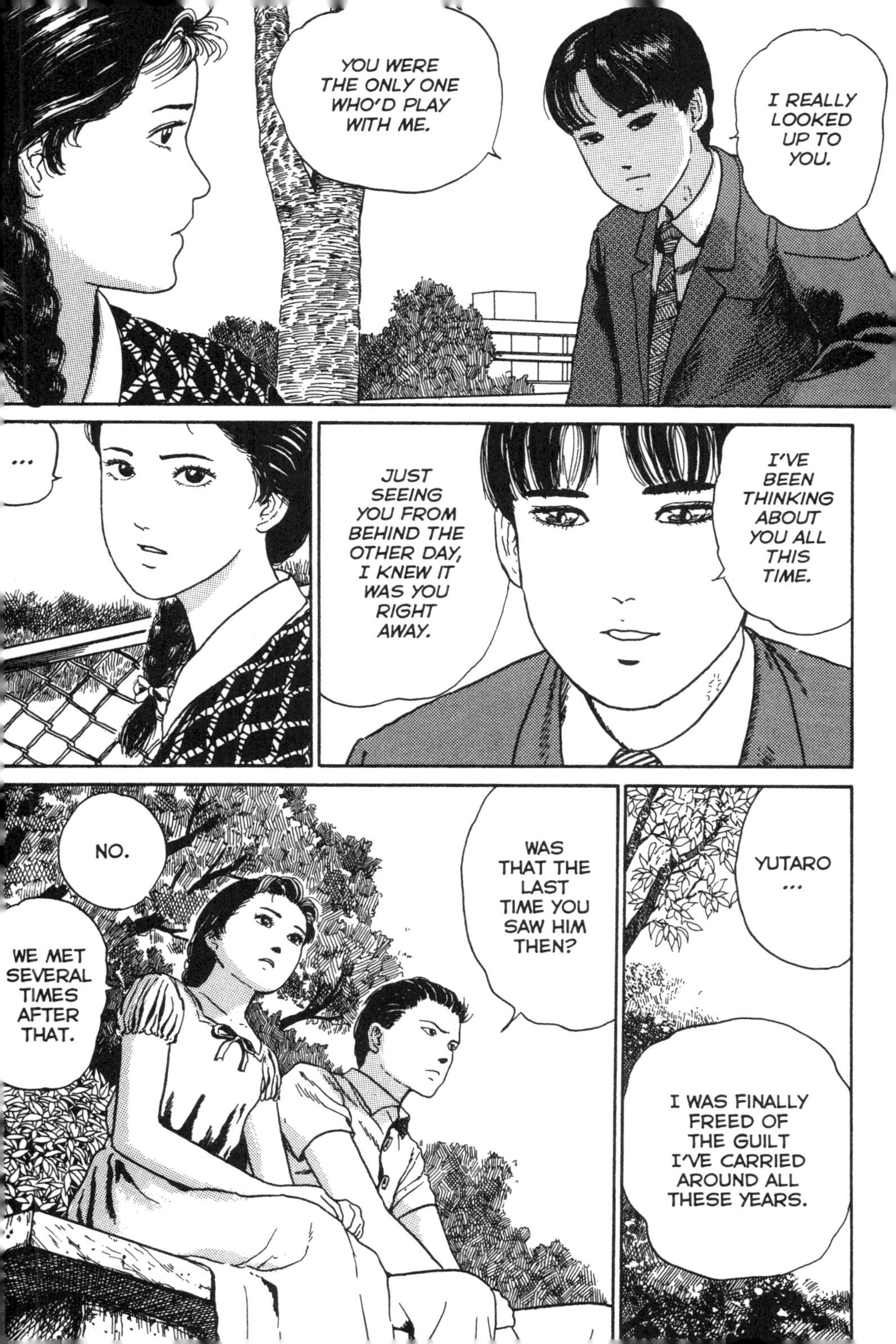
I REALLY LOOKED UP TO YOU.
YOU WERE THE ONLY ONE WHO'D PLAY WITH ME.
I'VE BEEN THINKING ABOUT YOU ALL THIS TIME.
JUST SEEING YOU FROM BEHIND THE OTHER DAY, I KNEW IT WAS YOU RIGHT AWAY.
...
YUTARO ...
I WAS FINALLY FREED OF THE GUILT I'VE CARRIED AROUND ALL THESE YEARS.
WAS THAT THE LAST TIME YOU SAW HIM THEN?
NO.
WE MET SEVERAL TIMES AFTER THAT.

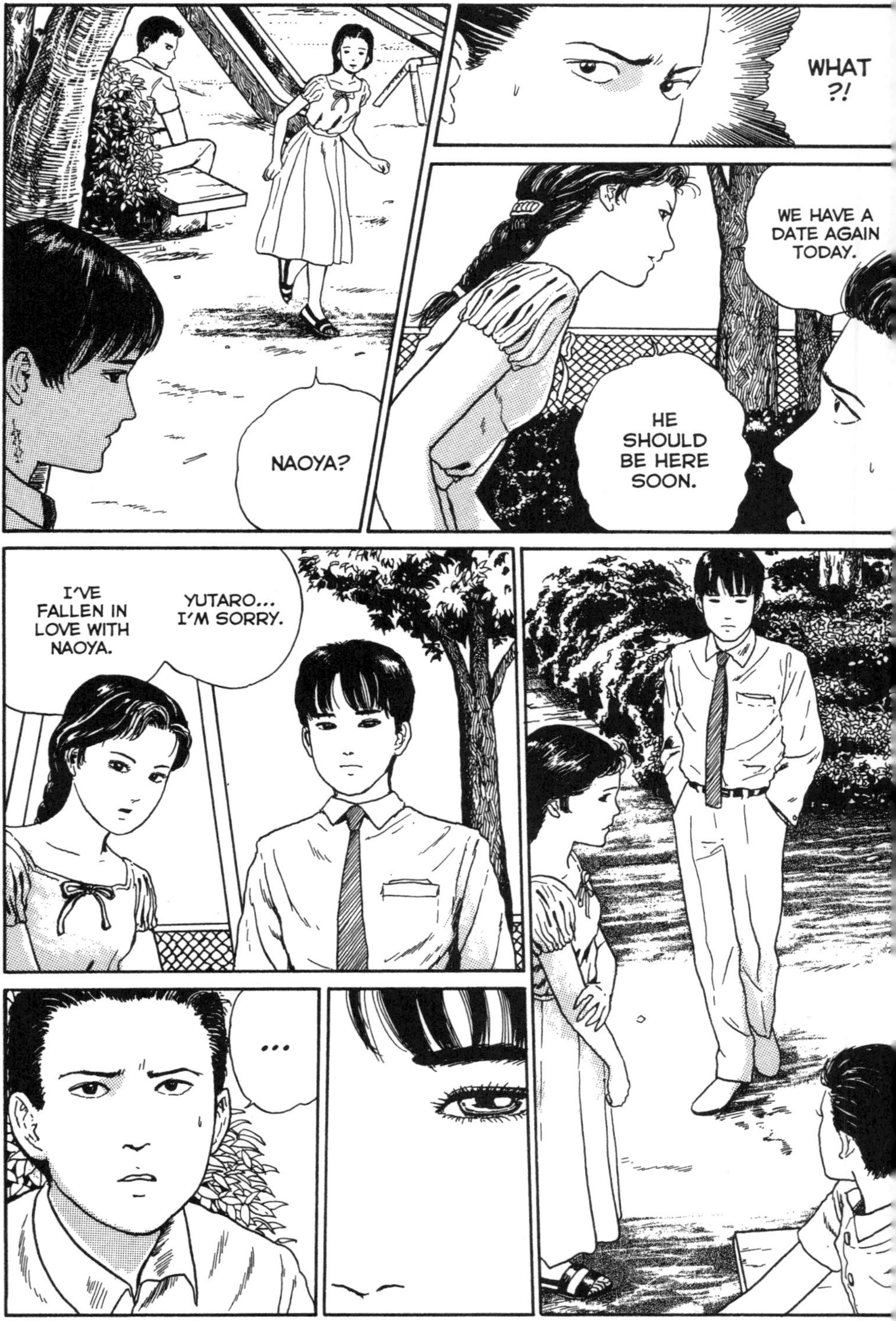
WHAT ?!
WE HAVE A DATE AGAIN TODAY.
HE SHOULD BE HERE SOON.
NAOYA?
YUTARO... I'M SORRY.
I'VE FALLEN IN LOVE WITH NAOYA.
...

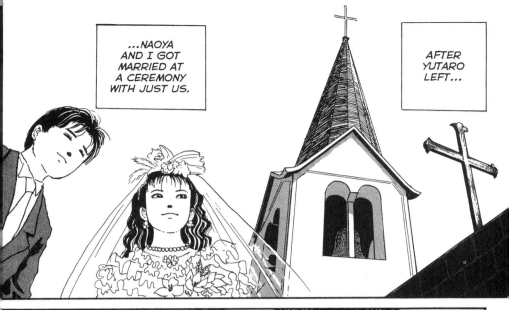

AFTER YUTARO LEFT...
...NAOYA AND I GOT MARRIED AT A CEREMONY WITH JUST US.
EVENTUALLY, WE HAD AN ADORABLE BABY BOY, HIROSHI.
I FIRMLY BELIEVED OUR HAPPINESS WOULD GO ON FOREVER.
BUT IT DIDN'T LAST THAT LONG.
NOT LONG AFTER HIROSHI WAS BORN, NAOYA DISAPPEARED.
HE SAID HE WAS OFF TO WORK AND NEVER CAME HOME AGAIN.
I PUT IN A MISSING PERSON REPORT, BUT THEY FOUND NO TRACE OF HIM.

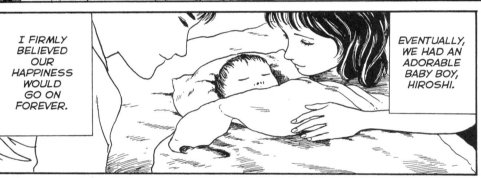

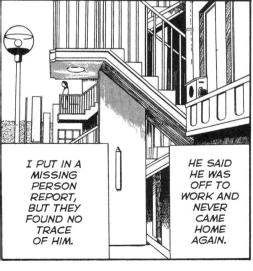

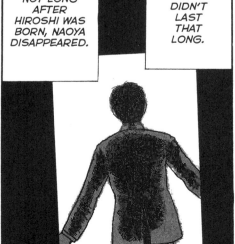

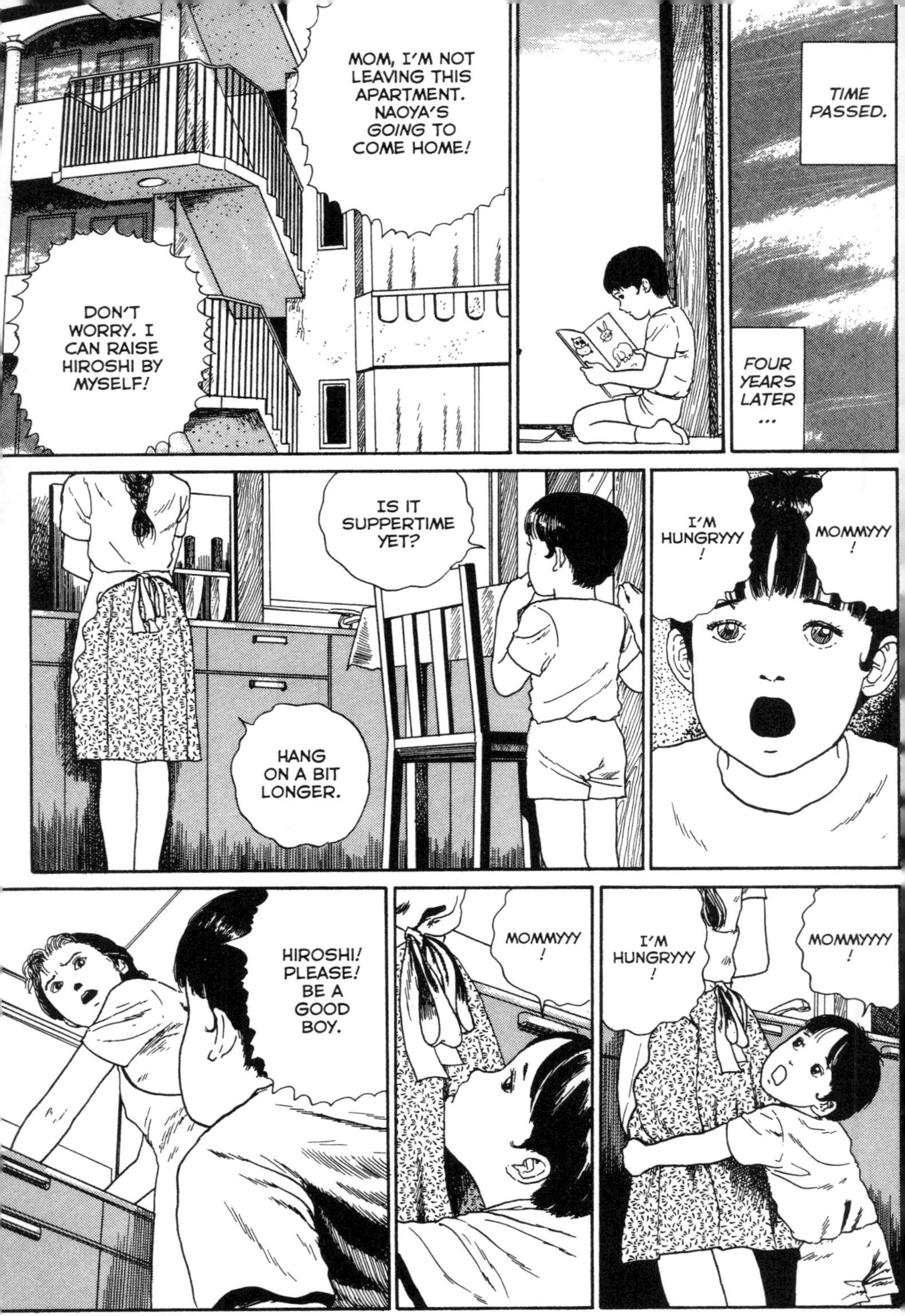
TIME PASSED.
FOUR YEARS LATER ...
MOM, I'M NOT LEAVING THIS APARTMENT. NAOYA'S *GOING* TO COME HOME!
DON'T WORRY. I CAN RAISE HIROSHI BY MYSELF!
MOMMYYY!
I'M HUNGRYYY!
IS IT SUPPERTIME YET?
HANG ON A BIT LONGER.
MOMMYYY!
I'M HUNGRYYY!
MOMMYYY!
HIROSHI! PLEASE! BE A GOOD BOY.

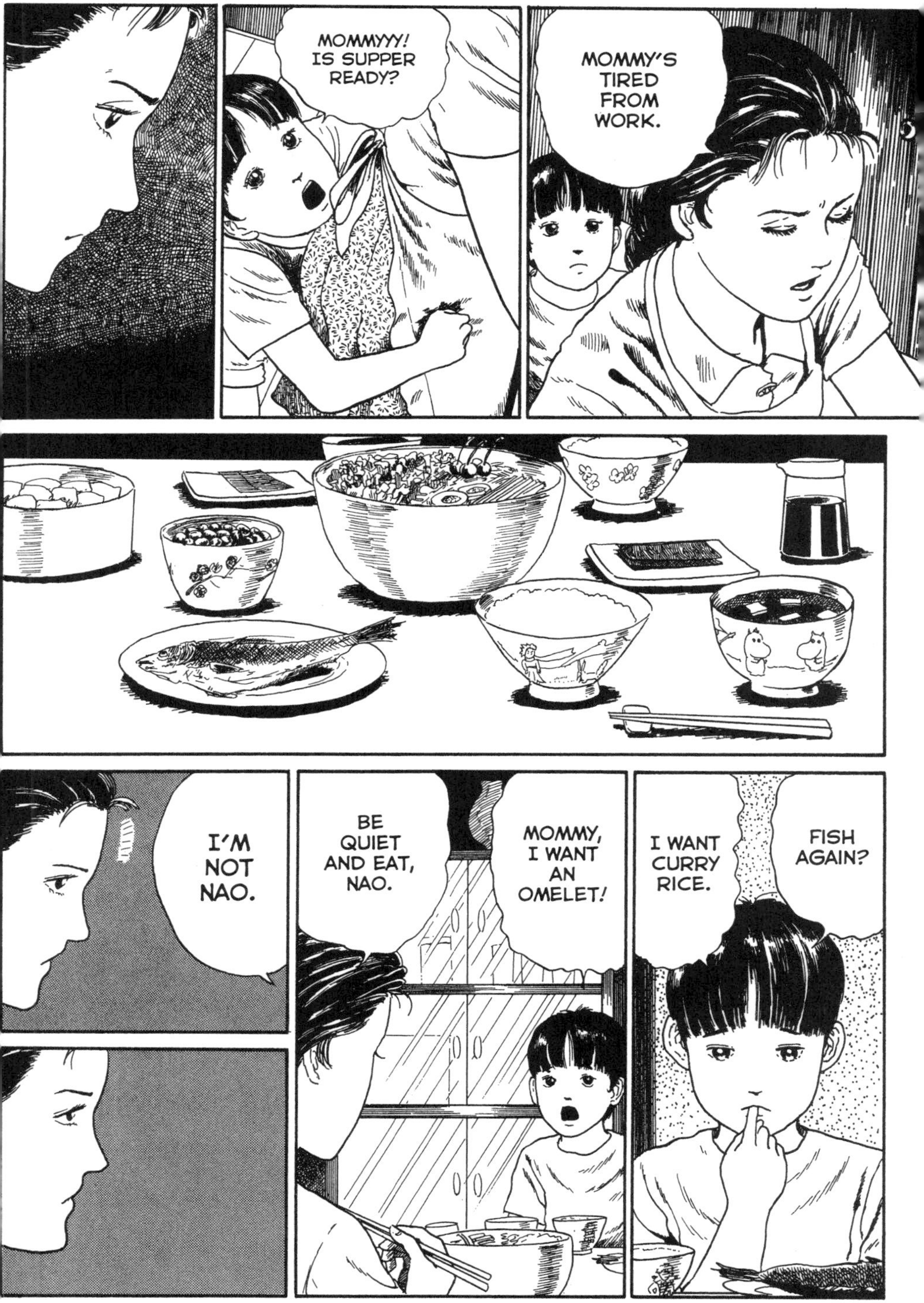
MOMMY'S TIRED FROM WORK.
MOMMYYY! IS SUPPER READY?
FISH AGAIN?
I WANT CURRY RICE.
MOMMY, I WANT AN OMELET!
BE QUIET AND EAT, NAO.
I'M NOT NAO.

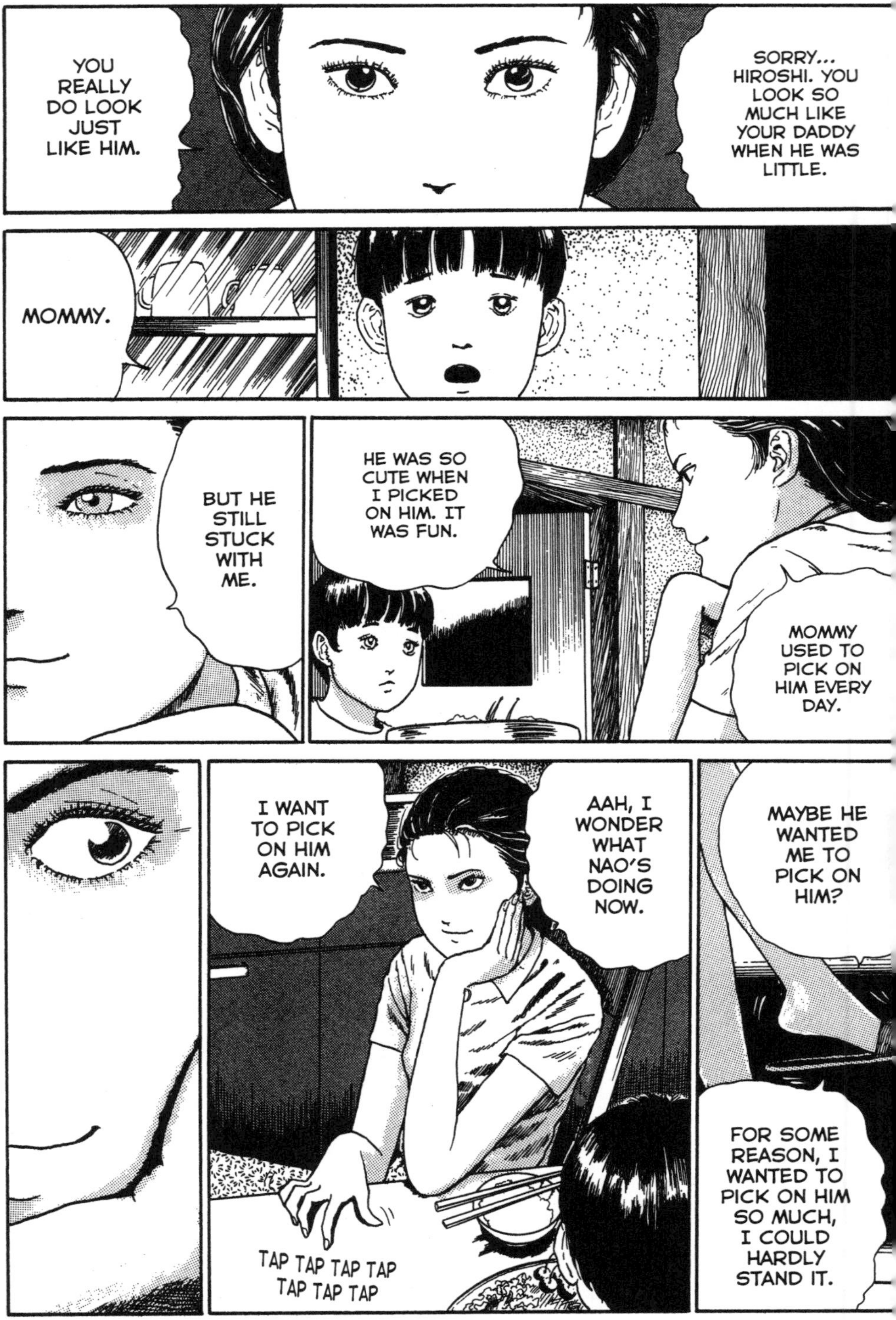
SORRY... HIROSHI. YOU LOOK SO MUCH LIKE YOUR DADDY WHEN HE WAS LITTLE.
YOU REALLY DO LOOK JUST LIKE HIM.
MOMMY.
MOMMY USED TO PICK ON HIM EVERY DAY.
HE WAS SO CUTE WHEN I PICKED ON HIM. IT WAS FUN.
BUT HE STILL STUCK WITH ME.
MAYBE HE WANTED ME TO PICK ON HIM?
FOR SOME REASON, I WANTED TO PICK ON HIM SO MUCH, I COULD HARDLY STAND IT.
AAH, I WONDER WHAT NAO'S DOING NOW.
I WANT TO PICK ON HIM AGAIN.
TAP TAP TAP TAP TAP TAP TAP

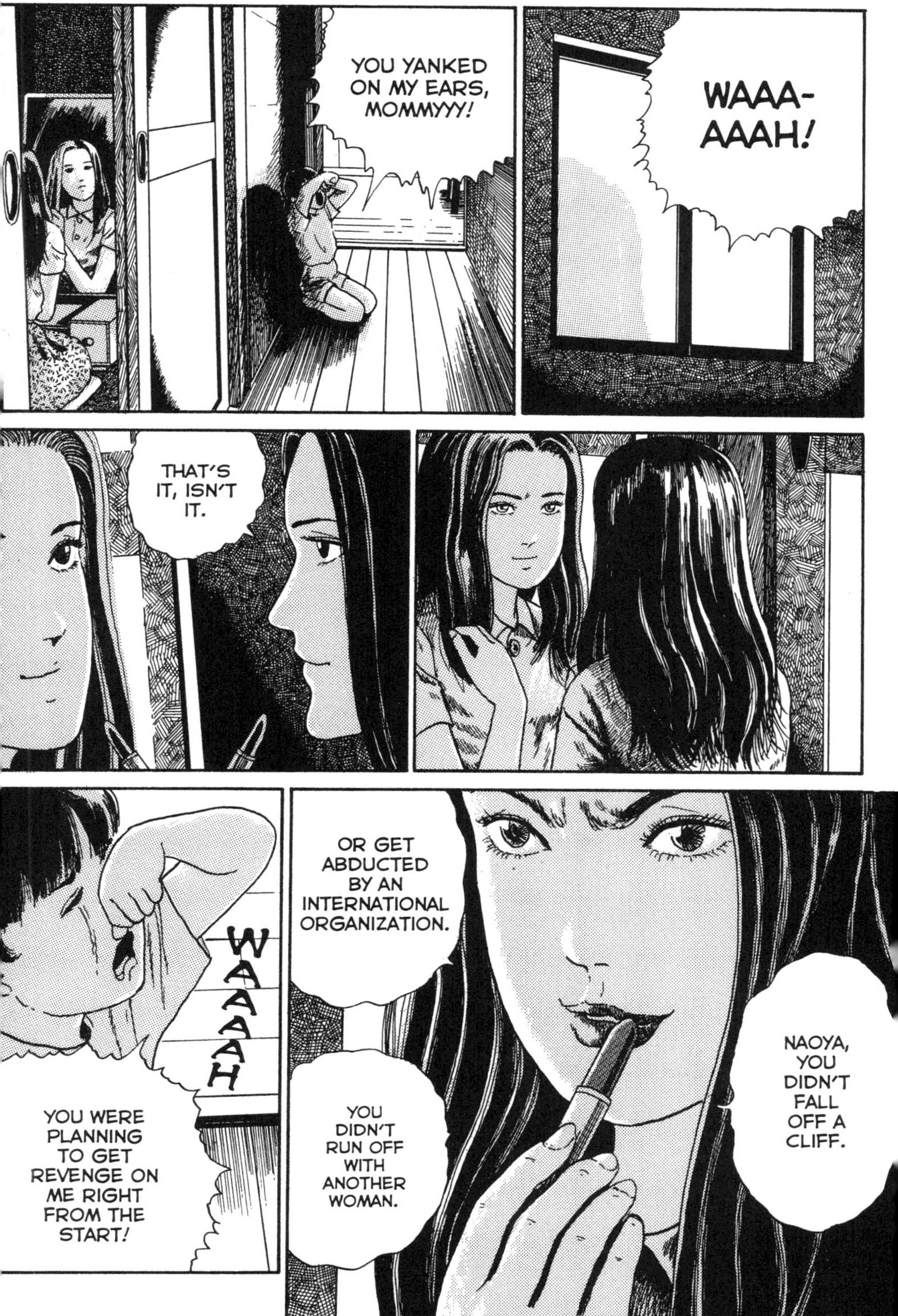
WAAA-AAAH!
YOU YANKED ON MY EARS, MOMMYYY!
THAT'S IT, ISN'T IT.
NAOYA, YOU DIDN'T FALL OFF A CLIFF.
YOU DIDN'T RUN OFF WITH ANOTHER WOMAN.
OR GET ABDUCTED BY AN INTERNATIONAL ORGANIZATION.
WAAAAH
YOU WERE PLANNING TO GET REVENGE ON ME RIGHT FROM THE START!

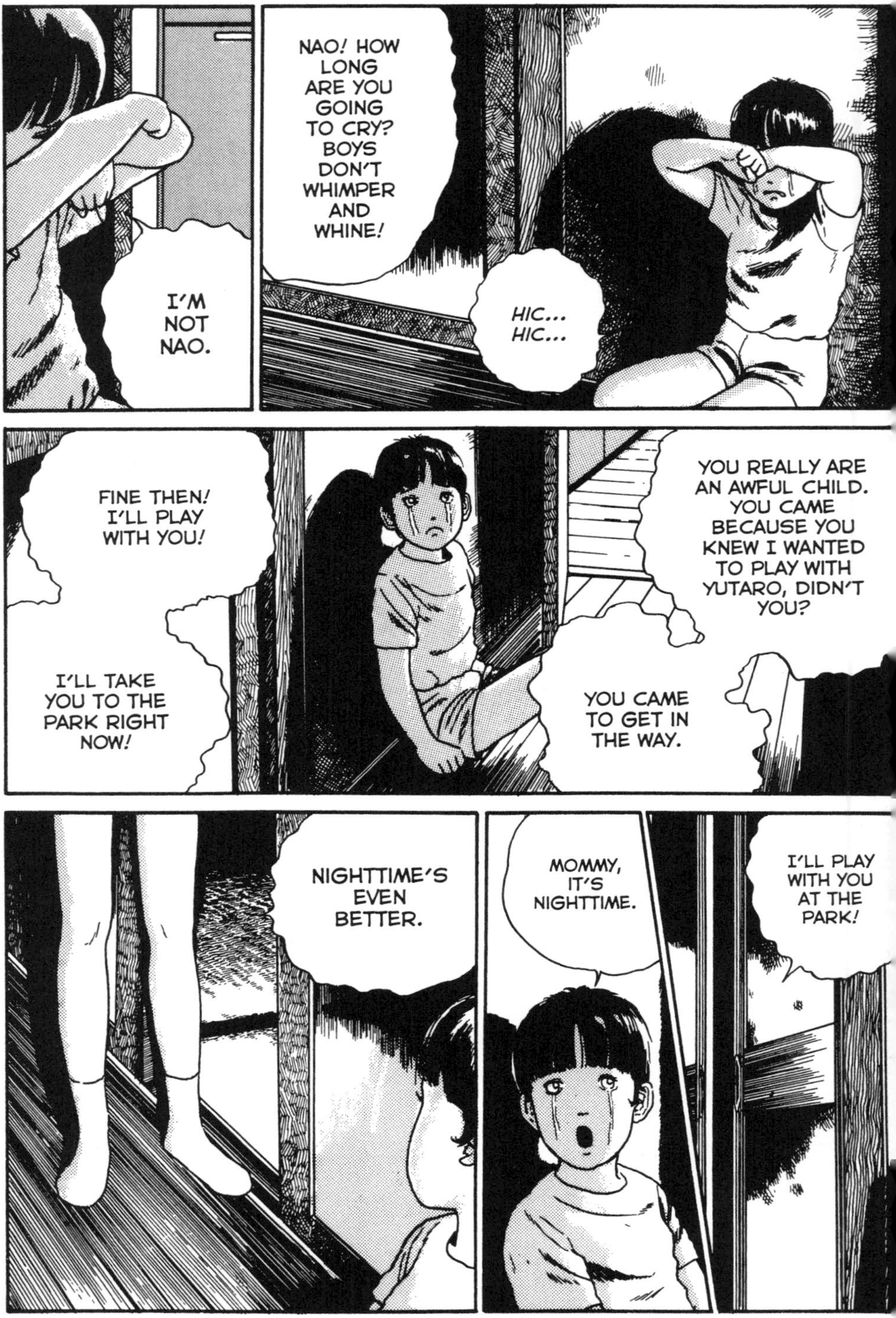
NAO! HOW LONG ARE YOU GOING TO CRY? BOYS DON'T WHIMPER AND WHINE!
HIC... HIC...
I'M NOT NAO.
YOU REALLY ARE AN AWFUL CHILD. YOU CAME BECAUSE YOU KNEW I WANTED TO PLAY WITH YUTARO, DIDN'T YOU?
YOU CAME TO GET IN THE WAY.
FINE THEN! I'LL PLAY WITH YOU!
I'LL TAKE YOU TO THE PARK RIGHT NOW!
I'LL PLAY WITH YOU AT THE PARK!
MOMMY, IT'S NIGHTTIME.
NIGHTTIME'S EVEN BETTER.

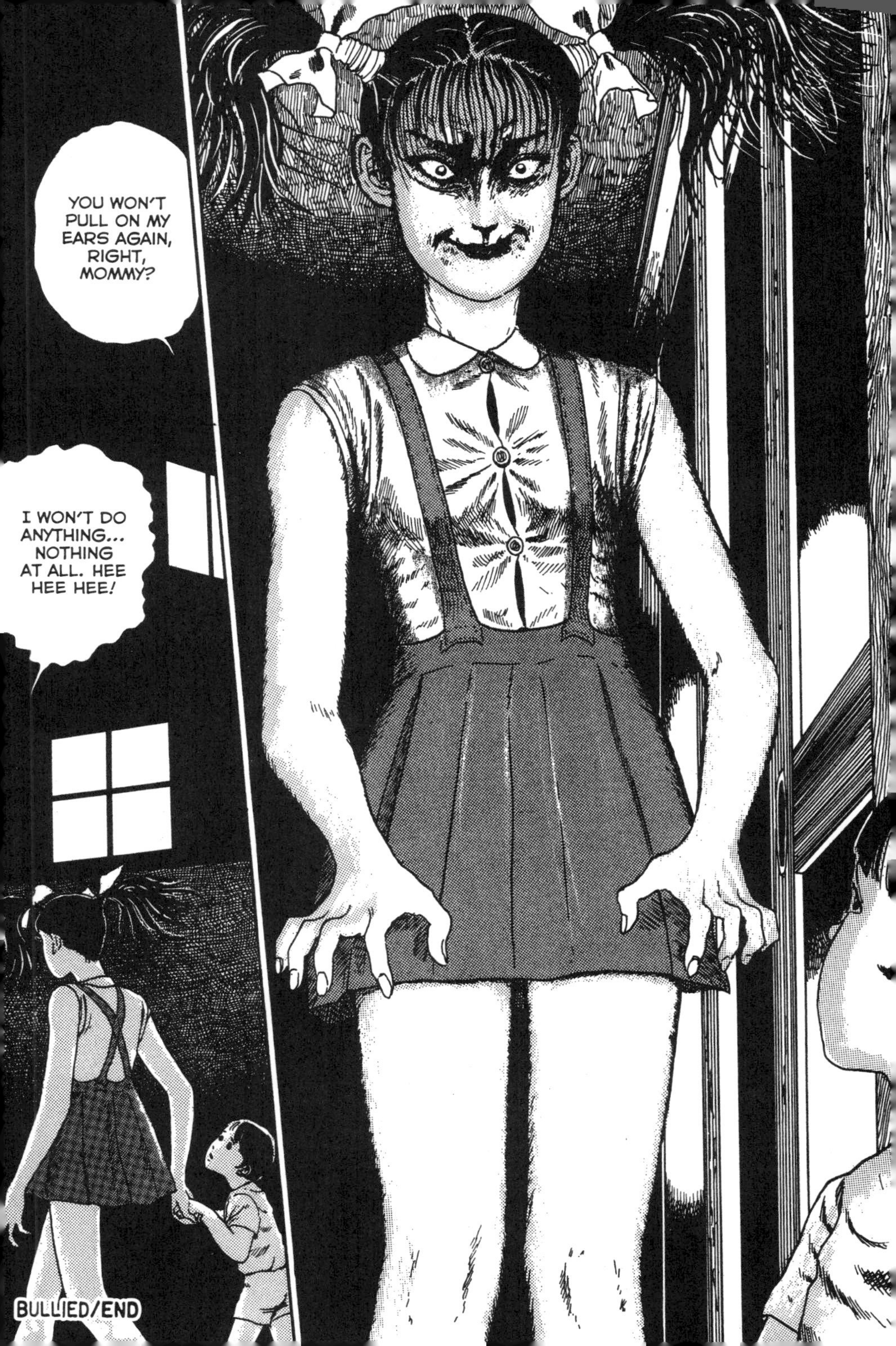
YOU WON'T PULL ON MY EARS AGAIN, RIGHT, MOMMY?
I WON'T DO ANYTHING... NOTHING AT ALL. HEE HEE HEE!
BULLIED/END

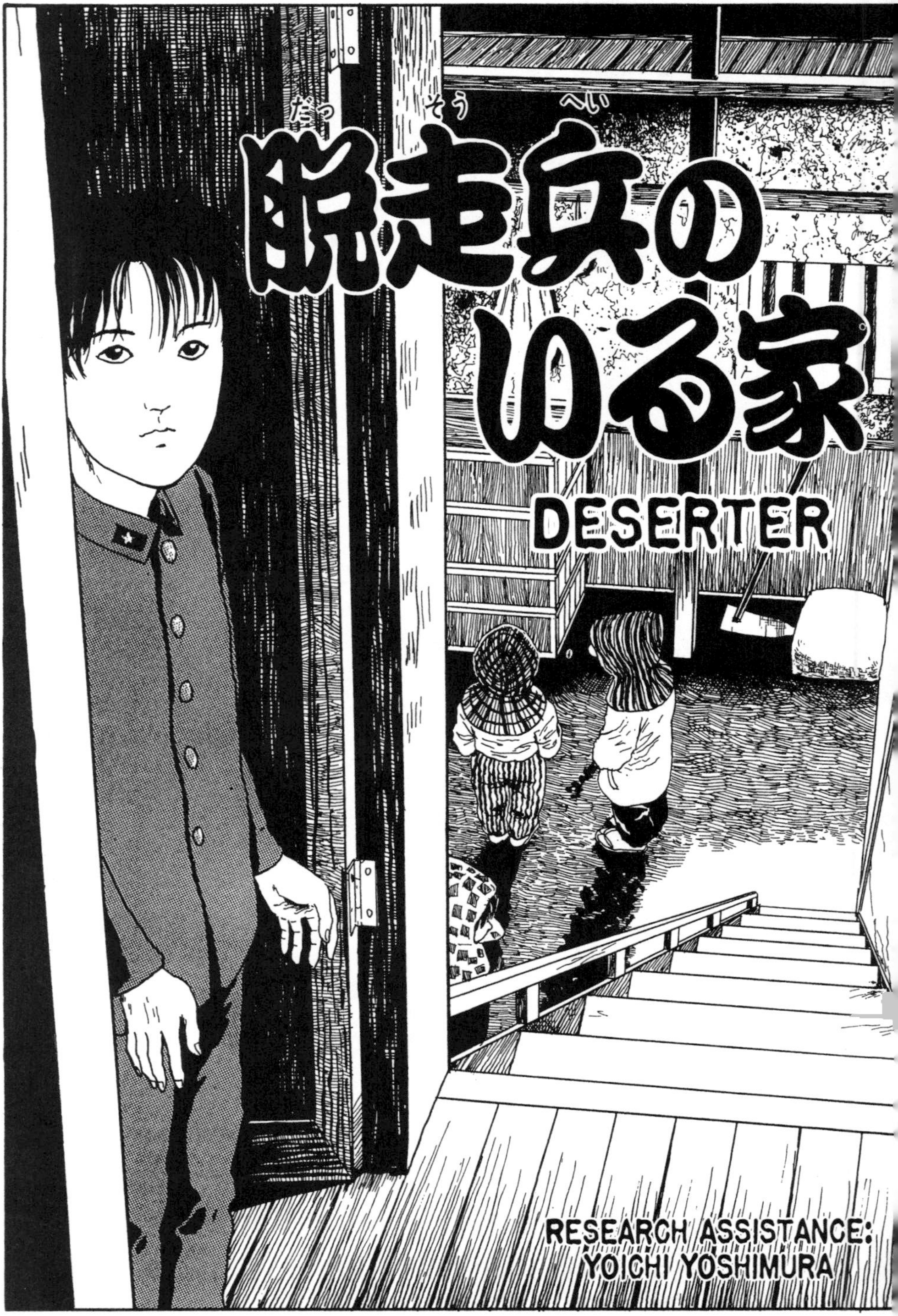

だっそうへい
脱走兵のいる家
DESERTER
RESEARCH ASSISTANCE:
YOICHI YOSHIMURA

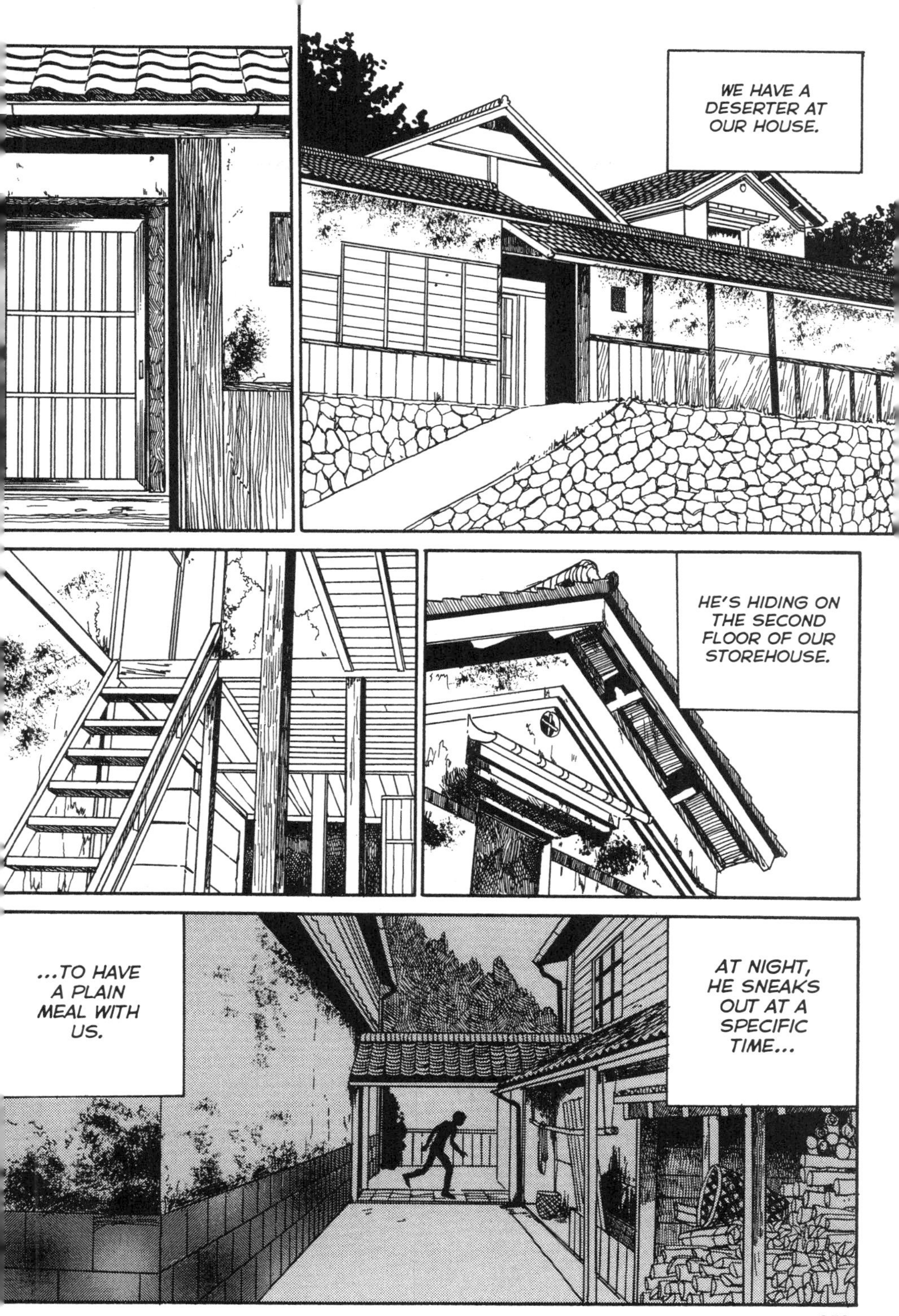
WE HAVE A DESERTER AT OUR HOUSE.
HE'S HIDING ON THE SECOND FLOOR OF OUR STOREHOUSE.
AT NIGHT, HE SNEAKS OUT AT A SPECIFIC TIME...
...TO HAVE A PLAIN MEAL WITH US.

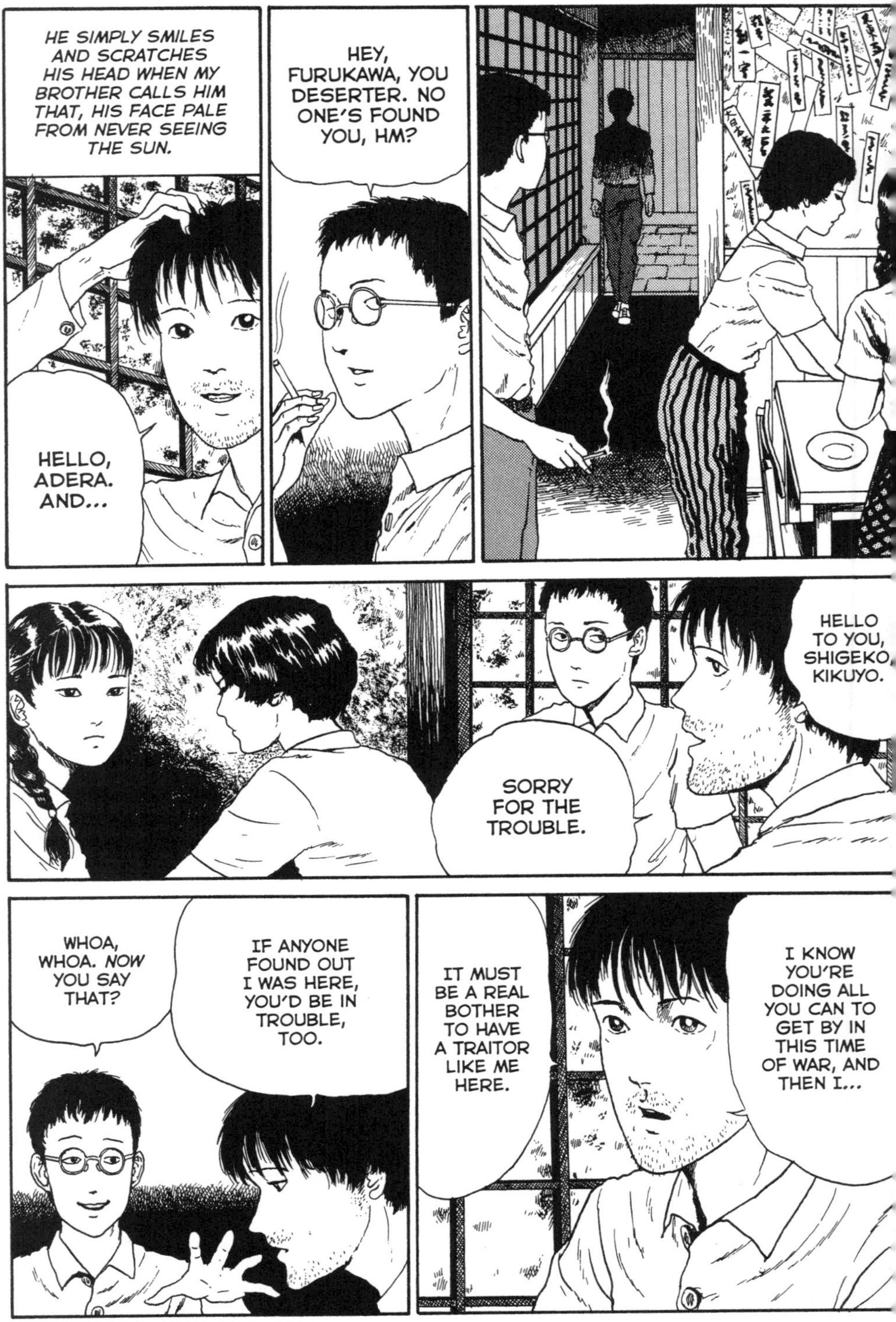
HEY, FURUKAWA, YOU DESERTER. NO ONE'S FOUND YOU, HM?
HE SIMPLY SMILES AND SCRATCHES HIS HEAD WHEN MY BROTHER CALLS HIM THAT, HIS FACE PALE FROM NEVER SEEING THE SUN.
HELLO, ADERA. AND...
HELLO TO YOU, SHIGEKO, KIKUYO.
SORRY FOR THE TROUBLE.
I KNOW YOU'RE DOING ALL YOU CAN TO GET BY IN THIS TIME OF WAR, AND THEN I...
IT MUST BE A REAL BOTHER TO HAVE A TRAITOR LIKE ME HERE.
IF ANYONE FOUND OUT I WAS HERE, YOU'D BE IN TROUBLE, TOO.
WHOA, WHOA. *NOW* YOU SAY THAT?

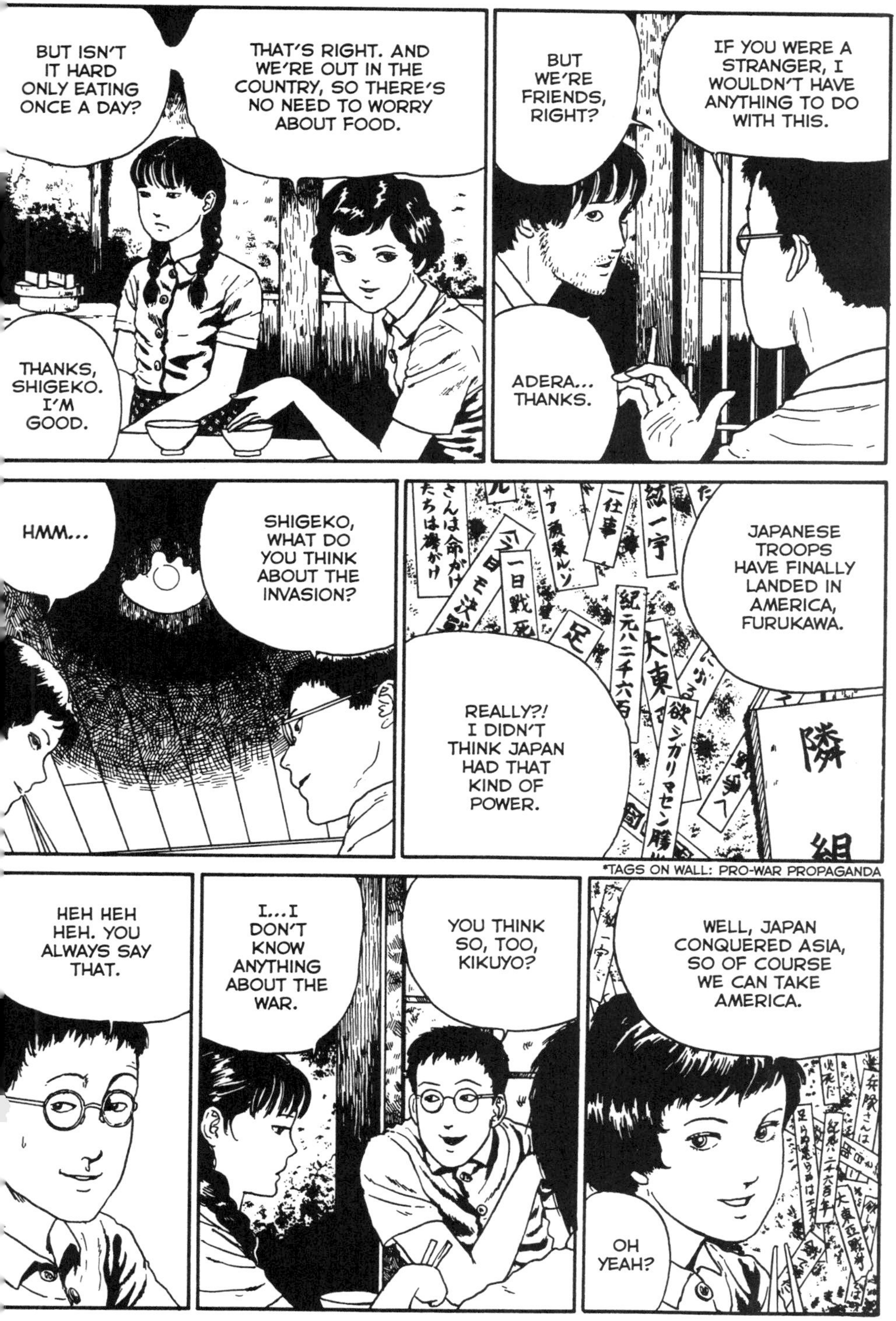
IF YOU WERE A STRANGER, I WOULDN'T HAVE ANYTHING TO DO WITH THIS.
BUT WE'RE FRIENDS, RIGHT?
ADERA... THANKS.
THAT'S RIGHT. AND WE'RE OUT IN THE COUNTRY, SO THERE'S NO NEED TO WORRY ABOUT FOOD.
BUT ISN'T IT HARD ONLY EATING ONCE A DAY?
THANKS, SHIGEKO. I'M GOOD.
JAPANESE TROOPS HAVE FINALLY LANDED IN AMERICA, FURUKAWA.
REALLY?! I DIDN'T THINK JAPAN HAD THAT KIND OF POWER.
SHIGEKO, WHAT DO YOU THINK ABOUT THE INVASION?
HMM...
WELL, JAPAN CONQUERED ASIA, SO OF COURSE WE CAN TAKE AMERICA.
OH YEAH?
YOU THINK SO, TOO, KIKUYO?
I...I DON'T KNOW ANYTHING ABOUT THE WAR.
HEH HEH HEH. YOU ALWAYS SAY THAT.

*TAGS ON WALL: PRO-WAR PROPAGANDA

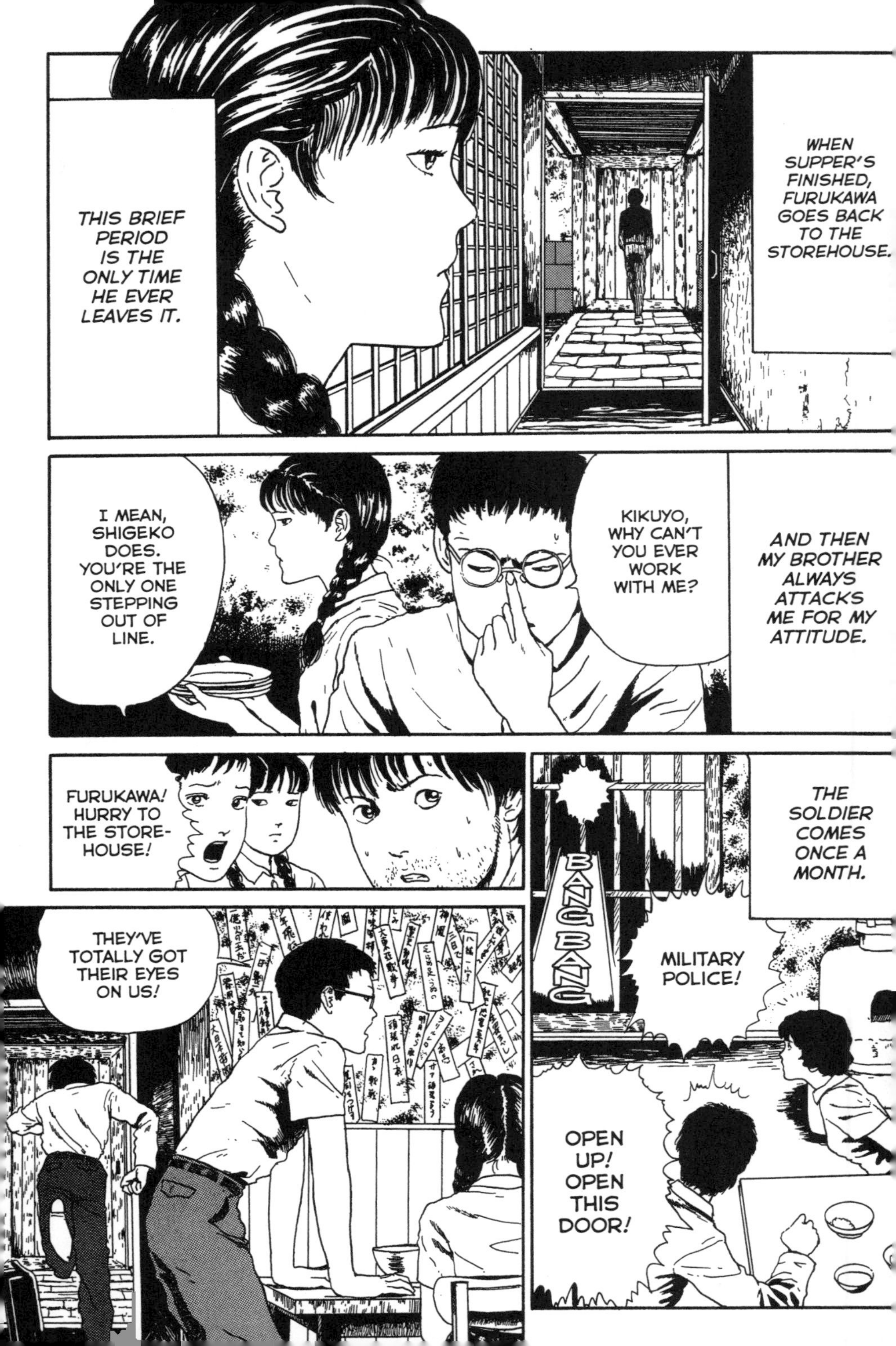
WHEN SUPPER'S FINISHED, FURUKAWA GOES BACK TO THE STOREHOUSE.
THIS BRIEF PERIOD IS THE ONLY TIME HE EVER LEAVES IT.
AND THEN MY BROTHER ALWAYS ATTACKS ME FOR MY ATTITUDE.
KIKUYO, WHY CAN'T YOU EVER WORK WITH ME?
I MEAN, SHIGEKO DOES. YOU'RE THE ONLY ONE STEPPING OUT OF LINE.
THE SOLDIER COMES ONCE A MONTH.
BANG BANG
MILITARY POLICE!
OPEN UP! OPEN THIS DOOR!
FURUKAWA! HURRY TO THE STORE-HOUSE!
THEY'VE TOTALLY GOT THEIR EYES ON US!

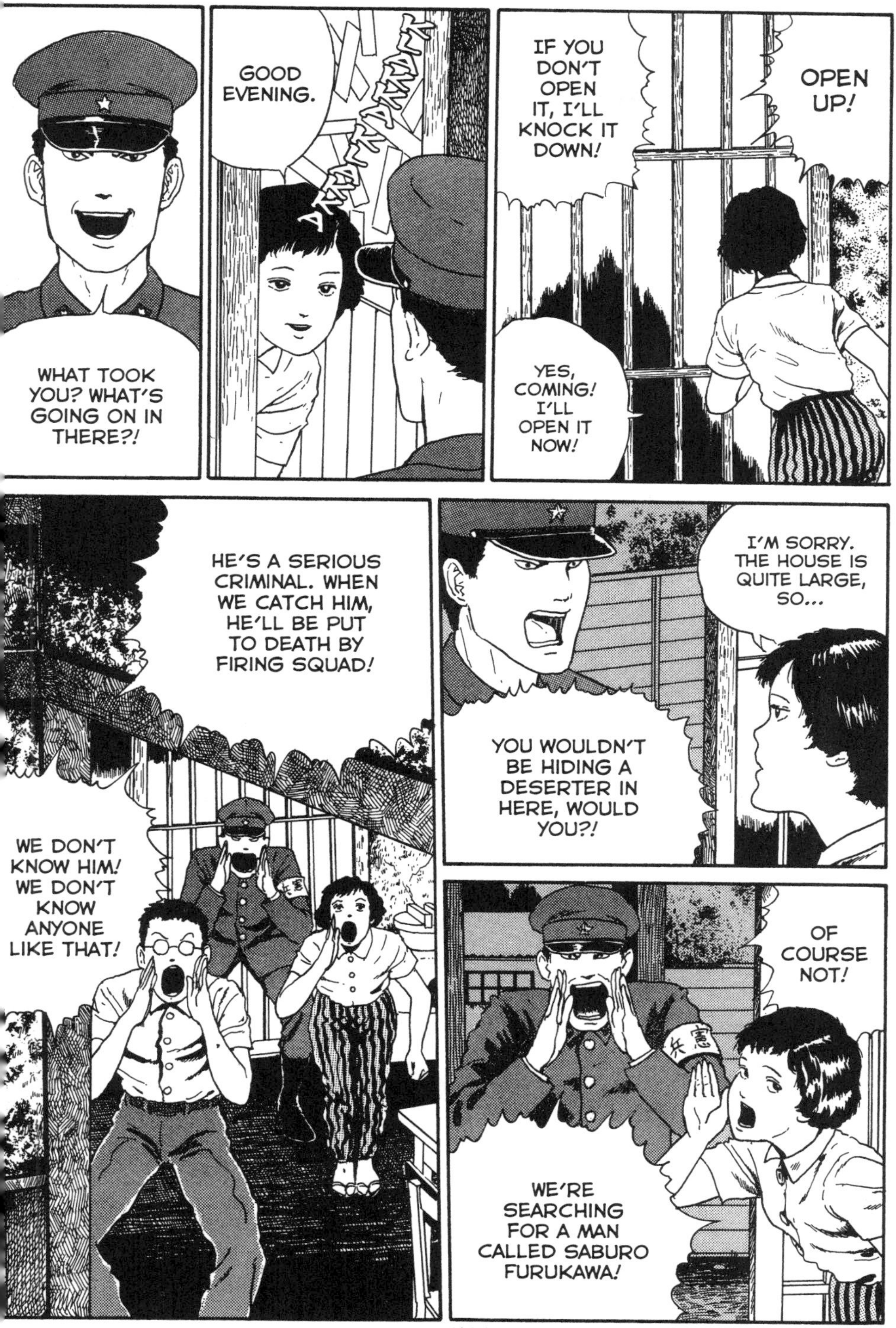
OPEN UP!
IF YOU DON'T OPEN IT, I'LL KNOCK IT DOWN!
YES, COMING! I'LL OPEN IT NOW!
GOOD EVENING.
WHAT TOOK YOU? WHAT'S GOING ON IN THERE?!
I'M SORRY. THE HOUSE IS QUITE LARGE, SO...
YOU WOULDN'T BE HIDING A DESERTER IN HERE, WOULD YOU?!
OF COURSE NOT!
WE'RE SEARCHING FOR A MAN CALLED SABURO FURUKAWA!
HE'S A SERIOUS CRIMINAL. WHEN WE CATCH HIM, HE'LL BE PUT TO DEATH BY FIRING SQUAD!
WE DON'T KNOW HIM! WE DON'T KNOW ANYONE LIKE THAT!

*ARMBAND: MILITARY POLICE

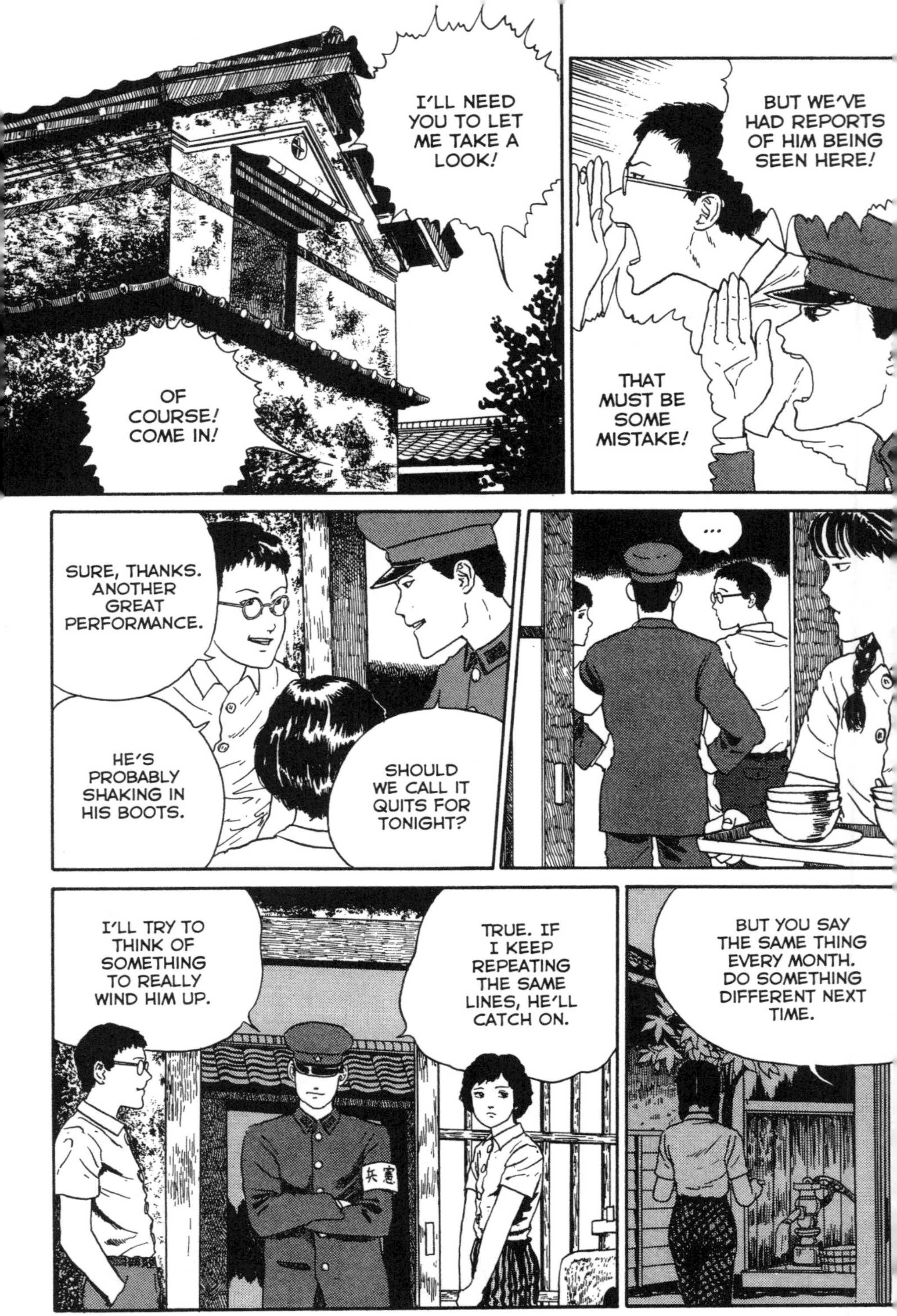
BUT WE'VE HAD REPORTS OF HIM BEING SEEN HERE!
THAT MUST BE SOME MISTAKE!
I'LL NEED YOU TO LET ME TAKE A LOOK!
OF COURSE! COME IN!
...
SURE, THANKS. ANOTHER GREAT PERFORMANCE.
SHOULD WE CALL IT QUITS FOR TONIGHT?
HE'S PROBABLY SHAKING IN HIS BOOTS.
BUT YOU SAY THE SAME THING EVERY MONTH. DO SOMETHING DIFFERENT NEXT TIME.
TRUE. IF I KEEP REPEATING THE SAME LINES, HE'LL CATCH ON.
I'LL TRY TO THINK OF SOMETHING TO REALLY WIND HIM UP.

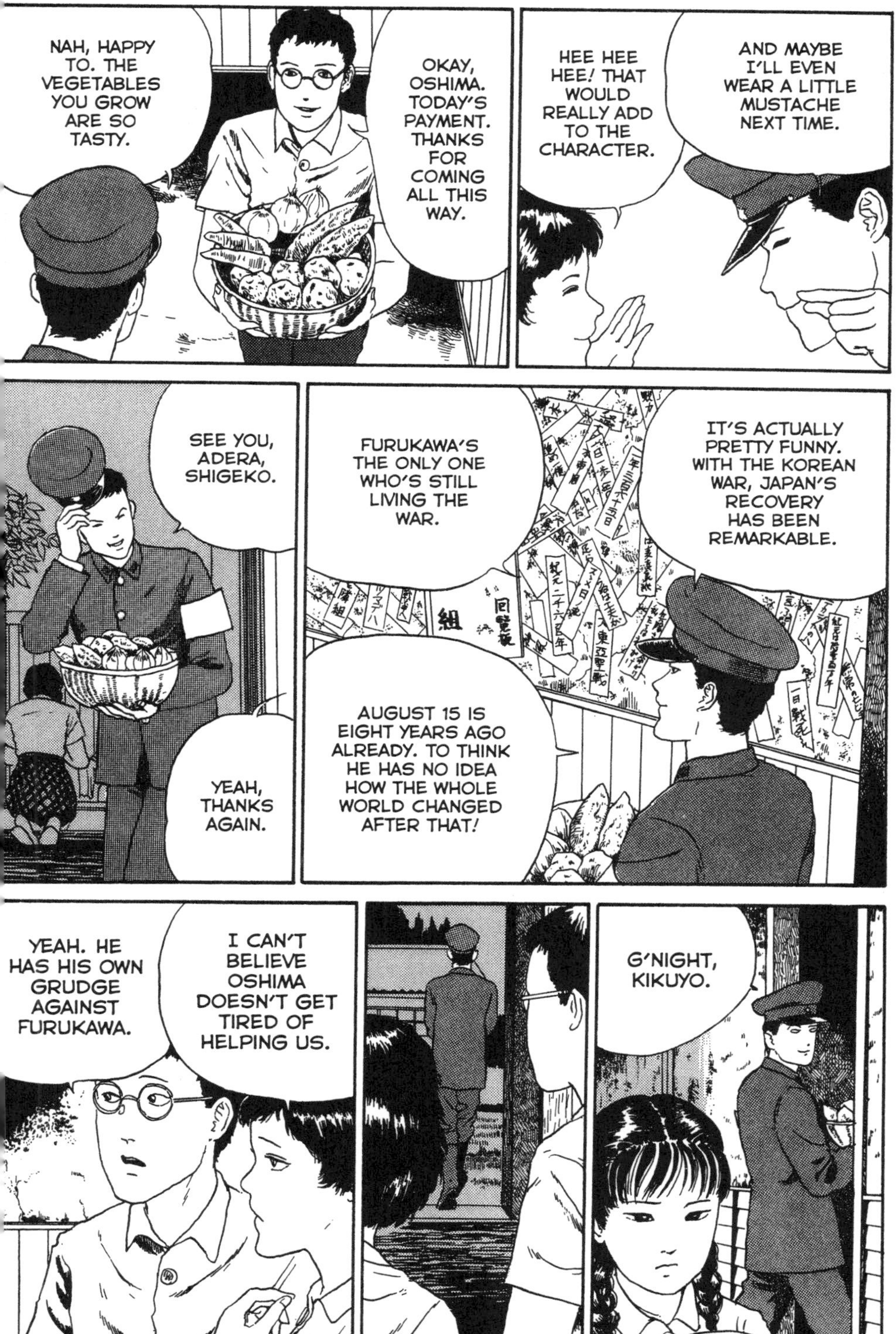
AND MAYBE I'LL EVEN WEAR A LITTLE MUSTACHE NEXT TIME.
HEE HEE HEE! THAT WOULD REALLY ADD TO THE CHARACTER.
OKAY, OSHIMA. TODAY'S PAYMENT. THANKS FOR COMING ALL THIS WAY.
NAH, HAPPY TO. THE VEGETABLES YOU GROW ARE SO TASTY.
IT'S ACTUALLY PRETTY FUNNY. WITH THE KOREAN WAR, JAPAN'S RECOVERY HAS BEEN REMARKABLE.
FURUKAWA'S THE ONLY ONE WHO'S STILL LIVING THE WAR.
AUGUST 15 IS EIGHT YEARS AGO ALREADY. TO THINK HE HAS NO IDEA HOW THE WHOLE WORLD CHANGED AFTER THAT!
SEE YOU, ADERA, SHIGEKO.
YEAH, THANKS AGAIN.
G'NIGHT, KIKUYO.
I CAN'T BELIEVE OSHIMA DOESN'T GET TIRED OF HELPING US.
YEAH. HE HAS HIS OWN GRUDGE AGAINST FURUKAWA.

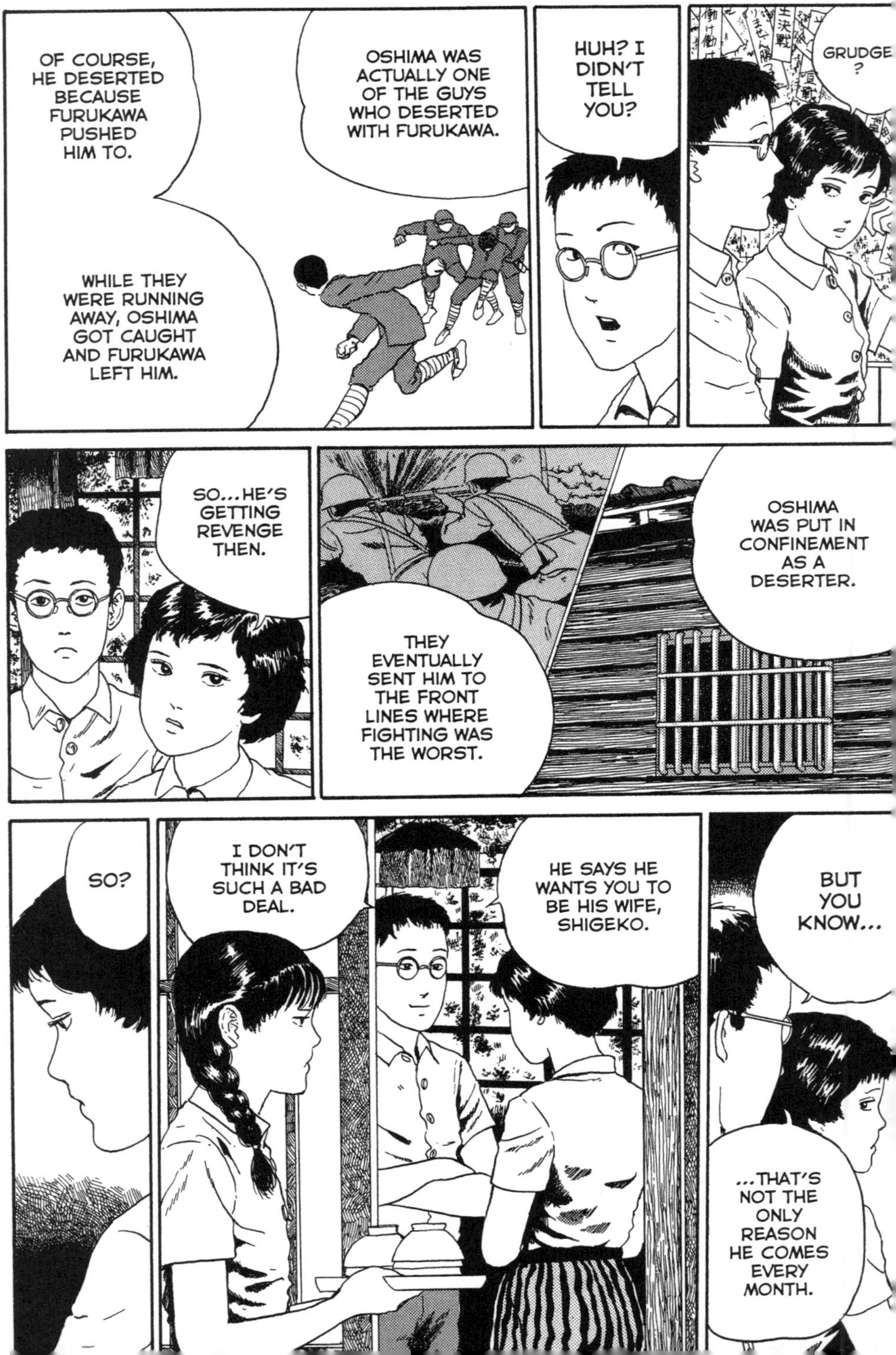
GRUDGE?
HUH? I DIDN'T TELL YOU?
OSHIMA WAS ACTUALLY ONE OF THE GUYS WHO DESERTED WITH FURUKAWA.
OF COURSE, HE DESERTED BECAUSE FURUKAWA PUSHED HIM TO.
WHILE THEY WERE RUNNING AWAY, OSHIMA GOT CAUGHT AND FURUKAWA LEFT HIM.
OSHIMA WAS PUT IN CONFINEMENT AS A DESERTER.
THEY EVENTUALLY SENT HIM TO THE FRONT LINES WHERE FIGHTING WAS THE WORST.
SO...HE'S GETTING REVENGE THEN.
BUT YOU KNOW...
...THAT'S NOT THE ONLY REASON HE COMES EVERY MONTH.
HE SAYS HE WANTS YOU TO BE HIS WIFE, SHIGEKO.
I DON'T THINK IT'S SUCH A BAD DEAL.
SO?

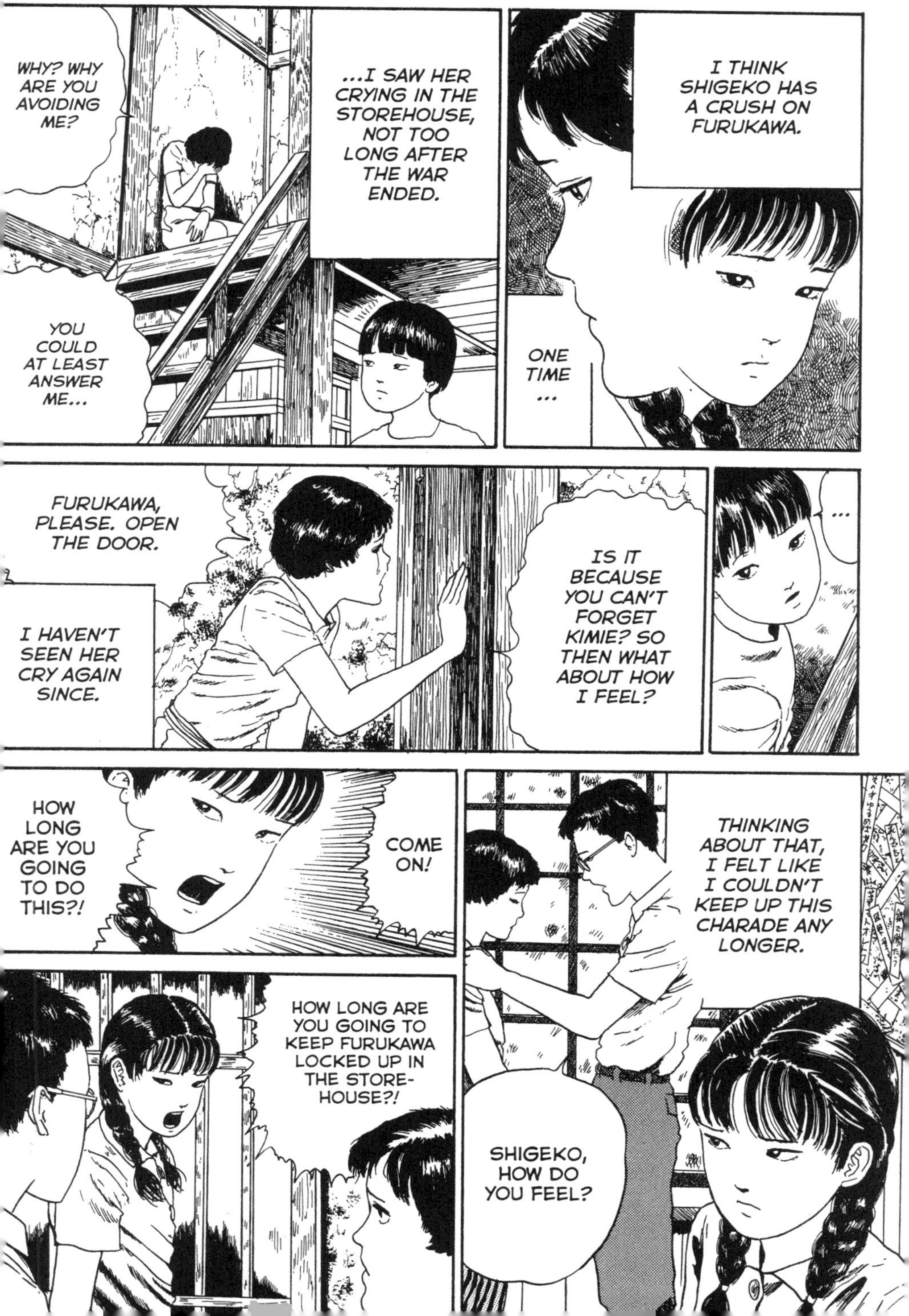
I THINK SHIGEKO HAS A CRUSH ON FURUKAWA.
ONE TIME ...
...I SAW HER CRYING IN THE STOREHOUSE, NOT TOO LONG AFTER THE WAR ENDED.
WHY? WHY ARE YOU AVOIDING ME?
YOU COULD AT LEAST ANSWER ME...
...
IS IT BECAUSE YOU CAN'T FORGET KIMIE? SO THEN WHAT ABOUT HOW I FEEL?
FURUKAWA, PLEASE. OPEN THE DOOR.
I HAVEN'T SEEN HER CRY AGAIN SINCE.
THINKING ABOUT THAT, I FELT LIKE I COULDN'T KEEP UP THIS CHARADE ANY LONGER.
SHIGEKO, HOW DO YOU FEEL?
COME ON!
HOW LONG ARE YOU GOING TO DO THIS?!
HOW LONG ARE YOU GOING TO KEEP FURUKAWA LOCKED UP IN THE STORE-HOUSE?!

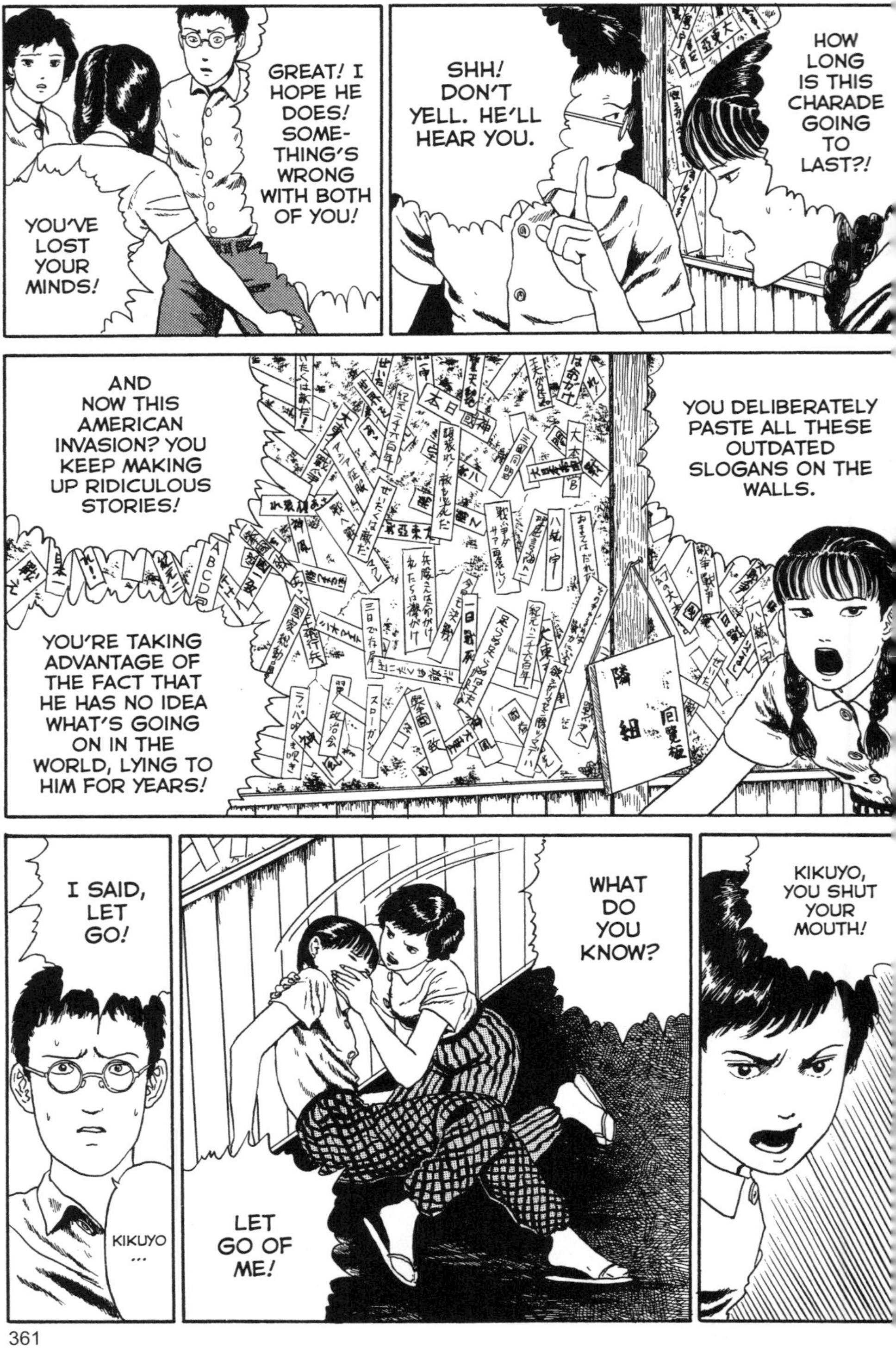
HOW LONG IS THIS CHARADE GOING TO LAST?!
SHH! DON'T YELL. HE'LL HEAR YOU.
GREAT! I HOPE HE DOES! SOME-THING'S WRONG WITH BOTH OF YOU!
YOU'VE LOST YOUR MINDS!
YOU DELIBERATELY PASTE ALL THESE OUTDATED SLOGANS ON THE WALLS.
AND NOW THIS AMERICAN INVASION? YOU KEEP MAKING UP RIDICULOUS STORIES!
YOU'RE TAKING ADVANTAGE OF THE FACT THAT HE HAS NO IDEA WHAT'S GOING ON IN THE WORLD, LYING TO HIM FOR YEARS!
隣組 回覧板
KIKUYO, YOU SHUT YOUR MOUTH!
WHAT DO YOU KNOW?
LET GO OF ME!
I SAID, LET GO!
KIKUYO ...

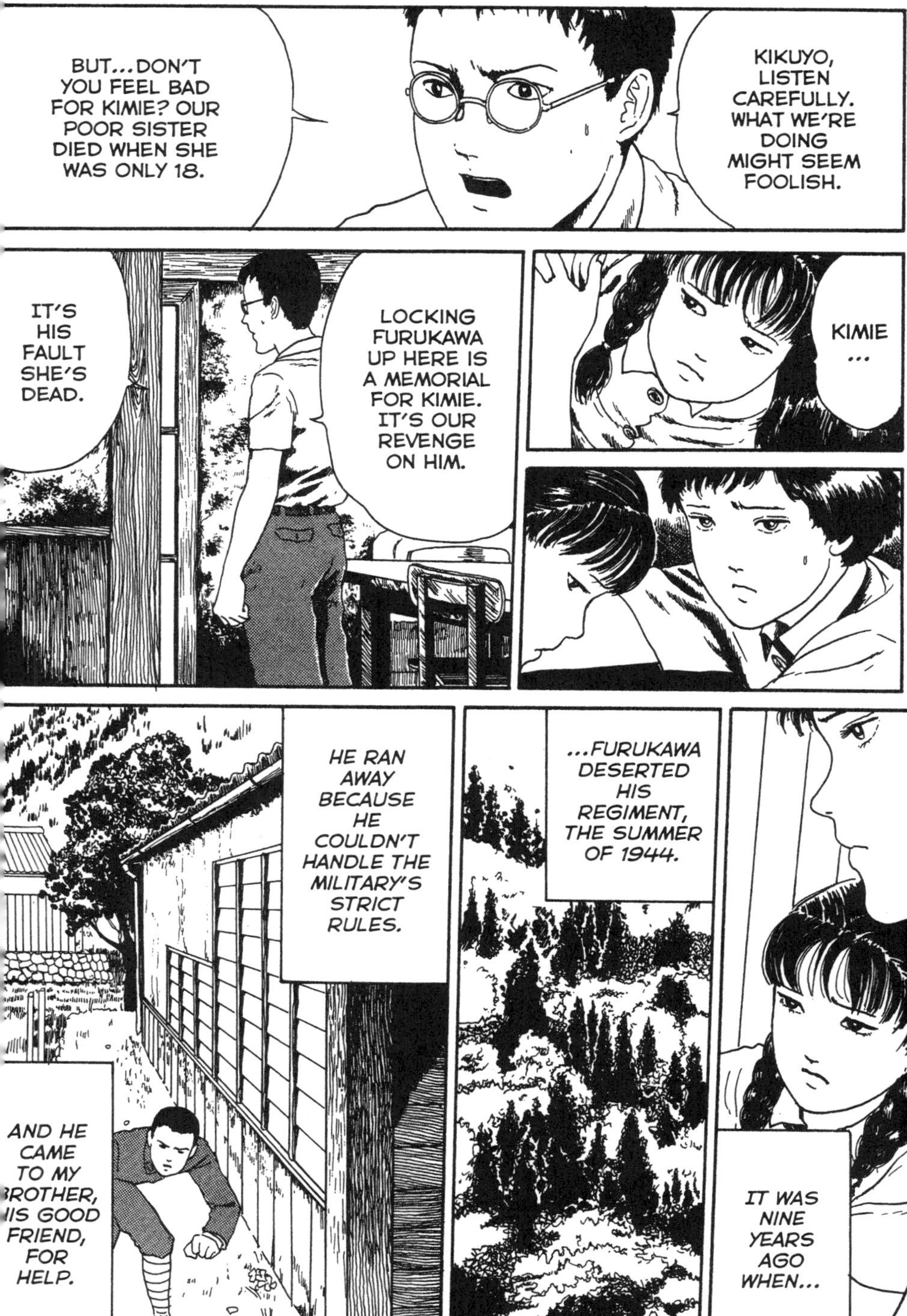
KIKUYO, LISTEN CAREFULLY. WHAT WE'RE DOING MIGHT SEEM FOOLISH.
BUT...DON'T YOU FEEL BAD FOR KIMIE? OUR POOR SISTER DIED WHEN SHE WAS ONLY 18.
KIMIE ...
LOCKING FURUKAWA UP HERE IS A MEMORIAL FOR KIMIE. IT'S OUR REVENGE ON HIM.
IT'S HIS FAULT SHE'S DEAD.
IT WAS NINE YEARS AGO WHEN...
...FURUKAWA DESERTED HIS REGIMENT, THE SUMMER OF 1944.
HE RAN AWAY BECAUSE HE COULDN'T HANDLE THE MILITARY'S STRICT RULES.
AND HE CAME TO MY ROTHER, IS GOOD FRIEND, FOR HELP.

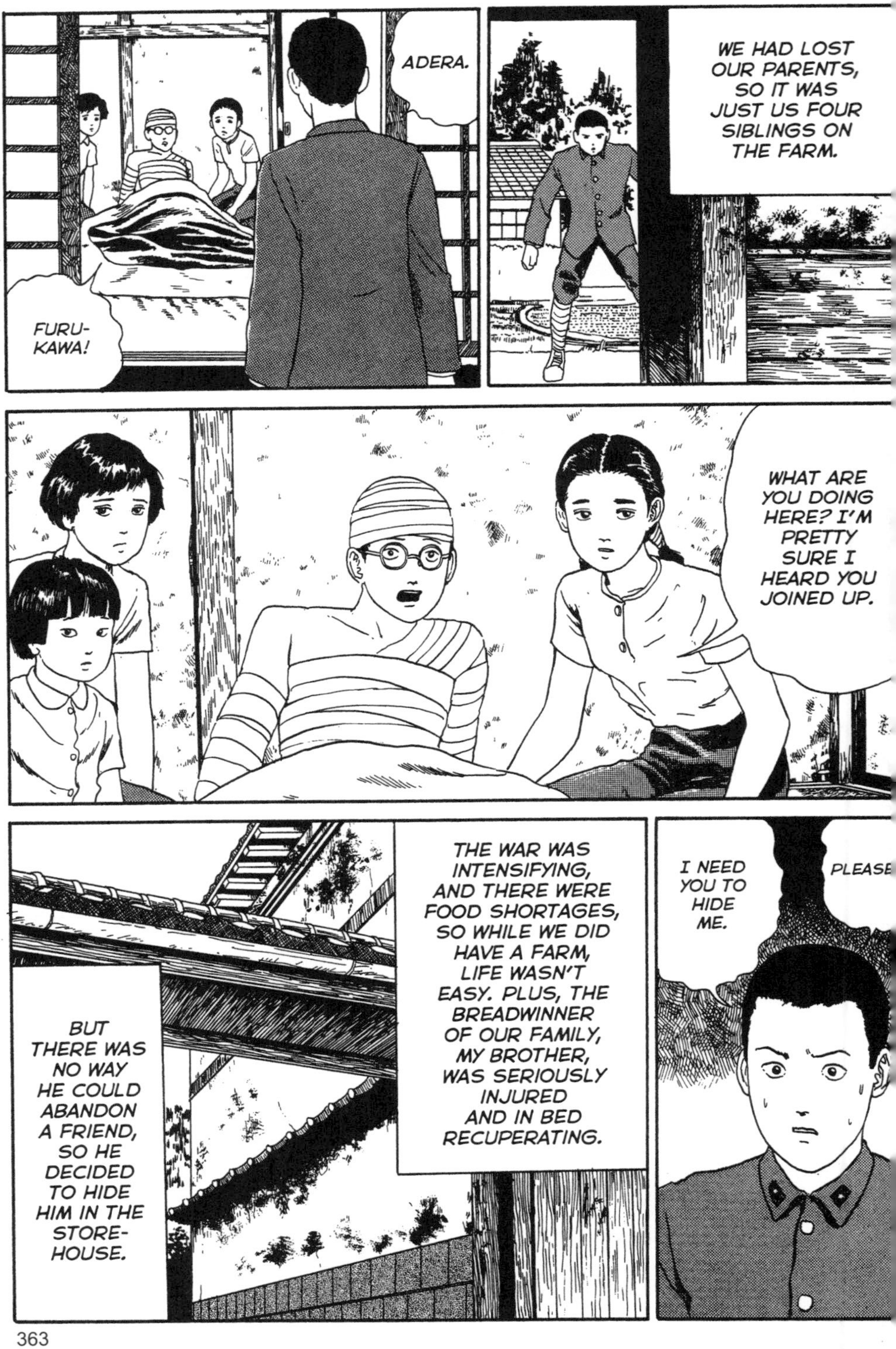
WE HAD LOST OUR PARENTS, SO IT WAS JUST US FOUR SIBLINGS ON THE FARM.
ADERA.
FURU-KAWA!
WHAT ARE YOU DOING HERE? I'M PRETTY SURE I HEARD YOU JOINED UP.
PLEASE
I NEED YOU TO HIDE ME.
THE WAR WAS INTENSIFYING, AND THERE WERE FOOD SHORTAGES, SO WHILE WE DID HAVE A FARM, LIFE WASN'T EASY. PLUS, THE BREADWINNER OF OUR FAMILY, MY BROTHER, WAS SERIOUSLY INJURED AND IN BED RECUPERATING.
BUT THERE WAS NO WAY HE COULD ABANDON A FRIEND, SO HE DECIDED TO HIDE HIM IN THE STORE-HOUSE.

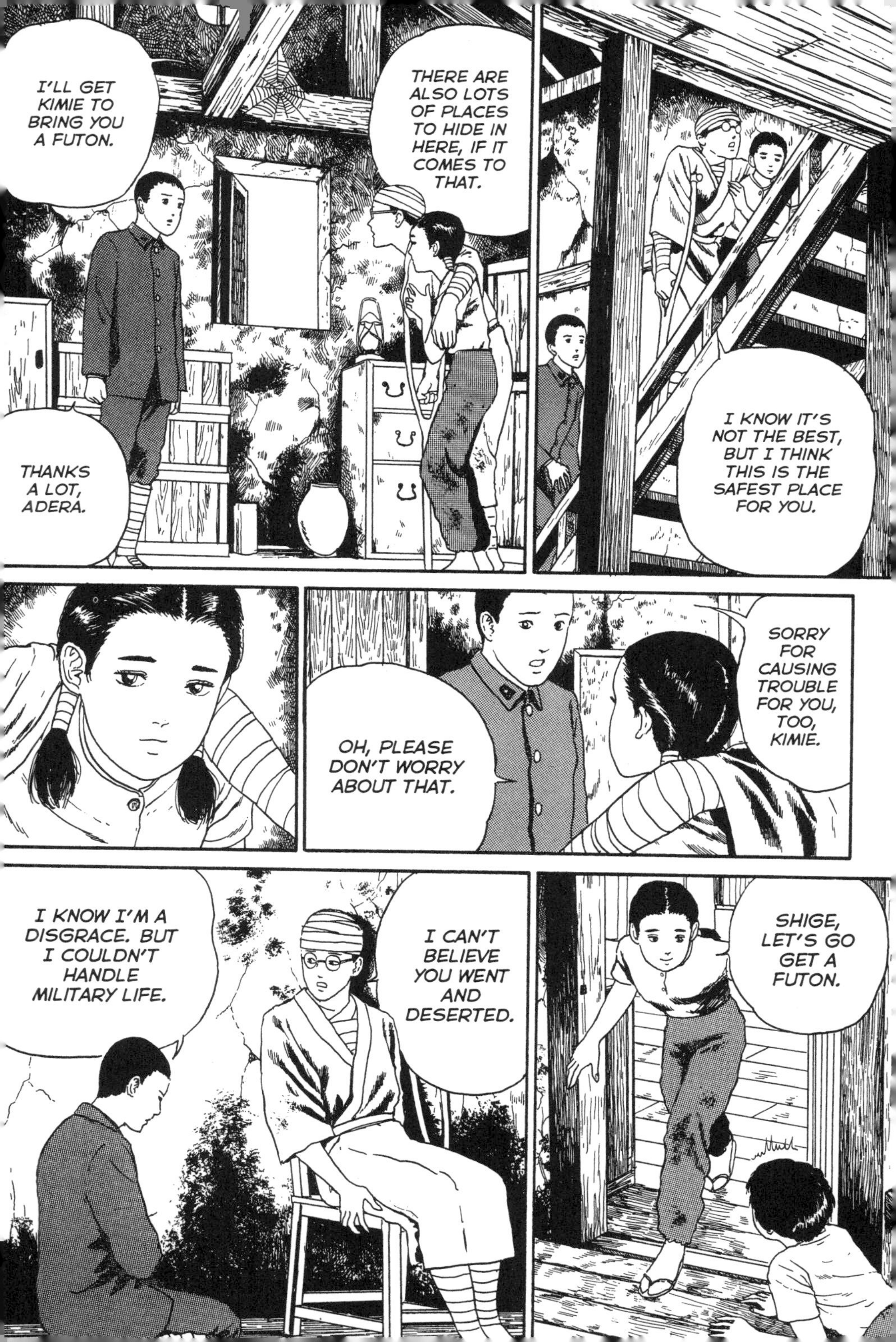
I KNOW IT'S NOT THE BEST, BUT I THINK THIS IS THE SAFEST PLACE FOR YOU.
THERE ARE ALSO LOTS OF PLACES TO HIDE IN HERE, IF IT COMES TO THAT.
I'LL GET KIMIE TO BRING YOU A FUTON.
THANKS A LOT, ADERA.
SORRY FOR CAUSING TROUBLE FOR YOU, TOO, KIMIE.
OH, PLEASE DON'T WORRY ABOUT THAT.
SHIGE, LET'S GO GET A FUTON.
I CAN'T BELIEVE YOU WENT AND DESERTED.
I KNOW I'M A DISGRACE. BUT I COULDN'T HANDLE MILITARY LIFE.

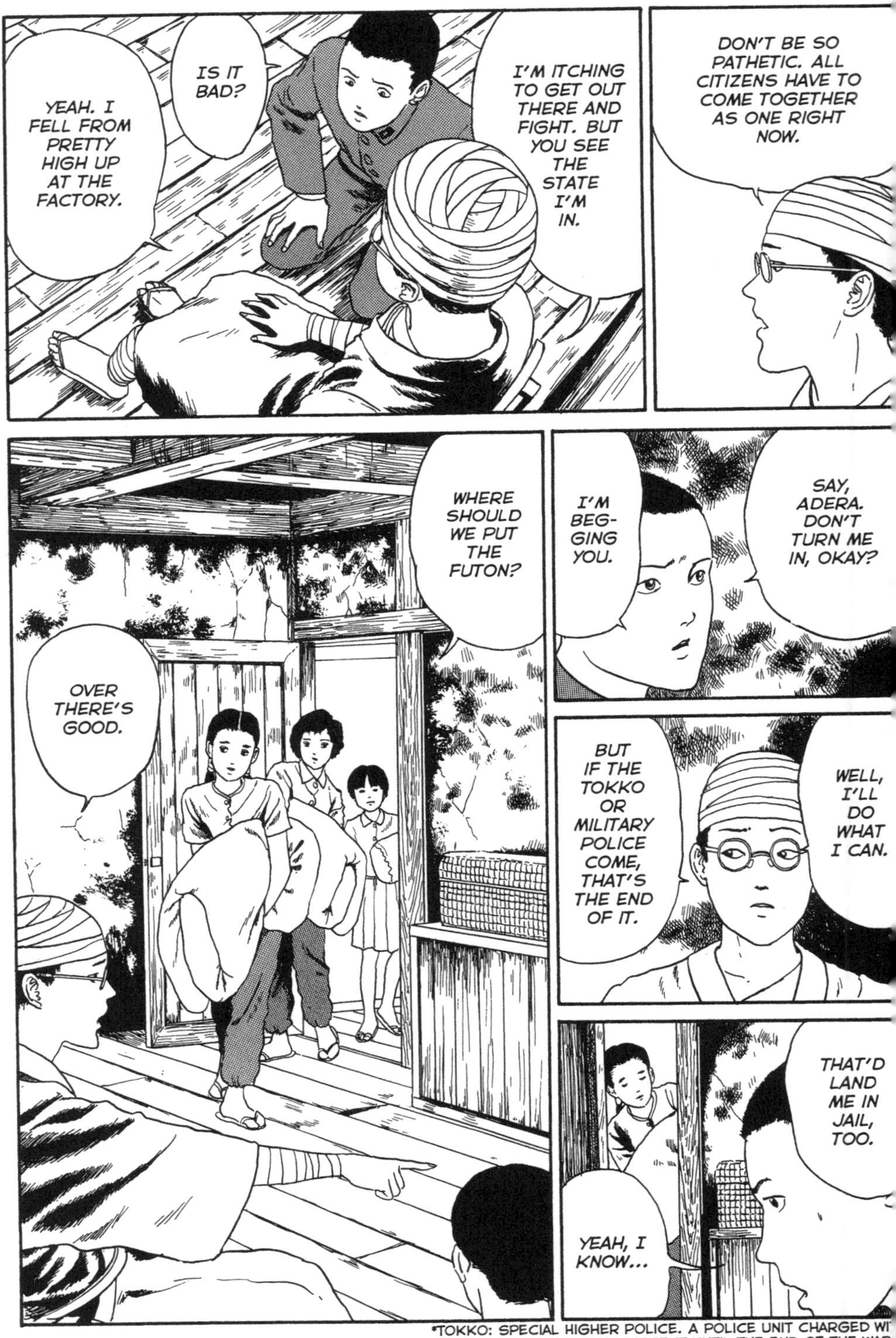
DON'T BE SO PATHETIC. ALL CITIZENS HAVE TO COME TOGETHER AS ONE RIGHT NOW.
IS IT BAD?
YEAH. I FELL FROM PRETTY HIGH UP AT THE FACTORY.
I'M ITCHING TO GET OUT THERE AND FIGHT. BUT YOU SEE THE STATE I'M IN.
SAY, ADERA. DON'T TURN ME IN, OKAY?
I'M BEG-GING YOU.
WELL, I'LL DO WHAT I CAN.
BUT IF THE TOKKO OR MILITARY POLICE COME, THAT'S THE END OF IT.
THAT'D LAND ME IN JAIL, TOO.
YEAH, I KNOW...
WHERE SHOULD WE PUT THE FUTON?
OVER THERE'S GOOD.

*TOKKO: SPECIAL HIGHER POLICE. A POLICE UNIT CHARGED WI
DEALING WITH POLITICAL DISSENT UNTIL THE END OF THE WAR

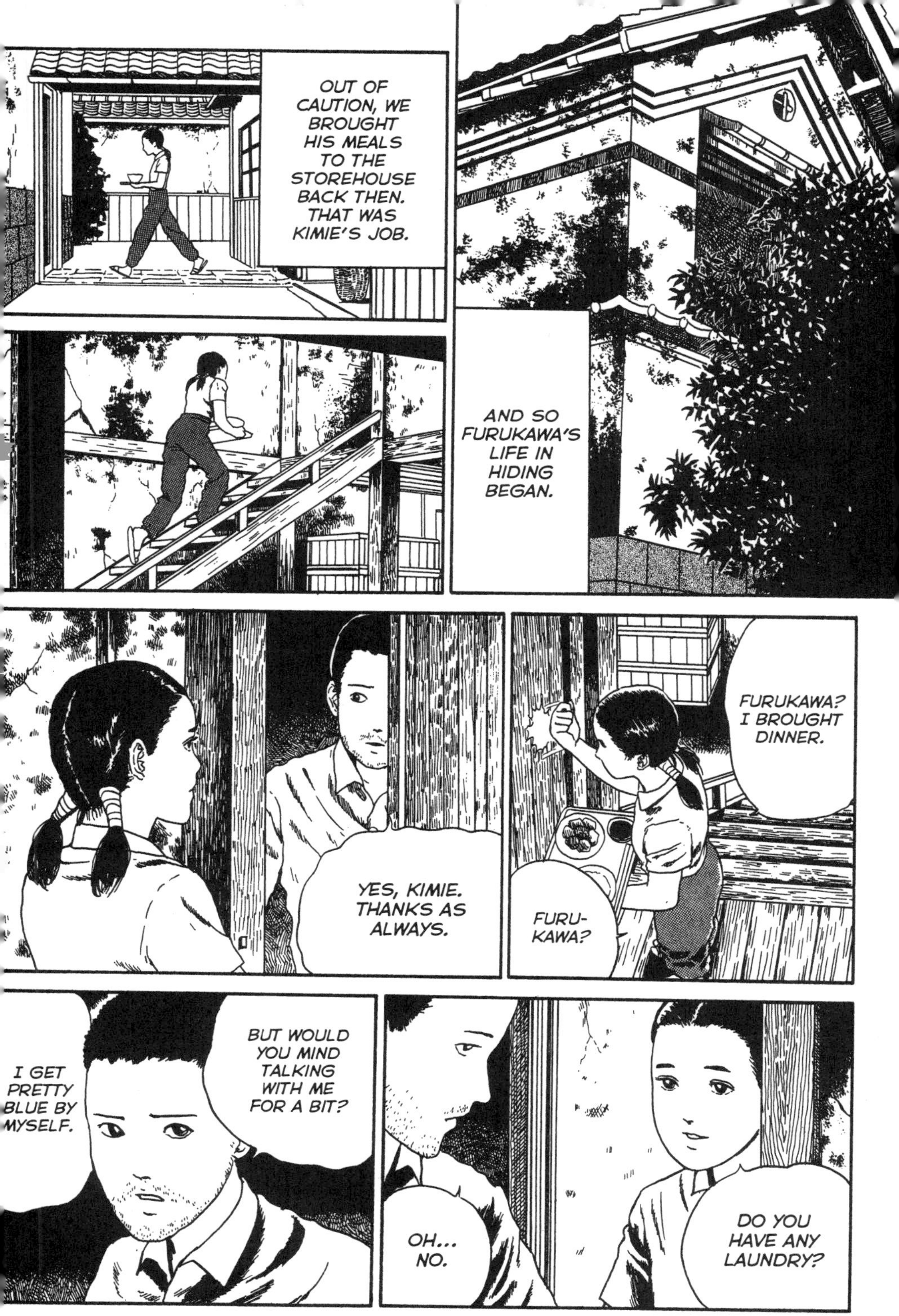
AND SO FURUKAWA'S LIFE IN HIDING BEGAN.
OUT OF CAUTION, WE BROUGHT HIS MEALS TO THE STOREHOUSE BACK THEN. THAT WAS KIMIE'S JOB.
FURUKAWA? I BROUGHT DINNER.
FURU-KAWA?
YES, KIMIE. THANKS AS ALWAYS.
DO YOU HAVE ANY LAUNDRY?
OH... NO.
BUT WOULD YOU MIND TALKING WITH ME FOR A BIT?
I GET PRETTY BLUE BY MYSELF.

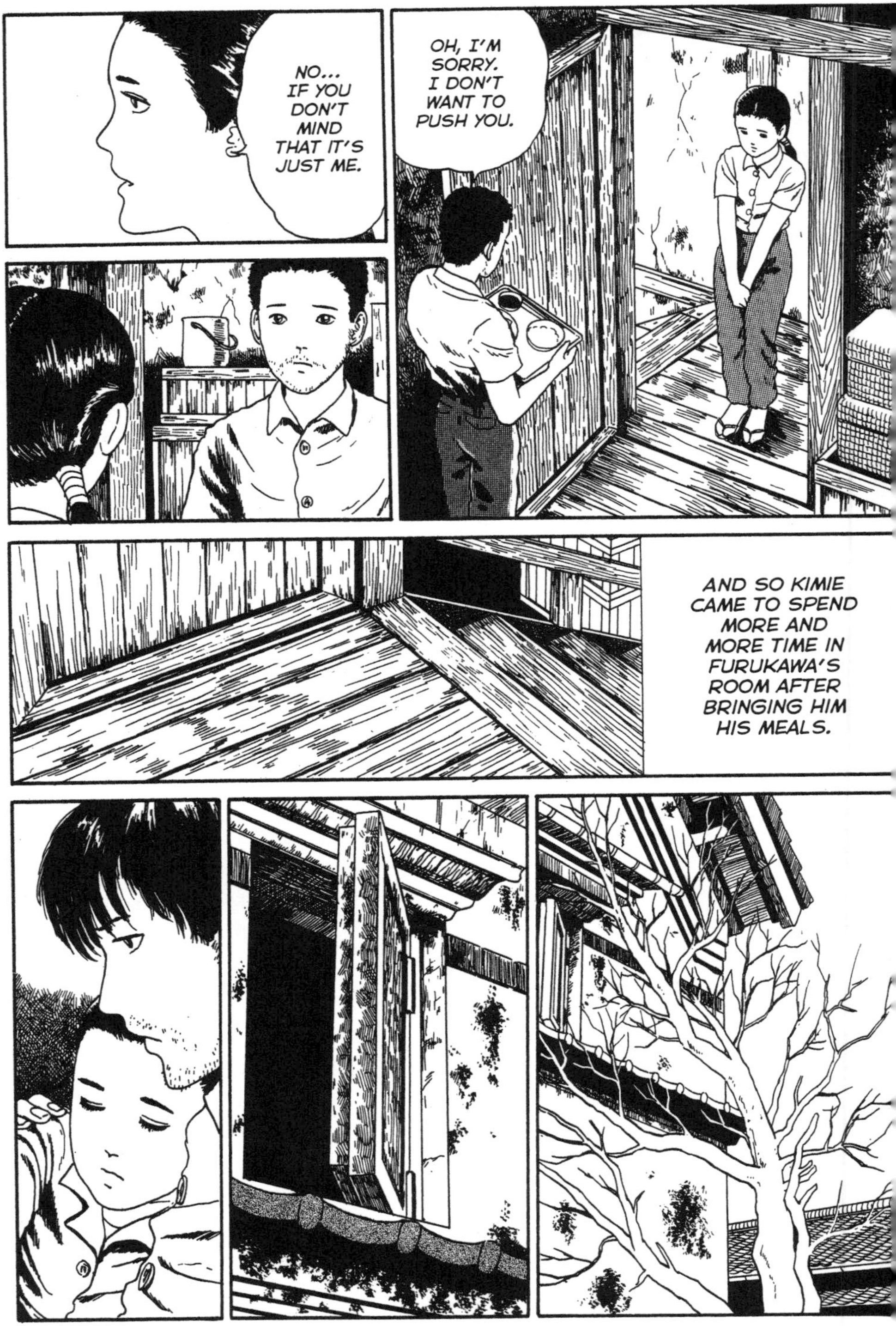
OH, I'M SORRY. I DON'T WANT TO PUSH YOU.
NO... IF YOU DON'T MIND THAT IT'S JUST ME.
AND SO KIMIE CAME TO SPEND MORE AND MORE TIME IN FURUKAWA'S ROOM AFTER BRINGING HIM HIS MEALS.

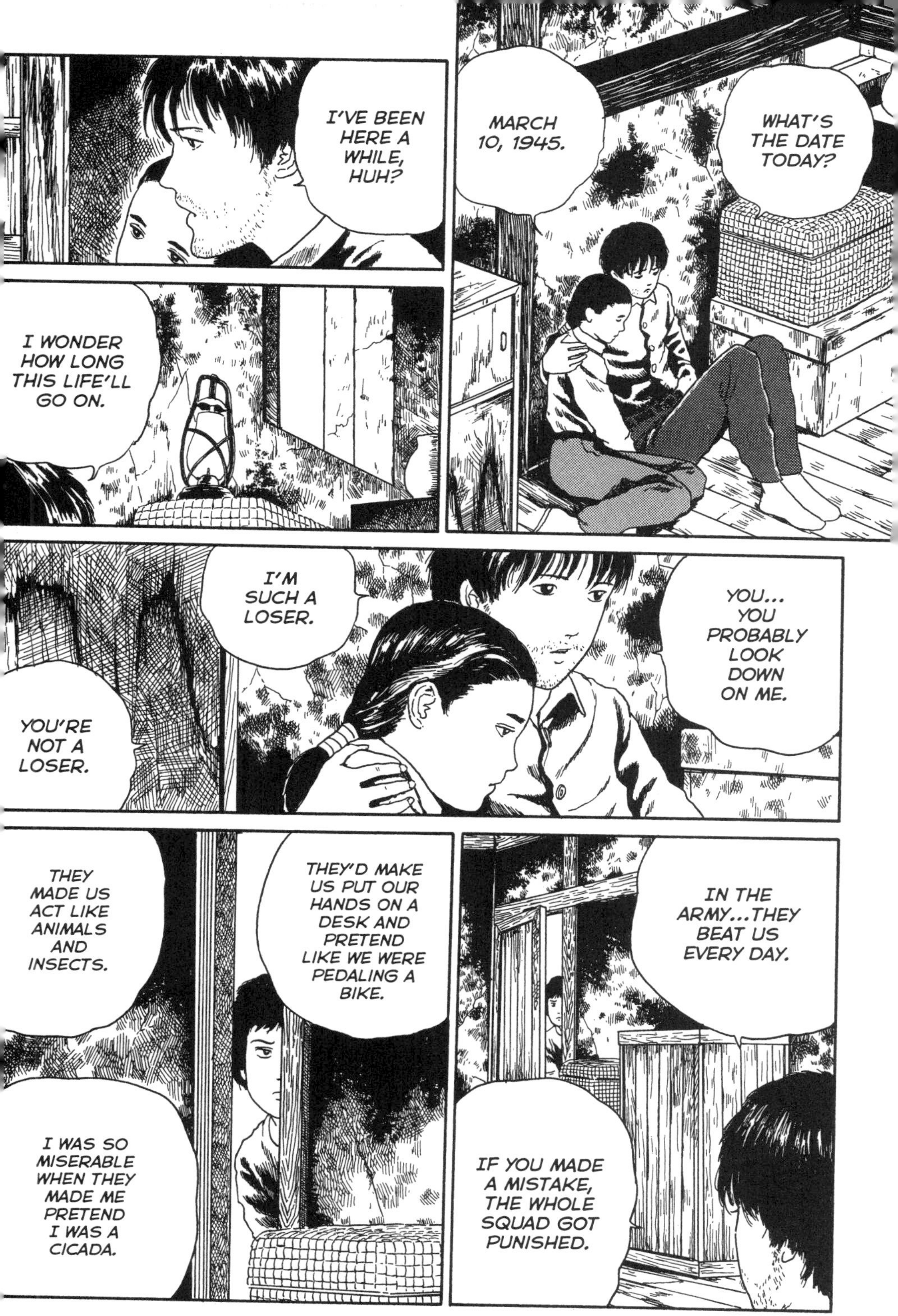
WHAT'S THE DATE TODAY?
MARCH 10, 1945.
I'VE BEEN HERE A WHILE, HUH?
I WONDER HOW LONG THIS LIFE'LL GO ON.
YOU... YOU PROBABLY LOOK DOWN ON ME.
I'M SUCH A LOSER.
YOU'RE NOT A LOSER.
IN THE ARMY...THEY BEAT US EVERY DAY.
IF YOU MADE A MISTAKE, THE WHOLE SQUAD GOT PUNISHED.
THEY'D MAKE US PUT OUR HANDS ON A DESK AND PRETEND LIKE WE WERE PEDALING A BIKE.
THEY MADE US ACT LIKE ANIMALS AND INSECTS.
I WAS SO MISERABLE WHEN THEY MADE ME PRETEND I WAS A CICADA.

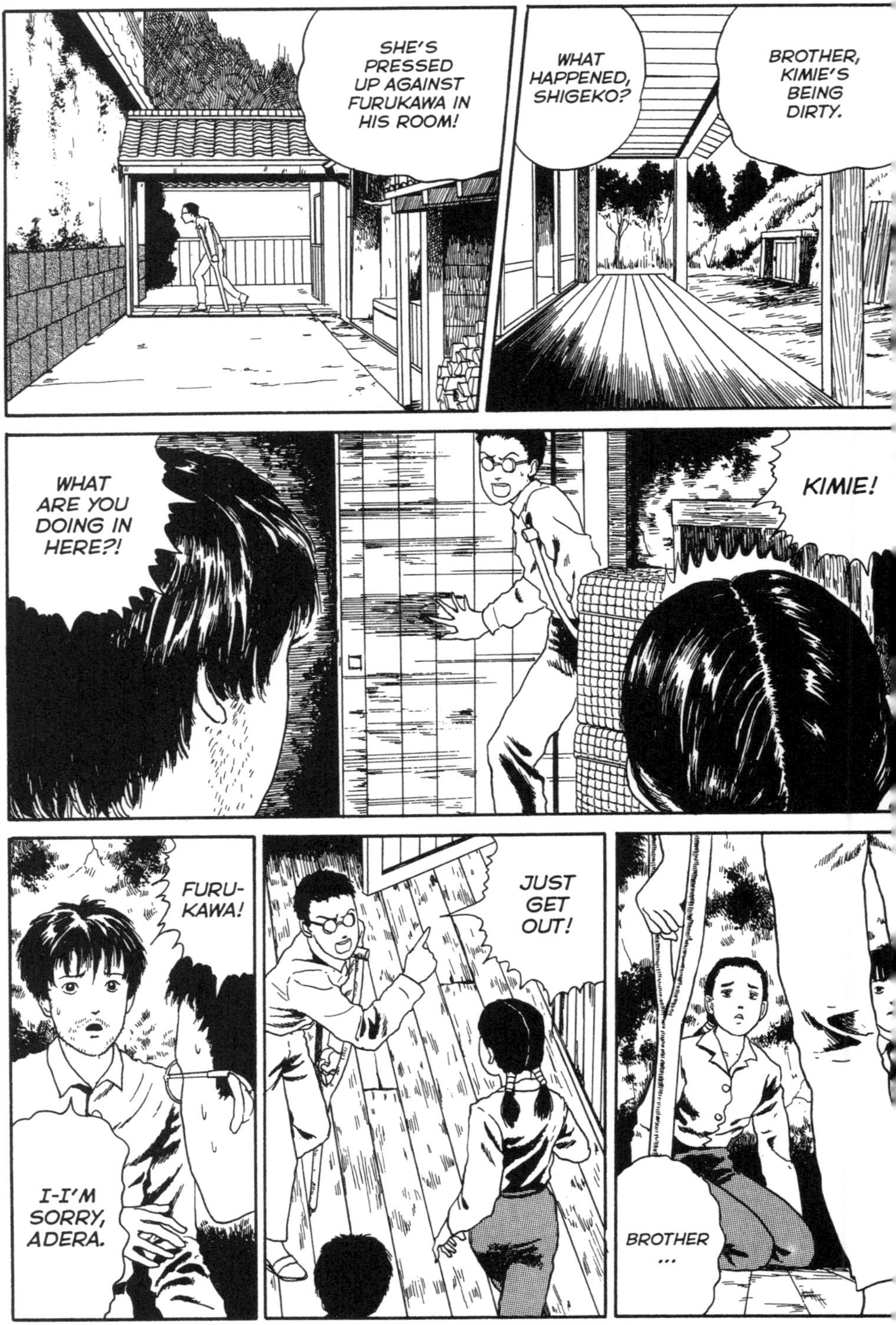
BROTHER, KIMIE'S BEING DIRTY.
WHAT HAPPENED, SHIGEKO?
SHE'S PRESSED UP AGAINST FURUKAWA IN HIS ROOM!
KIMIE!
WHAT ARE YOU DOING IN HERE?!
BROTHER ...
JUST GET OUT!
FURU-KAWA!
I-I'M SORRY, ADERA.

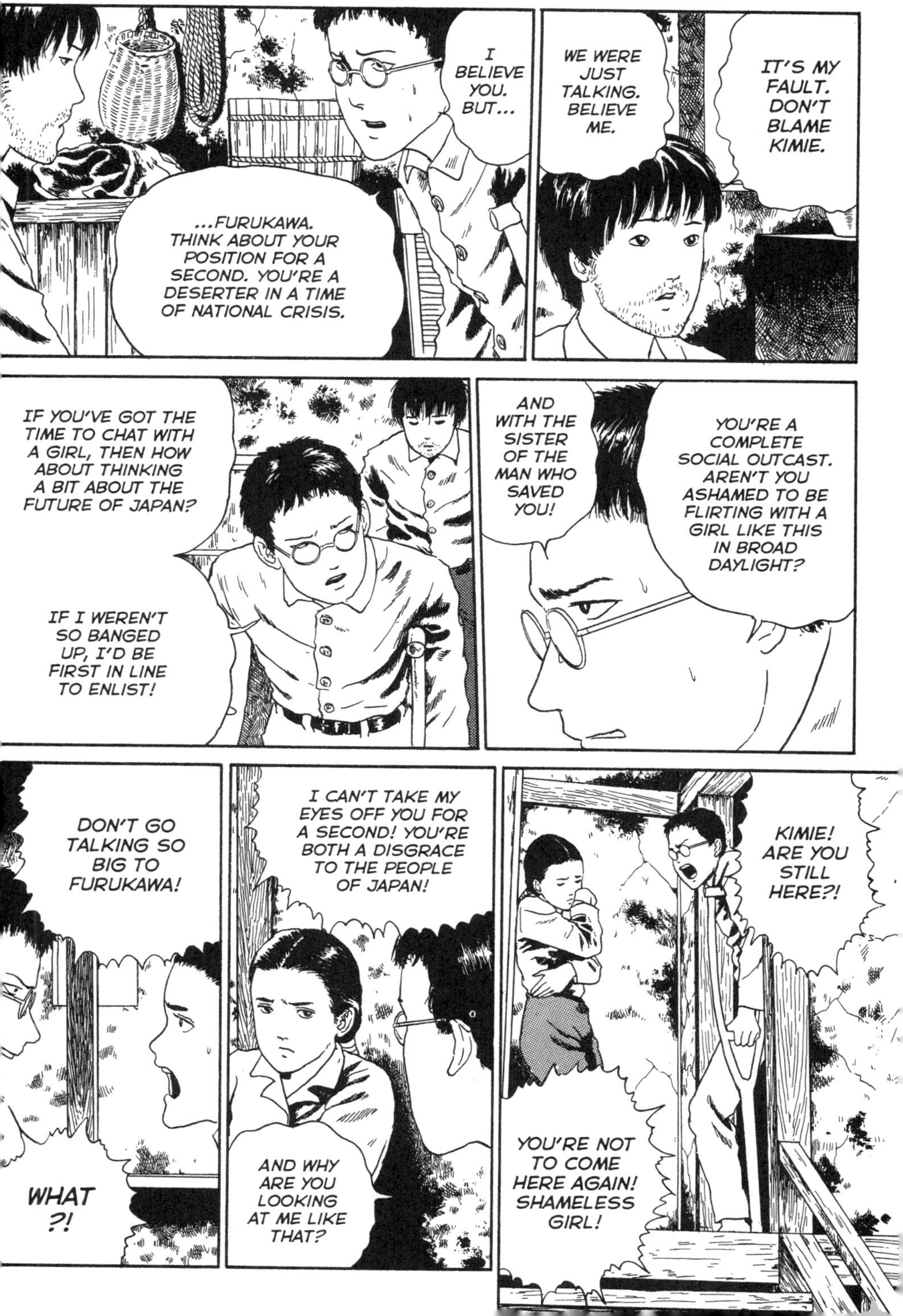
IT'S MY FAULT. DON'T BLAME KIMIE.
WE WERE JUST TALKING. BELIEVE ME.
I BELIEVE YOU. BUT...
...FURUKAWA. THINK ABOUT YOUR POSITION FOR A SECOND. YOU'RE A DESERTER IN A TIME OF NATIONAL CRISIS.
YOU'RE A COMPLETE SOCIAL OUTCAST. AREN'T YOU ASHAMED TO BE FLIRTING WITH A GIRL LIKE THIS IN BROAD DAYLIGHT?
AND WITH THE SISTER OF THE MAN WHO SAVED YOU!
IF YOU'VE GOT THE TIME TO CHAT WITH A GIRL, THEN HOW ABOUT THINKING A BIT ABOUT THE FUTURE OF JAPAN?
IF I WEREN'T SO BANGED UP, I'D BE FIRST IN LINE TO ENLIST!
KIMIE! ARE YOU STILL HERE?!
YOU'RE NOT TO COME HERE AGAIN! SHAMELESS GIRL!
I CAN'T TAKE MY EYES OFF YOU FOR A SECOND! YOU'RE BOTH A DISGRACE TO THE PEOPLE OF JAPAN!
AND WHY ARE YOU LOOKING AT ME LIKE THAT?
DON'T GO TALKING SO BIG TO FURUKAWA!
WHAT ?!

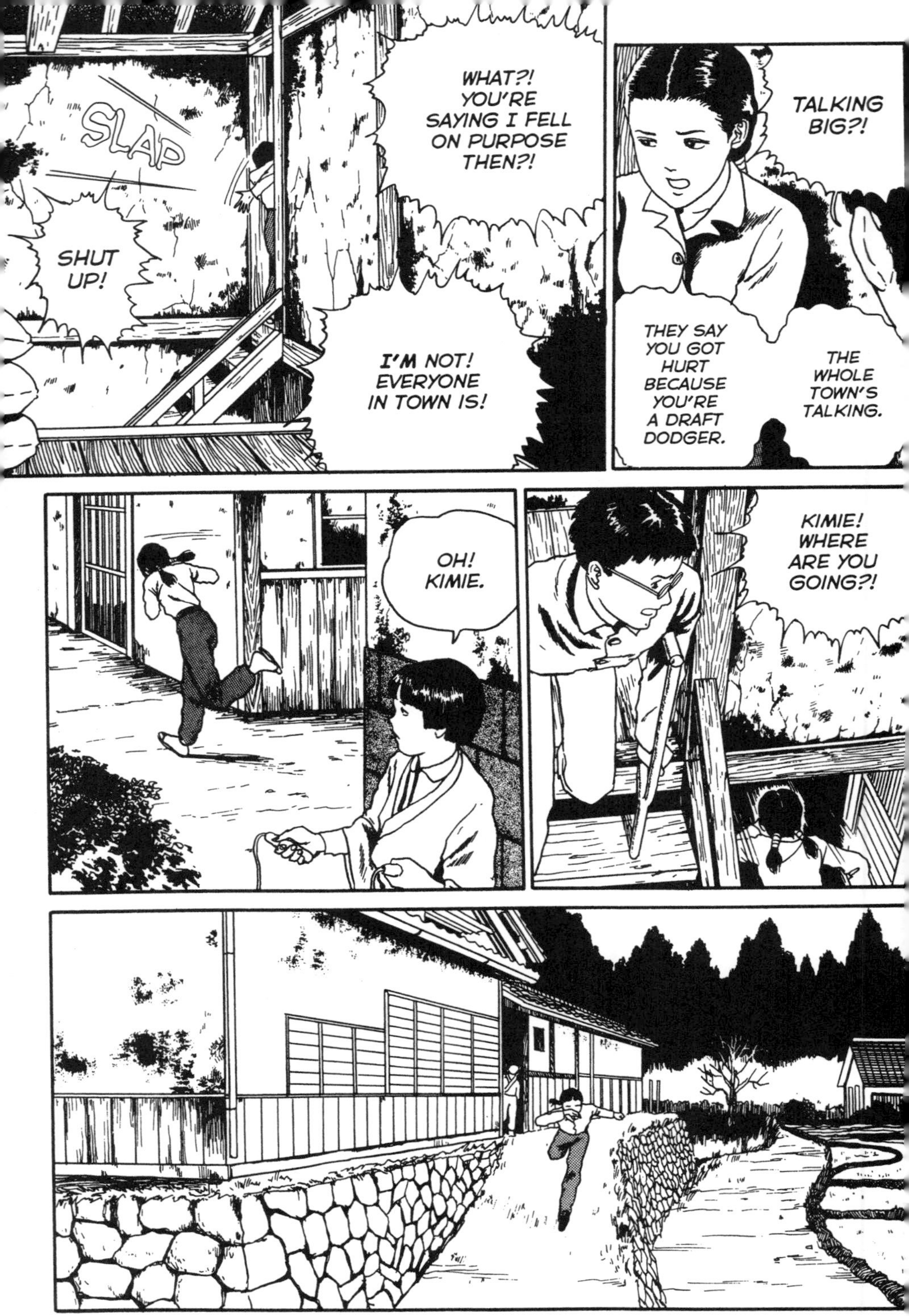
TALKING BIG?!
THE WHOLE TOWN'S TALKING.
THEY SAY YOU GOT HURT BECAUSE YOU'RE A DRAFT DODGER.
WHAT?! YOU'RE SAYING I FELL ON PURPOSE THEN?!
I'M NOT! EVERYONE IN TOWN IS!
SLAP
SHUT UP!
KIMIE! WHERE ARE YOU GOING?!
OH! KIMIE.

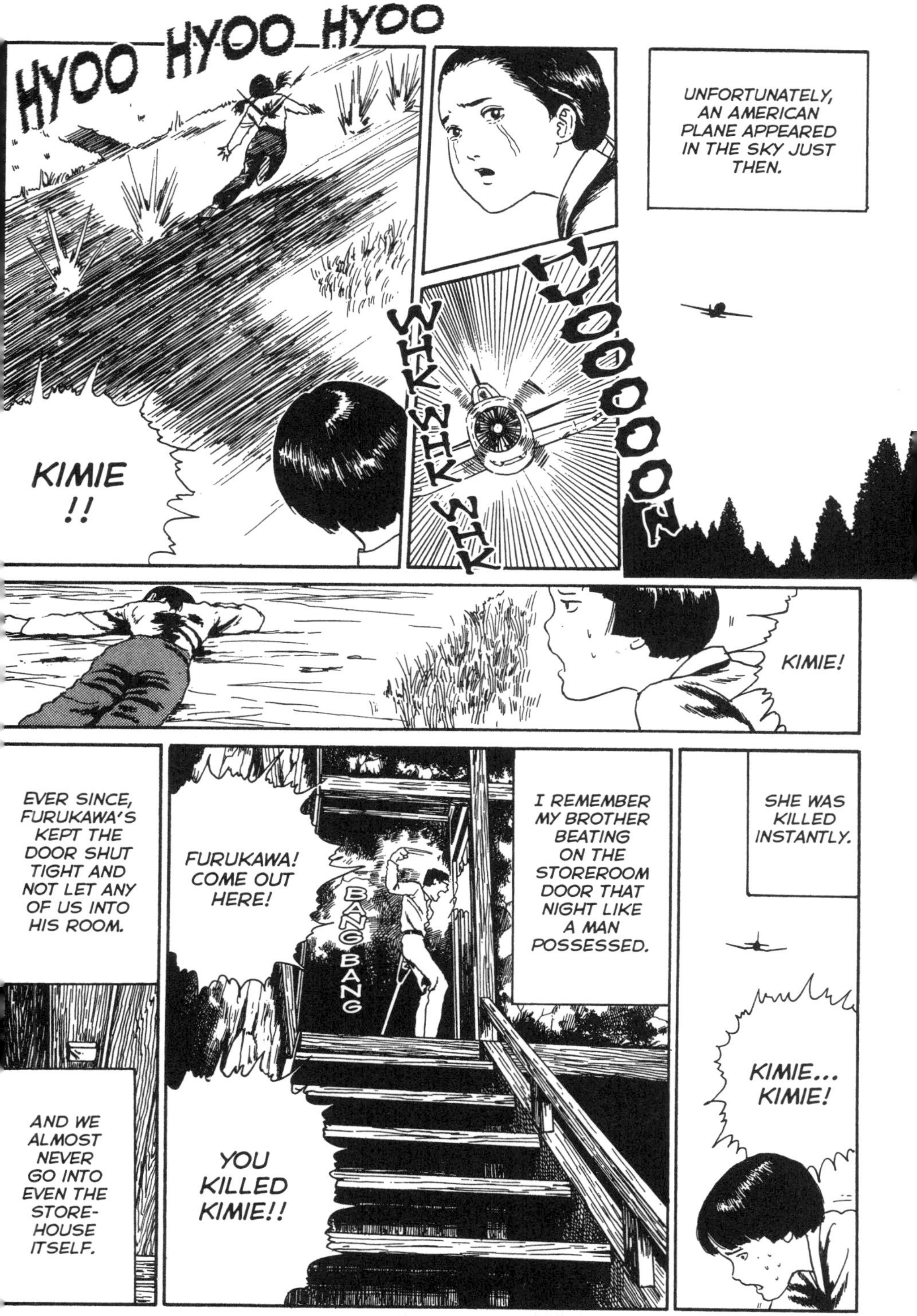
UNFORTUNATELY, AN AMERICAN PLANE APPEARED IN THE SKY JUST THEN.
VOOOOOOON
WHK WHK WHK
HYOO HYOO HYOO
KIMIE !!
KIMIE!
SHE WAS KILLED INSTANTLY.
KIMIE... KIMIE!
I REMEMBER MY BROTHER BEATING ON THE STOREROOM DOOR THAT NIGHT LIKE A MAN POSSESSED.
FURUKAWA! COME OUT HERE!
BANG BANG
YOU KILLED KIMIE!!
EVER SINCE, FURUKAWA'S KEPT THE DOOR SHUT TIGHT AND NOT LET ANY OF US INTO HIS ROOM.
AND WE ALMOST NEVER GO INTO EVEN THE STORE-HOUSE ITSELF.

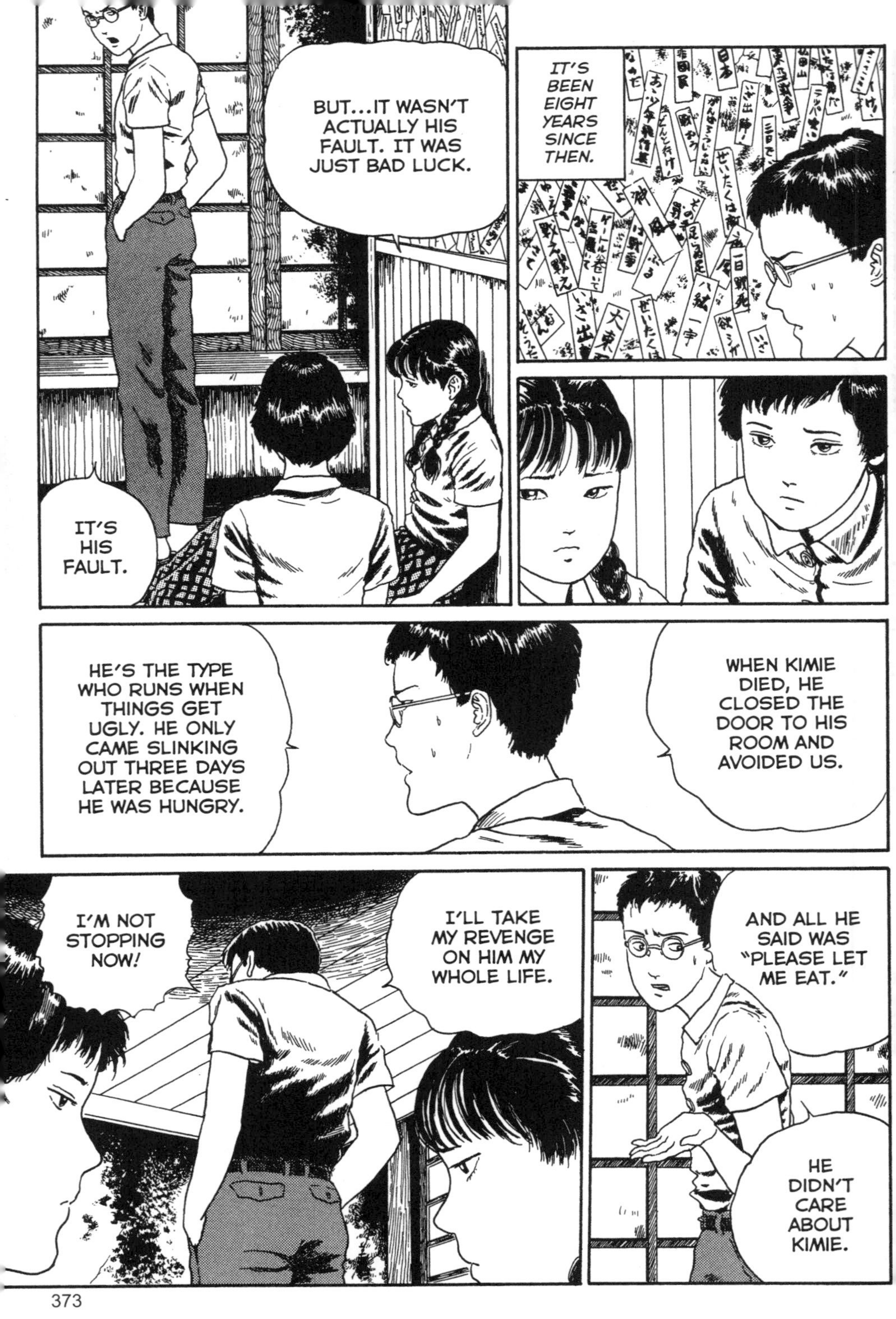
IT'S BEEN EIGHT YEARS SINCE THEN.
BUT...IT WASN'T ACTUALLY HIS FAULT. IT WAS JUST BAD LUCK.
IT'S HIS FAULT.
WHEN KIMIE DIED, HE CLOSED THE DOOR TO HIS ROOM AND AVOIDED US.
HE'S THE TYPE WHO RUNS WHEN THINGS GET UGLY. HE ONLY CAME SLINKING OUT THREE DAYS LATER BECAUSE HE WAS HUNGRY.
AND ALL HE SAID WAS "PLEASE LET ME EAT."
HE DIDN'T CARE ABOUT KIMIE.
I'LL TAKE MY REVENGE ON HIM MY WHOLE LIFE.
I'M NOT STOPPING NOW!

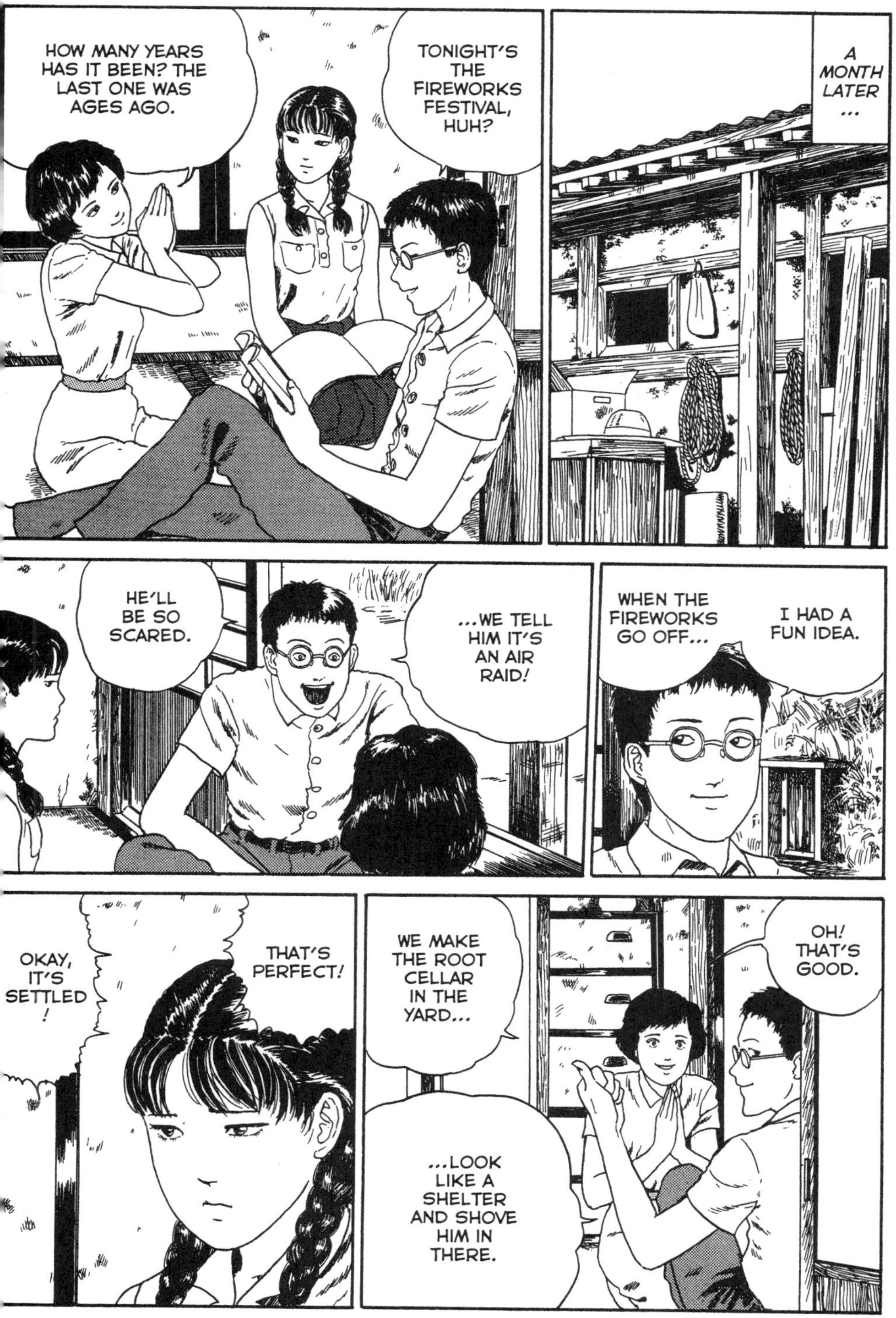
A MONTH LATER ...
TONIGHT'S THE FIREWORKS FESTIVAL, HUH?
HOW MANY YEARS HAS IT BEEN? THE LAST ONE WAS AGES AGO.
I HAD A FUN IDEA.
WHEN THE FIREWORKS GO OFF...
...WE TELL HIM IT'S AN AIR RAID!
HE'LL BE SO SCARED.
OH! THAT'S GOOD.
WE MAKE THE ROOT CELLAR IN THE YARD...
...LOOK LIKE A SHELTER AND SHOVE HIM IN THERE.
THAT'S PERFECT!
OKAY, IT'S SETTLED!

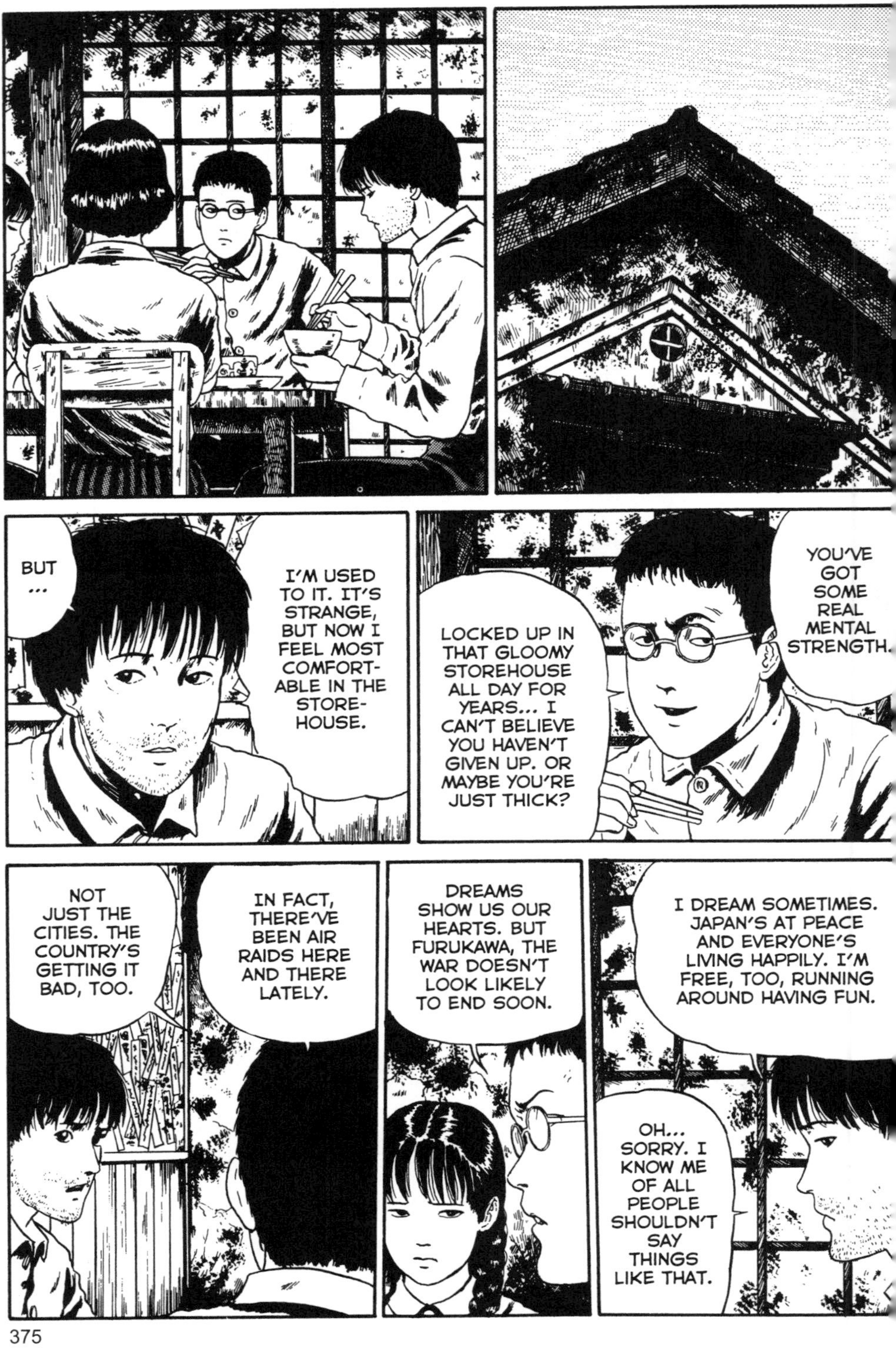
YOU'VE GOT SOME REAL MENTAL STRENGTH.
LOCKED UP IN THAT GLOOMY STOREHOUSE ALL DAY FOR YEARS... I CAN'T BELIEVE YOU HAVEN'T GIVEN UP. OR MAYBE YOU'RE JUST THICK?
I'M USED TO IT. IT'S STRANGE, BUT NOW I FEEL MOST COMFORT-ABLE IN THE STORE-HOUSE.
BUT ...
I DREAM SOMETIMES. JAPAN'S AT PEACE AND EVERYONE'S LIVING HAPPILY. I'M FREE, TOO, RUNNING AROUND HAVING FUN.
OH... SORRY. I KNOW ME OF ALL PEOPLE SHOULDN'T SAY THINGS LIKE THAT.
DREAMS SHOW US OUR HEARTS. BUT FURUKAWA, THE WAR DOESN'T LOOK LIKELY TO END SOON.
IN FACT, THERE'VE BEEN AIR RAIDS HERE AND THERE LATELY.
NOT JUST THE CITIES. THE COUNTRY'S GETTING IT BAD, TOO.

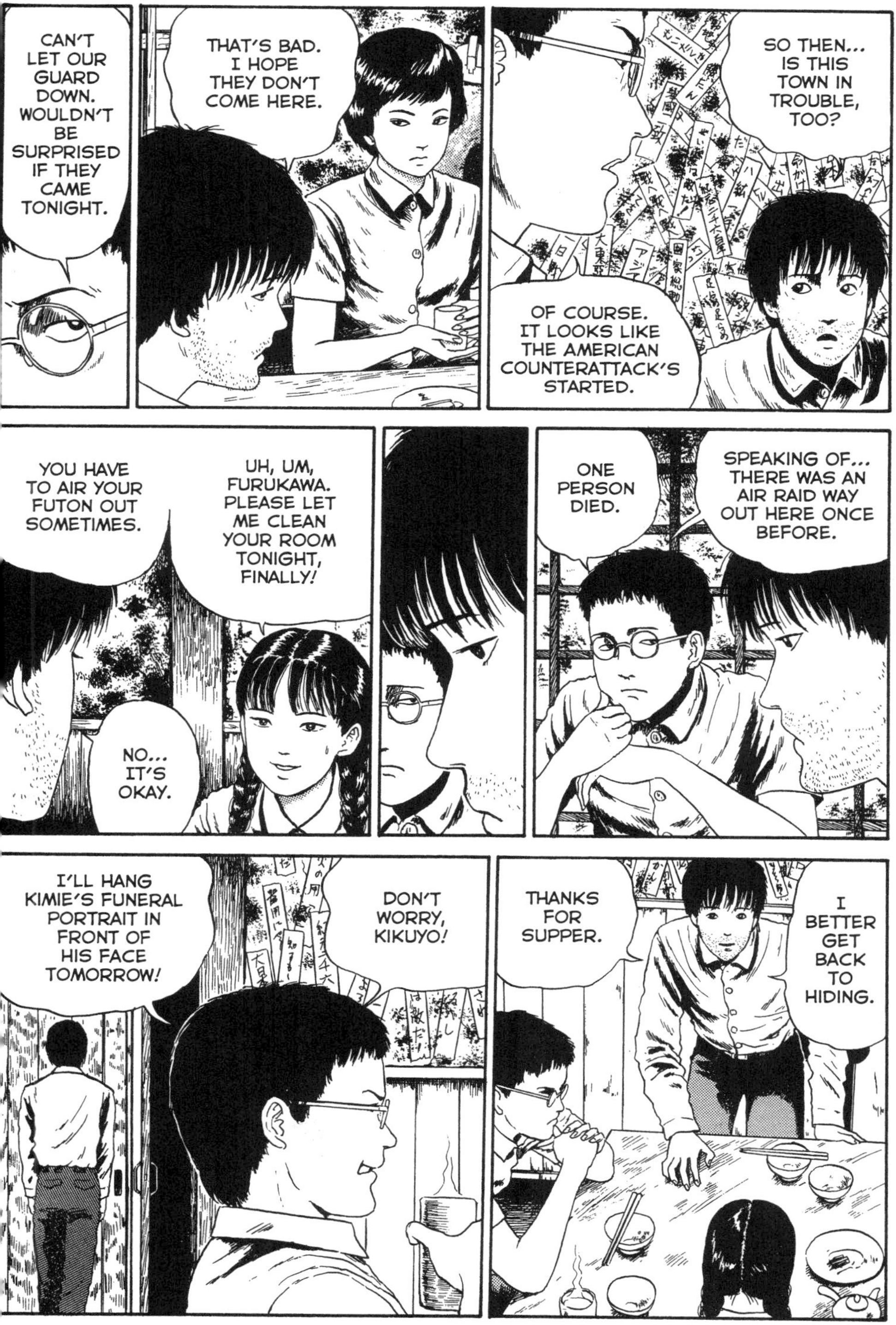
SO THEN... IS THIS TOWN IN TROUBLE, TOO?
OF COURSE. IT LOOKS LIKE THE AMERICAN COUNTERATTACK'S STARTED.
THAT'S BAD. I HOPE THEY DON'T COME HERE.
CAN'T LET OUR GUARD DOWN. WOULDN'T BE SURPRISED IF THEY CAME TONIGHT.
SPEAKING OF... THERE WAS AN AIR RAID WAY OUT HERE ONCE BEFORE.
ONE PERSON DIED.
UH, UM, FURUKAWA. PLEASE LET ME CLEAN YOUR ROOM TONIGHT, FINALLY!
YOU HAVE TO AIR YOUR FUTON OUT SOMETIMES.
NO... IT'S OKAY.
I BETTER GET BACK TO HIDING.
THANKS FOR SUPPER.
DON'T WORRY, KIKUYO!
I'LL HANG KIMIE'S FUNERAL PORTRAIT IN FRONT OF HIS FACE TOMORROW!

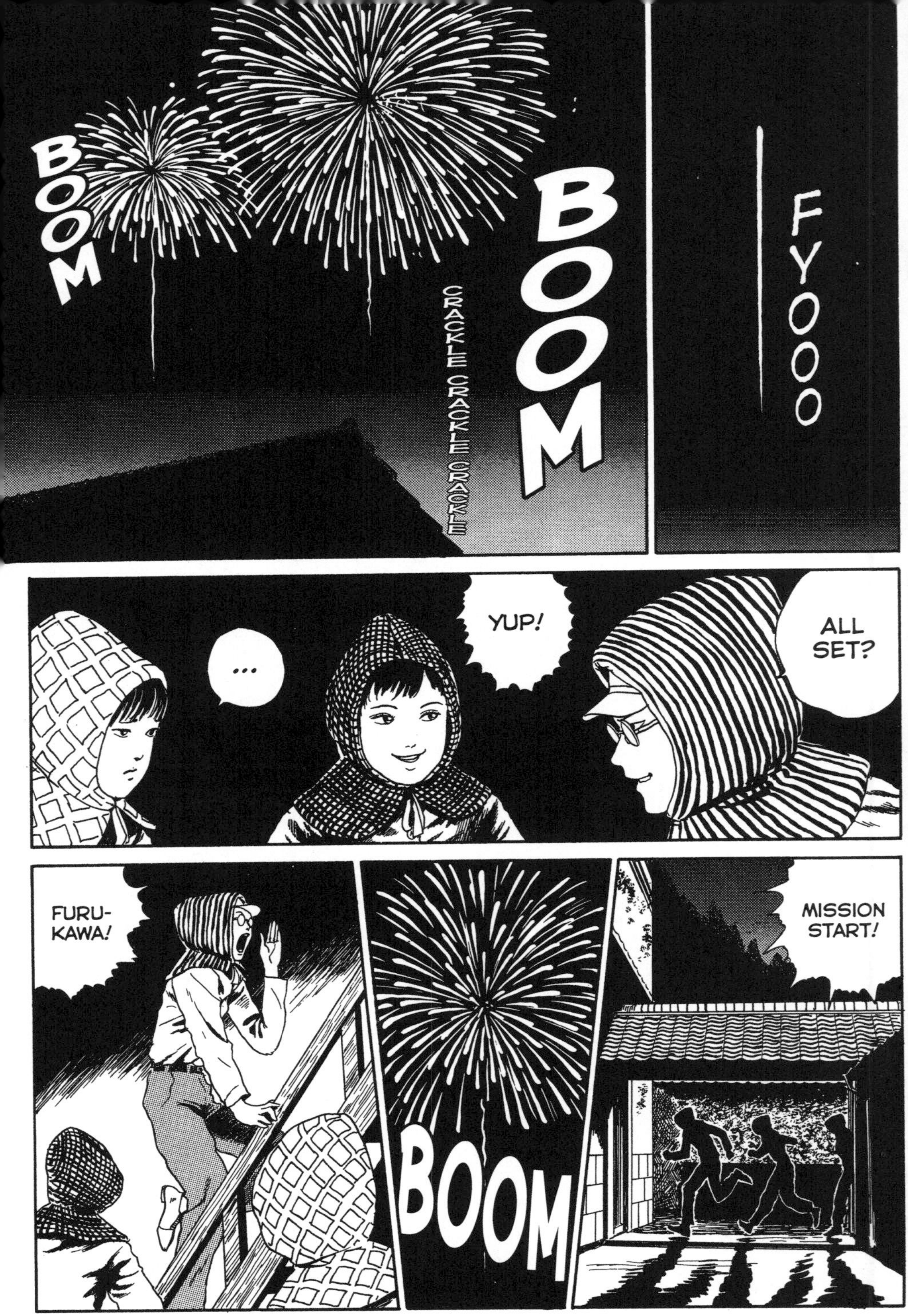
FYOOO
BOOM
CRACKLE CRACKLE CRACKLE
BOOM
ALL SET?
YUP!
...
MISSION START!
BOOM
FURU-KAWA!

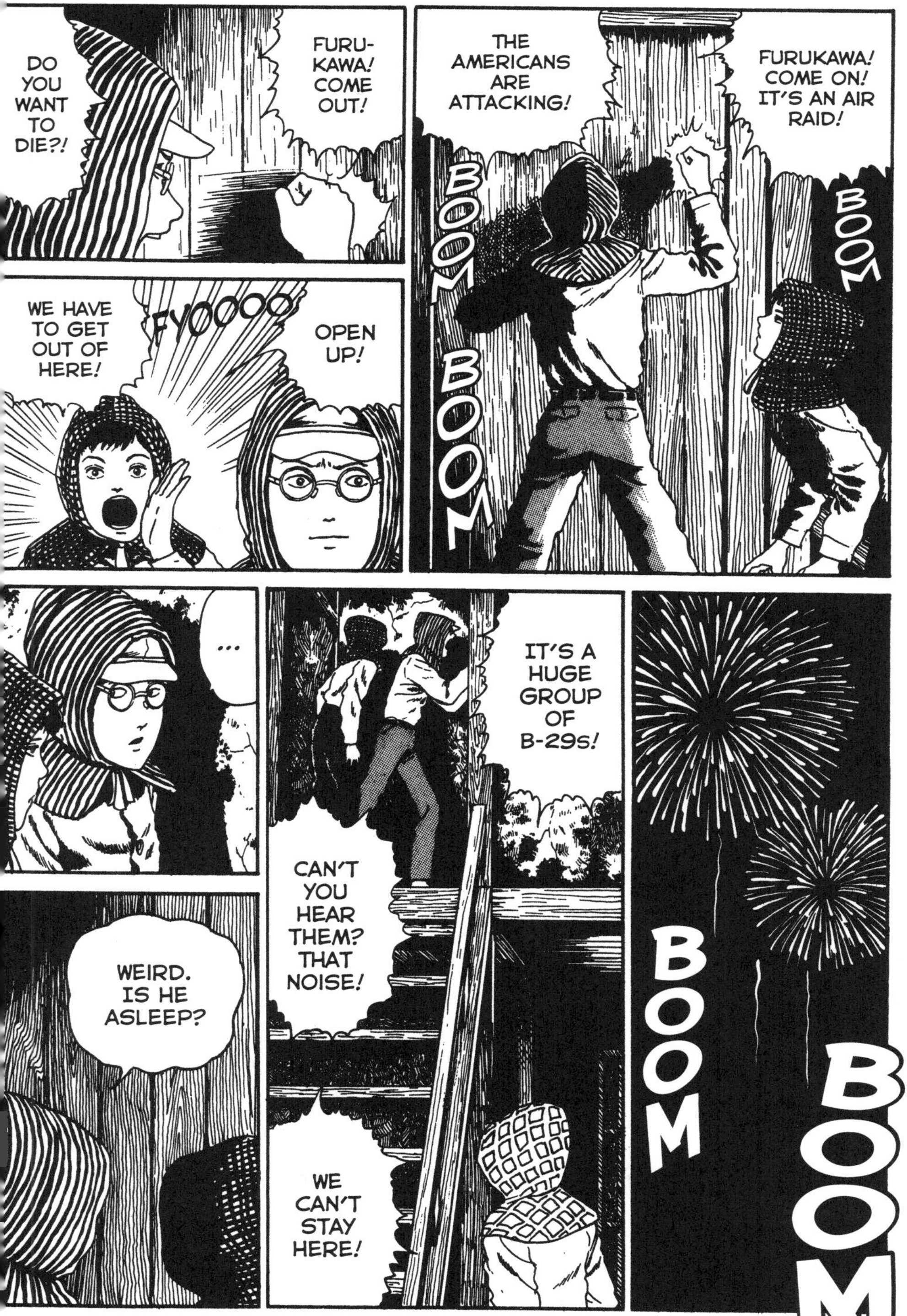
FURUKAWA! COME ON! IT'S AN AIR RAID!
BOOM
THE AMERICANS ARE ATTACKING!
BOOM BOOM
FURU-KAWA! COME OUT!
DO YOU WANT TO DIE?!
OPEN UP!
FYOOOO
WE HAVE TO GET OUT OF HERE!
BOOM
BOOM
IT'S A HUGE GROUP OF B-29s!
CAN'T YOU HEAR THEM? THAT NOISE!
WE CAN'T STAY HERE!
...
WEIRD. IS HE ASLEEP?

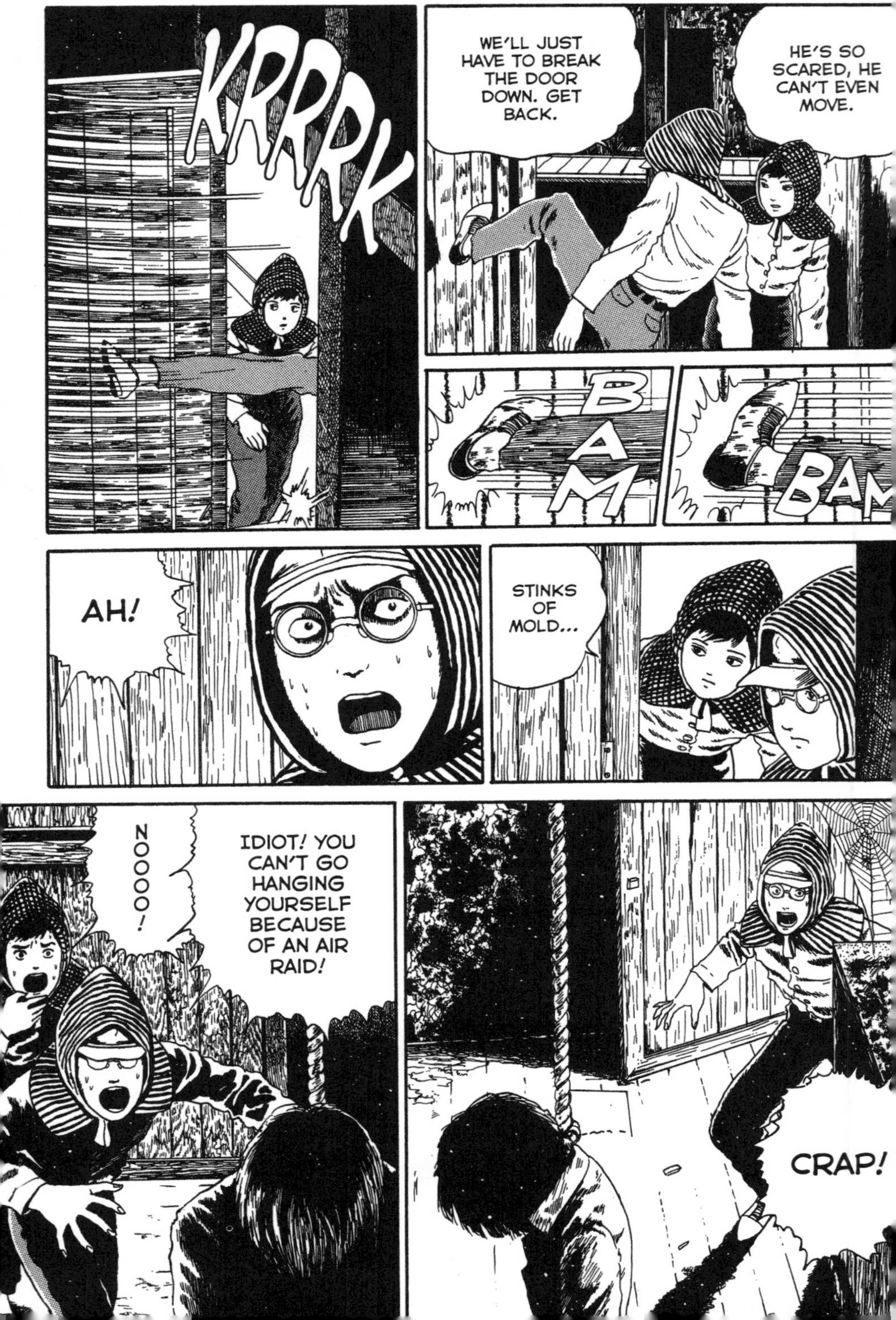
HE'S SO SCARED, HE CAN'T EVEN MOVE.
WE'LL JUST HAVE TO BREAK THE DOOR DOWN. GET BACK.
BAM
BAM
KRRRK
STINKS OF MOLD...
AH!
CRAP!
IDIOT! YOU CAN'T GO HANGING YOURSELF BECAUSE OF AN AIR RAID!
NOOOOO!

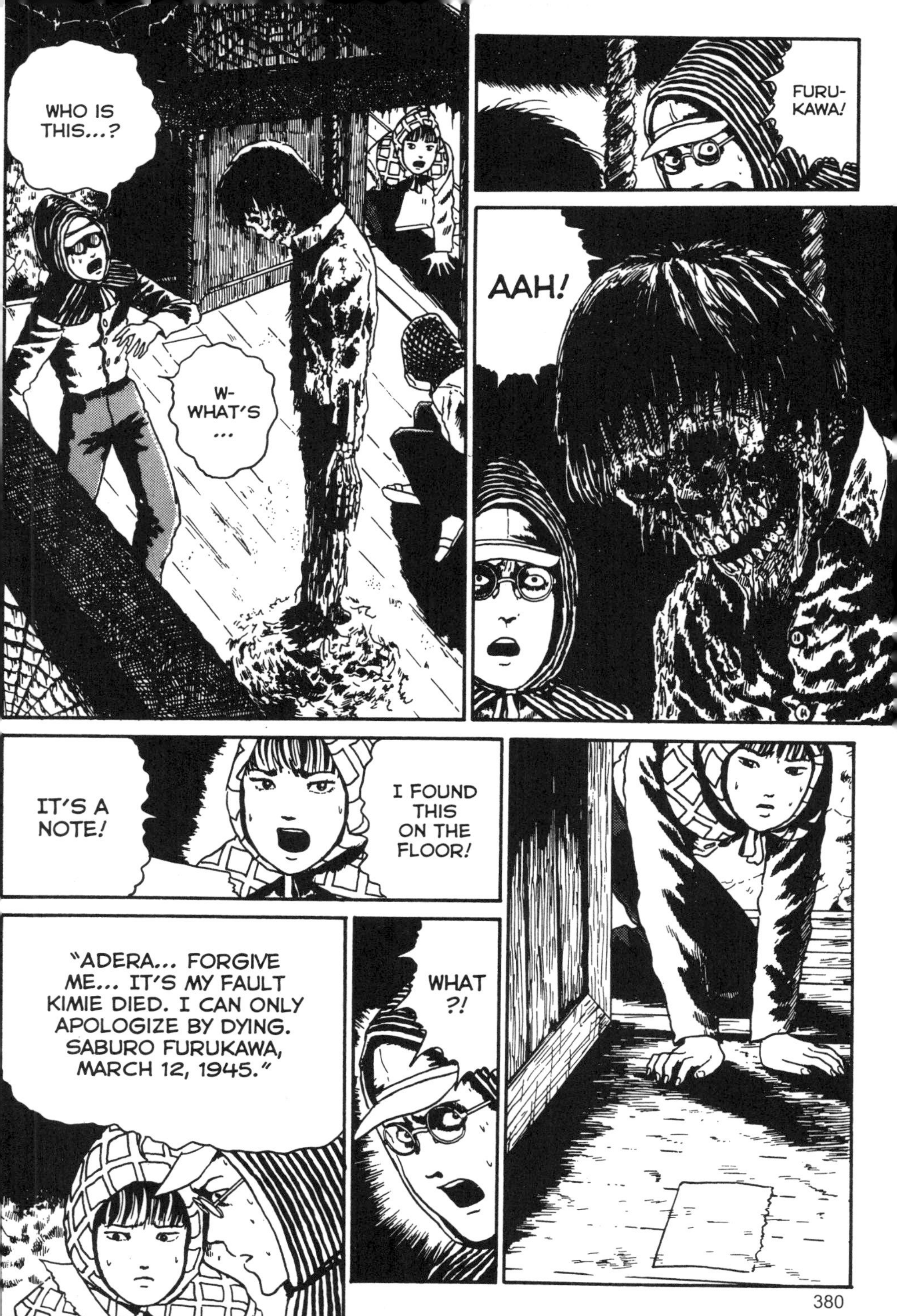
FURU-KAWA!
AAH!
WHO IS THIS...?
W-WHAT'S ...
I FOUND THIS ON THE FLOOR!
IT'S A NOTE!
WHAT ?!
"ADERA... FORGIVE ME... IT'S MY FAULT KIMIE DIED. I CAN ONLY APOLOGIZE BY DYING. SABURO FURUKAWA, MARCH 12, 1945."

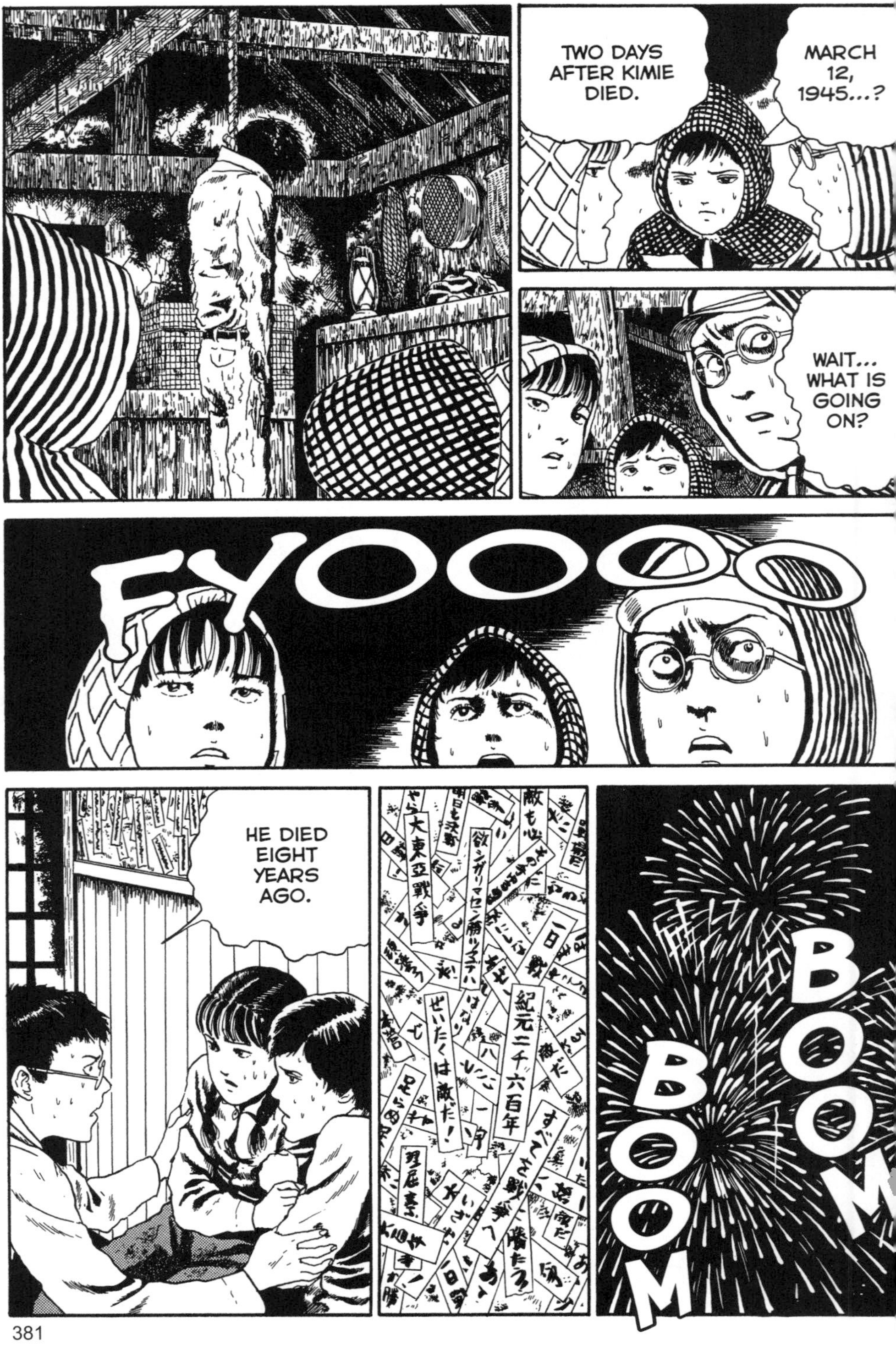
MARCH 12, 1945...?
TWO DAYS AFTER KIMIE DIED.
WAIT... WHAT IS GOING ON?
FYOOOO
BOOM
BOOM
大東亞戰爭
欲シガリマセン勝ツマデハ
紀元二千六百年
ぜいたくは敵だ!
HE DIED EIGHT YEARS AGO.

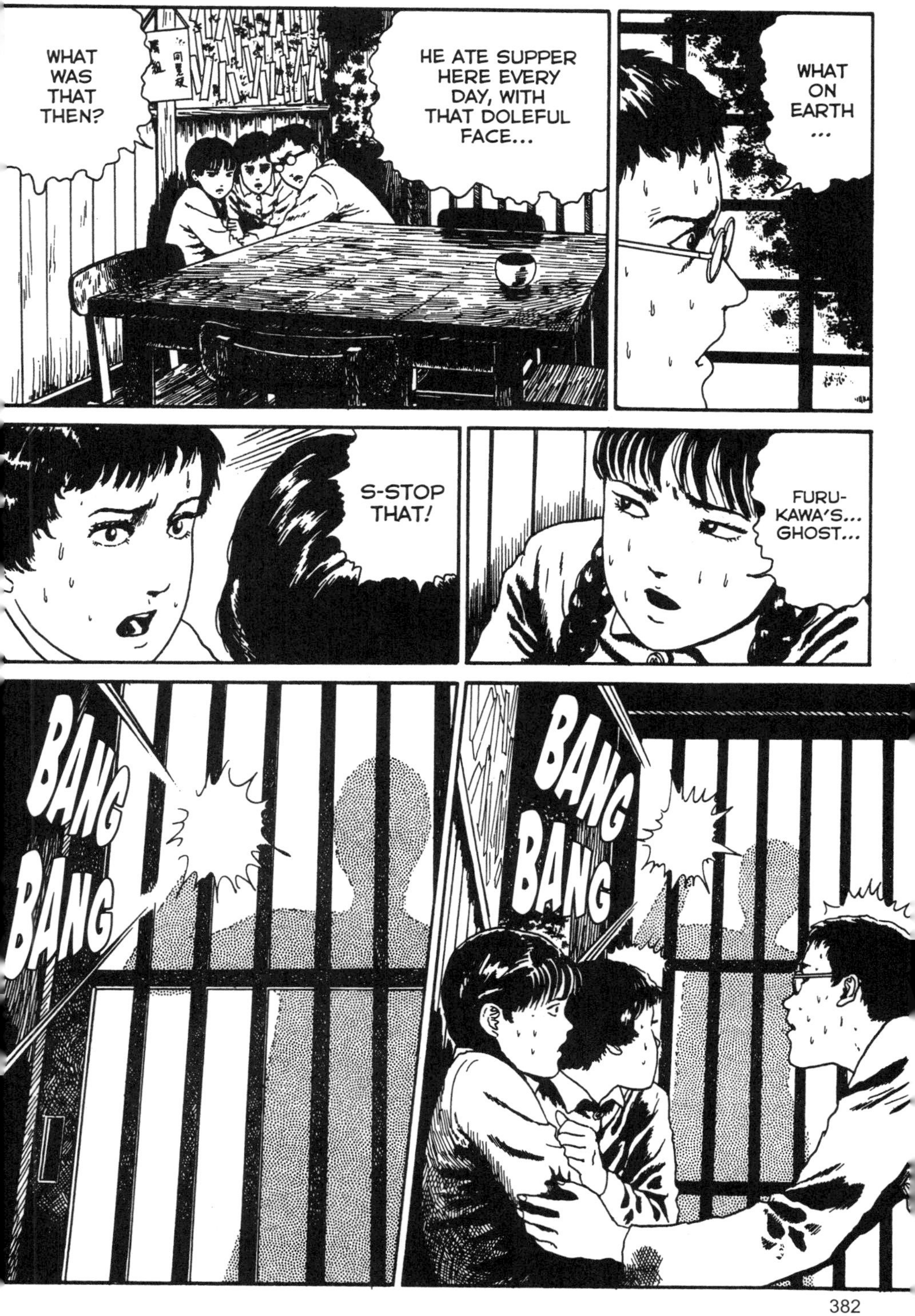
WHAT ON EARTH ...
HE ATE SUPPER HERE EVERY DAY, WITH THAT DOLEFUL FACE...
WHAT WAS THAT THEN?
FURU-KAWA'S... GHOST...
S-STOP THAT!
BANG BANG
BANG BANG

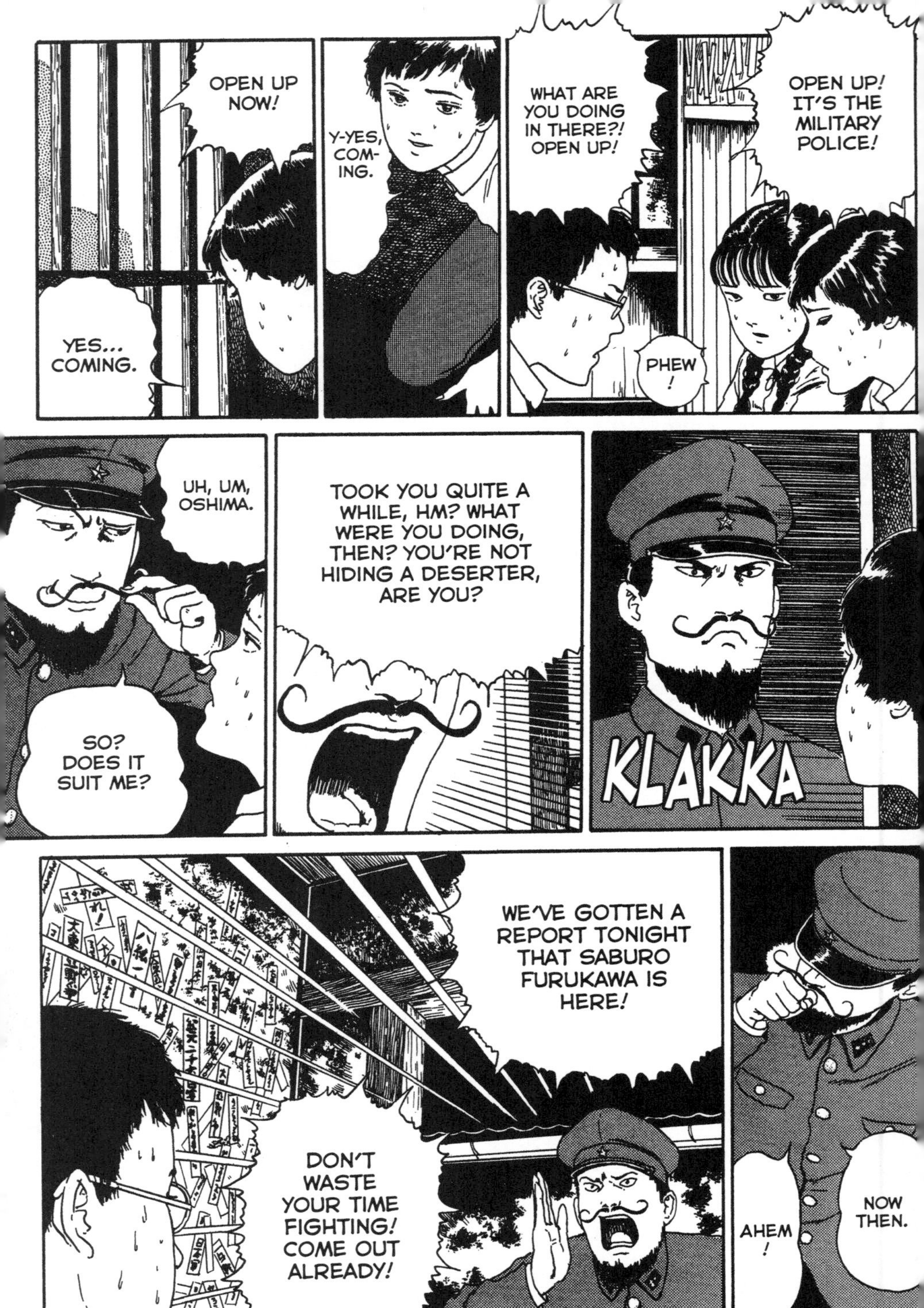
OPEN UP! IT'S THE MILITARY POLICE!
WHAT ARE YOU DOING IN THERE?! OPEN UP!
PHEW!
Y-YES, COM-ING.
OPEN UP NOW!
YES... COMING.
KLAKKA
TOOK YOU QUITE A WHILE, HM? WHAT WERE YOU DOING, THEN? YOU'RE NOT HIDING A DESERTER, ARE YOU?
UH, UM, OSHIMA.
SO? DOES IT SUIT ME?
NOW THEN.
AHEM!
WE'VE GOTTEN A REPORT TONIGHT THAT SABURO FURUKAWA IS HERE!
DON'T WASTE YOUR TIME FIGHTING! COME OUT ALREADY!

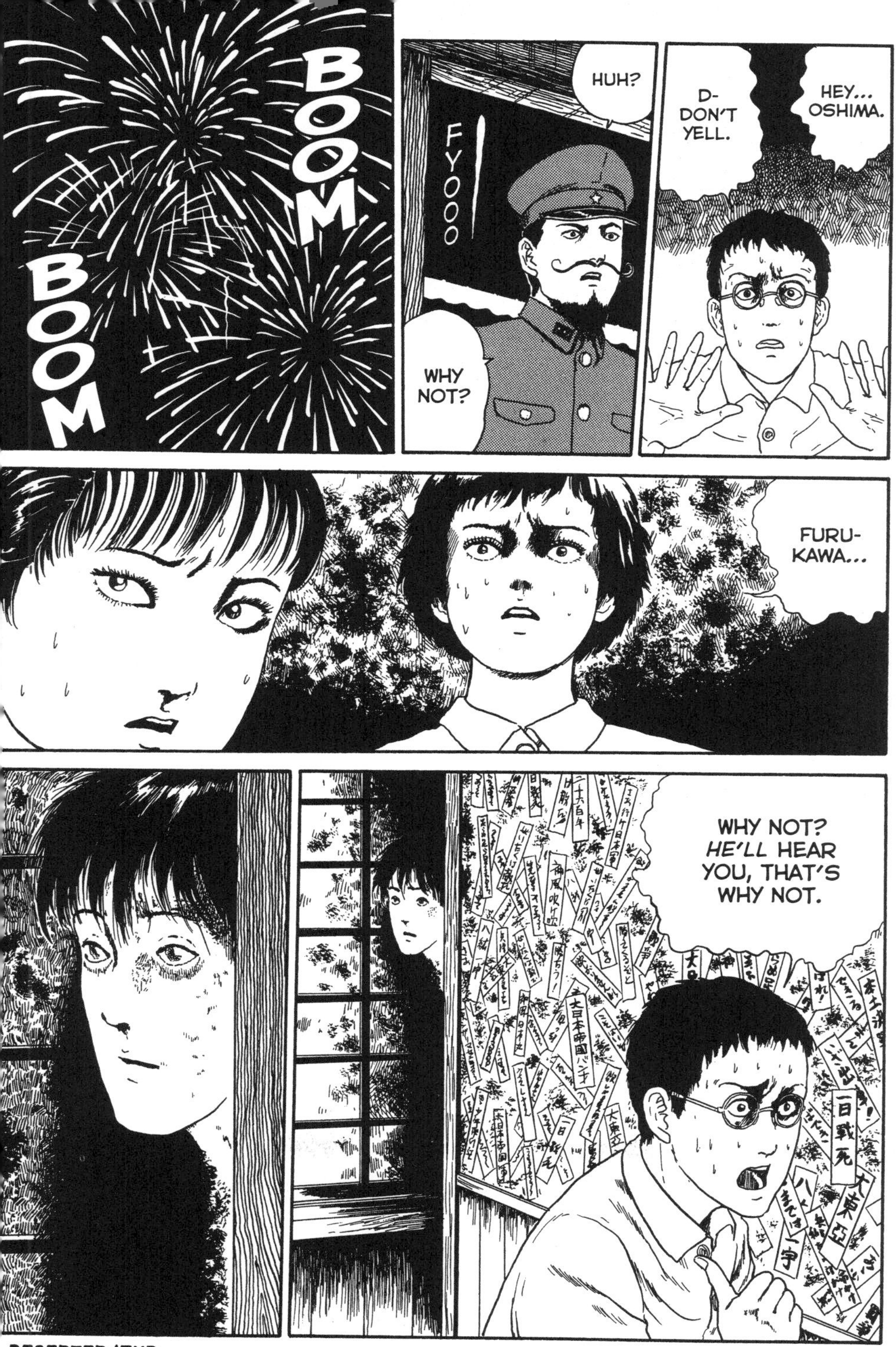
HEY... OSHIMA.
D- DON'T YELL.
HUH?
FYOOO
WHY NOT?
BOOM
BOOM
FURU-KAWA...
WHY NOT? *HE'LL* HEAR YOU, THAT'S WHY NOT.

DESERTER/END

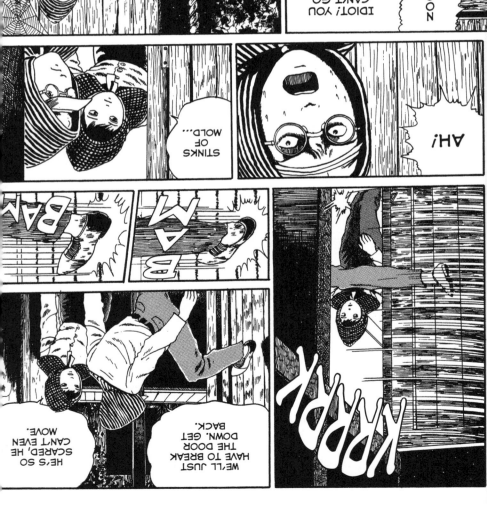

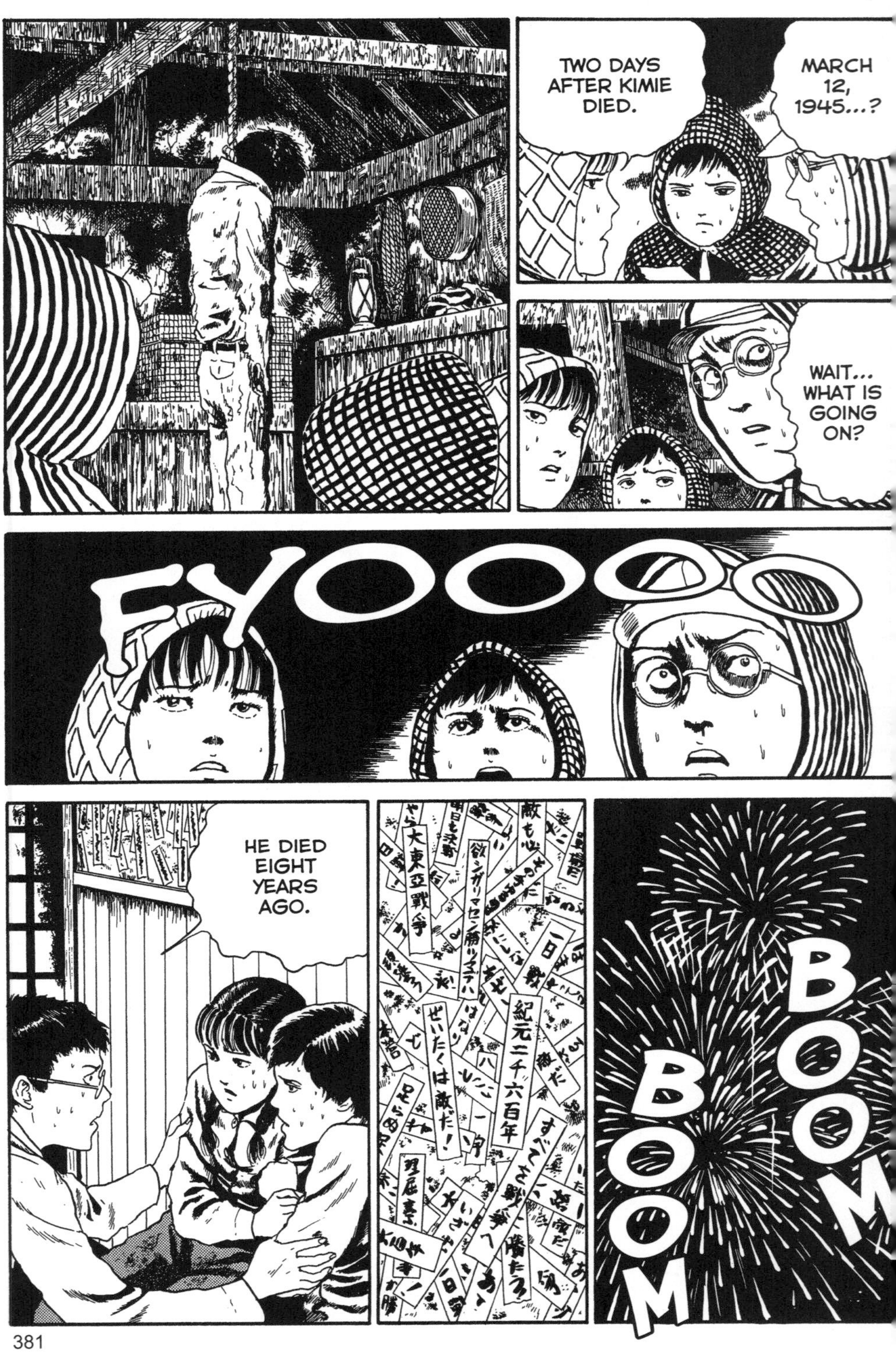
MARCH 12, 1945...?
TWO DAYS AFTER KIMIE DIED.
WAIT... WHAT IS GOING ON?
FYOOOO
BOOM
BOOM
紀元二千六百年
欲シガリマセン勝ツマデハ
ぜいたくは敵だ!
大東亜戦争
HE DIED EIGHT YEARS AGO.

FURU-
KAWA'S....
GHOST....

S-STOP
THAT!

...
WHAT
ON
EARTH

HE ATE SUPPER
HERE EVERY
DAY, WITH
THAT DOLEFUL
FACE...

WHAT
WAS
THAT
THEN?

BOOM
BOOM

FYOOO

HUH?

WHY NOT?

D- DON'T YELL.

HEY... OSHIMA.

FURU- KAWA...

WHY NOT? *HE'LL* HEAR YOU, THAT'S WHY NOT.

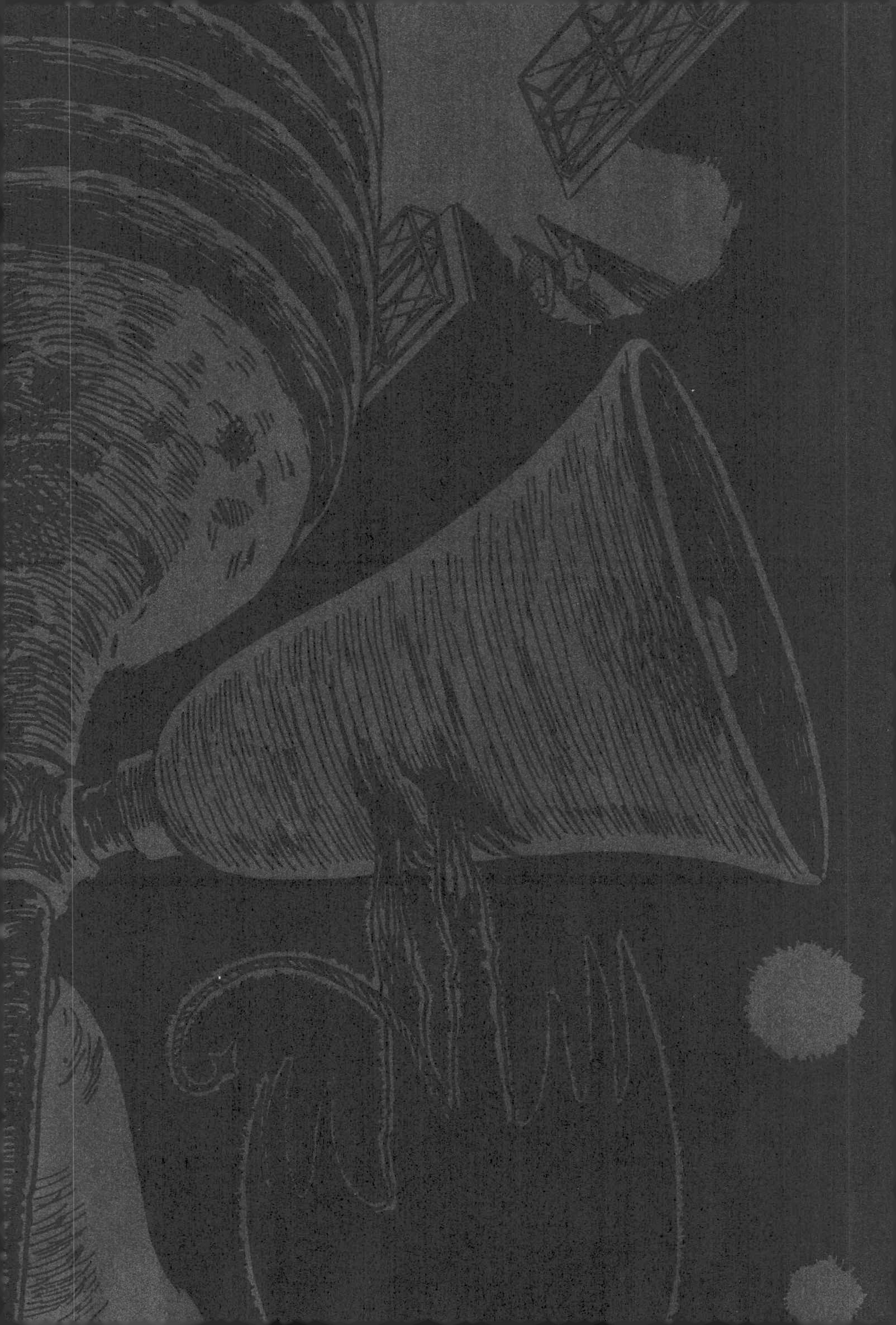

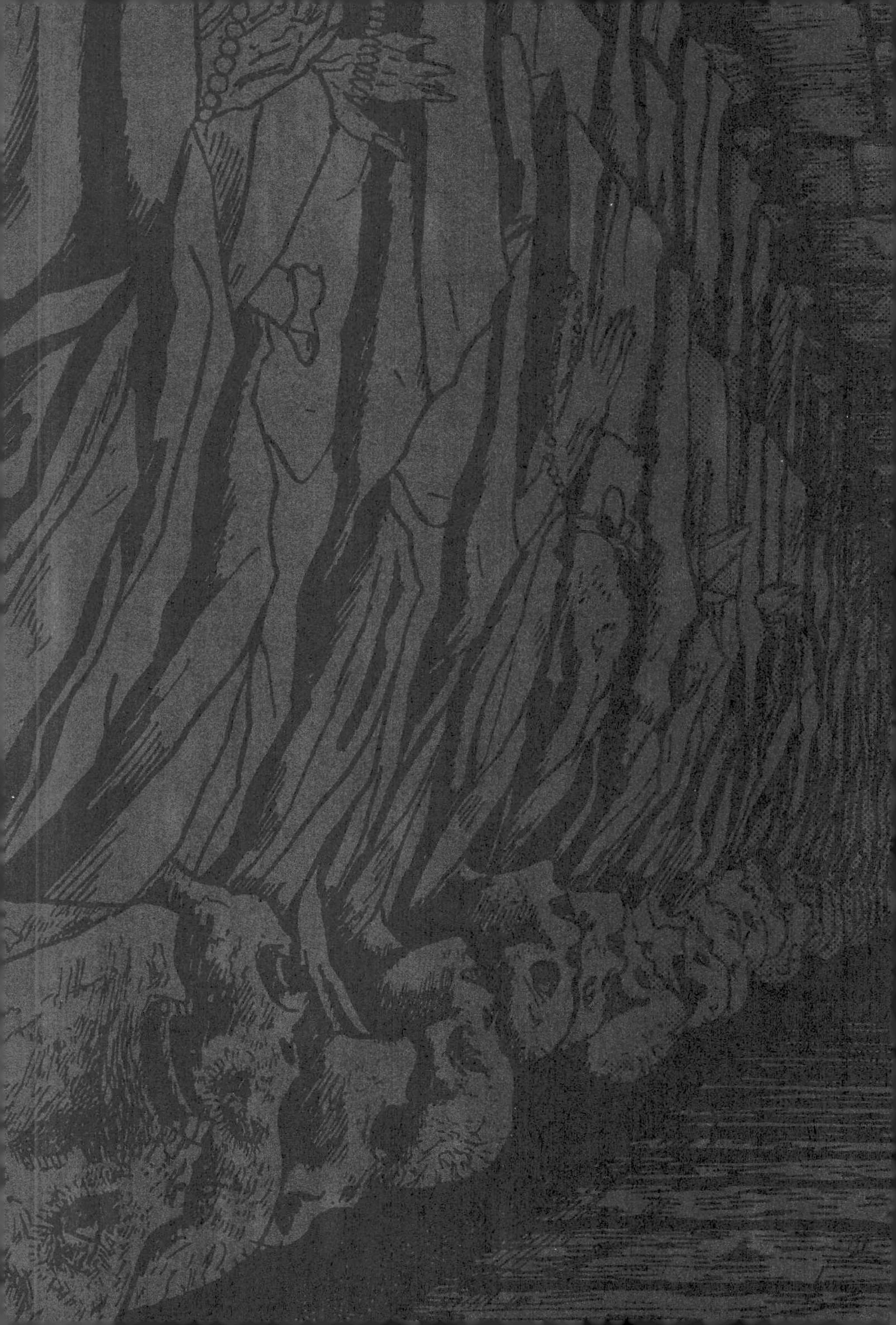

ABOUT THE AUTHOR

Junji Ito made his professional manga debut in 1987 and since then has gone on to be recognized as one of the greatest contemporary artists working in the horror genre. His titles include *Tomie* and *Uzumaki*, which have been adapted into live-action films; *Gyo*, which was adapted into an animated film; and his books *Fragments of Horror*, *Frankenstein*, *Lovesickness*, *No Longer Human*, *Remina*, *Shiver*, *Smashed*, and *Venus in the Blind Spot*, all of which are available from VIZ Media. Ito's influences include classic horror manga artists Kazuo Umezz and Hideshi Hino, as well as authors Yasutaka Tsutsui and H.P. Lovecraft.

He is a three-time Eisner Award winner. In 2019 his collection *Frankenstein* won in the "Best Adaptation from Another Medium" category, and in 2021 he was awarded "Best Writer/Artist," while *Remina* received the award for "Best U.S. Edition of International Material (Asia)."

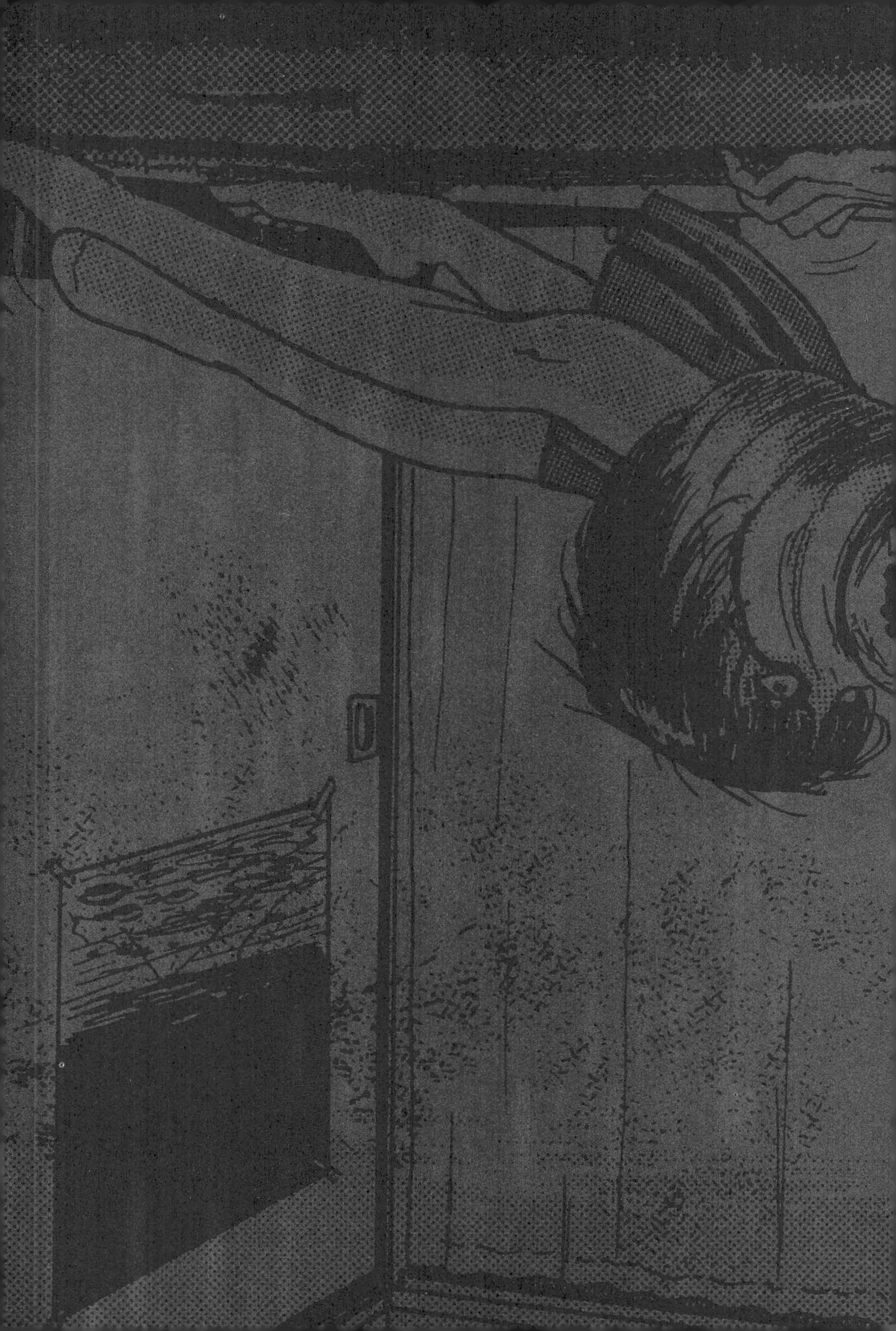

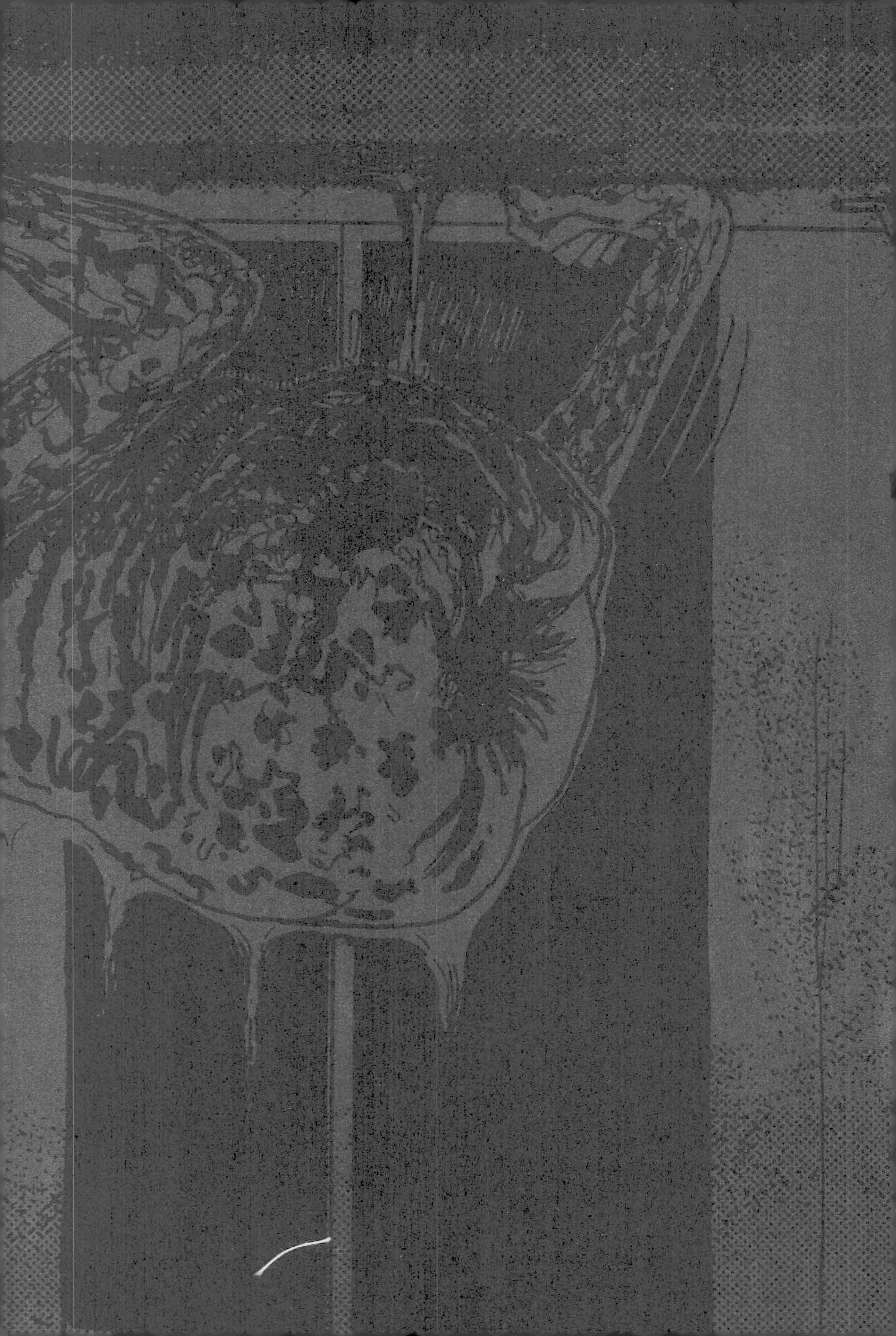

DESERTER

JUNJI ITO STORY COLLECTION

Story & Art by Junji Ito

Ito Junji Kessakushu 5: Dassouhei no iru ie
© JI Inc. 2011
Originally published in Japan in 2011 by Asahi Shimbun
Publications Inc., Tokyo. English translation rights arranged
with Asahi Shimbun Publications Inc., Tokyo through
TOHAN CORPORATION, Tokyo.

Translation & Adaptation: Jocelyne Allen
Touch-Up Art & Lettering: Eric Erbes
Cover & Graphic Design: Adam Grano
Editor: Masumi Washington

Printed in the U.S.A.

Published by VIZ Media, LLC
P.O. Box 77010
San Francisco, CA 94107

10 9 8 7 6 5 4 3 2
First printing, December 2021
Second printing, December 2021

VIZ SIGNATURE

viz.com

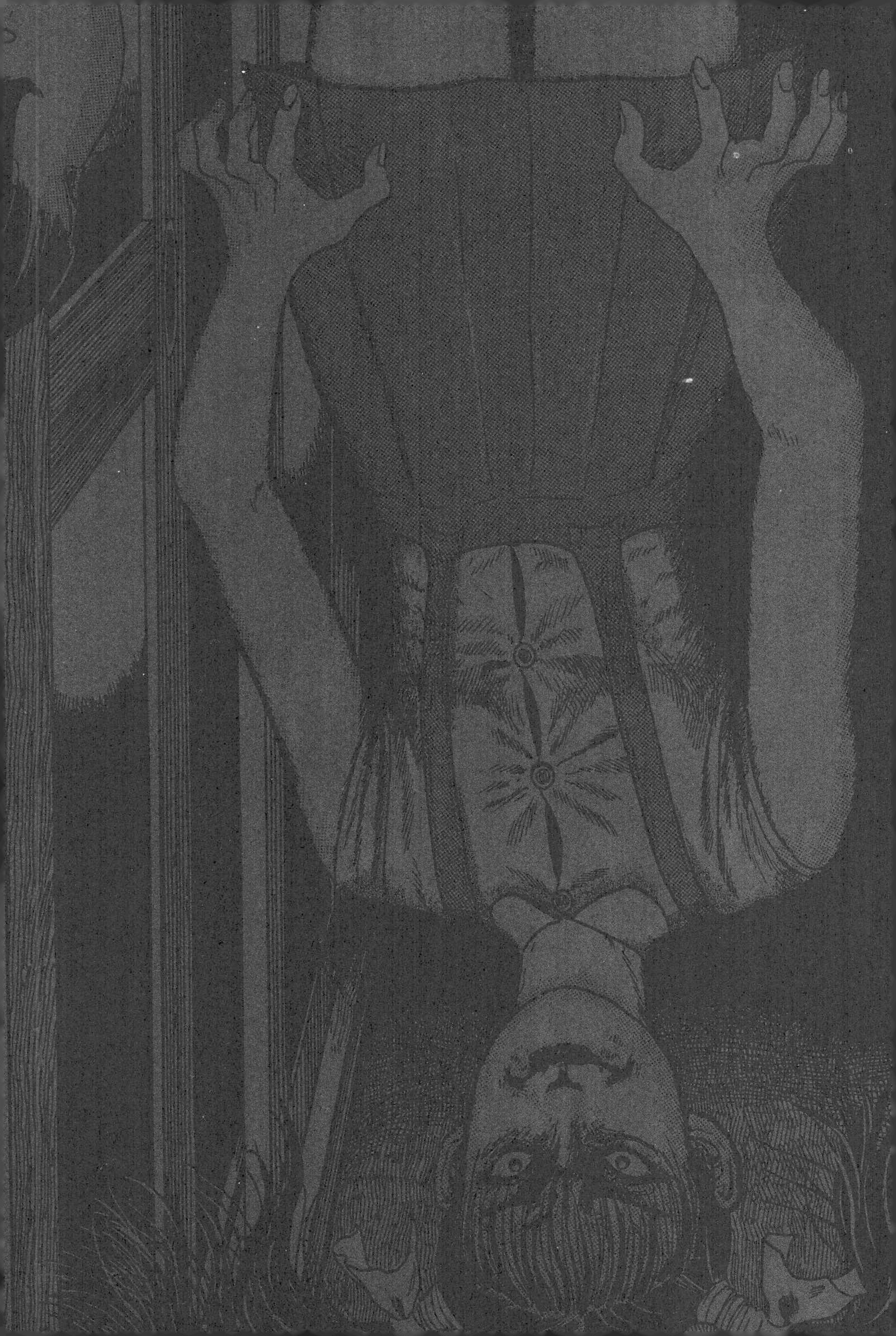